Microsoft® FoxPro® 2.5 for Windows

The Master Reference

Also by John Fitzsimmons and Robin Stark:
Microsoft FoxPro 2.5 for DOS: The Master Reference

Microsoft® FoxPro® 2.5 for Windows

The Master Reference

John C. Fitzsimmons
Robin Stark

Windcrest®/McGraw-Hill

New York San Francisco Washington, D.C. Auckland Bogotá
Caracas Lisbon London Madrid Mexico City Milan
Montreal New Delhi San Juan Singapore
Sydney Tokyo Toronto

Notices

Microsoft™, Windows®, FoxPro®, MS-DOS® Microsoft Corporation

FIRST EDITION
FIRST PRINTING

Published by Windcrest, an imprint of McGraw-Hill, Inc.
The name "Windcrest" is a registered trademark of McGraw-Hill, Inc.

Library of Congress Cataloging-in-Publication Data

Fitzsimmons, John.
Microsoft FoxPro 2.5 for Windows : the master reference / by John C. Fitzsimmons and Robin Stark.
p. cm.
Includes index.
ISBN 0-07-060991-8 (pbk.)
1. Database management. 2. FoxPro for Windows. I. Stark, Robin. II. Title.
QA76.9.D3F5938 1994
005.75'65—dc20 93-48075
CIP

Editorial team: Jennifer Holt DiGiovanna, Acquisitions Editor
Robert E. Ostrander, Executive Editor
Aaron G. Bittner, Book Editor
Production team: Katherine G. Brown, Director
Patsy D. Harne, Desktop Operator
Linda L. King, Proofreading
Design team: Jaclyn J. Boone, Designer
Brian Allison, Associate Designer
Cover design by Stickles Associates, Bath, Pa.
Cover photograph © Orion Press/Westlight.

WR1
0609918

Contents

Introduction

Having worked with FoxPro for Windows since its early beta version, and as the co-author of *Microsoft FoxPro 2.5 for DOS:The Master Reference*, I realized that a FoxPro for Windows book was in order. While FoxPro for Windows is similar to its DOS brother, it extends further to take full advantage of the Windows environment. You can now integrate graphics into databases, access Windows API functions, and harness the power of Dynamic Data Exchange and Object Linking and Embedding. And now that FoxPro exists on two different platforms, development of cross-platform applications can be a reality.

As with our DOS version, the purpose of this book is to replace the seven FoxPro manuals with one detailed reference book. *Microsoft FoxPro 2.5 for Windows: The Master Reference* is a book that can be useful for new or seasoned users of FoxPro.

The book contains twelve chapters and is structured to move you through FoxPro one step at time. Chapter 1 takes you through the FoxPro interface, so that you can become proficient at window control and menu operations. Chapter 2 contains a complete listing of all FoxPro commands, with detailed syntax listings, a full description, and good examples. Chapter 3 details a subset of FoxPro commands, the SET commands. In chapter 4, you'll find a complete listing of all FoxPro functions, again with good examples.

While *Microsoft FoxPro 2.5 for Windows: The Master Reference* is primarily a reference book, you'll find a great introduction to programming in chapter 5. The important issues of programming, including standards and conventions, flow control, and decision making are detailed. Chapters 6 through 10 focus on the application development tools: the Screen Builder, Menu Builder, RQBE Window, Report Writer, and the Project Manager.

FoxPro version 2.5a introduces cross-platform and international capabilities such as accented character conversion and foreign language indexing support. These capabilities are discussed in chapter 11. In chapter 12, you'll learn how to implement the capabilities of Windows DDE and OLE into your FoxPro applications.

Finally, we're providing you with *Microsoft FoxPro 2.5 for Windows: The Master Reference* on a disk. The enclosed disk contains a Windows help-style version of this book. Now while you're tooling away in FoxPro, the press of a key will display these pages right before your eyes. You can even copy out the examples and paste them directly into FoxPro.

In 1991 I, along with many others, got my first glimpse of FoxPro for Windows at the closing of the annual FoxPro Developers Conference in Toledo, Ohio. 1992 was proclaimed the Year of the Fox, and we all waited anxiously for new versions of FoxPro, including Windows and Macintosh. One year later Fox Software, originators of FoxPro, was acquired by Microsoft. I, among others, wondered just what was in store for the FoxPro product line. Microsoft listened to the developer community, and responded. FoxPro for Windows is the premier Windows database development system today.

If you are a user of earlier versions of FoxPro, or even another type of dBase application, you should find *Microsoft FoxPro 2.5 for Windows: The Master Reference* just the reference that you need to take full advantage of the new features of FoxPro for Windows.

FoxPro stands alone at the top of the database mountain. This book is your first step in getting there.

John C. Fitzsimmons

1
The FoxPro user interface

The FoxPro user interface is the best place for a beginner to become familiar with database management. The user interface lets you work entirely from pop-up menus, selecting commands and functions with a few keystrokes or mouse movements. With the interface, you can design your database, create reports and mailing labels, and perform a wide variety of operations that formerly required programming skills. This chapter is designed to teach you the basics of FoxPro for Windows, including interface controls and how to navigate through FoxPro's menu system.

This book assumes the reader has some knowledge of Microsoft Windows and a graphical user interface. Consult your Windows documentation for any information not provided in this chapter.

Interface basics

FoxPro is an event-driven, "windowing" application. Each action you perform or menu option you select is an event, and multiple events can occur at the same time. FoxPro uses menus and windows for all of its operations, including data entry, help, dialogs, and development tools. When a FoxPro dialog appears, you'll most likely be required to perform some type of action. You can use FoxPro productively with either a standard keyboard or mouse.

Using the mouse

While FoxPro can be used with a keyboard, it is much more efficient when using a mouse. FoxPro uses the standard Windows *mouse pointer*, which by default is an arrow that points to the top left corner of the screen. When using the mouse, the position of the mouse cursor determines how the mouse action is interpreted.

While many mouse devices come with many buttons, FoxPro only recognizes the actions of the left and right buttons. Throughout this book you will see references to using the mouse. The following describes how to use a mouse in FoxPro:

Position Position the mouse cursor over a menu or dialog option.

Click Press the left mouse button once.

Double-click Press the left mouse button twice, in succession.

Drag Press the left mouse button, hold it, and move the mouse. Release the mouse button to end the action.

Using the mouse in a FoxPro dialog or data entry screen causes the object cursor (the keyboard cursor) to disappear. You can redisplay it by pressing the Tab key on the keyboard.

If you do not install a mouse driver before starting Windows, FoxPro will use the standard Windows mouse driver. Refer to your mouse documentation on loading the appropriate mouse drivers and handling the mouse.

Using the keyboard

The keyboard is used in FoxPro to enter data, activate hot keys and menu shortcuts, break program execution, and more. All functions you can accomplish with a mouse you can do with the keyboard.

FoxPro can be used with any IBM-compatible keyboard. Many old keyboards only have 10 function keys, and FoxPro is designed to use 12 function keys. Some keyboards have the function keys along the top, while others are on the side. The keys you will use most often are the Enter, Escape (Esc), Shift, Control (Ctrl), and Alternate (Alt) keys. You should familiarize yourself with the placement of these keys, along with the Backspace, Caps Lock, Delete, and arrow keys.

You can use the keyboard to emulate the mouse in certain operations, such as selecting options in a menu or list. The following describes mouse functions and their corresponding keyboard functions.

Position Use the Tab, Enter or arrow keys.

Click Press the Spacebar once.

Double-click Press the Spacebar twice, or press the Enter key.

Interface windows

When you start FoxPro, the desktop screen appears, as shown in Fig. 1-1. This screen has the FoxPro logo, a Command window, and a system menu bar. If you know the commands and functions you want to use, you can simply type them in the Command window to execute their actions.

The Command window is an example of a FoxPro system window. Figure 1-2 shows the Command window and points out the parts of a standard FoxPro window. Other user windows such as program, text, report and label windows can be opened from the File menu when you choose the Open option. If you have several user windows open at once, their names will all be listed on the Window menu, with the frontmost window selected. Other system windows such as the Trace and Debug windows can be activated by selecting them from the Program menu. You can move another window to the front by selecting it from the menu or clicking on it. Windows can be sized, moved, and manipulated in other ways as described in the next section.

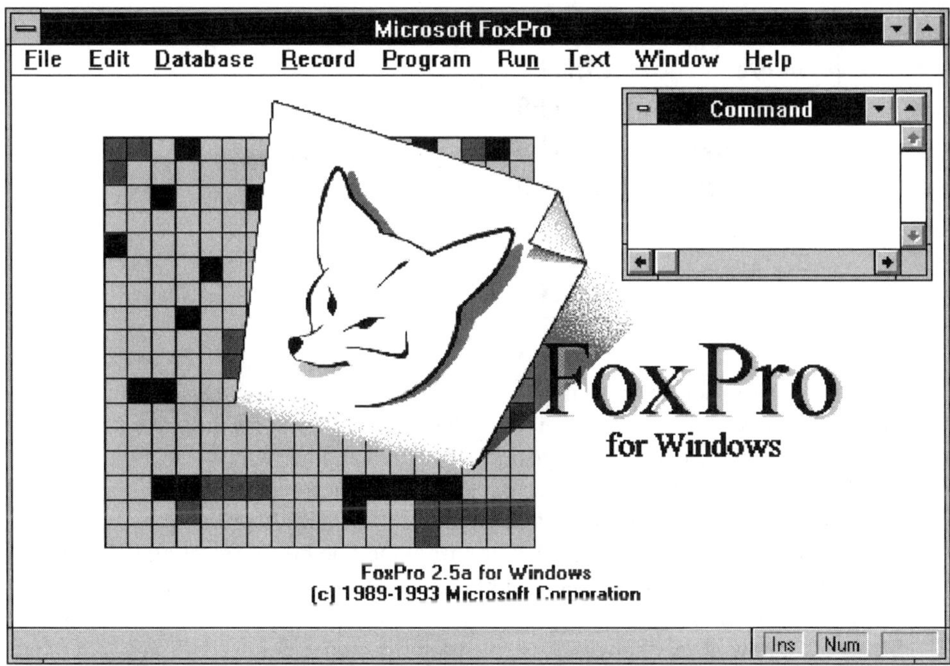

1-1 Sign-on screen.

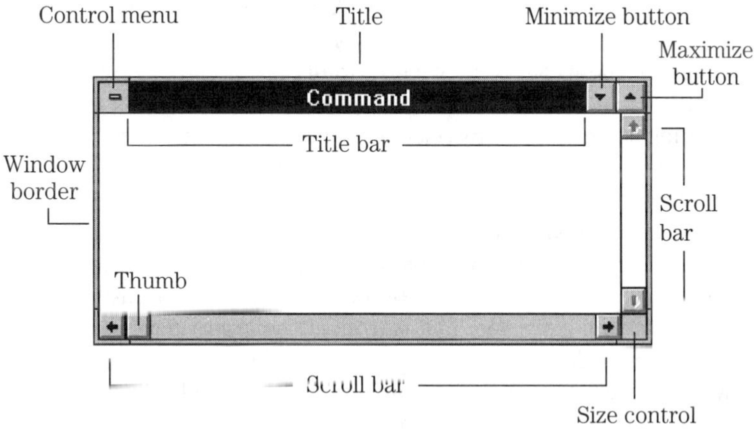

1-2 Command Window.

Controlling windows

All FoxPro system windows have a control menu (see Fig. 1-3) that can be used to move, close or size the window. To move a window using the mouse, click on the title bar of the window, drag the window to the desired location and release the mouse. Windows can be moved using the keyboard by utilizing the window's control menu.

Restore	Ctrl+F5
Move	Ctrl+F7
Size	Ctrl+F8
Minimize	Ctrl+F9
Maximize	Ctrl+F10
Close	Ctrl+F4
Next Window	Ctrl+F6

1-3 Window control menu.

Open the control menu by clicking on it and select Move (or use the shortcut key Ctrl-F7). Use the arrow keys to move the window, then press Enter to fix the window in place. If you want to move a window that is positioned behind another window without bringing it forward, hold down the Shift key, click on any visible portion of the title bar, and drag.

The easiest way to close most system windows is by simply pressing Escape. Other ways to close windows include selecting Close from the File menu, selecting Close from a window's control menu (or use the shortcut key Ctrl-F4), or by double-clicking on the window's control menu box.

Sizing a window is very simple. First, position the mouse pointer over any part of the window edge. This causes the mouse pointer to change to a double arrow. Next, click and drag the selected edge of the box. This will increase or decrease the size of the window. To resize a window using the keyboard, open the control menu by clicking on it and select Size (or use the shortcut key Ctrl-F8). Use the arrow keys to size the window, then press Enter to fix the window in place.

Minimizing a window causes the window to disappear and be replaced by an icon at the bottom of the screen. Windows can be minimized by clicking on the minimize button (triangle is pointing downward), or by selecting Minimize from the window's control menu (or use the shortcut key Ctrl-F9). Maximizing a window causes the window to expand and fill the entire screen, sometimes even overflowing the main FoxPro title bar. Windows can be maximized by clicking on the maximize button (triangle is pointing upward), or by selecting Maximize from the window's control menu (or use the shortcut key Ctrl-F10). Once a window has been minimized or maximized, the window can easily be restored to its previous size by selecting the restore button (triangle pointing up and down), or by selecting Restore from the window's control menu (or use the shortcut key Ctrl-F5).

Some system windows such as the Command, Debug, and browse windows are displayed with horizontal and vertical scroll bars that let you scroll the window to see more information that is not showing. With a mouse, click the arrows at either end of the scroll bar along the edge of the window. To view information more rapidly, drag the square-shaped thumb. Click once in the page up or page down area to see the preceding or following page. With the keyboard, use the arrow keys to scroll, and PgUp and PgDn to move up or down one page. Press Ctrl-Home to go to the top of the window, and End to go to the bottom.

Other window control functions are detailed in the Window menu section later in this chapter.

See also The Window menu

Interface menus

You can type commands in the Command window if you are already familiar with FoxPro's command language. For beginners, the System menu is the door to operating FoxPro's database management system. The FoxPro System menu consists of the following options:

- File
- Edit
- Database
- Record
- Program
- Run
- Window
- Help

Each menu option is called a *menu pad*. Certain FoxPro operations, such as browsing a database, modifying a screen or report, or activating the calculator, will add and remove pads to the base System menu. When you select a menu pad, a pop-up containing a list of options appears beneath the pad. Some of the options might appear dimmed, and you cannot select them. These items are disabled because some other operation must be performed before they can be chosen.

Some of the pop-up menu options are followed by ellipses (...). This indicates that a dialog box will appear when you select the option. This dialog box will ask you for further information about the activity you want to perform. Some of the items in a dialog box might also include ellipses. This means that another dialog box will appear when the option is selected.

Using menus with a mouse

To select a menu pad with the mouse, position the cursor over the desired pad and click. This causes a list of options to pop down. Select an option from the pop-up list by positioning the cursor over the desired option and click, or drag the cursor to the desired option and release the mouse. When the option is selected, the action is performed, or if the item has an ellipsis, a dialog box appears.

Using menus with the keyboard

Most functions are easier with the mouse; others can be done more quickly when you know the keystrokes and therefore don't have to look up from your work to find items on the screen.

The system menu bar can be accessed by simply pressing the Alt or F10 key, which highlights the File pad. Move the menu cursor using the ← and → keys to the desired pad, and press Enter.

Each menu pad has an associated hot key that is highlighted and is usually the first letter of the menu-pad text. You can activate a selective menu pad by holding the Alt key and pressing the pad's hot key. To select an option from the menu pop-up, press the item's hot key, or use the ↑ and ↓ keys to highlight the option you want and then press the spacebar. If you want to leave the menu without selecting an option, press Esc, Alt, or F10.

Once you are familiar with interface menu options, you can select them by pressing Alt or F10, the menu hot key, and the option hot key without stopping to look at the menu. Some menu items can be selected from the keyboard by pressing the Ctrl key and a function key. These special shortcut keys are listed to the right of the menu options on the menu listing (Help is F1).

Dialog boxes

When you select a menu item that's followed by ellipses, a dialog box will appear. Dialog boxes also appear during other operations that require more information from you. You can press Esc to exit most dialog boxes without providing any information.

To move around a dialog box with the keyboard, press Tab until the control you want is highlighted. You can point to the desired control with the mouse and click to select it. Each type of control has its own requirements for executing an action. These are described in the following sections.

Push button *Push buttons* are gray boxes with shadow borders. Each button contains words or a picture that associates the button with its action. Figure 1-4 shows a set of push buttons. Activating the push button executes the action described or opens a dialog box if there are ellipses after the text. Push buttons must be highlighted or pointed to and then selected by pressing Enter or clicking with the mouse. If the push button has an associated hot key, pressing Alt plus the hot key letter will "push" the button.

A push button that is surrounded by a solid black border is the default button. The default push button can be activated by pressing Enter when the cursor is on any control other than a push button. When the cursor is on a push button, that button automatically becomes the default button.

1-4 A push button set.

Scrollable list *Scrollable lists* contain items such as directories, files, or fields. Figure 1-5 shows a scrollable list. To scroll down the list, click the arrow at either end of the scroll bar or use the ↑ and ↓ keys. You can use PgUp and PgDn to see more pages in the list, as well as Home and End to move to the top and bottom of the lists. You can also find items in the list with the keyboard by entering the first few characters of the item you want. Once you've located an item, you can select it by clicking on it with the mouse pressing the spacebar.

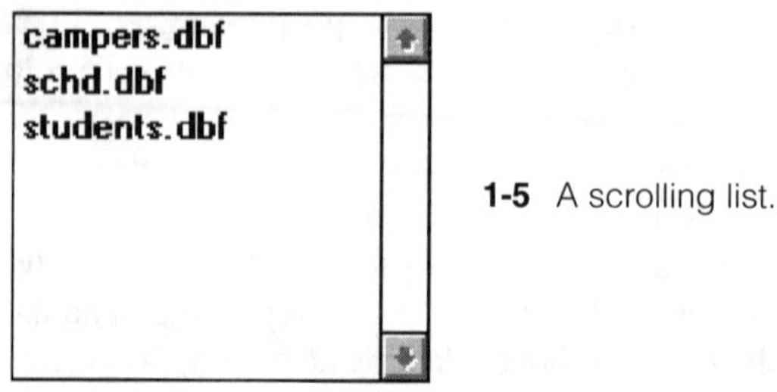

1-5 A scrolling list.

Radio button A *radio button* is an empty circle followed by text. Only one radio button in a group can be chosen at a time. Figure 1-6 shows a set of radio buttons.

Click to choose an item in the radio button list. When the button is on, a bullet appears inside the circle. When you choose a radio button, any other previously chosen button in the group is automatically deselected.

Today
Tomorrow
Next Week

1-6 A radio button set.

Check box A *check box* is an empty square followed by text. Figure 1-7 shows a check box. When a check box is highlighted, you can turn its settings on or off by clicking on it. When a check box is turned on, an X shows in the square.

If the text is followed by ellipses, choosing the check box opens a dialog box. When you complete the dialog box and choose OK, the check box shows an X. More than one box can be checked at one time.

1-7 A check box control.

Text box A *text box* is an area where you can enter text. Point to the text area with the mouse or tab to it using the keyboard, and then enter text. Figure 1-8 shows a text box.

text goes here

1-8 A text box.

Pop-up control A *pop-up control* is a rectangle with an underlined arrow to the side. A pop-up contains a list of options from which one option can be selected. Pop-ups are similar to a scrolling list, but only the selected option is displayed. Figure 1-9 shows a pop-up control. To select an item in the pop-up using the mouse, click on the pop-up and drag the highlight bar to the desired item and release the mouse.

If you are using a keyboard, use the Tab key to select the pop-up control. Once selected, press the Spacebar or use Alt-↑ or Alt-↓ to open the pop-up list. Use the ↑ and ↓ keys to highlight the desired item and press the spacebar. You can also use PgUp and PgDn to scroll a long list of pop-up items. The Home and End keys take you to the top and bottom of the list. Items in the list can also be found with the keyboard by entering the first few characters of the item you want.

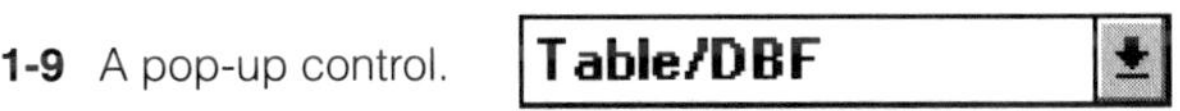

1-9 A pop-up control.

Spinner control A *spinner control* is a numeric incrementer that contains a numeric value along with an up and down value control. Figure 1-10 shows a spinner control. To change the value of a spinner, click on the ↑ to increment the value, or the ↓ to decrement the value.

You can also select the text box that contains the numeric value and enter a new value using the keyboard. Use the ↑ and ↓ keys to change the value.

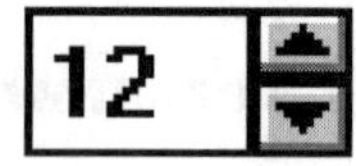

1-10 A spinner control.

Alerts

If you ask FoxPro to do something impossible, or if you start to do something that will overwrite existing information, an alert box appears to warn you or tell you of your error. You can remove the alert from the screen by clicking the mouse button or by pressing any key with the exceptions of the function keys and the Ctrl, Shift, or Alt keys. Some alerts will also require you to make a choice, such as OK or Cancel. You can't ignore these; you must make an appropriate selection to continue.

Text editing in the Interface

You can edit text in FoxPro's Browse and Edit windows, data entry screens, Program, Text, Memo, Report and Screen Layout windows, and in dialog boxes. Some text editing procedures can be accomplished from the Edit menu (i.e., Cut, Copy, Paste, Select All), and others use cursor movement keys.

When editing program, text, and memo fields a Text menu pad will appear on the FoxPro system menu. The options available in the Text menu can be used to further customize the appearance of the text. See The Text menu later in this section for more information on the Text menu.

Cursor movement

To edit text, you must place the cursor where you want to make changes. The cursor appears as a flashing vertical bar. The Insert key toggles between Insert and Overwrite modes and status of the Insert key is displayed in the status bar. When you type a character in Insert mode ("Ins" is displayed in the status bar), it appears at the cursor position, and existing text is moved one character to the right. When you type text in Overwrite mode, existing text is replaced by your entry.

With the keyboard, use any of the movement keys described as follows:

Key	Moves cursor
→/←	One character to the right/left.
↑/↓	Up/down one line.

PgUp/PgDn	Up/down one window of text.
Home/End	To the beginning/end of the current line.
Ctrl-→/←	One word to the right/left.
Ctrl-Home/End	To beginning/end of text.

With a mouse, you can position the editing cursor by pointing and clicking or by scrolling using the scroll bars at the right and bottom edges of the window. To use the scroll bars, click on the appropriate arrow or drag the thumb to scroll quickly. Then point and click on the cursor position you want. When the cursor is in the desired position, type the text you want to enter. When editing text, FoxPro automatically wraps words at the end of each line. Press Enter to start a new paragraph.

Selecting text

When you want to move or copy blocks of text, you must first select the text. Place the cursor at the beginning of the text you want to select. The keystrokes for selecting are listed here. They are the same keystrokes for cursor movement, with the Shift key added. To use the selection keystrokes, press and hold each necessary key until the final key is pressed. For instance, to select a word, hold down Shift, press and hold Ctrl, and press the appropriate arrow:

Keys	Selects
Shift-←/→	One character at a time.
Shift-↑/↓	One line at a time.
Shift-Ctrl-←/→	From the cursor to the beginning/end of the word.
Shift-Ctrl-Home/End	From the cursor to the beginning/end of the text.
Ctrl-A	All text.

To deselect text, press any cursor movement key. You can also select and deselect text quite easily with the mouse. Just place the cursor on the appropriate line and then:

Mouse action	Selects
Double-click	A word.
Triple-click	A line.
Double-click, drag	Word by word.
Triple-click, drag	Line by line.
Reposition cursor, Shift click	All text from original cursor location to Shift-click location.

To deselect text with the mouse, drag back over selected text before you release the mouse button. After releasing the mouse button, Shift-click at the position in the text where you want the selection to end. Deselect all selected text by placing the pointer outside the selected text and clicking.

FoxPro also utilizes the Windows "drag-and-drop" capabilities which let you select text, drag the selection to a new location, and drop the selection into place. To use drag-and-drop first select a block of text. Then position the mouse pointer over any section of the selected text and click the mouse; the mouse pointer now has a small box at the bottom. Drag the pointer to another location and release the mouse.

Deleting text

You can delete text with three keys. Press the backspace key to delete the character immediately to the left of the cursor. If text is selected, backspace will delete the entire selection. Ctrl-backspace deletes the word in which the cursor is positioned. When the cursor is in a blank space following a word, Ctrl-backspace deletes the space and the word. The Delete key will erase the character immediately to the right of the cursor position. If text is selected, Delete will erase the selection.

The Text Menu

The Text Menu is available when the cursor is in a text or memo editing window, and it contains the following options:

Font... Displays the Windows Font dialog. The Font dialog is common among many Windows applications and is used to select a font, font style and size. Refer to your Windows documentation for more information on changing a font.

Enlarge font Enlarges the font size for all text in the current window to the next point size. The ability to enlarge a font depends upon the font being used.

Reduce font Reduces the font size for all text in the current window file to a lower point size. The ability to reduce a font depends upon the font being used.

Single space Changes the line spacing for all text in the current window to single spacing.

1½ space Changes the line spacing for all text in the current window to one and one-half spacing.

Double space Changes the line spacing for all text in the current window to double spacing.

Indent Indents all selected text to the next tab stop.

Undent Moves all selected text that is indented back to the previous tab stop.

Spelling... Activates the FoxPro spell checker dialog, which can be used to spell check text files and memo fields.

The FoxPro menu system

Now that you know how to get around FoxPro's User Interface, you are ready to begin executing actions. This section covers each menu separately, starting with the menu you are most likely to use first, and continuing in this order:

- File menu
- Window menu
- Database menu
- Edit menu
- Record menu
- Program menu
- Help menu
- Run menu

The beginning of each menu section has a short tutorial designed to help you get a feel for the uses of the menu options. Following that, each menu option is defined in the order that it appears on the menu.

The File menu

The options on the File menu (see Fig. 1-11) let you create, save, open, close, and print your files. For practice, create a new file to keep track of the campers attending the Sierra Sylvestri Summer Camp.

New...
Open...
Close
Save
Save As...
Revert
Print Setup...
Print...
Exit

1-11 The File menu.

First, open a new file. Choose New from the File menu by either pressing Alt-F and then Enter, or pointing to the File menu and clicking on the New option. You should see that the Table/DBF radio button is selected. Choose OK to open a new database file. A structure box will appear. Describe the fields you want to include in your database with the following steps:

1. Type `fname` in the text box and press Tab.
2. Press Tab again to accept the Character description.
3. Type `12` in the Width column and press Tab.
4. Type `lname`, press Tab twice, enter 12 as the width, and press Tab.
5. Type `City` and press Tab twice.
6. Enter `12` and press Tab.
7. Type `Age` and Tab once.
8. Press the spacebar in the Type column. Select Numeric from the pop up to indicate your entries in this field must be numeric.
9. Enter `2` in the Width column.
10. Type `Camp`, press Tab twice, and enter `17` in the Width column. Choose OK, and a Save As dialog box appears. Type `Campers` in the text box and choose Save.

Now you have a named database with five fields, but there are no records in it. Select Yes at the "Input data records now" message box to display an append screen in which you can enter records into the Campers database. You can see your field names on the left side of the browse screen. Enter five names into the database, as shown in Fig. 1-12. Notice that it is not necessary to press Enter in the Age field because FoxPro automatically moves the cursor to the next field when the current field is filled.

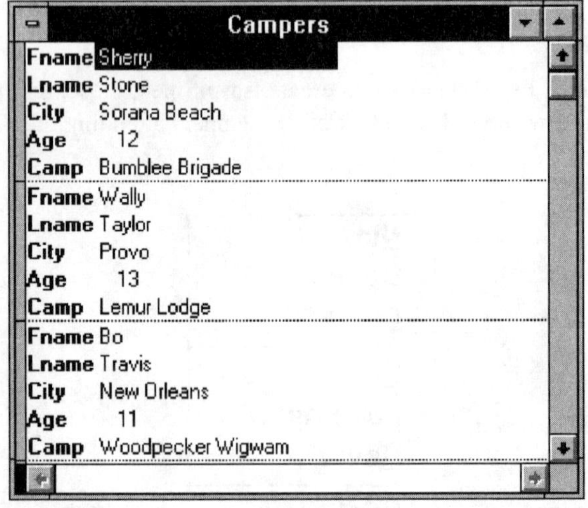

1-12 New database with records entered.

Close the append window by choosing File Close. This does not actually close the Campers file; try opening it and see what happens:

1. Choose File Open.
2. Select Campers from the menu.

As you can see, FoxPro will not allow you to select the Campers file. That is because it is already open. If you want to see the records again, you can choose Browse from the Database menu, or Append from the Record menu, or a number of other options that will display the contents of the Campers file. Because the Campers file is already open, you will not need to indicate the file name every time you want to perform an action.

To close the Campers file, choose View from the Window menu and select the Close push button or, if you are finished working in FoxPro, choose Quit from the File menu. Each option in the File menu is described in the following sections.

File New...

File New lets you create a new file in FoxPro. As shown in Fig. 1-13, selecting it opens a dialog box with a list of radio buttons. Choose Cancel to exit the dialog box without creating a new file. Choose OK after you have selected a file type that you want to create.

File New Table/DBF

When you choose the Table/DBF radio button in the New File dialog box, an empty Structure dialog appears. You define the fields you want to include in your database in four columns in the text box. Type the name of the first field under the Name heading. When

1-13 New File dialog box.

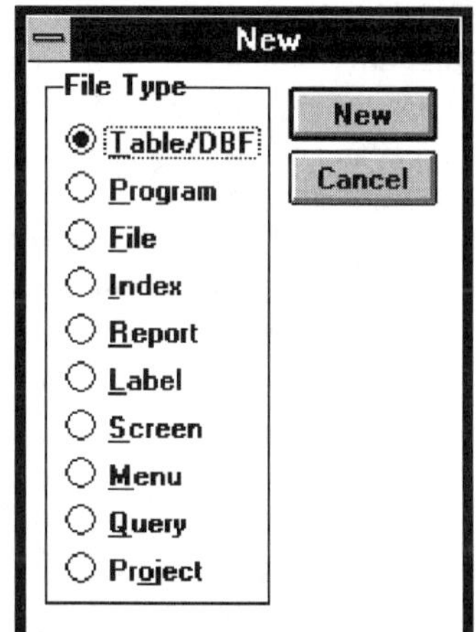

you press Enter, the default field type and width will appear. Tab to the Type column to select a field type from the pop-up. Type options are:

Type	**Specifications**	**Width restrictions**
Character	Any type of data	Up to 254
Numeric	Numeric data only	Up to 20, including the ± sign and decimal
Float	Scientific data	Up to 20, including the ± sign and decimal
Date	Dates only	8
Logical	Accepts T or F	1
Memo	Any type of data	Expands to accept data entered; limited only by disk space
General	Windows OLE objects	Expands to accept data entered; limited only by disk space

Enter the width and decimal places, if applicable. Figure 1-14 shows the CAMPERS .DBF file structure.

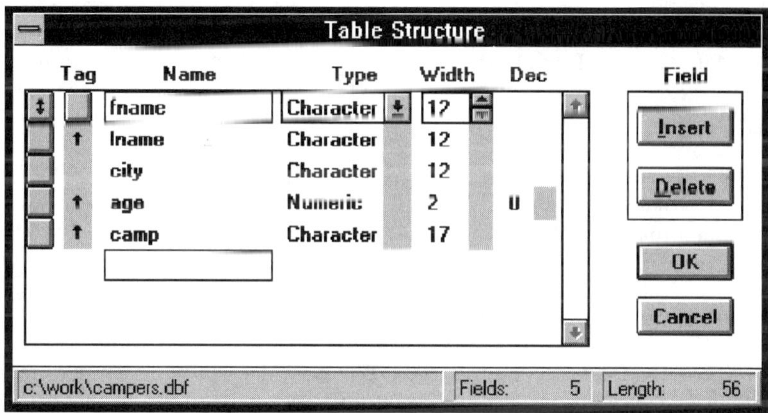

1-14 Structure dialog box for Campers.dbf.

You can insert and delete fields in the database structure. To insert a field, place the cursor on the field above which you want to add a new field. Choose the Insert push button. A field named Newfield appears with a character type and a width of 10. Type the field name, select the type, and enter the width you want for the field. To delete a field, select it and choose the Delete push button.

You can also change the order of the fields in the database. Using the mouse, position the cursor over the double-headed arrow button to the left of the current field. Click and drag the field to its new position. With the keyboard, Tab until the field you want to move is highlighted. Press Ctrl-↑ to move the field up and Ctrl-↓ to move the field down. Press Enter to fix the field in place.

While you are defining or modifying a database structure, you can also create a structural compound index file for the database. Indexes are used to control the viewing and reporting order of a database, and for quickly locating certain records. The Tag column to the immediate left of each field name is used to create an index "tag" for that field.

To create an index, Tab until the Tag box is highlighted. Press the spacebar and a ↑ appears; an ascending index has just been created for that field. Press the spacebar again and a ↓ appears; a descending index has been created. Pressing the spacebar a third time removes the index reference for that particular field. If you are using a mouse, position the mouse pointer over the Tag box and click. Each double click of the mouse performs the same action of the spacebar description above. See the File New Index discussion in this chapter for more information on indexes.

When you are finished defining the database structure, choose OK, and a Save As dialog box will appear. Type the new name of the database in the text box and choose Save. A message box appears, asking if you want to input data records now. Choose No to return to the Interface screen. If you choose Yes, an Append screen appears. You can also access this screen by choosing Append from the Record menu or Browse from the Database menu. To append records, type data in the appropriate fields, and press Enter to move to the next field. A blank record is always added to the existing list of records.

When you append records, a Browse menu is added to the menu bar. The options on this menu let you view your database in different formats and edit your records. See the section on The Browse menu in this chapter for further information on browsing records. See chapter 12, Using DDE and OLE in FoxPro, for more information on placing data in a general field.

See also Database Browse, File Save As, Record Append, File New Index, The Browse menu, Using DDE and OLE in FoxPro

File New Program

When you choose the Program radio button in the File New dialog box, an empty program editing window titled Untitled.prg is opened. Enter your program in the window and save the file. It will automatically be given a .PRG file extension. See chapter 5 for information on programming.

File New File

When you choose the File radio button to the File New display box an empty text editing window named Untitled is opened. Enter any text in the window and then save the file and close the window. No extension is assigned to the file name unless you specify one.

File New Index

The Index radio button is enabled only if a database is open in the active work area. Indexing (see Fig. 1-15) allows you to set the viewing or reporting order of records in the active database (you can activate one of several open databases in the View window).

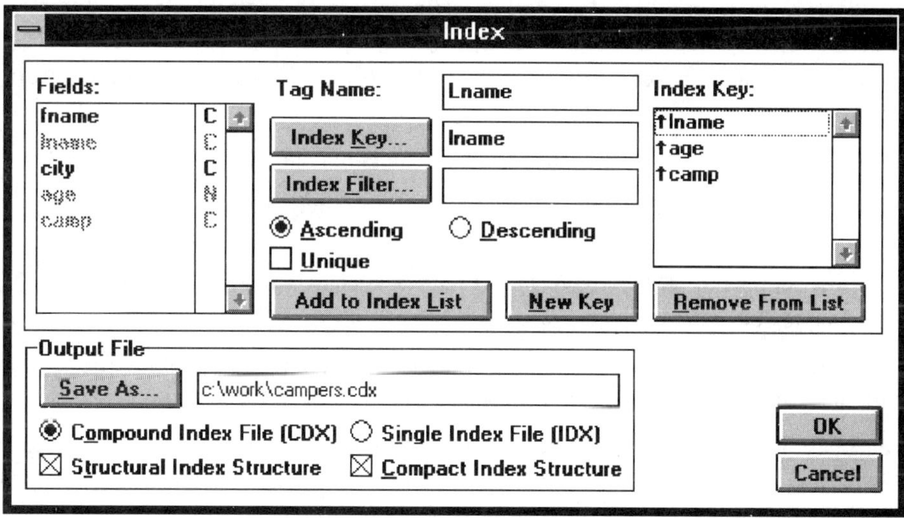

1-15 Index dialog box.

When you select the Index radio button, the Index dialog box is displayed, which allows you to create indexes for the current database. Two types of indexes can be created. Compound index files (.CDX) contain multiple index orders (for instance, last name order, zip order, and Camp name order) and if the compound index is structural (the index file has the same name as the database file), the index is opened when the database file is opened. Single index files (.IDX) contain one index order (for instance last name) and must be explicitly opened with the USE or SET INDEX commands. The following options are presented when creating new indexes:

Fields Displays a scrolling list of fields in the current database file available for indexing. All fields, other than Memo and General type, can be indexed.

Tag Name Specifies the index tag name of the index. When building a compound index (.CDX), each index expression is given a tag to reference the index key by. This option is only available when building compound indexes.

Index Key... Displays the Expression Builder dialog, which allows you to create an index using a valid FoxPro expression. You can also enter the expression in the text box. The Expression Builder is detailed after this section.

Index Filter... Displays the Expression Builder, which allows you to build a valid FoxPro expression limiting the records included in the index to only those records that match the expression. You can also enter the expression in the text box. The Expression Builder is detailed after this section.

Ascending/Descending This radio button allows you to select the order in which the records appears. Ascending is top to bottom and descending is bottom to top. By default all indexes are created in ascending order. If you initially create an index as ascending or descending, it is not necessary to rebuild the index if you want the order reversed. The SET ORDER command supports an ASCENDING|DESCENDING argument, which automatically reverses the index order. This option is only available when creating compound indexes (.CDX).

Unique Check this option if you want the index to only include the first record of all records that have identical values in the index key.

Add to Index List Moves the index expression and tag name to the Index Key list.

New Key Resets the Tag Name, Index Key, Index Filter, Ascending/Descending, and Unique options for building a new index tag.

Remove from List Removes the selected index expression from the Index Key list, allowing you to delete the index tag, or modify the index expression.

CDX/IDX This radio button allows you to choose between a single index file, or compound index file. The CDX option is checked by default when creating a new index.

Structural When checked the compound index file is created with the same name as the database file, with a .CDX extension. This option is checked by default and is only available when creating a compound index file.

Compact When checked, creates a compact index file. This option can only be changed when creating a single index file. All compound index files are compact by default.

Save as... Displays the Save As dialog, allowing you to select the name of the new index file. This option is only available when creating a single index file, or compound index file that is not structural.

Index Key list Displays a scrolling list of indexes for the current database file.

Creating an index is very simple. To select a field to index, move to the Fields list and select the field to index on. Selecting the field fills in the Index Key and Tag Name text boxes with the field name. If this is the desired index expression, select the Add to Index List button to move the index tag to the Index Key list. To index on a valid FoxPro expression other than the base field name, select the Index Key... push button to activate the Expression Builder, or simply type in the expression in the text box. When your index is complete, select the OK button to save the index and all changes that were made.

If you are using FoxPro version 2.5a or above along with other versions of FoxPro 1.x or FoxBase, you should use the noncompact single index file for compatibility. Otherwise, use compound index files when creating indexes.

See also Database Setup, The Expression Builder, USE, SET INDEX, SET ORDER

The Expression Builder

The Expression Builder lets you build expressions that FoxPro uses to complete certain commands and to execute specific actions. Some expressions are simple: a field name is an expression when it is used to indicate the index key. Complex expressions combine a number of variables to express a command. They might include combinations of field names, memory variables, constants, functions, and operators. The expressions you build when you choose the For... and While... push buttons of certain dialogs will often be somewhat complex.

The Expression Builder makes it easy for you to build these complex expressions. When you need an expression, you can type it in the text box and choose Verify to make sure it is a valid expression. Then you can choose OK. But if you are not sure how each of the elements of the expression must be entered, you can use the available controls to help you build the expression.

The String, Math, Logical, and Date options each contain pop-up lists of functions available for use in building expressions. (See chapter 2, FoxPro Commands, and chapter 4, FoxPro Functions, for descriptions of commands and functions.) When you choose an item from one of these pop-ups, it is entered in the expression box along with its type of parameter, which is selected. For example, if you wanted to index the campers in the Campers database, but you only wanted to include those campers over the age of 11, you would need a For... expression indicating the field name in which age appears, a logical operator, and the comparison value. These elements, Age, and 11, are shown in the example in Fig. 1-16.

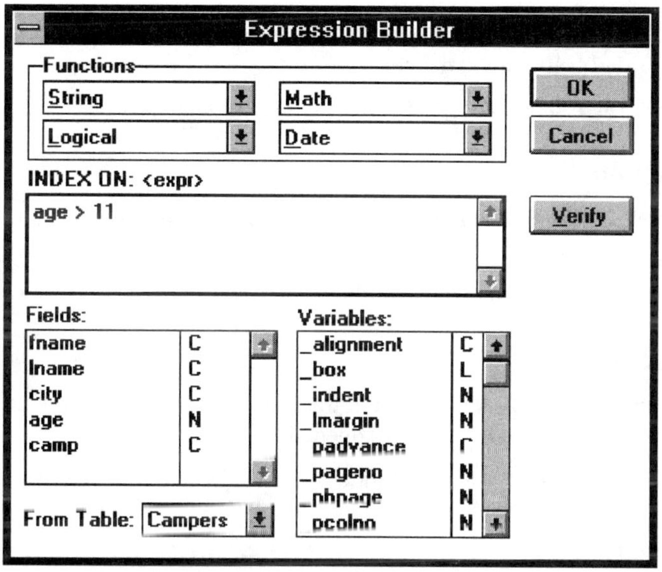

1-16 The Expression Builder.

When you enter an item in the Expression box, whether by typing or by selecting it from a pop-up, you can use standard editing techniques to edit the expression. You can combine selecting items from list boxes and pop-ups with typing the data you need.

The Field list contains the field names of the current database. The Variables list contains all memory variables that have been defined before the Expression Builder dialog was activated. When you choose a variable from the list, it is added to the expression in the expression box. Variables are usually used when you are programming in FoxPro.

The From Table pop-up shows the database that's currently selected. If more than one database is open, you can use the From Table pop-up to select fields from other databases for use in the expression.

Choose Verify when you have completed entering your expression and you want to verify that it is a valid FoxPro expression. If the expression is not valid, FoxPro will display a message. Press any key or click the mouse to remove the message. Choose OK to save your changes and return to the previous dialog box.

Finally, the options available in each pop-up, along with the variables in the Variables list, can be controlled by changing the Expression Builder preferences from the Preferences option of the Edit menu.

See also GETEXPR, Edit Preferences

File New Report

When you choose the Report radio button in the File New dialog box, an empty report form layout window titled Untitled.frx is opened.

See also Chapter 9, Using the Report Writer and Label Designer

File New Label

When you choose the Label radio button in the File New dialog box, an empty label form layout window titled Untitled.lbx is opened.

See also Chapter 9, Using the Report Writer and Label Designer

File New Screen

When you choose the Screen radio button in the File New dialog box, an empty screen design layout window titled Untitled.scx is opened.

See also Chapter 6, Using the Screen Builder

File New Menu

When you choose the Menu radio button in the File New dialog box, an empty menu design layout window titled Untitled.mnx is opened.

See also Chapter 7, Using the Menu Builder

File New Query

When you choose the Query radio button in the File New dialog box, an empty RQBE editing window titled Untitled.qpr is opened.

See also Chapter 8, Using the RQBE window

File New Project

When you choose the Project radio button in the File New dialog box, an empty project design layout window titled Untitled.pjx is opened.

See also Chapter 10, Using the Project Manager

File Open...

When you choose File Open, the dialog box shown in Fig. 1-17 displays a list of files or directories along with other options. The first time you choose File Open, the current default drive and directory appear in their pop-ups. All files or directories under the displayed parent directory are listed in the scrollable list box. If you change the drive or directory, the change will remain current throughout this FoxPro session unless you change it.

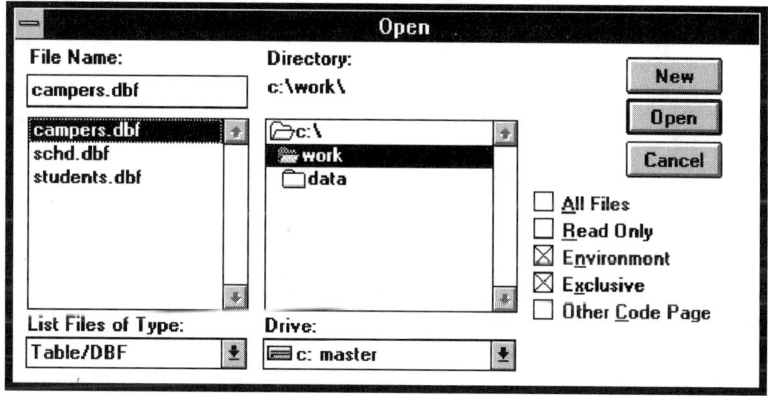

1-17 File Open dialog box.

Change drives by opening the pop-up and selecting a new drive. Change parent directories by selecting from the directory list. To change subdirectories, choose the subdirectory in the scrollable list box. The subdirectory name appears in the directory pop-up, and all the files in that directory appear in the list box.

The files in the list box all contain the file extension for the file type displayed in the type box. For example, when Table/DBF is selected in Type, all files listed show the .DBF extension. To change file types, open the Type pop-up. Selecting each file type generates a different kind of action.

Table/DBF Displays all files with a .DBF extension. A database file is opened in the current work area. If a database is already open in the current work area, it is closed before the new database is opened.

Program Displays all files with an extension of .PRG, .SPR, .MPR, or .QPR. A program source file is opened in a text editing window.

File Displays all files with no extension, or a .TXT extension. A text file is opened in a text editing window.

Index Displays all files with an extension of .CDX or .IDX. This option is enabled only if there is a database open in the current work area.

Report Displays all files with an .FRX or .FRM extension. A report file is opened in a Report layout window. See the Using the Report Writer and Label Designer chapter (chapter 9) for editing reports.

Label Displays all files with an .LBX or .LBL extension. A label file is opened in a Label layout window. See the Using the Report Writer and Label Designer chapter (chapter 9) for editing labels.

Screen Displays all files with an .SCX extension. A screen file is opened in a Screen builder window. See the Using the Screen Builder (chapter 6) chapter for editing screens.

Menu Displays all files with an .MNX extension. A menu file is opened in a Menu builder window. See the Using the Menu Builder chapter (chapter 7) for editing menus.

Query Displays all files with a .QPR extension. A query file is opened in the RQBE builder window. See the Using the RQBE window chapter (chapter 8) for editing queries.

Project Displays all files with a .PJX extension. A project file is opened in a Project builder window. See the Using the Project Manager chapter (chapter 10) for editing projects.

View Displays all files with a .VUE, .LBV, or .FRV extension. A .VUE file contains a FoxPro environment setting. Opening a view file causes all open databases and indexes to be closed and the environment contained in the view file is restored.

If you want to see all the files in the current directory, regardless of type, check the All Files check box. Attempting to open an incorrect file type will cause an error.

To open a database, program or text file as read-only, check the Read Only check box. This allows the file to be opened and viewed, but not changed. The Environment check box is available when opening a Screen, Report or Label file. Opening a Screen, Report or Label file when Environment is checked will restore any environment setting saved with the file. Deselecting the Environment option is equivalent to using the NOENVIRONMENT clause with the appropriate MODIFY SCREEN, MODIFY REPORT, or MODIFY LABEL commands.

When opening a database, use the Exclusive check box to open a database file exclusively. Selecting the Exclusive check box option is equivalent to using the EXCLUSIVE clause with the USE command, while deselecting the Exclusive check box is equivalent to using the SHARE clause with the USE command. The Other Code Page check box is discussed in chapter 11, Cross-platform and international capabilities.

Once you have selected the appropriate file type, choose the file you want from the list box and choose Open. To create a new file, choose New. This dialog box is described under File New. To exit the dialog box without opening a file, choose Cancel.

See also File New, Window View

File Close

Choose this option to close the active window. This does not necessarily close the file associated with the window, as in the case of the View window. When you use File Close to close the View window, the files listed in the work area list remain open. You can close all active windows by holding down the Shift key when activating the File menu pad. This causes the File Close option to change to File Close All. Mouse users can also close a window by clicking on the close box in the upper left corner of the window.

See also Window View

File Save

This option saves any changes you have made to items in the active window (not any open windows behind it). The document remains open. If the active document has not been named or is a new file, the Save As dialog box appears when you select Save. Save is disabled if you have made no changes since the document was last saved or when a window other than an editing window is frontmost (e.g., Browse, Command).

See also File Save As

File Save As...

In the Save As dialog box in Fig. 1-18, you can name and save a new file, or rename and save a current file under the new name. To name a new file, type the name in the text box and select Save. If the file has already been named, that name will show in the text box. If this is the first time the file has been saved, its new name appears at the top of the window and the file is saved. If you are renaming an existing file, that file is closed and the new title appears at the top of the new window. If you have made changes since you last saved the old file, those changes appear in the new file, but not in the old one.

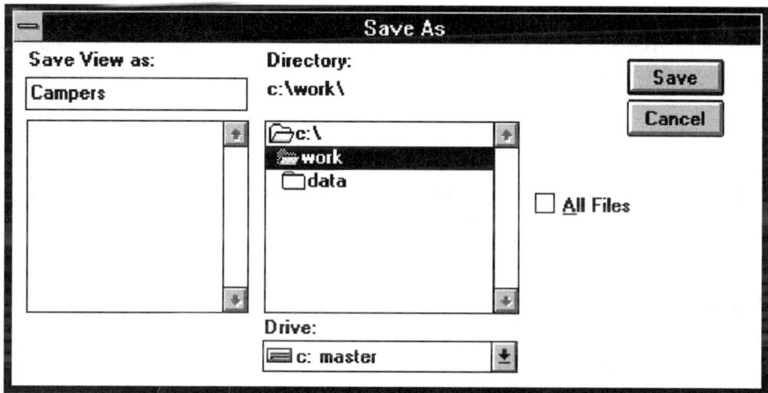

1-18 File Save As dialog box.

If you are saving a text file, you must provide the appropriate extension (i.e., .TXT) if you want it included in the file name. Program files are automatically assigned a .PRG extension. If you choose Save As... when the View window is active, you can save the current environment as a .VUE file. This file contains settings such as names of all files in use, relations that have been established, etc. To exit the Save As... dialog box without saving or renaming a file, choose Cancel or press Esc.

See also File Open, Window View

File Revert

If you have made changes to the currently displayed memo field or text, program, report, label, or screen file since it was last saved, you can choose Revert to discard those changes and revert to the last saved version of the file.

Before it replaces the current version, FoxPro asks if you want to discard the changes. If you choose Yes, the document reverts to the old version; if you choose No, the current changes remain on screen.

File Print Setup...

Activates the Windows Print Setup dialog, which lets you control where printed output goes and how the output is formatted. The options presented in this dialog will differ among certain printers. Consult your printer manual and Windows documentation for more information.

File Print

You can print the contents of a window or file using the Print option. The Print dialog box contains a pop-up from which you can select the contents of the clipboard, the Command window, any open editing window, or the currently defined user window.

To print a file that is currently unopened, choose the File... push button and select the file to be printed. When the Line Numbers box is enabled, checking it will automatically add line numbers to the output. Selecting Page Eject Before will cause a blank page to be ejected from the printer before the selected file is printed. Selecting Page Eject After will force the last page to be ejected from the printer automatically. Choose OK to print your selection, or Cancel to exit without printing.

File Exit

The Exit option ends your FoxPro session and returns you to the Program Manager, or the last active Windows application.

The Window menu

The Window menu (see Fig. 1-19) lets you activate, hide, and cycle among FoxPro and user-defined windows. It can also be used to activate the FoxPro Command and View windows. Each FoxPro system window, for example the Command and View windows, has a control menu of its own. See the section on Controlling Windows in this chapter for more information on moving, sizing and closing windows.

If you have more than one window open on the screen, you can size the windows so they all fit on the screen. This may not work very well if you have several windows. Another way to work with many windows open is to put one behind the other. Try this with the View window.

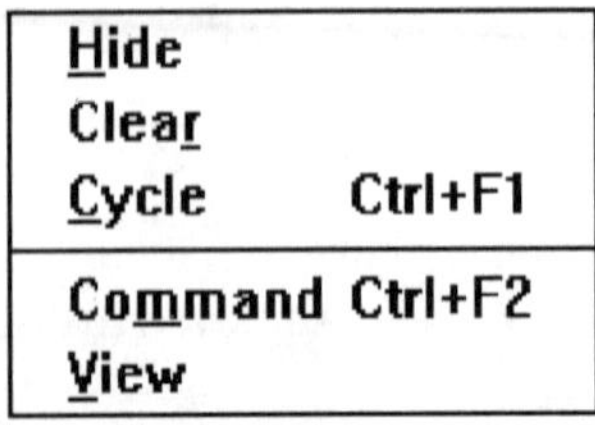

1-19 The Window menu.

First, open the View window. Open the Window menu and select View. The View window opens in front of the Command window. Because the Command window keeps track of all your operations, you might want to have a look at the commands you have executed. To do this, activate the Command window by pressing Ctrl-F2 (the hot key). Now the Command window is in front of the View window.

Another way to change windows is to use the Cycle option. When you choose Cycle, the current window moves to the back and the next window is visible. This is handy when you have several windows on the screen because you can save opening the menu to select each window—just press Ctrl-F1 to see the next window. The remaining Window options, in addition to the ones just covered, are described in detail in the following sections.

Window Hide

You can hide a window if you want to remove it from view without closing or deactivating it. A hidden window continues to be listed at the bottom of the Window menu.

When you select Hide from the Window menu, the active window is hidden from view. If you have more than one window open, you can hide them all by pressing the Shift key when you choose the Window menu. This replaces the Hide option with Hide All. Use the Show All option to unhide the windows. To unhide a single window, choose the name of the window from the Window menu. System windows such as View and Command are always listed as options on the Window menu.

Window Clear

Use Clear to remove all text and graphics from the current output window. For example, selecting Clear from the Window menu immediately after starting FoxPro clears the desktop of the sign-on logo. You can also clear the current output window by issuing the CLEAR command.

Use the Edit menu Clear option to remove selected text and objects from an editing window.

See also Edit Clear, CLEAR

Window Cycle

Use Cycle when you want to cycle through your open windows. Each time you choose Cycle, the front window moves to the back and the following window becomes active and visible. Windows cycle in the order they were opened. You can also cycle through windows using the Next Window option from a window's control menu.

Shortcut key: Ctrl-F1 from the Window menu
Ctrl-F6 from the window control menu

Window Command

Select Command to activate the FoxPro Command window. The Command window is used to enter FoxPro commands interactively and also displays all the actions generated when you make menu selections in the interface.

Some commands that you enter into the Command window may cause the window to scroll horizontally due to the length of the command. If you want to keep a lengthy command inside the viewable portion of the Command window, simply enter a portion of the command, followed by a semicolon (;), and press the Enter key. Continue the rest of the command on the next line. When the entire command has been entered, press Enter to execute the command.

Scroll the Command window to see previously executed actions. You can re-execute an action by moving the cursor to the desired line and pressing Enter. Previously entered commands can also be edited before they are executed.

Shortcut key: Ctrl-F2

See also Window Hide

Window View

The View window allows you to control many aspects of the FoxPro environment without a need for programming. You can open database files, set indexes and relations, and change the value of many environment controls. To open the View window shown in Fig. 1-20, select View from the Window menu. The scrolling list on the left is used to open and select database files, and the scrolling list on the right displays relational links between database files.

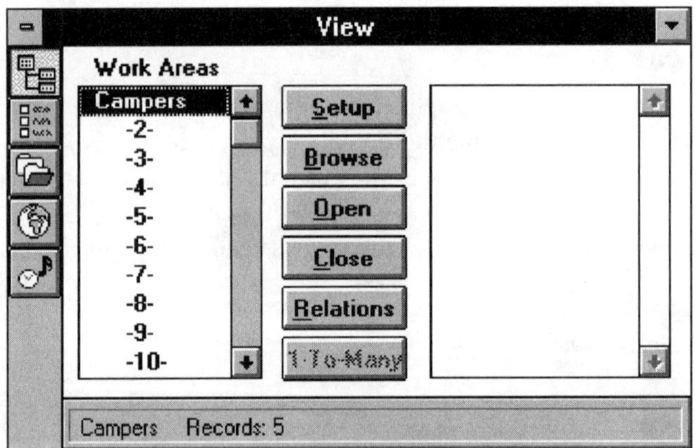

1-20 View window.

Situated between the two scrolling lists are six push buttons that are used to control the FoxPro environment, open, edit, and close database files, and set relations between database files. The five graphical push buttons in the upper left corner of the View window are used to control the FoxPro environment and are described below.

View This button is used to return to the main view window. When you are in one of the panels called up by On/Off, Files, or Misc., selecting View closes the current panel and displays the View window.

On/Off The On/Off panel (see Fig. 1-21) contains 21 check boxes with setting controls for FoxPro. When you check a box, the option is ON, otherwise it is OFF. For example,

1-21 On/Off panel.

checking on HELP makes FoxPro Help available to you. Each of these settings has an associated SET ... ON/OFF command and are described in chapter 3.

Files The Files panel (see Fig. 1-22) allows you to change certain default settings. All of these controls have an associated SET ... ON/OFF|TO command and are described in chapter 3.

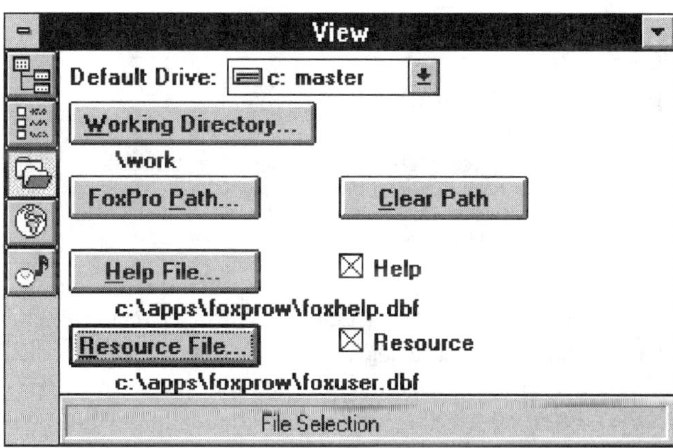

1-22 Files panel.

Default drive This pop-up displays the current default drive. Select the pop-up to see a list of available drives, and choose the one you want to use (see SET DEFAULT).

FoxPro path... Displays the Select Directory dialog, allowing you to specify a directory path for FoxPro to search through to find a file that is not in the default directory. Choose the drive, directory, and/or subdirectories from the pop-up and the scrollable list. The path you choose is displayed at the top of the box. When the path is correct, choose Select, and the path appears in the Files panel. Multiple paths can be selected by choosing this option a number of times. You can deactivate this path by choosing the Clear Path push button (see SET PATH).

Help file... Displays the Open File dialog, allowing you to specify the current help file to be displayed when you press F1 or choose Help from the Help menu. The default file is FOXHELP.DBF. Select the file you want from the list box and choose Open. To activate the selected help file, ensure the Help check box is checked. (see SET HELP).

Resource file... Displays the Open File dialog, allowing you to specify the resource file you want to use with FoxPro. This is a file that contains resource information such as window size and location, color sets, text file preference settings, etc. You can create additional resource files for different color schemes. Choose a file from the list box in the dialog box and choose Open. The resource file name appears in the files panel. To activate the selected resource file, ensure the Resource check box is checked. (see SET RESOURCE).

International The International panel (see Fig. 1-23) contains a variety of check and text boxes for determining certain international formats and values in FoxPro. All of these controls have an associated SET ... ON/OFF|TO command and are described in chapter 3.

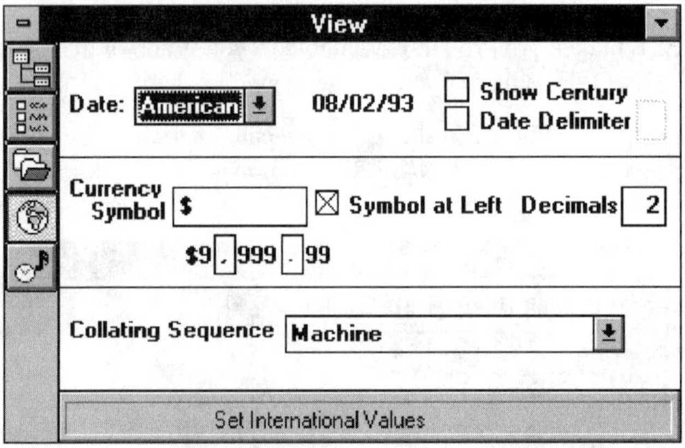

1-23 International panel.

Date The Date pop-up contains a list of date formats from which you can choose. When you select a new date format, the date to the right of the pop-up is displayed in that format, and all FoxPro date expressions are displayed in the selected format (see SET DATE).

Show Century When selected, causes FoxPro date expressions to be displayed with all four digits in the year (see SET CENTURY).

Date Delimiter Checking Date Delimiter allows you to change the standard date delimiter, which is a slash (/) (see SET MARK).

Currency Symbol For currency formats, indicate the number of places to follow the decimal point in the Decimals box. Type the symbol you want to use in the Symbol box, and check the Symbol at Left check box if you want the symbol to appear at the left of a currency value. A sample of your currency format is shown below the text boxes (see SET CENTURY).

Collation sequence A collation sequence is used in determining how supported international characters and languages are indexed and sorted. The Collation Sequence setting can only be changed if a CODEPAGE value is specified in the FoxPro configuration file, which is normally CONFIG.FPW. International indexing and sorting is discussed in the SET COLLATE section of chapter 3, FoxPro SET commands.

Misc The Misc panel (see Fig. 1-24) contains a variety of check and text boxes for determining certain formats and values in FoxPro. All of these controls have an associated SET ... ON/OFF|TO command and are described in chapter 3.

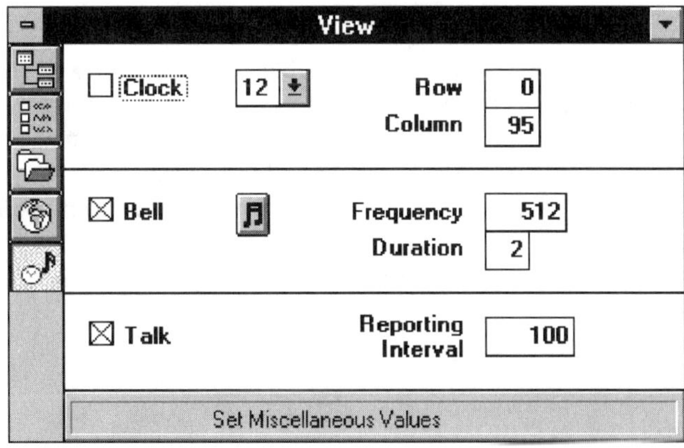

1-24 Misc panel.

Clock When selected, displays the system clock at the specified position. The 12/24 pop-up allows you to change between 12- and 24-hour display formats (see SET CLOCK).

Bell When checked, turns on and allows to adjust the tone of the computer's speaker. Select the musical note button to hear the bell you have set (see SET BELL).

Talk When checked, processing status information is displayed at regular intervals on your screen. The default Reporting Interval is 100, but you can specify an interval from 1 to 32,767 (see SET TALK).

The scrolling list at the left of the View window (see Fig. 1-20) is the work area list. A FoxPro database file is opened in a work area. FoxPro supports up to 225 work areas, which means you can have up to 225 database files open at any one time.

If you are using a keyboard, a work area can be selected by scrolling to the desired work area and pressing the Spacebar. This highlights the work area, flagging it as the active work area. Pressing Enter at the active work area displays the Open File dialog, allowing you to select a database file to open. If you are using a mouse, simply click on a work area to make it active, or double click to make it active and display the Open File dialog.

If you press Enter while at a work area in use, a Browse window will be displayed; otherwise the Open File dialog will appear, assuming you want to browse a database. The six push buttons in the middle of the View window are used to open and manipulate data base files.

Setup Displays the Setup dialog, allowing you to modify the database structure, add or modify indexes, and control field and filter settings. See Database Setup in this chapter for more information or setting up a database.

Browse Displays the records of the current database in a window, and adds a Browse option to the system menu. See Database Browse in this chapter for more information on browsing a database.

Open Displays the Open File dialog, allowing you to select a database file to open in the current work area. If you select a database and then OK, the file is opened in the current work area, and the name of the database is displayed in the work area list.

Close Closes the database in the selected work area and the work area designator is displayed in the work area list.

Relations FoxPro's relational powers let you relate any two databases that have a common field. A relation temporarily connects records so you can view all relevant information of related records at once. For example, Sierra Sylvestri Campers have scheduled activities for each day at the camp. Setting up a relation between the list of campers and the schedule of activities can save some scanning for a camper who wants to know what activity is scheduled for today.

To set relations, first open the controlling database in a free work area. This is the database to which another database will be related. The controlling database can be indexed or sorted in any order. In this example, CAMPERS.DBF is the controlling database, and it's indexed on the Lname (last name) field for the campers' convenience.

Next, open the related database in a free work area. Figure 1-25 shows, for example, the SCHD.DBF database with the activity schedule. The related database must be sorted or indexed on the common field that will be used to relate the two databases. Because the field they have in common is Camp, the SCHD.DBF database has an index on Camp, and it is active. Now select the CAMPERS database and choose the Relations push button. The file name CAMPERS appears in the Relations box with an arrow pointing to it. This indicates that it is the controlling database.

Select the related database, SCHD, and enter or select the field name Camp in the Expression Builder. Since this common field exists in both files, the expression box will default to Camp. Choose OK, and you will see an arrow point from the CAMPERS file name to the SCHD file name in the Relations box, as shown in Fig. 1-26. This shows the direction of the relation. You can continue relating databases in this manner, as long as you have common fields, and the related database is indexed or sorted on the related field.

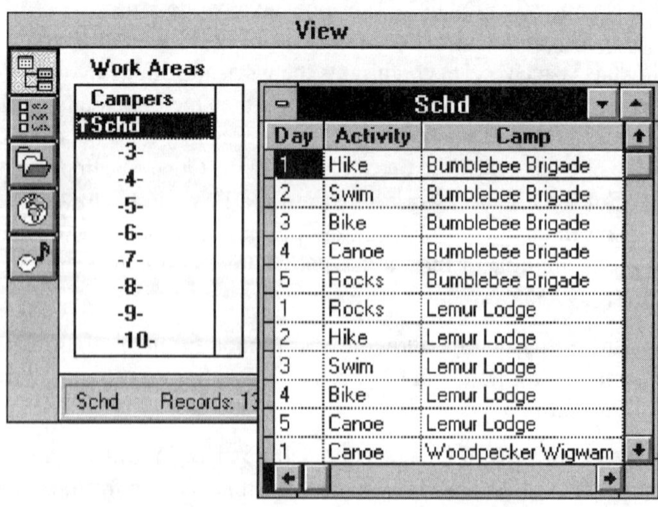

1-25 Schd.dbf database.

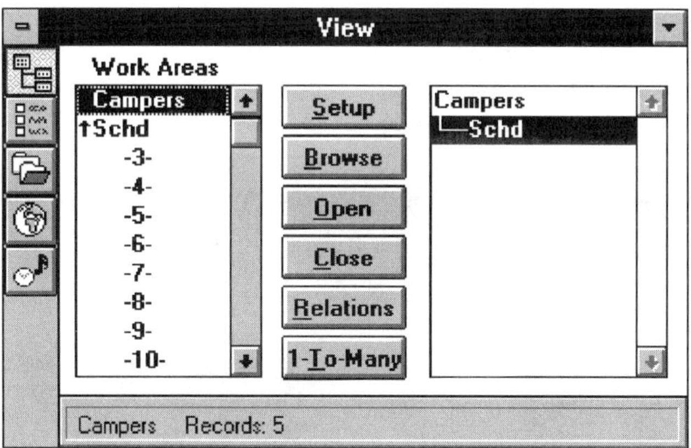

1-26 Relations set between Campers and Schd.

1-To-Many FoxPro allows you to set relation types of 1-to-1, 1-to-many, and many-to-1. All 3 types of relations can be set following the steps above. However the 1-to-many relation requires one more step. To create a 1-to-many relationship, follow the steps described above. Once the relation is set, select the 1-To-Many push button which displays the dialog shown in Fig. 1-27.

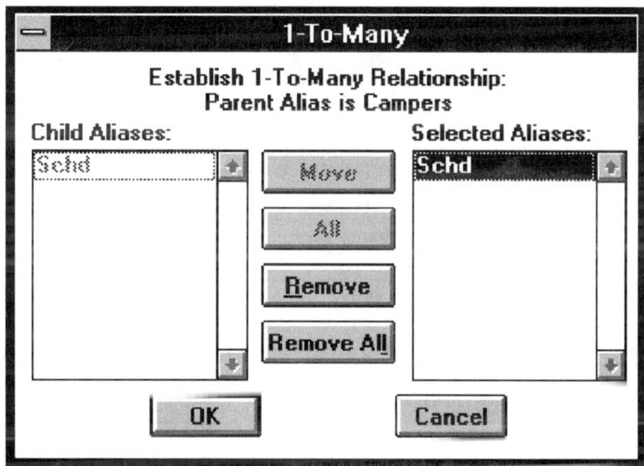

1-27 1-to-Many dialog.

The Child Aliases list on the left will contain the alias of all databases that are a target of the selected source database. Move the desired database(s) to the Selected Aliases list. Do this by highlighting the alias then activating the Move push button, or by double clicking on the alias name. You can remove databases from a 1-to-many relationship by selecting the alias from the Selected Aliases list and activating the Remove push button, or by double-clicking on the alias name.

To see how the relation works, browse the CAMPERS database. Suppose that it is day 1 and that camper Wally Taylor wants to know what he will be doing today. Select his name in the CAMPERS database. Now return to the View window and select the SCHD work area. Choose Browse. When the Browse window opens, the first record with Lemur Lodge, Wally's camp, is highlighted. According to the information in Fig. 1-28, Wally and the other Lodgers will be climbing rocks today.

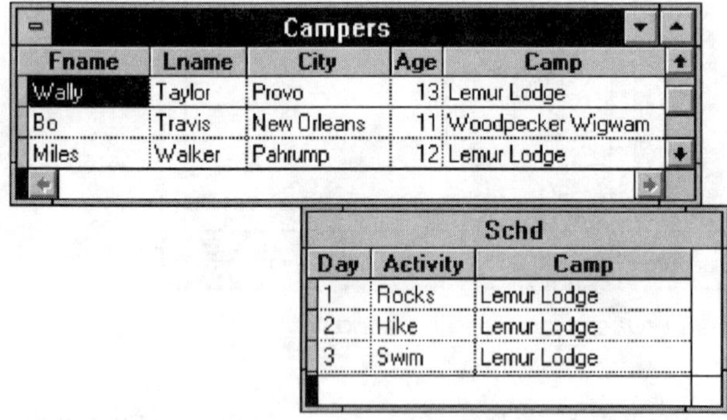

Campers

Fname	Lname	City	Age	Camp
Wally	Taylor	Provo	13	Lemur Lodge
Bo	Travis	New Orleans	11	Woodpecker Wigwam
Miles	Walker	Pahrump	12	Lemur Lodge

Schd

Day	Activity	Camp
1	Rocks	Lemur Lodge
2	Hike	Lemur Lodge
3	Swim	Lemur Lodge

1-28 Related records in related database.

If you want to change the *relational expression* (the field name that connects the databases), you can do so by selecting the related database and choosing a new field name. To remove relations, choose the related database in the Relations list. When the Expression Builder appears, erase the field name from the expression box and choose OK.

The Database menu

The Database menu (see Fig. 1-29) contains options that let you manipulate entire databases in a variety of ways.

Use the Campers database you created with the File menu to use some of the options on the Database menu. First, open the Campers database using File Open or the Open push button in the View window.

Now choose Setup from the Database menu. Use the Setup dialog box in Fig. 1-30 to create an index file for the Campers file:

1. Choose Add.
2. Select New in the Open dialog box.
3. In the Index dialog box, select Lname from the Fields list and then Add to Index List to create the index key.
4. Select the ( ) IDX radio button, as this will be an .IDX file.
5. Select Save As, change the index file name to LNAME.IDX, and choose OK.
6. Select OK from the Index dialog to create the index.

Now you can see the index name, Lname, in the Setup dialog. It has a key in front of it. This indicates it is the active index. Browse the database to see how the index works. See File New Index in this chapter for more information on creating indexes.

Choose Database Browse. The campers are listed in alphabetical order by their last names. Sorting a file is different from creating an index. Sorting creates a new data file and indexing creates an index file. Press Esc to close the Browse window and choose Sort (see Fig. 1-31) from the Database menu . Sort the Campers database on the Fname field.

1. Highlight the Fname field and press Enter. It appears in the Sort Order box.
2. Make sure the Ascending radio button is on.
3. Enter `Fname` in the Save As text box. Indexes and sort files do not have to be named with the same name as their index or sort expressions, but it's a good way to keep them straight. When you create indexes and sort files for several databases, you will want to use names that reflect both the original database and the index key, if possible.
4. Choose OK.

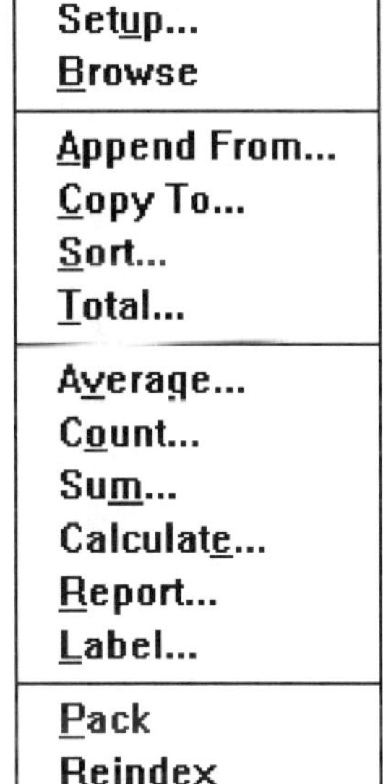

1-29 The Database menu

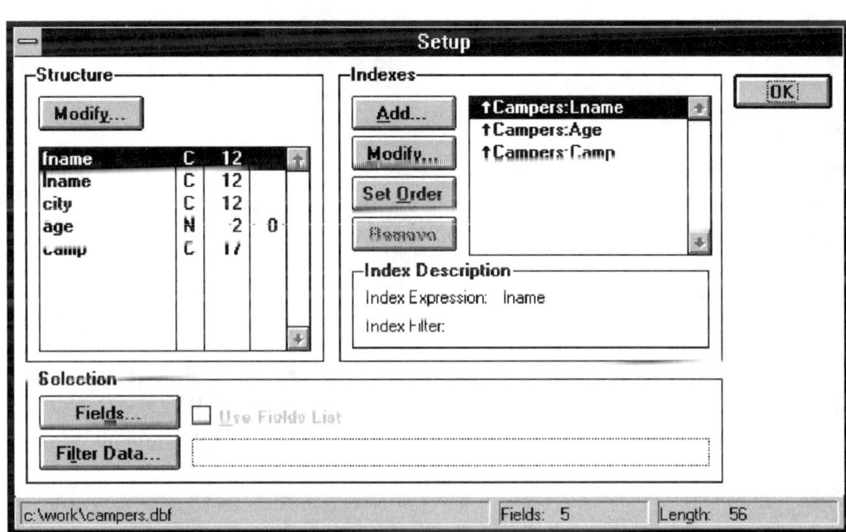

1-30 Database Setup dialog box.

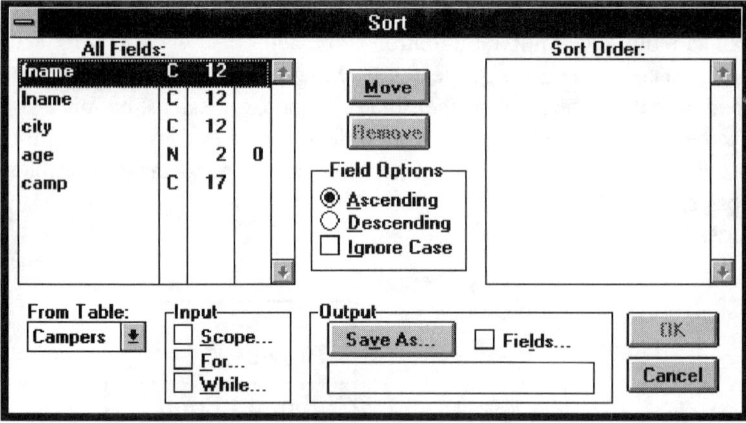

1-31 Sort dialog box.

If you were to browse the Campers database now, you would still see the names alphabetized by last name. That is because sorting creates a whole new file. To see the Campers file sorted, use File Open to open the Fname file. Notice that it has the .DBF file extension, just like a normal database. Now choose Browse from the Database menu. The campers are in order by first name. Find out the average age of the campers.

1. Choose Average from the Database menu.
2. Enter `Age` in the Expr text box.
3. Choose OK.

You will see the average age in the lower left corner of your screen. Now you are ready to find out more about the additional elements involved in Setup, Sort, and the other options on the Database menu.

See also File New, File Open, Window View

Database Setup...

Use this option to set up the current work area. If no database is in use when you choose Setup, the Open File dialog appears so you can select and open a database. Then the Setup dialog box, shown in Fig. 1-30, will appear.

Structure The Structure list box in the upper left portion of the dialog box lists the fields in the current database.

Modify If you want to change the structure of the database, choose the Modify push button, and the Modify Structure dialog box appears as shown in Fig. 1-14. See the File New Table/DBF section in this chapter for more information on modifying the database structure.

Indexes If there are any indexes currently open, they appear in the Indexes list. An index orders a database according to the index expression. There is no limit to the number of indexes a single database can have open at once.

Add... To open an existing index or create a new index file, choose the Add... push button. This brings up the Open dialog box, where you can select the index to open, or select New to create a new index. Once an index has been created or opened, the index name appears in the Indexes list box. You can continue to open indexes for the current database. The index with a key next to it designates the controlling index.

When you choose an index name in the Indexes list box, the index expression and filter appear in the index description below the list. See the File New Index section in this chapter for more information on creating indexes.

Modify... If you want to change the index key for an index, select that index in the Indexes list and then choose the Modify push button in the Index box. This calls up the Index dialog that you used when you created the index. Choose OK when you have made the modifications you want, and answer Yes if you want to save the changes permanently. See the File New Index section in this chapter for more information on modifying indexes.

Set Order If you have more than one index open for the current database, or a compound index file is open, the index (or tag) with the key next to its name in the Indexes box is the one determining the order of the records in the database. To use a different existing index to order your records, choose the index in the Indexes list and select Set Order. If you choose the index that is currently active, the Set Order push button changes to No Order. If you choose No Order, no indexes will be active.

Remove Open indexes appear in the Indexes box in the Setup dialog box. When you select an index in the list and choose Remove, the index name is removed from the list and closed. If the index being removed is a single index file the index is closed. If the index being removed is a tag from a compound index file, the tag is permanently removed from the index file.

Fields... The Fields Picker dialog box shown in Fig. 1-32 lets you determine which fields will show when your database is displayed. The current database is displayed in the From Table pop-up in the lower left corner of the Fields Picker dialog box. You can change databases by selecting another from the pop-up. All the fields in the current database appear in the All Fields list box. Initially, the Selected Fields box is empty. This is where the fields

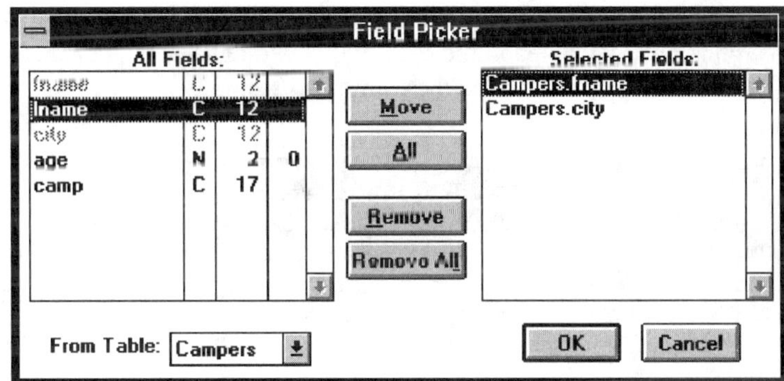

1-32 Fields Picker dialog box.

you choose are displayed. The four push buttons in the middle of the box determine the display of the database:

Move When you select a database field from the All Fields box and choose Move, that field appears in the Selected Fields box (if Move is disabled, it is because you have not yet selected a field).

All If you want all the fields to be displayed, choose All (or exit the dialog box by choosing Cancel).

Remove Use the Remove button after selecting a field in the Selected Fields box to remove it from the selected display. This button is only enabled if you have selected a field in the box.

Remove All Choose Remove All to delete all fields from the Selected Fields box.

When you have selected the fields you want to display, choose OK. To exit the dialog without selecting new fields, choose Cancel. If any fields are selected, the Use Fields List check box is checked. You can clear the fields list by selecting Remove All in the Field Picker dialog, or by issuing the command SET FIELDS TO.

Filter Data... You can create a filter that allows only certain records to be available for processing in your database. Choose Filter Data and enter the condition that filters out records in the Expression Builder (see File New for details on the Expression Builder). For example, if you only want to process records on campers from the Bumblebee Brigade, the filter expression would be `Camp = "Bumblebee Brigade"`.

When you display your database, only the records that meet the filter condition appear. The other records still exist; they are just not shown. To clear any active filter, simply remove the filter expression from the Expression Builder.

See also File New, SET ORDER, SET FIELDS, SET FILTER

Database Browse

Selecting Browse displays the records of the current database in a window, allowing you to make changes to the data. The window used to display the records contains many controls for manipulating the view of the data. The name of the database appears in the window title as shown in Fig. 1-33. There are four ways to open a Browse window in the interface:

- Choose Browse from the Database menu.
- Choose the Browse push button in the View window when a database is open.
- Double click on a work area in the View window that has an open database.
- Enter the BROWSE command in the Command window.

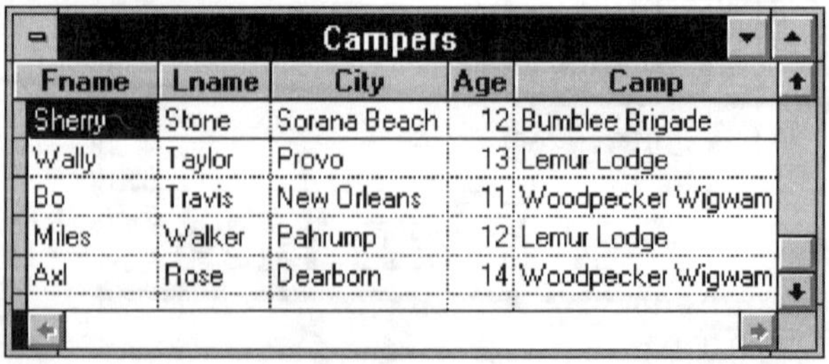

Campers

Fname	Lname	City	Age	Camp
Sherry	Stone	Sorana Beach	12	Bumblee Brigade
Wally	Taylor	Provo	13	Lemur Lodge
Bo	Travis	New Orleans	11	Woodpecker Wigwam
Miles	Walker	Pahrump	12	Lemur Lodge
Axl	Rose	Dearborn	14	Woodpecker Wigwam

1-33 Browse window.

If you choose the Browse option from the Database menu when no database is open, the Open dialog box appears. Select the database you want to browse and choose Open.

You can move around the records in your Browse window to view and edit particular fields. Press the Tab key to select successive fields to the right. When you Tab on the last field, the cursor moves to the first field in the database. The ↑ and ↓ arrows move from row to row, and PgDn and PgUp move page by page. Press End to move to the end of your entry in a field, and press Home to move to the first character in the field. You can also use the scroll bars on the right and bottom of the Browse window. To close a Browse window, choose Close from the File menu, press Ctrl-W, or select Close from the browse window control panel.

See also Window Command, Window View

When a browse window is active, a Browse option is added to the active menu. The Browse menu is discussed following the Database menu.

Database Append From...

This option lets you add records to the current database from another database or file. When Append From... is selected, the dialog shown in Fig. 1-34 is displayed. The following options are available:

From... Selecting the From... push button activates the Open dialog, allowing you to select a file to copy records from. Select the desired file and choose OK. The text box below the From... push button is filled in with the path and name of the selected file. You can also type the name of the file into the text box.

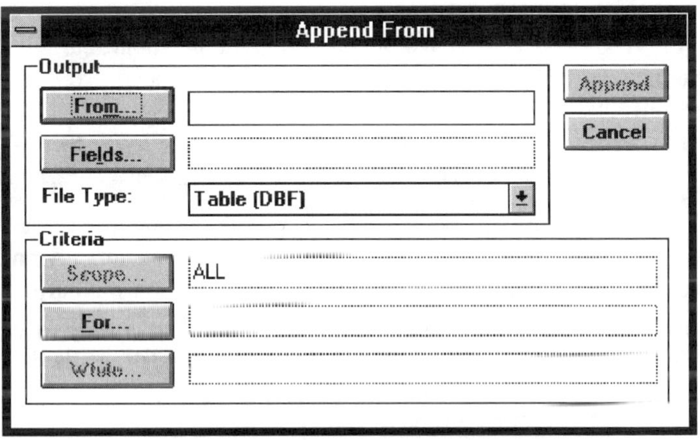

1-34 Append From dialog box.

The From... file doesn't have to be a database. You can select another file type from the File Type pop-up. The optional file types are:

Table/DBF	Standard FoxPro database with a .DBF extension.
Delimited with Tabs	A text file in which each field is separated by a Tab.
Delimited with Commas	A text file in which each field is separated by a comma.

Delimited with Spaces	A text file in which each field is separated by one space.
SDF	A text file in which the records have a fixed length and end with a carriage return and line feed.
SYLK	Symbolic Link Interchange Format.
DIF	Visicalc's Data Interchange Format.
XLS	Microsoft Excel, versions 2.0, 3.0 and 4.0.
MOD	Microsoft Multiplan version 4.01.
WRK	Lotus Symphony, version 1.0.
WR1	Lotus Symphony, version 1.1 or 1.2.
WKS	Lotus 1-2-3, version 1.x.
WK1	Lotus 1-2-3, version 2.x.
WK3	Lotus 1-2-3, version 3.x.
PDOX	Borland's Paradox version 3.5 and 4.0.
RPD	Ashton Tate's RapidFile version 1.2.
FW2	Ashton Tate's Framework II.

Fields... The Field Picker dialog box (see Fig. 1-32) lets you pick the fields of the database to be appended to. It is the same dialog box used in the Setup option on the Database menu. See the Database Setup section in this chapter for more information on selecting fields.

Scope, For, and While These three push-buttons allow you to control which database records are affected by the action. The Scope, For, and While options are contained in many FoxPro database action dialogs and can be used separately or together. Only the For option is available in this dialog.

Scope... Acts on certain records in the active database, relative to the record pointer. The Scope dialog shown in Fig. 1-35 contains the following options:

All Affects all records and is the same as not specifying a scope.

Next Affects a range of records, beginning with the current record and continuing for the number of records specified in the text box. Specify Next 1 to affect only the current record.

Record Affects only the record number specified in the text box.

Rest Affects all records beginning with the current record, to the end of the database file.

For... Selecting For... activates the Expression Builder. Enter a valid FoxPro expression. FoxPro will evaluate each record in the database, and act only on those records that match the For... expression. For example, `Lname > "B"` would affect only records with a last name entry that starts with C or higher. Choose fields and operators in the Expression Builder, or enter the For... clause in the Expression Builder text box.

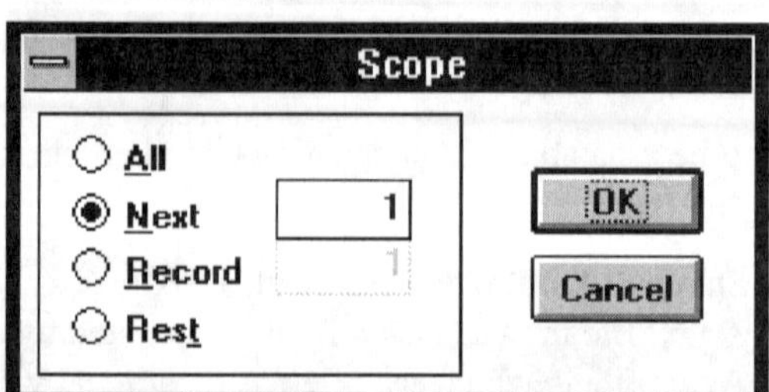

1-35 Scope dialog box.

While... Selecting While... activates the Expression Builder. Enter a valid FoxPro expression. As long as each record in the database matches the While expression, the action is taken. When a record is encountered that does not match the expression, the action is stopped. When both the For... and While... options are used together, the While... expression takes precedence.

See also Database Setup

Database Copy to...

The Copy To... option lets you copy records from the current database into a new file. When Copy to... is selected, the dialog shown in Fig. 1-36 is displayed. The following options are available:

Save as... Selecting the Save as... push button activates the Save File dialog, allowing you to select a file to copy records to. Select the desired file and choose OK. The text box below the Save as... push button is filled in with the path and name of the selected file. You can also type the name of the file into the text box.

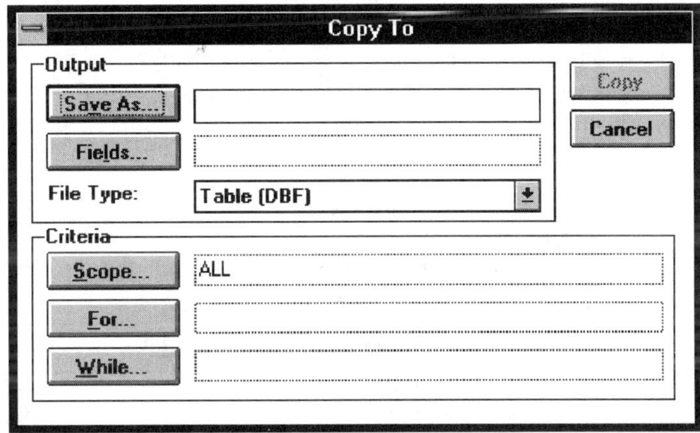

1-36 Copy To dialog box.

You can save the current file to a file other than a database. Choose one of the following from the Type pop-up:

Database	Standard FoxPro database with .DBF extension.
Delimited with Tabs	A text file in which each field is separated by a Tab.
Delimited with Commas	A text file in which each field is separated by a comma.
Delimited with Spaces	A text file in which each field is separated by one space.
SDF	A text file in which the records have a fixed length and end with a carriage return and line feed.
SYLK	Symbolic Link Interchange Format.
DIF	Visicalc's Data Interchange Format.
XLS	Microsoft Excel, versions 2.0, 3.0 and 4.0.

MOD	Microsoft Multiplan version 4.01.
WRK	Lotus Symphony, version 1.0.
WR1	Lotus Symphony, version 1.1 or 1.2.
WKS	Lotus 1-2-3, version 1.x.
WK1	Lotus 1-2-3, version 2.x.

Fields... The Field Picker dialog box (see Fig. 1-32) lets you pick the fields you want to be appended into the database. It is the same dialog box used in the Setup option on the Database menu. See the Database Setup section in this chapter for more information on selecting fields.

Scope, For, and While Three push-buttons are below the Save as... push button, which allow you to control which database records are affected by the action. See the Database Append From section in this chapter for more information on Scope, For, and While.

Database Sort...

This option lets you create a new database sorted in the order you indicate in the Sort... dialog box, as shown in Fig. 1-31. The current database is displayed in the From Table pop-up. The pop-up lists only open databases and is disabled if only one database is open.

The fields in the current database are listed in the All Fields list. Memo and general fields are disabled because a database cannot be sorted on these types of fields. The column to the right of the field name lists the first letter of the type of the field, and the next column shows the field length. The column on the right shows the number of decimal places used in the field.

Move To determine the order of the new database, you must select fields from the All Fields list, and press Enter or choose Move to move them into the Sort Order box. If, for example, you want campers to be listed in alphabetical order according to their last names, you would put the Lname field in the Sort Order box.

Field Options To indicate that the order should go from A–Z rather than Z–A, turn on the Ascending radio button (selected by default) in the Field Options box. If some names are entered with initial capitals and others in lowercase, check the Ignore Case box. Otherwise, uppercase records will be sorted first. FoxPro's international capabilities also allow you to sort a database on the translation of accented characters that may be used in different language versions of FoxPro. See chapter 11 for more information on the international capabilities of FoxPro.

You can continue choosing fields for the Sort Order box. You might want the secondary order to be first name, so you would move that into the second line of the Sort Order list. You must list fields in their order of importance: If you list the Fname field first, names will be in order alphabetically by first name first, then by last name.

To remove a field from the Sort Order list, choose the field and select Remove. The three Input check boxes allow you to limit the records to be included in the new database by specifying a scope, or For or While expression. See the Database Append From section in this chapter for more information on Scope, For, and While.

Save As... Type the name of the new database in the Save As text box, or choose the Save As... push button to activate the Save As dialog.

Fields... When the Fields... check box is checked, only the fields you select in the Field Picker dialog box (see Fig. 1-32) are contained in the sorted database. See the Database Setup section in this chapter for more information on using the Field Picker dialog.

See also Database Setup

Database Total...

Total... (see Fig. 1-37) sums numeric values for all records that match a given expression. The totaled results are stored in a database file.

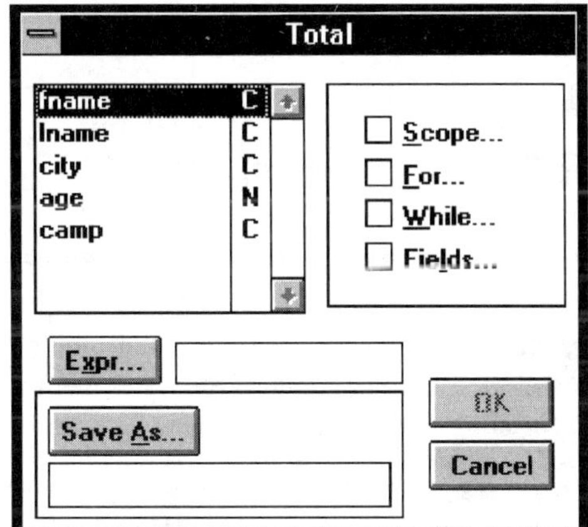

1-37 Total dialog box

The Total dialog box contains a scrollable list of the fields in the current database. You select one of these fields or type a field name in the Expr... text box. The field or expression you total on should match the index key expression of the active index or the database sort order. When you execute Total without specifying Scope, For, While, or Fields, all numeric fields in the database that contain duplicate values in the Expr... field are totaled. For instance, if the Lname field is the index key, Total will sum the ages of campers who have the same last name.

Expr... Selecting the Expr... push button activates the Expression Builder, which allows you to create a valid FoxPro expression for totaling the database on. You can also type the expression directly into the Expr... text box without activating the Expression Builder.

Save As... Type the name of the new database in the Save As text box, or choose the Save As... push button to activate the Save As dialog. This is the file where the new database with totaled fields will be saved.

Scope, For, While and Fields These options, found in the box on the right side of the screen, can be used to limit the records included in the totaling process. See the Database Append From section in this chapter for more information on Scope, For, and While, and the Database Setup section in this chapter for more information on using the Field Picker dialog.

See also Database Append From, Database Setup, Database Sum

Database Average...

You can use the Average option shown in Fig. 1-38 to average the numeric values in your database fields.

Expr... Selecting the Expr... check box activates the Expression Builder, which allows you to create a valid FoxPro expression for averaging the database on.

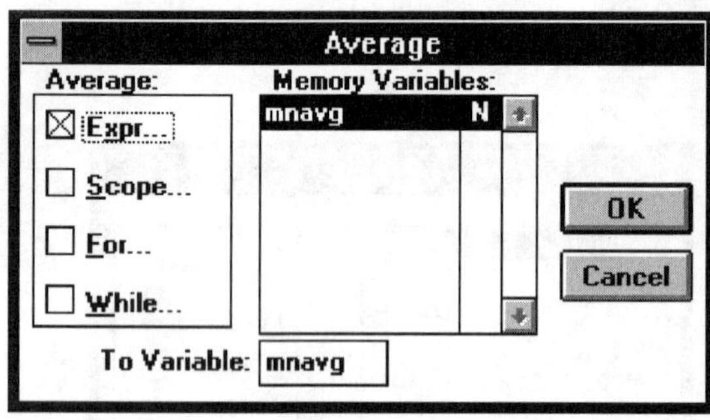

1-38 Average dialog box.

Scope, For, and While These check boxes, found in the Average box, can be used to limit the records included in the averaging process. See the Database Append From section in this chapter for more information on Scope, For, and While.

Memory Variables To store the resulting average value to a memory variable, enter the name of the variable in the To Variable text box, or select a variable from the Memory Variables list. If you specify a new variable name, that variable will be displayed in the Memory Variables list after the average computation has been completed.

Choose OK to compute the average, or choose Esc or Cancel to exit without making the computation. If you have SET TALK ON, the average will show on screen when you execute the option.

See also Database Append From, Window View

Database Count...

The Count option (see Fig. 1-39) lets you count the number of records that meet your criteria.

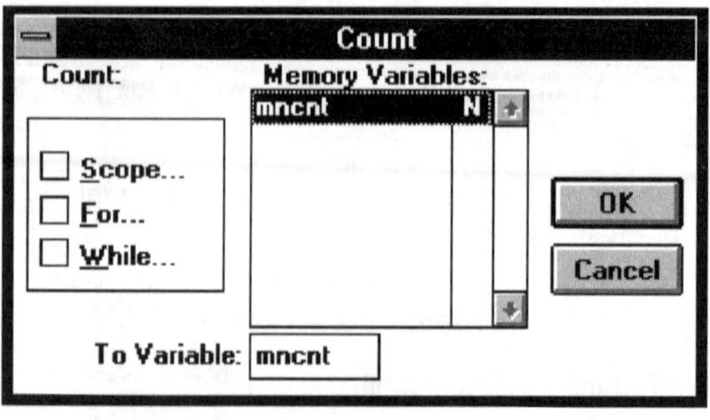

1-39 Count dialog box.

Scope, For, and While These check boxes, found in the Count box, can be used to limit the records included in the counting process. See the Database Append From section in this chapter for more information on Scope, For, and While.

Memory Variables To store the resulting count value to a memory variable, enter the name of the variable in the To Variable text box, or select a variable from the Memory Variables list. If you specify a new variable name, that variable will be displayed in the Memory Variables list after the count computation has been completed.

Choose OK to compute the count, or choose Esc or Cancel to exit without making the computation. If you have set Talk On in the On/Off panel of the View window, the count will show on screen when you execute the option.

See also Database Append From, Window View

Database Sum...

The Sum option sums the values in numeric fields in your database (see Fig. 1-40).

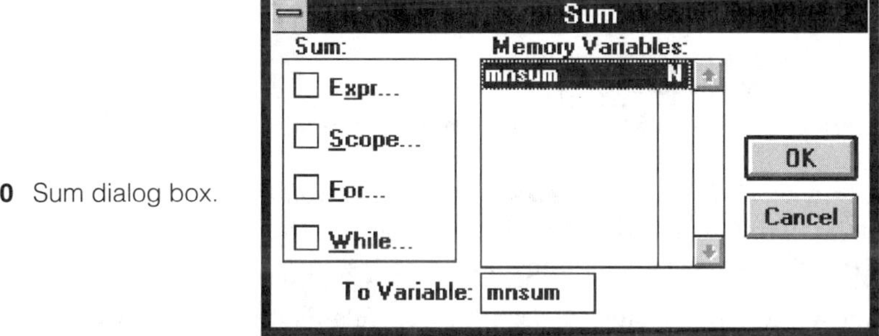

1-40 Sum dialog box.

Expr... Selecting the Expr... check box activates the Expression Builder, which allows you to create a valid FoxPro expression for summing the database on.

Scope, For, and While These check boxes found in the Sum box can be used to limit the records included in the summing process. See the Database Append From section in this chapter for more information on Scope, For, and While. Selecting the Expr... check box activates the Expression Builder, which allows you to create a valid FoxPro expression for summing the database on.

Memory Variables To store the resulting sum value to a memory variable, enter the name of the variable in the To Variable text box, or select a variable from the Memory Variables list. If you specify a new variable name, that variable will be displayed in the Memory Variables list after the sum computation has been completed.

Choose OK to compute the sum, or choose Esc or Cancel to exit without making the computation. If you have set Talk On in the On/Off panel of the View window, the sum will show on screen when you execute the option.

See also Database Append From, Database Total, Window View

Database Calculate...

The Database Calculate option (see Fig. 1-41) lets you use FoxPro commands and functions to help you perform financial and statistical operations on fields.

Expr... Selecting the Expr... check box activates the Expression Builder, which allows you to create a valid FoxPro expression for the calculation. The Calculate Expression Builder is different from other Expression Builders; it has only one pop-up (Math), and there are fewer options here than usual. You can combine any of these options to create an expression string. When you build the expression, you can string together multiple expressions by separating each one with a comma. See chapter 2 on commands and chapter 4 on functions for descriptions of how these expressions work.

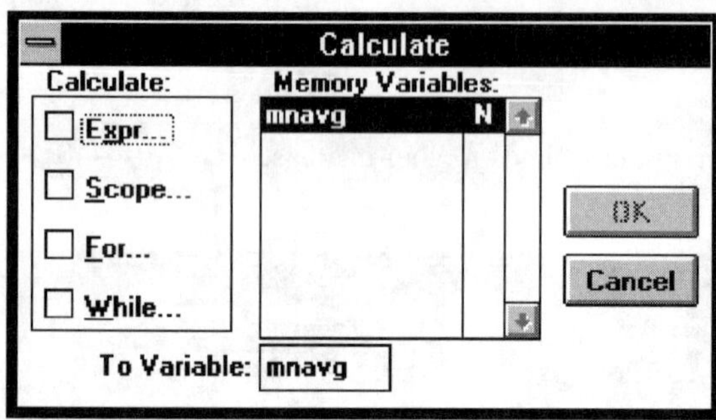

1-41 Calculate dialog box.

Scope, For, and While These check boxes that are found in the Calculate box can be used to limit the records included in the calculation process. See the Database Append From section in this chapter for more information on Scope, For, and While.

Memory Variables To store the resulting calculation(s) to memory variables, enter the name(s) of the variable in the To Variable text box, or select a variable from the Memory Variables list. If you specify new variable names, those variables will be displayed in the Memory Variables list after the sum computation has been completed. If you have strung together multiple expressions for the calculation, you must string together an equal number of variables in the To Variable text box.

Choose OK to process the calculation, or choose Esc or Cancel to exit without making the calculation. If you have set Talk On in the On/Off panel of the View window, the calculation will show on screen when you execute the option.

See also Database Append From, chapter 2, FoxPro Commands, chapter 3, FoxPro Functions

Database Report...

Use the Report... option on the Database menu to print predefined reports for selected databases. The Report dialog is shown in Fig. 1-42. (The More >> push button must be selected to expand the Report dialog.) The following options are available:

Form... You can enter the name of the report in the text box, or select the Form... push button to activate the Open File dialog, which displays a list of report files. If a report

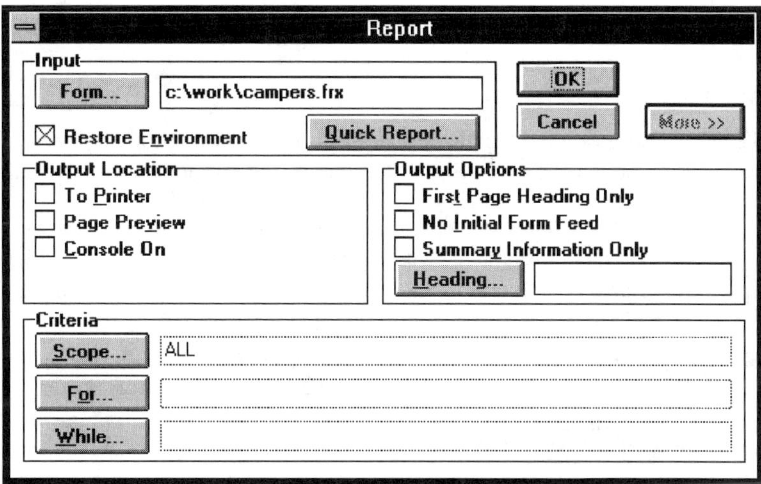

1-42 Report dialog box.

form is already open when Report is selected, its name will automatically appear in the text box.

Restore Environment If the selected report has a saved environment setting, turn on this option to restore that environment before the report is printed. Saving a report environment is discussed in chapter 9, Using the Report Writer and Label Generator.

Quick Report... Selecting this option displays the Quick Report dialog, allowing you to instantly create a new report. Creating a quick report is discussed in chapter 9, Using the Report Writer and Label Generator.

First Page Heading Only If you check the First Page Heading Only box, the report is printed with Page Headers on the first page only.

No Initial Form Feed Check this box if you do not want to eject a blank page before the report prints.

Summary Information Only Check this box to print summary information only.

Heading... Use this option to add a heading line to each page of the report. Enter the heading text in the text box or select the Heading push button to activate the Expression Builder.

To Printer Check this box if you want to send the report output to a printer.

Page Preview Check this box to get an on-screen preview of the report before printing it.

Console On Check this box to see the report on screen while it is printing.

Scope, For, and While These push buttons that are found in the Criteria box can be used to limit the records included in the report output. See the Database Append From section in this chapter for more information on Scope, For, and While.

When you choose OK, the report is run. Choose Cancel or press Esc to exit the dialog box without running the report.

See also Database Append From, chapter 8, Using the Report Writer and Label Designer

Database Label

Use the Label... option on the Database menu to print predefined labels for selected databases. The Label dialog is shown in Fig. 1-43. The following options are available:

Form... You can enter the name of the label file in the text box, or select the Form... push button to activate the Open File dialog, which displays a list of label files. If a label form is already open when Label is selected, its name will automatically appear in the text box.

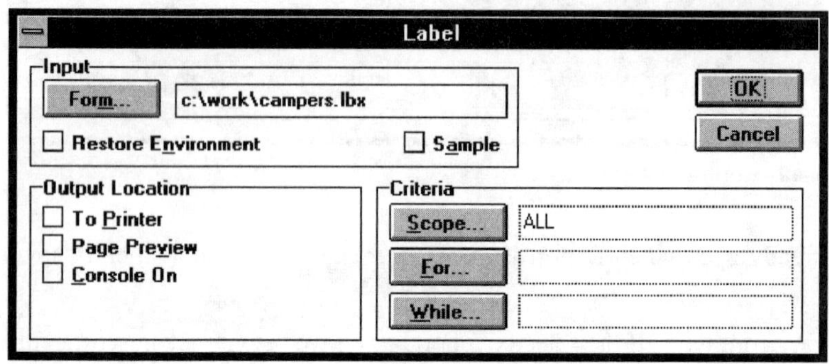

1-43 Label dialog box.

Restore Environment If the selected label has a saved environment setting, turn on this option to restore that environment before the label is printed. Saving a label environment is discussed in chapter 9, Using the Report Writer and Label Generator.

Sample If you check the Sample box, a single sample prints so you can check the alignment of your printer. The asterisks on the label show the size and placement of fields. After you print a sample, FoxPro asks if you want more samples. You can continue choosing Yes and printing more samples until your printer alignment is correct. When you are ready to run all the labels, choose Do Labels. You can choose Cancel or press Esc to leave the dialog box without running labels.

To Printer Check this box if you want to send the label output to a printer.

Page Preview Check this box to get an on-screen preview of the label before printing it.

Console On Check this box to see the label on screen while it is printing.

Scope, For, and While These push buttons that are found in the Criteria box can be used to limit the records included in the report output. See the Database Append From section in this chapter for more information on Scope, For, and While.

When you choose OK, the labels are generated. Choose Cancel or press Esc to exit the dialog box without generating the labels.

See also Chapter 9, Using the Report Writer and Label Designer, Database Append From

Database Pack

Pack is used to permanently remove deleted records from the current database. Database records can be "marked" for deletion by selecting Toggle Delete from the Browse menu, Delete from the Record menu, or by using the DELETE command.

Before a database can be packed, it must be opened exclusively, otherwise FoxPro will generate an "Exclusive open of file is required" error. Packing a database is an operation that cannot be reversed. Always make a backup before you pack your database.

See also Browse Toggle Delete, Record Delete, SET EXCLUSIVE, USE, DELETE

Database Reindex

Reindex is used to rebuild the index file of the current database. Occasionally, index files become corrupted or out of date. If you notice that your open index file does not seem to be working properly, choose Reindex to reconstruct the index(s). A database can also be reindexed using the REINDEX command.

Before a database can be reindexed, it must be opened exclusively, otherwise FoxPro will generate an "Exclusive open of file is required" error.

See also SET EXCLUSIVE, USE, REINDEX

The Browse menu

Whenever a Browse window is active, the Browse menu pad is added to the menu bar (see Fig. 1-44). The Browse menu pad also appears in the menu bar when you append records after creating a new file or by choosing the Record Append option.

Browse Append/Change

If you open the Browse menu just after opening your Browse window, the database is displayed in Browse mode, which is record by record, and the first option available in the

Change
Grid
Link Partitions
Change Partition Ctrl+H
Font...
Size Field
Move Field
Resize Partitions
Goto...
Seek
Toggle Delete Ctrl+T
Append Record Ctrl+N

1-44 The Browse menu.

Browse menu is Change. When you choose Change, the display changes to field by field, and field names and contents are listed vertically instead of horizontally. This is shown in Fig. 1-45.

If you used the Append option from the Record menu to go to append mode, the Change option is named Append when you are in Browse mode. If you open the Browse menu while you are in append mode, the option appears as Browse. Choosing Browse changes the format of your database so that fields are listed horizontally.

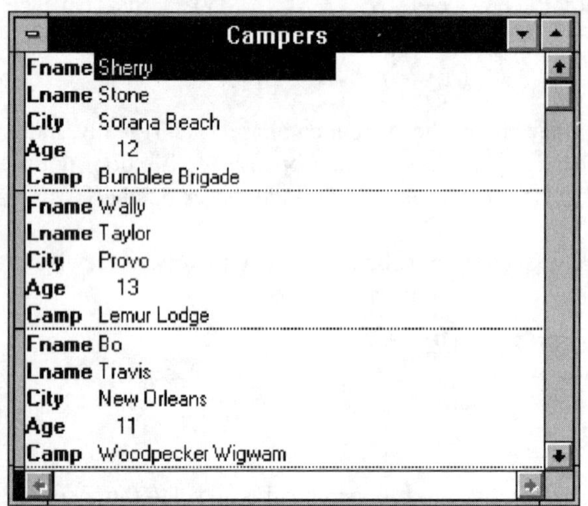

1-45 Records shown in append mode.

Browse Grid

Toggles Grid mode. When Grid is "on," fields are separated by a vertical line and the Grid option is preceded by a check mark character. Selecting Grid when the grid lines are visible removes them from the browse windows and toggles Grid mode to "off."

Browse Link Partitions

Toggles Link mode in split windows. If you have used Resize Partitions to create partitions in your Browse window, you can toggle "on" Link Partitions to display a vertical scroll bar in both partitions. When Link Partitions is "on," both partitions will scroll together vertically. Toggle Link Partitions "off" to scroll each partition independently of the other.

See also Browse Resize Partitions

Browse Change Partition

When you have two partitions, choosing Change Partition lets you activate the currently inactive partition by moving the cursor into that partition. If you are using a mouse, you can change partitions by clicking the mouse on the desired position.

Shortcut key: Ctrl-H

See also Browse Resize Partitions

Browse Font...

Displays the Windows Font dialog. The Font dialog is common among many Windows applications and is used to select a font, font style and size for all records in the Browse window. Refer to your Windows documentation for more information on changing a font.

Browse Size Field

Size Field is used to change the viewing width of fields in the browse window. In Browse mode, choose Size and use the ← or → keys to stretch or shrink the selected field. Press Enter to fix the size of the field.

If you are using a mouse, you can size a field by moving the mouse pointer directly over the grid to the right of the field. Click the mouse and drag the field to the desired size. Changing the size of a field in a browse window does not actually change the physical size of the field in the database.

Browse Move Field

Move Field is used to change the position of fields in the browse window. Relocate a field by placing the cursor in the desired field and choosing Move Field from the Browse menu. Use the arrow keys to drag the field to its new position and press Enter. You can move a field in Browse or Change mode.

If you are using a mouse, you can move a field by positioning the mouse pointer directly over the column heading of the desired field. Click the mouse and drag the field to its new location. Changing the location of a field in a browse window does not actually change the physical location of the field in the database.

Browse Resize Partitions

Resize Partitions is used to "split" a browse window into two partitions or resize a browse window that was previously split. When you choose Resize Partitions, the window splitter appears, as shown in Fig. 1-46. Use the ← or → keys to move the splitter to the right of the fields you want to remain in view, and press Enter. The window splitter disappears and the partitions are resized.

If you are using a mouse, you can resize a partition by positioning the mouse pointer directly over the window splitting control. Click the mouse and drag the partition to the desired location.

You can partition the Browse window so you can scroll part of the database while the other portion stays in place. This is useful when you want to scroll through several fields but you want to keep the name field (usually at the left end of the database) in view. Splitting a browse window does not actually change the physical structure of the database.

See also Browse Change Partition, Browse Unlink Partitions

Browse Goto...

Goto allows you to move the record pointer to a desired record in the database. The Goto... dialog box has four radio buttons as shown in Fig. 1-47.

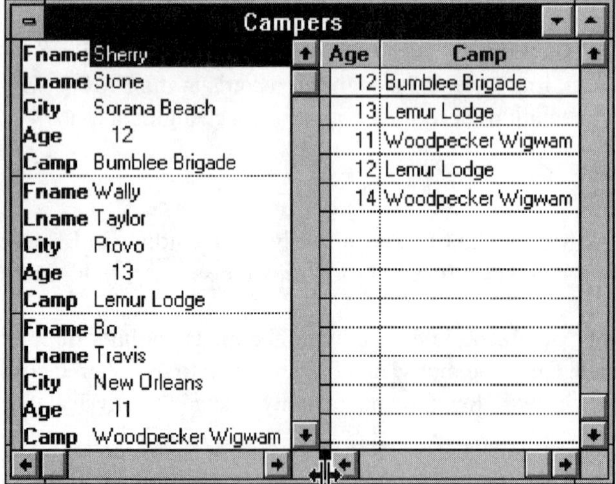

1-46 Browse window splitter.

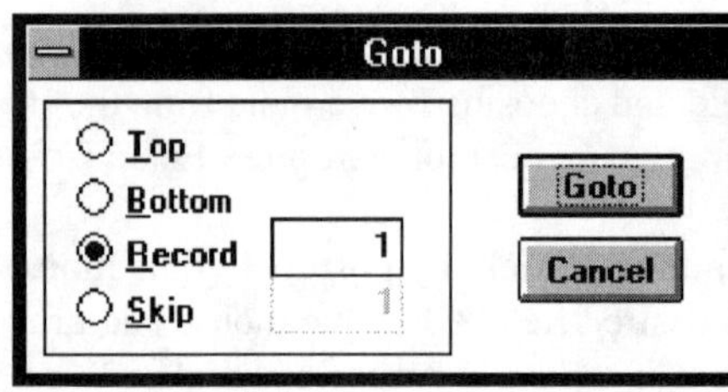

1-47 Goto dialog box.

Top Moves the record pointer to the first record in the database.

Bottom Moves the record pointer to the last record in the database.

Record Moves the record to the specified record number. Enter the record number in the text box. If the value entered in the text box does not match a record in the database, FoxPro displays the error "Record is out of range."

Skip Moves the record pointer a specified number of records past the current record. Enter a negative value to move the record pointer backwards.

When you've selected the radio button you want, choose Goto. Choose Cancel or press Esc to leave with moving the cursor.

Browse Seek...

If the database being browsed has an active index, the Expression Builder is displayed, which allows you to build an expression and search for a record matching the expression. This operation is the same as Record Seek.

See also Record Seek

Browse Toggle Delete

Toggle Delete "marks" a record for deletion. When you want to remove a record from a database, you must first mark it for deletion. Select the record to be deleted and choose

Toggle Delete. Deleted records are identified by a black box in the delete column at the beginning of the record. Deleted records are not actually removed until you pack the database using the Database Pack option. If you are using a mouse, you can delete a record by positioning the mouse pointer over the delete column of the desired record and click.

Shortcut key: Ctrl-T

See also Database Pack

Browse Append Record

Append Record adds a blank record to the end of the database. Because a blank record is automatically added when you complete entry of a record in a new database, Append Record is not available when you are browsing a file just created with the File New option.

Shortcut key: Ctrl-N

The Edit menu

The Edit menu (see Fig. 1-48) provides options for editing text and Windows OLE objects in different types of FoxPro windows. Edit the Memo field in the CMPSCHD database shown in Fig. 1-49. Choose Database Browse to view the database in a Browse window. You are going to put a description in the first hike record. First, open the memo field by placing the cursor on the memo field, and pressing Ctrl-PgDn or double clicking with the mouse.

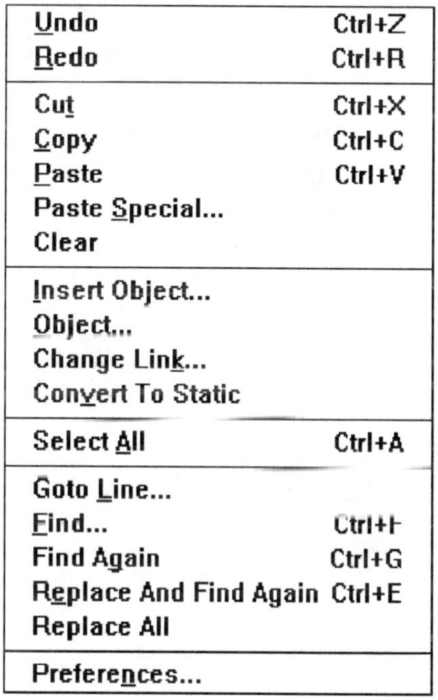

Undo	Ctrl+Z
Redo	Ctrl+R
Cut	Ctrl+X
Copy	Ctrl+C
Paste	Ctrl+V
Paste Special...	
Clear	
Insert Object...	
Object...	
Change Link...	
Convert To Static	
Select All	Ctrl+A
Goto Line...	
Find...	Ctrl+F
Find Again	Ctrl+G
Replace And Find Again	Ctrl+E
Replace All	
Preferences...	

1-48 The Edit menu.

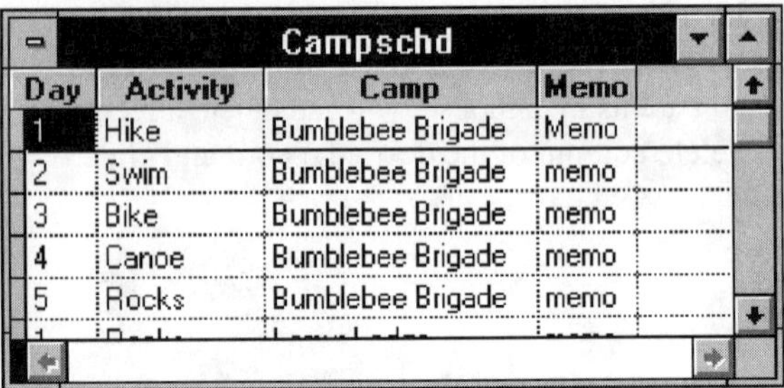

Day	Activity	Camp	Memo
1	Hike	Bumblebee Brigade	Memo
2	Swim	Bumblebee Brigade	memo
3	Bike	Bumblebee Brigade	memo
4	Canoe	Bumblebee Brigade	memo
5	Rocks	Bumblebee Brigade	memo

1-49 Cmpschd database.

Now type the text shown in Fig. 1-50 into your memo window. Use normal typing methods. When you finish, place the cursor at the top of the memo window. Try using some of the options on the Edit menu. Suppose the hiking path really runs south from the Wigwam.

1. Choose Find... from the menu.
2. In the Look For text box, type `north`.
3. In the Replace With text box, type `south`.
4. Choose Find.
5. Choose Replace All from the Edit menu.

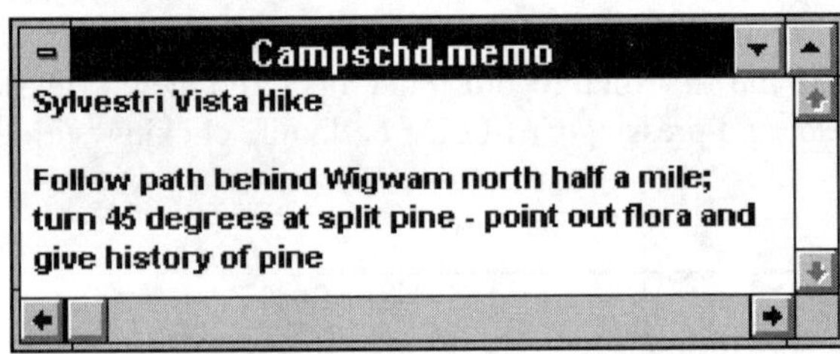

1-50 Text in a memo window.

North becomes south. Now change it back:

1. Choose Undo from the menu.
2. Change south back to north again.
3. Choose Redo from the menu.

Now that you are absolutely sure you got the direction right, put the hike description in another hike record.

1. Choose Select All from the menu. All the text in the memo window becomes highlighted.
2. Choose Copy from the menu.
3. Close the window by pressing Ctrl-W.

In the Browse window, place the cursor on the memo field of the next hike record and open the window. Copy the text into the window by choosing Paste from the menu: the text appears in the window. When you copied it from the original memo field, FoxPro stored it on a clipboard. When you selected Paste, FoxPro copied the clipboard into the window.

You can cut or copy and paste single characters, words, lines, paragraphs, or whatever you like. The keystrokes to use for selecting text are listed here:

Keystrokes	Selects
Shift-arrow (←/→)	One character at a time.
Shift-arrow (↑/↓)	One line at a time.
Shift-Ctrl-arrow (←/→)	From cursor to beginning/end of word.
Shift-Ctrl-End	From cursor to end of text.
Shift-Ctrl-Home	From cursor to beginning of text.
Ctrl-A	All text.

Press any cursor movement key to deselect. With a mouse, you can select text by dragging through it. There are also a few shortcuts for selecting with a mouse:

To select	Action
A word	Point to the word and double click.
A line	Point to the line and triple click.
Word by word	Point to the first word, double click and drag.
Line by line	Point to the first line, triple click and drag.
Segment of text	Point to the beginning of the segment, then Shift-click at the end of the segment.

Deselect by dragging in the opposite direction before you release the mouse button. After you release the mouse button, you can deselect by Shift-clicking in the selected text at the point where you want the selection to end. Clicking in the window anywhere outside the selected area deselects the entire selection. The Edit menu options are described in detail in the following sections.

Edit Undo

If you change your mind about an action you performed, you can choose Undo to reverse it. FoxPro remembers everything you have done since the beginning of your session, so you can choose Undo repeatedly to reverse successive actions all the way back to your first action. In Undo and Redo, actions are:

- Pressing Delete or Backspace.
- Selecting text and pressing Delete or Backspace.
- Selecting and starting to type replacement text.
- Moving the cursor and typing.
- Using any other keystrokes before pressing the spacebar and typing.
- Choosing any of these Edit menu options: Cut, Paste, Clear, or Replace All.

You can Undo actions after you have saved them, but if you close a file and reopen it, Undo is disabled until you perform new actions. To undo an Undo, you must choose Redo from the Edit menu. If you choose Undo after undoing an action, the action immediately previous to the Undo is undone. In a Browse window, Undo is available within fields. Each time you move to a new field, you start over; Undo is disabled until you make new changes in the field.

Shortcut key: Ctrl-Z

See also Edit Redo

Edit Redo

Redo undoes an Undo. In other words, if you perform an action and then choose Undo, the action is reversed. If you then choose Redo, the action is restored. Redo only works on undone actions. You cannot, for example, cut and paste a line of text and then choose Redo to paste it again. You can choose Redo repeatedly to undo Undo actions starting with the most recent and working back to the first. If Undo has not been used, Redo is not available for selection.

Shortcut key: Ctrl-R

See also Edit Undo

Edit Cut

Use Cut when you want to remove text or an object from an editing window. The text or object that is cut is stored in the FoxPro clipboard. Each type of FoxPro for Windows editing screen, text, reports, screens, and menus, has its own clipboard. For example, if you cut an object from a screen builder window, you can paste that object only onto another screen layout and not a text or report layout window.

To restore the text or object, move the cursor to the new position and choose Paste. Any text or object that is placed onto the FoxPro clipboard is also sent the Windows clipboard, and can be inserted into other Windows applications. Consult your Windows documentation for more information.

Shortcut key: Ctrl-X

See also Edit Copy, Edit Paste

Edit Copy

Copy copies the selected text or object and stores it in the FoxPro clipboard. Copy is similar to Cut, yet the original text or object remains in place in the file and on screen. Each type of FoxPro editing screen, text, reports, screens, and menus, has its own clipboard. For example, if you copy an object from a report layout window, you can paste that object only onto another report layout and not a text or screen builder window.

Use Paste to copy the text from the clipboard into the new cursor position. Any text or object that is placed onto the FoxPro clipboard is also sent to the Windows clipboard, and can be inserted into other Windows applications. Consult your Windows documentation for more information.

Shortcut key: Ctrl-C

See also Edit Cut, Edit Paste

Edit Paste

Paste inserts objects from the FoxPro clipboard or text from the Windows clipboard at the cursor position. Use this option after cutting or copying FoxPro text or objects with the Cut or Copy menu options. When you use Cut or Copy, text and objects are stored on a clipboard. Each type of FoxPro editing screen, text, reports, screens, and menus, has its own clipboard. For example, if you copy a field object from a report layout, you can paste that field object only into another report layout and not a screen layout or program file.

You can choose Paste repeatedly to paste the same clipboard text as many times as you like. If you copied text from another Windows application, Paste can be used to paste that text into a FoxPro text or program file. Any text or object that is placed onto the FoxPro clipboard is also sent to the Windows clipboard, and can be inserted into other Windows applications. Consult your Windows documentation for more information.

Shortcut key: Ctrl-V

See also Edit Copy, Edit Cut, Paste Special

Edit Paste Special...

Use Paste Special to link a Windows OLE object on the Windows clipboard into a FoxPro general field. Paste Special is only available when the cursor is in a general field editing window and a Windows OLE object is on the Windows clipboard.

When Paste Special is selected, the dialog shown in Fig. 1-51 appears. The Source information displays the Windows application and file that is being inserted into the general field. The Data Type list displays the available formats for the object. The format you select depends upon what you want to do with the object. Selecting a specific application format allows you to open the source application and edit the object once it has been pasted into the general field.

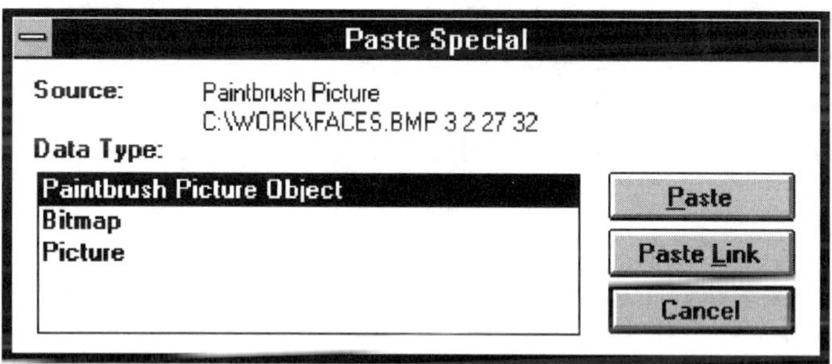

1-51 Paste Special dialog box.

Select Paste to embed the object. To create an OLE link for the object, select Paste Link. Consult your software application and Windows documentation for more information.

See also Edit Object, Edit Insert Object, chapter 12, Using DDE and OLE in FoxPro

Edit Clear

Deletes the selected text or object from the screen without placing it on the clipboard. Choosing Clear is the same as pressing the Delete key. If you choose Clear without selecting any text or objects, the current output window is erased. If Clear is selected when a general field editing window is frontmost, any embedded object in the field is removed, including all links.

See also Chapter 12, Using DDE and OLE in FoxPro

Edit Insert Object...

Use Insert Object to embed a Windows OLE object that is not on the Windows clipboard into a FoxPro general field. Insert Object is only available when the cursor is in a general field editing window. Unlike Paste Special, a Windows OLE object does not have to be on the Windows clipboard. When Insert Object is selected, the dialog shown in Fig. 1-52 appears.

1-52 Insert Object dialog box.

The Object Type list contains a listing of all Windows applications on the computer that can create OLE objects. To create a new object, select the desired application and choose OK. This will start the application or make it active if it is already running. Once your object is created you can update the object with the appropriate menu option from the application and return to FoxPro. The object is now embedded in the general field.

If the OLE object you wish to embed already exists in file format, select the File button to display the Insert Object From File dialog. Select the desired file and then Insert to embed the object in the general field. Consult your software application and Windows documentation for more information.

See also Edit Object, Edit Paste Special, chapter 12, Using DDE and OLE in FoxPro

Edit Object...

The Object option changes to reflect the type of OLE object and its parent application that is linked to the general field of the current record. For example, if the general field contains a Paintbrush picture, the Object menu option will be displayed as Edit Paintbrush Picture Object. In many cases, selecting this option will launch the linked application with the contents of the general field displayed.

This option is only available when a general field editing window that contains a linked Windows OLE object is frontmost. Consult your software documentation for more information on the choices that may appear in the Object option.

See also Edit Insert Object, Edit Paste Special, chapter 12, Using DDE and OLE in FoxPro

Edit Change Link...

Use Change Link to update the link of a Windows OLE object that was inserted into a FoxPro general field with the Paste Link option. Change Link allows you to edit the link of a Windows

OLE object from the source application and is useful in fixing a broken link that may occur if you have changed the name or location of a linked file. This option is only available when a general field editing window that contains a linked Windows OLE object is frontmost.

See also Edit Insert Object, Edit Paste Special, chapter 12, Using DDE and OLE in FoxPro

Edit Convert to Static

Use Convert to Static to flag a Windows OLE object embedded in a general field as "read-only." When Convert to Static is used, the object in the memo field remains, all links are closed, and the object's parent application cannot be launched to change the object.

If the object is a picture it remains in the general field. If the object is a Microsoft Word document or Microsoft Excel spreadsheet, only the icon remains in the general field. This option is only available when a general field editing window that contains a linked Windows OLE object is frontmost.

See also Edit Insert Object, Edit Paste Special, chapter 12, Using DDE and OLE in FoxPro

Edit Select All

Select All selects all the text or objects in the active editing window. In a Browse window, this option selects all text in the current field including blanks.

Shortcut key: Ctrl-A

See also Edit Cut, Edit Paste

Edit Goto Line...

When you choose Goto Line..., a dialog box appears. Enter the line number you want to go to, and choose Goto. The cursor will be moved to that line number. Goto Line... is only enabled if you have unchecked the Wrap Words box in the Preferences... dialog box.

See also Edit Preferences

Edit Find...

You can find or replace specific text with this option. Open the file in which you want to find text, and choose Find.... The dialog box shown in Fig. 1-53 will appear, containing the following options.

Look For Enter the text to search for in the text box. You can also find Enter, Tab, backslash, and line-feed characters by typing:

Character	Entry
Enter	\r
Tab	\t
Backslash	\\
Line feed	\n

Replace With If you want to replace text, enter the replacement data in the text box. While you can use Find in a Browse window, the dialog box does not contain a Replace

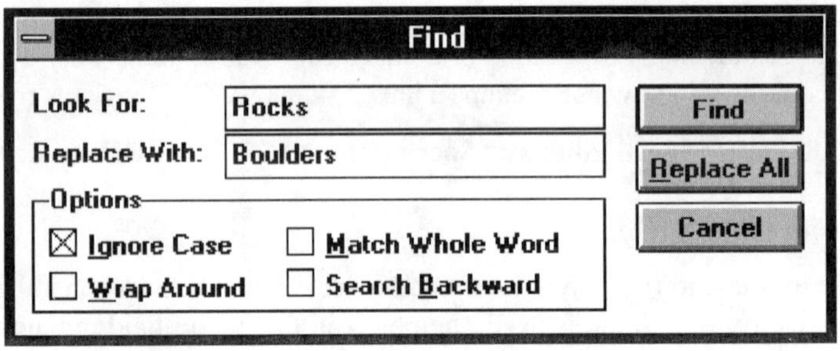

1-53 Find dialog box.

With box. Use Record Replace to replace information in the Browse window. When you choose Find, the text specified in Look For is located, and the replacement is not performed until you choose Replace and Find Again.

Ignore Case Check this option to locate both upper- and lowercase occurrences of the specified text. For example, with Ignore Case checked, if the search text is Mad Max, FoxPro will find any occurrence of Mad Max, or mad max.

Match Whole Word Check this option to search for an exact match of the specified text. For example, with Match Whole Word checked, only sham will be found if sham is the Look For text. With Match Words unchecked, sham will also find shambolic, shaman, unashamed, etc., if you have used them in your text.

Wrap Around When Wrap Around is checked, the entire file is searched, starting at the cursor position, to the end of the file, and then back to the cursor position from the top of the file, for the specified text without repositioning the cursor to the beginning of the file.

Search Backward When Search Backward is checked, the search is from the cursor position to the beginning of the file. When Search Backward is not checked, the search is from the cursor position to the end of the file.

When you are ready to begin searching, choose Find. The first occurrence of the text is highlighted for editing, and you must select Replace or Replace All to replace the text. Choose Cancel or press Esc to leave the dialog box without finding text.

Shortcut key: Ctrl-F

See also Edit Find Again, Edit Replace All, Edit Replace and Find Again, Record Replace

Edit Find Again

Find Again is only available if you have used the Find option to find the first occurrence of specified text. To find the next occurrence, choose Find Again. FoxPro continues to search from the current cursor position. When there are no more occurrences of the text, a Not Found message appears.

Shortcut key: Ctrl-G

See also Edit Find

Edit Replace and Find Again

After you have found the first occurrence of text to be replaced using the Find option, you can choose Replace and Find Again to replace the text with the replacement text and find the next occurrence. If you decide not to replace this occurrence of the text, you can choose Find Again to find the next occurrence without making the replacement.

Shortcut key: Ctrl-E

See also Edit Find, Edit Find Again

Edit Replace All

After you have used Find to find the first occurrence of text you want to replace, you can choose Replace All to replace every occurrence of that text in the active file.

See also Edit Find, Edit Replace and Find Again

Edit Preferences...

The Preferences... dialog box contains a number of settings you can use to control the display and editing preferences when editing text files, or when the Expression Builder and Calculator windows are active. The dialog shown in Fig. 1-54 is displayed when editing database memo fields. Other options will appear in the Preferences dialog for different types of files.

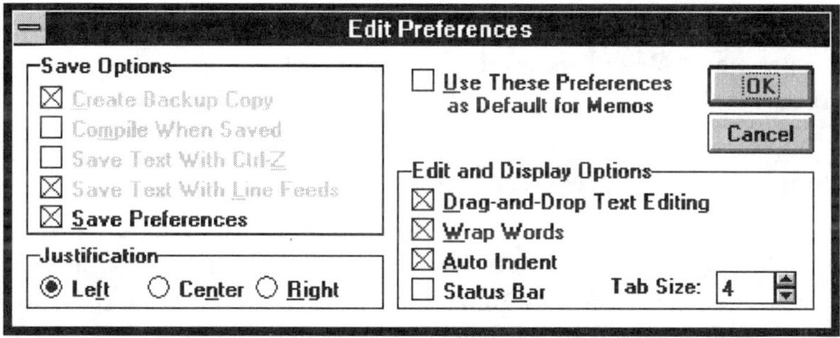

1-54 Preferences dialog box.

Create Backup Copy Check this option to create a backup file (.BAK) when you save an edited text or program file.

Compile When Saved When checked, all source code files will automatically be compiled when saved. See Program Compile in this chapter for more information on compiling programs.

Save Text with Ctrl-Z Check this option to place a Ctrl-Z character (→) at the end of a text file. Some applications require a Ctrl-Z character when reading a text file to determine the logical end of the file.

Save Text with Line Feeds Check this option to add a carriage return and line feed to the end of all lines when a text or program file is saved.

Save Preferences Check this box to store the preference settings in the resource file so they remain the same each time you open a file or window.

Use These Preferences If you check this box, all settings become the default for new text, program, or memo-editing windows.

Left justify When selected, all text in the current window is aligned to the left margin.

Center justify When selected, all text in the current window is aligned to the center.

Right justify When selected, all text in the current window is aligned to the right margin.

Drag-and-Drop Text Editing When checked, allows you to "drag" selected text to a new location and "drop" it into place using the mouse. Drag-and-drop is similar to using the Cut and Paste options from the Edit menu.

Wrap Words Check this option if you want text in the current window to wrap to the next line automatically when it reaches the right margin of the window.

Auto Indent Auto indent automatically indents the current line by the same amount as the previous line. When both Auto Indent and Wrap Words are checked, all wrapped text is indented by the same amount as the first line of the paragraph.

Status Bar Check this option to display the cursor line and column position in the status bar when editing a program (.PRG) file. The status bar may also display the status of the Insert, CapsLock, and NumLock keys. If Wrap Words is also checked, the line number is not displayed. The status bar also indicates "Modified" if the current program file has been changed since it was last saved.

Tab size Enter the number of spaces that each Tab character will advance. The value entered can range from 0 to 50.

Expression Builder Preferences

When Preferences is selected from the Edit menu and the Expression Builder is the active window, a dialog appears that allows you to control which functions and variables are available when using the Expression Builder.

In the Function Popups list, the available options for the selected type of function (Math, String, Logical and Date) are displayed. Each function that has a bullet next to it will appear in the appropriate pop-up. Remove or add a function by selecting the function and pressing Enter, or double-click on the function. Select the All push button to make all functions available, or Clear to make none of the functions available.

The Field Aliases options determine whether a selected database field is prefaced with its alias (or database) name. When the Show System Memory Variables box is checked, all system memory variables will be available in the Variables list.

The Record menu

The Record menu (see Fig. 1-55) allows you to work with individual records in your databases. Let's follow the mischievous Woodpecker Wigwam as they replace the CAMP field name information for their rivals, the Bumblebee Brigade.

Append
Change

Goto...
Locate...
Continue Ctrl+K
Seek...

Replace...
Delete...
Recall...

1-55 The Record menu.

With the Campers database open, the Wigwam leader chooses Replace from the Record menu. In the dialog box, he unscrupulously enters the replacement information. He looks around, and then he:

1. Selects the field name in which information will be replaced: Camp.
2. Enters the replacement text, `"Bumbling Brickheads"` in the With box.
3. Checks the For check box and presses Enter to enter a For clause in the Expression Builder. The Woodpeckers enter: `Camp = "Bumblebee Brigade"` Without a For clause, all the Camp field information would be changed to Bumbling Brickheads.
4. Chooses OK to return to the Replace dialog box, and chooses Replace again. By typing Browse in the Command window, he and the other Woodpeckers get a good laugh seeing all the Bumblebees listed as Bumbling Brickheads.

This was so much fun the saboteurs decided to get rid of the Lemur Lodge altogether. To do this, they:

1. Choose Delete from the Record menu.
2. Check the For box and press Enter to call up the Expression Builder. To get rid of the Lemur Lodge, they build the expression `Camp = "Lemur Lodge"`.
3. Choose OK to return to the Delete dialog, and choose Delete.

When the feckless leader of the Woodpeckers types Browse in the Command window to see the new version of the database, he goes crazy: The Lemurs are still there! The Delete option only marks the records for deletion; they are not actually erased until you choose Pack from the Database menu.

To save some poor unsuspecting Camp office worker from accidentally wiping out the Lemur Lodge records, you could choose Recall from the Record menu, choose a scope of All, and choose Recall from the dialog box. This unmarks all the records marked for deletion. See if you can have this much fun with the rest of the Record menu.

Record Append

Append adds a blank record to the end of the active database in Append mode. Append mode lists fields and records vertically in the Append window.

In Browse mode, fields are listed horizontally. If you choose Record Append in Browse mode, the window changes to Append mode as it adds the blank record. When you are in Append mode, each field label begins with ». To switch back to Browse mode, choose Browse from the Browse menu. When you finish entering records, choose File Close, press Ctrl-W, or double-click on the close box with the mouse.

See also Browse Append/Change, File Close

Record Change

Choose Change to display the active database vertically so you can edit records, as shown in Fig. 1-56. When you choose Change, the Browse menu is added to the menu bar. Choose Browse to view records with the fields listed horizontally. You can also edit records in Browse mode.

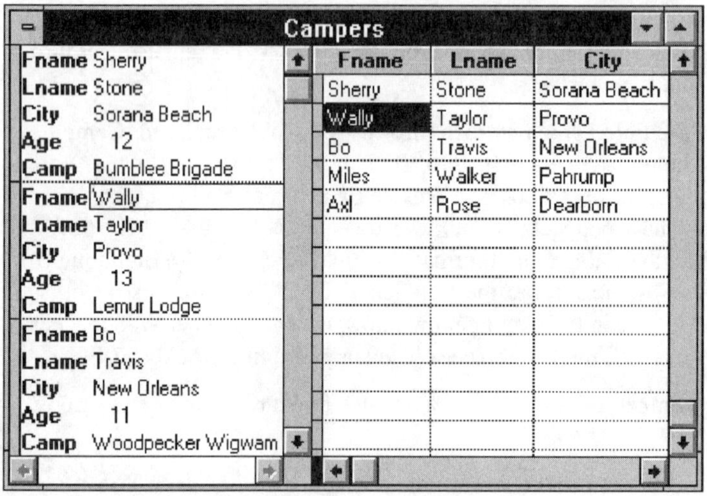

1-56 Append mode (left) and Browse mode (right).

You can choose Change from the Browse menu to return to Change mode, or choose Change from the Record menu. When you finish entering records, choose File Close, press ctrl-W, or double-click on the close box with the mouse.

See also File Close

Record Goto...

Choose Goto... to position the cursor on a record in the database. This operation is the same as Browse Goto.

See also Browse Goto

Record Locate...

Using the dialog shown in Fig. 1-57, you can locate a record in the database using a valid FoxPro Scope, For or While expression. See the Database Append From section in this chapter for more information on Scope, For, and While.

1-57 Locate dialog box.

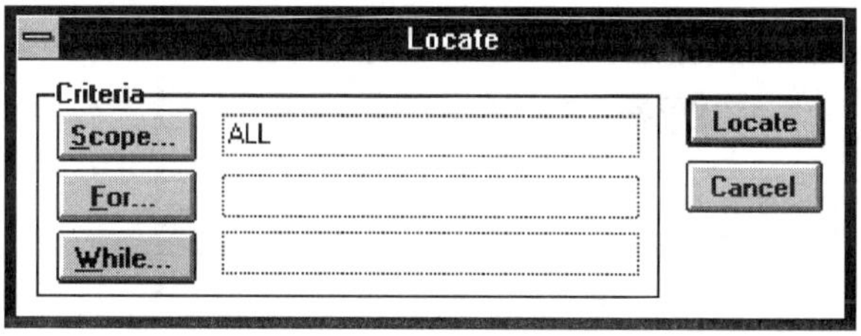

When all your conditions are set, choose Locate. The cursor moves to the first record that meets your conditions. To find the next record, choose Continue from the Record menu. If no records match your conditions, the cursor moves to the end of the file or the last record in the specified Scope. Choose Cancel or press Esc to leave the dialog box with locating records.

See also Database Append From, Record Continue

Record Continue

Choose this option to find the next record that meets the criteria specified in Record Locate. This option is only available if a preceding Locate command was successful.

Shortcut key: Ctrl-K

See also Record Locate

Record Seek...

Seek... locates a record in the database using the active index. When you select Seek..., the Expression Builder appears. The expression you enter must be based on the active index key. For example, if the active index tag is Lname and its key expression is UPPER(Lname), the Seek expression must include the uppercase value of Lname.

When you choose OK, FoxPro searches the index for the location of a matching record. In a Browse window, the record is highlighted. If no records match the expression, the last record in the file is selected. This option is only available if the database has an active index.

Record Replace

The Replace option (see Fig. 1-58) lets you replace data in a field. The Replace dialog box contains a list of the fields in the database shown in the From Table pop-up. Select the appropriate database, and then select the field in which you want to replace data.

With... Type the replacement data in the With... text box, or select the With... push button to activate the Expression Builder. The expression you enter must match the data type of the field you are replacing.

If you want to replace the information in particular records, use any combination of the Scope, For or While check boxes to specify criteria. See the Database Append From section in this chapter for more information on Scope, For, and While.

See also Database Append From

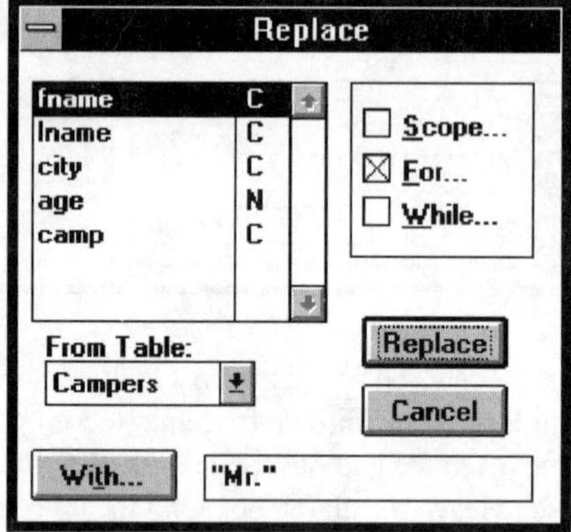

1-58 Replace dialog box.

Record Delete...

This option lets you mark records for deletion. If you have already opened a Browse window with a database, the easiest way to mark single records is to use Browse Toggle Delete. Marking records for deletion does not actually remove them from the database. To do this you must choose Pack from the Database menu.

When you choose Delete..., a dialog box (see Fig. 1-59) appears. If you want to delete only certain records, use any combination of the Scope, For or While check boxes to specify criteria. See the Database Append From section in this chapter for more information on Scope, For, and While.

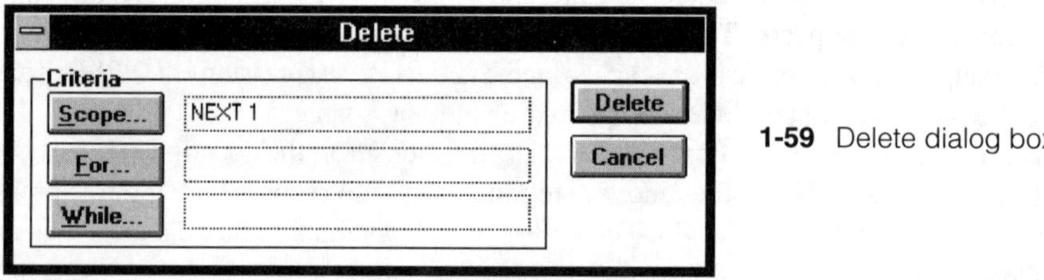

1-59 Delete dialog box.

When you have completed your definitions, choose Delete. To exit the dialog box without deleting records, choose Cancel or press Esc.

See also Database Append From, Browse Toggle Delete, Database Pack

Record Recall...

This option lets you unmark records that have been marked for deletion, before they are removed from the database. If you have already opened a Browse window with a database, the easiest way to recall single records is select the Browse Toggle Delete option when the record pointer is on a deleted record.

When you choose Recall..., a dialog box similar to Fig. 1-59 appears. If you want to recall only certain records, use any combination of the Scope, For or While check boxes to specify criteria. See the Database Append From section in this chapter for more information on Scope, For, and While. When you have completed your definitions, choose Recall. To exit the dialog box without recalling deleted records, choose Cancel or press Esc.

See also Browse Toggle Delete, Record Delete, Database Pack

The Program menu

The Program menu shown in Fig. 1-60 is used to execute and manipulate FoxPro program files.

Do... Ctrl+D
Cancel
Resume Ctrl+M

Debug
Trace

Compile...
Generate...
Macros...

Beautify...
FoxDoc

1-60 The Program menu.

Program Do...

Do... lets you execute a program file. The Do... dialog box contains a list of FoxPro source code files and FoxPro applications including .PRG, .APP, .SPR, .MPR, .QPR, and .EXE files. Select the appropriate drive, directory, and file you want to run and choose Do.

If you want to interrupt a program while it is running, press Escape. In the dialog box that appears, you can choose Cancel to stop running the program and close the file.

Choose Suspend to stop running the program but keep the file open. You can continue running the program if you choose Resume from the Program menu. Choose Ignore to ignore the interruption and proceed with the program execution.

Shortcut key: Ctrl-D

See also Program Resume, Window Trace

Program Cancel

Choose Cancel when you want to cancel execution of a program after choosing Suspend to interrupt the program. This option is only available after you have chosen Suspend and if the menu is active.

See also Program Do..., Window Trace

Program Resume

The Resume option resumes execution of a suspended program. Resume is only available after you choose Suspend to interrupt the running of a program and if the menu is active.

Shortcut key: Ctrl-M

See also Program Do..., Window Trace

Program Debug

The Debug window (see Fig. 1-61) lets you monitor the value of variables and expressions and set break points in programs you have written. To monitor values, Tab to the left partition of the window, or click there with the mouse and type the variable or expression you want to monitor. When you execute your program, the Debug window displays the values in the right partition of the window. You can type up to 16 debugging variables in the Debug window, and they can be related to more than one module or program.

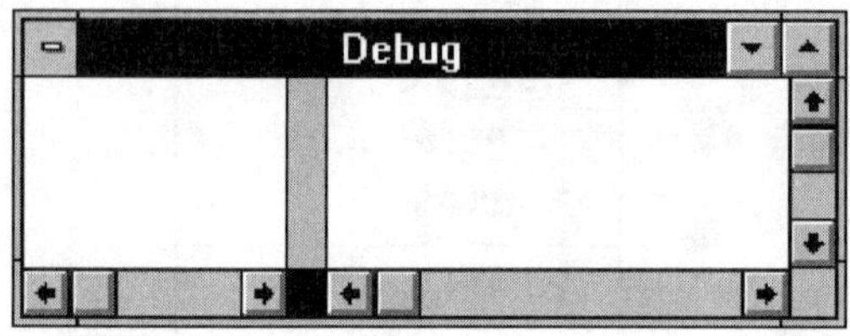

1-61 Debug window.

A break point column separates the left and right partitions of the Debug window. To set a program break, mark a spot on the column by clicking to the right of the variable or expression that sets the break condition. With the keyboard, Tab until you see a highlighted block in the break point column, and use the ↑ and ↓ keys to move the block next to the variable or expression you want. Press the spacebar and a bullet appears to indicate a break point is set. You can remove a break point by clicking on it or pressing the spacebar when the cursor is positioned on it.

The program is suspended when the value of a variable or expression at a break point changes, and the message "Do suspended" appears on the screen. You can choose Cancel or Resume from the Program menu or from the Trace window to cancel or resume execution of the program.

See also Program Cancel, Program Resume, Program Trace

Program Trace

You can watch your program executing in the Trace window shown in Fig. 1-62. Each program line is highlighted as it is executed. Use the Trace window to set break points within programs, similar to setting break points with variables using the Debug window. When a break point is encountered in a program, program execution is suspended and the Trace window is displayed with the current program line highlighted.

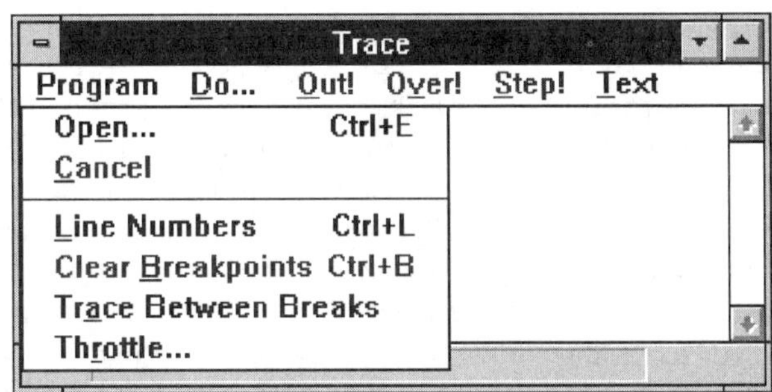

1-62 Trace window.

The Trace window contains its own menu of 6 menu pads: Program, Do..., Out, Over, Step, and Text. The Out, Over and Step options are only enabled when a program is running. The Program pop-up contains the following options:

Open... Displays the Open File dialog, which allows you to open a source code file in the Trace window.

Cancel When selected, cancels a suspended program.

Line Numbers When checked, displays line numbers next to each line of the program displayed in the Trace window.

Clear Break points When checked, removes all break points that you may have inserted into a number of source code files.

Trace Between Breaks When checked, all lines of the current program are displayed in the Trace window as they are executed. When not checked, only those lines that have break points will be displayed in the Trace window, as those lines are encountered. This option is set on by default. You can also use the SET TRBETWEEN command to perform the same action.

Throttle... When selected, the Execution Throttle dialog is displayed. This dialog allows you to specify the speed, in seconds, at which program lines are executed. If the value is greater than 0, each program line will be executed every specified second.

Program/Procedure names When a program is executed, its name appears in a list at the bottom of the Program pop-up. As other programs and procedures are called, their names are added to the list. The current program or procedure is always the first name in the list, the program that called the current program is next, and so on. Selecting the name of a program other than the current one will display that program or procedure in the Trace window. You can use the Home key to return to the first program in the list.

You can set break points in the Trace window to suspend program execution. Position the cursor on the desired line and click with the mouse or press the spacebar to set a break point. A bullet appears to the left of the line, and the program will stop running when the break point is reached. You can choose Cancel or Resume from the Program menu or by selecting the push buttons in the Trace window.

To remove a break point, click or press the spacebar on that line. Break points references are stored in the FoxPro resource file (usually FOXUSER.DBF). This allows you to set the break points only once and have them active for any future FoxPro session. If a source-code file that contains break points is recompiled, the break point references will be removed.

The Do... option will begin executing the program displayed in the Trace window. If no program is displayed, the Open File dialog appears, allowing you to select a source-code file to run. Once a program has been executed and subsequently suspended, Do... changes to Resume. Selecting Resume continues program execution at the line where it was suspended.

The Out option continues execution of the current program, without displaying it in the Trace window, even if Trace Between Breaks is checked. Program execution stops at the program line immediately following the line that called the current program. This allows you to not have to wait and watch while a subroutine or lower level program is executed.

The Over option allows you to "step" over a program line that calls another program or procedure. If the line being stepped over calls another program or procedure, it is executed without being displayed in the Trace window.

The Step option executes a program one line at a time. Use the Text... option to change the font used in the Trace window. If you are running a program or application that contains no debug information (see Program Compile), the message "Source is not available" is displayed in the Trace window.

If you press Esc while a program is suspended and the Trace window is active, a dialog box appears. Choose Cancel to stop, or choose Ignore to continue execution.

See also Program Cancel, Program Resume, Program Debug, Program Compile, SET TRBETWEEN

Program Compile...

In the Compile dialog box (see Fig. 1-63) you can select one or more FoxPro source-code files to be compiled. When a source-code file is compiled, an object file is created with the same name as the source-code file, but with a different extension. When you run a program, FoxPro uses the object file to interpret the commands. Listed below are source-code file extensions and their related object file extensions.

Source code	Object code
.PRG	.FXP
.SPR	.SPX
.MPR	.MPX
.QPR	.QPX

The Files to Compile list in the dialog box displays all the program and format files in the current directory. Change the drive or directory by making selections in the Drives pop-up and Current Directory list. The following options are available in the Compile dialog (The More >> push button must be selected to expand the Compile dialog.)

Files To Compile Select from the list the source-code files to compile. Clicking on a single file will highlight that file. To select multiple files, use a combination of Shift + click or Ctrl + click.

Show All Files When selected, displays all files in the current drive and directory.

Tag All/Tag None Select the Tag All push button to tag all files in the list, and Tag None to deselect any tagged files in the list. If all files are tagged and you want to deselect a file, Shift-click on the appropriate file.

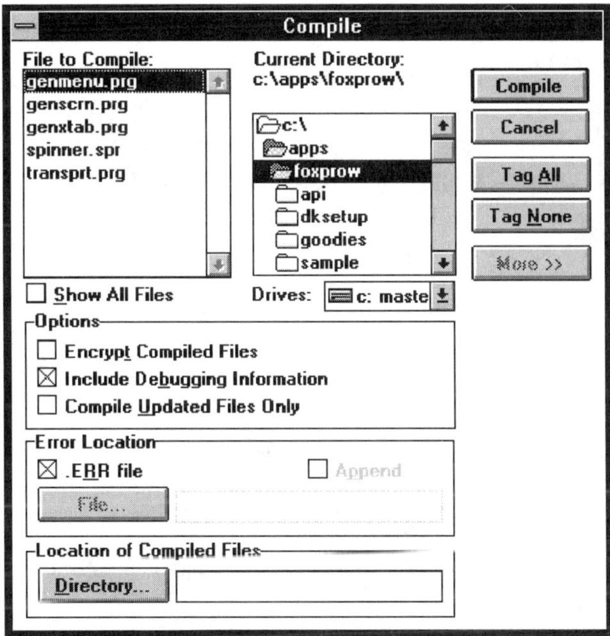

1-63 Compile dialog box.

Options These check boxes allow you to control which selected files are compiled, if the resulting files are encrypted, and whether or not the compiled programs contain debugging information.

Encrypt Compiled Files When checked, FoxPro will scramble and encrypt the resulting file.

Include Debugging Information When checked, FoxPro will include the information that allows you to trace your program through the trace window. If any program files are compiled without debugging information, any attempt to trace the execution will result in a "Source code not available" message in the trace window.

Compile Updated Files Only When checked, FoxPro will only compile those selected program files that have been changed since they were last compiled.

Error Location Lets you create an error file that will contain all command and function errors the FoxPro encounters during the compiling process.

.ERR file When checked, FoxPro will log errors for each source code file in a file with the same name as the source-code file, giving it an extension of .ERR.

File... If selected, you can tell FoxPro what file to log all errors to. Enter the file name in the text box, or select the File... push button to display the Open File dialog. The Append option will add to the file if it already exits, otherwise a new one will be created.

Append When checked, adds to the file if it already exits, otherwise a new one will be created.

Location of Compiled Files If you want to save the resulting files in a different directory than the source files, enter the directory name in the text box. Select the Directory... push button to display the Select Directory dialog, which allows you to select a drive and directory.

Select the Compile push button when you are ready to begin the compilation process.

See also Program Compile

Program Compile

When any source-code file editing window is frontmost, the Compile... option displays as Compile. Choosing Compile simply compiles the open source-code file.

If FoxPro finds errors as the program is compiling, the line with the error is highlighted in the editing window and a dialog box tells you your error. Choose Ignore to ignore the error and continue compiling. If you choose Ignore All, FoxPro ignores this error and any that follow. Choose Cancel to stop compilation. If you SET LOGERRORS ON before you choose Compile, FoxPro stores the errors messages it finds in an .ERR file with the same name as the program file.

See also Program Compile..., SET LOGERRORS

Program Generate

The Generate option is used with the Screen Builder and Menu Builder tools to generate source-code files from screen and menu layouts.

See also Chapter 6, Using the Screen Builder, chapter 7, Using the Menu Builder

Program Macros...

Macros are like FoxPro's hot keys. When you press a macro key combination, a predefined set of actions is automatically performed. You can create macros with the Macros... menu option. Macros definitions can be saved to a file. When FoxPro is started, any macros in the DEFAULT.FKY file will automatically be restored.

The Macros dialog box (see Fig. 1-64) contains a scrollable list of macros available for use. F2 through F9 are default macros. When FoxPro is first started, the default macros F2 through F9 issue the following FoxPro commands:

Macro	Command
F2	SET
F3	LIST
F4	DIR
F5	DISPLAY STRUCTURE
F6	DISPLAY STATUS
F7	DISPLAY MEMORY
F8	DISPLAY
F9	APPEND

The macro settings of the F2–F9 keys can be changed for a FoxPro session using the SET FUNCTION command. See chapter 2 for more information on these commands.

Record Choose this option to create a macro by recording the keystrokes as you run them. The Macro Key Definition dialog shown in Fig. 1-65 appears. When the cursor is in the Defined Key text box, you must press a key combination that will be the hot key for the

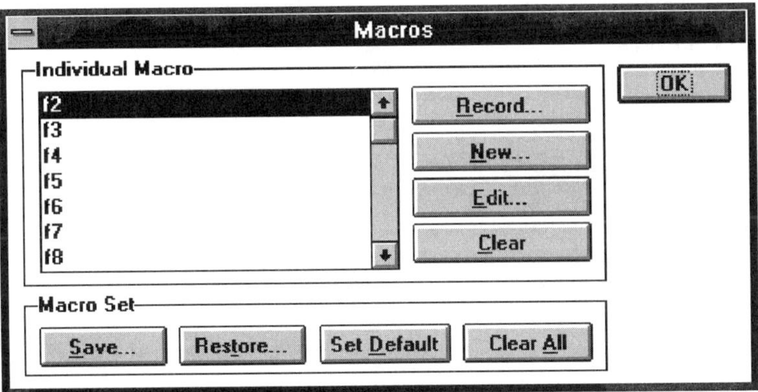

1-64 Macros dialog box.

1-65 Record Macro dialog box.

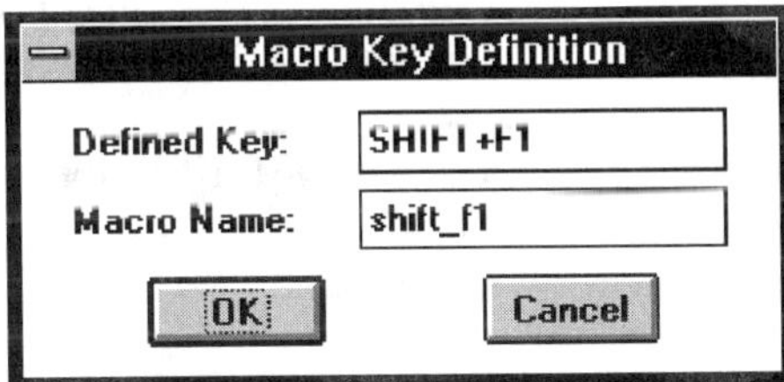

macro. See the New Macro section above for valid key combinations. Once a key combination is entered, the Macro Name text box is automatically filled in, replacing the plus sign (+) with an underscore (_). You can change the macro name without changing the hot key character(s).

Once you have defined the macro hot keys and name, select the OK push button to begin recording the macro, or Cancel to exit the dialog without recording. If you try to define a macro that already exists, a message box appears prompting you to overwrite or append to the existing macro. You can choose Overwrite to replace the existing macro or Append keystrokes to add the new commands to the end of the existing macro.

When you are finished recording the macro, press Shift-F10. The Stop Recording dialog box appears. An example is shown in Fig. 1-66. If you made an error and you want to erase what you have done, choose Discard. The Insert Literal button literally inserts the next keystroke you type into your macro. If you would like the macro to pause during execution, choose Insert Pause and specify either a keystroke or number of seconds to resume playback. Once a macro has paused, you can resume entering commands or selecting menu options until the macro continues. When you are ready for the macro to continue, press Shift-F10.

If you decide you want to keep going with the macro you started, choose Continue, and you can continue recording the defined macro. Choose OK if you are finished and you want the macro to be saved and available for use. FoxPro does not record mouse movements or button clicks in a macro.

New... Choose this button to manually create a new macro. The Macro Edit dialog shown in Fig. 1-67 appears. You must press a key combination that will be the hot key for the macro. You can combine Ctrl, Alt, or Function with letter keys. Combinations that are allowed are listed below:

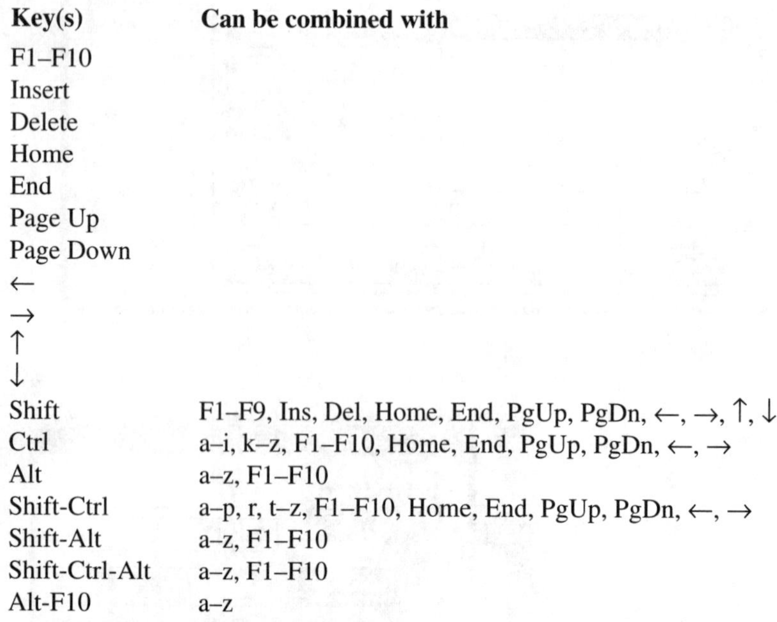

Key(s)	**Can be combined with**
F1–F10	
Insert	
Delete	
Home	
End	
Page Up	
Page Down	
←	
→	
↑	
↓	
Shift	F1–F9, Ins, Del, Home, End, PgUp, PgDn, ←, →, ↑, ↓
Ctrl	a–i, k–z, F1–F10, Home, End, PgUp, PgDn, ←, →
Alt	a–z, F1–F10
Shift-Ctrl	a–p, r, t–z, F1–F10, Home, End, PgUp, PgDn, ←, →
Shift-Alt	a–z, F1–F10
Shift-Ctrl-Alt	a–z, F1–F10
Alt-F10	a–z

1-66 Macro Stop Recording dialog box.

1-67 New Macro dialog box.

You can create and save several macros using the same keystrokes, as long as you save them in different files. Of course, only one macro per keystroke set can be available for use at a time.

When you press the combination you want to use, it appears in the Defined Key text box. A macro name also appears in the Macro Name text box. You can accept this name or type a new one. Typically, you will use the macro keystrokes (with an underline replacing the hyphen) as the macro name. Macro names can be up to 20 characters long. In FoxPro, you must use a plus sign (+) between key names, such as Shift and Ctrl (Shift + Ctrl), and do not leave any spaces between key names and the plus sign.

The Macro Contents text box is where you enter the keystrokes and commands to evaluate when your macro is executed. Enclose all valid FoxPro keystrokes in curly braces ({}). FoxPro keystrokes can be found in the ON KEY LABEL section in chapter 2.

Select OK to save the macro. If you have defined a macro key that already exists, FoxPro will prompt you to overwrite the existing macro. Your new macro is now displayed in the macros list.

Edit The macro Edit option allows you to manually edit a previously recorded macro. When this option is selected the New Macro dialog shown in Fig. 1-67 appears. This allows you to change the Defined Key or the Macro Name without rerecording the macro. The macro contents lists all the literal text and keyboard functions that were entered when the macro was recorded. To change the macro, simply move your editing cursor to the desired area and make the appropriate change. All keyboard commands such as Enter, Spacebar, Escape, etc. are enclosed in curly brackets ({}).

Clear and Clear All When you create a macro, it appears in the scrollable list and you can use it to perform the actions you recorded. If you quit FoxPro after creating a new macro without saving it, the macro is erased.

Pressing Clear before the macro is saved also erases the macro. If you have saved the macro, however, pressing Clear simply clears it from the scrollable list. You can use the Restore push button, described below, to restore the file in which you saved the macro, and it will appear again on the scrollable list. Clear clears the selected macro from the list. Clear All clears all the macros on the list.

Save... If you have created a set of macros that you will want to use again in other FoxPro sessions, use the Save push button to save the macro definitions to a file. When you choose Save, the Save As dialog box appears. Choose the directory in which you want to save the macro file, and enter the file name in the text box. When you save a macro file, all the macros listed in the scrollable list are saved to the specified file with an .FKY file extension.

Choose OK when you are ready to save the macros, or choose Cancel to exit Save As without saving the file. If you use Clear or Clear All after saving macros, you can create new macros with the same hot keys. You can save and clear these macros and restore the previously saved macros using the Restore push button.

Restore... Restore activates the File Open dialog. Enter the name of a valid FoxPro macro file to restore and select Open. If you choose Restore when there is already a list of active macros in the Macro dialog box, the macros in the restored file are added to the list. If any of the restored macros use the same hot keys as the current list, the newly restored macro replaces the existing one. The original macro, however, is not deleted from the file or altered in any way.

Set Default When this option is selected, all current macro definitions are saved to the startup macro file, DEFAULT.FKY. FoxPro will save this file in the same directory where your FOXUSER file is stored, or in the current directory if there is no FOXUSER file. Choose OK to confirm your action.

Program Beautify...

Use Beautify to change the appearance of a program file. If you have a certain style to writing program code, such as all commands upper- or lowercase, the Beautification Options dialog (see Fig. 1-68) can be used to quickly update a program to your style. The following options are available:

Make Key Words Key words consist of FoxPro commands and functions. Select UPPER CASE to change all key words to uppercase, lower case to change all key words to lowercase, or No Change to leave all keywords unchanged.

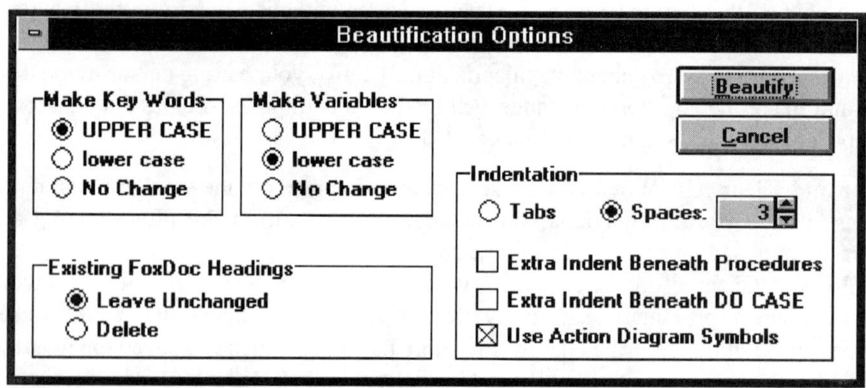

1-68 Beautify dialog box.

Make Variables Variables consist of FoxPro system variables, user-defined variables, procedure and function names, and unknowns. Select UPPER CASE to change all variables to uppercase, lower case to change all variables to lowercase, or No Change to leave all variables unchanged.

Tabs/Spaces When a program is beautified, all control structure code (IF/ENDIF, DO WHILE/ENDDO, SCAN/ENDSCAN, etc.) is automatically indented based on the setting of the Tabs/Spaces radio button. If Tabs is selected, program code is indented one Tab stop. The number or Tab spaces is determined by the setting of the _tabs system memory variable. If Spaces is selected, program code is indented the specified number of spaces to a maximum of nine spaces.

Extra Indent Beneath Procedures When checked, all program code beneath a procedure or function is automatically indented. The amount of indentation is dependent on the Tabs/Spaces setting.

Extra Indent Beneath DO CASE When checked, all program code between a DO CASE/ENDCASE structure is indented. The amount of indentation is dependent on the Tabs/Spaces setting.

Use Action Diagram Symbols When checked, action diagram symbols for control structures and their terminators (IF/ENDIF, DO WHILE/ENDDO, SCAN/ENDSCAN, etc.) are displayed to provide a quick visual check on the organization of a program file. The diagram symbols are actually placed into the program file and must be removed before compiling. This can be accomplished by reversing the action from the Beautify dialog or by choosing Undo from the Edit menu. This option is only available when the current program file is being edited using the FoxFont font.

Existing FoxDoc Headings If the current program file utilizes FoxDoc headings, you can choose to leave them unchanged or delete them automatically by selecting the appropriate radio button.

Since no changes are made to the actual program file until it is saved, you can use the Beautification Options dialog as many times as necessary to create the desired program file. When you are ready to save your program, select Save or Save As... from the File menu.

Program FoxDoc

FoxDoc is an application system documenter that can be used to document a FoxPro application.

The Help menu

Use the options on the Help menu (see Fig. 1-69) to find out more about FoxPro or call additional desktop programs that you have installed.

Contents
Search for Help on...
How to Use Help
About FoxPro...
Calculator
Calendar/Diary
Filer
Puzzle

1-69 The Help menu.

Help Contents

The FoxPro Help system is context-sensitive: accessing the help system displays information for the dialog or menu function that is selected. FoxPro offers two types of help systems: the Windows style help (see Fig. 1-70), or the familiar FoxPro .DBF style help (see Fig. 1-71). This section documents the .DBF style help since it is common among all FoxPro platforms. Consult your Windows documentation for more information on using the Windows style help.

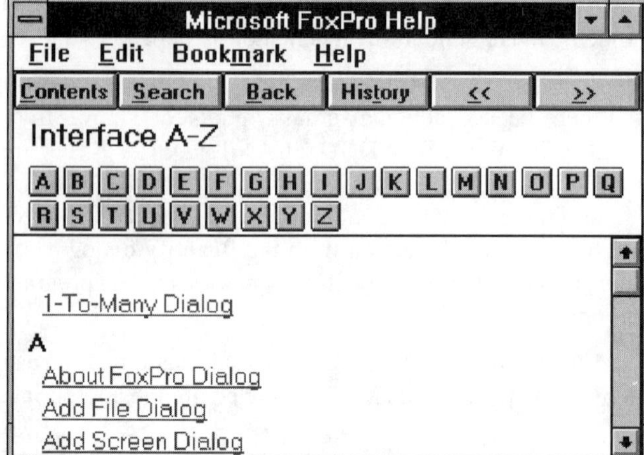

1-70 Windows style help.

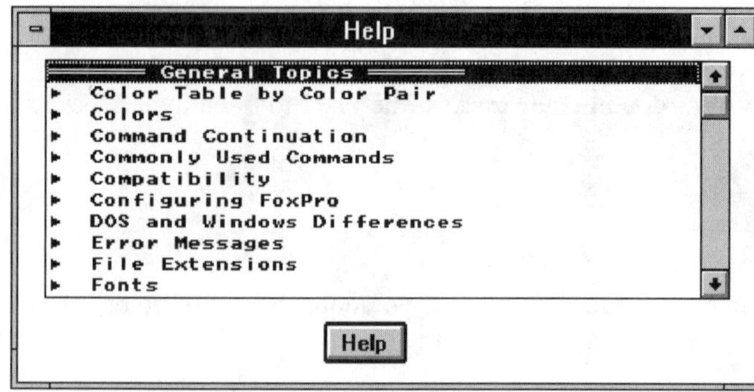

1-71 FoxPro .DBF style help.

The Help window shown in Fig. 1-71 is a standard FoxPro window and initially displays a list of all available help topics. You can scroll through the list or type the first few letters of the topic you would like to see. To view the help text of any topic press Enter or double click on the topic. Once help text is displayed you can navigate through the help by using displayed controls:

Topics Returns the help window back to the topics list.

Next Displays the help text for the next topic.

Previous Displays the help text for the previous topic.

Look Up Highlighting any text in the window and selecting the Look Up push button will search through all available help topics for one matching your text.

See also Select an item in the pop-up and help for that topic will be displayed.

You can scroll through the help text with the arrow, PgUp, PgDn, Home, and End keys. The FoxPro help system is context-sensitive: selecting Help at any dialog will instantly display the Help window with text for that dialog.

You can also select and copy Help text to the clipboard and paste the text into other files in FoxPro. The default help text can be changed by turning off the help system using the SET HELP OFF command, opening the FOXHELP.DBF database, and then browsing the text detail memo field.

Shortcut key: F1

See also Edit Copy, SET HELP

Help Search for Help on...

Search for Help on is only enabled when using Windows style help and can be used to search for help topics.

Help How to Use Help

How to Use Help is only enabled when using Windows style help and can be used to display information on using the Windows help system.

Help About FoxPro...

The About FoxPro dialog consists of seven different screens which provide a variety of information concerning FoxPro and the current session. You can navigate through the screens using the Next and Prior push buttons. Select the Done push button to remove the dialog.

Help Calculator

The FoxPro Calculator is a desktop accessory that looks like a standard pocket calculator. You can perform calculations by choosing the calculator buttons with the mouse. From the keyboard, type the equation as it would be written. All the keys have keyboard equivalents except:

Keystroke	Calculator button
Q	$\sqrt{\ }$
R	MR
N	@
A	M+
Z	MC
S	M–

To calculate, for example, the square root of 27 times 16 divided by 3, type

```
27*16/3Q=
```

The result is 12.

You can edit text in the display panel, and copy and paste into other documents. You can also copy numeric values from other documents into the display panel.

See also _calvalue, _calcmem

Calculator Preferences If you choose Preferences from the Edit menu, you can change preferences in the Calculator Preferences dialog box. The three NumLock State radio buttons determine whether NumLock on your keyboard is turned on or off. If the first radio button is on, NumLock simply remains the way it was when you choose Calculator from the System menu.

If you turn on Remember NumLock state, the Calculator reverts to whichever state NumLock was in last time you used it. If you choose the third button, NumLock turns on automatically when you use the Calculator.

The three Decimal Places radio buttons determine the type of decimal place used in calculator functions. When you choose OK, your preferences takes effect. When you exit the Calculator, NumLock returns to the state it was in before you called the Calculator.

See also Edit Preferences

Help Calendar/Diary

The Calendar/Diary is a complete calendar and diary. When you choose this option, the Calendar/Diary dialog opens. The left half of the window in Fig. 1-72 displays the current month with today's date selected. The right half of window is the diary section, where you can enter text related to the selected date. When you open the calendar, a Diary menu appears at the right end of the menu bar. Keyboard users can use the menu to select options that correspond to the push buttons in the window.

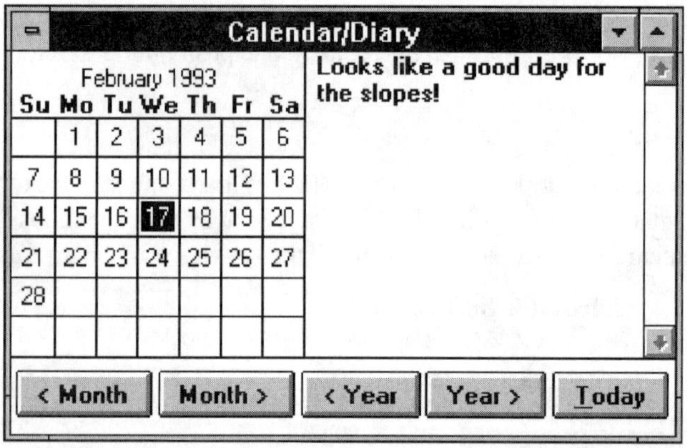

1-72 Calendar/Diary.

To change the selected day in the calendar, use the arrow keys or click on the date you want to select. To change the month, choose PgUp to move backward and PgDn to move forward, or use the Month push buttons at the bottom of the window. To move backward and forward by year, use Shift-PgUp or Shift-PgDn, or choose the Year push buttons. Select the Today push button to return to the calendar displays to today's date.

To make a diary entry, select the appropriate day and press Tab or click in the Diary panel. You can enter as much text as you like—there is no limit—and you can use standard FoxPro editing techniques to edit text (See the Edit menu description). To return to the calendar, press Shift-Tab or click in the calendar with the mouse.

Eventually you will have enough old entries that valuable space on your disk is wasted. You can periodically delete entries by selecting a day on the calendar and choosing Delete...

from the Diary menu. A message asks if you want to delete all entries prior to the day. Choose Yes to delete the entries, or No to return to the Calendar without making deletions. You can close the Calendar window by choosing File Close, pressing Esc, or clicking the close box.

See also Edit menu, _diarydate

Help Filer...

The FoxPro Filer desk accessory lets you manipulate all the files and directories on your hard disk without leaving FoxPro. Many of FoxPro's Filer functions are similar to the Windows File Manager utility. When you choose Filer from the System menu, the Filer dialog shown in Fig. 1-73 is activated.

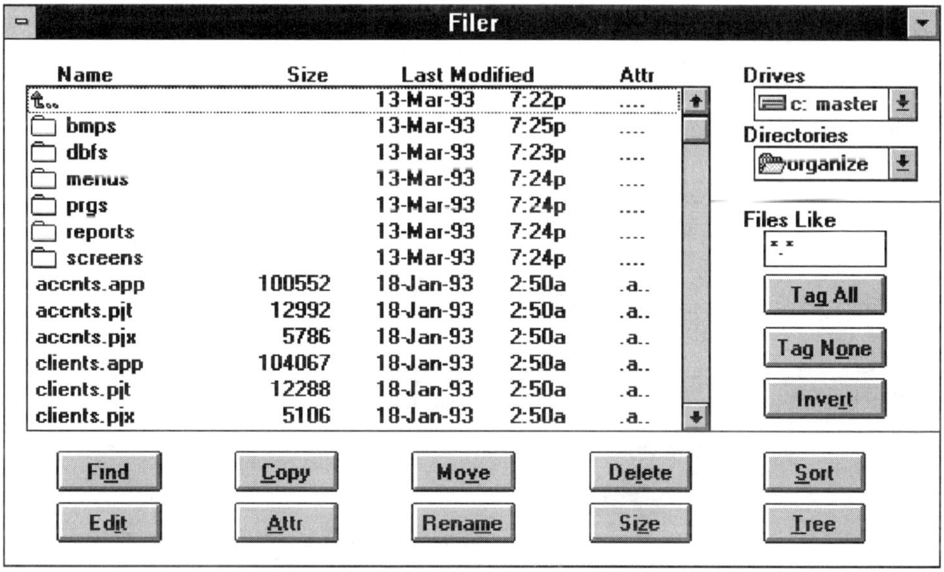

1-73 The Files panel.

Files list The scrollable list in the Files panel contains all the files in the current drive and directory. Use the Drives and Directories pop-ups to change the drive or directory and to display the appropriate files. You can also change directories by choosing a folder icon in the scrollable list. The [..] is the parent directory, so you move up the directory tree when you choose it in the list. If the current directory is the root directory, no parent directory is displayed in the list.

Files Like You can limit which files appear in the scrollable list by specifying a file description in the Files Like text box. You can enter any portion of the file name and use the wildcard asterisk to display files with the characters you have typed, plus any other characters. For example, entering CAMP*.* would list all files that begin with CAMP, including CAMPERS.DBF, CAMP.CDX, etc. If you want to indicate more than one specification, simply separate the phrases with a semicolon. For example, to list all .DBF and all .IDX files, you would enter *.DBF;*.IDX. Do not put spaces between the specifications. Press Enter to list the files you have specified.

Tag All and Tag None When you select a file on which you want to perform an operation, the file is highlighted. You can tag individual files by Tabbing to the scrollable list and highlighting the desired file. Press the spacebar or click with the mouse to tag the file.

To tag multiple files, highlight the first file, hold down the Shift key and use the ↑ or ↓ keys, or point with the mouse to highlight and select the files you want. If you continue to hold down the Shift key and click on → back to a tagged file, the file is untagged. The Shift key lets you toggle between tagged and untagged. Tagged files remain tagged until you untag them, change drives, switch to the Tree panel, or exit the Filer dialog. You have two tag options available:

Tag All Choose Tag All to tag all the files in the scrollable list. This is most useful when you have specified files using Files Like.

Tag None Untags all the tagged files in the list. Unlike Tag All, Tag None untags all tagged files in all directories, regardless of whether the files are shown in the scrollable list.

Invert Choose Invert to untag all tagged files and tag all untagged files in the current directory. This is handy when you want to tag all but a few files. Tag those files, then choose Invert to switch the tagging.

Find Use Find to tag files of a certain description in a number of different directories. In the Find dialog box, enter the file name or portion of the file name with asterisks that you want to find. This text box works the same way as the Files Like text box. Enter *.PRG as shown in Fig. 1-74 to find all program files, or *.PRG;*.SPR to find all program and screen code files. The Filer searches through the current directory.

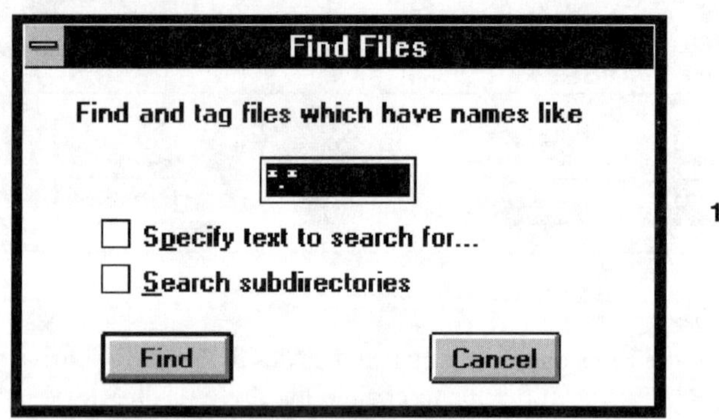

1-74 Filer Find dialog box.

Specify text to search for... You can further specify which files will be found in this dialog box. When you enter text strings of up to 256 characters in one or more of the text boxes, the Filer will tag files that contain those strings. Choose the Any radio button to tag a file that has at least one of the strings you entered. If you want to tag only files that contain all of the specified strings, turn on the All radio button.

The other options are:

Ignore case If you want the Filer to ignore case as it searches for strings, check this box. If one of your strings is Batter my heart three personed God, a file that contains batter my heart three personed god will also be tagged.

Match words If you have entered a short word, you can check Match words to ensure that only files with the exact words are tagged, and not files that contain your string within a word. For example, if your string is con, files with unconscious, connubial, or concentric will be tagged unless Match words is checked. When you have entered your specifications, choose OK to return to the Find dialog box. Choose Cancel or press Esc to exit without making specifications.

Search subdirectories Check this box if you want Find to search the current directory and all its subdirectories. If you want to search an entire drive, choose the root directory in the Directories pop-up and check Search subdirectories.

When you are ready to tag files, choose Find. If you have specified a large number of files or you are currently on a network, this will take some time. When the search is complete, you are returned to the Files panel, and the tagged files matching your description(s) are highlighted in the scrollable list.

Copy You can copy tagged files to a new location with this option. The original file is left intact, and you can rename the copy during the process. Figure 1-75 shows the dialog box. Enter the new name or extension in the text box at the top of the Copy dialog box. The default, *.*, copies the files without changing the name. If you enter, for example, *.new, all the files will have the NEW extension in their new location.

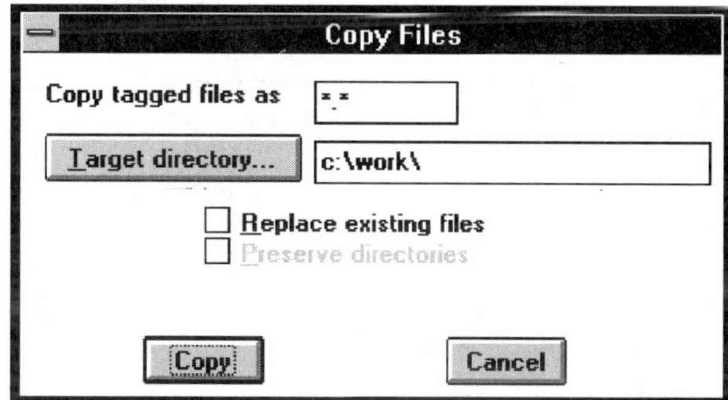

1-75 Filer Copy dialog box.

Target Directory You can enter the target directory in this text box, or choose the push button or menu option, and select a directory in the dialog box that appears. Use the Drive and Directory pop-ups to indicate the desired location for the copied files. When you choose Select, you are returned to the Copy dialog box and the new drive and directory appear in the Target directory text box.

Replace existing files If you check this box, any files in the target directory with the same name as your entry in the Copy tagged files as text box will be overwritten. If you do not check this box and files exist with the same name as the copy name, a message box asks if you want to overwrite the existing files. Choose Yes to overwrite the files, or No to stop the operation and return to the Files panel.

When you are ready to copy the tagged files, choose Copy. Files that are currently open cannot be tagged or copied. After the operation is performed, the original files remain tagged, but the new files are not tagged.

Move Move works exactly the same way as Copy except that the tagged files are erased from their original location in the process. The Move dialog box contains the same options as the Copy dialog box, described in the preceding paragraphs.

Delete Delete removes tagged files from your hard disk. When you choose this option, a dialog box similar to Fig. 1-76 appears:

Delete The Delete dialog box asks if you are sure you want to delete the file named in the text box. Choose Delete to delete this file. This is the default button. If there are other tagged files, the next file name appears in the box.

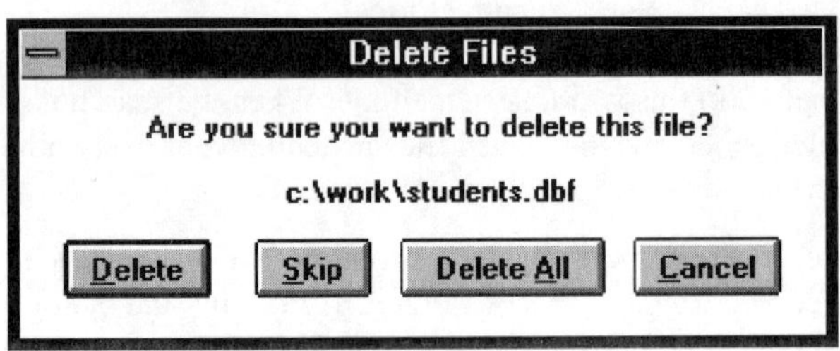

1-76 Delete dialog box.

Skip If you choose Skip, the file is not deleted, and the next tagged file appears.

Delete All Choose this option to delete the displayed file and all the others you have tagged without confirming deletions with the dialog box. It is a good idea to make a backup before you delete all tagged files, especially since Delete All erases tagged files in all directories, not just the directory displayed in the Files panel. You can stop the deletion by pressing Esc. Choose Cancel to return to the Files panel without deleting any files.

Edit When you choose Edit, text editing windows open for all tagged files. You can tag as many files as your computer's memory and the DOS FILES = parameter allow. If an error message appears, you need to untag some files before you can continue. Once the editing windows are open, you can use normal FoxPro editing techniques or options from the Edit menu to edit the windows.

Attr The far right column of the scrollable list in the Files panel shows the DOS attributes of each file. You can change these attributes by selecting a file or a group of files and choosing the Attr push button or menu option. The Attributes dialog box in Fig. 1-77 displays the name of the currently selected file and its current attributes. Use the four check boxes to change the attributes.

Read Only Read Only files can be viewed but not changed (even by the Filer). You can use the Filer to overwrite a Read Only file, but you are prompted for confirmation first.

Attributes

Do you want to change the attributes of

c:\work\students.dbf

☐ Read Only ☐ Hidden File
☒ Archived ☐ System File

Change | Change All | Cancel

1-77 Attributes dialog box.

Archived Files that have been modified or newly created have the Archived attribute. Many backup programs only back up files that are archived. After the file is backed up, the Archived attribute is removed.

Hidden You can hide files so that they do not appear in a DOS directory listing by checking this box. You cannot move, delete, rename, or overwrite hidden files.

System DOS operating files should have the System attribute. This protects the file from being moved, deleted, renamed, or overwritten.

Change and Change All You can apply the attributes you have selected to the file displayed in the dialog box, or to all the tagged files. Choose Change (the default) to change the current file. If you choose Change All, all the tagged files will be given the selected attributes. Keep in mind that Change All changes all tagged files in all directories, not just the current directory. Press Esc to stop a Change All execution. Choose Cancel before you begin an operation to return to the Files panel without changing any attributes.

Rename Choose this option to rename files that are tagged. The file name of the first tagged file appears twice in the Rename dialog box. You can edit the name in the To box, or type a new name as shown in Fig. 1-78. Choose Rename when you are ready to rename the file.

If a file already exists with the name you entered, a message box asks if you want to continue. If you choose Yes, the next tagged file appears in the Rename dialog, and this file name is left unchanged. Choose No to stop the operation and return to the Files panel.

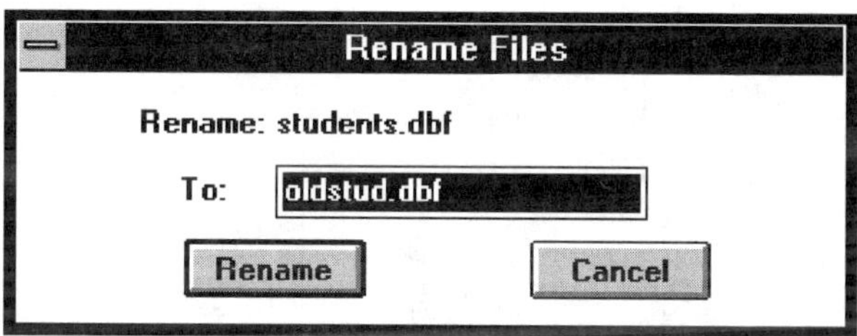

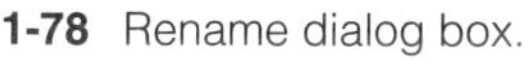
1-78 Rename dialog box.

Size When you are moving or deleting files on your disk, you want to know how much room you will be freeing. The Size dialog box gives you this information. The top half of the box shows the number of tagged files in all directories (not just the current directory), and the number of bytes in those files. The bottom half of the box displays the actual space occupied.

Your DOS allocates disk space in units called clusters. The number of bytes in a cluster depends on the system. If your system allocates 2048 bytes per cluster, then the minimum amount of space reserved for a file is 2048, even if the file only uses 113 bytes. A file containing 2049 bytes will use two clusters for 4096 bytes. The number of clusters used by your tagged files is multiplied by the cluster value to show the actual number of bytes occupied.

Sort You can sort files in a directory to change the order in which they appear in the scrollable list. If you use the Files Like box, only the specified files will be sorted. Otherwise, all files in the directory appear in the new order you select. The Sort dialog box contains two sets of radio buttons. The default selection is Name and Ascending. Choosing Name sorts the files in alphabetical order. Ascending sorts them from A–Z, Descending from Z–A.

Size sorts files according to the number of bytes they use. Choose Ascending to sort from smallest to largest, Descending for largest to smallest. Sort files in date order by choosing the Date radio button. Ascending puts the files in order from the oldest to the newest, Descending from the newest to the oldest.

Attributes sorts files by attribute. Ascending attribute order is r, a, s, h. Descending order is h, s, a, r. When you are ready to sort, choose OK. Files are displayed in the order you chose. Choose Cancel to leave the Sort dialog without changing the file order.

Tree Choose this option to bring up the Tree panel (see Fig. 1-79). This panel lets you perform most of the same operations available in the Files panel, but it performs them on entire directories rather than specific files. Always make a backup before you do anything in the Trees panel. To leave the Trees panel without taking action, press Esc or click the close control.

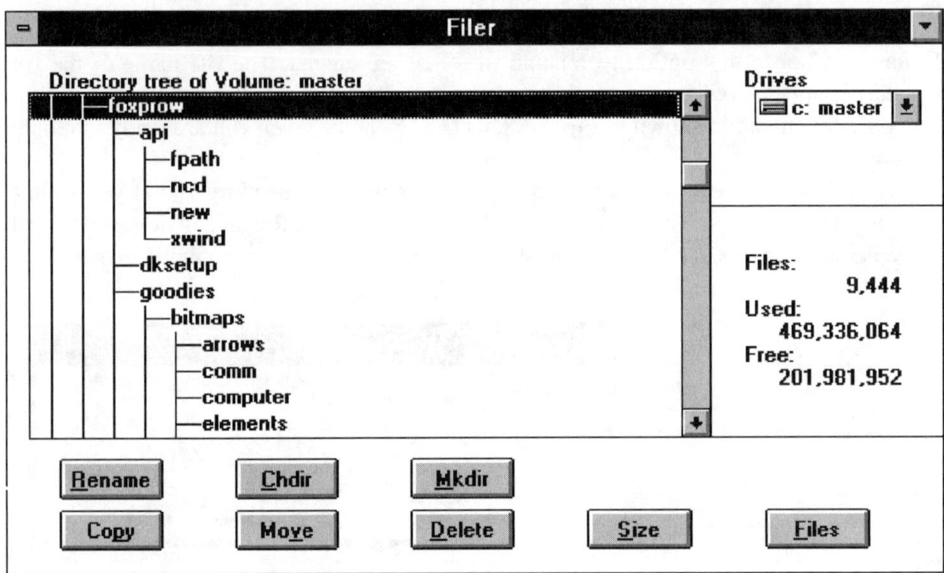

1-79 The Tree panel.

Drive The first time you choose Tree, the scrollable list displays the directories and subdirectories for the current drive. You can use the scroll bar or the ↑ or ↓ to see any directories that do not fit in the list window.

To change the drive, open the Drives pop-up and select the drive you want displayed in the list box. Beneath the Drives pop-up, you will see the number of files on that drive, the space they occupy, and the amount of free space.

Tagging directories Before you can perform operations on the files in directories, you must tag them, just as you do in the Files panel. When you execute an operation, it is performed only on the files in tagged directories. To tag directories, Tab to the scrollable list. Use the ↑ or ↓ keys to highlight the directory you want, or point with the mouse. Then press the spacebar, or click.

To tag more than one directory at a time, hold down the Shift key and select the directories you want to tag. Dragging the mouse with the Shift key held down allows you to tag consecutive directories. You can use the Shift key as a toggle to untag directories. When you press Shift and then press the spacebar or click, a tagged directory is untagged. Use the following push buttons to perform operations on tagged directories.

Rename You can rename directories using the Rename dialog box. The dialog used to rename directories is similar to the one used to rename files (see Fig. 1-78). When you choose this push button, the name of the first tagged directory appears in the dialog box. Type a new name in the text box and choose OK. Directory names must follow standard DOS conventions: maximum 8 characters with an extension of up to 3 characters.

If you have tagged more than one directory, directories appear one after the other in the dialog box to be renamed. If you try to rename a directory with a name that already exists under the same parent directory, you will be denied access to the file. When you rename a directory, none of the files in the directory is affected. The directory will move to the appropriate alphabetical position on the directory tree, under the same parent directory as the original name.

Change Directory This is a convenient way to change the default working directory to avoid having to type the entire path when you want to work on a file in the directory. To change directories, select the directory where you want FoxPro to look when no path is specified and choose ChDir. The bullet that marks the current directory moves to the directory you selected.

Make Directory To make a new directory, select the directory that will be its parent directory and choose Mkdir. The Make Directory dialog box appears. Type the new directory name in the text box and choose Mkdir. If you try to use an existing name, a message box asks if you want to return to the Make Directory dialog to make a new directory in another tagged parent (Yes), or to the Tree panel (No). Choose Cancel to leave the Make Directory dialog box without creating a new directory.

Copy Use this push button to copy the tagged directory into another directory. Files that are currently open cannot be copied. In the Copy dialog box shown in Fig. 1-80, enter the name of the directory into which you want to copy the tagged directory.

If you choose the Target Directory push button, you can select the target directory from the Target dialog box. If files are in the target directory with the same names as files in the directory to be copied, checking the Replace existing files box will overwrite the existing files in the target directory. If this box is not checked, an alert box asks if you want to overwrite files with the same name, and you can choose Yes to do so or No to skip the file and continue the operation.

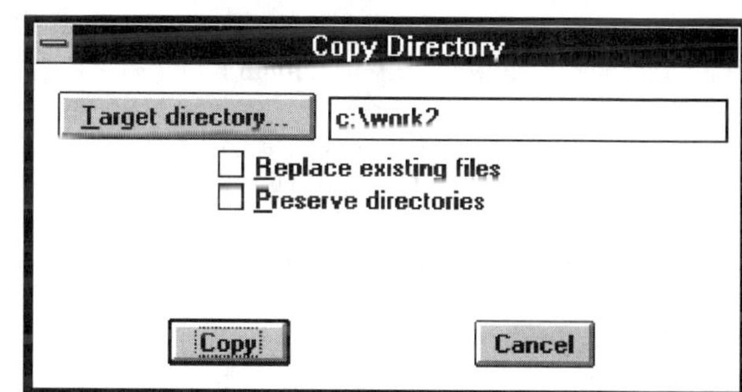

1-80 Copy Directory dialog box.

With Preserve directories, if you tag more than one directory, you can simply copy all the files in all the tagged directories to a single target directory, or you actually copy the directory structure as well. When you choose Preserve directories, all the directories below the tagged directory farthest from the root directory will be preserved in the copy. For example, your C: directory might contain the subdirectories Metal, Classics, and Blues; and your directory tree, with additional subdirectories, would look like this:

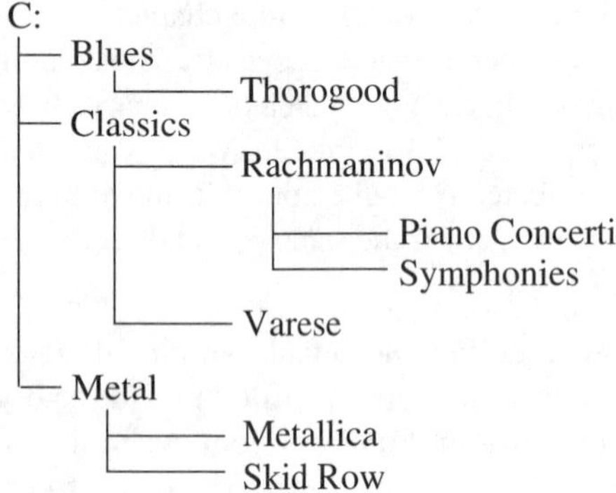

If you tag the Classics directory and the Symphonies subdirectory, and copy them to D:\Favorites, the new D: drive tree looks like this:

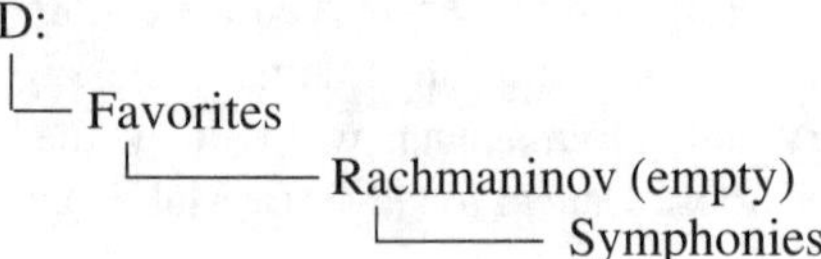

All files from tagged directories are copied, and the directory structure of directories above tagged directories is preserved. Because the Rachmaninov directory was not tagged, any files in that original directory were not copied. Because the Symphonies subdirectory was tagged, the Rachmaninov directory structure was copied intact.

Move Move works exactly the same way as Copy, except that the original tagged directories are deleted when you choose Move. You cannot move an open file. If you tag a parent directory but you do not tag all its subdirectories, the tagged subdirectories will be moved, but the parent will be copied.

Delete Be careful with this option and do a backup before you choose it! The tagged directory name appears at the top of the Delete dialog box.

Delete files only If you check this box, only the files in the tagged directory will be deleted. The directory itself will remain intact.

Remove all subdirectories When you tag a parent directory and check this box, all subdirectories and their files will be deleted. If you want to delete only specific subdirectories, tag them individually and make sure this box is not checked.

Delete Choose Delete to remove the directory displayed in the dialog box. If you have tagged other directories, they will appear consecutively each time you choose Delete.

Skip If you want to go on to the next directory without deleting the directory displayed in the dialog box, choose Skip.

Delete All If you are brave enough to delete all the tagged directories without confirmation, choose Delete All. A message asks if you are sure you want to do this. If you choose Yes, all the tagged directories and their files are erased forever. Choose Cancel before executing a Delete operation to leave the dialog box without taking action.

Size The Size dialog box is the same as the size dialog box in the Files panel. The top half of the box shows the number of files in the tagged directories and the number of bytes in those files. The bottom half of the box displays the actual space occupied. DOS allocates disk space in units called clusters. Depending on your system, DOS might allocate, say, 2048 bytes per cluster, in which case any file, no matter how small, uses at least 2048 bytes. A file containing 2049 bytes will use two clusters, or 4096 bytes.

Files Choose this option to return to the Files panel. (Refer to the beginning of this section for a description of the Files panel.)

See also FILER

Help Puzzle

Have fun! Hint: press Ctrl-End when you get stuck.

The Run menu

The Run menu is unique; it is not actually a part of the default system menu, but is added by a FoxPro startup application. When you first install FoxPro onto your computer, the application FOXRUN.APP is installed in the same directory as FoxPro. FOXRUN is an application written in FoxPro that adds the Run options to the menu.

New Query...	Performs the same action as File New Query.
Query...	Runs an existing RQBE file.
Screen...	Runs an existing screen code file.
Report...	Runs an existing report file.
Label...	Runs an existing report file.
Application...	Runs an existing application.

If you do not want the Run menu to appear, add the following line to your CONFIG.FP file:

```
STARTUP = ""
```

See also File New Query, Program Do..., Database Report...

2
FoxPro commands

You can issue FoxPro commands either interactively in the Command window or from within programs. Many of the commands (such as DO WHILE and IF) can be executed only within programs.

In this chapter, we've listed the commands in alphabetical order and described proper syntax for each one. Each command is followed by a short description, and then details for using it. The conventions used in this chapter are:

- All commands and optional clauses are displayed in uppercase.
- All optional clauses are enclosed in square brackets, [ ].
- Multiple-choice clauses are separated by a pipe, |. Only one option can be used.
- All required and optional arguments are in lowercase italics. The expression type of each parameter is very important. Character expressions are identified by *expC*, numeric by *row*, *col*, and *expN*, date by *expD*, and logical by *expL*. Parameters defined by *filename* must contain a valid DOS directory, path and filename. Any other type of parameter can be any valid FoxPro expression. Some commands require more than one parameter of the same type. These are identified sequentially.
- Some commands support an indefinite list of parameters that can be repeated. Those parameters are followed by ellipses (...).
- The scope parameter accepts one of the following: ALL, NEXT *expN*, RECORD *expN*, and REST.

Many FoxPro commands support the use of optional FONT [expC [,expN]] and STYLE [expC1|expC2] clauses that can be used to display output in different font types and sizes. The font, expC, must be an available Windows font, otherwise a substitute font with similar characteristics will be used. Specify the font size with expN. If no size is specified, a 10 point font is used.

Use the STYLE clause to define the style for the font specified with the FONT clause. The style, expC1, must be a valid style for the defined font, otherwise a substitute style with similar characteristics will be used. When a font is specified and the STYLE clause is omitted, the standard font style is used. Font style characters can be combined to create different styles. Unless specified elsewhere, the available font styles for all commands using a FONT and STYLE clause are listed below:

Character	Font Style
B	Bold
I	Italic
N	Normal
O	Outline
Q	Opaque
S	Shadow
–	Strikeout
T	Transparent
U	Underline

=

```
= expression
```

Description The command evaluates the expression.

Operational rules This command is particularly useful with functions that perform an operation, such as the AINS( ) function, which inserts a row into any array. Many user-defined functions also perform operations. This command is the most efficient way to run such a function when you do not have to store the result to a memory variable or use the ? command, which displays the expression.

Example

```
= AINS(options,1)
```

See also ?

\ and \\

`\ expression` and `\\expression`

Description These commands output lines of text to the screen or to a file.

Operational rules If SET TEXTMERGE is ON and has been set to a filename, the text is sent to a file; otherwise it appears on the screen. This command is similar to the TEXT ... ENDTEXT command in that text does not have to be enclosed in quotes. You can embed an expression in the text by enclosing it in the text merge delimiters, << >>. The delimiters can be changed with the SET TEXTMERGE DELIMITERS command.

The \ command issues a carriage return before printing the line of text, so it is one line below the previous item displayed. The \\ command prints at the current screen or file position. The \ command by itself displays a blank line. You can use the NOSHOW keyword of SET TEXTMERGE to suppress screen output.

Examples The following program sends the displayed message to a file named INVITE .TXT.

```
USE MAILLIST ORDER ZIP
```

```
SET TEXTMERGE TO Invite
SCAN
   \Dear <<MAILLIST.Fname>>,
   \
   \ Please come to our party Saturday night at 8:00 p.m.
   \ Yours, Corky
ENDSCAN
SET TEXTMERGE TO
```

When run, the program writes the following the INVITE.TXT:

```
Dear Harry,
Please come to our party Saturday night at 8:00 p.m.
Yours, Corky
```

See also TEXT ... ENDTEXT, SET TEXTMERGE

? and ??

```
? expression [PICTURE expC] [FUNCTION codes] [AT expN] [FONT
expC [,expN]] [STYLE expC1|expC2]
```

Description These commands display the contents of the expression list.

Operational rules The ? command displays an expression on the screen or sends it to the printer. A carriage return is issued before displaying or printing the expression, so it is positioned one line below the previous item displayed. The ?? command prints at the current screen or printer position. The ? command by itself displays a blank line.

If SET PRINTER is ON, the expression is sent to the printer and is also displayed on the screen if SET CONSOLE is ON. You can use the PICTURE and FUNCTION clauses to define the display of the expressions. See the @ ... SAY/GET section for a list of valid PICTURE and FUNCTION codes. Use the AT option to define the column where the expression will display. Use the FONT and STYLE clauses to display the output in different font types and sizes.

Examples

```
? Fname FUNCTION "@T", Lname PICTURE "@!"
John SMITH
? Fname FUNCTION "@T", Lname AT 50
John                               Smith
```

See also @ ... SAY/GET, SET PRINTER, SET CONSOLE

???

```
??? expression
```

Description This command sends an expression to the printer without changing the position of the printer head.

Operational rules The ??? command is helpful to use when you need to send printer control codes at the beginning of a printout. The ? and ?? commands can be used to perform the same function, but they might move the printer head, disturbing the layout of the printout. Control codes can be designated in several ways, namely:

- The CHR( ) function. For example: CHR(27) + "E"
- The ASCII number: "{27}{69}"
- The character, such as: "{ESC}{69}"
- A combination. For example: "{27}E"

Example The following command would reset a Hewlett Packard laser printer.

```
??? "{27}E"
```

See also @ ... SAY/GET, CHR( )

@ ... SAY/GET

@ *row*, *col* SAY *expression* [PICTURE *expC*] [FUNCTION *codes*] [SIZE *expN1*, *expN2*] [FONT *expC* [, *expN*]] [STYLE *expC*] [COLOR SCHEME *expN1*|COLOR *color pair*] GET *expression* [PICTURE *expC*] [FUNCTION *codes*] [SIZE *expN1*, *expN2*] [FONT *expC* [,*expN*]] [STYLE *expC*] [DEFAULT *value*] [ENABLE|DISABLE] [MESSAGE *expC*] [[OPEN] WINDOW *window name*] [RANGE *expLow*,*expHigh*] [VALID *expL*|*expN*] [ERROR *expC*] [WHEN *expL*] [COLOR SCHEME *expN*|COLOR *color pair*]

Description This command displays information formatted for the screen or printer and creates fields for input screens.

Operational rules The @ ... SAY command displays *expression* at *row*, *col* in the current output window or sent to the printer if SET DEVICE TO is PRINTER. The @ ... GET command allows you to change the value of expression at *row*, *col* of the active window. GETs are activated with the READ command.

The location of *row*, *col* is relative to the main font of the defined window. You can also specify decimal fractions in *row*, *col* for more precise position. The display and masking of @ ... SAY/GET expressions can be controlled with the PICTURE and FUNCTION clauses. Some PICTURE clauses and FUNCTION codes accomplish the same task and you can use a combination of both. FUNCTION codes can be part of a PICTURE clause but the FUNCTION clause can only contain FUNCTION codes.

The following optional codes can be used with the FUNCTION clause or preceded with an @ in the PICTURE clause to display output in these various ways. To combine functions, place them together with the @ sign (i.e.: @T!).

A Allows alphabetic characters only.
B Left align numeric data.
C A CR (credit) shows after a positive number (use with SAY only).
D Uses the current SET DATE format for date output.
E Edits as a European date (DD/MM/YY) (SET DATE TO BRITISH).
I Output is centered in the field.
J Right justifies output.
K Entire field is selected for editing when the cursor moves into the field.
L Leading zeros are displayed in numbers.

M Specifies a list of items which the user can choose from in a GET field. Items must be separated with commas. When editing, the user can press the spacebar to scroll the choices of items.

R Specifies a format string that will be displayed in a GET field but not be saved. This can be used with character data only.

S*n* Specifies a number n that defines how long the display will be. If the field is longer, it will horizontally scroll when edited. This can also be done with the SIZE clause.

T Trims leading and trailing blanks from the field.

X A DB (debit) shows after a negative number (use with SAY only).

Z Numeric fields that are zero display as blanks.

(Negative number display surrounded by parentheses (SAY only).

! Alphabetical characters converted to uppercase.

^ Displays numbers in scientific notation.

$ Displays numbers in currency format specified with SET CURRENCY. If SET CURRENCY is LEFT this code can only be used with GET.

Use the PICTURE clause to change displays such as uppercase conversion, and comma mode. Below is a list of picture template symbols that are used when editing data.

A	Allows only letters.
L	Allows logical data only.
N	Allows letters or digits.
X	Allows any character.
Y	Allows only Y or N.
!	Converts to uppercase.
9	Allows only digits and signs.
#	Allows only digits, blanks and + or –.
$	Displays a dollar sign, $, in place of leading zeros and can only be used in a GET if SET CURRENCY is LEFT.
*	Displays an asterisk, *, in place of leading zeros.
,	Displays commas between thousands.
.	Decimal point position.

Additional PICTURE and FUNCTION codes are available for GET controls such as check boxes, invisible and push buttons, lists, pop ups, and radio buttons.

*C	Creates a check box.
*I	Creates an invisible button.
&	Creates a list.
^	Creates a pop-up.
*	Creates a push button.
*R	Creates a radio button.
N	Specifies a nonterminating control.
T	Specifies a terminating control.
H	Specifies a button set to be horizontal.
V	Specifies a button set to be vertical.
\\	Disables a control.

\! Specifies the default push button.
\? Specifies the Escape push button.

The @ ... SAY/GET command supports a number of other options and arguments that allow you to control the appearance of input and output expressions and to test the validity of data input with a GET:

RANGE *expLow, expHigh* The RANGE clause verifies that the entry is between the range of two expressions. If it is not, an error message appears which alerts the user to the valid range of entries.

VALID *expL|expN* The VALID clause checks whether *expL* is true (.T.) before allowing the user to move on to the next field. This clause is particularly useful when *expL* is a user-defined function. A custom error message can be added to the end of the VALID statement using the ERROR clause. If the VALID clause is followed by a numeric expression (most often a user-defined field that evaluates as a numeric), the return value determines how the verification will behave. If the value is 0, the cursor remains in the field and an error message is displayed. If the value is a positive number, the cursor advances that number of fields (GET statements) for the next input field. If the value is negative, the cursor moves back that number of fields.

WHEN *expL* The cursor will only go to this field for editing if *expL* evaluates as true (.T.).

DEFAULT *value* If the GET expression is a memory variable that has not been initialized before GET is issued, the DEFAULT clause will initialize expression to value. If DEFAULT is not used and the GET expression does not exist in memory, FoxPro will display a "Variable not found" error.

MESSAGE *expC* By default the message, *expC*, is displayed in the status bar at the bottom of the screen when the cursor moves to this GET statement. If the status bar has been turned off (SET STATUS BAR OFF), the message is displayed at the last line of the screen.

[OPEN] WINDOW *window name* This function is used for editing memo fields in a user-defined window. The window *window name* must be defined before the GET is issued. Precede this clause with the word OPEN, and the window will be open by default. The user must still press Ctrl-Home to edit the memo even if the window is open.

SIZE *expN1, expN2* This clause allows you to change the size of the GET display. The default size is one row with the width of the expression that is being edited. The height, *expN1*, is in rows. The width, *expN2*, is in columns relative to the font specified with the FONT clause. If no font is specified, the main window font is used.

COLOR *color pair* Allows you to specify a custom color pair different than the default @ ... SAY/GET color setting of the active color scheme.

COLOR SCHEME *expN* Allows you to specify the @ ... SAY/GET color setting of a specific color scheme.

ENABLE|DISABLE When GET fields are disabled, they appear in the disabled color pair of the current color scheme and the cursor skips over the field. The default is ENABLE.

The colors of a GET field are derived from the current window or screen. You can change the default colors by specifying a predefined color scheme or a color pair list. Specifying a color pair list allows you to use colors that are not included in the default color scheme. To change the default GET color pairs, set the color pairs according to the following table:

1	Not used
2	GET editing region
3	Not used
4	Not used
5	Message
6	Selected text in GET editing region
7	Not used
8	Not used
9	Not used
10	Disabled GET editing region

The first half of the color pair specifies the foreground color, the second half the background color.

If you use the Screen Builder to create your data entry screens, you may not have to use this command at all. The Screen Builder automatically generates the commands for @ ... SAY/GET.

Examples

```
@ 3,1 SAY "Database of California Clients" FONT "MS Sans Serif", 8
@ 5,1 SAY "Enter Last Name" GET Lname PICTURE "@!"
@ 5,50 SAY "First Name" GET Fname PICTURE "@!"
@ 7,1 SAY "Address:" GET Address
@ 8,1 SAY "City:" GET City
@ 8,10 SAY "State:" GET State PICTURE "@!" DEFAULT "CA"
@ 8,18 SAY "Zip:" GET Zip PICTURE "99999" RANGE "90000","97000"
@ 10,1 SAY "Phone:" GET Phone PICTURE "(999)999-9999"
@ 12,1 SAY "Cust. Code:" GET Code VALID LEFT(Code,1) $ "A,D,L";
ERROR "Code must begin with A, D or L"
@ 14,1 SAY "Taxable? " GET Tax PICTURE "Y" VALID IIF(TAX="Y",1,2)
@ 15,1 SAY "Tax ID # " GET Taxid PICTURE "999-99-9999"
@ 17,1 SAY "Year to-Date Sales $ " GET Sales
READ
```

See also READ, Using the Screen Builder

@ ... SAY BMPs & OLE Objects

```
@ row, col SAY filename BITMAP| general field [STYLE expC]
[SIZE expN1, expN2] [CENTER] [ISOMETRIC|STRETCH]
@ row, col SAY general field VERB expN|expC [NOWAIT]
```

Description This command displays bitmap (.BMP) pictures and OLE objects formatted for the screen or printer.

Operational rules The first form of this @ ... SAY command displays a Windows bitmap file specified in *filename* or a Windows OLE object that is embedded in *general field* in the current output window, or sent to the printer if SET DEVICE TO is PRINTER. The top left corner of the picture is determined by the values of *row*, *col*. The position of *row* is determined by the height of the font specified for the current output window. The position of *col* is determined by the width of the same font. When displaying a bitmap the filename must be delimited with quotes or square brackets, followed immediately by the BITMAP keyword.

Use the STYLE clause to determine whether the image is displayed in opaque mode—text and objects behind the picture are hidden, or transparent mode—text and objects behind the picture show through. Specify Q in *expC* for opaque or T for transparent.

Use the SIZE clause to specify the size of the image to display. The height, *expN1*, is a multiple of the height of the font for the current output window and the width, *expN2*, is a multiple of the width of the font for the current output window. If the size specified is too small to display the image, the image is clipped. This can be avoided by using the ISOMETRIC or STRETCH clause. When ISOMETRIC is used, the image is scaled within the specified area and proportionally. When STRETCH is used, the image is stretched vertically, horizontally, or both ways to fill the specified area. Use the CENTER clause to center the image within the area specified with the SIZE clause. If no size is specified, the image is centered within the current output window.

The second form of this @ ... SAY command is used to activate the parent application of the OLE object embedded in *general field* and execute a command verb. This can be anything from editing a Microsoft Word document to "playing" a sound object. Each Windows OLE application (server) contains a command verb for all of the application's actions. When using FoxPro, you can issue the command RUN/N REGEDIT /V to activate the Windows Registration Info Editor. This displays the command verbs and corresponding number for all installed OLE applications. See your Windows and application software documentation for more information.

Use the VERB clause to execute a command verb for an OLE object. The command verb can be either a numeric expression, *expN*, or a character expression, *expC*. Some Windows applications need to be manually exited before control will return to FoxPro. Including the NOWAIT clause will force some applications to automatically exit and return to FoxPro. See the Using DDE and OLE in the FoxPro chapter (chapter 12) for further information on OLE capabilities.

See also APPEND GENERAL, CREATE SCREEN, MODIFY GENERAL, SET PALETTE, SHOW GETS, Using DDE and OLE in FoxPro

@ ... GET Check Boxes

See @ ... SAY/GET

Description This command creates a GET check box.

Operational rules Check boxes allow a field to be marked True or False (Yes or No). The box is displayed at *row* and *col* on the screen. The GET expression can be a field or memory variable. If it is a logical expression, it will be .T. when the check box is marked, .F. otherwise. If it is numeric, it will be 1 when marked, 0 otherwise. The value of the GET expression is changed by clicking anywhere on the check box prompt.

To create a check box, you must use the appropriate FUNCTION and/or PICTURE clauses of @ ... GET. The FUNCTION clause is *C and then the prompt for the box. The PICTURE clause is @*C and the prompt. To use both, the FUNCTION clause must contain *C and the PICTURE clause must contain the prompt.

The T and N options set whether checking or unchecking the box should terminate the READ. To terminate the READ, place a T directly after the C. The N option is the default. It sets a box to not terminate the READ. A *hot key* is an underlined letter that allows the status of the check box to be changed from anywhere on the editing screen by selecting Alt plus the hot key letter. To assign a hot key, place \< in front of the desired letter in the prompt.

You can also create "picture" check boxes in FoxPro. A picture check box is created by placing a Windows bitmap (.BMP) picture at the location of the check box object. To create a picture check box, substitute the FUNCTION clause specified above with *CB or the PICTURE clause with @*CB. Follow the FUNCTION/PICTURE clause by a space and the file name of the picture file to display. A picture check box has three states: up (unchecked), down (checked), and disabled, and treats variables the same as a text check box. Use the SHOW GETS command to change the picture displayed when checking or unchecking the check box. Picture check boxes cannot have hot keys.

The colors of a check box are derived from the current window or screen. You can change the default colors of a check box by specifying a predefined color scheme or a color pair list. Specifying a color pair list allows you to use colors that are not included in the default color scheme. To change the default list color pairs, set the color pairs according to the following table:

1	Not used
2	Not used
3	Not used
4	Not used
5	Message
6	Not used
7	Not used
8	Not used
9	Enabled check box
10	Disabled check box

The first half of the color pair specifies the foreground color, the second half the background color.

If you use the Screen Builder to create your data entry screens, you may not have to use this command at all. The Screen Builder automatically generates the commands that create check boxes.

Examples

```
@ 2,16 GET phone_ret ;
   PICTURE "@*C Return phone call" ;
   SIZE 1,21 DEFAULT 0
READ CYCLE
```

See also @ ... SAY/GET, READ, SHOW GETS, Using the Screen Builder

@ ... GET Invisible Buttons

See @ ... SAY/GET

Description This command creates a GET invisible button set.

Operational rules Invisible buttons are much like push buttons in that the user selects a particular button, excluding the rest. The main difference is that invisible buttons do not have prompts like push buttons do. Instead, they are just rectangular regions of the screen. Invisible buttons can be sized to a height greater than 1 row and can be used for creating large push buttons.

The area is displayed at *row* and *col* on the screen. The GET variable may be a numeric field or memory variable. Its value will correspond to the button chosen. The first button is 1, the next 2, etc. To create invisible buttons, you must use the appropriate FUNCTION and/or PICTURE clauses. The FUNCTION clause is *I, and the PICTURE clause is @*I. If more than one button is to be created, a semicolon must be specified to separate each button prompt. To use both clauses, the FUNCTION clause must contain *I and the PICTURE clause contains the number of semicolons.

The T and N options set whether a button should terminate the READ. To terminate the READ if a button is chosen, place a T directly after the I. The N option is the default. It sets a button to not terminate the READ. The H and V options set whether the buttons are in a horizontal or vertical row. The default is vertical.

The colors of a push button are derived from the current window or screen. You can change the default colors of a push button by specifying a predefined color scheme or a color pair list. Specifying a color pair list allows you to use colors that are not included in the default color scheme. To change the default list color pairs, set the color pairs according to the following table:

1	Not used
2	Not used
3	Not used
4	Not used
5	Not used
6	Selected invisible button
7	Not used
8	Not used
9	Not used
10	Not used

The first half of the color pair specifies the foreground color, the second half the background color.

If you use the Screen Builder to create your data entry screens, you may not have to use this command at all. The Screen Builder automatically generates the commands that create invisible buttons.

Example This example creates an invisible button 16 characters wide and 3 lines high. The result is a push-button region from column 10 to column 25 and row 2 to row 4. It then lays a prompt over the button.

```
@ 2,10 GET mbutton ;
   PICTURE "@*IVN " SIZE 3,16,1 DEFAULT 0
@ 3,0 SAY "Click here" SIZE 1,10, 0
READ CYCLE
```

See also @ ... SAY/GET, READ, Using the Screen Builder

@ ... GET Lists

See @ ... SAY/GET

Description This command creates a GET scrolling list.

Operational rules Lists allow the user to pick an option from a scrolling list of multiple options. The list is displayed at *row* and *col* on the screen.

The GET expression can be a field or memory variable. If the expression is numeric, it becomes the number of the item chosen. If it is a character, it becomes the character equivalent of the list item. The list GET supports an additional clause of FROM *array* [RANGE *expN1*[,*expN2*]|POPUP *popup name*. The elements that define the list can come from an existing array by specifying the array with FROM *array* or from an existing pop-up by specifying the pop-up with POPUP *popup name*. The default size of the list is determined by the widest item in the list, and the number of rows below the list. Use the SIZE *expN1*, *expN2* clause to change the size of the list area. The height, *expN1*, is in rows. The width, *expN2*, is in characters.

If the GET list uses an array, the optional RANGE clause can be used to limit which elements of the array will appear in the list. The RANGE *expN1* argument determines the starting array element for the list. If a starting element is specified with *expN1*, *expN2* determines the number of elements to include in the list. If the array used is two-dimensional, only those elements in the same column as *expN1* are included in the list.

Pop-ups are created using the DEFINE POPUP command. If the items in the list use a pop-up that included the SCROLL keyword, a scroll bar is placed on the right side of the list when the list contains more items than can be displayed at once.

The colors of the list are derived from the current window or screen. You can change the default colors of a list by specifying a predefined color scheme or a color pair list. Specifying a color pair list allows you to use colors that are not included in the default color scheme. To change the default list color pairs, set the color pairs according to the following table:

1	Disabled option
2	Enabled option
3	Border and scroll bar
4	Not used
5	Message
6	Selected item
7	Not used
8	Not used
9	Enabled list
10	Disabled list

The first half of the color pair specifies the prompt color, the second half the background color.

If you use the Screen Builder to create your data entry screens, you may not have to use this command at all. The Screen Builder automatically generates the commands that create lists.

Examples The first example is a list that was defined using the POPUP clause. The program sets up a list of all available data files. The user chooses the file, and the program opens it. The SCROLL option in the DEFINE POPUP command creates a scroll bar on the right of the list that can be used by a mouse.

```
** DATAFILES.PRG
** program that allows the user to pick a database
CLEAR
memfile = " "
DEFINE POPUP datafiles PROMPT FILES LIKE *.DBF SCROLL
@ 5,1 GET memfile POPUP datafiles ;
   SIZE 15,20 DEFAULT " "
READ CYCLE
USE (memfile)
```

When run, the program displays a list of all data files on the default directory. The size of the list area is 15 rows by 20 characters.

The second example is a list that was defined by an array. The program is a list of three predetermined data files. The user chooses the file, and the program opens it.

```
** DATA2.PRG
** program that allows the user to pick a database
CLEAR
DIMENSION datafile(3)
memfile = " "
datafile(1) = "STUDENTS.DBF"
datafile(2) = "TEACHERS.DBF"
datafile(3) = "PARENTS.DBF"
@ 5,1 GET memfile FROM datafile SIZE 5,15
READ CYCLE
USE (memfile)
```

See also @ ... SAY/GET, READ, DEFINE POPUP, Using the Screen Builder

@ ... GET Popups

See @ ... SAY/GET

Description This command creates a GET pop-up.

Operational rules Pop-ups display a list of options which the user can choose from. The list of options is only displayed when the cursor is at that particular field on the screen. When the cursor is elsewhere, the pop-up displays as a rectangle with an underlined down arrow. The pop-up is displayed at *row* and *col* on the screen.

The GET variable can be a memory variable or field. If the expression is numeric, it becomes the number of the item chosen. If it is a character, it becomes the character equivalent of the selected pop-up item. The pop-up GET supports an additional clause FROM *array*. Use this to fill the pop-up with the elements of *array*. To create a pop-up, you must use the FUNCTION and/or PICTURE clauses. The FUNCTION clause is ^, followed by the list of items separated with semicolons. The PICTURE clause is @^ followed by the list. To use both clauses, the FUNCTION clause must contain ^ while the PICTURE clause contains the list of items.

The T and N options set whether activating the pop-up should terminate the READ. To terminate the READ, place a T directly after the ^ in clause. The N option is the default. It sets a pop-up to not terminate the READ. A *hot key* is an underlined letter that allows an option to be chosen from anywhere in the pop-up list. To assign a hot key, place \< in front of the desired letter in the prompt.

The default size of the pop-up box is determined by the widest item in the list, and the number of items. Use the SIZE *expN1*, *expN2* clause to change the size. Because the length is always determined by the number of items, it will ignore the number placed in *expN1*. A pop-up GET supports an optional second parameter for the COLOR SCHEME clause which allows you to control the colors of pop-up options and the border of the pop-up. The colors of the pop-up are derived from the current window or screen. You can change the default colors of a pop-up by specifying a predefined color scheme or a color pair list with COLOR SCHEME *expN1*, [*expN2*].

The color scheme specified in *expN1* controls the colors of the pop-up face when a pop-up is enabled or disabled, and the pop-up message. The color scheme specified in *expN2* controls the color of the pop-up border and the options displayed in the pop-up. Specifying a color pair list allows you to use colors that are not included in the default color scheme. To change the default pop-up color pairs, set the color pairs according to the following table:

Color pair	*expN1*	*expN2*
1	Not used	Disabled options
2	Not used	Enabled options
3	Not used	Border
4	Not used	Not used
5	Message	Not used
6	Selected pop-up	Selected option
7	Not used	Hot keys
8	Not used	Not used
9	Enabled pop-up	Not used
10	Disabled pop-up	Not used

The first half of the color pair specifies the foreground color, the second half the background color.

If you use the Screen Builder to create your data entry screens, you may not have to use this command at all. The Screen Builder automatically generates the commands that create pop-ups.

Examples The first example is a screen with two pop-ups used in editing a student's record. The first pop-up determines the Sex field (Male, Female, Unknown). The second determines the grade of the student. Hot keys are set for the options in the first pop-up:

```
choices = "Freshman;Sophomore;Junior;Senior"
@ 3,1 SAY "Student Database - Personal Information "
@ 5,1 SAY TRIM(Fname) + " " + Lname
```

```
@ 7,1 SAY "Sex:" GET sex FUNCTION "^ /<Male;/<Female;/Unknown"
@ 7,40 SAY "Class:" GET class FUNCTION "^" PICTURE choices
READ CYCLE
```

The second example is the same program for editing the class field, the only difference being that the items in the list are defined by an array.

```
CLEAR
DIMENSION mclass(4)
mclass(1) = "Freshman"
mclass(2) = "Sophomore"
mclass(3) = "Junior"
mclass(4) = "Senior"
@ 3,1 SAY "Student Database – Personal Information "
@ 5,1 SAY TRIM(Fname) + " " + Lname
@ 7,40 SAY "Class:" GET class FROM mclass FUNCTION "^"
READ CYCLE
```

See also @ ... SAY/GET, READ, DEFINE POPUP, Using the Screen Builder

@ ... GET Push Buttons

See @ ... SAY/GET

Description This command creates GET push buttons.

Operational rules Push buttons are most often used to determine an action. For instance, many FoxPro dialog boxes terminate with the push buttons OK and Cancel.

The GET variable may be a memory variable or field. If the expression is numeric, it becomes the number of the item chosen. If it is a character, it becomes the character equivalent of the list item. To create a push button, you must use the FUNCTION and/or PICTURE clauses. The FUNCTION clause is *, followed by the list of push button prompts separated by semicolons. The PICTURE clause is @* followed by the list. To use both clauses, the FUNCTION clause must contain * while the PICTURE clause contains the list of items.

The T and N options set whether activating the push button should terminate the READ. To terminate the READ, place a T directly after the *. The N option is the default. It sets a button to not terminate the READ. The H and V options set whether the buttons are in a horizontal or vertical row. The default is vertical.

A *hot key* is an underlined letter that allows an option to be chosen from anywhere on the editing screen by selecting Alt plus the hot key letter. To assign a hot key, place \< in front of the desired letter in the prompt. The default button is the one that displays with a solid black border around the button. To set a default button, place \! before the prompt. To assign a button that is chosen when Esc is hit, precede the prompt with \?. The action of a default button can be changed with the SET KEYCOMP command.

The width and height of a button is determined by the width and height of the widest prompt and the font specified with the FONT clause. If no font is specified the main window font is used. Use the SIZE clause to size a push button set. Specify the height of a push button with *expN1*, the width with *expN2*, and the number of columns between each button with *expN3*.

You can also create "picture" push buttons in FoxPro. A picture push button is created by placing a Windows bitmap (.BMP) picture at the location of each push button prompt. To create a picture push button, substitute the FUNCTION clause specified above with *B or the PICTURE clause with @*B. Follow the FUNCTION/PICTURE clause by a space and the file name of the picture file to display. A picture push button has three states: up (unselected), down (selected), and disabled; it treats variables the same as a text push button does. Use the SHOW GETS command to change the picture displayed when selecting a picture push button. Picture push buttons cannot have hot keys.

Because the colors of push buttons cannot be changed in FoxPro, specifying color schemes or color pairs have no effect on push buttons other than messages (color pair 5). You must use the Windows Control Panel to change the colors of push buttons. See your Window documentation for more information on using the Control Panel.

If you use the Screen Builder to create your data entry screens, you may not have to use this command at all. The Screen Builder automatically generates the commands that create push buttons.

Examples The example is a screen with push buttons that will determine the order that a report will be printed in—*Alpha*, *Zip*, or *Class*. Hot keys are set for the first letter of each option, with the Zip option being the default push button. The buttons are set in a horizontal layout instead of the vertical default.

```
@ 3,1 SAY "Student Roster"
morder = ""
@ 15,1 SAY "Choose the sort order for the listing:"
@ 17,1 GET morder ;
   PICTURE "@*HN \<Alpha;\!\<Zip;\<Class" ;
   SIZE 1,7,2 DEFAULT 1
READ CYCLE
SET ORDER TO (morder)
```

See also @ ... SAY/GET, READ, SHOW GETS, SET KEYCOMP
Using the Screen Builder

@ ... GET Radio Buttons

See @ ... SAY/GET

Description This command creates GET radio buttons.

Operational rules Radio buttons are much like push buttons, in that they determine one choice out of a list. When an option is selected, a bullet is displayed inside a circle next to the chosen option.

The GET variable may be a memory variable or field. If the expression is numeric, it becomes the number of the item chosen. If it is a character, it becomes the character equivalent of the list item. A radio button option can be selected by clicking on any part of the option.

To create a radio button, you must use the FUNCTION and/or PICTURE clauses. The FUNCTION clause is *R, followed by the list of radio button prompts, separated with semicolons. The PICTURE clause is @*R followed by the list. To use both clauses, the FUNCTION clause must contain *R while the PICTURE clause contains the list of prompts.

The T and N options set whether selecting a radio button area should terminate the READ. To terminate the READ, place a T directly after the *R. The N option is the default. It sets a button area to not terminate the READ. The H and V options set whether the buttons are in a horizontal or vertical row. The default is vertical.

A *hot key* is a highlighted letter that allows an option to be chosen from anywhere on the editing screen by pressing Alt plus the hot key letter. To assign a hot key, place \< in front of the desired letter in the prompt.

The default size of each radio button option is determined by the width of the widest prompt and the font specified with the FONT clause. If no font is specified the main window font is used. Use the SIZE clause to size a radio button set. Specify the height of a radio button with *expN1*, the width with *expN2*, and the number of columns between each button with *expN3*.

You can also create "picture" radio buttons in FoxPro. A picture radio button is created by placing a Windows bitmap (.BMP) picture at the location of each radio button prompt. To create a picture radio button, substitute the FUNCTION clause specified above with *RB or the PICTURE clause with @*RB. Follow the FUNCTION/PICTURE clause by a space and the file name of the picture file to display. A picture check box has three states: up (unselected), down (selected), and disabled, and treats variables the same as a text radio button. Use the SHOW GETS command to change the picture displayed when selecting a picture radio button. Picture radio buttons cannot have hot keys.

The colors of the radio buttons are derived from the current window or screen. You can change the default colors of a radio button by specifying a predefined color scheme or a color pair list. Specifying a color pair list allows you to use colors that are not included in the default color scheme. To change the default radio button color pairs, set the color pairs according to the following table:

1	Not used
2	Not used
3	Not used
4	Not used
5	Message
6	Selected radio prompt
7	Hot keys
8	Not used
9	Enabled radio prompt
10	Disabled radio prompt

The first half of the color pair specifies the prompt color, the second half the background color.

If you use the Screen Builder to create your data entry screens, you may not have to use this command at all. The Screen Builder automatically generates the commands that create radio buttons.

Examples The example is a screen with radio buttons that will determine the order that a report will be printed in—*Alpha*, *Zip* or *Class*. Hot keys are set for the first letter of each option. The buttons are set in a horizontal layout instead of the vertical default. They are four spaces apart from each other instead of the one space default.

```
@ 3,1 SAY "Student Roster"
```

```
morder = " "
@ 15,1 SAY "Choose the sort order for the listing:"
@ 17,1 GET morder ;
   PICTURE "@*RHN Alpha;Zip;Class" ;
   SIZE 1,9,7 DEFAULT 1
READ CYCLE
SET ORDER TO (morder)
```

When run, the program will display:

```
Choose the sort order for the listing:
   ( ) Alpha   ( ) Zip   ( ) Class
```

See also @ ... SAY/GET, READ, Using the Screen Builder

@ ... GET Spinners

`@ row,col GET expression SPINNER expN1 [,expN2 [,expN3]]`

Description This command creates a GET spinner control.

Operational rules A spinner control is used to increment a numeric value. The spinner consists of a text box, an ↑ for increasing the value, and a ↓ for decreasing the value. The value of a spinner GET can be changed by clicking on the up or down arrow control, or by using the ↑ and ↓ keys on the keyboard when the spinner text box is selected.

The GET variable may be a memory variable or field and must be a numeric value. The GET command for a spinner control requires the SPINNER clause, unlike other GET controls which simply use a FUNCTION/PICTURE clause.

When you change the value of a spinner variable, you can specify with *expN1* the value to increase or decrease the spinner variable. For example, if *expN1* is 3, clicking on the ↑ or ↓ arrow changes the value of the expression by 3. Use *expN2* to control the lowest value that can be selected with the spinner control, and use *expN3* to control the highest value selected with the spinner control. The values specified in *expN2* and *expN3* do not affect a value entered into the spinner text box via the keyboard. You must use a combination of the RANGE and VALID clauses to control the low and high values entered into the text box.

Examples The first example creates a spinner control with a maximum value of 10, incremented by 1. The second example creates a spinner control with a maximum value of 50, incremented by 1.5.

```
@ 1.5,1.0 GET m.counter SPINNER 1.000, 1, 10 PICTURE "@K" ;
   SIZE 0.923, 6.200 FONT "MS Sans Serif", 8
@ 1.5,1.0 GET m.counter SPINNER 1.5, 1, 50 PICTURE "@K" ;
   SIZE 0.923, 6.200 FONT "MS Sans Serif", 8
```

See also @ ... SAY/GET, READ, Using the Screen Builder

@ ... EDIT Text Edit Region

`@ row, col EDIT expression SIZE expN1, expN2 [, expN3] [FUNCTION codes] [FONT expC [,expN] [STYLE expC] [DEFAULT value] [ENABLE|DISABLE] [MESSAGE expC] [VALID expL|expN [ERROR expC]] [WHEN expL] [NOMODIFY] [SCROLL] [TAB] [COLOR SCHEME expN|COLOR color pair]`

Description This command creates a text editing region.

Operational rules Text editing regions are used with memo fields and long character expressions. A rectangular box is displayed where the entire field can be edited. All of the commands available in the FoxPro editor can be used in a text editing region. The EDIT *expression* can be a memory variable or field.

To create a text editing region, you must use the SIZE *expN1*, *expN2* clause. An optional third number *chars* can be used in the clause to determine the number of characters of *expression* that can be edited. If the height is set to one, a special text editing region is created that scrolls horizontally. Otherwise, the text will word wrap and scroll down as it is typed into the area.

The I and J FUNCTION codes determine special alignment. Use FUNCTION 'J' to right justify text, FUNCTION 'I' to center text. Other supported clauses of the @ ... EDIT command are:

DEFAULT *value* If the EDIT expression is a memory variable that has not been initialized before EDIT is issued, the DEFAULT clause will initialize *expression* to *value*. If DEFAULT is not used and the EDIT expression does not exist in memory, FoxPro will display a "Variable not found" error.

ENABLE|DISABLE When EDIT fields are disabled, they appear in the disabled color pair of the current color scheme and the cursor skips over the field. The default is ENABLE.

MESSAGE *expC* By default the message, *expC*, is displayed in the status bar at the bottom of the screen when the cursor moves to this GET statement. If the status bar has been turned off (SET STATUS BAR OFF), the message is displayed at the last line of the screen.

VALID *expL*/*expN* The VALID clause checks whether *expL* is true (.T.) before allowing the user to move on to the next field. This clause is particularly useful when *expL* is a user-defined function. A custom error message can be added to the end of the VALID statement using the ERROR clause. If the VALID clause is followed by a numeric expression (most often a user-defined field that evaluates as a numeric), the return value determines how the verification will behave. If the value is 0, the cursor remains in the field and an error message is displayed. If the value is a positive number, the cursor advances that number of fields (EDIT statements) for the next input field. If the value is negative, the cursor moves back that number of fields.

WHEN *expL* The cursor will only go to this field for editing if *expL* evaluates as true (.T.).

NOMODIFY This clause sets the @ ... EDIT field to be read-only and no changes can be made to the expression.

SCROLL This clause creates a scroll bar on the right side of the EDIT area that can be used by a mouse to scroll through the field. The scroll bar is only displayed if the text is too large to fit in the region.

TAB Text editing regions are exited by pressing Tab or Ctrl-Tab. The TAB clause causes the Tab key to insert a tab instead of exiting the region. When the clause is active, Ctrl-Tab is the only key that exits the region. The NOTAB clause is the default.

SIZE *expN1*, *expN2* This clause allows you to change the size of the GET display. The default size is one row with the width of the expression that is being edited. The height, *expN1*, is in rows. The width, *expN2*, is in columns relative to the font specified with the FONT clause. If no font is specified, the main window font is used.

COLOR *color pair* Allows you to specify a custom color pair other than the default @ ... EDIT color setting of the active color scheme.

COLOR SCHEME *expN* Allows you to specify the @ ... EDIT color setting of a specific color scheme.

If you use the Screen Builder to create your data entry screens, you may not have to use this command at all. The Screen Builder automatically generates the commands that create edit regions.

The colors of an edit region are derived from the current window or screen. You can change the default colors of an edit region by specifying a predefined color scheme or a color pair list. Specifying a color pair list allows you to use colors that are not included in the default color scheme. To change the default edit region color pairs, set the color pairs according to the following table:

1	Not used
2	Enabled text editing region
3	Scroll bar in dim, controls in background color
4	Not used
5	Message
6	Selected text editing region
7	Not used
8	Not used
9	Not used
10	Disabled text editing region

The first half of the color pair specifies the prompt color, the second half the background.

Examples The example is a screen with a text editing region that allows for editing of a memo field. The region is 5 rows high by 60 characters across. A scroll bar is created for getting to text that has scrolled off of the screen.

```
** STUDENT.PRG ** program fills out a student's narrative Information
@ 3,1 SAY "Student Database - Narrative Information "
@ 5,1 SAY TRIM(Fname) + " " + Lname
@ 7,1 SAY :Enter Narrative:"
@ 8,1 EDIT narr ;
   SIZE 6,60,0 DEFAULT " " SCROLL
READ CYCLE
```

See also @ ... SAY/GET, READ, Using the Screen Builder

@ ... BOX

`@ row1,col1,row2,col2 BOX expC`

Description This command creates a box on the screen.

Operational rules This @...BOX command draws a box in the rectangular area made up of corner *row1, col1* through the opposite corner *row2, col2*.

The optional character argument *expC* defines the characters to be used in drawing the box. The string can be up to 9 characters, each character defining each corner, each side, and the fill character. The default is a single line.

Examples The example draws a single line box at the bottom half of the screen:

```
@ 10, 1 TO 15, 75 BOX
```

See also @ ... SAY/GET

@ ... CLEAR

@ *row1,col1* [CLEAR|CLEAR TO *row2,col2*]

Description This command clears a rectangular area of the screen.

Operational rules The @ ... CLEAR command erases the rectangular area made up of corner *row1, col1* through the bottom right corner of the screen. Use the CLEAR TO option to clear through the bottom right corner *row2, col2*.

See also @ ... SAY/GET, CLEAR

@ ... FILL

@ *row1,col1* FILL TO *row2,col2* [COLOR SCHEME *expN*|COLOR *color pair*]

Description This command colors in a rectangular area of the screen.

Operational rules The @ ... FILL command colors in a rectangular area made up of corner *row1, col1* through the opposite corner or *row2, col2*.

The optional argument COLOR attribute defines the color of the box. The attribute codes are listed under the SET COLOR command. The argument COLOR SCHEME *expN* defines the color according to a predefined color scheme.

Examples

```
@ 1, 1 FILL TO 5, 30 COLOR r/b
```

See also @ ... SAY/GET

@ ... MENU

@ *row,col* MENU *array,expN1* [*,expN2*][TITLE *expC*][SHADOW]

Description This command creates and displays a pop-up menu.

Operational rules The *row, col* locations specify the top left corner of the pop-up relative to the current output window. The options available in the menu are taken from *array*. Use the *expN1* clause to determine how many items are available on the menu when the menu pop-up is activated; use *expN2* to determine how many options can be displayed in the pop-up at one time. TITLE *expC* will display an optional title at the top of the menu. If you want the menu pop-up box to have a shadow, include the SHADOW clause.

Examples

```
DIMENSION SORTS(3)
Sorts(1) = "Alpha"
Sorts(2) = "Zip"
Sorts(3) = "Other"
@ 3,3 MENU Sorts, 3 TITLE "Choose an order to sort by"
READ MENU TO Choice
DO CASE
   CASE Choice = 1
      SET ORDER TO MAILALPH
   CASE Choice = 2
      SET ORDER TO MAILZIP
   CASE Choice = 3
      ACCEPT "Enter Expression to Sort By " TO Other
      INDEX ON EVALUATE(Other) TAG Temp
      GO TOP
ENDCASE
```

See also DEFINE POPUP

@ ... PROMPT

`@ row,col PROMPT expC [MESSAGE expC]`

Description This command, along with MENU TO creates a light-bar type menu.

Operational rules A series of PROMPT options will display *expC* at *row*, *col*. The optional MESSAGE clause will display a message when the item is selected. Selecting one of the PROMPT *expC* options will save the value of the selection to a memory variable.

Examples

```
@ 3,1 PROMPT "Alpha" MESSAGE "Sort in Alphabetical Order"
@ 3,10 PROMPT "Zip" MESSAGE "Sort by Zip Code"
@ 3,20 PROMPT "Order" MESSAGE "Sort in User-Defined Order"
MENU TO Choice
DO CASE
   CASE Choice = 1
      SET ORDER TO MAILALPH
   CASE Choice = 2
      SET ORDER TO MAILZIP
   CASE Choice = 3
      ACCEPT "Enter Expression to Sort By " TO Other
      INDEX ON EVALUATE(Other) TAG Temp
      GO TOP
ENDCASE
```

See also MENU TO

@ ... TO

`@ row1,col1 TO row2,col2 [DOUBLE|PANEL|border string] [PATTERN expN] [PEN expN1 [,expN2]] [STYLE expC] [COLOR SCHEME expN|COLOR color pair]`

Description This command creates a box on the screen allowing more options than the @ ... BOX command.

Operational rules The @ ... TO command draws a box in the rectangular area made up of corner *row1*, *col1* through the opposite corner to *row2*, *col2*.

The optional arguments DOUBLE, PANEL, or *border string* define the character to be used in drawing the box. The default is a single line. You can specify a string of characters in *border string* that contains the elements of the border. The string elements must appear in proper order such as: end, end, side, side, corner, corner, corner, corner.

Use the optional PATTERN clause to specify a fill pattern for the box. The value of *expN* can range from 0 to 7. See the chapter on Using the Screen Builder (chapter 7) for a diagram of the available patterns. The PEN clause can be used to control the border of the box. You must specify a pen width with *expN1* and a pen type with *expN2*. Listed below are available pen types.

Pen Width	*expN1* value	Pen Type	*expN2* value
Hairline	0	None	0
1 point	1	Dotted	1
2 point	2	Dashed	2
3 point	3	Dash-dot	3
4 point	4	Dash-dot-dot	4
5 point	5		
6 point	6		

The STYLE clause determines the curvature of the object. By specifying a value from 0 to 99 with *expC*, you can create square corners (with a value of 0), or a circle (with a value of 99). The higher the value, the more the corners are curved. You can also include T in *expC* to make the object transparent.

The box is drawn using the SAY color pair of the COLOR SCHEME of the current output window. To draw the box in a color other than the COLOR SCHEME of the current output window, use COLOR *color pair* or COLOR SCHEME *expN*.

Examples The first example draws a single line box at the bottom half of the screen. The second example draws a colored double line box.

```
@ 10, 1 TO 15, 75
@ 1, 1 TO 5, 30 DOUBLE COLOR B/R
```

See also @ ... SAY/GET, @ ... BOX

ACCEPT

ACCEPT [*expression*] TO *memvar*

Description This command displays the prompt and pauses until the user enters something.

Operational rules The ACCEPT command is most often used in programs where the amount of data to be entered is small and appearance isn't important. Each ACCEPT command halts the program until the user types in an answer and presses Enter. The ACCEPT command is easier to use than full-screen editing commands such as @ ... GET, because:

- The memory variable does not have to be initialized before issuing the command.
- Screen coordinates do not have to be set. (ACCEPT displays the prompt in the same manner as the ? command).

However, the ACCEPT command is not as powerful as the full-screen editing commands, especially since the entry cannot be formatted or validated. Memory variables created by the ACCEPT command are always of the character type. The variable becomes the length of the entry typed in.

If the optional *expression* is not used, the ACCEPT command simply pauses and waits for the user to enter something.

Examples The following program prompts the user to enter their name. The memory variable Mname becomes the length of the entry:

```
ACCEPT "Enter Your Name " TO MNAME
? "Hi there ", MNAME
```

See also @ ... SAY/GET

ACTIVATE MENU

ACTIVATE MENU *menu name* [NOWAIT] [PAD *pad name*]

Description This command displays a user-defined menu.

Operational rules User-defined menus are menus that show a list of options. The user can navigate through the options with the arrow keys or mouse. An option can be selected from the menu by clicking on it.

Menus are defined with the DEFINE MENU and DEFINE PAD commands. The ON PAD and ON SELECTION PAD commands define the operations to be performed when an option is selected. Once the definitions are set, you can use ACTIVATE MENU to display the menu on screen. Use DEACTIVATE MENU to erase a menu from the screen.

The optional NOWAIT clause displays the menu and continues with program execution. Otherwise the menu must be deactivated for program execution to continue. Use the optional PAD *pad name* clause to define which menu item should be highlighted first. The default is the first pad.

See DEFINE MENU for a program that creates a menu.

See also DEFINE MENU

ACTIVATE POPUP

ACTIVATE POPUP *popup name* [AT *row,col*] [BAR *expN*] [NOWAIT] [REST]

Description This command displays a user-defined pop-up menu.

Operational rules User-defined pop-ups are menus that show a list of options. The user can navigate through the options with the arrow keys or mouse. An option can be selected from the menu by clicking on it. Pop-ups are defined with the DEFINE POPUP command. Pop-ups defined with DEFINE POPUP are very similar to menus defined with DEFINE MENU. Menus can be vertically or horizontally oriented while pop-ups are always vertical. Use DEACTIVATE MENU to erase a menu from the screen.

The NOWAIT option causes the pop-up to be displayed, and continues program execution. Use the AT *row*, *col* option to define where on the current output screen the pop-up is to be activated. This position takes precedence over that of the DEFINE POPUP setting. Use BAR *expN* to automatically select a particular bar of the pop-up menu. The command ACTIVATE POPUP BAR 3 automatically selects the third bar.

If the pop-up has been defined using the PROMPT FIELD clause of DEFINE POPUP, activating the pop-up will cause the first option in the list to be selected, even if the current record of the database does not match the PROMPT FIELD expression. Use the REST key word to initially select the option that matches the current record of the database.

Pop-up menus are designed with the DEFINE POPUP and DEFINE BAR commands. The ON SELECTION POPUP command defines the operations to be performed when a bar from the pop-up menu is selected. Once the definitions are set, you can use ACTIVATE POPUP to call it up. Use DEACTIVATE POPUP to remove a pop-up menu from the screen. See DEFINE BAR for a program that creates a pop-up menu within a bounce-bar menu.

See also DEFINE BAR

ACTIVATE SCREEN

```
ACTIVATE SCREEN
```

Description This command directs output to the default FoxPro desktop screen.

Operational rules Windows are defined with the DEFINE WINDOW command and activated with ACTIVATE WINDOW. The ACTIVATE SCREEN command allows you to direct all screen output back to the main FoxPro window without removing any existing windows. Press Alt-Ctrl-Shift to display the currently active window.

See also DEFINE WINDOW, ACTIVATE WINDOW

ACTIVATE WINDOW

```
ACTIVATE WINDOW [window list]|ALL [IN [WINDOW] window
name|SCREEN] [BOTTOM|TOP|SAME] [NOSHOW]
```

Description This command displays a user-defined window on the screen.

Operational rules Windows are defined with the DEFINE WINDOW command. Use ACTIVATE WINDOW to then display it. All screen output is directed to the front most active window. Multiple windows can be activated at once by including the window names in window list. Each *window name* in the list must be separated by a comma.

Use the optional keyword ALL to activate all defined windows. Use the BOTTOM and TOP keywords to place them behind (BOTTOM) or in front (TOP) of other windows. The SAME option places a window where it was before being hidden. The NOSHOW option does not show the window on screen, although output is still directed there.

The IN WINDOW *window name* will activate a window as a child inside of the WINDOW *window name* and it cannot be moved outside of the parent window.

See also DEFINE WINDOW

APPEND

```
APPEND [BLANK]
```

Description This command adds new records to the active database.

Operational rules The APPEND command adds a new record and brings up a browse editing screen. Each new record is added onto the bottom of the file. If a format screen has been set, that format is used instead of the basic edit screen format.

APPEND BLANK adds a record to the database without displaying the edit screen.

See also EDIT

APPEND FROM

```
APPEND FROM filename|? [FIELDS field list] [FOR expL] [[TYPE]
[DELIMITED [WITH TAB|WITH expC|WITH BLANK] | DIF | FW2 | MOD |
PDOX | RPD | SDF | SYLK | WK1 | WK3 | WKS | WR1 | WRK |XLS]]
```

Description This command adds records from a file to the current database.

Operational rules When appending from a file, the optional file types are:

Type	Description
DELIMITED	Variable length fields separated with a comma.
DELIMITED WITH *expC*	Variable length fields separated with *expC*.
DELIMITED WITH BLANK	Variable length fields separated with a space.
DELIMITED WITH TAB	Variable length fields separated with Tab.
DIF	Visicalc's Data Interchange Format.
FW2	Ashton Tate's Framework II.
MOD	Microsoft Multiplan version 4.01.
PDOX	Borland's Paradox versions 3.5 and 4.0.
RPD	Ashton Tate's RapidFile version 1.2.
SDF	Fixed length ASCII file.
SYLK	Symbolic Link interchange format.
WK1	Lotus 1-2-3, version 2.x.
WK3	Lotus 1-2-3, version 3.x.
WKS	Lotus 1-2-3, version 1.x.
WR1	Lotus Symphony, version 1.1 or 1.2.
WRK	Lotus Symphony, version 1.0.
XLS	Microsoft Excel, versions 2.0, 3.0 and 4.0.

The optional FOR *expL* argument appends only the records that match a certain criteria. Use the FIELDS *field list* clause to select the fields that will be appended. Use APPEND FROM ? to pull up the Open File dialog and choose a file. By default FoxPro expects you to append new records from another DBF file. You cannot append an open database file from another open database file. The source DBF file must be closed before it can be appended from.

When data from a worksheet is read in (DIF, WKS, XLS, etc.), each row becomes a record, and each column a field. If one of the optional file types is used, FoxPro assumes the default extension of the file name. For example, Lotus version 1.0 files are assumed to end with a .WKS extension, ASCII files assume a .TXT extension. Enter the extension if it is not the default. If the file name does not have an extension, be sure to use a period (.) after the file name.

Example

```
USE MAILLIST
APPEND FROM MAIL  && add records from another FoxPro file
APPEND FROM MAIL  FOR State="CA" && add records that match criteria
APPEND FROM MAIL  SDF && add records from fixed ASCII file
APPEND FROM MAIL  DELIM && add records from comma delimited file
APPEND FROM MAIL  DELIM WITH / && add records with fields
separated with /
APPEND FROM MAIL  FIELDS Fname,Lname,City
```

See also APPEND, IMPORT

APPEND FROM ARRAY

APPEND FROM ARRAY *array* [FOR *expL*] [FIELDS *field list*]

Description This command adds records from an array into the current database.

Operational rules When appending from a single dimension array, each array element represents a field of one record. When appending from a two-dimensional array, each column represents a field, and each row represents a record. If the array contains more elements than there are database fields, they are ignored.

Use the FOR *expL* clause to select records to be appended. The condition statement must be based on the field names that the array variables will be read into, not the array name. The FIELDS clause allows you to select which fields will be updated with the new records.

Example

```
USE MAILLIST
APPEND FROM ARRAY Data FIELDS Name, Zipcode
```

See also APPEND

APPEND GENERAL

APPEND GENERAL *field* FROM *file* [LINK] [CLASS *ole class*]

Description This command places the contents of *file* into the specified general field of the current database file.

Operational rules FoxPro general fields are used to store Windows OLE objects. Appending a general field replaces any objects that are in the general field.

Use the optional LINK clause to create a link between the file and the general field. When a link is created, only certain elements of the OLE file are stored in the general field. If changes are made to the file that is linked, the changes are updated in the general field. If no link exists, the entire contents of the file are embedded into the general field and any changes made to the file will not be updated.

Use the CLASS clause to force the object inserted into the general field to be treated as an *ole class* object. This is useful when embedding a file with an extension other than the default. For example, the default extension of a Microsoft Excel spreadsheet file is .XLC. To append a spreadsheet from another application and create an OLE link for Microsoft Excel, the following command might be used:

```
APPEND GENERAL info FROM "C:\WORK\NUMBERS.WK1" CLASS EXCELCHART
```

Consult your Windows and application software documentation for more information on OLE class types. See the chapter on Using DDE and OLE in FoxPro (chapter 13) for more information on storing Windows OLE objects in a general field.

Example

```
USE STUDENTS
APPEND GENERAL image FROM "DAVE.BMP"
```

See also @ ... SAY BMPs & OLE Objects, MODIFY GENERAL, chapter 12, Using DDE and OLE in FoxPro

APPEND MEMO

APPEND MEMO *memo field* FROM *file* [OVERWRITE]

Description This command places the contents of *file* into the specified memo field of the current database file.

Operational rules The optional OVERWRITE argument replaces the entire contents of the memo field. If this option is not used, the command simply appends the memo data to the end of the current memo.

Almost any type of data can be appended to a memo field, including text and binary.

Example

```
USE MAILLIST
APPEND MEMO Comments FROM MAIL.TXT  (adds memos from Mail.txt)
```

See also COPY MEMO

AVERAGE

AVERAGE [*expression*] [*scope*] [FOR *expL*] [WHILE *expL*] [TO *memvar list*|TO ARRAY *array*][NOOPTIMIZE]

Description This command computes the arithmetic mean of the numeric fields of a data file.

Operational rules If no arguments are provided, FoxPro displays the average of each numeric field in the current database. You can provide a field list to specify the field(s) to be summed.

To create memory variables whose values are the averages, use the TO *memvar list* or TO ARRAY *array*. When calculating to an array, the array must be declared as single dimension, and each field in the field list updates the next row of the array. You can use the optional FOR *expL*, WHILE *expL*, and scope arguments to include only a subset of the records in the calculation. Use the optional NOOPTIMIZE clause to disable Rushmore technology when averaging a database.

Examples

```
AVERAGE
AVERAGE Wage, Bonus TO Awage, Abon
AVERAGE Wage TO Awage FOR State = "CA"
AVERAGE Wage, Bonus, Comm TO ARRAY Mamount
```

The last example assumes that Mamount has been declared as a one-dimensional array. After the AVERAGE, Mamount(1) is equal to the average of the Wage field.

See also DECLARE

BROWSE

```
BROWSE [FIELDS field list] [FONT expC [,expN]] [STYLE expC]
[FOR expL] [FORMAT] [FREEZE field] [KEY expr1 [, expr2]] [LAST]
[LEDIT] [REDIT] [LOCK expN] [LPARTITION] [NOAPPEND] [NODELETE]
[NOEDIT|NOMODIFY] [NOLGRID] [NORGRID] [NOLINK] [NOMENU]
[NOOPTIMIZE] [NOREFRESH] [NORMAL] [NOWAIT] [PARTITION expN]
[PREFERENCE name] [REST] [SAVE] [TIMEOUT expN] [TITLE expC]
[VALID [:F] expL [ERROR expC]] [WHEN expL] [WIDTH expN]
[[WINDOW window name] [IN [WINDOW] window name|IN SCREEN]]
[COLOR SCHEME expN|COLOR color pair]
```

Description This command displays a list of records in an editing window.

Operational rules The BROWSE command is very useful in FoxPro. It can provide you with the means to easily and quickly edit large blocks of records. BROWSE can also be used to simply display a list of records for viewing or selecting. When browsing a file the records appear in list format, one record per row. Full screen editing is in effect with the addition of the following keys:

- Ctrl-left arrow (horizontally scroll left)
- Ctrl-right arrow (horizontally scroll right)

You can use the arrow keys or a mouse to scroll through the records being browsed. A browse window can be closed with Ctrl-W, which saves your changes, or Ctrl-Q, which aborts all changes to the selected field.

The optional FIELDS *field list* arguments restrict the fields or field order displayed in the BROWSE command. The SET FIELDS command can also set the fields list. Within the FIELDS clause several optional switches may be used. Precede the switch with slash (/) or colon (:). The switches are:

/expN Field is displayed with a width of *expN*.

/B=expr1, expr2 Field falls between the range (boundaries) of *expr1* and *expr2*.

/H=expr Specifies the field heading *expr* over the field (the default is the name of the field).

/R Field is read only.

/V=expr If *expr* is not true (.T.), an error message is displayed in the status bar and the field is not exited.

/V=expr*:E=*expC *expC* is displayed as the error message.

***/V=expr*:F** Validation check is run whether or not the field is changed (forced valuation). The default is for validation only if the field is edited.

/W=expL Field can only be edited when *expL* is evaluated as true (.T.).

/P Specifies a PICTURE option for each field. See the @ ... SAY/GET command for a list of PICTURE and FUNCTION codes.

Example

```
BROWSE FIELDS Names /P = '@!', Income /P = '99,999,999'
```

Use multiple verification switches by entering the /V only once. For example, /V = *expr1*:F:W/*expr2* only allows verification if the field has been edited, and only allows editing when *expr2* is true (.T.). The FIELDS clause can also support calculated fields. A calculated field contains information that cannot be edited and is created with any valid FoxPro expression. For example if the SALARY.DBF database contained the numeric fields Base and Taxrate the command:

```
BROWSE FIELDS SALARY.Base, SALARY.Taxrate, Taxes=Base * Taxrate
```

would display the value of Base multiplied by Taxrate. The FORMAT clause allows you to use a format file within the Browse mode. The fields from the format file will be chosen for the BROWSE screen, and all PICTURE, RANGE, WHEN, and VALID clauses from the file are in effect.

The BROWSE command has many optional arguments and clauses that make it a very powerful full-screen editing tool:

FOR *expL* Displays only records that match the condition *expL*. If *expL* is not an optimizable clause, the BROWSE command may run slowly.

FREEZE *field* Only allows field to be edited although other fields can be viewed.

KEY *expr1* Specifies a key value (or range of values) *expr1*, *expr2* for records that are to be displayed in the Browse window. The database must have an index tag that matches the key expression.

LAST Displays the browse with the same attributes and setting when the database was last browsed.

LEDIT When the window is split, set the left partition into Change mode. Much like choosing Change from the Browse menu pop-up.

REDIT When the window is split, set the right partition into Change mode.

LOCK *expN* If the value of *expN* is greater than 0 the browse window will be split into two partitions with *expN* fields displayed in the left partition and the partition is locked so no other fields can be viewed. If *expN* is equal to 0 the browse is not partitioned and the partition functions are disabled.

LPARTITION When used in conjunction with the PARTITION option, it splits the Browse window and places the cursor in the left partition. (The default is for the cursor to be placed in the right partition).

NOAPPEND Prevents records from being added to the database.

NODELETE Prevents records from being deleted from the database.

NOEDIT|NOMODIFY Prevents records from being edited (may only be viewed).

NOLGRID|NORGRID When the window is split, turns off the vertical field separators in the left|right window (like choosing Grid Off from the BROWSE menu).

NOLINK When the window is split, as one partition is scrolled, the other does not scroll (the default is for partitions to scroll in tandem).

NOMENU Prevents access to the BROWSE menu pop-up.

NOOPTIMIZE Disables Rushmore optimization (the default is for Rushmore to be enabled).

NOREFRESH Prevents the Browse window from being refreshed. Browse windows are refreshed at the rate determined by SET REFRESH. This clause is useful when the Browse is for read-only use; the clause improves performance.

NORMAL Ignores user-defined window characteristics which would affect the display of the Browse screen and positions the browse window in the top left corner of the current output window.

NOWAIT When called from a program, the program continues executing after the BROWSE command is executed. By default program execution will stop on the BROWSE command until the Browse window is exited.

PARTITION *expN* Splits the Browse window at column *expN*. This is the same as using the window splitter with the mouse, or choosing Resize Partitions from the Browse menu.

PREFERENCE *name* Uses the Browse screen settings and attributes saved last time with the PREFERENCE clause. If PREFERENCE *name* does not exist it will be created and saved in the current resource file.

REST Use REST to prevent the record pointer from being moved to the top of the file when the Browse window is opened.

SAVE Leaves the Browse window and any memo editing windows active. The SAVE option has no effect when used in the command window.

TIMEOUT *expN* Waits *expN* seconds for input. If that time has elapsed, it closes the Browse window. This option is available only within programs.

TITLE *expC* Changes the title of the browse window to *expC*.

VALID [:F] *expL* [ERROR *expC*] After editing a record, if expression *expL* is false, the cursor will not move off the record and an "Invalid input" message is displayed. You can display your own error message when VALID returns false by including the ERROR *expC* clause and the expression *expC* is displayed as the error message. By default the expression *expL* is only validated when data has changed. Use the :F argument to force validation anytime the record pointer changes.

WHEN *expL* When you move to a record and the expression *expL* is false, the record becomes read-only.

WIDTH *expN* Limits the maximum width of all fields to *expN*.

WINDOW *window name* The Browse window will take on the characteristics, such as color, size and DEFINE WINDOW options of WINDOW *window name*.

IN WINDOW *window name*|SCREEN The Browse window will be displayed as a child window inside of *window name* and cannot be moved outside the parent window. The SCREEN clause places the Browse window on the FoxPro desktop screen.

COLOR *color pair* Defines the color of the Browse window.

COLOR SCHEME *expN* Chooses a predefined color scheme for the Browse window.

Multiple databases can be browsed together when a link is established using the SET RELATION command. Include the command SET SKIP to define a one-to-many relationship and see all records from the child database. For instance, suppose there is a data file of students related to a file of classes and there are 30 students per class. If the class file is the parent database, the student file is the child database. When fields from both files are displayed in Browse mode, and SET SKIP has been activated, it shows one record for the parent database and multiple records for the child.

If both files are displayed in the Browse mode, press Ctrl-↓ to move to the next parent record. Press Ctrl-↑ to move to the previous parent record. Also, fields from multiple databases can be viewed in one Browse window by prefacing the field name with the database Alias (Example BROWSE FIELDS Class.Name, Student.Number)

Examples

```
BROWSE
BROWSE NOAPPEND NODELETE
BROWSE FIELDS Lname,Fname,City,Zip FONT "MS Sans Serif", 8
BROWSE FIELDS Name /R,Sex /P="!"/V=Sex$"MF":E="Must be M or F"
```

See also APPEND, EDIT, SET RELATION, SET SKIP

BUILD APP

`BUILD APP` *`filename`* `FROM` *`project`*

Description This command creates an .APP application file from a project file.

Operational rules The project file must contain all of the files needed in the application. Creating an application file can also be accomplished using the Project Manager.

See also CREATE PROJECT, Using the Project Manager

BUILD EXE

`BUILD EXE` *`filename`* `FROM` *`project`*`[STANDALONE] [EXTENDED]`

Description This command creates a compact or stand-alone executable .EXE file from a project file.

Operational rules This command requires that the FoxPro Distribution Kit be installed with FoxPro. You must specify the project name from which the EXE is built. By default a compact EXE file requiring FoxPro runtime libraries is created. Use the STANDALONE option to create an EXE that does not require FoxPro runtime libraries. To take advantage of all FoxPro Extended functions, include the EXTENDED clause.

See also BUILD APP, Using the Project Manager

BUILD PROJECT

```
BUILD PROJECT project file [FROM file list]
```

Description This command creates a project file (.PJX) that contains information regarding all files of a project.

Operational rules A project file is a database that contains information regarding all files that are used in an application. Project files are used with the BUILD APP command for building an executable (.APP/.EXE) file.

The file types that may be used in the file list are programs, menus, reports, labels, screen, and library files. The project database may be opened and changed with the MODIFY PROJECT command. If changes have been made to any of the files in the file list, use BUILD PROJECT or rebuild the project file from the Project Manager.

See also CREATE PROJECT, Using the Project Manager

CALCULATE

```
CALCULATE option list [scope] [FOR expL] [WHILE expL] [TO
memvar list|TO ARRAY array] [NOOPTIMIZE]
```

Description This command performs a calculation of all or a subset of records in the current database.

Operational rules The CALCULATE command displays the answer to the calculations. Valid calculations for the option list are: AVG( ), CNT( ), MAX( ), MIN( ), NPV( ), STD( ), SUM( ), and VAR( ).

Keep in mind that if SET TALK is OFF, the calculation will not display on the screen. The optional TO *memvar list* initializes a memory variable that is equal to the calculation. Use a *memvar list* or *array name* if more than one calculation is in the option list. The array must already be declared, and must be a one-dimensional array. The optional FOR *expL*, WHILE *expL*, and *scope* arguments are used to calculate only records that match a specified criteria. Use the optional NOOPTIMIZE clause to disable Rushmore when performing calculations.

Example

```
CALCULATE MAX(Grade)
CALCULATE MIN(Sales) FOR Salesman = "JONES"
CALCULATE STD(Grade) TO Stdgrad
CALCULATE MAX(Grade), MIN(Grade), STD(Grade) to Mxgrad, Mngrad,
Sdgrad
CALCULATE MAX(Grade), MIN(Grade), STD(Grade) to Mxgrad
```

The last example assumes that Mxgrad is a one-dimensional array that has been declared.

See also COUNT, RECCOUNT( )

CALL

```
CALL module [WITH expC|memvar] [SAVE|NOSAVE]
```

Description This command runs a binary program previously loaded into memory.

Operational rules FoxPro can run binary (assembly language and machine language) programs. To do this you must:

1. Load the program into memory with the LOAD command.
2. Run the program with the CALL command.
3. Release it from memory with the RELEASE MODULE command.

Binary programs are useful in instances where a function must be performed that FoxPro cannot do. For instance, certain screen graphics manipulation and file maintenance on non-FoxPro files can be done with binary programs. You can pass variables to the program using the WITH *expC|memvar* option.

If the binary library writes directly to video RAM, use the SAVE option so FoxPro will not overwrite anything written to the screen with the library. FoxPro's API functions are more advanced than LOAD and CALL functions and should be used in place of LOAD and CALL libraries.

See also LOAD, SET LIBRARY

CANCEL

```
CANCEL
```

Description This command halts a program and returns to the command window.

Operational rules The CANCEL command stops a program without exiting the FoxPro system. The user is exited to the command window. All data files remain open, while all memory variables that were created in the canceled program are released. If the command is issued from the runtime version, the user is exited to DOS.

This command is equivalent to choosing the Cancel option from the prompt Cancel, Suspend, Ignore that is displayed when an error is encountered in a program, or when the user presses Esc while running a program.

See also SUSPEND, ON SHUTDOWN

CHANGE

The CHANGE command is equivalent to EDIT.

See also EDIT

CLEAR

```
CLEAR [OPTION]
```

Description This command is used to clear the screen, the memory, the open databases, or other elements from FoxPro.

Operational rules The CLEAR command without any arguments clears the screen. The following arguments are available:

ALL Releases all user-defined memory variables, arrays, user-menus, pop-ups and windows. This command also closes all open databases and indexes and sets the current work area to 1.

FIELDS Clears any fields that may have been included in SET FIELDS TO.

GETS Removes any impending @ ... GET from memory.

MACROS Releases all keyboard macros. Save any defined macros before releasing them.

MEMORY Releases all public and private variables from memory.

MENUS Releases all user-defined menus from memory.

POPUPS Releases all user-defined pop-ups from memory.

PROGRAM Removes any programs from FoxPro's memory buffer.

PROMPT Releases any menu prompts that have been defined with @ ... PROMPT.

READ [ALL] Clears the current READ and returns program control to the previous READ (if any). The optional ALL clause will terminate all READ levels and return control to the command window.

TYPEAHEAD Removes all characters from the keyboard buffer.

WINDOWS Removes all user-defined windows from memory.

See also CLOSE

CLOSE

```
CLOSE [OPTION]
```

Description This command is used to close any file currently open.

Operational rules The CLOSE command ensures that the contents of a currently open file have been saved. To close one database file, issue the USE command while in that SELECTed area. The following arguments are available:

ALL Closes all open database and index files, text, program and memo editing windows, and files opened with the FCREATE( ) and FOPEN( ) functions. CLOSE ALL does not close any FoxPro desk accessories or program debugging windows.

ALTERNATE Closes the file specified in SET ALTERNATE TO.

DATABASE Closes all open database and index files only and sets the active work area to 1.

FORMAT Closes the format file for the currently selected database.

INDEXES Closes all indexes for the currently selected work area.

PROCEDURE Closes the file specified in SET PROCEDURE TO.

See also CLEAR

CLOSE MEMO

`CLOSE MEMO` *`memo field`*`[,`*`memo field`*`]|ALL`

Description This command is used to close any database memo field editing windows.

Operational rules To close a specific memo field editing window, specify the field with memo field. Use CLOSE MEMO ALL To close all open memo field editing windows.

See also MODIFY MEMO

COMPILE

`COMPILE` *`filename|skel`* `[ENCRYPT|NODEBUG]`

Description This command is used to compile a source code program file to an .FPX object code file.

Operational rules FoxPro requires that program files are compiled into object code before running. FoxPro uses the object code files to allow the programs to run much faster. These files, unlike source code files, cannot be edited with MODIFY COMMAND.

FoxPro automatically compiles programs when DO *program name* is issued in the program file but no compiled file exists or the program file is more recent than the compiled file. The program (.PRG, .SPR, .MPR) file is compared to the object code (.FPX, .SPX, .MPX) file. If the two are different, then it recompiles the object code. Use SET DEVELOPMENT OFF to turn off automatic compiling.

The COMPILE command checks for errors in the source code. If an error is found, the command displays the line number of the error and allows you to abort the compile process. If a program file is compiled with the ENCRYPT option, the resulting object code file contains a higher level of security for your application. Because of the process used to encrypt the file, most compression routines such as PkZip and LhArc cannot compress the encrypted FoxPro object files. To remove debugging ability from your application use the NODEBUG option. This disables the ability to trace program execution in the Trace window.

See also SET DEVELOPMENT, MODIFY COMMAND

CONTINUE

`CONTINUE`

Description This command is used to locate the next record that matches the criteria used in the LOCATE command.

Operational rules The LOCATE command is used to find the first record that matches a specified criteria. If the criteria is based on a field that is indexed, the SEEK command will find the record much faster than the LOCATE command.

To find the next record that matches the criteria, use the CONTINUE command. If no other records match the criteria, the record pointer moves to the end of file, and the EOF( ) function returns a value of true (.T.).

Example

```
USE MAILLIST
LOCATE FOR Lname = "SMITH"
? Lname, Fname
SMITH JOHN
CONTINUE
? Lname, Fname
SMITHSON ANDY
```

See also LOCATE

COPY FILE

`COPY FILE filename1 TO filename2`

Description This command makes a duplicate copy of any type of file.

Operational rules The COPY FILE command is equivalent to the DOS COPY command. The DOS command is actually faster than COPY FILE, and it can be accessed from FoxPro through the RUN command. However, some users cannot access the RUN command because they do not have enough memory. In this case, COPY FILE can be substituted.

Example

```
COPY FILE MAIL.FRM TO MAIL2.FRM
```

See also RUN|!

COPY INDEXES

`COPY INDEXES index file list|ALL [TO cdx file]`

Description This command copies a list of index files into a new or existing compound index (.CDX) file.

Operational rules Compound indexes contain multiple index "tags" allowing for many indexes to be maintained through one file. If the compound index file does not exist, it is created. If it does exist, the new index tag is simply added to the current list of tags. If the optional TO *cdx file* is not used, FoxPro automatically creates a file with the same name as the .DBF file but with a .CDX extension. Use the optional to ALL option instead of the *index file list* and it will add all open .IDX index files to the .CDX file.

Examples

```
COPY INDEX Mailzip  (adds MAILZIP.IDX to MAILLIST.CDX)
COPY INDEX Mailzip TO Mail2  (adds MAILZIP.IDX to MAIL2.CDX)
```

See also COPY TAG

COPY MEMO

```
COPY MEMO memo field TO filename [ADDITIVE]
```

Description This command copies the data from a memo file to a text file.

Operational rules If *filename* does not exist, FoxPro creates it with a default extension of .TXT. If the file does exist, it is overwritten unless the optional ADDITIVE argument is used. ADDITIVE appends the memo field text to the bottom of *filename*.

Example

```
COPY MEMO Comment TO Narrative.TXT
COPY MEMO Comment TO Narrative ADDITIVE
```

See also APPEND MEMO

COPY STRUCTURE

```
COPY STRUCTURE TO filename [FIELDS field list] [[WITH]
CDX|[WITH] PRODUCTION]]
```

Description This command copies only the structure of the current database to *filename*.

Operational rules The new file is a FoxPro database with a .DBF extension. It will not contain any records. The optional FIELDS *field list* argument copies only the specified fields to the new database. If the original file has a structural index file, the WITH CDX and WITH PRODUCTION options create a structural index for the new database containing all index tags from the source file.

Examples

```
COPY STRUCTURE TO Mail2
COPY STRUCTURE TO Mail2 FIELDS Lname,Fname,City
```

See also APPEND

COPY STRUCTURE EXTENDED

```
COPY TO filename STRUCTURE EXTENDED
```

Description This command copies the structure of the current database to another database.

Operational rules The TO *filename* database is created with the structure of the source database file and consists of the following fields:

Field	Contents
FIELD_NAME	Field names from selected database
FIELD_TYPE	C = Character
	N = Numeric
	F = Float
	D = Date
	L = Logical
	M = Memo

Field	Contents
	G = General
	P = Picture
FIELD_LEN	Width of field
FIELD_DEC	Number of decimal places in numeric fields.

Once the TO *filename* has been created, a new database file can be created using the CREATE FROM command.

See also CREATE FROM

COPY TAG

```
COPY TAG tag name [OF cdx file] TO idx file
```

Description This command copies a tag from a compound index file to a single index (.IDX) file.

Operational rules Compound indexes contain multiple index "tags" allowing for many indexes to be maintained through one file. If the optional OF *cdx file* is not used, FoxPro searches all open structural index files for a matching index TAG. If compound index tags using *tag name* of all open compound index files exist, you must use the OF *cdx file* to access the proper index.

Example

```
COPY TAG Zip TO MAILZIP  (creates MAILZIP.IDX)
COPY TAG Zip OF Mail2 TO MZIP  (creates MZIP.IDX from
MAIL2.CDX)
```

See also DELETE TAG

COPY TO

```
COPY TO filename [FIELDS field list] [scope] [FOR expL] [WHILE
expL] [[WITH] CDX]|[[WITH] PRODUCTION] [NOOPTIMIZE] [[TYPE]
[FOXPLUS | DIF | MOD | SDF | SYLK | WK1 | WKS | WR1 | WRK | XLS
| DELIMITED [WITH delimiter|WITH BLANK|WITH TAB]]]
```

Description This command copies the records from the current database file to *filename*.

Operational rules Unless a type is specified, the new file is a FoxPro database with a .DBF extension. When copying to a file, the optional file types are:

Type	Description
DELIMITED	Variable length fields separated with commas.
DELIMITED WITH *expC*	Variable length fields separated with *expC*.
DELIMITED WITH BLANK	Variable length fields separated with a space.
DELIMITED WITH TAB	Variable length fields separated with Tab.
DIF	Visicalc's Data Interchange Format.
MOD	Microsoft Multiplan version 4.01.
SDF	Fixed length field ASCII file.

SYLK	Symbolic Link interchange format.
WK1	Lotus 1-2-3, version 2.x.
WK3	Lotus 1-2-3, version 3.x.
WKS	Lotus 1-2-3, version 1.x
WR1	Lotus Symphony, version 1.1 or 1.2.
WRK	Lotus Symphony, version 1.0.
XLS	Microsoft Excel, version 2.0.
FOXPLUS	Only needed if the FoxBase file contains a memo field, as FoxPro memo fields are structured differently.

You can use the optional FOR *expL*, WHILE *expL*, and scope arguments to include only a subset of the records to copy.

The optional FIELDS *field list* argument copies only the specified fields to the new database. If the original file has a structural index file, the WITH CDX and WITH PRODUCTION options create a structural index for the new database. Use the NOOPTIMIZE option to disable Rushmore when copying a database.

Example

```
COPY TO Mail2 FOR LNAME = "S"(copies for specified criteria)
COPY TO Mail2 NEXT 100(copies next 100 records)
COPY TO Mail2 SDF(copies to a fixed ASCII file)
COPY TO Mail2 DELIMITED(copies to a variable length file)
COPY TO Mail2 Lname, Fname, City(copies to a three-field file)
```

See also APPEND, EXPORT

COPY TO ARRAY

```
COPY TO ARRAY array [FIELDS field list] [scope] [FOR expL]
[WHILE expL] [NOOPTIMIZE]
```

Description This command copies the records from the current database file to an array.

Operational rules The array must be declared before issuing this command. If the array is two-dimensional, each record is given a row in the array. If the array is one-dimensional, then FoxPro simply adds in each field from each record. The copying stops at the last field and record, or when all dimensions are filled, whichever comes first.

The optional FOR *expL*, WHILE *expL*, and *scope* arguments are used to copy only records that match a specified criteria. The optional FIELDS *field list* argument copies only the specified fields to the array. Use the optional NOOPTIMIZE clause to disable Rushmore when copying database records to any array.

Example

```
USE MAILLIST
DECLARE Mail[5,6]
COPY TO ARRAY Mail FOR ZIP = "92111"
5 records copied
? Mail[1,1] + Mail[1,2]
John  Smith
```

```
? Mail[2,1] + Mail[2,2]
Joe  Schmo
```

See also APPEND FROM ARRAY

COUNT

```
COUNT scope [FOR expL] [WHILE expL] [TO memvar] [NOOPTIMIZE]
```

Description This command counts the number of records in the current database.

Operational rules The COUNT command displays the number of records counted. Keep in mind that if SET TALK is OFF, the count does not display on the screen. The optional TO *memvar* initializes a memory variable that is equal to the number of records counted.

The optional FOR *expL*, WHILE *expL*, and *scope* arguments are used to count only records that match a specified criteria. Use the optional NOOPTIMIZE clause to disable Rushmore when counting database records.

Example

```
COUNT FOR Zip = "92111"
COUNT TO Zcount WHILE UPPER(Lname) = "SMITH"
```

See also CALCULATE, RECCOUNT()

CREATE

```
CREATE [filename|?]
```

Description This command creates the structure for a FoxPro database file.

Operational rules A FoxPro database file is defined by its field names, the type of each field, the length of each field, and whether the field is to be indexed. The default extension for a database file is .DBF. A database can have up to 255 fields. Field names can be from 1 to 10 characters and can contain letters, numbers, and the underline character (_). Field names must begin with a letter. Each field must be one of the following types: Character, numeric, floating point number, logical, date, picture, general, or memo.

Character field widths can be from 1 to 254 in length. Numeric fields can be up to 20 digits. Date fields are automatically 8, picture, general and memo fields are 10, and logical fields are 1. Data entered in a picture, general or memo field is not stored in the .DBF file, but is a second file with the extension .FPT. If no file name is specified or you use ?, a dialog will ask you for the database file name.

See also MODIFY STRUCTURE

CREATE COLOR SET

```
CREATE COLOR SET color set name
```

Description This command creates a new color set from the current color settings.

Operational rules All color pairs of the current color scheme are saved in the color set *color set name*. A color set name can be up to 10 characters long and must begin with a character or underscore (_). Color sets that are created with CREATE COLOR SET are stored in the current FoxPro resource file and can be loaded using the SET COLOR SET command.

See also SET COLOR SET, SET COLOR TO

CREATE CURSOR (SQL)

CREATE CURSOR *dbf_name* (*fieldname*, *type* [(*precision*[, *scale*])])|FROM ARRAY *array*

Description This command creates a temporary database file.

Operational rules Cursor tables in FoxPro are temporary database files that exist in memory until closed. Cursor tables have all the same attributes of a normal FoxPro DBF and the same restrictions. Each field in the database is defined with a field name, type, precision and scale. These definitions can be identified in the CREATE CURSOR command or they can exist in ARRAY *array*.

The *dbf_name* argument specifies the name of the cursor table and can contain any valid DOS path and filename or expression. The field name, type, precision, and scale all must follow the rules of any FoxPro database structure. Some data types such as numeric and character require that you specify a width and number of decimal places. The table below represents the values for field type, precision and scale:

Type	Precision	Scale	Description
C	n		Character string of width n
D			Date
F	n	d	Float of width n with d decimal places
L			Logical
M			Memo
N	n	d	Numeric of width n with d decimal places
G			General
P			Picture

If a scale is not specified for numeric or floating point fields the scale will be zero. A cursor table is always created and opened exclusively, regardless of the SET EXCLUSIVE setting. FoxPro creates a unique temporary DOS file handle for the cursor table.

Example

```
CREATE CURSOR STUDENTS (Lname C(20), Fname C(10), Class N(5,2))
Notes M(10))
? ALIAS()
STUDENTS
DISPLAY STRUCTURE
Structure for table:          c:\foxpro25\00981927.tmp
Number of data records:       0
Date of last update:          01/02/93
Field  Field Name   Type        Width   Dec  Index
  1      LNAME      Character    20
  2      FNAME      Character    10
```

```
  3      CLASS      Numeric      5      2
** Total **                     36
```

See also CREATE TABLE

CREATE FROM

`CREATE [filename1] FROM [filename2]`

Description This command creates a database file from a special type of database that contains the structure in its records.

Operational rules The CREATE FROM command creates a new database using the structure contained in *filename2*. The COPY TO STRUCTURE EXTENDED command creates a database file which contains the structure of a new database file. The structured file is made up of four fields: FIELD_NAME, FIELD_TYPE, FIELD_LEN, and FIELD_DEC. This database has one record for each field in the current file. *filename1* specifies the name of the new target database while *filename2* is the database that contains the structural information.

Structure extended files can be used to create structures of new files within programs. The program can make decisions on the structure (such as adding or deleting fields, or changing names and lengths) through editing the extended file, and then creating the file with CREATE FROM. This allows the user to create or modify a structure without using the full-screen CREATE or MODIFY STRUCTURE commands.

See also COPY TO STRUCTURE EXTENDED

CREATE LABEL

```
CREATE LABEL [filename|?] [NOWAIT] [SAVE] [[WINDOW window name]
[IN [WINDOW] window name|IN SCREEN]]
```

Description This command uses the FoxPro label generator to create a format for mailing labels.

Operational rules When in the label generator, you set the dimensions of the label, the number of labels to print across the page, and then the contents of each label (fields and templates). If you use the optional ? argument in place of *filename*, FoxPro then brings up the dialog box that allows you to enter a name. If *filename* already exists, the CREATE LABEL command does not overwrite it. Instead, it allows you to modify the file. The default extension of label format files is .LBX.

The optional NOWAIT clause will continue program execution after the label has been created. To open the label template in a specific window other than the FoxPro screen, use the IN WINDOW *window name* option. The *window name* window must be defined using the DEFINE WINDOW command before opening the label. The SAVE clause leaves the label design window open after another window has been activated.

Use the LABEL command to print the labels. Labels printed with this command automatically omit blank lines for records that have no contents in particular fields.

See also LABEL

CREATE MENU

```
CREATE MENU [filename|?] [NOWAIT] [SAVE] [[WINDOW window name]
[IN [WINDOW] window name|IN SCREEN]]
```

Description This command activates the FoxPro Menu builder which helps you build menus and pop-ups.

Operational rules The menu builder creates a menu (.MNX) file that contains information regarding the menu created in the menu builder. The menu file may be opened with the MODIFY MENU command and changed. This command is equivalent to choosing New... from the File menu, and specifying a Menu file.

If the file name is not included, the menu file is temporarily named UNTITLED and must be named when saved. The optional ? argument can be used to get the Open File dialog box where you can choose from a list of .MNX files or enter a new name.

Use the WINDOW *window name* clause to place the menu layout within a window. It will take on all characteristics of the window. Use IN WINDOW *window name* to open the menu layout in the parent window. The menu layout must be smaller than the parent, and stay within the parent window's boundaries. The IN SCREEN option is the default. This causes the menu builder to be placed on the screen instead of within a window.

See also MODIFY MENU, Using the Menu Builder

CREATE PROJECT

```
CREATE PROJECT [filename|?] [NOWAIT] [SAVE] [WINDOW window
name] [IN [WINDOW] window name|IN SCREEN]
```

Description This command activates the FoxPro Project manager which helps you build a project file.

Operational rules A project database (.PJX) contains information regarding a group of files that are all used in one application. The .PJX file is a database that contains information regarding all the files in the project. Project files are used with the BUILD APP command for building an .APP file and for building .EXE files. The file can be opened with the MODIFY PROJECT command and changed.

CREATE PROJECT is equivalent to choosing New... from the File menu, and specifying a Project file. If the file name is not included, the project file is temporarily named UNTITLED and must be named when saved. The optional ? argument can be used to get the Open File dialog where you can choose from a list of .PJX files or enter a new name.

Use the WINDOW *window name* clause to place the Project window within another window. It will then take on all of the characteristics of that window. Use IN WINDOW *window name* to open the Project window inside a parent window. The Project window must be smaller than the parent and stay within the parent window's boundaries. The IN SCREEN option is the default. This causes the Project window to be placed on the screen instead of within a window.

See also MODIFY PROJECT, Using the Project Manager

CREATE QUERY

```
CREATE QUERY [filename|?]
```

Description This command activates the RQBE window, which helps you create a query.

Operational rules When in the RQBE window you define the field to select by, the comparison operator (Like, Exactly Like, More Than, Less Than, etc.) and the comparison. You can select multiple criteria by connecting them with AND (the default) or OR. You can also select the method to output the query (Browse, Report, Label, Cursor, etc.)

The RQBE window builds an SQL SELECT command. The SELECT command allows you to specify the query and then FoxPro determines the most optimal way to retrieve the information.

CREATE QUERY is equivalent to choosing New... from the File menu, and specifying a Query file. The query is stored in a program file with a .QPR extension. The file can be opened with the MODIFY QUERY command and changed. To run a query, use DO *query filename*. If the file name is not included, the query file is temporarily named UNTITLED and must be named when saved. The optional ? argument can be used to get the Open File dialog where you can choose from a list of .QPR files or enter a new name.

See also MODIFY QUERY, Using the RQBE Window and SQL

CREATE REPORT

```
CREATE REPORT [filename|?] [NOWAIT] [SAVE] [[WINDOW window
name] [IN [WINDOW] window name|IN SCREEN]]
```

Description This command activates the FoxPro Report generator to create a report format (.FRX) file.

Operational rules When in the report generator, you set the dimensions of the report, headings, contents of the body of the report, and subtotal groupings.

If you omit *filename*, FoxPro asks for the name when you save the file. If you use the optional ? argument in place of *filename*, FoxPro then brings up the dialog box that allows you to enter a name. If *filename* already exists, the CREATE REPORT command does not overwrite it. Instead, it allows you to modify the file.

CREATE REPORT is equivalent to choosing New... from the File menu, and specifying a Report file. The report is stored in a database file with an .FRX extension. The file can be opened with the MODIFY REPORT command and changed. If the file name is not included, the report file is temporarily named UNTITLED and must be named when saved. The optional ? argument can be used to get the Open File dialog where you can choose from a list of .FRX files or enter a new name. Print reports using the REPORT command.

See also REPORT, Using the Report Writer

CREATE REPORT (quick report)

```
CREATE REPORT filename1|? FROM filename2 [FORM | COLUMN]
[FIELDS field list] [ALIAS] [NOOVERWRITE] [WIDTH expN]
```

Description This command creates a FoxPro report without using the Report generator.

Operational rules The report that is created using this command is similar to selecting the Quick Report... option from the Report menu. If you omit *filename*, FoxPro asks for the name when you save the file. If you use the optional ? argument in place of *filename*, FoxPro then brings up the dialog box that allows you to enter a name. If *filename* already exists and the NOOVERWRITE clause is used, the CREATE REPORT command does not overwrite it.

The FROM *filename2* is the name of a database file from which the report will be generated. Specifying FORM creates the report and the database fields are arranged from top to bottom in the Detail band. The COLUMN option arranged the fields from left to right in the Detail band. This is the default if FORM|COLUMN is not specified.

Use the FIELDS *field list* option to specify which fields to include on the report. The ALIAS option will preface the fields placed on the report with the database name. By default the width of the report is 80 characters and can be changed by specifying WIDTH *expN*. The report created using this command can be opened and modified using the MODIFY REPORT command. Print reports using the REPORT command.

See also Using the Report Writer

CREATE SCREEN

```
CREATE SCREEN [filename|?] [NOWAIT] [SAVE] [WINDOW window name]
[IN [WINDOW] window name|IN SCREEN]
```

Description This command activates the FoxPro Screen builder which helps you create custom data entry screens.

Operational rules The Screen builder allows you to create custom screen layouts and easily define pop-ups, radio buttons, and other objects. CREATE SCREEN is equivalent to choosing New... from the File menu, and specifying a screen file. The screen's information is stored in a file with an .SCX extension. The screen file can be opened with the MODIFY SCREEN command and changed.

If the file name is not included, the screen file is temporarily named UNTITLED and must be named when saved. The optional ? argument can be used to get the Open File dialog where you can choose from a list of .SCX files or enter a new name.

Use the WINDOW *window name* clause to place the Screen template window within another window. It will take on all characteristics of that window. Use IN WINDOW *window name* to open the screen builder inside a parent window. The Screen template window must be smaller than the parent, and stay within the parent window's boundaries. The IN SCREEN option is the default. This causes the screen template to be placed on the screen instead of within a window.

See also MODIFY SCREEN, Using the Screen Builder

CREATE SCREEN (quick screen)

```
CREATE SCREEN filename1|? FROM filename2 [ROW | COLUMN] [FIELDS
field list] [ALIAS] [NOOVERWRITE] [SIZE height, width] [SCREEN]
```

Description This command creates a FoxPro data editing screen without using the Screen Builder.

Operational rules The screen that is created using this command is similar to selecting the Quick Screen... option from the Screen menu. If you omit *filename*, FoxPro asks for the name when you save the file. If you use the optional ? argument in place of *filename*, FoxPro then brings up the dialog box that allows you to enter a name. If *filename* already exists and the NOOVERWRITE clause is used, the CREATE SCREEN command does not overwrite it.

The FROM *filename2* is the name of a database file from which the screen will be generated. Specifying ROW creates the report and the database fields are arranged from top to bottom on the screen. The COLUMN option arranges the fields from left to right on the screen. This is the default if ROW|COLUMN is not specified.

Use the FIELDS *field list* option to specify which fields to include on the screen. The ALIAS option will preface the fields placed on the screen with the database name. By default the height and width of the window created is 24 × 80 characters and can be changed by specifying SIZE *height*, *width*. Editing screens created using this command are placed in windows. Using the SCREEN clause places the editing screen on the FoxPro desktop. The screen created using this command can be opened and modified using the MODIFY SCREEN command.

See also MODIFY SCREEN, Using the Screen Builder

CREATE TABLE (SQL)

```
CREATE TABLE dbf_name (field name, type [(precision[,
scale])])|FROM ARRAY array
```

Description This command creates a FoxPro database file.

Operational rules A table created with CREATE TABLE is a FoxPro database (.DBF) file. The CREATE TABLE command is exactly like the CREATE CURSOR command except databases created using CREATE TABLE are saved on disk after they are closed. All databases created using the CREATE TABLE command have all the same attributes of a normal FoxPro DBF and the same restrictions.

Each field in the database is defined with a field name, type, precision and scale. These definitions can be identified in the CREATE TABLE command or they can exist in ARRAY array. The *dbf_name* specifies the name of the table and can contain any valid DOS path and filename or expression. The *field name*, *type*, *precision*, and *scale* all must follow the rules of any FoxPro database structure. Some data types such as numeric and character require that you specify a width and number of decimal places. The table below represents the values for field type, precision and scale:

Type	Precision	Scale	Description
C	n		Character string of width n
D			Date
F	n	d	Float of width n with d decimal places
L			Logical
M			Memo
N	n	d	Numeric of width n with d decimal places
G			General
P			Picture

If a scale is not specified for numeric or floating point fields the scale will be zero. A new database is always created and opened exclusively, regardless of the SET EXCLUSIVE setting.

Example

```
CREATE TABLE STUDENTS (Lname C(20), Fname C(10), Class N(5,2))
Notes M(10))
? ALIAS()
STUDENTS
DISPLAY STRUCTURE
Structure for table:           c:\foxpro25\students.dbf
Number of data records:        0
Date of last update:           01/02/93
Field   Field Name   Type        Width  Dec  Index
  1       LNAME      Character   20
  2       FNAME      Character   10
  3       CLASS      Numeric      5      2
** Total **                      36
```

See also CREATE CURSOR, CREATE

CREATE VIEW

```
CREATE VIEW view file
```

Description This command creates a view (.VUE) file from the FoxPro environment.

Operational rules A view file saves information regarding the following environment settings:

- Open data, index, alternate and format files, and their work areas.
- Current selected work area.
- Relationships set between files.
- Open format files.
- Current filter conditions including SET FIELDS and SET FILTER.
- Current help and resource files.
- Settings of SET DEFAULT and SET PATH.

To quickly restore all these settings with one command, use SET VIEW TO view file. The CREATE VIEW command creates a file named view file with a DOS extension of .VUE file from the current settings.

See also SET VIEW

DEACTIVATE MENU

DEACTIVATE MENU *menu name* [, *menu name2* ...]|ALL

Description This command removes a user-defined menu from the screen.

Operational rules Menus are defined with the DEFINE MENU and DEFINE PAD commands. Use ACTIVATE MENU to then display them. DEACTIVATE MENU *menu name* erases the specified menu from the screen, but does not clear it from memory. This can be accomplished with CLEAR ALL or RELEASE MENUS commands.

Specify *menu name* of the menu to deactivate, or use the ALL option to remove all menus from the screen. If you are using the FoxPro *_msysmenu* function, issuing the command SET SYSMENU TO DEFAULT will remove your user-defined menu and restore the default FoxPro menu. See DEFINE MENU for a program that creates a user-defined menu.

See also DEFINE MENU

DEACTIVATE POPUP

`DEACTIVATE POPUP` *`popup name`*`|ALL`

Description This command removes a user-defined pop-up from the screen.

Operational rules Pop-up menus are designed with the DEFINE POPUP and DEFINE PAD commands. Use ACTIVATE POPUP to then display them. DEACTIVATE POPUP *popup name* erases the specified popup from the screen, but does not clear it from memory. This can be accomplished with CLEAR ALL or RELEASE POPUP commands. Specify the name of the pop-up to deactivate with *popup name*, or use the ALL option to remove all pop-ups from the screen. See DEFINE BAR for a program that creates a user-defined pop-up menu.

See also DEFINE BAR

DEACTIVATE WINDOW

`DEACTIVATE WINDOW` *`window name[, window name2 ...]`* `|ALL`

Description This command removes a window from the screen.

Operational rules Windows are designed with the DEFINE WINDOW command. Use ACTIVATE WINDOW to then display them. DEACTIVATE WINDOW *window name* erases the specified window from the screen, but does not clear it from memory. This can be accomplished with CLEAR ALL or RELEASE WINDOWS command. Specify the name of the window to deactivate with *window name*, or use the ALL option to remove all windows from the screen.

See also DEFINE WINDOW

DECLARE

`DECLARE` *`array(expN1 [, expN2])`*

Description This command initializes an array in memory.

Operational rules You must declare arrays before using them. Arrays are special memory variables that have multiple values. An array is set up like a table. When storing values to an array, you define which number of the table you are storing to. The DECLARE statement declares the maximum number of values to be stored in each dimension of the array.

An array can be single- or multi-dimensional. The first number is called the row number. If the array is two dimensional, there is a second number which is called the column number. You may declare more than one array at a time. Array dimensions may be entered in square brackets ([ ]) or parentheses.

To define an array element use the STORE or = command, just like defining any other memory variable. All data in an array is initially equal to .F. To change the size of an array, use the DECLARE command again. Changing the size of any array does not affect any values the array may hold. The DECLARE command is identical to DIMENSION.

Example

```
DECLARE Subtotal[5,2]     && declare an array named Subtotal
Subtotal[1,1] = 100
STORE 200 TO Subtotal(1,2)
DECLARE Marray(3,3), Marray2(4,2), Marray3(6,6)
```

See also STORE

#DEFINE ... #UNDEF

```
#DEFINE constant name expression
#UNDEF constant name
```

Description These commands are used to create compile-time constants.

Operational rules The #DEFINE and #UNDEF commands are "preprocessor" directives that replace the name of a memory variable or array with an actual value. A constant value is one that never changes. You can reduce the amount of memory used in a program by referencing a constant value rather than a variable or array.

When FoxPro compiles a program that uses #DEFINE, all occurrences of *constant name* are replaced with *expression*. This action only affects the compiled source code file (.FXP, .SPX, .MPX, .QPX) and does not change the text within the source program. Because these commands are evaluated at the time a source file is compiled, *expression* should not be a memory variable or array element unless it has been initialized before the source code is compiled. The specified *constant name* must reference a valid FoxPro variable or array.

The #DEFINE command replaces all occurrences of *constant name* only in the source file it is used in. This means that the memory variable or array that is replaced with expression is available only to the program that creates the constant. The #UNDEF command is used to stop the replacement.

Examples The following is a typical FoxPro program:

```
mstop = 10
FOR mni = 1 TO mstop
   WAIT WINDOW "The current value is " + ALLTRIM(STR(mni))
ENDFOR
```

Using the #DEFINE command, the program code would look like the following:

```
#DEFINE mstop 10
#UNDEF
FOR mni = 1 TO mstop
   WAIT WINDOW "The current value is " + ALLTRIM(STR(mni))
ENDFOR
```

When compiled, FoxPro replaces all occurrences of *mstop* with 10. The resulting compiled code would "read"

```
FOR mni = 1 TO 10
   WAIT WINDOW "The current value is " + ALLTRIM(STR(mni))
ENDFOR
```

See also #IF ... #ENDIF

DEFINE BAR

DEFINE BAR *expN|system option name* OF *popup name* PROMPT *prompt* [BEFORE *expN*|AFTER *expN*] [KEY *label* [, *expC*]] [MESSAGE *expC*] [SKIP [FOR *expL*]] [COLOR SCHEME *expN*|COLOR *color pair*]

Description This command defines the contents of a pop-up menu.

Operational rules Each option in a user-defined menu is called a bar. DEFINE BAR allows you to define the options that exist within the pop-up menu. Each pop-up option is given a line number starting with one. The pop-up name is defined with the DEFINE POPUP command. The actual option is defined using the prompt keyword.

To define a menu where each option has a pop-up menu that contains additional options, issue the following commands:

1. DEFINE MENU to name the menu.
2. DEFINE PAD to name and position each option in the menu.
3. ON PAD to activate each pop-up for each pad.
4. DEFINE POPUP to name and position each pop-up menu.
5. DEFINE BAR to position each option within the pop-up menu.

To activate the menu, the following commands must be issued ON SELECTION to call the procedure that runs each bar option from the pop-up menu, then the ACTIVATE MENU displays the menu (with pop-ups) on screen.

To define a hot key, place \< before the appropriate letter in the prompt. A separating bar may be placed between options by using a prompt of \-. You may also use the option KEY *label* to define a hot key. When the KEY option is used, the label is displayed as text next to the bar. The key label must be a valid key label name (see the ON KEY LABEL command). You can define the text to be displayed by using the KEY label text command.

Use the optional MESSAGE *expC* clause to display a message at the bottom of the screen when this particular option is highlighted. Use the optional SKIP clause if you want the option displayed, but disabled. For example, use the SKIP FOR *expL* to disable the option only when *expL* is True (.T.).

The COLOR and COLOR SCHEME clauses allow you to set your own colors in the pop-up menu. Use the options BEFORE *expN* and AFTER *expN* to determine where the bar will be displayed in the pop-up. These must be used in conjunction with the RELATIVE keyword in the DEFINE POPUP command. The BEFORE clause causes the pop-up to appear before pop-up *expN*, and AFTER causes the pop-up to appear after pop-up *expN*. When the RELATIVE keyword is not used, undefined bar numbers are reserved blank bars within the pop-up.

For instance, the following pop-up would have Guests as the top pop-up, and no blank bar is reserved for bar 2.

```
DEFINE POPUP Whch RELATIVE FROM 3,2
DEFINE BAR 1 OF Whch PROMPT "Members"
DEFINE BAR 3 OF Whch PROMPT "Guests" BEFORE MFIRST
```

The following pop-up Whch2 would have Prospects as the middle pop-up, before Guests. Again, no blank bar is reserved for bar 3 because the RELATIVE keyword is used.

```
DEFINE POPUP Whch RELATIVE FROM 3,2
DEFINE BAR 1 OF Whch PROMPT "Members"
DEFINE BAR 2 OF Whch PROMPT "Guests" BEFORE MFIRST
DEFINE BAR 4 OF Whch PROMPT "Prospect" BEFORE 2
```

If you use the Menu Builder to create your menus, you may not have to use this command at all. The Menu Builder automatically generates the commands that define menus and pop-ups.

Example The following program creates the menu and pop-up options. This program only sets up the pop-up for the leftmost option, Add.

```
DEFINE MENU Mail
DEFINE PAD Add OF Mail PROMPT "Add " AT 2,2
DEFINE PAD Edit OF Mail PROMPT "Edit" AT 2,20
DEFINE PAD List OF Mail PROMPT "List" AT 2,38
DEFINE PAD Exit OF Mail PROMPT "Exit" AT 2,56

ON PAD Add OF Mail ACTIVATE POPUP Wchfil

DEFINE POPUP Wchfil FROM 3,2
DEFINE BAR 1 OF Wchfil PROMPT "\<Members"  && M is the hot key
DEFINE BAR 2 OF Wchfil PROMPT "Guests"
DEFINE BAR 3 OF Wchfil PROMPT "/-"  && separating line
DEFINE BAR 4 OF Wchfil PROMPT "Prospect" KEY "Alt-F2"
ON SELECTION POPUP Wchfil DO Chooser WITH BAR()

ACTIVATE MENU Mail

PROCEDURE Chooser
PARAMETER Barchoice
DO CASE
   CASE Barchoice = 1
      USE MEMBERS
   CASE Barchoice = 2
      USE GUESTS
   CASE Barchoice = 4
      USE PROSPECT
ENDCASE
APPEND
RETURN
```

See also DEFINE POPUP, ON KEY LABEL, Using the Menu Builder

DEFINE BOX

```
DEFINE BOX FROM column1 TO column2 HEIGHT expN [AT LINE expN]
[SINGLE|DOUBLE|border string]
```

Description This command sets coordinates and borders of a box to be printed around text.

Operational rules The default border of the box is a single line box. The optional SINGLE, DOUBLE, and *border string* allow you to change the border characters. See SET BORDER regarding the layout of the border definition string. Use the AT LINE *expN* to specify the line to begin the box.

To print the box, the system variable *_box* must be set to true (.T.).

Examples

```
DEFINE BOX FROM 2 TO 60 HEIGHT 10 DOUBLE
```

See also SET BORDER

DEFINE MENU

```
DEFINE MENU menu name [BAR [AT LINE expN]] [IN [WINDOW] window
name|IN SCREEN] [KEY key label] [MESSAGE expC] [NOMARGIN]
[COLOR SCHEME expN|COLOR color pair]
```

Description This command creates a user-defined menu in memory.

Operational rules Before a menu can be designed, it must be defined. DEFINE MENU simply allows you to name the menu. Use DEFINE PAD to set each of the options and their coordinates.

To define and display a user-defined menu, the following commands must be issued:

1. DEFINE MENU to name the menu.
2. DEFINE PAD to name and position each option in the menu.
3. ON SELECTION PAD to assign the commands that will be run when a pad is selected.
4. ACTIVATE MENU to display the menu.

Use the optional KEY *key label* clause to define a key that activates the menu. The key label must be a valid key label name (see the ON KEY LABEL command). Use the optional MESSAGE *expC* to display a message in the status bar or at the bottom of the screen when the menu is activated.

Use the WINDOW *window name* or IN WINDOW *window name* clause to place the menu bar within a window. It will take on all characteristics of that window. Use BAR to create a bar menu that scrolls through the options if the number of pads exceeds the size of the defined menu screen or window. You may specify the screen or window row in which a menu bar is placed with the BAR AT LINE *expN* clause.

Use NOMARGIN to eliminate the extra space placed to the left of each menu pad. The COLOR and COLOR SCHEME clauses allow you to set your own colors in the pop-up menu.

If you use the Menu Builder to create your menus, you may not have to use this command at all. The Menu Builder automatically generates the commands that define menus.

Example The following program creates a menu and activates various options.

```
DEFINE MENU Mail
DEFINE PAD Add OF Mail PROMPT "Add" AT 2,2
DEFINE PAD Edit OF Mail PROMPT "Edit" AT 2,20
DEFINE PAD List OF Mail PROMPT "List" AT 2,38
DEFINE PAD Exit OF Mail PROMPT "Exit" AT 2,56

ON SELECTION PAD Add OF Mail APPEND
ON SELECTION PAD Edit OF Mail EDIT
ON SELECTION PAD List OF Mail DO Lister
ON SELECTION PAD Exit OF Mail QUIT
ACTIVATE MENU Mail
```

See also DEFINE PAD

DEFINE PAD

DEFINE PAD *pad name* OF *menu name* PROMPT *expC* [AT *row, column*] [BEFORE *pad name*|AFTER *pad name*] [KEY *key label* [, *expC*]] [SKIP [FOR *expL*]] [MESSAGE *expC*] [COLOR SCHEME *expN*|COLOR *color pair*]

Description This command defines the options that will be displayed in a user-defined menu.

Operational rules Use DEFINE PAD to set each of the options and their coordinates of a menu that has been named with DEFINE MENU. The AT clause and coordinates are optional. If you do not include them, FoxPro will place the first option in the left corner of row one. Each subsequent option will be one space to the right. There is no limit to the pads that may be defined, other than the computer's memory limits.

Use the optional MESSAGE *expC* to display a message in the status bar or at the bottom of the screen when the pad is selected. Use the optional SKIP clause if you want the option displayed, but unable to be chosen (the option display in half intensity).

Use the SKIP FOR *expL* to disable the option only when *expL* is true (.T.). Disabled options can be highlighted but not selected. To define a hot key, place \< before the appropriate letter in prompt. You can also use the optional KEY *key label* clause to define a hot key. When the KEY option is used, the key label is displayed as text next to the bar. The key label must be a valid key label name (see the ON KEY LABEL command).

The COLOR *color pair* and COLOR SCHEME *expN* clauses allow you to set your own colors for an individual pad. Use the options BEFORE *pad name* and AFTER *pad name* to determine where the pad will be displayed in the menu. The BEFORE clause causes the pad to appear before *pad name*, and AFTER causes the pad to appear after *pad name*. When these clauses are used in conjunction with the BAR keyword in the DEFINE MENU command, they determine the physical placement of a pad in the menu. When the BAR keyword is not used, they determine the activation order, but the physical placement of the pads is determined by the order in which they were created.

For instance, the following menu would have the List option displayed before Edit:

```
DEFINE MENU Mail
DEFINE PAD Add OF Mail PROMPT "Add "
DEFINE PAD Edit OF Mail PROMPT "Edit"
DEFINE PAD List OF Mail PROMPT "List" BEFORE Edit
```

See DEFINE MENU for a program that creates a bounce-bar menu.

Examples

```
DEFINE PAD Add OF Mail PROMPT "Add " AT 2,2
DEFINE PAD Add OF Mail PROMPT "\<Add " && A is hot key
DEFINE PAD Add OF Mail PROMPT "Add " MESSAGE "Add Records To
Mail.dbf"
```

If you use the Menu Builder to create your menus, you may not have to use this command at all. The Menu Builder automatically generates the commands that define menus and pads.

See also DEFINE MENU

DEFINE POPUP

DEFINE POPUP *popup name* [FROM *row1, col1*] [TO *row2, col2*] [IN [WINDOW] *window name*|IN SCREEN] [KEY *key label*] [MARGIN] [MESSAGE *expC*] [MOVER] [MULTISELECT] [PROMPT FIELD *expr*|PROMPT FILES [LIKE *skel*]|PROMPT STRUCTURE] [RELATIVE] [SCROLL] [TITLE *expC*] [COLOR SCHEME *expN*|COLOR *color pair*]

Description This command sets the placement and contents of a pop-up menu.

Operational rules DEFINE POPUP designs a pop-up menu that is displayed vertically. You can call pop-up menus that display whenever an option from a user-defined menu is highlighted. This creates a "menu within a menu."' The coordinates FROM *row1*, *col1* define the placement of the top left corner of the pop-up. See DEFINE BAR for a complete program that displays a user-defined menu with pop-up menus.

Use the optional MESSAGE *expC* to display a message in the status bar or at the bottom of the screen when the pop-up is selected. Use the TITLE *expC* to display a title that displays centered at the top border of the pop-up. You do not need to provide the optional TO *row2*, *col2* for the bottom corner coordinates of the menu. FoxPro will choose a best fit determined by the number and width of bars within the pop-up menu, set with the DEFINE BAR command.

The PROMPT FIELD, PROMPT FILES, and PROMPT STRUCTURE clauses are used when you want the options of the pop-up to be the contents of a database, files on a disk or the structure of a database. You might not use DEFINE BAR if you are going to use any of the PROMPT options. PROMPT FIELD displays the contents of *expr* in each record of the database file in the pop-up window. PROMPT FILES displays a list of the files (you can use the optional LIKE skel clause) contained in the current directory. PROMPT STRUCTURE displays all fields in the specified database.

Use the WINDOW *window name* or IN *window name* clause to place the pop-up window within a window. It takes on all characteristics of that window. Use the option KEY *key label* to define a hot key that activates the pop-up. The key label must be a valid key label name (see the ON KEY LABEL command). The COLOR *color pair* and COLOR SCHEME *expN* clauses allow you to set your own colors in the pop-up menu.

Use MARGIN to place an extra space to the left and right of each option. If this option is used in conjunction with check marks, the marks are displayed one space left of the option. Without the MARGIN clause, the check marks overwrite the first character of the prompt.

The MOVER clause allows the options in the pop-up to be rearranged by the user. To do this, a double-headed arrow is placed to the left of each option. The options can be rearranged by using the mouse (click on the arrow and drag the option up or down) or the keyboard (select the option and press Ctrl-↓ or Ctrl-↑.

The MULTISELECT clause allows multiple options to be chosen from a pop-up. When an option is chosen from this type of pop-up, the option is highlighted. Multiple options can be selected by the mouse (hold down Shift or Ctrl and click the options) or the keyboard (hold down Shift or Ctrl and press Enter or the spacebar). See the MARGIN clause regarding placement of the check marks. MULTISELECT is not available if the pop-up is defined as PROMPT FIELD, PROMPT FILE or PROMPT STRUCTURE.

The RELATIVE keyword allows you to control where options in the pop-up are placed. When the RELATIVE keyword is not used, undefined bar numbers are reserved blank bars within the pop-up. See the DEFINE BAR command for examples of how the BEFORE and AFTER keywords can change the placement of bars in the pop-up when used in conjunction with RELATIVE.

The SCROLL keyword places a scroll bar to the right of the pop-up. Scroll bars allow you to use a mouse to move quickly through the pop-up. The scroll bar is only displayed when the pop-up is too long to fit in the screen or active window.

If you use the Menu Builder to create your menus, you may not have to use this command at all. The Menu Builder automatically generates the commands that define menus and pop-ups.

Examples

```
DEFINE POPUP Whchfile FROM 3,2
DEFINE POPUP Whchfile FROM 3,2 TO 8,12
DEFINE POPUP Whchfile SCROLL FROM 3,2 PROMPT FILES LIKE M*
DEFINE POPUP Statepop FROM 3,2 PROMPT FIELD States
```

See also DEFINE BAR

DEFINE WINDOW

DEFINE WINDOW *window name1* FROM *row1, col1* TO *row2, col2*|AT *row1, col1* SIZE *row2, col2* [IN [WINDOW] *window name2*|IN SCREEN|IN DESKTOP] [FONT *expC* [,*expN*]] [STYLE *expC*] [TITLE *expC*] [HALFHEIGHT] [DOUBLE|PANEL|NONE|SYSTEM | *border string*] [CLOSE|NOCLOSE] [FLOAT|NOFLOAT] [GROW|NOGROW] [MDI| NOMDI] [MINIMIZE] [ZOOM|NOZOOM] [ICON FILE *expC*] [FILL FILE *bmp filename*] [COLOR SCHEME *expN*|COLOR *color pair*]

Description This command creates and sets the attributes of a user-defined window.

Operational rules Windows are defined using the DEFINE WINDOW command and activated using the ACTIVATE WINDOW or SHOW WINDOW commands. You can define multiple windows, but output is directed to the most recently activated one.

You can choose from either the FROM|TO or AT|SIZE clauses to define the size of the window. When using FROM|TO, the top left row and column positions of the window are based on the font and style of *window name1*'s parent window. A parent window is another user-defined window or the main FoxPro desktop window. When using AT|SIZE, the size and location of the window is based on the font and style of *window name1*, as specified with the FONT and STYLE clauses.

The DEFINE WINDOW command supports a number of optional clauses that are described below.

window name1 Defines the window reference name.

FROM *row1*, *col1* Determines the top left coordinates of the window. Row and column positions can be fractional for accurate positioning.

TO *row2*, *col2* Determines the bottom right coordinates of the window when used with the FROM clause. Row and column positions can be fractional for accurate positioning.

AT *row1*, *col1* Determines the top left coordinates of the window. Row and column positions can be fractional for accurate positioning.

SIZE *row2*, *col2* Determines the bottom right coordinates of the window when used with the AT clause. Row and column positions can be fractional for accurate positioning.

IN [WINDOW] *window name2* Defines *window name1* as a child window inside *window name2*. A child window cannot be moved outside the coordinates of its parent window. When using the IN clause, coordinates specified with the FROM|TO and AT|SIZE clauses are relative to the size of *window name2*.

IN SCREEN Places *window name1* on the main FoxPro desktop window.

IN DESKTOP Places *window name1* in the Windows desktop which is outside the main FoxPro desktop window. The coordinates of *window name1* are relative to the main Windows desktop. When a window is defined as IN DESKTOP, that window will always be the frontmost window while FoxPro is active.

FONT *expC* [,*expN*] This clause defines the type and size of the font for the window.

STYLE *expC* This clause defines the style for the font specified with the FONT clause.

TITLE *expC* When used, the expression *expC* is centered in the title bar of the window.

HALFHEIGHT Creates a title bar that is half the size of a normal Windows title bar. This clause is useful when running FoxPro for DOS applications in Windows. The HALFHEIGHT clause takes precedence over the SYSTEM and FONT clauses.

DOUBLE|PANEL|NONE|SYSTEM|*border string* The default border for a window is a single line box. Use these options to define another type of border for the window. Specifying DOUBLE, PANEL or *border string* places a wide border around the window. Use SYS-

TEM to give the window the same controls as a FoxPro system window. Specifying NONE removes any border from the window.

CLOSE|NOCLOSE Specifying CLOSE allows the window to be closed by the user and activates the Close option in the window's control menu. NOCLOSE is the default and prevents a window from being closed by the user.

FLOAT|NOFLOAT Specifying FLOAT allows the window to be moved by the user and activates the Move option in the window's control menu. NOFLOAT is the default and prevents a window from being moved by the user.

GROW|NOGROW Specifying GROW allows the window to be resized by the user and activates the Size option in the window's control menu. NOGROW is the default and prevents a window from being resized by the user.

MDI|NOMDI Specifying MDI gives the window Multiple Document Interface capabilities. When a window is defined as MDI, maximizing the window causes the window to completely fill the main FoxPro window and places the window's title bar in the main FoxPro title bar. When a window is defined as NOMDI, the window can only be maximized to a position directly under the main FoxPro title bar. An example of an MDI window is a browse window. An example of a NOMDI window is the Command window. NOMDI is the default.

MINIMIZE Specifying MINIMIZE allows the window to be minimized by the user and activates the Minimize option in the window's control menu.

ZOOM|NOZOOM Specifying ZOOM allows the window to be maximized by the user and activates the Maximize option in the window's control menu. NOZOOM is the default and prevents a window from being maximized by the user.

ICON FILE *expC* When a window is minimized it is displayed as an icon on the FoxPro desktop. By default the icon is the same used by FoxPro. You can specify a custom icon to be displayed by including the name of the icon file in *expC*.

FILL FILE *bmp filename* Use this clause to display a graphic image in the background of the window. When specifying FILL FILE, the image contained in *bmp filename* is replicated to fill the background of the window. The number of replications is relative to the size of the image and the size of the window.

COLOR SCHEME *expN* Specifying a COLOR SCHEME displays the using of the User Window color pair of color scheme *expN*.

COLOR *color pair* Specifying a color pair displays the window in the colors of *color pair*.

If you use the Screen Builder to create your data entry screens, you may not have to use this command at all. The Screen Builder automatically generates the commands that define windows and control their attributes.

Examples

```
DEFINE WINDOW Wind1 FROM 3,2 TO 10,78 TITLE "Data Entry Window"
DEFINE WINDOW Wind1 FROM 3,2 TO 10,78 COLOR GR/B, B/GR, W
DEFINE WINDOW Wind1 FROM 3,2 TO 10,78 SYSTEM MDI
```

See also SET BORDER, ACTIVATE WINDOW

DELETE

```
DELETE [scope] [FOR expL] [WHILE expL] [NOOPTIMIZE]
```

Description This command marks a record for deletion from the current database file.

Operational rules To delete a record from the database file, mark all records to be deleted with the DELETE command or through the Edit or Browse screens. Then issue the PACK command. The PACK command actually removes the records. It makes a copy of the data file without the records marked for deletion, so it can take a while to run. The PACK command renumbers the records.

The DELETE command is equivalent to pressing Ctrl-T or choosing Toggle Delete while editing or browsing. Records marked for deletion display an asterisk when listed and a bullet when in Browse mode. The SET DELETED ON command tells FoxPro to ignore deleted records when displaying, editing, and listing. This allows deleted records to appear removed without having to PACK.

You can use the optional FOR *expL*, WHILE *expL*, and *scope* arguments to include only a subset of the records in the calculation. Use the NOOPTIMIZE clause to disable Rushmore when deleting records.

Example

```
DELETE
DELETE FOR UPPER(State) = "NY"
DELETE NEXT 5
```

See also PACK, RECALL

DELETE FILE

```
DELETE FILE [filename|?]
```

Description This command removes an entire file from the disk.

Operational rules The DELETE FILE command is equivalent to the ERASE command. You cannot erase a file that is currently open. The DELETE FILE command does not allow wild cards (? and *) to delete multiple files at one time, so you might prefer to use the DEL command from DOS. To run a DOS command while at the command window, use ! or RUN. The optional ? argument can be used to get a listing of files from which you can choose.

Example

```
DELETE FILE MAILLIST.DBF
ERASE MAILLIST.DBF
DELETE FILE ?
! DEL MAILLIST.*
Pfile = "PRODUCTS.DBF"
DELETE FILE (Pfile)
```

See also RUN|!, ERASE

DELETE TAG

```
DELETE TAG tag name [OF cdx file]|ALL [OF cdx file]
```

Description This command removes a tag from a compound index (.CDX) file.

Operational rules Compound indexes contain multiple index "tags" allowing for many indexes to be maintained through one file. The compound index file must be open when this command is issued.

If the optional OF *cdx file* is not used, FoxPro automatically looks for a file with the same name as the .DBF file but with a .CDX extension. If that file isn't found, it then searches other open .CDX files for the corresponding tag name.

Use the optional to ALL clause to delete all tags. If the currently selected database has a structural index file, all tags are removed, the .CDX file is deleted from the disk, and the database is no longer flagged as having such a file. Use ALL OF *cdx file* to remove all tags from a compound index other than the structural one.

Example

```
DELETE TAG Zip OF Mailzip   (deletes Zip from MAILLIST.CDX)
```

See also COPY TAG

DIMENSION

The DIMENSION command is equivalent to the DECLARE command.

See also DECLARE

DIR | DIRECTORY

```
DIR | DIRECTORY [ON drive] [[LIKE] [path] [skel]] [TO PRINTER
[PROMPT]|TO FILE filename]
```

Description This command displays a list of files on disk.

Operational rules The DIRECTORY command works very much like the DOS directory command. However, if no clause is included, it only shows database (.DBF) files. Otherwise, it allows use of the DOS wild cards (? and *). You can specify the drive to search by using the ON *drive* option and the type of files to display with the LIKE *path* option.

DIRECTORY output defaults to displaying on the screen. Use the TO PRINTER option to print to the printer, or the TO FILE *filename* to print to an ASCII file. When sending output to the printer, the optional PROMPT keyword can be used to access the Windows Printer Setup dialog before printing.

Example

```
DIR  && shows all .DBF files
DIR A:*.*  && shows all files from the A drive
DIR *.FRX  && shows all .FRX files
DIR TO PRINT  && prints the directory of .DBF files
```

See also RUN|!

DISPLAY

```
DISPLAY [[FIELDS] field list] [scope] [FOR expL] [WHILE expL]
[OFF] [TO PRINTER [PROMPT]|TO FILE filename] [NOCONSOLE]
[NOOPTIMIZE]
```

Description This command displays the contents of the current database.

Operational rules The DISPLAY command is equivalent to a LIST command. The only difference is that when DISPLAY is issued, only one screen is displayed at a time, and the user is requested to `Press a key to continue ....` The LIST command lists the entire contents without pausing between screens.

You can use the optional FOR *expL*, WHILE *expL*, and *scope* arguments to include only a subset of the records in the display. If the optional FIELDS *field list* is not used, all fields of the database will be displayed. If the combined width of the selected fields exceeds the width of the screen display, the information will wrap around the screen. By default the record number of each record being displayed is displayed at the far left. Use the OFF option to suppress displaying the record number.

Output from this command defaults to printing on the screen. Use the TO PRINTER option to print to the printer, or the TO FILE *filename* to print to an ASCII file. When sending output to the printer, the optional PROMPT keyword can be used to access the Windows Printer Setup dialog before printing. If the display is sent to the printer or to a file, use the NOCONSOLE option to suppress displaying the records on the screen. Use the NOOPTIMIZE clause to disable Rushmore when displaying records.

See also LIST

DISPLAY FILES

```
DISPLAY FILES [ON drive] [LIKE skel] [TO PRINTER [PROMPT]| TO
FILE filename]
```

Description This command displays information about specified files.

Operational rules The DISPLAY FILES command is equivalent to the LIST FILES command. The only difference is that when DISPLAY FILES is issued, only one screen is displayed at a time, and the user is requested to `Press a key to continue ....` The LIST FILES command lists the entire contents without pausing between screens. You can specify the drive to search by using the ON *drive* option and the type of files to display with the LIKE *skel* option.

Output from this command defaults to printing on the screen. Use the TO PRINTER option to print to the printer, or the TO FILE *filename* to print to an ASCII file. When sending output to the printer, the optional PROMPT keyword can be used to access the Windows Printer Setup dialog before printing.

See also LIST FILES

DISPLAY MEMORY

```
DISPLAY MEMORY [LIKE skel] [TO PRINTER [PROMPT]|TO FILE
filename] [NOCONSOLE]
```

Description This command displays the current contents of memory variables and arrays.

Operational rules The DISPLAY MEMORY command is identical to the LIST MEMORY command. The only difference is that when DISPLAY MEMORY is issued, only one screen is displayed at a time, and the user is requested to `Press a key to continue` .... The LIST MEMORY command lists the entire contents without pausing between screens. You can specify the variables to display with the LIKE *skel* option.

Output from this command defaults to printing on the screen. Use the TO PRINTER option to print to the printer, or the TO FILE *filename* to print to an ASCII file. When sending output to the printer, the optional PROMPT keyword can be used to access the Windows Printer Setup dialog before printing. If the display is sent to the printer or to a file, use the NOCONSOLE option to suppress displaying the information on the screen.

See also LIST MEMORY

DISPLAY STATUS

```
DISPLAY STATUS [TO PRINTER [PROMPT]|TO FILE filename] [NOCONSOLE]
```

Description This command displays the status of the FoxPro environment.

Operational rules The DISPLAY STATUS command is equivalent to the LIST STATUS command. The only difference is that when DISPLAY STATUS is issued, only one screen is displayed at a time, and the user is requested to `Press a key to continue` .... The LIST STATUS command lists the entire contents without pausing between screens.

Output from this command defaults to printing on the screen. Use the TO PRINTER option to print to the printer, or the TO FILE *filename* to print to an ASCII file. When sending output to the printer, the optional PROMPT keyword can be used to access the Windows Printer Setup dialog before printing. If the display is sent to the printer or to a file, use the NOCONSOLE option to suppress displaying the status on the screen.

See also LIST STATUS

DISPLAY STRUCTURE

```
DISPLAY STRUCTURE [IN expN|expC] [TO PRINTER [PROMPT]|TO FILE
filename] [NOCONSOLE]
```

Description This command displays the structure of a database file.

Operational rules The DISPLAY STRUCTURE command is equivalent to the LIST STRUCTURE command. The only difference is that when DISPLAY STRUCTURE is issued, only one screen is displayed at a time, and the user is requested to `Press a key to continue` .... The LIST STRUCTURE command lists the entire contents without pausing between screens. By default FoxPro will display the structure of the currently selected database file. Use IN *expN*|*expC* to display the structure of a database in another work area where *expN* is the work area number and *expC* is the database alias.

Output from this command defaults to printing on the screen. Use the TO PRINTER option to print to the printer, or the TO FILE *filename* to print to an ASCII file. When sending output to the printer, the optional PROMPT keyword can be used to access the Windows Printer Setup dialog before printing. If the display is sent to the printer or to a file, use the NOCONSOLE option to suppress displaying the structure on the screen.

See also LIST STRUCTURE

DO

```
DO program [WITH parameters] [IN filename]
```

Description This command executes a program or procedure.

Operational rules The DO command, when issued from the command window, calls the main module of the program. Use DO program within a command file to call other programs. Each program that is called extends one level lower. When you use DO to run a program, the program command file is executed until:

- The RETURN command is encountered.
- The program is CANCELed.
- Another DO program is issued.
- The end of the program file is reached.
- The QUIT command is executed.

Use the RETURN command to return to the calling program. The program then continues execution at the line below the last DO command.

A procedure or function that exists in another file can be executed with the IN *filename* option. This is useful when a number of procedures exist in one or more program files. If a procedure file has been specified with SET PROCEDURE TO, the IN *filename* is not required, as FoxPro will automatically search the procedure file for *filename*.

Lower level programs can access memory variables initialized in upper level programs. However, memory variables initialized in lower level programs are local to that program, and cannot be accessed from higher levels. To change a variable's value in a lower level program (or procedure) and pass that value back to the calling program, set the variable as a parameter. Include the WITH *parameters* clause in your DO statement.

Examples

```
DO Mainmenu
DO Heading WITH Title, Pageno
DO Count_money IN Procs.prg
```

See also PARAMETERS, SET PROCEDURE, and PROCEDURE

DO CASE

```
DO CASE
   CASE expression
      statements
   CASE expression
      statements
   CASE expression
      statements
   OTHERWISE
```

```
    statements
ENDCASE
```

Description This command is used within programs to provide conditional processing.

Operational rules If the *expression* is true (.T.), then the program processes all statements between the CASE and next CASE statement. The program only processes the first condition that is true. The DO CASE command must end with an ENDCASE statement. It is good programming technique to indent all commands within the CASE statements. For example:

```
DO CASE
   CASE Choice = "1"
      DO Addit
   CASE Choice = "2"
      DO Print
   CASE Choice = "3"
      QUIT
   OTHERWISE
      CANCEL
ENDCASE
```

The DO CASE command must be used in situations where each case is mutually exclusive. In other words, instances where only one of the CASE statements can be true. This CASE statement is an example.

The DO CASE is different from the IF in that you can have more than two possible expressions to process. You can use the OTHERWISE command as the last case to handle situations when none of the cases are true.

See also IF ... ENDIF

DO WHILE

```
DO WHILE condition
   statements
   [LOOP]
   [EXIT]
ENDDO
```

Description This command is used within programs to provide a looping capability with conditional processing.

Operational rules If the *condition* is true (.T.), then the program will continue processing all commands between the DO and ENDDO statement until condition is not true (.F.). It is good programming technique to indent all commands within the DO and ENDDO statements. For example:

```
DO WHILE Mem < 10
   ? Mem
   Mem = Mem + 1
ENDDO
```

The LOOP command can be used within a DO WHILE to return to the beginning of the loop. Use the EXIT command to exit the loop and continue processing the program at the command line below ENDDO.

Example The following command skips through the MAILLIST database, and displays one record at a time. If a record has N in the Active field, the record is not displayed. Although this is a valid program, a simpler program could be written that performs the same function with the SCAN FOR command:

```
USE MAILLIST
DO WHILE !EOF()
   IF Active = "N"
      SKIP
      LOOP
   ENDIF
   CLEAR
   ? Fname, Lname, Phone
   ACCEPT "Display another? " TO Cont
   IF Cont = "N"
      EXIT
   ENDIF
   SKIP
ENDDO
```

See also DO CASE and SCAN

EDIT

EDIT [FIELDS *field list*] [*scope*] [FOR *expL*] [WHILE *expL*] [FONT *expC* [,*expN*]] [STYLE *expC*] [FREEZE *field name*] [KEY *expr1* [, *expr2*]] [LAST] [LEDIT] REDIT] [LPARTITION] [NOAPPEND] [NODELETE] [NOEDIT|NOMODIFY] [NOLINK] [NOMENU] [NOOPTIMIZE] [NORMAL] [NOWAIT] [PARTITION *expN*] [PREFERENCE *name*] [REST] [SAVE] [TIMEOUT *expN*] [TITLE *expC*] [VALID [:F] *expL* [ERROR *expC*]] [WHEN *expL*] [WIDTH *expN*] [[WINDOW *window name*] [IN [WINDOW] *window name*|IN SCREEN]] [COLOR SCHEME *expN*|COLOR *color pair*]

Description This command displays an editing window to add/edit records to a database.

Operational rules The EDIT command displays an editing window with the fields displayed vertically (BROWSE displays fields horizontally). The EDIT command is very similar to the BROWSE command. You can move from record to record in the Edit window with the ↑ and ↓ keys or move forward or backward through a group of records with the PgUp or PgDn key. To move to the next or previous field, press Tab or Shift+Tab. The EDIT command is equivalent to selecting Change from the Browse menu pad.

The optional FIELDS *field list* arguments restrict the fields or field order displayed in the EDIT command. The SET FIELDS command can also set the fields list. Within the FIELDS clause several optional switches may be used. Precede the switch with slash (/) or colon (:). The switches are:

/expN Field is displayed with a width of *expN*.

/B=*expr1, expr2* Field falls between the range (boundaries) of *expr1* and *expr2*.

/H=*expr* Specifies the field heading *expr* over the field (the default is the name of the field).

/R Field is read only.

/V=*expr* If *expr* is not true (.T.), an error message is displayed and field not exited.

/V=*expr*:E=*expC* *expC* is displayed as the error message.

/V=*expr*:F Validation check is run whether or not the field is changed (forced valuation). The default is for validation only if the field is edited.

/W=*expL* Field can only be edited when *expL* is evaluated as true (.T.).

/P Specifies a PICTURE option for each field. See the @ ... SAY/GET command for a list of PICTURE and FUNCTION codes. Example:

```
EDIT FIELDS Names /P = '@!', Income /P = '99,999,999'
```

Use multiple verification switches by entering the /V only once. For example, /V = *expr1*:F:W*expr2*/ only allows verification if the field has been edited, and only allows editing when *expr2* is true (.T.). The FIELDS clause can also support calculated fields. A calculated field contains information that cannot be edited and is created with any valid FoxPro expression. For example, if the SALARY.DBF database contained the numeric fields Base and Taxrate, the command:

```
EDIT FIELDS SALARY.Base, SALARY.Taxrate, Taxes=Base * Taxrate
```

would display the value of Base multiplied by Taxrate.

The FORMAT clause allows you to use a format file within the Edit mode. The fields from the format file will be chosen for the BROWSE screen, and all PICTURE, RANGE, WHEN, and VALID clauses from the file are in effect.

The EDIT command has many optional arguments and clauses that make it a very powerful full-screen editing tool:

scope Chooses a subset of records to edit. Valid conditions are ALL, NEXT *expN*, RECORD *expN*, and REST.

FOR *expL* Displays only records that match the condition *expL*. If *expL* is not an optimizable clause, the EDIT command may run slowly.

WHILE *expL* Records are displayed in the editing window as long as the expression *expL* is true (.T.).

FONT *expC* [,*expN*] This clause defines the type and size of the font used.

STYLE *expC* This clause defines the style for the font specified with the FONT clause.

FREEZE *field* Only allows *field* to be edited although other fields can be viewed.

KEY *expr1* Specifies a key value (or range of values) *expr1*, *expr2* for records that are to be displayed in the Edit window. The database must have an index tag that matches the key expression.

LAST Displays the editing window with the same attributes and setting when the database was last edited with the EDIT or CHANGE commands.

LEDIT When the window is split, set the left partition into Browse mode. Much like choosing Browse from the Browse menu pop-up.

REDIT When the window is split, set the right partition into Browse mode.

LPARTITION When used in conjunction with the PARTITION option, it splits the Edit window and places the cursor in the left partition. (The default is for the cursor to be placed in the right partition).

NOAPPEND Prevents records from being added to the database.

NODELETE Prevents records from being deleted from the database.

NOEDIT|NOMODIFY Prevents records from being edited (may only be viewed).

NOLGRID|NORGRID When the window is split, turns off the vertical field separators in the left|right window (like choosing Grid Off from the BROWSE menu).

NOLINK When the window is split, as one partition is scrolled, the other does not scroll (the default is for partitions to scroll in tandem).

NOMENU Prevents access to the EDIT menu pop-up.

NOOPTIMIZE Disables Rushmore optimization (the default is for Rushmore to be enabled).

NORMAL Ignores user-defined window characteristics which would affect the display of the Edit screen and positions the editing window in the top left corner of the current output window.

NOWAIT When called from a program, the program continues executing after the EDIT command is executed. By default program execution will stop on the EDIT command until the Edit window is exited.

PARTITION *expN* Splits the Edit window at column *expN*. This is the same as using the window splitter with the mouse, or choosing Resize Partitions from the Browse menu.

PREFERENCE *name* Uses the Edit screen settings and attributes saved last time with the PREFERENCE clause. If PREFERENCE *name* does not exist, it will be created and saved in the current resource file.

REST Use REST to prevent the record pointer from being moved to the top of the file when the Edit window is opened.

SAVE Leaves the Edit window and any memo editing windows active. The SAVE option has no effect when used in the command window.

TIMEOUT *expN* Waits *expN* seconds for input. If that time has elapsed, it closes the Edit window. This option is available only within programs.

TITLE *expC* Changes the title of the editing window to *expC*.

VALID [:F] *expL* [ERROR *expC*] After editing a record, if expression *expL* is false, the cursor will not move off the record and an "Invalid input" message is displayed. You can display your own error message when VALID returns false by including the ERROR *expC* clause and the expression *expC* is displayed as the error message. By default the expression *expL* is only validated when data has changed. Use the :F argument to force validation anytime the record pointer changes.

WHEN *expL* When you move to a record and the expression *expL* is false, the record becomes read-only.

WIDTH *expN* Limits the maximum width of all fields to *expN*.

WINDOW *window name* The Edit window will take on the characteristics, such as color, size, and DEFINE WINDOW options of WINDOW *window name*.

IN WINDOW *window name*|SCREEN The Edit window will be displayed as a child window inside of *window name* and cannot be moved outside the parent window. The SCREEN clause places the Edit window on the FoxPro desktop screen.

COLOR *color pair* Defines the color of the Edit window.

COLOR SCHEME *expN* Chooses a predefined color scheme for the Edit window.

You can edit multiple databases by establishing a link using the SET RELATION command. Include the command SET SKIP to define a one-to-many relationship and see all records from the child database. For instance, suppose there is a data file of students related to a file of classes and there are 30 students per class. If the class file is the parent database, the student file is the child database. When fields from both files are displayed in Browse mode, and SET SKIP has been activated, it shows one record for the parent database and multiple records for the child.

If both files are displayed in the Edit mode, press Ctrl-↓ to move to the next parent record. Press Ctrl-↑ to move to the previous parent record. Also, fields from multiple databases can be viewed in one Edit window by prefacing the field name with the database Alias (Example EDIT FIELDS Class.Name, Student.Number)

Examples

```
EDIT
EDIT NEXT 10
EDIT NOAPPEND NODELETE
EDIT FIELDS Lname,Fname,City,Zip FONT "MS Sans Serif", 8
EDIT FIELDS Name /R,Sex /P="!"/V=Sex$"MF":E="Must be M or F"
```

See also APPEND, BROWSE, SET RELATION, and SET SKIP

EJECT

```
EJECT
```

Description This command advances the paper in a printer to the next page.

Operational rules The EJECT command will send a form feed (ASCII character 12) to the printer to advance the paper to the top of the next page. However, if the system memory variable *_padvance* has been set to LINEFEEDS, the correct number of linefeeds to advance the page will be sent instead.

EJECT will reset PROW() and PCOL() to zero. EJECT PAGE, unlike the EJECT command, affects the *_pageno* and *_plineno* system variables. Use EJECT PAGE when the ON PAGE handler is in effect.

See also EJECT PAGE

EJECT PAGE

```
EJECT PAGE
```

Description This command advances the paper in a printer to the next page, and takes in consideration printer system variables.

Operational rules The EJECT PAGE command will send a form feed unless the system variable *_padvance* has been set to LINEFEEDS, in which case the correct number of linefeeds will be sent to advance the paper to the top of the next page.

EJECT PAGE, unlike the EJECT command, affects the *_pageno* and *_plineno* system variables. Use EJECT PAGE when the ON PAGE handler is in effect.

See also ON PAGE, EJECT

ERASE

The ERASE command is equivalent to the DELETE FILE command.

See also DELETE FILE

EXIT

```
EXIT
```

Description This command is used to leave a loop.

Operational rules The EXIT command must be used within the DO...ENDDO, FOR...ENDFOR, and SCAN...ENDSCAN commands. EXIT causes the program to go to the bottom of the loop and proceed with the next command.

Example

```
USE MAILLIST
SCAN
   CLEAR
   ? Fname, Lname, Phone
   ACCEPT "Display another? " TO Cont
   IF UPPER(Cont) = "N"
      EXIT
   ENDIF
ENDSCAN
```

See also DO WHILE, SCAN, FOR ... ENDFOR

EXPORT

```
EXPORT TO filename [FIELDS field list] [scope] [FOR expL]
[WHILE expL] [NOOPTIMIZE] [TYPE]| DIF | MOD | SYLK | WK1 | WKS
| WR1 | WRK | XLS |
```

Description This command copies the records from the current database file to *filename*.

Operational rules Exporting data from a FoxPro database allows you to use the data with other software. If no extension is specified for *filename*, the default extension for the specified TYPE is used.

When exporting data, the optional file types are:

Type	Description
DIF	Visicalc's Data Interchange Format.
MOD	Microsoft Multiplan version 4.01.
SYL	Symbolic Link interchange format.
WKS	Lotus 1-2-3, version 1.x
WR1	Lotus Symphony, version 1.1 or 1.2.
WRK	Lotus Symphony, version 1.0.
XLS	Microsoft Excel, version 2.0.

You can use the optional FOR *expL*, WHILE *expL*, and *scope* arguments to include only a subset of the records in the export. The optional FIELDS *field list* argument copies only the specified fields to the new file. Use the NOOPTIMIZE option to disable Rushmore when exporting records.

Example

```
EXPORT TO Mail2 WK1 NEXT 100 && copies next 100 records
EXPORT TO Mail2 DIF Lname, Fname, City  && copies to a three-
field file
```

See also COPY TO

EXTERNAL

```
EXTERNAL ARRAY | LABEL | LIBRARY | MENU | PROCEDURE
| REPORT | SCREEN file list|array list
```

Description This command tells the FoxPro Project manager where undefined references in a project can be found.

Operational rules A project database (.PJX) contains information regarding a group of files that are all used in one application. Project files are used with the BUILD APP command for building an .APP file and for building .EXE files.

Sometimes the group of files include undefined references to other files. This is most common when name expressions and macro substitution are used in programs. Use the EXTERNAL command to alert the project manager to the location of these files. The command must include one of the following keywords and the corresponding *file list* or *array list*. The file name extension default is based on that of the keyword:

Keyword	File
ARRAY	Array definition
LABEL	Label definition file
LIBRARY	API Library file
MENU	Menu definition file

Keyword	File
PROCEDURE	Procedure file
REPORT	Report definition file
SCREEN	Screen definition file

Example

```
EXTERNAL REPORT Budget
mreport = "Budget"
REPORT FORM (mreport) TO PRINT
```

See also SET PROCEDURE

FILER

```
FILER [LIKE skel] [NOWAIT] [IN [WINDOW] window name|SCREEN]
```

Description This command provides access to the FoxPro file maintenance desk accessory.

Operational rules The LIKE *skel* option will display only those files matching the DOS skel. The file skeleton can contain any valid DOS name, including wild cards. If the Filer utility is being called from a program, the NOWAIT option will cause the program to continue after the FILER command is executed.

Use the WINDOW *window name* or IN WINDOW *window name* clause to place the Filer screen within a window. It will take on all characteristics of that window. The SCREEN option is the default and places the Filer window on the FoxPro desktop screen.

See also The FoxPro User Interface

FIND

```
FIND literal
```

Description This command moves to the first record in the current database that matches *literal*.

Operational rules FIND searches the current master index for *expression*. This command is very much like the SEEK command, except that SEEK searches for an expression instead of a literal. When the argument is a literal, you do not place quotes around it. Therefore, if it is a character memory variable, it should be preceded with an ampersand (&). There is no way to use FIND with a numeric memory variable.

If a match is found, the record pointer moves to that record. Use SKIP to find the next record that matches. If no records match, FOUND( ) will be set to false, and the record pointer will be moved to the end of the file (EOF( ) is true). However, if SET NEAR is ON, the pointer will go to the nearest record in the index.

Example

```
USE MAILLIST ORDER Mlname
Find Smith
Record 2
Mname = "Brown"
Find &Mname
Record 7
```

See also SEEK

FLUSH

```
FLUSH
```

Description This command sends all buffers to the disk.

Operational rules The FLUSH command sends all data in RAM to the disk so that if the program is exited incorrectly (the power goes off or the computer gets reset before exiting FoxPro) no data will be lost. The CLOSE FILES command also flushes the buffers, but the FLUSH command is more efficient if you wish to continue using the files.

See also CLOSE

FOR ... ENDFOR

```
FOR memvar = expN1 TO expN2
   [STEP expN3]
   statements
   [EXIT]
   [LOOP]
ENDFOR|NEXT
```

Description This command is used within programs to run a looping process a specified number of times.

Operational rules All statements between the FOR and ENDFOR commands are executed the number of times between *expN1* and *expN2*.

The *memvar* does not need to be defined before issuing the command. It evaluates to *expN1* the first time through the loop and is automatically incremented by one when it hits the ENDFOR and loops back to the FOR. The loop continues until *memvar* reaches *expN2*. The optional clause STEP *expN3* causes the counter to increment by *expN3* instead of by one. The incrementer can be either a positive or negative number.

It is good programming technique to indent all commands within the FOR and ENDFOR statements. For example:

```
FOR Mem = 1 TO 10
   ? Mem
ENDFOR
```

The LOOP command can be used within a FOR command to increment *memvar* and return to the beginning of the loop. Use the EXIT command to exit the loop and continue processing the program at the command line below ENDFOR.

Example The following command skips through ten records of the MAILLIST database, displaying each record on the screen. If a record has N in the Active field, the record is not displayed. Although this is a valid program, a simpler program could be written that performs the same function with the SCAN FOR command:

```
USE MAILLIST
FOR Mem = 1 TO 10
   IF Active = "N"
      SKIP
      LOOP
   ENDIF
```

```
   CLEAR
   ? RECNO(), Fname, Lname, Phone
   SKIP
ENDFOR
?
INPUT "Enter Number to Edit" GET Memrec
EDIT Memrec
```

See also DO WHILE, SCAN

FUNCTION

`FUNCTION` *`function name`*

Description This command identifies a user-defined function (UDF) program.

Operational rules If a certain function must be performed more than once in a program, it is easier to create a user-defined function with the FUNCTION command. User-defined functions are created just like procedures, except that they are called from within commands, instead of being called in a separate command.

Functions begin with the FUNCTION command, and end with RETURN. A user-defined function can have multiple arguments and can pass back a value to the calling program.

Example In the following program, the heading program calls a user-defined function that prints the heading centered on the page, depending on the width of the paper:

```
Mhead = "Income Analysis"
? CENTERIT(Mhead,75)
                      Income Analysis

FUNCTION centerit
PARAMETERS Heading, Width
PRIVATE Mcenter
Mcenter = SPACE(Width/2 - LEN(Heading)/2)) + Heading
RETURN Mcenter
```

See also PARAMETERS

GATHER

`GATHER FROM` *`array`*`|MEMVAR [FIELDS` *`field list`*`] [MEMO]`

Description This command replaces the fields in the current record of the active database with corresponding memory values.

Operational rules The value of each field of one record can be placed into memory with the SCATTER command. Use the GATHER command to update the database with the values in memory after they have changed. When gathering from an array, each array element represents a field. To gather from a memory variable, it must have been created with the SCATTER command. This is very useful in programs that edit a record in a data file.

Before the edit session, SCATTER the record to a memory variable. Then, if the user exits with a key defined as the "abort" key, use the GATHER command to set all fields back to their previous values. You can also edit memory variables created with the SCATTER command and then use GATHER to update the database. Use the FIELDS *field list* option to define the fields to be replaced. The optional MEMO clause must be used if the SCATTER command used the MEMO option.

Example

```
USE MAILLIST
SCATTER MEMVAR MEMO
@ 3,1 SAY "Database of Clients"
@ 3,60 SAY "Press ESC to Abort"
@ 5,1 SAY "Enter Last Name" GET m.Lname PICTURE "@!"
@ 5,50 SAY "First Name" GET m.Fname PICTURE "@!"
@ 7,1 SAY "Address:" GET m.Address
@ 8,1 SAY " City:" GET m.City
@ 8,15 SAY " State:" GET m.State PICTURE "@!"
@ 8,30 SAY "Zip:" GET m.Zip PICTURE "99999"
READ
IF LASTKEY() != 27
   GATHER MEMVAR MEMO
ENDIF
```

See also SCATTER

GETEXPR

```
GETEXPR [prompt] TO memvar [TYPE expC [; error]]
[DEFAULT expC]
```

Description This command calls up the FoxPro Expression Builder to help you create a memory variable.

Operational rules The GETEXPR command is especially useful for setting user-defined criterion within programs. The expression builder walks the user through the steps of setting up the criteria. GETEXPR can be used to create any type of memory variable, although it always returns it in string form to *memvar*. The *prompt* expression will be displayed on the Expression Builder and can be used to remind you of the type of expression to build.

To designate the type of variable, use the TYPE *expC* clause where type can be C, N, L, or D. This allows FoxPro to verify that the expression created is of type *expC*. Place an optional *error* message after the TYPE clause with the syntax TYPE *expC* ; *error* where *error* is the error message. Set a default variable with the DEFAULT *expC* clause. *expC* will be displayed as the initial expression.

Example

```
USE MAILLIST
GETEXPR "Enter selection criteria" TO Crit TYPE "L" DEFAULT
"State='CA'"
SET FILTER TO &Crit
LIST OFF Fname, Lname, City
```

See also STORE

GO|GOTO

```
GO|GOTO [RECORD] expN1 [IN expN2|IN expC]
GO|GOTO TOP|BOTTOM [IN expN2 | IN expC]
```

Description This command moves to the specified record.

Operational rules The GOTO command by default moves the record pointer in the current database. Alternate arguments are BOTTOM and TOP. GOTO TOP moves to the top of the database file, which is record number 1 in a nonindexed file, or the first record in an indexed file. GOTO BOTTOM moves to the bottom of the database file, which is the last record number in a nonindexed file, or the last record in an indexed file. To reach the end of the file (where EOF() is true), issue GOTO BOTTOM, and then SKIP. The record number will display as one more than RECCOUNT().

The optional argument IN *expN*|*expC* allows you to move the record pointer in a database other than the current work area. *expN* is the work area number and *expC* is the database alias.

Example

```
GOTO BOTTOM
GO 5
GO 5 IN MAILLIST
```

See also SEEK

HELP

```
HELP [topic] [IN [WINDOW] window name|IN [WINDOW] SCREEN]
[NOWAIT]
```

Description This command activates the FoxPro help screen.

Operational rules When in the help screen, you will get a screen full of help regarding a particular *topic*. You can then highlight additional keywords, and press Enter to get screens of information regarding other topics. The optional *topic* argument allows you to get a screen of information regarding a particular topic.

FoxPro for Windows offers two types of help systems: the Windows style help and the familiar FoxPro .DBF style help. The style of help displayed when issuing the HELP commands is determined by the setting of SET HELP TO. Only the *topic* parameter is supported when using Windows style help. All other HELP clauses and parameters are supported for .DBF style help.

Use the WINDOW *window name* or IN WINDOW *window name* clause to place the Help screen within a window. It will take on all characteristics of that window. The SCREEN option is the default and places the Help screen on the FoxPro desktop screen.

If help is invoked in a program, use the NOWAIT option to continue program execution after the Help window is displayed. FoxPro uses the FOXHELP.HLP file for Windows style help and FOXHELP.DBF for .DBF style help as the default help file. You can change the help file with the SET HELP TO command and can also control which topics are available with the SET TOPIC command.

Example

```
HELP
HELP "USE"
```

See also SET HELP, SET TOPIC

HIDE MENU

`HIDE MENU` *`menu name`*`[, `*`menu name`*` ...]|ALL [SAVE]`

Description This command hides a user-defined menu from the screen.

Operational rules Menus are designed with the DEFINE MENU command. Use ACTIVATE MENU to then display them on screen. HIDE MENU *menu name* removes the menu from the screen and menu *menu name* can be redisplayed using the SHOW MENU command. Hiding a menu is not the same as deactivating it. Use the ALL clause in place of *menu name* to hide all active menus. The SAVE option leaves an image of the menu on screen or in a window.

See also ACTIVATE MENU

HIDE POPUP

`HIDE POPUP` *`popup name`*`[, `*`popup name`*` ...]|ALL [SAVE]`

Description This command hides a user-defined pop-up from the screen.

Operational rules Pop-ups are designed with the DEFINE POPUP command. Use ACTIVATE POPUP to then display them on screen. HIDE POPUP *popup name* removes the pop-up from the screen and pop-up *popup name* can be redisplayed using the SHOW POPUP command. Hiding a pop-up is not the same as deactivating it. Use the ALL clause in place of *popup name* to hide all active pop-ups. The SAVE option leaves an image of the pop-up on screen or in a window.

See also ACTIVATE POPUP

HIDE WINDOW

`HIDE WINDOW [`*`window name`*`[, `*`window name2`*`] ...]|ALL [IN [WINDOW]` *`window name`*`|IN [WINDOW] SCREEN]`

Description This command hides a user-defined window from the screen.

Operational rules Windows are designed with the DEFINE WINDOW command. ACTIVATE WINDOW to then display them on screen. HIDE WINDOW *window name* removes the window from the screen and window *window name* can be redisplayed using the SHOW WINDOW command. This command is the same as choosing Hide from the Window menu. Hiding a window is not the same as deactivating it. Use the ALL clause in place of *window name* to hide all active windows.

Windows can be hidden within other windows by specifying IN WINDOW *window name*. The FoxPro desktop screen can be hidden by issuing the command HIDE WINDOW SCREEN.

See also ACTIVATE WINDOW

#IF ... #ENDIF

```
#IF expN1|#IF expL1
    statements1
[#ELIF expN2|#ELIF expL2
    statements2
#ELIF expNn|#ELIF expLn
    statements3]
[#ELSE
    statements4]
#ENDIF
```

Description These commands are used to determine what program code to include when creating an object file.

Operational rules The #IF and #ENDIF commands are used to conditionally specify the source code that is included in a compiled program. When a program containing #IF ... #ENDIF is compiled, FoxPro logically determines what code to include in the object code based on the value of the logical or numeric expressions. The logic of these commands is similar to the standard IF | ELSE | ENDIF and DO CASE commands combined. In simple FoxPro terms these commands state:

```
IF this expression is true
   use this code and exit
   DO CASE
      CASE this expression is true
        use this code and exit
      CASE this expression is true
        use this code and exit
ENDCASE
ELSE && When all other possibilities fail
   use this code
ENDIF
```

If *expN1* is greater than 0 or *expL1* is true (.T.), FoxPro includes all program code after the initial #IF statement, exits the #IF ... #ENDIF structure, and continues program compilation beginning with the first line after the #ENDIF statement. If the evaluation is 0 or false (.F.), all successive #ELIF arguments are evaluated until *expNn* or *expLn* is nonzero or true. When an #ELIF argument returns true, all statements after that #ELIF are included and the #IF structure is exited.

If the initial #IF values and all #ELIF values are false, FoxPro will default to including the code after the #ELSE argument, if it is included. If you use memory variable or arrays for *expN* and *expL* values, be sure that the variable or array is #DEFINEed, since variables are not evaluated when source code is compiled.

Example In the following example, the #IF ... #ENDIF structure determines which version of FoxPro compiles the program and then displays the appropriate message.

```
#IF "WINDOWS" $ UPPER(VERSION())
   ? "Welcome to FoxPro for Windows"
#ELIF "MAC" $ UPPER(VERSION())
   ? "Welcome to FoxPro for Macintosh"
#ELIF "UNIX"' $ UPPER(VERSION())
   ? "Welcome to FoxPro for Unix"
#ELSE
   ? "Welcome to FoxPro for DOS"
#ENDIF
```

See also #DEFINE

IF ... ENDIF

```
IF expL
   statements
[ELSE
   statements]
ENDIF
```

Description These commands are used within programs to provide conditional processing.

Operational rules If the expression *expL* is true (.T.), then the program will process all commands between the IF and ENDIF statement. If *expL* is false (.F.), then the program continues processing after the ENDIF statement. It is good programming technique to indent all commands within the IF and ENDIF statements. For example:

```
IF Mprn = "P"
   SET PRINT ON
   EJECT
ENDIF
```

The optional ELSE is useful in situations where one procedure should be performed if one condition is true, with a different procedure if the condition is false. If *expL* evaluates to false (.F.) the statements after the ELSE are executed. Although IF statements can be nested (just remember each IF must have a companion ENDIF), it is often better to use the DO CASE command if many conditions are to be tested.

Example

```
ACCEPT "Display to Screen, Printer, or File? (S/P/F)" TO Mprn
IF Mprn = "P"
   SET PRINT ON
   EJECT
ELSE
   IF Mprn = "F"
      SET ALTERNATE TO Prnfile
      SET ALTERNATE ON
   ELSE
```

```
      SET CONSOLE ON
   ENDIF
ENDIF
```

See also DO CASE

IMPORT

`IMPORT FROM` *`filename`* `[TYPE] FW2 | MOD | PDOX | RPD | WK1 | WK3 | WKS | WR1 | WRK | XLS`

Description This command creates a new database file from another type of file.

Operational rules When importing from a file, the optional file types are:

Type	**Description**
FW2	Ashton Tate's Framework II.
MOD	Microsoft Multiplan version 4.01.
PDOX	Borland's Paradox version 3.5.
RPD	Ashton Tate's RapidFile version 1.2.
WK1	Lotus 1-2-3, version 2.x.
WK3	Lotus 1-2-3, version 3.x.
WKS	Lotus 1-2-3, version 1.x.
WR1	Lotus Symphony, version 1.1 or 1.2.
WRK	Lotus Symphony, version 1.0.
XLS	Microsoft Excel, version 2.0.

A new database is created with the same name as the file the data is imported from. A .DBF extension is assigned to the new FoxPro database. The TYPE clause is optional, however you must specify a file type.

See also APPEND FROM

INDEX

`INDEX ON` *`expression`* `TO` *`idx file`*`|TAG` *`tag name`* `[OF` *`cdx file`*`] [FOR` *`expL`*`] [COMPACT] [ASCENDING|DESCENDING] [UNIQUE] [ADDITIVE]`

Description This command creates indexes to display records.

Operational rules The INDEX ON command creates an index file that controls the display order of the records. Unlike the SORT command, INDEX ON does not physically change the order of the records database.

You can index a file on one field, multiple fields, an expression, or by fields within functions. If you are combining character fields and numeric fields, you must convert the numeric field to a string with the STR( ) function. The following are examples of each:

INDEX ON UPPER(Lname) TAG Mname (sorts ignoring case)

INDEX ON Lname+Fname TAG Mname (sorts by Fname within Lname)

INDEX ON STR(Dept,2)+Lname TAG Mname (sorts by first 2 characters of Dept and Lname)

INDEX ON Lname TO MNAME.IDX (sorts by Lname field)

FoxPro works best using the structural compact index (.CDX) type. This allows you to create multiple index "tags" that are stored in one file. Using the TO *idx file* option creates an .IDX index that can only store one index tag. The COMPACT keyword is only for single .IDX index files and creates compact indexes. The down side of this is that each open .IDX file requires its own DOS file handle. Also single index .IDX files are not opened when a database is opened, as are multiple index .CDX files. Using the TAG *tag name* option simply adds the new index expression and *tag name* to the current .CDX file.

Multiple index files are automatically opened with the database and are updated whenever a value changes. Single index files must be opened by a user or a program and updated manually. To keep a single index correctly updated, it must be open at all times that data is appended or edited. You can open the index when you open the data file with the USE file INDEX file command, or with the SET INDEX TO command. If you do change data when the index is not open, you will need to open it and REINDEX the file.

If no .CDX file exists when INDEX ON and TAG *tag name* are used, FoxPro will automatically create a structural compact index file that is the same name of the database file. To add TAG *tag name* into a .CDX file other than the database's, use the OF *cdx file* option.

By default all indexes are created in ascending order. You can use the DESCENDING option to create indexes that are descending. If an index is created in ascending order, it is not necessary to reindex or recreate the index. You can use SET ORDER TO ... ASCENDING | DESCENDING to change the order.

The FOR criteria filters out records that do match the criteria. Keep in mind that with that index open, you cannot access records if they are not in the filter. This is a very good clause to use if you are making a temporary index for any situation that filters out records because it makes access much faster.

The UNIQUE argument causes it to include only the first records that contain a particular key. For instance, if the file is indexed on City, the index only takes the first entry for each city. This is helpful when getting lists of all unique entries for a certain field.

When you create an index file or files for database with INDEX, any previously opened .IDX index files are closed. If the ADDITIVE key word is included, previously opened .IDX index files remain open.

Examples

```
INDEX ON Amount TO MAMT.IDX
INDEX ON Amount TAG Mamt FOR City = "San Diego"
INDEX ON Date TAG Mdate UNIQUE          && only puts in the first
                                        record of each date
INDEX ON {12/31/2199}-Date TAG Mdate   && dates in descending
                                        order
```

To index a numeric field in descending order, use the key of 1**numeric field*. To sort a date field in descending order, use the key of {12/13/2199} - *expD*. Both of these expressions evaluate to numbers.

See also USE, SET INDEX TO, SET ORDER TO

INPUT

```
INPUT [prompt] TO memvar
```

Description This command displays the prompt and pauses until the user enters something.

Operational rules The INPUT command is most often used in programs where few questions are to be prompted on the screen. Each INPUT command halts the program until the user types in an answer and presses Enter. The INPUT command is easier to use than full-screen editing commands such as @ ... GET, because:

- The memory variable does not have to be initialized before issuing the command.
- Screen coordinates do not have to be set. (INPUT displays the prompt in the same manner as the ? command).

However, the INPUT command is not as powerful as the full-screen editing commands, especially because the entry cannot be formatted or validated. Memory variables created by the INPUT command are numeric if a number is entered; otherwise they are of the character type. The variable becomes the length of the entry typed in.

The ACCEPT command is just like INPUT, except the memory variable will always be a character.

Examples The following program prompts the user to enter their name and age. The memory variable Mname becomes the length of the entry. It is a character variable because the user typed in a string. The memory variable Mage becomes numeric as long as the user types in a number.

```
INPUT "Enter Your Name: " TO Mname
? "Hi there ", Mname
INPUT "Enter Your Age: " TO Mage
? "Are you really ", Mage, "?"
```

See also ACCEPT

INSERT

```
INSERT [BEFORE] [BLANK]
```

Description This command allows the user to add new records to the database at the position of the current record.

Operational rules The INSERT command brings up the full-screen edit mode, just like the APPEND command. The record is added one below the current record. For instance, if the pointer is at record 10, the new record is inserted as record 11, and the numbers of all records following are increased by one. If the file is indexed, INSERT works like APPEND in that the new record is added to the end of the database.

When a record is inserted near the top or into the middle of a database, nearly the entire database must be rebuilt by rewriting every record. This can be an extremely lengthy process on large files. Try using alternate methods such as APPEND BLANK and INSERT INTO.

Use the BEFORE clause to insert records at the current record number instead of one record after. Use BLANK to insert a record without going into the full-screen edit mode. When inserting a blank record, all fields of the record will be blank. If the BLANK option is not used and SET CARRY is on, the new record will contain the same data as the previous record.

See also EDIT, APPEND BLANK, INSERT INTO (SQL)

INSERT INTO (SQL)

```
INSERT INTO dbf name [(field name1 [, field name2 [, ...]])]
VALUES (expr1 [, expr2 [, ...]])
```

or

```
INSERT INTO dbf name FROM ARRAY array|FROM MEMVAR
```

Description This command adds a new record to a database.

Operational rules This INSERT INTO command appends a record to the end of a database. Unlike the INSERT command which will only insert a record into the current database, INSERT INTO can append a record to a database in another work area or one that is not even open. The new record includes data listed in the INSERT command or included in the specified *array*.

INSERT INTO *dbf name* specifies the name of the database file to which a record will be appended. *dbf name* can include a path and can be a name expression. If *dbf name* isn't already open, it is opened exclusively in a new work area and the record is appended however, the new work areas is not selected. If *dbf name* is open, INSERT appends the record to the database. If the database is open in a work area other than the current work area, it isn't selected after the record is appended.

You can use *field name1, field name2...* to specify certain fields to update and the fields can be listed in any order. If no fields are listed, then VALUES *expr1*, *expr2...* must be specified for ALL fields. You must specify values in the field order of the database.

Use the FROM ARRAY *array* option to insert a record using values in an array. The structure of the array must match the structure of the database being updated and each element of the array must contain a value that is the same type as its corresponding field.

If you SCATTER database information into memory, you can create a new record using the FROM MEMVAR option. This copies data from memory variables into the new record in the specified database. Data is copied only into fields that have corresponding memory variables.

See also SELECT (SQL)

JOIN

```
JOIN WITH expN|WITH expC TO filename FOR expL [FIELDS field
list] [NOOPTIMIZE]
```

Description This command makes a new database file out of two database files.

Operational rules The new database file specified with TO *filename* will be made up of all of the fields in the active database, plus all of the fields in the joined database specified in WITH *expN|expC*. *expN* is the number of the work area that the second database is open and *expC* is the alias name of the second database. For every time a record in the active database matches a record in the second database, you have one record in the new database. The JOIN command can take a very long time to run if both databases are large files.

To limit the records added to the new database use the FOR clause. JOIN evaluates the FOR *expL* for each record. If *expL* is true (.T.), a new record is created in the new file. Use of the FOR clause makes the JOIN command Rushmore optimizable if an optimized expression is used in *expL*.

The field order of the new database is all of the fields from the first database plus all of the fields from the second database, up to the 255-field limit. To change the field order, or restrict the fields in the new database, use the optional argument FIELDS *field list*. Use the optional NOOPTIMIZE clause to disable Rushmore when joining databases.

Example In this example, a new file named Salename is made up of each sales record, which includes the sales information from Sales and the name of the client from MAIL-LIST.

```
USE MAILLIST IN 1
USE SALES IN 2
JOIN WITH Sales TO Salename FOR A.Clicode = B.Clicode FIELDS;
   A.Clicode, A.Name, B.Date, B.Amount
```

See also SELECT (SQL)

KEYBOARD

KEYBOARD *expC* [PLAIN]

Description This command allows you to put characters into the keyboard buffer, which are then played out at the next input command.

Operational rules The KEYBOARD command is very useful in creating demonstration programs because you can make the keyboard type things automatically. The characters to be played, *expC*, stay in the buffer until a command that looks for input is issued. The KEYBOARD command is also very useful in program when you need to push the user in the right direction.

The characters in *expC* can be literal or expressions. If any ON KEY LABEL assignments are active, a keyboarded character will set off the ON KEY LABEL routine. Using the PLAIN keyword allows you to stuff characters defined with ON KEY LABEL into the buffer without executing ON KEY LABEL routines.

Example In the example given here, if the user answers Y to the first question, the program types in the name and address onto the screen.

```
ACCEPT "Do you want the program to enter the data? " TO Demo
IF UPPER(Demo) = "Y"
   KEYBOARD "George Jetson"+CHR(13)+"Los Gatos"+CHR(13)+"CA
92111"
ENDIF
@ 5,1 SAY "Enter Name" GET Name
@ 6,1 SAY " City:" GET City
@ 6,30 SAY " State:" GET State PICT "!!"
@ 6,40 SAY "Zip:" GET Zip
READ CYCLE
```

See also ON KEY LABEL

LABEL

```
LABEL [FORM label file|?] [ENVIRONMENT] [scope] [FOR expL]
[WHILE expL] [NOCONSOLE] [NOOPTIMIZE] [PDSETUP] [PREVIEW]
[SAMPLE] [TO PRINTER [PROMPT]|TO FILE filename]
```

Description This command prints labels for a data file. The label format must already be created with the CREATE LABEL command.

Operational rules The CREATE LABEL command allows you to set the label dimensions, number of labels across, and contents of the label within a label definition (.LBX) file. The argument ? can be used in place of the *label file* name. FoxPro displays a list of .LBX files to choose from.

To run the labels, make sure the data file is your active file, and issue the LABEL command. If no data files are open and you saved the work environment with the label, you can use the ENVIRONMENT option so FoxPro will open the necessary files.

You can use the optional FOR *expL*, WHILE *expL*, and *scope* arguments to include only a subset of the records to print. Labels default to printing on the screen. Use the TO PRINTER option to print to the printer, or the TO FILE *filename* to print to an ASCII file. When sending output to the printer, the optional PROMPT keyword can be used to access the Windows Printer Setup dialog before printing. If the report is sent to the printer or to a file, use the NOCONSOLE option to suppress printing of the report on the screen.

The PDSETUP clause only affects labels that were created in FoxPro for DOS and have not been converted to FoxPro for Windows. If the DOS label being printed contains a printer driver setup, you must use the PDSETUP option to load the required setup. The SAMPLE option prints a sample label, allowing you to set up the printer just right. After it prints the sample, it asks `Do you want more samples?`. It continues this process until you enter N.

The PREVIEW option displays a group of labels (one screenful) on the screen letting you verify that the label definition is set up correctly. After exiting the preview screen, the LABEL command must be issued again (without PREVIEW) to actually begin printing the labels. Use the NOOPTIMIZE option to disable Rushmore when printing labels.

Example

```
LABEL FORM Mlabel ENVIRONMENT
LABEL FORM Mlabel TO PRINT
LABEL FORM Mlabel PREVIEW FOR State = "CA"
LABEL FORM Mlabel NEXT 100 TO FILE Labels (creates Labels.Txt)
```

See also CREATE LABEL

LIST

```
LIST [FIELDS fields list] [scope] [FOR expL1] [WHILE expL1]
[OFF] [NOCONSOLE] [NOOPTIMIZE] [TO PRINTER [PROMPT]|TO FILE
filename]
```

Description This command list the contents of the current database.

Operational rules The LIST command is equivalent to a DISPLAY command. The only difference is that when DISPLAY is issued, only one screen is displayed at a time, and the user is requested to `Press a key to continue ....` The LIST command lists the entire contents without pausing between screens.

You can use the optional FOR *expL*, WHILE *expL*, and scope arguments to include only a subset of the records in the output. If the optional FIELDS *field list* is not used, all fields of the database will be displayed. If the combined width of the selected fields exceeds the width of the screen display the information will wrap around the screen. By default the record number of each record being displayed is displayed at the far left. Use the OFF option to suppress displaying the record number.

Lists default to printing on the screen. Use the TO PRINTER option to print to the printer, or the TO FILE *filename* to print to an ASCII file. When sending output to the printer, the optional PROMPT keyword can be used to access the Windows Printer Setup dialog before printing. If the list is sent to the printer or to a file, use the NOCONSOLE option to suppress displaying the records on the screen. Use the NOOPTIMIZE clause to disable Rushmore when listing records.

See also DISPLAY

LIST FILES

```
LIST FILES [ON drive] [LIKE skel] [TO PRINTER [PROMPT]|TO FILE
filename]
```

Description This command lists all files from a directory that match a parameter.

Operational rules The default list is a list of .DBF files, along with their size, number of records, and last update date. Use LIKE *skel* to get a list of files other than the *.DBF default. Skeletons follow the wild card conventions of DOS:

- An asterisk (*) represents any combination of characters.
- A question mark (?) represents any one character.

You can LIST files on a drive other than the current drive by using the ON *drive* option. The files list default to printing on the screen. Use the TO PRINTER option to print to the printer, or the TO FILE *filename* to print to an ASCII file. When sending output to the printer, the optional PROMPT keyword can be used to access the Windows Printer Setup dialog before printing.

Examples

```
LIST FILES
LIST FILES LIKE *.prg
LIST FILES LIKE *.* ON B: TO PRINTER
```

See also DISPLAY FILES

LIST MEMORY

```
LIST MEMORY [LIKE skel] [TO PRINTER [PROMPT]|TO FILE filename]
[NOCONSOLE]
```

Description This command lists the current contents of memory variables and arrays.

Operational rules The LIST MEMORY command is identical to the DISPLAY MEMORY command. The only difference is that when LIST MEMORY is issued, the entire contents are displayed without pausing between screens. You can specify the variables to display with the LIKE *skel* option.

The memory variable list defaults to printing on the screen. Use the TO PRINTER option to print to the printer, or the TO FILE *filename* to print to an ASCII file. When sending output to the printer, the optional PROMPT keyword can be used to access the Windows Printer Setup dialog before printing. If the report is sent to the printer or to a file, use the NOCONSOLE option to suppress printing of the list on the screen.

See also DISPLAY MEMORY

LIST STATUS

```
LIST STATUS [TO PRINTER [PROMPT]|TO FILE filename] [NOCONSOLE]
```

Description This command lists the status of the FoxPro environment.

Operational rules The LIST STATUS command is identical to the DISPLAY STATUS command. The only difference is that when DISPLAY STATUS is issued, only one screen is displayed at a time, and the user is requested to `Press a key to continue ...`. The LIST STATUS commands lists the entire contents without pausing between screens.

The status list defaults to printing on the screen. Use the TO PRINTER option to print to the printer, or the TO FILE *filename* to print to an ASCII file. When sending output to the printer, the optional PROMPT keyword can be used to access the Windows Printer Setup dialog before printing. If the report is sent to the printer or to a file, use the NOCONSOLE option to suppress printing of the status on the screen.

See also DISPLAY STATUS

LIST STRUCTURE

```
LIST STRUCTURE [IN expN|expC] [TO PRINTER [PROMPT]|TO FILE
filename] [NOCONSOLE]
```

Description This command lists the structure of a database file.

Operational rules The LIST STRUCTURE command is equivalent to the DISPLAY STRUCTURE command. The only difference is that when DISPLAY STRUCTURE is issued, only one screen is displayed at a time, and the user is requested to `Press a key to continue ...`. The LIST STRUCTURE commands lists the entire contents without pausing between screens. By default FoxPro will display the structure of the currently selected database file. Use IN *expN*|*expC* to display the structure of a different work area.

The structure list defaults to printing on the screen. Use the TO PRINTER option to print to the printer, or the TO FILE *filename* to print to an ASCII file. When sending output to the printer, the optional PROMPT keyword can be used to access the Windows

Printer Setup dialog before printing. If the list is sent to the printer or to a file, use the NOCONSOLE option to suppress printing of the status on the screen.

See also DISPLAY STRUCTURE

LOAD

```
LOAD filename [SAVE] [NOSAVE]
```

Description This command loads a binary program into memory.

Operational rules FoxPro can run binary (assembly language and machine language) programs. To do this you must:

1. Load the program into memory with the LOAD command.
2. Run the program with the CALL command.
3. Release it from memory with the RELEASE MODULE command.

Binary programs are useful in instances where a function must be performed that FoxPro cannot do. For instance, certain screen graphics manipulation and file maintenance on non-FoxPro files can be done only through binary programs.

If the binary library writes directly to video RAM, use the SAVE option so FoxPro will not overwrite anything written to the screen with the library. Unless it is necessary, don't include SAVE, because it takes FoxPro some time to scan and save the screen contents upon each return from the binary routine.

FoxPro's API functions are more advanced than LOAD and CALL functions and should be used in place of LOAD and CALL libraries when possible.

See also CALL, SET LIBRARY

LOCATE

```
LOCATE FOR expression [scope] [WHILE expL] [NOOPTIMIZE]
```

Description This command searches for a record based on conditions.

Operational rules LOCATE searches the file sequentially, starting from the top. This command is very much like the SEEK command, except that SEEK searches using an index, so it is much faster, especially with large files.

Rushmore optimizes a query created with LOCATE FOR if the FOR expression is an optimizable expression. For best performance, use an optimizable expression in the FOR clause. The *scope* argument allows you to limit the number of records that match the FOR condition. Use WHILE *expL* if you need to loop through a subset of records without using CONTINUE.

If a match is found, the record pointer moves to that record. If TALK is SET ON, the resulting record number will be displayed on screen. Use CONTINUE to find the next record that matches the condition. If no records match, FOUND( ) is set to false (.F.), and the record pointer is moved to the end of the file (EOF( ) is true).

Example

```
USE MAILLIST
LOCATE FOR UPPER(Lname) = "Smith"
```

```
Record = 5
LOCATE FOR Lname = "Smith" .AND. State = "CA"
Record = 7
CONTINUE
End of LOCATE scope
? EOF()
.T.
```

See also SEEK

MENU

```
MENU BAR array1, expN1
MENU expN2, array2, expN3 [, expN4]
READ MENU BAR TO memvar1, memvar2 [SAVE]
```

Description These commands create and activate a user-defined menu.

Operational rules The three FoxPro menu-creation commands are: MENU BAR, which defines a user-defined menu, MENU, which defines pop-up menus within the menu options, and READ MENU, which activates the menu.

The main menu, defined by MENU BAR is a horizontal menu. Each option in a Fox-Pro-type menu is called a bar. It is possible to design a vertical pop-up menu that is displayed whenever one of the bars in the main menu is highlighted with the cursor. Once the pop-up menu is displayed, the user can move the cursor to any of the options in the bar pop-up, creating a "menu within a menu."

To define a menu where each option has a pop-up menu that contains additional options, the following commands must be issued:

1. Set array variables as each menu option.
2. Set a different array for each pop-up menu option.
3. MENU BAR installs the bounce bar using the array values.
4. MENU installs the pop-up using the pop-up array values.
5. READ MENU activates the entire menu system.

The MENU BAR *array1* is a two-dimensional character string array. Each menu option is defined with the second dimension of 1. Define a message for each option with the second dimension of 2. The number of menu options is defined with *expN1*.

Each menu defined by the MENU command is a vertical pop up. The pop-ups are used in conjunction with a horizontal bar menu (defined with MENU BAR) where a certain pop-up menu is displayed whenever the corresponding bar of the main menu is highlighted.

The first parameter of MENU, *expN2*, is the position on the bar menu where the pop-up will be displayed. The MENU *array2* array is a one-dimensional character string array. Each menu option is defined as a number of the array. The number of options within the pop-up is defined with *expN3*.

A fourth optional parameter, *expN4* defines the number of options to display on the screen at one time. In cases where there are many options, you might not want them all to show in the menu. FoxPro allows the user to scroll to options not displayed.

If you use the Menu Builder to create your menu, you may not have to use these commands at all. The Menu Builder automatically generates the commands that create menus and pop-ups.

Example The following program creates the menu and pop-up options in the DEFINE BAR example, shown earlier. This program only sets up the pop-up for the leftmost option, Add.

```
DIMENSION OPTIONTOP(4,2)

OPTIONTOP(1,1) = "Add "
OPTIONTOP(2,1) = "List"
OPTIONTOP(3,1) = "Exit"
OPTIONTOP(1,2) = "Append Records into Database "
OPTIONTOP(2,2) = "List Records "
OPTIONTOP(3,2) = "Exit to DOS"

DIMENSION POPS(4)

POPS(1) = "Members"
POPS(2) = "Guests"
POPS(3) = "Prospect"

ROW = 1
COL = 1

MENU BAR OPTIONTOP, 3
MENU 1,POPS, 3
READ MENU BAR TO ROW,COL
```

See also Using the Menu Builder

MENU TO

MENU TO *memvar*

Description This command activates a light bar menu created with the @ ... PROMPT command.

Operational rules The MENU TO command displays a light bar menu that the user can choose options from. Define the options and positions of the menu using the @ ... PROMPT command. If the *memvar* is one of the menu options, the cursor begins by highlighting that option. If it is not a valid option, the cursor defaults to the first option. The menu option selected is returned to *memvar*.

Examples

```
@ 3,1 PROMPT "Alpha" MESSAGE "Sort in Alphabetical Order"
@ 3,10 PROMPT "Zip" MESSAGE "Sort by Zip Code"
@ 3,20 PROMPT "Order" MESSAGE "Sort in User-Defined Order"
SET MESSAGE TO 22
MENU TO Choice
```

```
DO CASE
   CASE Choice = 1
      SET ORDER TO MAILALPH
   CASE Choice = 2
      SET ORDER TO MAILZIP
   CASE Choice = 3
      ACCEPT "Enter Expression to Sort By " TO Other
      INDEX ON EVALUATE(Other) TAG Temp
      GO TOP
ENDCASE
```

See also @ ... PROMPT

MODIFY COMMAND|FILE

MODIFY COMMAND|FILE [*filename*|?] [AS *expN*] [NOEDIT] [NOWAIT] [NOMENU] [RANGE *expN1*, *expN2*] [[WINDOW *window name1*] [IN [WINDOW] *window name2*|IN SCREEN]] [SAME] [SAVE]

Description This command invokes the FoxPro text editor.

Operational rules Program (.PRG) files are edited using MODIFY COMMAND and text (.TXT) files with MODIFY FILE. If *filename* is not specified FoxPro will display the Open File dialog so you can choose a file to modify. The NOEDIT clause opens *filename* as read-only, so it cannot be modified. If the editor is invoked in a program, using the NOWAIT clause will continue program execution after the editing screen is opened. The NOMENU clause can be used to prevent the Text menu pad from appearing in the main menu.

The RANGE option lets you open a text editing window with a range of characters selected. Characters are selected starting at the position specified with *expN1* up to (but not including) the *expN2* character. If *expN1* is equal to *expN2*, no characters are selected, and the cursor is placed at the position specified with *expN1*.

The AS clause is used to open the file in a different code page so that any accented characters in the file will be translated. Specify a valid code page with *expN*. See chapter 11 for more information on code pages and character translation.

Use the WINDOW *window name* clause to place the editing screen within a window. It will take on all characteristics of the window. Use IN WINDOW *window name* to open the editing screen in a parent window. The editing screen window must be smaller than the parent, and stay within the parent window's boundaries. The IN SCREEN option is the default. This causes the editing screen to be placed on the FoxPro desktop screen instead of within a window.

The SAME clause causes a previously activated editing window that is minimized or hidden to be restored in the background, without activating the window. The SAVE option leaves an image of the editing window on screen after the editing window has been closed. SAVE can only be used in a program and has no effect when issued from the Command window.

The FoxPro editor is invoked unless an alternative one has been set in the CONFIG.FP file. Use the command TEDIT = *program* to call an alternate editor. For example, TEDIT = WS would call up WordStar (WS.EXE) as the editor.

See also DO

MODIFY GENERAL

```
MODIFY GENERAL general field1 [,general field2 ...] [NOMODIFY]
[NOWAIT] [WINDOW window name1] [IN [WINDOW] window name2|IN
SCREEN]
```

Description This command opens a window for editing a general field.

Operational rules The MODIFY GENERAL command is equivalent to editing a record and pressing Ctrl-PgDn or double-clicking when at the general field. MODIFY GENERAL is very useful in programs because the program can control how the user will get into the memo editor; they are not forced to use the Ctrl-PgDn method.

General fields are used to store Windows OLE objects. See the chapter on Using DDE and OLE in FoxPro for more information on storing and editing OLE objects in a general field. Multiple general fields editing windows can be opened by listing more than one general field in the MODIFY GENERAL statement. The NOMODIFY clause opens *general field* as read-only, so it cannot be modified. The NOWAIT clause allows the program to continue processing while the general field is open. Otherwise, the program halts execution until the general field window is closed.

Use the WINDOW *window name1* clause to place the editing window within a window. It will take on all characteristics of the window. Use IN WINDOW *window name2* to open the editing window in a parent window. The general field editing window must be smaller than the parent, and stay within the parent window's boundaries. The IN SCREEN option is the default. This causes the editing window to be placed on the FoxPro desktop screen instead of within a window.

Examples

```
MODIFY GENERAL Faces
MODIFY GENERAL Faces, Badges
MODIFY GENERAL Faces NOWAIT
```

See also APPEND GENERAL, Using DDE and OLE in FoxPro

MODIFY LABEL

```
MODIFY LABEL [filename|?] [[WINDOW window name1] [IN [WINDOW]
window name2|IN SCREEN]] [NOENVIRONMENT] [NOWAIT] [SAVE]
```

Description This command opens a label format (.LBX) file for editing.

Operational rules For more details, see CREATE LABEL. Use the NOENVIRONMENT option to prevent the environment saved with the label from being restored. The SAVE option leaves an image of the label on screen after the report layout window has been closed. SAVE can only be used in a program and has no effect when issued from the Command window.

See also CREATE LABEL

MODIFY MEMO

```
MODIFY MEMO memo field1[, memo field2 ...] [NOEDIT] [NOWAIT]
[NOMENU] [RANGE expN1, expN2] [[WINDOW window name1] [IN
[WINDOW] window name2|IN SCREEN]] [SAME] [SAVE]
```

Description This command opens a window for editing a memo field.

Operational rules The MODIFY MEMO command is equivalent to editing a record and pressing Ctrl-PgDn or double-clicking when at the memo field. MODIFY MEMO is very useful in programs because the program can control how the user will get into the memo editor—they are not forced to use the Ctrl-PgDn method.

Multiple memo fields can be edited by listing more than one memo field in the MODIFY MEMO statement. The NOEDIT clause opens *memo field* as read-only, so it cannot be modified. The NOWAIT clause allows the program to continue processing while the memo is open. Otherwise, the program halts execution until the memo window is closed. The NOMENU clause can be used to prevent the Text menu pad from appearing in the main menu.

The RANGE option lets you open a text editing window with a range of characters selected. Characters are selected starting at the position specified with *expN1* up to (but not including) the *expN2* character. If *expN1* is equal to *expN2*, no characters are selected, and the cursor is placed at the position specified with *expN1*.

Use the WINDOW *window name1* clause to place the memo editing window within a window. It will take on all characteristics of the window. Use IN WINDOW *window name2* to open the memo editing window in a parent window. The memo editing window must be smaller than the parent, and stay within the parent window's boundaries. The IN SCREEN option is the default. This causes the memo editing window to be placed on the FoxPro desktop screen instead of within a window.

The SAME clause causes a previously activated memo editing window that is minimized or hidden to be restored in the background, without activating the window. The SAVE clause leaves an image of the memo editing window on screen after the memo editing window has been closed. SAVE can only be used in a program and has no effect when issued from the Command window.

Example

```
MODIFY MEMO Narrative
MODIFY MEMO Narrative, History
MODIFY MEMO Narrative NOWAIT
```

See also CLOSE MEMO

MODIFY MENU

MODIFY MENU [*filename*|?] [[WINDOW *window name1*] [IN [WINDOW] *window name2*|IN SCREEN]] [NOENVIRONMENT] [NOWAIT] [SAVE]

Description This command opens a menu (.MNX) file for editing.

Operational rules For more details, see CREATE MENU. Use the NOENVIRONMENT option to prevent the environment saved with the menu from being restored. The SAVE option leaves an image of the menu on screen after the menu window has been closed. SAVE can only be used in a program and has no effect when issued from the Command window.

See also CREATE MENU

MODIFY PROJECT

```
MODIFY PROJECT [filename|?] [[WINDOW window name1] [IN [WINDOW]
window name2 |IN SCREEN]] [SAVE]
```

Description This command opens a project (.PJX) file for editing.

Operational rules For more details, see CREATE PROJECT. The SAVE option leaves an image of the menu on screen after the project window has been closed. SAVE can only be used in a program and has no effect when issued from the Command window.

See also CREATE PROJECT

MODIFY QUERY

```
MODIFY QUERY [filename |?] [NOWAIT]
```

Description This command opens a query (.QPR) file for editing.

Operational rules For more details, see CREATE QUERY.

See also CREATE QUERY

MODIFY REPORT

```
MODIFY REPORT [filename|?] [[WINDOW window name1] [IN [WINDOW]
window name2|IN SCREEN]] [NOENVIRONMENT] [NOWAIT] [SAVE]
```

Description This command opens a report (.FRX) file for editing.

Operational rules For more details, see CREATE REPORT. Use the NOENVIRONMENT option to prevent the environment saved with the report from being restored. The SAVE option leaves an image of the menu on screen after the report window has been closed. SAVE can only be used in a program and has no effect when issued from the Command window.

See also CREATE REPORT

MODIFY SCREEN

```
MODIFY SCREEN [filename|?] [[WINDOW window name1] [IN [WINDOW]
window name2|IN SCREEN]] [NOENVIRONMENT] [NOWAIT] [SAVE]
```

Description This command opens a screen (.SCX) file for editing.

Operational rules For more details, see CREATE SCREEN. Use the NOENVIRONMENT option to prevent the environment saved with the screen from being restored. The SAVE option leaves an image of the menu on screen after the screen window has been closed. SAVE can only be used in a program and has no effect when issued from the Command window.

See also CREATE SCREEN

MODIFY STRUCTURE

```
MODIFY STRUCTURE
```

Description This command allows you to change the definition of a FoxPro database file.

Operational rules This command is the same as CREATE, except it is used on existing database file structures. Make sure that there is enough room on your disk for the new file plus the space used by the old file (roughly double the .DBF file space). For more details, of file structures, see CREATE.

See also CREATE

MODIFY WINDOW

Description This command allows you to change the attributes of a user-defined window.

Operational rules This command is used to change the definition of a user-defined window created with the DEFINE WINDOW command without redefining the window. The following attributes of an existing user-defined window can be modified:

```
window name
FROM|TO
AT|SIZE
FONT
STYLE
TITLE
HALFHEIGHT
DOUBLE|PANEL|NONE|SYSTEM
CLOSE|NOCLOSE
FLOAT|NOFLOAT
GROW|NOGROW
MINIMIZE|NOMINIMIZE
ZOOM|NOZOOM
ICON FILE
FILL FILE
COLOR SCHEME
COLOR
```

Changes to the window take affect immediately after the MODIFY WINDOW command is issued. If you are changing the colors of a window, issue the CLEAR command to redisplay the window in the specified colors. See the DEFINE WINDOW command description in this chapter for more information on the appropriate use of the clauses listed above.

See also DEFINE WINDOW

MOVE POPUP

MOVE POPUP *popup name* TO *row, col*|BY *change row, change col*

Description This command moves a pop-up to a new location on the screen.

Operational rules You can issue the new coordinates of the pop-up with TO *row*, *col*. An alternate method is to move the pop-up relative to its current position. To do this, replace TO *row*, *col* with BY *change row*, *change col*. You can move the pop-ups of the system menu by using the name of the system menu pop-up (*_msystem*, *_mfile*, *_medit*, *_mdata*, *_mrecord*, *_mprog* or *_mwindow*). To return them to their original locations, use SET SYSMENU TO DEFAULT.

Example The first example moves the pop-up to row 5, column 20. The second example moves the File pop-up (from the system menu) down 5 rows and over 10 columns from its current position.

```
MOVE POPUP Mpop TO 5, 20
MOVE POPUP _mfile BY 5,10
```

See also DEFINE WINDOW

MOVE WINDOW

```
MOVE WINDOW window name TO row, col|BY expN1, expN2 [CENTER]
```

Description This command moves a window to a new location on the screen.

Operational rules Use this command to reposition a window on the screen. You can issue the new coordinates of the window with TO *row*, *col*. An alternate method is to move the window relative to its current position. To do this, replace TO *row*, *col* with BY *change row*, *change column*. Use the optional CENTER clause to position the specified window in the center of the FoxPro desktop screen, or its parent window.

Examples The first example moves the window to row 5, column 20; the second example moves the window up two rows from its current position:

```
MOVE WINDOW Mwind TO 5, 20
MOVE WINDOW Mwind BY 1, 0
```

See also DEFINE WINDOW

NOTE | && | *

```
NOTE [comments] | * [comments] | && [comments]
```

Description This command allows the user to type lines of comment in a program file.

Operational rules It is always a good practice to place notes and comments in program files. This documents the program and makes it easier to understand if you must go back to it to make changes, or for someone else who looks at it.

When FoxPro encounters the note command, it ignores the rest of the text on that line when executing a program. The asterisk (*) can be used in place of NOTE. To make your note extend past one line, place a semicolon at the end. The other comment command is two ampersands (&&). These can be placed after a command, on the same line. Enter the text after the ampersands.

Example

```
************* ************************
NOTE Maillist.prg — Mailing List Program
* Last Updated: 5/1/89
NOTE — Maillist.prg prints selected records in a name & phone
format
USE MAILLIST ORDER Mzip && open file and index, etc.
```

See also MODIFY COMMAND

ON BAR

ON BAR *expN* OF *popup name1* [ACTIVATE POPUP *popup name2*|ACTIVATE MENU *menu name*]

Description This command activates a pop-up or menu when a bar *expN* or pop-up name is chosen.

Operational rules The ON BAR command is used in conjunction with a pop-up. When the user selects a particular option from the pop-up menu, ON BAR defines the next pop-up or menu that is to be called. A pop-up that displays and activates another pop-up is called a hierarchical pop-up. To call commands or procedures from a pop-up, use ON SELECTION BAR or ON SELECTION POP-UP.

The ON BAR command must be followed by either ACTIVATE POPUP *popup name2* or ACTIVATE MENU *menu name*, depending on whether a sub-popup or sub-menu is being defined. When a pop-up option has a sub-menu or sub-popup attached to it, an arrow is placed to the right of the option. The MARGIN keyword of DEFINE POPUP should be used in defining the pop-up options; otherwise the arrow might overwrite the last character of the option's prompt.

Example The example creates a pop-up that allows the user to pick a printer brand off of a menu of available printers. The first pop-up provides the choices of dot matrix or laser. If the user chooses dot matrix, another pop-up appears, listing a choice of three dot matrix printers. If the user chooses laser, a pop-up with two choices appears.

```
DEFINE POPUP Mprint FROM 2,20 MARGIN MESSAGE "Choose your type
of printer"
DEFINE BAR 1 OF Mprint PROMPT "\Dot Matrix"
DEFINE BAR 2 OF Mprint PROMPT "\Laser"
ON BAR 1 OF Mprint ACTIVATE POPUP Dotty
ON BAR 2 OF Mprint ACTIVATE POPUP Laser

DEFINE POPUP Dotty FROM 2,20 MESSAGE "Choose your dot matrix
printer"
DEFINE BAR 1 OF Dotty PROMPT "\Epson"
DEFINE BAR 2 OF Dotty PROMPT "\Okidrata"
DEFINE BAR 3 OF Dotty PROMPT "\Toshiga"

DEFINE POPUP Laser FROM 2,20 MESSAGE "Choose your laser
printer"
```

```
DEFINE BAR 1 OF Laser PROMPT "\Hewlett Packard"
DEFINE BAR 2 OF Laser PROMPT "\Canyawn"
ON SELECTION POPUP ALL DO Prnchoice
ACTIVATE POPUP Mprint
```

```
PROCEDURE Prnchoice
? "The printer you chose was the "+PROMPT()
WAIT "Is that Correct? " TO Mchk
```

See also DEFINE WINDOW

ON ERROR

ON ERROR [*command*]

Description This command is used to trap errors within a program.

Operational rules Use the ON ERROR command to trap errors so that the program does not fall out with a FoxPro error message. This command should be placed at the beginning of the main program, and it remains effective until an error or another ON ERROR command is encountered. Disable the trap by issuing ON ERROR without the *command* argument. Several functions can be useful in conjunction with this command. ERROR( ) returns the number of the error. MESSAGE( ) returns the description of the error.

Example The following program calls the procedure Errmess if an error occurs.

```
SET PROCEDURE TO Mailpro
ON ERROR DO Errmess WITH ERROR(), MESSAGE()
USE MAILLIST ORDER Mzip

PROCEDURE errmess
PARAMETERS merror,mmsg
SET PRINT OFF

DO CASE
   CASE ERROR() = 126 OR ERROR() =125
      ? "Please put your printer on line"
      WAIT
OTHERWISE
      ? "The following error has occurred", MESSAGE()
      ? "Number ", ERROR()
   WAIT
ENDCASE

SET PRINT ON
RETRY
RETURN TO MASTER
```

See also ERROR( )

ON ESCAPE

ON ESCAPE [*command*]

Description This command calls *command* if the Escape key is pressed within a program.

Operational rules Use the ON ESCAPE command to detect when the user presses the Esc key so that the program does not fall out with the FoxPro abort message. This command has precedence over any ON KEY traps that have been set. SET ESCAPE OFF disables this command. You can also disable the trap by issuing ON ESCAPE without the *command* argument.

Example The following program calls the program Escmess if the Esc key is pressed:

```
ON ESCAPE DO Escmess
USE MAILLIST ORDER Mzip
SET PRINT ON

PROCEDURE escmess
SET PRINT OFF
? "Program aborted, press any key to return to the main menu"
?
WAIT ""
RETURN TO MASTER
```

See also ON KEY

ON KEY

ON KEY [*command*]

Description This command calls *command* if any key is pressed within a program.

Operational rules You may only have one ON KEY in effect. If ON ESCAPE is in effect, pressing Esc triggers that command instead of the ON KEY *command*. If it is not in effect, the Esc key triggers the ON KEY command. Disable the trap by issuing ON KEY without the *command* argument.

Example

```
? "Press any key to abort printing"
ON KEY DO Keyabort
USE MAILLIST ORDER Mzip

PROCEDURE Keyabort
SET PRINT OFF
? "Printing has been aborted"
WAIT
RETURN TO MASTER
```

See also ON ERROR

ON KEY =

ON KEY [= *expN*] [*command*]

Description This command calls *command* if the specified key is pressed within a program.

Operational rules The ON KEY = command allows you to set a particular command for the specified key. Only one ON KEY = can be set at a time. This command only works when used in conjunction with the READ command. This command can be used for pulling up help screens and setting macros (automatic keystrokes) for entry screens.

The *expN* is the ASCII character of the key. The following table shows the *expN* to be used for nonprintable characters:

Key code	Keys
272–281	Alt-Q,W,E,R,T,Y,U,I,O,P
286–294	Alt-A,S,D,F,G,H,J,K,L
300–306	Alt-Z, X,C,V,B,N,M
315–324	F1 to F10 function keys
327	Home
328	↑
329	PgUp
331	←
333	→
335	End
336	↓
337	PgDn
338	Ins
339	Del
340–349	Shift F1 to Shift F10
350–359	Ctrl-F1 to Ctrl-F10
360–369	Alt-F1 to Alt-F10
370	Ctrl-Print Screen
371	Ctrl-←
372	Ctrl-→
373	Ctrl-End
374	Ctrl-PgDn
375	Ctrl-Home
376–385	Alt--1 to Alt-10
386	Alt--
387	Alt-=
388	Ctrl-PgUp

Example In this example, the ON KEY command is used for bringing up a context-sensitive help screen. The VARREAD( ) function displays the name of the GET expression where the F1 key was pressed. Before the help screen is retrieved, the current screen is saved to a memory variable, so it can be refreshed once the help box is exited:

```
USE MAILLIST
ON KEY = 315 DO Helpit
@  1,1 SAY "Press F1 to get help for a particular field"
@  3,1 GET Code
@  4,1 GET Desc
READ
```

```
*** Helpit.Prg
SAVE SCREEN TO Mscreen
@ 12,0 CLEAR
@ 12,1, 21,78 BOX
DO CASE
   CASE VARREAD() = "CODE"
      @ 15, 5 SAY "Help for Code Field . . . "
   CASE VARREAD() = "DESC"
      @  15,5 SAY "Help for Desc Field . . . "
ENDCASE
WAIT ""
RESTORE SCREEN FROM Mscreen
RETURN
```

See also VARREAD( ), ON KEY LABEL

ON KEY LABEL

`ON KEY [LABEL key label] [command]`

Description This command calls command if the specified key is pressed within a program.

Operational rules ON KEY LABEL allows you to set a particular command for each specified *key label*. Multiple ON KEY LABEL commands may be set at a time. This command can be used for pulling up help screens and setting "macros" (automatic keystrokes) for entry screens. Disable the trap by issuing ON KEY LABEL *key label* without the command argument.

You can easily change and restore ON KEY LABEL settings by using PUSH KEY and POP KEY. To change the setting of an ON KEY LABEL without clearing it issue the command PUSH KEY then issue the new ON KEY LABEL command. This puts the previous ON KEY LABEL setting onto a stack in memory. When you need to restore the previous ON KEY LABEL setting, issue the command POP KEY.

Since FoxPro is under the control of Windows, some ON KEY LABEL functions cannot be trapped when executing Windows; for example, using the left mouse button to open a window control menu, clicking in a scroll bar, pressing Ctrl-Esc to activate the Task List, etc.

The *key label* is the letter of the key. The following table shows the key label to be used for nonprintable characters:

Key label	Keys
LEFTARROW	←
RIGHTARROW	→
UPARROW	↑
DNARROW	↓
HOME	Home
END	End
PGUP	PgUp
PGDN	PgDn
DEL	Del
BACKSPACE	Backspace

SPACEBAR	Spacebar
INS	Ins
TAB	Tab
BACKTAB	Shift-Tab
ENTER	Enter
LBRACE	{
RBRACE	}
F1 to F12	F1 to F12 function keys
CTRL+F1 to CTRL+F12	Ctrl-F1 to Ctrl-F12
SHIFT+F1 to SHIFT+F9	Shift-F1 to Shift-F9
SHIFT+F11 to SHIFT+F12	Shift-F11 to Shift-F12
ALT+F1 to ALT+F12	Alt-F1 to Alt-F12
ALT+0 to ALT+9	Alt-0 to Alt-9
ALT+A to ALT+Z	Alt-A to Alt-Z
ALT+PGUP	Alt-PgUp
ALT+PGDN	Alt-PgDn
CTRL+LEFTARROW	Ctrl-←
CTRL+RIGHTARROW	Ctrl-→
CTRL+HOME	Ctrl-Home
CTRL+END	Ctrl-End
CTRL+PGUP	Ctrl-PgUp
CTRL+PGDN	Ctrl-PgDn
CTRL+A to CTRL+Z	Ctrl-A to Ctrl-Z
RIGHTMOUSE	Right mouse
LEFTMOUSE	Left mouse
MOUSE	Mouse
ESCAPE	Escape

Example In this example, the ON KEY LABEL command is used for bringing up two types of help screen. If the user presses F1 they get a context-sensitive help screen. If they press Alt-F1 they get a general help screen. Before either help screen is retrieved, the current screen is saved to a memory variable with SAVE SCREEN, so it can be refreshed once the help box is exited (using RESTORE SCREEN).

```
USE MAILLIST
ON KEY LABEL F1 DO Helpit ON KEY LABEL ALT-F1 DO Genhelp
@ 1,1 SAY "Press F1 to get help for a field, ALT-F1 for general
help"
@ 3,1 GET Code
@ 4,1 GET Desc
READ

*** Helpit.Prg
SAVE SCREEN TO Mscreen
@ 12,0 CLEAR
@ 12,1, 21,78 BOX
DO CASE
   CASE VARREAD() = "CODE"
```

```
      @ 15, 5 SAY "Help for Code Field . . . "
   CASE VARREAD() = "DESC"
      @ 15,5 SAY "Help for Desc Field . . . "
ENDCASE
WAIT " "
RESTORE SCREEN FROM Mscreen
RETURN

*** Genhelp.Prg
SAVE SCREEN TO Mscreen
@ 12,0 CLEAR
@ 12,1, 21,78 BOX
@ 15,5 SAY "General help for screen editing . . . "
WAIT
RESTORE SCREEN FROM Mscreen
RETURN
```

See also VARREAD(), INKEY()

ON PAD

ON PAD *pad name* OF *menu name1* [ACTIVATE POPUP *popup name*] [ACTIVATE MENU *menu name2*]

Description This command specifies the menu pop-up or menu bar that is activated when you choose a specific menu pad.

Operational rules The ON PAD command is used in conjunction with a menu created with the DEFINE MENU and DEFINE PAD commands. When the user selects a particular option, the ON PAD command calls a sub-menu (pop-up or menu bar) to appear.

The optional ACTIVATE POPUP *popup name* argument allows the user to then use the arrow keys to move among the bars of the pop-up menu, creating a sub-pop-up menu. Use ACTIVATE MENU *menu name2* to activate another menu bar. See the DEFINE POPUP command for an example of a menu program.

See also DEFINE POPUP

ON PAGE

ON PAGE [AT LINE *expN command*]

Description This command calls *command* when line *expN* is reached on a printed page.

Operational rules The ON PAGE command can be used to print page breaks and headers after every *expN* number of lines. Previous versions of FoxPro did not have this command, and users were forced to check for line numbers using memory variables. If the routine is to eject the page, use the EJECT PAGE command (not the EJECT command).

Set ON PAGE before turning on the printer with SET PRINT ON or SET DEVICE TO PRINT. To disable the ON PAGE trap, issue the ON PAGE command without an argument.

Example

```
USE MAILLIST ORDER Mzip
SET PRINT ON
ON PAGE AT LINE 58 DO Header
DO Header
SCAN
   ? Lname,Fname
ENDSCAN
ON PAGE

PROCEDURE Header
EJECT PAGE
? "Mailing List by Zip Code"
?  REPLICATE("- ",35)
RETURN
```

See also SET PRINTER, EJECT PAGE

ON READERROR

ON READERROR [*command*]

Description This command calls *command* if an error occurs during a READ.

Operational rules The errors that occur during the READ are invalid data entries, entries outside of the RANGE specification, and entries that do not meet the VALID conditions. FoxPro automatically provides an error message for these instances, but ON READERROR allows you to run your own error handling routines.

This command should be placed at the beginning of the program, and it remains effective until an error or another ON READERROR command is encountered. Disable the trap by issuing ON READERROR without the command argument.

See also ON KEY

ON SELECTION BAR

ON SELECTION BAR *expN* OF *popup name* [*command*]

Description This command executes *command* when bar *expN* of pop-up *popup name* is selected.

Operational rules The ON SELECTION BAR command is used in conjunction with a menu created with the DEFINE POPUP command. If the user chooses bar number *expN*, ON SELECTION BAR defines the command or procedure that will then be performed.

Disable the branching by issuing ON SELECTION BAR without the command argument.

This command is similar to ON SELECTION POPUP which assigns a command to an entire pop-up menu. To assign a sub-menu (pop-up or menu) to appear when a particular option is chosen, use ON BAR.

Example

```
ON SELECTION BAR 1 OF items DO Getitem.PRG
ON SELECTION BAR 3 OF system QUIT
```

See also ON BAR, ON SELECTION POPUP

ON SELECTION MENU

ON SELECTION MENU *menu name*|ALL [*command*]

Description This command executes *command* when the user selects any option from menu *menu name*.

Operational rules The ON SELECTION MENU command is used in conjunction with a menu created with the DEFINE MENU command. When the user selects something from the menu, ON SELECTION MENU defines the command or procedure that will then be performed. The ON SELECTION MENU command must be issued before activating the menu with ACTIVATE MENU. The ON SELECTION PAD command takes precedence over an ON SELECTION MENU.

You can use ALL in place of *menu name* to select the same command for all menus. Disable the branching by issuing ON SELECTION MENU without the command argument.

See also DEFINE MENU

ON SELECTION PAD

ON SELECTION PAD *pad name* OF *menu name* [*command*]

Description This command executes *command* when the user has selected pad *pad name* of menu *menu name*.

Operational rules The ON SELECTION PAD command is used in conjunction with a menu created with the DEFINE MENU and DEFINE PAD commands. When the user selects a particular option from the pad, ON SELECTION defines the command or procedure that will then be performed. The ON SELECTION PAD command must be issued before activating the menu with ACTIVATE MENU.

The command can utilize the MENU( ), PAD( ), and PROMPT( ) functions which determine the last selected option. Disable the branching by issuing ON SELECTION PAD without the command argument. See the DEFINE MENU section for an example of a menu that utilizes ON SELECTION PAD.

See also DEFINE MENU

ON SELECTION POPUP

ON SELECTION POPUP *popup name*|ALL [*command*]

Description This command executes command when the user has selected an option from pop-up menu *popup name*.

Operational rules The ON SELECTION POPUP command is used in conjunction with a menu created with the DEFINE POPUP command. When the user selects a particular option from the pop-up menu, ON SELECTION POPUP defines the command or procedure that is then performed. The ON SELECTION POPUP command must be issued before activating the pop-up with ACTIVATE POPUP.

You can use ALL in place of *popup name* to select the same command for all pop-ups. Disable the branching by issuing ON SELECTION POPUP without the command argument. See the DEFINE POPUP section for an example of a menu that utilizes ON SELECTION POPUP.

See also DEFINE POPUP

ON SHUTDOWN

```
ON SHUTDOWN [command]
```

Description This command executes *command* when you attempt to quit FoxPro, or exit Windows while FoxPro is active.

Operational rules If you try to exit FoxPro when a READ is in effect a "Cannot exit FoxPro" dialog is activated. This can be avoided by issuing an ON SHUTDOWN command. If you have decided to exit Windows while FoxPro is active and an application is running, you might want to issue a command that safely closes all data files before the system is shut down.

PACK

```
PACK [MEMO] [DBF]
```

Description This command permanently removed all records marked for deletion from the active database file.

Operational rules To delete a record from the database file:

1. Mark all records to be deleted.
2. Issue the PACK command.

PACK makes a copy of the data file without the old records, so it may take a while to run. PACK will renumber the records as deleted records are removed. Make sure that there is enough room on your disk for the new file plus the space used by the old file (roughly double the .DBF file space).

The SET DELETED ON command tells FoxPro to ignore deleted records when displaying, editing, and listing. This allows deleted records to appear as if they have already been removed without having to PACK.

The MEMO keyword causes only the memo (.FPT) file to be packed; all unused space is deleted and the file is reduced in size. The keyword DBF causes only the database to be packed, but the memo file is not packed. When no keyword is used, both data file and memo file (if there is one) are packed.

See also DELETE

PARAMETERS

`PARAMETERS` *`parameter list`*

Description This command is used to pass data values and memory variables to a subprogram, procedure, or user-defined function, where those variables can be changed and passed back.

Operational rules The PARAMETERS statement of the called program must be the first executable statement of the procedure or function. When using PARAMETERS, call the procedure, program or function by defining the parameter list using WITH *parameter list*. The variables in the calling parameter list must match the number of items in the PARAMETERS parameter list. The names of the variables do not need to match.

The way an array is passed in the PARAMETER statement is determined by UDFPARMS. The entire array is passed if UDFPARMS is set to REFERENCE or the array name is prefaced with @. If UDFPARMS is set to VALUE, only the first element of the array is passed.

It's possible to pass fewer parameters than called for with the PARAMETERS statement. You can't, however, attempt to pass more paramaters than called for with the PARAMETERS statement.

Example

```
USE MAILLIST ORDER Mzip
SET PRINT ON
Line = 99
SCAN
   IF Line > 60
      DO Header with Line, "Mailing List by Zip Code"
   ENDIF
   ? Lname,Fname
   Line = Line+1
ENDSCAN

PROCEDURE Header
PARAMETERS Lineno, Title
EJECT PAGE
? "Page #",Lineno
?
? Title
?
? REPLICATE("-",75)
Line = 5
RETURN
```

See also PROCEDURE, PARAMETERS()

PLAY MACRO

`PLAY MACRO` *`macro name`* `[TIME` *`expN`*`]`

Description This command performs a saved macro.

Operational rules Macros are sets of keystrokes that FoxPro automatically performs for you. Run a macro by pressing the keystroke that you specified for calling the macro. Macros are created using the SAVE MACROS command.

To call a macro from a program, use PLAY MACRO. This causes the keystrokes to perform as if someone had pressed the key combination that runs the macro. The macro is then played the first time that input is requested in the program (for instance at an ACCEPT, @ ... GET, or EDIT command).

If multiple PLAY MACRO commands are pending, it performs them in reverse order. In other words, the most recent PLAY MACRO is performed first. The TIME option allows you to specify a delay of *expN* seconds between 0 and 10. Time is delayed *expN* seconds between each keystroke of the macro. You can keep separate sets of macros in a macro library file. To make a macro library current, use the RESTORE MACROS command.

See also RESTORE MACROS

POP KEY

```
POP KEY [ALL]
```

Description This command restores ON KEY LABEL settings.

Operational rules ON KEY LABEL settings that were pushed onto a memory stack using PUSH KEY are restored using POP KEY. POP KEY is used in conjunction with PUSH KEY to save ON KEY LABEL settings in memory, make changes to the settings, and then restore them later. Using the ALL clause clears all current ON KEY LABEL settings and removes any ON KEY LABEL settings from the memory stack.

See also PUSH KEY

POP MENU

`POP MENU` *`menu name`* `[TO MASTER]`

Description This command restores a menu from the stack.

Operational rules Menus can be placed on a stack using the PUSH MENU command. This command allows you to make changes to the menu and use it temporarily in its changed state. POP MENU is then used to pull the menu from the stack, restoring it back to its original state. Use the TO MASTER clause to restore the first menu pushed on the stack and clear the stack.

Menus are designed with the DEFINE MENU command. Once the definitions are set, you can use ACTIVATE MENU to call it up. Use DEACTIVATE MENU to remove a menu from the screen, and see DEFINE MENU for a program that creates a user-defined menu.

See also DEFINE MENU, PUSH MENU

POP POPUP

`POP POPUP` *`popup name`*

Description This command pulls a pop-up from the stack.

Operational rules Pop-up menus can be placed on a stack using the PUSH POPUP command. This command allows you to make changes to the pop-up and use it temporarily in its changed state. POP POPUP is then used to pull the pop-up from the stack, restoring it back to its original state.

Pop-up menus are designed with the DEFINE POPUP and DEFINE BAR commands. Once the definitions are set, you can use ACTIVATE POPUP to call it up. Use DEACTIVATE POPUP to remove a pop-up menu from the screen. See DEFINE BAR for a program that creates a pop-up menu within a user-defined menu.

See also DEFINE BAR
PUSH POPUP

PRINTJOB ... ENDPRINTJOB

```
PRINTJOB
   statements
ENDPRINTJOB
```

Description These commands utilize FoxPro printing system memory variables while printing.

Operational rules The PRINTJOB ... ENDPRINTJOB commands are used to initialize the printer and set the printing environment before sending output to the printer. When the PRINTJOB command is executed, a number of FoxPro system variables are activated and codes are sent to the printer. The following actions occur when PRINTJOB is executed:

1. FoxPro sends starting printer control codes, stored in the system memory variable _pscode, to the printer.
2. FoxPro ejects a page if the system memory variable _peject is set to BEFORE or to BOTH.
3. FoxPro sets the system memory variable _pcolno to 0. _pcolno stores the printer column number.

The following actions occur when ENDPRINTJOB is executed:

1. FoxPro sends ending printer control codes to the printer to reset the printer to the configuration it had before PRINTJOB was issued. The ending printer control codes are stored in the system memory variable _pecode.
2. FoxPro ejects a page if the system memory variable _peject is set to AFTER or to BOTH.
3. Execution loops back to PRINTJOB to print another copy of the report if the _pcopies system memory variable is set to a value higher than 1 (the default). The number of copies is determined by the value of the system memory variable _pcopies. When the number of copies printed equals the value of _pcopies, FoxPro exits the loop. Program control then begins with the command immediately following ENDPRINTJOB.

These commands can only be utilized with FoxPro built-in reporting capabilities (such as the REPORT FORM command) and must be called within a program.

Examples

```
USE MAILLIST ORDER Mzip
SET PRINT ON
_pcopies = 3
_peject = "both"
PRINTJOB
   ON PAGE AT LINE 58 DO Header
   SCAN
      ? Lname,Fname
   ENDSCAN
ENDPRINTJOB
SET PRINT OFF

PROCEDURE Header
? "Page #",_pageno
? REPLICATE ("-",75)
RETURN
```

See also ON PAGE

PRIVATE

PRIVATE *memvar list*
PRIVATE ALL [LIKE *skel1*|EXCEPT *skel2*]

Description This command is used to hide memory variables and arrays.

Operational rules Private memory variables allow two variables with the same name in different programs. One memory variable can be in a lower level program, and the other can be in the program that called it. If the value of the variable in the lower level program is changed, it will not affect the value of the variable in the calling program. Memory variables created in programs default to being private variables.

Unlike the PUBLIC command, PRIVATE does not create variables; it only hides them. Use the ALL LIKE clause to declare all variables of *skel1* to be private. The optional EXCEPT is used with ALL LIKE to exclude variables of *skel2* from the ALL LIKE *skel1* list. Both *skel1* and *skel2* can contain the wild card characters ? and *.

Examples

```
PRIVATE Date, Amount, Time
PRIVATE ALL
PRIVATE LIKE D* EXCEPT Date
```

See also PUBLIC

PROCEDURE

PROCEDURE *procedure name*

Description This command identifies a procedure program.

Operational rules If a certain procedure must be performed more than once, it is easier to create a common procedure with the PROCEDURE command. Procedures begin with the PROCEDURE command, and can end with an optional RETURN. All FoxPro procedures and user-defined functions automatically return an implicit true value. A procedure can have multiple arguments and can pass back a value to the calling program.

PROCEDURE *procedure name* must be no longer than 10 characters in length and begin with a letter or underscore. With the SET PROCEDURE TO command you can specify a program file that contains an unlimited number of procedures in it. When you call a procedure with the DO or = command, FoxPro searches for the procedure in the following order:

1. The file containing DO *procedure name* is searched.
2. The file opened with SET PROCEDURE (if one is set) is searched.
3. FoxPro looks through the programs in the execution chain. Program files are searched beginning with the most recently executed program and continuing back to the first executed program.
4. FoxPro looks for a stand-alone program file. If a program file with the same name as the file name specified with DO is found, the program is executed. If a matching program file name isn't found, an error message "File doesn't exist" is returned.

Example In the following program, the heading program calls a user-defined function that prints the heading centered on the page, depending on the width of the paper:

```
Mhead = "Income Analysis"
? CENTERIT(Mhead,75)
                        Income Analysis

PROCEDURE centerit
PARAMETERS Heading, Width
PRIVATE Mcenter
Mcenter = SPACE(Width/2 - LEN(Heading)/2)) + Heading
RETURN Mcenter
```

See also PARAMETERS

PUBLIC

```
PUBLIC memvar list
PUBLIC [ARRAY] array1(expN1 [, expN2]) [,array2 (expN3 [,
expN4])] ...
```

Description This command is used to declare global memory variables and arrays.

Operational rules Public memory variables allow you to make changes to a memory variable in a lower level program or subroutine and pass those changes back to the calling program. Variables and arrays that are defined in the Command Window are automatically PUBLIC, while variables created in programs are only available to the initializing program and lower-level programs.

Public memory variables are logical types (.T. or .F.) until they are initialized to some other type. It is important that you do not declare a memory variable PUBLIC after it has been initialized. Therefore, it is a good idea to include the PUBLIC command for all variables at the beginning of the master program so it is given before any of the variables have been set. The argument ARRAY *array* can be used in place of *memvar list* to define and declare multi-dimensional arrays.

Examples

```
PUBLIC Mem
Mem = 5
Mem2 = 5
DO Subprog
? Mem, Mem2     && Mem is 10, but Mem2 is still 5

PROCEDURE Subprog
Mem = 10  && Mem is public; it equals 10 in both programs
Mem2 = 10 && Mem2 is private; it stays 5 in Main.Prg
RETURN
```

See also PRIVATE

PUSH KEY

PUSH KEY [CLEAR]

Description This command places all current ON KEY LABEL settings on the stack.

Operational rules Placing ON KEY LABEL settings on a "stack" allows you to make changes to the ON KEY LABEL settings and use them in their changed state. POP KEY is then used to pull the ON KEY LABEL settings from the stack, restoring all ON KEY LABEL settings back to their original state. ON KEY LABEL settings are placed on and removed from the stack in a "last in, first out" order. Use the CLEAR clause to save all current ON KEY LABEL settings to the stack and clear all settings.

See also POP KEY

PUSH MENU

PUSH MENU *menu name*

Description This command places a menu on the stack.

Operational rules Placing menus on a "stack" allows you to make changes to the menu and use it temporarily in its changed state. POP MENU is then used to pull the menu from the stack, restoring it back to its original state. Menus are placed on and removed from the stack in a "last in, first out" order.

Menus are designed with the DEFINE MENU command. Once the definitions are set, you can use ACTIVATE MENU to call it up. Use DEACTIVATE MENU to erase a menu from the screen. See DEFINE MENU for a program that creates a user-defined menu.

See also DEFINE MENU, POP MENU

PUSH POPUP

```
PUSH POPUP popup name
```

Description This command places a pop-up on the stack.

Operational rules Placing pop-ups on a "stack" allows you to make changes to the pop-up and use it temporarily in its changed state. POP POPUP is then used to pull it from the stack, restoring it back to its original state. Pop-ups are placed on and removed from the stack in a "last in, first out" order.

Example In the following example, the pop-up menu has three bars: Add, Edit, and Browse. The pop-up is pushed to the stack, and the second bar is removed with the RELEASE BAR command. The pop-up is then restored to its original state with the POP POPUP command.

```
DEFINE POPUP editor

DEFINE BAR 1 OF editor PROMPT "Add"
DEFINE BAR 2 OF editor PROMPT "Edit"
DEFINE BAR 3 OF editor PROMPT "Browse"

ACTIVATE POPUP editor NOWAIT

PUSH POPUP editor
RELEASE BAR 2 OF editor
WAIT
POP POPUP editor
```

See also DEFINE POPUP, POP POPUP

QUIT

```
QUIT
```

Description This command ends the current FoxPro session and exits.

Operational rules The command QUIT closes all files before exiting. FoxPro files can be damaged or destroyed if the computer is turned off or reset without quitting. To help prevent this from happening, close files with the CLOSE commands once you no longer need them during a FoxPro session. You can also call the FLUSH command periodically to dump memory buffers without closing files.

See also CLOSE, ON SHUTDOWN

READ

```
READ [CYCLE] [ACTIVATE expL] [DEACTIVATE expL] [MODAL] [WITH
window list] [SHOW expL] [VALID expL|expN] [WHEN expL] [OBJECT
expN] [TIMEOUT expN] [SAVE] [NOMOUSE] [LOCK|NOLOCK] [COLOR
color pair|COLOR SCHEME expN]
```

Description This command allows you to edit data and objects defined with the @ ... GET command.

Operational rules The @ ... GET command allows you to define data GET fields and objects such as check boxes and pushbuttons. When a READ is exited program control is returned to the line directly after the READ command. The READ can be exited in a number of ways; moving forward past the last object or backward past the first object exits READ (if the CYCLE clause isn't included with READ); pressing Escape, Ctrl-W or choosing a control that was defined to terminate the READ also exits the READ.

READ allows editing of all @ ... GET statements made since the last READ or CLEAR GETS command. The READ command has a number of optional clauses and arguments that make it powerful:

CYCLE Prevents the READ from terminating when the editing cursor is on the last GET object. This allows the user to cycle through all GETs and objects without terminating the READ.

ACTIVATE *expL* The ACTIVATE clause is evaluated when READ is first executed and when any READ window changes. The expression *expL* is usually a user-defined function or an expression. The READ window changes when another window involved in the READ is activated.

DEACTIVATE *expL* The DEACTIVATE clause is evaluated when any READ window changes. Before activating another window the current window must be deactivated. The expression *expL* expression is usually a user-defined function or an expression.

MODAL Prevents all active windows not involved in the current READ from being accessed. Using the MODAL clause also disables all menu options when using the FoxPro system menu. Use this clause when you require an action to be taken.

WITH *window list* All activated windows included in window list can be accessed if the MODAL clause is included with the READ.

SHOW *expL* The SHOW clause is evaluated when the READ is first executed and whenever SHOW GETS is issued.

VALID *expL|expN* The VALID clause is evaluated when the READ is first executed and when an attempt to terminate a READ is issued. The READ will be terminated if *expL* is true (.T.). If *expL* is false (.F.) the READ remains active and the cursor stays in the current GET field.

WHEN *expL* The WHEN is evaluated only when the READ is first executed. If the expression *expL* returns true (.T.) the READ will be issued; otherwise it will be ignored and program execution will continue with the first line after the READ command.

OBJECT *expN* Specifies which GET object the edit cursor is in when the READ is issued. Each GET that is issued before the READ is an object; and GETs such as push buttons and radio buttons contain multiple objects. The actual object number is determined by the order that the GETs were issued and the options available in each GET object.

TIMEOUT *expN* Waits *expN* seconds for input. If that time has elapsed, the read is exited and program execution continues with the first line after the READ. If the READ is terminated by the timeout clause, the READKEY( ) function will return a value of 20 (otherwise it returns 276) and any changes made to the current GET are ignored.

SAVE The SAVE clause saves the definition of all GETs issued before the READ. If GETs have been saved, they can be activated again with the READ command without re-issuing the GET commands again.

NOMOUSE If the NOMOUSE key word is included with the READ, all GETs involved with the READ cannot be selected with the mouse. While in an object however, the mouse can still be used for all available editing functions.

LOCK|NOLOCK If a database has been opened for shared use (multi-user) and the GET objects are database fields the READ command may attempt to lock the record involved with the READ. The LOCK key word is used to force FoxPro to attempt to automatically lock the record involved in the READ. If LOCK is attempted the record can only be edited once the lock is successful. The SET REPROCESS command determines how many times or for how long locking attempts are made. READ defaults to READ LOCK if LOCK or NOLOCK isn't included. If NOLOCK is included, the records used by objects are not locked. Instead, all objects that use fields in the records are made read-only and the control cannot be selected and is displayed in the disabled colors. If you issue READ NOLOCK and modify a memo field, the record is automatically locked.

COLOR *color pair*|COLOR *expN* The color of the current @ ... GET editing region can be specified by including the number of an existing color scheme in the COLOR SCHEME clause or a set of color pairs in the COLOR clause. When an object is selected, it assumes the colors of the second color pair in the color pair list. All other colors in the color pair list are ignored. If you omit the first color pair you must include a comma for the color pair.

When a READ command is issued, the Enter, Tab, and arrow keys moves from object to object. To exit a READ, press Esc, Ctrl-W, or select a terminating object.

Examples

```
USE MAILLIST
ACTIVATE WINDOW names
@ 5,1 SAY "Enter Last Name" Lname
@ 5,50 SAY "First Name" GET Fname
READ CYCLE MODAL
```

See also @ ... SAY/GET

READ MENU

READ MENU TO *memvar* [SAVE]

Description This command activates a pop-up menu defined with the @...MENU command.

Operational rules The READ MENU command activates a pop-up menu that the user can choose options from. See the @ ... MENU command regarding the setup of the menu.

Examples

```
DIMENSION SORTS(3)
Sorts(1) = "Alpha"
Sorts(2) = "Zip"
Sorts(3) = "Other"
```

```
@ 3,3 MENU Sorts, 3 TITLE "Choose an order to sort by"
READ MENU TO Choice
DO CASE
   CASE Choice = 1
     SET ORDER TO MAILALPH
   CASE Choice = 2
     SET ORDER TO MAILZIP
   CASE Choice = 3
     ACCEPT "Enter Expression to Sort By " TO Other
     INDEX ON EVALUATE(Other) TAG Temp
     GO TOP
ENDCASE
```

See also @...MENU

RECALL

RECALL [*scope*] [FOR *expL*] [WHILE *expL*] [NOOPTIMIZE]

Description This command "unmarks" records marked for deletion.

Operational rules The RECALL command can be used to un-delete records before they are permanently removed from a database. To delete a record from the database file, mark all records to be deleted and then issue the PACK command.

You can use the optional FOR *expL*, WHILE *expL*, and *scope* arguments to include only a subset of the records to recall. Use the optional NOOPTIMIZE clause to disable Rushmore when recalling deleted records.

Examples

```
RECALL
RECALL FOR State = "CA"
RECALL NEXT 100
RECALL ALL
```

See also DELETE

REGIONAL

REGIONAL *memvar list*
#REGION *number*

Description This command is used to define regional memory variables and arrays.

Operational rules The REGIONAL command is used to define variables and arrays, using identical names in a program, to different "regions" of a program. This allows the same variable name to be used without being changed. The REGIONAL command is similar to the PRIVATE command; however, REGIONAL is processed when a program is compiled.

A region is defined with the #REGION directive. If you use the screen builder, FoxPro generates the #REGION directive for the screen code. Once a region has been defined, you can declare variables and arrays to be regional within the currently defined region by specifying them in *memvar list*.

When a program using these commands is compiled, and variables and arrays with the same name are declared regional, FoxPro substitutes each occurrence of the variable with a unique name, beginning with the second occurrence. This is done by padding the variable or array name with the underscore character (_), up to 10 characters in length.

See also PRIVATE, #DEFINE

REINDEX

```
REINDEX [COMPACT]
```

Description This command rebuilds all open index (.IDX and .CDX) files.

Operational rules Index files usually must be reindexed if they were not closed properly. This occurs when the computer is turned off or reset without using the QUIT command. Index files will also need to be reindexed if they were not open when records were added or edited in the database. The optional COMPACT keyword creates compact indexes even if the originals were not compact. Compact indexing causes the files to be smaller, and for index operations (such as SEEK) to run faster.

See also INDEX

RELEASE

```
RELEASE memvar list
RELEASE ALL [LIKE skel1|EXCEPT skel2]
RELEASE LIBRARY library name
RELEASE MENUS [menu list [EXTENDED]]
RELEASE PAD pad name OF menu name|ALL OF menu name
RELEASE POPUPS [popup list [EXTENDED]]
RELEASE BAR expN OF popup name|ALL OF popup name
RELEASE WINDOWS [window list]
```

Description This command erases variables, windows, pop-ups, menus and libraries from memory.

Operational rules To delete select memory variables use RELEASE with the *memvar list*, or with the ALL, ALL LIKE *skel1*, or ALL EXCEPT *skel2* argument. RELEASE MODULE removes a FoxPro API library that has been loaded with the SET LIBRARY command.

You cannot erase menus, pop-ups, or windows unless they are no longer in use. When menus, pop-ups, windows, and pads are released, they are removed from memory and erased from the screen. The EXTENDED keyword is used with RELEASE MENUS and RELEASE POPUPS to release all subordinate pads, pop-ups, bars, and ON routines.

Examples

```
RELEASE ALL
RELEASE ALL LIKE S*
RELEASE ALL LIKE S* EXCEPT Stuff
RELEASE MENUS Main, Edit
RELEASE PAD 1 OF Editor
RELEASE BAR ALL OF Mpop
```

See also CLEAR MEMORY

RELEASE MODULE

```
RELEASE MODULE filename
```

Description This command releases a binary routine loaded with the LOAD command.

Operational rules Binary files that are placed in memory with LOAD can only be released from memory using the RELEASE MODULE command. Specify the routine to release with *filename*.

See also LOAD, CALL

RENAME

```
RENAME filename1 TO filename2
```

Description This command changes the name of a file.

Operational rules The RENAME command is used to change the name of a file. You must specify the file extension of each file or FoxPro will assume an extension of .DBF. Both *filename1* and *filename2* can contain drive and directory information. You cannot rename a file that is currently open. The RENAME command does not allow wild cards (? and *) to rename multiple files at one time, so you might prefer to use the RUN command.

Examples

```
RENAME MAILLIST.DBF TO MAIL.DBF
RENAME C:\DATA\MAILLIST.DBF TO C:\DATA\MAIL.DBF
```

See also RUN|!

REPLACE

```
REPLACE field WITH expression [ADDITIVE] [scope] [FOR expL]
[WHILE expL] [NOOPTIMIZE]
```

Description This command performs a "global find and replace" routine in the current database.

Operational rules Use the optional FOR *expL*, WHILE *expL*, and *scope* arguments to perform the operation in a subset of the data file. To replace a field in all records, use the ALL argument. Without one of these clauses, REPLACE only replaces the contents in the current record. You can provide a list of fields to be replaced in one command. Replacing several fields at one time is faster than issuing separate REPLACE commands.

The ADDITIVE clause is for replacing memo fields with an expression. ADDITIVE causes the expression to be appended to the memo. If you do not use this clause, using this command with memo fields will replace the current memo entry with *expression*. Use the optional NOOPTIMIZE clause to disable Rushmore when replacing data.

Examples

```
REPLACE ALL Wages WITH Wages * 1.1
REPLACE City WITH "San Jose", State WITH "CA" FOR City = "SJ"
```

```
REPLACE NEXT 100 City WITH UPPER(City)
REPLACE Narrative WITH Comment1 + Comment2 ADDITIVE
```

See also SCATTER, GATHER

REPORT

```
REPORT [FORM filename|?] [ENVIRONMENT] [scope] [FOR expL]
[WHILE expL] [HEADING expC] [NOEJECT] [NOCONSOLE] [NOOPTIMIZE]
[PDSETUP] [PLAIN] [PREVIEW] [TO PRINTER [PROMPT]|TO FILE
filename] [SUMMARY]
```

Description This command prints a report using a FoxPro report file (.FRX).

Operational rules The CREATE REPORT command allows you to set the report dimensions, headings, groupings, and contents of the report within a report (.FRX) file. The argument ? can be used in place of the *report filename*. FoxPro displays a list of .FRX files to choose from. To run the report, make sure the necessary data file is your active file, and issue the REPORT command. If no data files are open and you saved the work environment with the report, you can use the ENVIRONMENT option so FoxPro will open the necessary files.

Use the optional FOR *expL*, WHILE *expL*, and *scope* arguments to print the report for a subset of the data file. Include HEADING *expC* to specify text *expC* to be printed as an additional heading at the top of each report page. If your report has a page heading defined, you can specify the PLAIN option to print the page heading on the first page only. The PLAIN option takes precedence over HEADING if both are used.

By default FoxPro will issue a form feed prior to the first page of the report. This causes a blank page to be ejected from the printer. Use NOEJECT to suppress the form feed prior to printing the report. Reports default to printing on the screen. Use the TO PRINTER option to print to the printer, or the TO FILE *filename* to print to an ASCII file. When sending output to the printer, the optional PROMPT keyword can be used to access the Windows Printer Setup dialog before printing. If the report is sent to the printer or to a file, use the NOCONSOLE option to suppress printing of the report on the screen.

The PDSETUP clause only affects reports that were created in FoxPro for DOS and have not been converted to FoxPro for Windows. If the DOS report being printed contains a printer driver setup, you must use the PDSETUP option to load the required setup. The PREVIEW option displays the report and pertinent data (one screenful) on the screen letting you verify that the report definition is set up correctly. After exiting the preview screen, the REPORT command must be issued again (without PREVIEW) to actually begin printing the report.

Use the NOOPTIMIZE option to disable Rushmore. This is only relevant when the FOR clause is being used. An alternate method is to globally disable Rushmore by using the SET OPTIMIZE command. SUMMARY prints a summary report (subtotals only) even if it has been set to No in the CREATE REPORT generator.

Examples

```
REPORT FORM Mlist
REPORT FORM Mlist PREVIEW
```

```
REPORT FORM Mlist TO PRINT
REPORT FORM Mlist TO PRINT HEADING "Rotary Club Mailing"
REPORT FORM Mlist FOR State = "CA" PLAIN NOEJECT
REPORT FORM Mlist NEXT 100 TO FILE Mreport  && creates
Mreport.Txt
REPORT FORM Mlist ENVIRONMENT TO PRINT
```

See also CREATE REPORT

RESTORE FROM

RESTORE FROM *filename*|FROM MEMO *memo field* [ADDITIVE]

Description This command restores memory variables and arrays into memory.

Operational rules Memory variables and arrays are saved with the SAVE TO command, which saves all or a subset of current variables to a file or memo field. RESTORE causes all current variables to be released from memory unless the ADDITIVE option is included. If any current memory variables have the same name, they are overwritten with the new values. When variables are restored from within a program, they automatically become PRIVATE unless they were previously declared PUBLIC in the program.

Variables and arrays can be stored in a .MEM file and restored using RESTORE FROM *filename* where *filename* is a .MEM file. They can also be stored in the memo field of a FoxPro database and can be restored using RESTORE FROM *memo field* where *memo field* is the memo they are stored in.

Examples

```
RESTORE FROM Memfile
RESTORE FROM Memfile ADDITIVE
RESTORE FROM MEMO Settings.vars
```

See also SAVE TO

RESTORE MACROS

RESTORE MACROS [FROM *filename*|FROM MEMO *memo field*]

Description This command restores keyboard macros to memory.

Operational rules Macro definitions are saved with the SAVE MACRO command, which saves all or a subset of current keyboard macros to a file or memo field. Macros can be stored in a macro (.FKY) file and restored using RESTORE MACROS FROM *filename* where *filename* is an .FKY file. They can also be stored in the memo field of a FoxPro database and can be restored using RESTORE MACROS FROM MEMO *memo field* where *memo field* is the memo they are stored in.

Examples

```
RESTORE MACROS FROM  Macfile
RESTORE MACROS FROM MEMO Settings.macs
```

See also SAVE MACROS

RESTORE SCREEN

`RESTORE SCREEN [FROM memvar]`

Description This command restores a screen layout or window that has been saved with the SAVE SCREEN command.

Operational rules The RESTORE SCREEN command is useful in situations where you are overlaying the current screen with information, such as a help window. To erase the information and restore the screen to its previous display, use the following sequence of commands:

1. Issue the command SAVE SCREEN TO *memvar* to save the screen settings to *memvar*.
2. Display the information, and when you are done...
3. Use RESTORE SCREEN FROM *memvar* to restore the screen settings.

Example The following program displays a help box when the user presses the F1 key. Before the help is displayed, the screen layout is saved to the memory variable Mscreen. To return from the help screen, the program calls RESTORE SCREEN to restore it to its previous settings:

```
USE MAILLIST
ON KEY LABEL F1 DO Helpit
@ 1,1 SAY "Press F1 to get help "
@ 3,1 GET Code
@ 4,1 GET Desc
READ CYCLE

*** Helpit.Prg
SAVE SCREEN TO Mscreen
@ 12,0 CLEAR
@ 12,1, 21,78 BOX
@ 15,5 SAY "General help for screen editing . . . "
WAIT
RESTORE SCREEN FROM Mscreen
RETURN
```

The *memvar* that holds the screen or window definition is displayed as a type S variable if the LIST or DISPLAY MEMORY is issued.

See also SAVE SCREEN, HIDE WINDOW

RESTORE WINDOW

`RESTORE WINDOW window list|ALL FROM filename|FROM MEMO memo field`

Description This command restores window definitions to memory.

Operational rules The RESTORE WINDOW command can be used to redefine windows that were saved to a file or memo field. Window definitions are saved with the SAVE WINDOW command, which saves all or a subset of defined windows to a file or memo field. Windows can be stored in a window (.WIN) file and restored using RESTORE WINDOW FROM *filename* where *filename* is a .WIN file. They can also be stored in the memo field of a FoxPro database and can be restored using RESTORE WINDOW FROM MEMO *memo field* where *memo field* is the memo they are stored in.

RESTORE WINDOW causes all current windows with the same name as those restored to be released from memory. The current status of each window saved is included with the saved window definition and is preserved when it is restored. You can use the *window list* argument to restore only those windows in the list. Use the ALL clause to restore all windows to memory.

See also SAVE WINDOW

RESUME

```
RESUME
```

Description This command causes a program to resume processing after it has been suspended.

Operational rules When a program encounters an error or is broken with the Esc key, it asks the user whether they want to Cancel, Suspend, or Ignore. If the user chooses Suspend, the program drops out to the command window. All memory variables still exist, as does the file status. At this point, files and variables can be manipulated. If the user then chooses RESUME, the program resumes processing at the next command line.

If the user chooses Cancel, memory variables are erased, and the program cannot resume processing. SUSPEND can also be placed within a program to make it suspend the program and return to the Command Window, leaving memory variables intact.

See also SUSPEND, CANCEL

RETRY

```
RETRY
```

Description This command causes a program to resume processing, and re-execute the line from which it exited.

Operational rules The RETRY command is particularly useful in error handling routines. After the error has been encountered, a routine can fix it. By using RETRY, it can then go back and retry the command where the error occurred.

Example

```
SET PROCEDURE TO Mailpro
ON ERROR DO Errmess
USE MAILLIST ORDER Mzip
SET PRINT ON

PROCEDURE ERRMESS
SET PRINT OFF
DO CASE
```

```
    CASE ERROR() = 126 OR ERROR() = 125
       ? "Please put your printer on line"
       WAIT
       SET PRINT ON
       RETRY
    OTHERWISE
       ? "The following error has occurred", MESSAGE()
       WAIT
       RETURN TO MASTER
ENDCASE
RETURN
```

See also ON ERROR

RETURN

RETURN [*expr* | TO MASTER | TO *program name*]

Description This command causes a program or subroutine to return to the calling program.

Operational rules If the RETURN command is placed in the master program, it drops out to the command window. When placed in any other program, RETURN returns to the calling program, one line below the line that made the call.

The TO MASTER clause causes a return to the highest level calling program (usually the main menu in menu-based systems). The TO clause allows you to choose the *program name* to return to. You may issue RETURN expr to return a value to the calling program. You are not required to place RETURN at the end of a FoxPro program or procedure, because there is an implicit RETURN at the end.

See also DO

RUN | !

RUN [/N [*expN*]] *command*|*program name*
! [/N [*expN*]] *command*|*program name*

Description This command executes DOS commands and Windows applications.

Operational rules The RUN command can be used to execute a DOS command or application, execute a Windows Program Information File (.PIF), or launch another Windows application from FoxPro.

When the file or command specified in *command|program name* does contain a file extension, FoxPro attempts to locate an associated Windows PIF file along the DOS path. A PIF is used to execute DOS commands and applications and controls the settings of a DOS window in Windows, such as amount of memory used and the state of the DOS window. If no PIF file is found, FoxPro will use the default FOXRUN.PIF that is included with FoxPro. The settings of FOXRUN.PIF can be modified using the Window PIF Editor. Consult your Windows documentation for more information on PIF files.

The NOWAIT parameter, /N, is used to launch another Windows application from FoxPro. The optional numeric parameter *expN* is used to control the attributes of the application when it is launched. Be sure that no spaces are between the /N clause and *expN*.

To leave the application	*expN* should be
Active and normal size	1
Active and minimized	2
Active and maximized	3
Inactive and normal size	4
Inactive and minimized	7

Examples

```
RUN COMMAND
RUN FOXRUN.PIF
RUN /N \WINDOWS\WINWORD\WINWORD.EXE
RUN /N4 AMIPRO.EXE
```

See also DO

SAVE MACROS

SAVE MACROS TO *filename*|TO MEMO *memo field*

Description This command saves keyboard macro definitions to a file or memo field.

Operational rules Macro definitions can be stored in a macro file (.FKY) with the command SAVE MACROS TO *filename* where *filename* is the .FKY file. They can also be saved to a FoxPro database memo field with the command SAVE MACROS TO MEMO *memo field*. Macro definitions can be restored to memory with the RESTORE MACROS command.

See also RESTORE MACROS

SAVE SCREEN

SAVE SCREEN [TO *memvar*]

Description This command saves the settings of the current output window to memory.

Operational rules The SAVE SCREEN command is useful in situations where you are overlaying the current screen with information, such as a help window. To erase the information and restore the screen to its previous display, use the following sequence of commands:

1. Issue the command SAVE SCREEN TO *memvar* to save the screen settings to *memvar*.
2. Display the information, and when you are done,...
3. RESTORE SCREEN FROM *memvar* to restore the screen settings.

See the RESTORE SCREEN sections for an example of a program that uses these commands.

See also RESTORE SCREEN, SHOW WINDOW

SAVE TO

SAVE TO *filename*|TO MEMO *memo field* [ALL LIKE|EXCEPT *skel*]

Description This command saves memory variables and arrays to a file or memo field.

Operational rules The SAVE TO command can be used to save the values of all user-created variables, clear the memory, and restore them at any time. The value of memory variables and arrays can be saved to a memory file (.MEM) with the command SAVE TO *filename* where *filename* is the name of the .MEM file. They can also be saved to a FoxPro database memo field with the command SAVE TO MEMO *memo field*.

Use the ALL LIKE *skel* or ALL EXCEPT *skel* clauses to save a subset of current memory variables and arrays. Use the RESTORE command to load the variables into memory.

Examples

```
SAVE TO Memfile
SAVE TO Memfile ALL LIKE S* EXCEPT Stuff
SAVE TO MEMO Settings.vars
```

See also RESTORE FROM

SAVE WINDOW

SAVE WINDOWS *window list* | ALL TO *filename* | TO MEMO *memo field*

Description This command saves window definitions to a file or memo field.

Operational rules All defined windows in memory can be saved to a window file with the command SAVE WINDOWS or to a FoxPro database memo field with the command SAVE WINDOWS ... TO MEMO. You can use the window list argument to save only those windows in the list. Use the ALL clause to save all windows in memory.

The window file (.WIN) argument *filename* specifies the file in which to save the windows. The *memo field* argument specifies the memo field in which to save the windows.

See also RESTORE WINDOW

SCAN

```
SCAN [NOOPTIMIZE] [scope] [FOR expL] [WHILE expL]
   [statements]
   [LOOP]
   [EXIT]
ENDSCAN
```

Description This command processes all or selected records of a database.

Operational rules The SCAN command is much like the DO WHILE command when processing a database. However SCAN, unlike DO WHILE, automatically advances the record pointer with each loop, eliminating the need for the SKIP command. You can use the optional FOR *expL*, WHILE *expL*, and *scope* arguments to process only a subset of the data file.

As with the DO WHILE command, you can use the LOOP to loop back to SCAN and begin processing the next record. You can use the EXIT command to end the SCAN process and continue with program execution on the line immediately after the ENDSCAN command. Use the optional NOOPTIMIZE clause to disable Rushmore when scanning a database.

Example

```
USE MAILLIST
SCAN FOR State = "CA"
```

```
   IF Active = "N"     && skip records where Active = "N"
      LOOP
   ENDIF
   ? Lname, Fname
   REPLACE Printed WITH "Y"
ENDSCAN    && automatically go to next record
```

See also DO WHILE

SCATTER

SCATTER [FIELDS *field list*] [MEMO] TO *array* | TO *array* BLANK | MEMVAR | MEMVAR BLANK

Description This command stores the values of the fields in the current record to an array or group of memory variables.

Operational rules When scattering to an array, each array element represents a field. When scattering to a memory variable, FoxPro takes care of making sure each field gets saved. This command is very useful in programs for editing records in a data file. Before the edit session, SCATTER the record to a memory variable. Then, if the user exits with a key defined as the "abort" key, use the GATHER command to set all fields back to their previous values.

Use the FIELDS *field list* option to limit the fields to be scattered. Use the BLANK option to create a set of memory variables that do not contain the entries from the record, but instead are the same type and length of each field in the record. The value of each of these variables will be "blank." In other words, numeric variables will be zero, character variables will be spaces, logicals will be .F., and dates will be { / / }.

The contents of a memo field can also be scattered to memory using the MEMO clause. If the content of a memo field is too large to fit into the available memory, FoxPro will issue an "Insufficient memory" error and ignore the entire SCATTER command. If a memo field is not scattered its memory variable or array element is set to .F.

To reference a database field rather than its value in memory, preface the field name with the database alias and a period (i.e., Contacts.Name). To reference a value in memory rather than a database field, preface the variable name with "m" and a period (i.e., m.Name).

Example

```
USE MAILLIST
SCATTER MEMVAR
@ 3,1 SAY "Database of Clients"
@ $,60 SAY "Press ESC to Abort"
@ 5,1 SAY "Enter Last Name" GET m.Lname PICTURE "@!"
@ 5,50 SAY "First Name" GET m.Fname PICTURE "@!"
@ $+2,1 SAY "Address:" GET Address
@ $+1,1 SAY " City:" GET m.City
@ $,$+1 SAY " State:" GET m.State PICTURE "@!"
@ $,$+1 SAY "Zip:" GET m.Zip PICTURE "99999"
READ
IF LASTKEY() != 27
```

```
   GATHER MEMVAR
ENDIF
```

See also GATHER

SCROLL

SCROLL *row1, col1, row2, col2, expN1* [, *expN2*]

Description This command scrolls the area of a window to a specified location.

Operational rules The coordinates *row1*, *col1* define the upper left corner of the region, and *row2*, *col2* is the bottom right corner. *expN* defines how many lines are to be scrolled. If this parameter is positive, the region scrolls up. If it is negative, the region scrolls down.

SCROLL defaults to scrolling vertically. To scroll horizontally, include a second numeric expression, *expN2*. If this parameter is positive, the region scrolls *expN2* characters right. If it is negative, the region scrolls *expN2* characters left.

Example

```
SCROLL 1,0, 10, 50, 3
See also  MOVE WINDOW
```

SEEK

SEEK *expression*

Description This command searches the current database and moves to the first record that matches *expression.*

Operational rules The SEEK command uses the master index to look for expression. The expression must be of the same type as the key expression of the master index. If a match is found, the record pointer moves to that record. If no records match, FOUND( ) is set to false, and the record pointer is moved to the end of the file (EOF( ) is true).

If SET EXACT is OFF, the expression does not have to be complete. For instance, the command SEEK "S" will find the first record in the index that begins with S. If SET EXACT is ON, the expression must match exactly. If SET NEAR is ON and no match is found, the record pointer is placed at the first record whose key closely matches the expression.

Example

```
USE MAILLIST ORDER Mlname
SEEK "Smith"
Record 2
Mname = "Brown"
SEEK Mname
Record 7
```

See also FIND

SELECT

SELECT *expN|expC*

Description This command activates a database work area.

Operational rules FoxPro opens a database file in a "work area." Up to 25 database files can be opened at a time in the Standard version and 225 in the extended version. Work areas that are not in use are identified by numbers (1 through 25[225]); areas that are in use can be identified by numbers or the alias of the database in use.

The usual process for working with multiple files is to SELECT each work area and open a database in that work area with the USE command. To change the current work area, simply call the SELECT command where *expN* is the work area number or *expC* is the database alias.

To access fields from a database in another work area, precede the field name with the work area number or alias name and a period (.). The USE command supports an optional IN clause that allows you to specify the work area in which to open a database.

Example

```
SELECT A
USE MAILLIST
SELECT B
USE STATES
? A.Lname, A.Fname, State
Smith   Joe   California
SELECT A
SKIP
? Lname, Fname, B.State
Brown   Sue   California
```

See also USE

SELECT (SQL)

```
SELECT [ALL|DISTINCT] [alias.]item [AS column_name] [,
[alias.]item [AS column_name] ...] FROM database list [alias]]
[[INTO destination]|[TO FILE filename [ADDITIVE]|TO PRINTER
[PROMPT]|TO SCREEN]] [PREFERENCE name] [NOCONSOLE] [PLAIN]
[NOWAIT] [WHERE expL [AND expL ...] [AND|OR expL [AND|OR expL
...]]] [GROUP BY expression] [HAVING expL] [UNION [ALL] SELECT
command] [ORDER BY expression [ASC|DESC] [, expression
[ASC|DESC] ...]]
```

Description This is used to query databases and retrieve data.

Operational rules The SELECT command is an SQL (Structured Query Language) command. Because the SELECT command is very extensive, FoxPro has an RQBE window, which helps you put together the pieces of the command. See chapter 9 for more information on the RQBE window.

The SELECT command begins with either SELECT ALL or SELECT item. This selects the fields and/or items which are to be output. The item list can include fields, constants, formulas, or one of the column functions (AVG(field), COUNT(field), SUM(field), etc.). If items are coming from more than one file, it is a good idea to preface them with their alias and a period (.) to distinguish common fields and variables. The SELECT command has a number of optional clauses and arguments that make it very powerful:

ALL|DISTINCT ALL is the default. This will cause all records matching the query to be displayed. Including DISTINCT will remove duplicate records from the result. DISTINCT can only be used once per SELECT clause.

FROM *database list* This clause lists the database(s) to be used in the query. If a file isn't open, SELECT opens it in a work area. The file remains open when the SELECT command is complete. *alias* is a temporary name for a database specified within the *database list*. If an alias is used, it must be used for the entire SELECT statement.

INTO *destination* This clause determines where the result will be stored. If INTO is not used, the results are displayed in a Browse window. If both INTO and TO are used, TO is ignored. When INTO is used, the output is not displayed. The destination can be:

ARRAY *array* Memory variable array.

CURSOR *database* A temporary database named database. The temporary database remains open and can be used and manipulated, but it is erased when it is closed.

DBF *filename* | TABLE *filename* Outputs the results to a .DBF file named filename.

TO Use TO and not INTO to send the result to:

***filename* [ADDITIVE]** *filename* is an ASCII file. Include the ADDITIVE keyword if appending to the file that already exists.

PRINTER Sends the results to the printer. When sending output to the printer, the optional PROMPT keyword can be used to access the Windows Printer Setup dialog before printing.

SCREEN Displays the result on the FoxPro desktop screen if the NOCONSOLE option is not used.

PREFERENCE *name* Uses the Browse screen settings and attributes saved last time with the PREFERENCE clause. If PREFERENCE *name* does not exist, it will be created and saved in the current resource file.

NOWAIT When called from a program, the program continues executing after the results are displayed or sent to a file.

NOCONSOLE Prevents the result from displaying on the current output window.

PLAIN Prevents column headings from being displayed in the output.

WHERE *expL* The WHERE clause is used for two purposes: to join multiple databases in a query and to filter records involved in the query. If multiple databases are involved in the query, the WHERE *expL* expression must be used to establish a relation between the databases. The expression *expL* specifies the linking fields from each database. For instance, if Mail.dbf is linked to Statenam.dbf by the fields Mail.Statecod and Statenam.State, *expL* would be Mail.Statecod = Statenam.State. You can set more than one relationship by separating join conditions with the word AND keyword. If multiple databases are involved in the query and there is no join condition, every field in the first database is joined with every field in the second database. This could result in a time consuming effort. If only one database is involved in the query the WHERE *expL* clause is used to determine which records are involved in the query (i.e., a filter). A SELECT query can use as many filters as necessary provided each one is separated by the AND or OR operator. Filter conditions can use the normal comparison operators (=, <, >, <>, !, etc.). But they can also use the following operators:

- ALL (subquery)
- ANY (*subquery*) or SOME (*subquery*)
- BETWEEN *startrange* AND *endrange*
- EXISTS (*subquery*)
- IN (*valueset*)
- IN (*subquery*)
- LIKE *subquery*

The last five selections can be preceded with NOT to negate the criteria. Set more than one relationship by separating conditions with either AND or OR. You can also use HAVING in place of the WHERE keyword.

A subquery is a SELECT within a SELECT. When the word ALL is used, the field must meet the query for all values generated by the subquery. When the word ANY or SOME is used, the field just has to match one of the values generated by the subquery. The word EXISTS evaluates as True unless the subquery is the null set. The word IN is true if the field is found within the value set (values separated with commas) or subquery. LIKE can use the wild card characters % (single unknown character) and "?" (group of unknown characters) in the comparison.

GROUP BY *expression* This clause groups the output results of the query. The *expression* can be a numeric expression indicating the location of the column in the output database (from left to right is 1).

ORDER BY *expression* [ASC|DESC] Using the ORDER BY clause will sort the query option based on the expression. The *expression* can contain either a field from the FROM or a numeric expression indicating the location of the column in the output database (from left to right is 1). Use the optional DESC key word to order the results in descending order.

Examples

```
SELECT company.name, company.city;
   FROM company;
   HAVING company.state = "CA"
```

Displays all Californian companies and their cities from the COMPANY database.

```
SELECT company.name, company.city;
   FROM company INTO TABLE calcomp
```

Creates a database named calcomp.dbf of all Californian companies and their cities.

```
SELECT name, city;
   FROM company ORDER BY city, company WHERE state = "CA"
```

Displays all Californian companies sorted alphabetically within city.

```
SELECT company.name, taxes.rate;
   FROM company,taxes;
   WHERE company.city = taxes.city AND company.state = "CA"
```

Displays all Californian companies and their tax rate by looking up their city's tax rate in taxes.dbf.

```
SELECT company.name ;
   FROM company ;
   WHERE company.type IN("FINANCE","REAL ESTATE","LAW FIRM")
```

Displays all companies that have a type field of FINANCE, REAL ESTATE, or LAW FIRM.

```
SELECT company.name, taxes.rate ;
   FROM company,taxes ;
   WHERE company.city = taxes.city;
   AND taxes.rate BETWEEN .06 AND .065
```

Displays all companies and their tax rates for cities with rates between .06 and .065.

```
SELECT company.name ;
   FROM company ;
   WHERE company.city IN (SELECT company.city FROM company
   WHERE company.type = "LAW FIRM")
```

Displays all companies that are in a city where there is a LAW FIRM.

See also Chapter 8, Using the RQBE Window and SQL, INSERT (SQL)

SET

```
SET
```

Description This command opens the View window.

Operational rules The SET command can be used to open the FoxPro View window, which is a useful tool to open databases and set relations.

See also SET VIEW

SET COMMANDS

See the next chapter for details regarding all of the FoxPro SET commands.

SHOW GET

SHOW GET *object* [, *expN* [PROMPT *expC*]] [ENABLE|DISABLE] [LEVEL *expN*] [COLOR SCHEME *expN*|COLOR *color pair*]

Description This command redisplays a single GET field or object.

Operational rules GET objects (memory variables, field names, push buttons, pop-ups, etc.) often need to be redisplayed when their values are changed. The SHOW GET command is used to redisplay the new value of the GET. When a field or control is redisplayed you can change many of its characteristics such as the display prompt, disable or enable the GET, or change the color.

Unlike the SHOW GETS command, which changes all current GET objects, the SHOW GET command can only change one object. The object to change is specified with *object*. If the GET object is a radio, invisible, or push button, you can specify which button to change with *object*, *expN*.

Use the PROMPT clause to change the onscreen prompt of the object. PROMPT can only be used with radio and push buttons, and check boxes. The object will be changed to *expC*. If the GET object is a picture radio button, push button, or check box, you can specify a bitmap (.BMP) picture file to change the prompt. A total of three files can be included in *expC*, with each file name separated by a comma. The first picture is used when the GET object is enabled. The second picture is used when the GET object is selected. The third picture is used when the GET object is disabled.

Multiple READ levels can occur in FoxPro. This happens when a READ is issued and then another is issued without clearing the first READ. The SHOW GET command always defaults to the current READ level. To change a GET object of a READ level other than the current one, use the LEVEL option and specify *expN* as the READ level.

The COLOR *color pair* and COLOR SCHEME *expN* clauses allow you to set your own colors for the redisplayed object. Including ENABLE allows the redisplayed object to be selected. DISABLE prevents the object from being selected, and the object is displayed with the disabled color pair.

Example In the example below, a user-defined function disables a field when a person's record is marked Inactive.

```
@ 1,30 SAY "Student's Individual Record"
@ 3,1 SAY "Name: " GET Name
@ 5,1 SAY "Inactive? " GET Activ PICTURE "Y" VALID CHKACT()
@ 7,1 SAY "Grade: " GET Grade
READ CYCLE

FUNCTION chkact
IF Activ = "N"
   SHOW GET Grade DISABLE
ENDIF
RETURN
```

See also @ ... SAY/GET, SHOW GETS

SHOW GETS

SHOW GETS [ENABLE|DISABLE] [LEVEL *expN*] [OFF|ONLY] [WINDOW *window name*] [LOCK] [COLOR SCHEME *expN*|COLOR *color pair*]

Description This command redisplays all GET fields and objects of a READ.

Operational rules GET objects (memory variables, field names, push buttons, pop-ups, etc.) often need to be redisplayed when their values are changed. The SHOW GETS command is used to redisplay the new values of GETs.

The COLOR *color pair* and COLOR SCHEME *expN* clauses allow you to set your own colors for the redisplayed objects. Including ENABLE allows the redisplayed objects to be chosen. DISABLE prevents any of them from being chosen, and the objects are displayed with the disabled color pair.

Multiple READ levels can occur in FoxPro. This happens when a READ is issued and then another without clearing the first READ. The SHOW GETS command always defaults to the current READ level. To change the GET objects of a READ level other than the current one, use the LEVEL option and specify *expN* as the READ level.

When the SHOW GET command is issued, FoxPro does two things: updates all GET objects of the current READ (unless LEVEL *expN* is specified) and executes any program code defined in the READ SHOW clause. If the READ SHOW procedure does not need to be executed when updating GET objects, use the ONLY clause. This will cause FoxPro to only update all current GET objects. The OFF clause does exactly the opposite: it only executes the READ SHOW procedure and does not update current GET objects. Use the WINDOW *window name* clause to redisplay the objects in a particular window. Use the SHOW GET or SHOW OBJECT commands to redisplay a single GET object.

If a database has been opened for shared use (multi-user), the READ command may attempt to lock the record involved with the READ. The SHOW GETS command respects the READ command in locking records. If the READ command was issued with LOCK, then SHOW GETS will attempt to lock the record. If the READ command was issued with NOLOCK and you need to lock the record, use the optional LOCK clause with the SHOW GET command. The SHOW GET LOCK command will override a READ NOLOCK command.

Example In the example below, a user-defined function disables all fields when a person's record is marked Inactive.

```
@ 1,30 SAY "Student's Individual Record"
@ 3,1 SAY "Name: " GET Name
@ 5,1 SAY "Inactive? " GET Activ PICTURE "Y" VALID CHKACT()
@ 7,1 SAY "Grade: " GET Grade
READ CYCLE

FUNCTION chkact
IF Activ = "N"
   SHOW GETS DISABLE
ENDIF
RETURN
```

See also @ ... SAY/GET, SHOW GET

SHOW MENU

`SHOW MENU` *`menu name`* `[,` *`menu name2`* `...]|ALL [PAD` *`pad name`*`] [SAVE]`

Description This command displays a defined menu without activating it.

Operational rules The menu displays on the screen, but you cannot move the cursor through it or make selections. The optional PAD *pad name* defines the pad that is highlighted. You can show all defined yet inactive menus with the ALL keyword, or specify menus with *menu name*. See the DEFINE MENU section for an example of a program that sets up the menu.

See also DEFINE MENU

SHOW OBJECT

```
SHOW OBJECT expN [ENABLE|DISABLE] [LEVEL expN] [PROMPT expC]
[COLOR SCHEME expN|COLOR color pair]
```

Description This command redisplays a single GET object.

Operational rules Each GET that is issued for a particular READ is considered an object. However if the GET is an invisible, push or radio button, each option of the button is an object. For instance, if the following GET command is issued:

```
@ 17,1 GET morder FUNCTION "*H \<Alpha;\!\<Zip;\<Class"
```

The variable *morder* is one GET but contains three push button objects. SHOW OBJECT is identical to SHOW GET except that each object must be referenced by *expN*, where SHOW GET can be referenced by the GET variable. GET objects are numbered in the order that the cursor passes through them in a READ statement. *expN* must match the GET object's number.

The optional PROMPT *expC* clause is to change the onscreen prompt of push buttons, radio buttons, or check boxes. The object will be changed to *expC*. If the GET object is a picture radio button, push button, or check box, you can specify a bitmap (.BMP) picture file to change the prompt. A total of three files can be included in *expC*, with each file name separated by a comma. The first picture is used when the GET object is enabled. The second picture is used when the GET object is selected. The third file is used when the GET object is disabled.

The COLOR *color pair* and COLOR SCHEME *expN* clauses allow you to set your own colors for the redisplayed object. Including ENABLE allows the redisplayed object to be selected. DISABLE prevents the object from being selected, and the object is displayed with the disabled color pair.

Multiple READ levels can occur in FoxPro. This happens when a READ is issued and then another without clearing the first READ. The SHOW OBJECT command always defaults to the current READ level. To change a GET object of a READ level other than the current one, use the LEVEL option and specify *expN* as the READ level. Use the SHOW GETS command to redisplay all GET objects. Use SHOW GET *var* to refer to a GET object by the object's name.

Example In the example below, a user-defined function disables the field after the user has passed through it:

```
@ 2,1 SAY "Taxable? " GET Mtax VALID DISTAX()
@3,1 SAY "Rate" GET Mrate
READ CYCLE

FUNCTION distax
IF Mtax = "N"
   SHOW OBJECT 2 DISABLE
ENDIF
RETURN
```

See also @ ... SAY/GET, SHOW GET

SHOW POPUP

SHOW POPUP *popup name* [, *popup name2* ...] | ALL [SAVE]

Description This command displays a defined pop-up menu without activating it.

Operational rules The pop-up displays on the screen, but you cannot move the cursor through it or make selections. This command is most often used when designing menus so you can test the appearance of your pop-up menu. See the DEFINE POPUP section for an example of a program that sets up the pop-up menu.

See also DEFINE POPUP

SHOW WINDOW

SHOW WINDOW *window list* | ALL[IN [WINDOW] *window name*|IN SCREEN] [REFRESH] [TOP|BOTTOM|SAME]

Description This command displays a defined window without activating it.

Operational rules The SHOW WINDOW is used to display defined windows that are hidden or have not been activated. User-defined windows are created with the DEFINE WINDOW command and activated for output with ACTIVATE WINDOW. If windows are defined as hidden or haven't been activated, SHOW WINDOW displays the windows without activating them.

You can specify the windows to show in *window list*. Each specified window must be separated by a comma (,). You can also use this command to rearrange how the windows lay over each other. The TOP (over all others), BOTTOM (behind all others), and SAME (at previous position) clauses define which layer the window should be on.

You can place a list of window names in the parameter *window name*, or use the keyword ALL to display all defined windows. The REFRESH clause can be used to update Browse windows and memo field editing windows in a network environment.

See also DEFINE WINDOW

SIZE POPUP

SIZE POPUP *popup name* TO *expN1*, *expN2*|BY *expN3*, *expN4*

Description This command resizes a previously defined pop-up.

Operational rules The SIZE POPUP command allows you to change the size of the pop-up without having to issue the DEFINE POPUP command again. The height is measured in rows and the width in columns.

The TO *expN1*, *expN2* clause can be replaced with BY *expN3*, *expN4*. This changes the pop-up relative to its current size. If the argument(s) is positive, the pop-up size increases; if it is negative, the pop-up size decreases. See the DEFINE POPUP section for an example of a program that sets up a pop-up menu.

See also DEFINE POPUP

SKIP

```
SKIP [expN1] [IN expN2 | expC]
```

Description This command is used to move the record pointer in a database.

Operational rules If the database is not indexed, SKIP simply moves to the next record number. If the database is indexed, this is the next record in the index.

The optional *expN1* causes the pointer to skip *expN1* records. The number can be either positive, which causes it to move forward, or negative, which causes it to move backwards. If the pointer is at the bottom record and a SKIP is issued, the record pointer will move to the end of file, and EOF( ) will be true (.T.). If the pointer is at the top record and a SKIP –1 is issued, the record pointer moves to the beginning of file, and BOF( ) will be true (.T.).

The SET FILTER and SET DELETED ON commands are respected by the SKIP command. Use the IN *expN2|expC* alias option to skip in a work area other than the current one, where *expN2* is the work area number and *expC* is the database alias.

Example

```
USE MAILLIST
SKIP
Record 2
SKIP 2
Record 4
SKIP -1
Record 3
```

See also GO|GOTO

SORT

```
SORT TO filename ON field [/A|/D] [/C] [ASCENDING |DESCENDING]
[scope] [FOR expL] [WHILE expL] [FIELDS field list] [NOOPTIMIZE]
```

Description This command creates a new database file and sorts the records.

Operational rules The SORT command copies the data file, so it uses up the same amount of space. If records are added to the new sorted file, they are not maintained in the sorted order.

You can sort a file on multiple fields by specifying the fields with FIELDS *field list*. Fields may be followed by the following arguments:

- /A Sort in ascending order.
- /D Sort in descending order.
- /C Ignore differences between upper and lowercase.

To combine these arguments, use only one slash (for example, /DC). The arguments ASCENDING and DESCENDING are then used for all fields that do not have a slash argument. Use the optional FOR *expL*, WHILE *expL*, and *scope* arguments to process only a subset of the data file. Use the optional NOOPTIMIZE clause to disable Rushmore when sorting a database.

Examples The following commands each create a file named MNAME.DBF, which is a sorted version of the current file:

```
SORT TO Mname ON Lname
SORT TO Mname ON Lname, Fname /C
SORT TO Mname ON Zip /A, Amount /D
SORT TO Mname ON Lname FOR State = "CA"
```

See also INDEX

STORE

STORE *expr* TO *memvar list|array list*

Description This command creates and/or changes the value of a memory variable or array.

Operational rules Memory variables and arrays are most often used in programs, although they can be used from the command window. Memory variables are much like fields, in that they can be character, numeric, logical, or data type. The data type of a memory variable is established by its value. A variable's name can be from 1 to 10 characters. However, memory variables are not stored in a file, so they are lost when the FoxPro session is over.

The = command is equivalent to the STORE command, except you can only store a value to one memory variable at a time with =. STORE accepts either a memory variable, a memory variable list or an array list. These commands can also be used to set the values of array elements; however, the array must already have been initialized with the DECLARE or DIMENSION command.

Examples

```
Mtot = 0
Mtot = Mtot + 1
STORE "Smith" TO Mname
STORE Lname TO Mname
STORE 0 TO Gtot, Mtot, Ltot
STORE 500 TO Marray(1,2)
```

See also DECLARE =

SUM

SUM [*expr list*] [*scope*] [FOR *expL*] [WHILE *expL*] [TO *memvar list*|TO ARRAY *array*] [NOOPTIMIZE]

Description This command provides the totals of the numeric fields of a data file.

Operational rules If no arguments are provided, FoxPro displays the sum total of each numeric field in the database. You can provide an *expr* list to specify the field(s) to be summed.

To create memory variables whose values are the sums, use the TO *memvar list* or TO ARRAY *array*. When summing to an array, the array must be declared as single dimension, and each field in the field list updates the next row. You can use the optional FOR *expL*, WHILE *expL*, and *scope* arguments to include only a subset of the records in the calculation. Use the optional NOOPTIMIZE clause to disable Rushmore when summing a database.

Examples

```
SUM
SUM Wage, Bonus to Mwage, Mbon
SUM Wage TO Mwage FOR State = "CA"
SUM Wage, Bonus, Commsion TO ARRAY Mamount
```

The last example assumes that Mamount has been declared as a one-dimensional array. After the SUM, Mamount(1) is equal to the total of the Wage field, Mamount(2) is equal to the total of Bonus, etc.

See also DECLARE

SUSPEND

```
SUSPEND
```

Description This command suspends program execution.

Operational rules When a program encounters an error, it will ask the user whether they want to Cancel, Suspend, or Ignore. Using the SUSPEND command in programs is equivalent to when the user chooses Suspend at the error message. All memory variables still exist, as does the file status. At this point, files and variables can be manipulated. If the user then chooses RESUME, the program resumes processing at the next command line.

SUSPEND can be placed within a program to make it return to the command window. The CANCEL command also halts the program, but memory variables will be cleared, and the program cannot resume processing.

See also RESUME

TEXT ... ENDTEXT

```
TEXT
     expression
ENDTEXT
```

Description This command displays all text entered between the TEXT and ENDTEXT commands.

Operational rules The TEXT command is the easiest command for printing text on the screen or to a printer. Simply enter the text as you want it displayed. You do not need to surround character strings with quote marks, as you do with the ? command.

Memory variables, expressions, and functions are only evaluated if SET TEXTMERGE is ON; otherwise all entries are interpreted literally. When SET TEXTMERGE is ON, the delimiters defined with SET TEXTMERGE DELIMITERS must be used to surround expressions. The default delimiters are << and >>.

Text can also be output to a file opened or created with the FCREATE( ) or FOPEN( ) low-level file commands. If a file handle returned by FCREATE( ) or FOPEN( ) is stored to the _text system memory variable, output is directed to the corresponding low-level file.

Examples

```
TEXT
```

This is information that will display just as it looks. Notice that there are no quote marks around the strings or commands such as ? or ??.

Today's date is <<DATE( )>>
ENDTEXT

See also ?, \ and \\

TOTAL

```
TOTAL TO filename ON expr [FIELDS field list] [scope] [FOR
expL] [WHILE expL] [NOOPTIMIZE]
```

Description This command copies a database to a second database file that contains subtotals of each numeric field.

Operational rules Unless the optional FIELDS *fields list* clause is included, the new file will have the same structure as the active file. For each unique key-indexed field in the active file, you will have one record in the new file. The active file must be sorted or indexed by a key field before issuing the command.

The numeric fields in the new file contain the sum totals for each particular key. Character, date, and logical fields contain the information of the first record that matches the unique key. Memo fields are not copied to the new file.

You can use the optional FOR *expL*, WHILE *expL*, and *scope* arguments to include only a subset of the records in the new file. Use the optional NOOPTIMIZE clause to disable Rushmore when totaling a database.

Examples

```
USE Dues ORDER Member
? RECCOUNT( )
20
TOTAL ON Membcode TO Totdues
USE Totdues
LIST Membcode, Dues
Record #   MEMBCODE   DUES
1          A01        200.00
2          A02        150.00
3          A12        -50.00
4          B03        100.00
5          B05        150.00
```

See also SUM

TYPE

```
TYPE filename1 [AUTO] [WRAP] [TO PRINTER [PROMPT]|TO FILE file-
name2] [NUMBER]
```

Description This command displays the contents of a file.

Operational rules The TYPE command works just like the TYPE command from DOS. It is most often used when displaying the contents of a program (.PRG) or text (.TXT) file.

The TYPE command can be used on any ASCII type file. Files that are not standard ASCII do not display clearly with the TYPE command.

If *filename1* contains tab characters, use the optional AUTO clause to indent text preceded by a tab. Including WRAP in the TYPE command will enable word wrapping when the file is displayed. When word wrapping is enabled, a word that is too long to fit at the end of a line is automatically moved to the next line.

TYPE output defaults to printing on the screen. Use the TO PRINTER option to print to the printer, or the TO FILE *filename2* to print to an ASCII file. When sending output to the printer, the optional PROMPT keyword can be used to access the Windows Printer Setup dialog before printing. The NUMBER clause numbers each line of the file. Page numbers, the current date, and the name of the file display at the top unless SET HEADING is OFF.

Examples

```
TYPE MAILLIST.PRG
TYPE MAILLIST.PRG TO PRINTER
TYPE MAILLIST.PRG TO WRAP PRINTER NUMBER
```

See also LIST FILES

UNLOCK

UNLOCK [IN *expN*|*expC*|ALL]

Description This command releases a locked database or record.

Operational rules Databases and records are locking with the LOCK command. Locking a database or record prevents another user from updating the file. Unlocking a record or file allows the record or file to be changed by other users.

If the UNLOCK command is issued without any arguments, FoxPro will unlock the current record. If any databases are related, unlocking a record does not unlock related records. Use the ALL keyword to release all locks in all open work areas. To unlock a record or file in another work area, use IN *expN*|*expC* where *expN* is the work area number and *expC* is the database alias.

See also RLOCK()
FLOCK()

UPDATE

UPDATE ON *field* FROM *expN*|*expC* REPLACE *field1* WITH *expr1* [, *field2* WITH *expr2* ...] [RANDOM]

Description This command performs a global find and replace on field while relating two files.

Operational rules The UPDATE command sets a relationship between the active file, where the replace will occur, and work area *expN* or alias *expC*. The two files must each have key field, and *expN*|*expC* must be indexed on that field. The active file must also be indexed on the field unless the RANDOM clause is included.

If there are multiple records with the same key in the active file, then only the first record that matches is updated.

Example

```
SELECT 1
USE Dues ORDER Member
LIST
Record #  MEMBCODE  DUES
1         A01       40.00
4         A01       60.00
2         A02       50.00
3         A12       50.00
5         A12       50.00
SELECT 2
USE Members ORDER Membcode
UPDATE ON Membcode FROM Dues REPLACE Totdues WITH totdues +
Dues
LIST
Record #  MEMBCODE  DUES
1         A01       100.00
4         A02       -50.00
2         A12       100.00
```

See also SET RELATION

USE

```
USE [filename|?] [IN expN1] [AGAIN] [INDEX index file list|?
[ORDER [expN2|idx file|[TAG] tag name [OF cdx file]
[ASCENDING|DESCENDING]]]] [ALIAS alias] [EXCLUSIVE] [SHARE]
[NOUPDATE]
```

Description This command opens a database (.DBF) file in a work area.

Operational rules The file is opened in the current work unless the IN *expN1* option is included. If a file is already open in that area, it is closed so that the new one can be opened. To close a file in a work area without opening a new file, issue USE without a file name.

The optional ? argument can be used in place of *filename*. FoxPro then provides a list of all .DBF files, which you can choose from. The following options are available for the USE command:

IN *expN1* Opens *filename* in work area *expN1*. USE ... IN 0 opens the database in the next available work area.

AGAIN Opens *filename* again if it is already open in another work area. This is useful for setting multiple relations to the same database file.

INDEX *index file list* Allows you to open index (.IDX and .CDX) files with the database file. The optional ? argument can be used in place of *index file list*. FoxPro then provides a list of all single and compound index files that you can choose from. Index files are numbered in the order that they are listed in *index file list*, tags in the order they were created. The first is the master. The master is the key order used for listings and with the SEEK command.

ORDER ***expN2|idx file|*****[TAG]** ***tag name*** **OF** ***cdx filename*** Determines the index file or tag that is to the controlling index. If no order is specified, the database will be in record order. An index can be referred to by its numerical order, file name, or tag name. *tag name* determines the tag name of the active compound index file that is to be master. *tag name* OF *cdx filename* determines the master tag name when there is more than one open compound index.

ASCENDING|DESCENDING Determines the order for the index specified with the ORDER clause.

ALIAS ***alias*** A database can be assigned an alias, or "handle", other than its DOS file name. If the alias is different than the file name, the alias must precede all commands that reference the database. If the database is being opened again or *alias* is already used, FoxPro will automatically assign it an alias based on the work area that the database is opened in. Work area aliases are assigned A through J and W11 through W25 (up to W225 in the Extended version). An alias name can consist of up to 10 characters.

EXCLUSIVE Opens the database so that no other users can access it. See SET EXCLUSIVE for more information on the exclusive use of databases.

SHARE Opens the database for shared use if SET EXCLUSIVE is ON. See SET EXCLUSIVE for more information on the exclusive use of databases.

NOUPDATE Prevents any changes to the database.

Example

```
USE MAILLIST ORDER MAILZIP DESCENDING
USE MAILLIST ORDER TAG ZIP
USE MAILLIST INDEX MAILNAME.IDX
USE MAILLIST IN 3
USE MAILLIST IN 3 EXCLUSIVE NOUPDATE
USE MAILLIST ALIAS MAIL IN 0
```

See also SELECT( ), INDEX

WAIT

`WAIT [expC] [TO memvar] [WINDOW [NOWAIT]] [CLEAR] [TIMEOUT expN]`

Description This command pauses the processing until a key is pressed.

Operational rules The WAIT command halts the program until the user presses a key. Use the TO *memvar* clause to create a character memory variable which stores the keyboard entry. If the optional prompt, *expC*, is not used, FoxPro displays Press any key to continue as the default message. To display no prompt, use the character string " " as the prompt. Prompts can be broken into multiple lines by placing a CHR(13) character at the end of each line.

Use the WINDOW keyword to display the message in a window in the upper right corner of the screen. Use WINDOW NOWAIT to display the message in a window that behaves like the FoxPro system messages. Pressing any key removes the window from the screen. NOWAIT does not discard the keystroke. TIMEOUT *expN* determines how many seconds can elapse without user input before the WAIT is terminated. TIMEOUT must be the last clause in the WAIT statement.

Examples

```
WAIT
WAIT "Do you want to print (Y/N)" TO PRN
WAIT " "
WAIT "Invalid Option Choice" WINDOW TIMEOUT 10
WAIT "You have the following options:" + CHR(13) + "1 for this"
+ ;
   CHR(13) + "2 for that"
```

See also ACCEPT

ZAP

`ZAP`

Description This command erases all records from the database file.

Operational rules Use ZAP in place of the commands DELETE ALL and PACK. ZAP is much faster and provides the verification question Zap ?. Use caution as the records of a zapped database cannot be retrieved.

See also DELETE, PACK

ZOOM WINDOW

ZOOM WINDOW *window name* MIN|MAX|NORM [AT *row1, col1*|FROM *row2, col2* [SIZE *expN1, expN2*|TO *row3, col3*]]

Description This command resizes a system or user-defined window.

Operational rules This command allows you to change the size of a system window (command, browse, text editing, etc.) or a window that you have created with DEFINE WINDOW. It is possible to place a window within another window. The inside window will take on all characteristics of the outer window. The larger window is called the parent, the smaller window the child. The child window must be smaller than the parent, and stay within the parent window's boundaries. The size can be one of a variety of size keywords. The keywords are:

MIN Reduces the window to an icon. This is the same as selecting Minimize from a window control menu.

MAX Expands to the full screen, (or if a child window, the full size of the parent).

NORM Returns a window to its normal size.

SIZE *expN1, expN2* Sizes the window to an *expN1* measured in rows, and *expN2* measured in columns.

The optional AT *row1, col1* and FROM *row2, col2* clauses allow you to move the window's location at the same time you change the size. The *row1, col1* represents the placement of the window's upper left corner. This clause performs the same operation as the MOVE WINDOW command. The AT and FROM clauses are ignored when the MIN or MAX clauses are used.

The clause TO *row3*, *col3* represents the placement of the window's bottom right corner. This clause is most often used in conjunction with the AT or FROM clauses.

Examples

```
ZOOM WINDOW Mwind MAX
ZOOM WINDOW Mwind SIZE 5,70 AT 0,0
```

3
FoxPro SET commands

The FoxPro SET commands are a special group of commands that change many of the environment settings, and control the way other commands, variables, and arrays are evaluated. The SET commands can be issued from the command window or from a program. In addition, the command SET by itself displays the View window, which allows you to control the state of open database files and the FoxPro environment, such as default drives and path settings.

In this chapter, the SET commands are listed in alphabetical order describing the proper syntax use of each. Each command is followed by a short description, and then details for using it. The conventions used in this chapter are:

- All commands and optional clauses are displayed in uppercase.
- All optional clauses are enclosed in square brackets, [ ].
- Multiple-choice clauses are separated by a pipe, |. Only one option can be used.
- All required and optional arguments appear in lowercase italic. The expression type of each parameter is very important. Character expressions are identified by *expC*, numeric by *row*, *col*, and *expN*, date by *expD*, and logical by *expL*. Parameters defined by *filename* must contain a valid DOS directory, path, and file name. Any other type of parameter can be any valid FoxPro expression. Some commands require more than one parameter of the same type. These are identified sequentially.
- Some commands support an indefinite list of parameters that can be repeated. These are followed by ellipses (...).
- The *scope* parameter accepts one of the following: ALL, NEXT *expN*, RECORD *expN*, and REST.

SET ALTERNATE

```
SET ALTERNATE ON|OFF
SET ALTERNATE TO [filename [ADDITIVE]]
```

Description This command sends output created with the ?, ??, LIST or DISPLAY commands to a text file.

Operational rules The SET ALTERNATE command is a two-step process. A text file must first be opened using SET ALTERNATE TO *filename*, followed by SET ALTER-

NATE ON. The SET ALTERNATE file is given the extension of .TXT if none is provided in *filename*. The output overwrites any data previously in the file; however, this can be avoided by using the ADDITIVE clause with SET ALTERNATE TO *filename*.

Through the command SET ALTERNATE OFF, the text file can remain open, although no output is saved to it. The commands CLOSE ALTERNATE or SET ALTERNATE TO with no file name closes the text file. Be sure to close the text file before using the file. The text file is a standard ASCII file that can be modified with the MODIFY COMMAND or MODIFY FILE command or a word processor. The default setting is OFF.

See also CLOSE, SET( )

SET ANSI

```
SET ANSI ON|OFF
```

Description This command controls how SQL strings are compared.

Operational rules When SQL makes comparisons between strings, it compares character by character until the shorter of the two strings is exhausted. However, if SET ANSI is ON, the shorter string is padded with blanks for the comparison. Using the == operator in a SELECT statement performs the same function as SET ANSI ON.

For example, if SET ANSI is ON, the following is false (.F.) because it pads the left expression with blanks:

```
"San" = "San Diego"
```

If SET ANSI is OFF, the following is true (.T.), because it stops the comparison at the third character:

```
"San" = "San Diego"
```

The default setting is ON.

See also SELECT (SQL), SET()

SET AUTOSAVE

```
SET AUTOSAVE ON|OFF
```

Description This command controls whether or not FoxPro flushes data buffers to disk.

Operational rules If SET AUTOSAVE is ON FoxPro saves each record to the disk after alterations have been made, thus reducing possibility of lost data. When AUTOSAVE is OFF, records are saved to the disk as the buffer is filled. The default setting is OFF.

See also FLUSH, SET()

SET BELL

```
SET BELL ON|OFF
SET BELL TO [frequency, duration]
```

Description The command controls the speaker bell and sound pitch.

Operational rules If SET BELL is ON, FoxPro will sound a "tone" at the following events:

- When you attempt to move outside a modal dialog.
- When a GET field is filled.
- An error occurs.

If SET BELL is OFF, no tone is heard. The *frequency* adjustment changes the pitch of the bell. It might be any number between 19 and 10,000 hertz. The default is 512 hertz. The *duration* adjustment changes the length of the bell. It can be any number between 1 and 19. The default is 2.

To sound a Windows waveform file, place the name of the file or a sound from the sounds section of the computer's WIN.INI file in *frequency* and specify 0 in the *duration* parameter. The default setting is ON.

Examples

```
SET BELL ON
SET BELL TO 600,10
SET BELL TO "C:\WINDOWS\LAFF.WAV"
```

See also SET()

SET BLOCKSIZE

```
SET BLOCKSIZE TO expN
```

Description This command controls how memo field files (.FPT) are stored on disk.

Operational rules Disk space is allocated for a memo field based on the value of *expN*. If *expN* is an integer between 1 and 32, disk space for the storage of memo fields is allocated in blocks of *expN* * 512 bytes. If *expN* is greater than 32, disk space is allocated in blocks of *expN* bytes. The size of memo field files can be shortened considerably if the BLOCKSIZE setting is greater than 32.

You can reset the BLOCKSIZE of a current file by changing the value of BLOCKSIZE and then using the COPY command to create a new database file. The new memo field file will be created using the current BLOCKSIZE setting. The default setting is 64.

See also PACK, SET()

SET BORDER

```
SET BORDER TO [SINGLE|DOUBLE|PANEL|NONE]
```

Description This command determines the borders for boxes, pop-ups and windows.

Operational rules The SET BORDER command is used to override the default border settings. The available border choices are:

SINGLE	Creates a single-line border.
DOUBLE	Creates a wide border.
PANEL	Creates a wide border.
NONE	Creates no border.

Issuing the command SET BORDER TO resets all default borders. The default setting is SINGLE.

See also @ ... BOX, @ ... TO, DEFINE WINDOW, SET()

SET BRSTATUS

```
SET BRSTATUS ON|OFF
```

Description This command controls the display of the Browse status bar.

Operational rules If SET BRSTATUS is ON and SET STATUS BAR is OFF, a DOS-style status bar showing current drive, current database, current record/total record and Insert, NumLock, and CapsLock settings is displayed. The status will not be displayed if SET BRSTATUS is OFF or if SET STATUS BAR is ON. The default setting is OFF.

See also SET STATUS BAR, SET STATUS, SET()

SET CARRY

```
SET CARRY ON|OFF
SET CARRY TO [field list [ADDITIVE]]
```

Description This command controls whether or not FoxPro carries data forward from the current record to a new record.

Operational rules If SET CARRY is ON, a new record created with the APPEND or INSERT command will bring forward all data in all fields from the current record to the new record. By default all fields will be carried forward. You can specify which fields to carry with SET CARRY TO *field list*. Only those fields specified in *field list* will be carried. Use the ADDITIVE clause to add on to the fields already specified with SET CARRY TO *field list*.

SET CARRY TO without an argument restores the default condition where all fields are updated. If SET CARRY is OFF, the SET CARRY TO command automatically sets CARRY to ON as well as defines the field list. The SET CARRY setting affects all open databases while the SET CARRY TO *field list* is specific to each work area. The default setting is OFF.

See also APPEND, SET()

SET CENTURY

```
SET CENTURY ON|OFF
```

Description This command controls the display and entry of the century in date type fields.

Operational rules If SET CENTURY is ON, all date type fields will be displayed with four digits. The default setting is OFF.

Examples

```
SET CENTURY ON
? DATE()
03/10/1993
```

```
SET CENTURY OFF
? DATE()
03/10/93
```

See also DATE(), YEAR(), SET()

SET CLEAR

```
SET CLEAR ON|OFF
```

Description This command controls whether the screen is cleared after quitting FoxPro and setting a format screen.

Operational rules The two commands this setting affects are QUIT and SET FORMAT TO. If SET CLEAR is OFF, the format screen superimposes on the current screen instead of clearing it. The default setting is ON.

See also CLEAR, SET()

SET CLOCK

```
SET CLOCK ON|OFF|STATUS
SET CLOCK TO [row,col]
```

Description This command controls the display and settings of the system clock on the screen.

Operational rules If SET CLOCK is ON FoxPro will display the system time at the top right corner of the screen. If SET CLOCK is STATUS the time is displayed in the Windows-style status bar at the bottom of the screen. You can also change the location of the clock by specifying a *row* and *col* position. Issuing SET CLOCK TO without any arguments restores the clock display to its default position. The clock format is hour:minutes:seconds.

See also SET HOURS, SET()

SET COLLATE

```
SET COLLATE TO expC
```

Description This command determines how FoxPro sorts and indexes a database file.

Operational rules When indexing or sorting a database, the setting of SET COLLATE determines the order of the records. FoxPro supports a variety of code paging and collation sequences to provide proper display and indexing of international characters. Use *expC* to specify the collation sequence. The following collating sequences are available.

General Used for English, Spanish and European languages. A GENERAL collation sequence removes the need to index on the UPPER() case value of a character field since no distinction is made between uppercase or lowercase letters.

Machine Standard setting for earlier versions of FoxPro and other Xbase products. Characters are ordered as they appear in the current code page. Use MACHINE when indexing with the UPPER() or LOWER() functions.

Spanish Used for traditional Spanish. When you specify SPANISH, "ch" is a single letter that sorts between "c" and "d," and "ll" sorts between "l" and "m."

Dutch Used for Dutch.

Iceland Used for Icelandic

Nordan Used for Norwegian and Danish

Swefin Used for Swedish and Finnish

When changing a collation sequence with the SET COLLATE command, only databases that are sorted or indexed after the command is issued are affected. If you create a single index file (.IDX) and SET COLLATE is TO MACHINE, a compact .IDX file is created. See chapter 1 for more information on creating index files.

You must specify a CODEPAGE sequence in your configuration file to use the SET COLLATE command. If you have not specified a CODEPAGE sequence in your configuration file a "To use this feature..." message appears. The default configuration file is normally CONFIG.FPW.

Example This example shows the difference between indexing with the GENERAL and MACHINE collation sequences.

```
USE NAMES
LIST
Record#  NAME
      1  ccC
      2  AaA
      3  AAA
      4  aaa
      5  AAAb
      6  Cbc
      7  BBBA
      8  aAa
      9  bbba

SET COLLATE TO "MACHINE"
INDEX ON name ORDER name
LIST
Record#  NAME
      3  AAA
      5  AAAb
      2  AaA
      7  BBBA
      6  Cbc
      8  aAa
      4  aaa
      9  bbba
      1  ccC
SEEK "b"
? RECNO()
9

SET COLLATE TO "GENERAL"
INDEX ON name ORDER name
LIST
```

```
Record#  NAME
      2  AaA
      3  AAA
      4  aaa
      8  aAa
      5  AAAb
      7  BBBA
      9  bbba
      6  Cbc
      1  ccC
SEEK "b"
? RECNO()
7
```

See also INDEX, chapter 11, Cross-platform and international capabilities

SET COLOR OF

SET COLOR OF NORMAL | MESSAGES | TITLES | BOX | HIGHLIGHT | INFORMATION | FIELDS TO [*color pair*]

Description This command controls the colors of user-defined menus and windows.

Operational rules The SET COLOR OF command can only be used to change the attributes of color schemes 1 and 2. *color pair* is one of 10 defined color pairs.

Example

```
SET COLOR OF FIELDS TO N/W
```

See also SET COLOR OF SCHEME, SET()

SET COLOR OF SCHEME

SET COLOR OF SCHEME *expN1* TO [SCHEME *expN2* | *color pair*]

Description This command changes the color pairs that make up a particular color scheme.

Operational rules The SET COLOR OF SCHEME command is used to change the colors of one predefined color scheme with the color pairs of another, or a custom color pair. If you do not specify SCHEME *expN2* or an optional *color pair*, color scheme *expN1* will take on the color attributes of the last color set that was loaded with the SET COLOR SET command.

Each FoxPro color scheme is made up of 10 pairs of colors. The order of the pairs is dependent on the scheme being used. FoxPro has 12 predefined and 10 user-customizable color schemes. The numbers of the schemes are:

1. User windows.
2. User menus.
3. Menu bar.
4. Menu pop-ups.
5. Dialogs.

6. Dialog pop-ups.
7. Alerts.
8. Windows.
9. Window pop-ups.
10. Browse.
11. Report.
12. Alert pop-ups.
13, 14. Reserved.
15–24. Custom.

For example, in scheme 1 (user windows), the 10 color pairs represent:

1. SAY fields.
2. GET fields.
3. Border.
4. Title, active.
5. Title, idle.
6. Selected item.
7. Clock.
8. Shadow.
9. Enabled control.
10. Disabled control.

When specifying a color pair list, use a comma to represent color pairs that you want to remain the same. You can also use Windows RGB values to specify a color pair list. An RGB color pair consists of six values, with each value separated by a comma. The first three colors of an RGB color pair determine the foreground color and the last three determine the background color. RGB color pair values can range from 0 through 255.

Some color elements of FoxPro such as window borders and push buttons can only be changed through the Windows Control Panel. Issue the command SET COLOR OF SCHEME *expN1* TO to restore the current Windows defaults.

Examples This example shows you how to use the SCHEME() and RGBSCHEME() functions to get the color pair list of any FoxPro color scheme, and then change the color scheme settings.

```
? SCHEME(1)        && User-defined windows; returns color pairs
W+/B,W+/BG,GR+/B,GR+/B,R+/B,W+/GR,GR+/RB,N+/N,GR+/B,R+/B,+
? RGBSCHEME(1)     && User-defined windows
RGB(0,0,0,255,255,255),RGB(0,0,0,192,192,192),RGB(0,0,0,255,255
,255),RGB...
```

The following example changes the fourth color pair (active window title) of color scheme 1, leaving all others unchanged.

```
SET COLOR OF SCHEME 1 TO , , , GR+/B*
? SCHEME(1)        && User-defined windows
W+/B,W+/BG,GR+/B,GR+/B*,R+/B,W+/GR,GR+/RB,N+/N,GR+/B,R+/B,+
SET COLOR OF SCHEME 1 TO , , , RGB(255,255,0,0,0,255)
? RGBSCHEME(1)     && User-defined windows
RGB(0,0,0,255,255,255),RGB(0,0,0,192,192,192),RGB(0,0,0,255,255
,255),RGB...
```

See also SET COLOR SET, SCHEME(), RGBSCHEME(), SET()

SET COLOR SET

```
SET COLOR SET TO [color set name]
```

Description This command loads the colors of a color set.

Operational rules The SET COLOR SET command loads the color settings of a predefined color set. Color set are created with the CREATE COLOR SET command and are stored in the current resource file (normally FOXUSER.DBF). If the optional *color set name* is not specified, the current color set is still active.

See also CREATE COLOR SET, SET()

SET COLOR TO

```
SET COLOR TO [[standard] [, [enhanced] [, [border]]]]
```

Description This command changes the colors of user-defined menus and windows.

Operational rules The SET COLOR TO command allows the color of the standard text, highlighted areas, borders, and backgrounds of color schemes 1 and 2 to be changed. SET COLOR TO not followed by an argument resets the display to "factory" settings.

Standard denotes the color of the background and the standard text. *Enhanced* is the color of the text and background of the highlighted areas. *Border* is the color of the border. The colors are represented by:

Color	FoxPro Color Symbol	Windows RGB Color
Black	N or blank	0,0,0
Blue	B+ or B*	0,0,255
Dark Blue	B	0,0,128
Green	G+ or G*	0,255,0
Dark Green	G	0,128,0
Cyan	BG* or BG+	0,255,255
Dark Cyan	BG	0,128,128
Red	R+ or R*	255,0,0
Dark Red	R	128,0,0
Magenta	RB+ or RB*	255,0,255
Dark Magenta	R	128,0,128
White	W+ or W*	255,255,255
Gray	W	192,192,192
Dark Gray	N+ or N*	128,128,128
Yellow	GR+ or GR*	255,255,0
Brown	GR	255,255,0
Blank	X	N/A

Example This example will produce blue text on a green background.

```
SET COLOR TO RGB(0,0,255,0,255,0)
```

See also SET COLOR OF SCHEME, SET COLOR SET, SET()

SET COMPATIBLE

```
SET COMPATIBLE ON | OFF | FOXPLUS | DB4
```

Description Controls compatibility with FoxBASE+ program commands.

Operational rules Use SET COMPATIBLE OFF if you run FoxBASE+ programs in FoxPro. This ensures that the commands LIKE(), PLAY MACRO, SELECT() and STORE (when STORE is used with arrays) will be interpreted correctly. If SET COMPATIBLE is ON while running a FoxBASE+ program, those commands and functions are interpreted for dBASE IV usage.

If you run dBASE IV programs in FoxPro SET COMPATIBLE must be ON to ensure the commands are interpreted correctly. Using the keywords FOXPLUS and DB4 are the same as ON and OFF respectively. The default setting is OFF.

See also SET()

SET CONFIRM

```
SET CONFIRM ON|OFF
```

Description This command controls whether a key must be pressed to exit a field.

Operational rules If SET CONFIRM is ON and you fill the contents of an input field (i.e., reach the last character), you must press the Enter or Tab keys to move to the next field. If SET CONFIRM is OFF, filling the field will automatically move the cursor to the next field.

The SET CONFIRM command also affects pop-ups created with the MENU command. If SET CONFIRM is OFF, pressing the first letter of a menu choice will automatically select and activate that option. SET CONFIRM ON forces you to press Enter or the spacebar to activate the option. The default setting is OFF.

See also @ ... SAY/GET, SET()

SET CONSOLE

```
SET CONSOLE ON|OFF
```

Description This command controls output to the active screen.

Operational rules Working only within a program, SET CONSOLE is used to prevent display of output to the screen: It cannot be used from the command window. Commands such as REPORT and LIST will display to the FoxPro desktop or the current output window if SET CONSOLE is OFF. Many FoxPro commands have a NOCONSOLE option that suppresses display to the screen regardless of the SET CONSOLE setting.

The SET CONSOLE setting also affects some FoxPro dialogs. If SET CONSOLE is OFF and a browse window is opened FoxPro will display an error. @ ... SAY commands always go to the DEVICE setting and are not affected by the status of SET CONSOLE. If an error occurs, SET CONSOLE is automatically reset to ON. The default setting is ON.

See also SYS(100), SET()

SET CURRENCY

```
SET CURRENCY TO [expC]
SET CURRENCY LEFT | RIGHT
```

Description This command controls the currency symbol and position of numeric expressions.

Operational rules The SET CURRENCY command only affects input fields using the $ PICTURE or FORMAT code. SET CURRENCY TO *expC* accepts a currency symbol of up to nine characters in length. You can use the SET CURRENCY TO command without any argument to reset the default to $.

If SET CURRENCY is LEFT the currency symbol will be displayed at the left side of the input field, while RIGHT will display the currency symbol at the right side of the input field. The default settings are $ and LEFT.

Examples

```
mamt = 123.45
@ 5,1 SAY mamt PICTURE "@$"
$123.45
SET CURRENCY RIGHT
@ 5,1 SAY mamt PICTURE "@$"
123.45$
```

See also SET DECIMALS, SET()

SET CURSOR

```
SET CURSOR ON|OFF
```

Description This command controls the cursor display during data input.

Operational rules If SET CURSOR is ON, a flashing cursor is displayed at all @ ... GET, @ ... EDIT, WAIT and INKEY() functions. SET CURSOR OFF to display no cursor. The default setting is ON.

See also SYS(2002), SET()

SET DATE

```
SET DATE [TO] AMERICAN | ANSI | BRITISH | FRENCH | GERMAN |
ITALIAN | JAPAN | USA | MDY | DMY | YMD
```

Description This command determines how dates are displayed.

Operational rules The SET DATE command allows you to control date expression input and date displays. The date conventions available are:

Setting	Display/input format
AMERICAN	MM/DD/YY
ANSI	YY.MM.DD
BRITISH/FRENCH	DD/MM/YY
GERMAN	DD.MM.YY

Setting	Display/input format
ITALIAN	DD-MM-YY
JAPAN	MM/DD/YY
USA	MM-DD-YY
MDY	MM/DD/YY
DMY	DD/MM/YY
YMD	YY/MM/DD

The default setting is AMERICAN.

Example

```
? DATE()
03/10/93
SET DATE ITALIAN
? DATE()
10-03-93
```

See also SET CENTURY, SET()

SET DEBUG

```
SET DEBUG ON|OFF
```

Description This command controls access to the Trace and Debug windows.

Operational rules When SET DEBUG is ON, you can access the Trace and Debug windows from the Window menu or by issuing the commands ACTIVATE WINDOW TRACE and ACTIVATE WINDOW DEBUG. If SET DEBUG is OFF, the Trace and Debug menus cannot be accessed from the Window menu, but can still be activated with the ACTIVATE WINDOW commands. The default setting is ON.

See also SET ECHO, SET()

SET DECIMALS

```
SET DECIMALS TO [expN]
```

Description This command determines the number of significant digits to the right of the decimal point in the display of numeric functions and calculations.

Operational rules The maximum number of decimal places specified with *expN* that can be displayed is 18 and the minimum is 0. The value determined by SET DECIMALS will only take effect if SET FIXED is ON. The default setting is 2.

Examples

```
SET FIXED ON
mamt = 1234.56789
? mamt
1234.57
SET DECIMALS TO 5
? mamt
1234.56789
```

See also SET FIXED, SET()

SET DEFAULT

```
SET DEFAULT TO [expC]
```

Description This command determines the drive and/or directory where FoxPro looks for and saves files.

Operational rules If the drive and/or directory specified in *expC* do not exist, FoxPro will warn you with an *"Invalid path or filename"* message. Two FoxPro SYS() functions, SYS(5) and SYS(2003), return the default drive and default directory with no drive designator, respectively. The default setting is the drive and directory that FoxPro is started in unless a different setting is specified in the CONFIG.FP configuration file.

Examples

```
SET DEFAULT TO D:\DATA
SET DEFAULT TO D
SET DEFAULT TO \FOX\DATA   && sub directory is in current drive
SET DEFAULT TO \    && change to root directory
```

See also SET PATH, SYS(5), SYS(2003), SET()

SET DELETED

```
SET DELETED ON|OFF
```

Description This command controls how deleted records are processed and displayed.

Operational rules Records can be marked for deletion with the DELETE command or from a Browse or Edit window. If SET DELETED is ON, no deleted records will be displayed in a browse window. This command also affects commands such as SEEK, LOCATE, LIST, REPORT, and EDIT. If SET DELETED is ON, you can still move the record pointer to a deleted record if the scope for a command points to a single record. If SET DELETED is OFF all records are available to be processed and displayed.

The INDEX and REINDEX commands always ignore the SET DELETED setting. If you test for the status of deleted records with commands that are optimized for Rushmore, index the database on the DELETED() function to get full optimization. The default setting is OFF.

See also DELETE, SET()

SET DELIMITERS

```
SET DELIMITERS ON|OFF
SET DELIMITERS TO expC|TO DEFAULT
```

Description This command controls delimiters around @ ... GET fields.

Operational rules If SET DELIMITERS is ON, all pending @ ... GET fields will be enclosed with a colon (:), which is the default. To use another character as the delimiter issue SET DELIMITERS TO *expC* where *expC* is the character to display. SET DELIMITERS TO DEFAULT will return the delimiter character to the colon. The default setting is OFF.

See also @ ... SAY/GET, SET()

SET DEVELOPMENT

```
SET DEVELOPMENT ON|OFF
```

Description This command controls whether FoxPro will compare source and object files when compiling source files.

Operational rules All source code files (.PRG, .SPR, .MPR, .QPR) are compiled into object code (.FXP, .SPX, .MPX, .QPX). The *object file* is a file containing an "execute only" form of FoxPro commands. Object files cannot be modified. Every time a FoxPro program is modified, an updated version of this executable object replaces the previous object file.

If SET DEVELOPMENT is ON, FoxPro will automatically compare the date and time stamps of the source and object files. If the source file has a date or time later than the object file, a new object file is created. This is useful in that you do not have to compile a program yourself after changing it.

If SET DEVELOPMENT is OFF, an updated object file is not created; moreover, the modifications of the program do not register until the program has been compiled. SET DEVELOPMENT ON always allows you to cancel a program during a READ if the Program menu pad is available. The default setting is ON.

See also COMPILE, MODIFY COMMAND, SET()

SET DEVICE

```
SET DEVICE TO SCREEN | TO PRINTER [PROMPT] | TO FILE filename
```

Description This command determines the output direction of @ ... SAY commands.

Operational rules The SET DEVICE command determines the destination of output from @ ... SAY commands to the screen, a printer, or a file. When SET DEVICE is set TO PRINTER, the output from @ ... SAY commands goes directly to the printer, and all @ ... GET commands are ignored. A page eject is issued if the coordinates of an @ ... SAY command are higher than the previous @ ... SAY command. SET DEVICE TO FILE sends all @ ... SAY commands to *filename*.

The default setting is TO SCREEN. This sends all @ ... SAY output to the desktop or the current window. When sending output to the printer, the optional PROMPT keyword can be used to access the Windows Printer Setup dialog before printing.

See also SYS(101), SET()

SET DISPLAY

```
SET DISPLAY TO CGA | COLOR | EGA25 | EGA43 | MONO | VGA25 | VGA50
```

Description This command determines the display mode on different monitors.

Operational rules This command is used to change the main FoxPro window font and the window display size. The effect of using this command may vary among different video cards and drivers. The SET DISPLAY command can only be used if the operating hardware can support the appropriate settings; otherwise the message "Display mode not available" is displayed. The following modes are supported:

CGA Switches the main window font to 9-point FoxFont.

COLOR Display mode is not available in Windows.

EGA25 Switches the main window font to 7-point FoxFont and changes the display mode to 25 lines.

EGA43 Switches the main window font to 9-point FoxFont and changes the display mode to 50 lines.

MONO Display mode is not available in Windows.

VGA25 Switches the main window font to 7-point FoxFont and changes the display mode to 25 lines.

VGA50 Switches the main window font to 9-point FoxFont and changes the display mode to 50 lines.

See also SET()

SET DOHISTORY

```
SET DOHISTORY ON|OFF
```

Description This command controls whether program commands are displayed in the command window.

Operational rules If SET DOHISTORY is ON, each command line of an executing program will be displayed in the command window. This will also result in very slow program execution as FoxPro builds a temporary file for the commands. The default setting is OFF.

See also SET ECHO, SET()

SET ECHO

```
SET ECHO ON|OFF
```

Description This command controls activation of the Trace window.

Operational rules The Trace window will be activated if the SET ECHO ON command is issued. The Trace window can also be activated with ACTIVATE WINDOW TRACE or from the Window menu. The Trace window can be activated with SET ECHO ON even if SET DEBUG is OFF. SET ECHO OFF closes the trace window. See the FoxPro User Interface chapter (chapter 1) for more information on using the Trace window. The default setting is OFF.

See also SUSPEND, SET()

SET ESCAPE

```
SET ESCAPE ON|OFF
```

Description This command controls program interruption using the Esc key.

Operational rules With SET ESCAPE ON, pressing the Esc key will cause FoxPro to interrupt program execution and display the Cancel, Suspend, Ignore alert. It is always a good idea to SET ESCAPE ON during application development; otherwise it may be necessary to reboot the computer. FoxPro ignores the Esc key if it is pressed with SET ESCAPE OFF. The default setting is ON.

See also ON ESCAPE, ON KEY LABEL, SET()

SET EXACT

```
SET EXACT ON|OFF
```

Description This command controls how string comparisons are made.

Operational rules When SET EXACT is OFF, a character string matches another as long as the comparison string is the same length or longer and contains the same characters as the model string. With SET EXACT ON, the comparison string must match the model string character for character. For instance, if SET EXACT is OFF, the command:

```
LIST FOR Lname = "S"
```

lists all records with an Lname that begins with S. If SET EXACT is ON, the comparison part of the criteria would have to have the same length as Lname, for instance:

```
LIST FOR Lname = "Smith   "     && Lname has a length of 8
```

The SET EXACT setting is ignored when character strings are compared with the == operator.

The default setting is OFF.

See also SET NEAR, SET()

SET EXCLUSIVE

```
SET EXCLUSIVE ON|OFF
```

Description This command controls shared use settings when database files are opened.

Operational rules SET EXCLUSIVE determines whether databases opened in a shared environment are available for exclusive use by one user or can be shared by other users. When SET EXCLUSIVE is ON, all databases opened cannot be accessed by other users, even for read-only use. Opening a database exclusively ensures that no other users will change the file. If SET EXCLUSIVE is OFF, all databases opened can be shared. The FoxPro commands INSERT, INSERT BLANK, MODIFY STRUCTURE, PACK, REINDEX and ZAP require exclusive use of a database file in a shared environment.

If the SET EXCLUSIVE setting is changed after databases have been opened, those files retain their SET EXCLUSIVE setting when they were opened. For example, if a database is opened with SET EXCLUSIVE ON and SET EXCLUSIVE is changed to OFF, the database is still in an exclusive state. If SET EXCLUSIVE is OFF, a database can still be opened exclusive with the USE ... [EXCLUSIVE] command without changing the status of SET EXCLUSIVE. The default setting is OFF.

See also USE, SET()

SET FIELDS

```
SET FIELDS ON|OFF
SET FIELDS TO [field list] | ALL]
```

Description This command controls which fields of a database can be accessed.

Operational rules Use SET FIELDS to define a list of fields that might be accessed by one or more files. The defined *field list* is used by all commands that have a field list option available in their use. For example:

```
SET FIELDS TO Lname, City
BROWSE
```

produces the same results as:

```
BROWSE FIELDS Lname, City
```

A field list must be identified before SET FIELDS ON is activated. SET FIELDS TO or SET FIELDS OFF strikes all fields from the active database from the field list, and SET FIELDS TO ALL includes all fields from the active database. The default setting is OFF.

See also BROWSE, SET()

SET FILTER

```
SET FILTER TO [expL]
```

Description This command determines which records of a database can be accessed.

Operational rules The SET FILTER TO command in effect "filters" out only those records of the current database that match the logical expression *expL*. SET FILTER TO without any argument deactivates the filter for the current database. SET FILTER TO *expL* specifies a condition for displaying records. The *expL* expression condition can be any valid FoxPro expression such as CITY = "Los Angeles" or BDAY = {09/12/68}. The filter is not evaluated until the record pointer is moved with commands such as SKIP or GOTO.

Be aware the filtering databases can result in extremely slow results. Use Rushmore optimizable commands such as SCAN, BROWSE, and REPORT whenever possible. This command has no default setting.

See also FILTER(), SET()

SET FIXED

```
SET FIXED ON|OFF
```

Description This command controls whether a fixed number of decimal places are displayed for numeric values.

Operational rules If SET FIXED is ON, the number of decimal places displayed is determined by the SET DECIMALS command. When SET FIXED is OFF the number of decimal places displayed for numerics is dependent on the specifics used in a numeric expression. Numeric database fields are displayed with the declared number of decimal places. The default setting is OFF.

See also SET DECIMALS, SET()

SET FORMAT

```
SET FORMAT TO [filename|?]
```

Description This command selects a format file (.FMT) to be used with the APPEND, BROWSE, CHANGE, EDIT, INSERT, or READ commands.

Operational rules The SET FORMAT command should be used for backward compatibility only. FoxPro 2.5 does not create format files; use the Screen builder tool to create multiple input screens. SET FORMAT TO *filename* opens the format file to process data entry. SET FORMAT TO ? displays a list of format files to open. CLOSE FORMAT or SET FORMAT TO closes the format file. This command has no default setting.

See also Using the Screen Builder, SET()

SET FULLPATH

```
SET FULLPATH ON|OFF
```

Description This command controls whether certain functions return a path with the file name.

Operational rules If SET FULLPATH is ON, the result returned by the CDX(), DBF(), IDX() and NDX() functions will include a path along with the filename. The default setting is ON.

Examples

```
SET FULLPATH ON
USE C:\CLASS\Students
? DBF()
C:\CLASS\STUDENTS.DBF
SET FULLPATH OFF
? DBF()
STUDENTS.DBF
```

See also DBF(), CDX(), SET()

SET FUNCTION

```
SET FUNCTION expN|key label TO [expr]
```

Description This command assigns a macro to a function key.

Operational rules The function keys F1 through F10 can be programmed to execute a macro when pressed. The function keys can be set from the command window, a program or the CONFIG.FP file. Shift-F1 through Shift-F9 and Ctrl-F1 through Ctrl-F10 can be programmed with macros as well. The Alt keys and Shift-F10 cannot be programmed. When programming function keys, a semicolon (;) denotes <Enter> (for pressing the Enter key) causing FoxPro to execute the command. Quotes can be used to denote text strings. See the ON KEY LABEL section for available key assignments.

The default key assignments are as follows:

Key	Assignment	Key	Assignment
F1	HELP	F6	DISPLAY STATUS
F2	SET	F7	DISPLAY MEMORY
F3	LIST	F8	DISPLAY
F4	DIR	F9	APPEND
F5	DISPLAY STRUCTURE	F10	Alt

See also FKLABEL(), SET()

SET HEADING

```
SET HEADING ON|OFF
```

Description This command controls column heading displays.

Operational rules If SET HEADING is ON, each field is displayed as a column heading when the AVERAGE, CALCULATE, DISPLAY, LIST, and SUM commands are executed. The default setting is ON.

See also DISPLAY, LIST, SET()

SET HELP

```
SET HELP ON|OFF
SET HELP TO [filename]
```

Description This command determines whether on-line help is available, and which help file to use.

Operational rules If SET HELP is ON, pressing the F1 key, issuing the HELP command or selecting Contents... from the Help menu will display a window of available help topics. The style of help, help topics and text available are determined by what is available in the SET HELP TO *filename* help file.

The help file must be a valid Windows help file (.HLP) or FoxPro database help file (.DBF). SET HELP TO without any argument sets the help file to the default FOXHELP.DBF file. The default settings are ON and TO FOXHELP.DBF.

Examples

```
SET HELP TO FOXHELP.HLP
SET HELP TO FOXHELP.DBF
SET HELP TO MYHELP.DBF
```

See also HELP, SET TOPIC, SET()

SET HELPFILTER

```
SET HELPFILTER [AUTOMATIC] TO [expL]
```

Description This command determines which help topics of the current help file can be accessed when using .DBF style help.

Operational rules The SET HELPFILTER command in effect "filters" out only those help records that match the logical expression *expL*. The *expL* expression should refer to fields in the help database. This command is very useful in creating a customized help system.

The help database, FOXHELP.DBF contains the following structure:

Field name	**Description**
Topic	List of help topics.
Details	Memo field that contains help text.
Class	Classifies the topic.

To remove the HELPFILTER, use the keyword AUTOMATIC or issue SET HELPFILTER TO. The default settings are ON and FOXHELP.DBF.

Examples

```
SET HELPFILTER TO Topic = 'INDEX'
SET HELPFILTER TO 'WINDOW' $ Topic
SET HELPFILTER TO 'WINDOW' $ Details
```

See also SET HELP, SET()

SET HOURS

```
SET HOURS TO [12|24]
```

Description This command determines the system clock display format.

Operational rules The system time can be displayed with the SET CLOCK ON command. SET HOURS TO 12 displays the time in a 12-hour format; SET HOURS TO 24 displays the time in a 24-hour format. The TIME() function always returns the current system time in 24-hour format, regardless of the SET HOURS TO setting. The default setting is 12.

See also SET CLOCK, SET()

SET INDEX

```
SET INDEX TO [file list|?] [ORDER expN|idx file|[TAG] tag name
[OF cdx file] [ASCENDING|DESCENDING]] [ADDITIVE]
```

Description This command opens index files for the current database.

Operational rules Both .IDX and .CDX type index files can be opened with SET INDEX. If a database has a structural compound index file, the index file is automatically opened when the database is opened. SET INDEX TO ? will display a list of .IDX and .CDX index files to open. If the ? is replaced by *file list*, those files are opened to be used with the active database file. The first index becomes the master index. To close all open indexes for the current work area, issue the command SET INDEX TO with no arguments. This will not close any structural compound indexes.

The ASCENDING and DESCENDING clause selects the order for the index. ASCENDING is the default. The ORDER clause allows you to choose a master index other than the first file (or first tag of a multiple index file). The following are all valid uses of the ORDER clause:

ORDER *expN* The variable *expN* refers to the index file as it appears in the index file list, or a tag in the order the tag was created.

ORDER ***idx file*** Refers to the name of the single index file.

ORDER [TAG] ***tag name OF cdx file*** Refers to the name of the tag within multiple index file *cdx file*.

This command has no default settings.

Examples

```
SET INDEX TO CUST.CDX ORDER ID
SET INDEX TO TEMP.IDX DESCENDING ADDITIVE
```

See also SET ORDER, SET COLLATE, USE, SET()

SET INTENSITY

```
SET INTENSITY ON|OFF
```

Description This command controls whether the @ ... GET fields are displayed with Windows color settings.

Operational rules When SET INTENSITY is ON the background of an @ ... GET editing region is displayed in the color setting of a Windows button face (usually gray). Windows color settings are controlled through the Windows Control Panel. Consult your Windows documentation for more information on using the Control Panel. The default setting is ON.

See also SET BLINK, SET()

SET KEYCOMP

```
SET KEYCOMP TO DOS|WINDOWS
```

Description This command is used to control keystrokes among different FoxPro platforms.

Operational rules When SET KEYCOMP is set TO DOS, certain keystrokes used to navigate through the interface, activate controls and select Browse text will emulate FoxPro for DOS.

A primary example is in the use of default push buttons. In FoxPro for Windows, a default push button can only be activated when the editing cursor is on any control other than a push button. When the editing control is on a push button, that button automatically becomes the default button. In FoxPro for DOS, a default push button can be activated at any time by pressing Ctrl-Enter. To emulate the DOS style, SET KEYCOMP TO DOS. Other examples are listed below.

Function	SET KEYCOMP TO WINDOWS	SET KEYCOMP TO DOS
Browse	Entering a field selects all text	Entering a field does not select all text.
Radio buttons	When the editing cursor is on a radio button, pressing Tab moves the cursor to the next object.	When the editing cursor is on a radio button, pressing Tab moves the cursor to the next radio button selection.

Function	SET KEYCOMP TO WINDOWS	SET KEYCOMP TO DOS
Hot keys	Hot keys can be activated at any place on the screen by pressing the hot key letter or Alt plus the hot key letter.	Hot keys can only be activated when the editing cursor is on a control.
Pop-ups	Open a pop-up by pressing the spacebar, Alt-↑ or Alt-↓. Options can be selected without opening the pop-up.	Open a pop-up by pressing Enter or the spacebar. Once a pop-up is open, use the arrow keys to select an option.

SET LIBRARY

`SET LIBRARY TO [`*`filename`*` [ADDITIVE]]`

Description This command controls access to an external API library.

Operational rules External API (Application Program Interface) libraries allows you to extend the capabilities of FoxPro. Any C or assembly language function can be incorporated into the FoxPro API. All functions in an external library can be accessed in the same manner as a FoxPro function. FoxPro assumes an extension of .FLL for this type of file. Use the keyword ADDITIVE to open additional API libraries without closing open libraries.

SET LIBRARY TO without arguments closes all open API libraries. Functions available in API libraries can be displayed with the DISPLAY STATUS or LIST STATUS commands. This command has no default settings.

See also LOAD, SET()

SET LOCK

`SET LOCK ON|OFF`

Description This command controls automatic file locking for some commands.

Operational rules If SET LOCK is ON, FoxPro will attempt to lock the current database when the following commands are issued:

AVERAGE *scope*	LIST
CALCULATE	LABEL
COPY TO	REPORT
COPY TO ARRAY	SORT
COUNT	SUM
DISPLAY *scope*	TOTAL
INDEX	JOIN *files*

The commands do not require that the database be locked before they are used. Locking the database keeps other users from updating the database while the commands are being processed. If SET LOCK is ON and the database cannot be locked, FoxPro will continue the locking attempt based on the value of SET REFRESH. Files can also be locked with the FLOCK() function. The default setting is OFF.

See also SET REFRESH, FLOCK(), SET()

SET LOGERRORS

```
SET LOGERRORS ON|OFF
```

Description This command controls whether compilation errors are saved to a file.

Operational rules FoxPro may encounter a program error when compiling a source file or building a project. If SET LOGERRORS is ON those errors found will be written to a file with the same name as the source, with an .ERR extension. When building a project or application, FoxPro will write the errors to a file with the same name as the project file. The default setting is ON.

See also COMPILE, SET()

SET MACKEY

```
SET MACKEY TO [expC]
```

Description This command determines the keyboard macro that displays the Macros dialog.

Operational rules When FoxPro is loaded the default Shift+F10 key combination displays the Macro dialog. The default can be changed by specifying a key or combination of key with *expC*. The available key combinations can be found under the ON KEY LABEL description. If SET MACKEY TO without an argument is issued, the Macros dialog cannot be accessed with any keyboard macro. The default setting is Shift+F10.

See also CLEAR MACROS, ON KEY LABEL, SET()

SET MARGIN

```
SET MARGIN TO expN
```

Description This command determines the left margin setting of printed output.

Operational rules When SET DEVICE TO is PRINTER the left margin column of printed output is determined by combining the _ploffset and _lmargin system variables. Use the SET MARGIN TO command to change the _ploffset value to *expN*.

The _ploffset value affects reports printed with the REPORT command while _lmargin does not. If a report printed with the REPORT command contains indented data, that is combined with _ploffset to determine the left margin of the printed page. The default setting is 0.

See also _lmargin, _ploffset, SET()

SET MARK OF

```
SET MARK OF MENU menu name TO expl
SET MARK OF PAD pad name OF menu name TO expL
SET MARK OF POPUP popup name TO expL
SET MARK OF BAR expN OF popup name TO expL
```

Description This command controls the display of a check mark character placed next to each option in a menu or pop-up.

Operational rules A check mark character is placed to the left of the option in a pop-up or menu when the logical expression *expL* is true (.T.). The check mark is removed when *expL* is false (.F.) The default setting for marks is the check mark (✓) and cannot be changed.

See also MRKBAR(), MRKPAD(), SET()

SET MARK TO

```
SET MARK TO [expC]
```

Description This command determines the date display delimiter of characters.

Operational rules A new delimiter can be set by enclosing the desired character in quotes. For example, SET MARK TO "-" will separate the month, day, and year by dashes. The default setting is the slash (/).

See also SET()

SET MEMOWIDTH

```
SET MEMOWIDTH TO expN
```

Description This command determines the display and output width of memo fields and character expressions.

Operational rules The width of expressions and memo fields that are greater than 254 characters and displayed in a window using the ?, ??, DISPLAY or LIST commands is determined by the value *expN*. If the expression is less than or equal to 254, the expression will wrap around the left and right margins of the window. Thc value of *expN* determines which column from the left margin to begin wrapping the expression. The width of the output is always determined by the font and font size of the output window.

The SET MEMOWIDTH setting has no effect if a memo field editing window is opened in a browse. However, the values returned by the ATCLINE(), ATLINE(), MEMLINES() and MLINE() functions are affected by the value of *expN*. The default setting is 50.

See also ATCLINE(), ATLINE(), MEMLINES(), MLINE(), SET()

SET MESSAGE

```
SET MESSAGE TO [expC]
SET MESSAGE TO [expN [LEFT|CENTER|RIGHT]]
SET MESSAGE WINDOW [window name]
```

Description This command controls the display of custom, menu and @ ... GET messages.

Operational rules By default the MESSAGE *expC* appears in the Windows-style status bar at the bottom of the main window. The display of the Windows-style status bar can be changed using the SET STATUS BAR command.

You can change the placement of the message with the SET MESSAGE TO *expN* command. The row number for the message is *expN*, where a row of 0 will display no message. Use the keywords LEFT, CENTER, or RIGHT to set the alignment of the message in this command. The *expN*, LEFT, CENTER and RIGHT arguments are ignored when the Windows-style status bar is displayed.

All messages are displayed on the FoxPro desktop screen unless another window has been specified with SET MESSAGE WINDOW *window name*. Use SET MESSAGE WINDOW with no argument to return the message display to the desktop. The default setting is centered at line 45 of the FoxPro desktop screen when the Windows-style status bar is off (SET STATUS BAR OFF).

See also SET STATUS, SET()

SET MULTILOCKS

```
SET MULTILOCKS ON|OFF
```

Description This command controls multiple record locking of a shared database.

Operational rules Records can be locked with the RLOCK() and LOCK() functions. SET MULTILOCKS must be ON to lock a set of records at one time. If a set of records is locked the command SET MULTILOCKS OFF will unlock all records in all work areas. To unlock a set of records in a single database you must use UNLOCK [IN] or UNLOCK on each record. The number of records that can be locked at one time is dependent on available memory and attempt to lock many records could result in the computer getting "locked up." The default setting is OFF.

See also UNLOCK, RLOCK(), FLOCK(), SET()

SET NEAR

```
SET NEAR ON|OFF
```

Description This command controls the record pointer position if a SEEK or FIND command fails.

Operational rules If SET NEAR is ON and a SEEK or FIND command is unsuccessful the record pointer will be positioned at the first record with the closest match to the SEEK or FIND expression. If SET NEAR is OFF, the record pointer will be at the end of the file (EOF()) and the FOUND() function will return false (.F.). The default setting is OFF.

See also SEEK, SET()

SET NOCPTRANS

```
SET NOCPTRANS TO [field list]
```

Description This command prevents code page translation of selected fields in the current database.

Operational rules All fields in the current database will be translated to the CODEPAGE setting specified in your FoxPro configuration file when the database is browsed, edited, or a memo field editing window is opened. You can specify which fields not to translate with *field list*.

Issue the command SET NOCPTRANS TO to make all fields in the current database available for translation. This command has no default setting.

See also Chapter 11, Cross-platform and international capabilities

SET NOTIFY

```
SET NOTIFY ON|OFF
```

Description Controls the display of some system messages.

Operational rules FoxPro system messages that are displayed in the status bar at the bottom of the screen will be suppressed if SET NOTIFY is OFF. Those messages include "Do canceled," "Suspended," and "records read." The default setting is ON.

See also SET MESSAGE, SET()

SET ODOMETER

```
SET ODOMETER TO [expN]
```

Description This command determines the interval display for commands that process records.

Operational rules If SET TALK is ON, commands such as COUNT, SUM and SELECT (SQL) display the process of records on the active screen. After every 100th record is processed the display is updated. The interval can be changed by specifying a range of 1 through 32,767 with *expN*. The default setting is 100.

See also SET TALK, SET()

SET OPTIMIZE

```
SET OPTIMIZE ON|OFF
```

Description This command controls the use of Rushmore optimization.

Operational rules FoxPro 2.5 is the fastest PC database available for data retrieval thanks to a technology known as Rushmore technology, which greatly speeds up commands that use the FOR clause. Sometimes, however, Rushmore must be disabled. This is in instances when the command is modifying an indexed field that is included in the query.

If the indexed field is used in an optimizable command, the Rushmore set will become outdated and may return erroneous results. SET OPTIMIZE OFF globally disables Rushmore, although most commands that take advantage of Rushmore also have NOOPTIMIZE clauses of their own. The default setting is ON.

See also SET ORDER, SET()

SET ORDER

```
SET ORDER TO [expN1|idx file|[TAG] tag name [OF cdx file] [IN
expN2|expC] [ASCENDING|DESCENDING]]
```

Description This command determines the active index of a database.

Operational rules A database can have more than one single index file (.IDX)or multiple index (.CDX) open at once. However, only one index or tag can be active at any time. Using an index on a database improves retrieval performance, determines the display and reporting order, and allows use of the SEEK command.

The argument determines the order of index files in a list. This order is important when using the SET INDEX TO and USE commands because the master (first) index is the one used in the SEEK, LIST, and REPORT commands. SET ORDER TO with no argument or with an argument of 0 restores the database file to its natural order with no index file as master. The following are all valid uses of the SET ORDER command:

SET ORDER TO *expN1* *expN1* refers to the tag or index file in ascending order as they are created and attached to a database.

SET ORDER TO *idx file* Refers to the name of the single index file.

SET ORDER TO [TAG] *tag name [OF cdx file]* Refers to the name of the tag within the multiple index file *cdx file*. The .CDX file is not needed unless more than one multiple index file with the same tag name is open.

IN *expN2*|*expC* SET ORDER controls the active index of the current work area. Use IN to change the active index of a database in a different work area. *expN2* is the number of the work area (1-25(225)) and *expC* is the alias of the database.

ASCENDING|DESCENDING Indexes are opened in their default ascending or descending order. The ASCENDING and DESCENDING clauses can be used to reverse the default order.

See also INDEX, SET COLLATE, SET()

SET PALETTE

```
SET PALETTE ON|OFF
```

Description This command determines whether the FoxPro color palette is used.

Operational rules SET PALETTE to ON to activate the default FoxPro color palette. When the FoxPro color palette is not active, the color palette of the last graphic image bitmap or Windows OLE object that was displayed in FoxPro is used when displaying subsequent images. If the color palette changes for the next image, that palette takes effect.

The default FoxPro palette can sometimes be used to better control the appearance of graphic images in FoxPro. This will vary among different video cards and drivers. The default setting is ON.

SET PATH

```
SET PATH TO [path]
```

Description This command determines a DOS path for FoxPro to search for files.

Operational rules FoxPro does not use the DOS path setting to search for files. The SET PATH command establishes a path for FoxPro to use when searching for files that are not in the current drive or directory specified with SET DEFAULT. The search path can be cleared SET PATH TO with no argument. Multiple paths can be specified in *path* by separating each one with a semicolon. There is no default setting for SET PATH.

Example

```
SET PATH TO C:\TEMP;D:\FOXTEMP
```

See also SET()

SET PDSETUP

```
SET PDSETUP TO [[expC [, expr1 [, expr2 ...]]] [WITH expr3 [,
expr4 ...]]]
```

Description This command determines which printer control setup to load when printing FoxPro for DOS reports and labels.

Operational rules A printer control setup is a combination of settings that include the type of printer, printer command codes, styles, margins and orientation. The printer setups are stored in a resource database file, usually the FOXUSER.DBF file. Printer setups can only be created and edited from FoxPro for DOS.

The printer setup name is specified in *expC*. When a printer setup is loaded *expC* is stored in the _pdsetup system variable. If *expC* cannot be located in the active resource file the current printer setup application specified in system variable _genpd is executed. You can place a dash (-) before *expC* to not invoke the printer setup application.

You can pass parameters to your custom printer setup application by including the *exprl, expr2,* ... arguments. The first line of your application must be a PARAMETERS statement to accept the parameters. Do not pass parameters if you use the FoxPro GENPD.APP as your printer setup application.

When a printer setup is loaded FoxPro loads the system array _pdparms into memory. This array contains all the vital information needed for controlling the printer. The dimensions and contents of the _pdparms array are controlled through the printer setup application. The _pdparms array cannot be cleared with the RELEASE ALL command. If you have a custom printer setup application including the WITH *expr3, expr4,* ... option causes FoxPro to add all expressions to the beginning of the *_pdparms* array. *expr3* would become the first element of the array and *expr4* would be the second. The FoxPro GENPD.APP printer setup application will ignore the WITH clause and all parameters.

All printer setups and _pdparms can be cleared by issuing SET PDSETUP TO. A printer setup is automatically loaded when starting FoxPro if one has been set as the default. This command has no default setting.

See also _genpd, SET()

SET POINT

```
SET POINT TO [expC]
```

Description This command determines the character denoting the decimal point in numeric values.

Operational rules Any single alphanumeric character can be specified for the decimal point. A space cannot be used for the decimal. The default can be restored by entering SET POINT TO without an argument. The default character is a period (.).

See also SET DECIMAL, SET()

SET PRINTER

```
SET PRINTER ON [PROMPT]|OFF
SET PRINTER TO [filename [ADDITIVE]|port]
SET PRINTER TO [\\machine name \printer name = dest] [FONT expC
[,expN]] [STYLE expC]
SET PRINTER TO [\\SPOOLER [\N] [\F = expN] [\B = banner] [\C =
expN] [\P = expN]] [\S = server] [\Q = queue]
```

Description This command controls output to a local or network printer, or a port.

Operational rules When SET PRINTER is ON, all output except @ ... SAY commands are sent to the printer. This includes commands such as DISPLAY, LIST, ? and ???. When sending output to the printer, the optional PROMPT keyword can be used to access the Windows Printer Setup dialog before printing. SET PRINTER TO *filename* specifies an ASCII text file to send the output to while SET PRINTER TO *port* will send the output to a valid parallel (LPT1, LPT2, LPT3) or the serial ports (COM1, COM2, COM3). If printing to a file, use the ADDITIVE clause to append to an existing file.

FoxPro also supports network printing. If printing on a network with multiple printers, the following options should be used:

\\ *machine name* *machine name* is the network name assigned to your workstation. This name is assigned by the network administrator and must be unique.

\ *printer name* *printer name* is a name assigned to the printer and is also assigned by the network administrator. LPT1, LPT2 or LPT3 is used to identify the destination (*dest*) of the installed printer.

\\SPOOLER This command is designed specifically for Novell Netware servers. The SPOOLER key word or any character string must be used but is ignored. The optional clauses are listed below. Don't leave spaces between any of the optional clauses when used.

\N Suppresses printing the banner page.

\F = *expN* Specifies the form number *expN* (0 through 255) that the output is printed on. This option is useful for producing different types of printed output, such as checks, invoices, letters, and so on.

\B = *banner* Specifies the heading that is printed on the banner page if one is printed. *banner* can contain up to 12 characters. The default heading is your network user name.

\C = *expN* Specifies the number of copies (1 through 255) queued to a network printer. The default is 1.

\P = *expN* Specifies the network printer where output is sent. *expN* is a number assigned to the printer by the network. The default is 0.

\S = *server* Specifies the network server to which the printer is attached. *server* should be a literal (not enclosed in quotes) rather than a string.

\Q = *queue* Specifies the queue name assigned to the printer you send output to. *queue* should be a literal (not enclosed in quotes) rather than a string.

FONT *expC [,expN]* This clause defines the type and size of the font used to print the output. The font, *expC*, must be an available Windows font; otherwise a substitute font with similar characteristics will be used. Specify the font size with *expN*. If no size is specified, a 10 point font is used.

STYLE *expC* This clause defines the style for the font specified with the FONT clause. The style, *expC*, must be a valid style for the defined font; otherwise a substitute style with similar characteristics will be used. The styles that are available for a font are determined by Windows. When a font is specified and the STYLE clause is omitted, the standard font style is used. Font style characters can be combined to create different styles. The available font styles that can be used are listed below:

Character	Font Style
B	Bold
I	Italic
N	Normal
O	Outline
Q	Opaque
S	Shadow
-	Strikeout
T	Transparent
U	Underline

SET PRINTER TO without any arguments will reset the printer to PRN. The default setting for SET PRINTER is OFF.

See also PRINTSTATUS(), SET()

SET PROCEDURE

```
SET PROCEDURE TO [filename]
```

Description This command sets a procedure file.

Operational rules A procedure file is a program that contains many separate procedures or functions. Procedures are used widely in programming for this reason. When a procedure or function is called, FoxPro will search for it in *filename* if it cannot be found in the current program.

If a file extension is not specified, FoxPro searches for and compiles, if necessary, the desired file with the .PRG extension. To close the current procedure file, issue SET PROCEDURE TO with no file name argument. This command has no default setting.

See also PROCEDURE, FUNCTION, SET()

SET READBORDER

```
SET READBORDER ON|OFF
```

Description This command determines if borders are places around GET editing fields.

Operational rules When SET READBORDER is ON, a border is placed around text editing @ ... GET fields. The default setting for is ON.

SET REFRESH

```
SET REFRESH TO expN1 [, expN2]
```

Description This command determines the update of browse displays when records are changed and the rate at which a database is flushed to disk.

Operational rules This command affects records displayed in a window opened with the BROWSE, CHANGE, or EDIT commands and memo field editing windows. *expN1* is the amount of time in seconds that FoxPro waits before updating the display. *expN2* specifies the interval at which records in memory are written back to the disk.

Both arguments must be between 0 and 3,600. If *expN2* is 0 the buffers are written to disk only when the browse window is closed. If no value is specified for *expN2*, it is given the same value as *expN1*. If *expN1* is set to 0, *expN2* is automatically set to 5. The default setting for this command is 0,5.

See also BROWSE, SET()

SET RELATION

```
SET RELATION TO [expr1 INTO expN1|expC1 [, expr2 INTO
expN2|expC2 ...] [ADDITIVE]]
```

Description This command sets linking relations between multiple databases.

Operational rules An active database file is linked to an open database file in another work area via a common field. The active database is considered the source and the INTO database the target. The target database must be indexed on the common field. SET RELATION TO without an argument removes the relation in use on the active database. Use the DISPLAY STATUS command to see all relationships currently set.

FoxPro supports three types of relations: one-to-one, one-to-many and many-to-one. In a one-to-one relation each record in the source file relates to no more than one record in the target. In a one-to-may relation each record in the source file relates to one or more records in the target. This is sometimes referred to as a parent-child relationship. In addition to SET RELATION, the SET SKIP command is required to create a one-to-many relationship; and in the many-to-one relation, multiple records in the source file relate to one record in the target.

expr1 is the expression that the databases are related on. This is usually the common field. INTO specifies the work area (*expN1*) or database alias (*expC1*) that is the target of the relation. Use the ADDITIVE clause to keep all existing relationships active. If the ADDITIVE clause is not specified, all current relationships will be closed.

Example The following program sets a relationship between two files. The common field is Clicode:

```
SELECT 1
USE SALES
SELECT 2
USE CLIENTS ORDER CODE
SELECT SALES
SET RELATION TO SALES.Clicode INTO CLIENTS
LIST Clicode, Amount, Date, B.Name
CLICODE   AMOUNT    B.NAME
A01       50.00     JIM JONES
A02       150.00    RUTH DOE
```

```
A01        200.00    JIM JONES
A03        100.00    HARRY CAREY
A02        50.00     RUTH DOE
```

See also SET SKIP, SET()

SET RELATION OFF

`SET RELATION OFF INTO` *`expN|expC`*

Description This command closes an active link between databases.

Operational rules SET RELATION OFF will break the relation between the active database and the database specified in work area *expN* or by its alias *expC*.

See also SET RELATION, SET()

SET REPROCESS

`SET REPROCESS TO` *`expN`* `[SECONDS]|TO AUTOMATIC`

Description This command determines how FoxPro will attempt to lock a record or file after an unsuccessful attempt.

Operational rules Attempting to lock a database or a record is not always a sure thing. Another workstation could have the file or record already locked. Use the SET REPROCESS command to control how long or how many times FoxPro will continue the locking procedure.

expN specifies how many attempts FoxPro will make. If the SECONDS option is used, *expN* specifies how many continuous seconds that a lock will be attempted. If *expN* is set to 0 and the initial lock attempt failed, FoxPro will attempt to lock the file or record until the Esc key is pressed. If Esc is pressed before a lock is made, FoxPro will display a dialog with "Record is in use by another." If *expN* is set to –1, FoxPro will attempt the lock indefinitely and the Esc key cannot stop the lock. Setting SET REPROCESS to –1 can result in problems if no other way is available to abort the lock process. It is better to use the AUTOMATIC clause in this case. Using AUTOMATIC will attempt a lock indefinitely but still allows you to press Esc to abort the lock process.

The status of ON ERROR comes into play when locking records and files. If an ON ERROR routine is set and an unsuccessful lock command fails, FoxPro will execute the ON ERROR routine. If the ON ERROR routine is executed, no other attempts will be made to lock the file or record. However, if the lock attempt is made by a function, the ON ERROR routine is ignored and the function will return a value of false (.F.). The default setting for this command is 0.

See also RLOCK(), FLOCK(), SET()

SET RESOURCE

```
SET RESOURCE ON|OFF
SET RESOURCE TO [filename]
```

Description This command controls the use and updating of a FoxPro resource file.

Operational rules A FoxPro resource file is a database that contains information about user-defined settings such as colors, window locations, sizes, etc. If a resource file is used and SET RESOURCE is ON, all windows opened and their screen coordinates, among other things, are saved for later use. A resource file also contains the settings of BROWSE LAST and BROWSE PREFERENCE.

The initial resource file is called FOXUSER.DBF. Specify a FoxPro database with *filename* to change the resource file. Issuing the command SET RESOURCE TO will automatically reset the resource file to FOXUSER.DBF change the setting of SET RESOURCE to ON. If the setting is set ON, then any changes made to the FoxPro environment are updated to or saved in the resource file. The default setting for this command is ON and FOXUSER.DBF.

See also SYS(2005), BROWSE, SET()

SET SAFETY

```
SET SAFETY ON|OFF
```

Description This command controls the display of warning messages when files will be overwritten.

Operational rules When SET SAFETY is ON, an attempt to save a file to a file of the same name will cause FoxPro to alert you that the file already exists and ask you to confirm overwriting the file. The commands ZAP and PACK also display a warning is SET SAFETY is ON. If SET SAFETY is OFF, existing files will be overwritten without a warning message.

The setting of SET SAFETY is very important when structural index files (.CDX) are used. When a database is opened that uses a .CDX index file, the index file is opened automatically. FoxPro accomplishes this by reading the database header to determine which index file to open, if any. If SET SAFETY is ON and you open a database file that has an associated CDX file and the CDX file cannot be found, FoxPro will alert you with "Structural CDX not found" and give you the options of Ignore or Cancel.

If Ignore is selected, the database header will be changed to reflect that the database has no CDX file. If Cancel is selected the database will not be opened. If the previous scenario occurs and SET SAFETY is OFF, FoxPro will automatically change the database header to reflect no CDX file without any warning. The default setting for this command is ON.

See also ON ERROR, SET()

SET SEPARATOR

```
SET SEPARATOR TO [expC]
```

Description This command determines the character that separates numeric values three digits to the left of the decimal point.

Operational rules The separator character can be only one character long. The default setting for this command is the comma (,).

See also SET DECIMALS, SET()

SET SKIP

```
SET SKIP TO [alias1 [, alias2] ...]
```

Description The command creates a one-to-many relationship between databases.

Operational rules When two database files are linked with the SET RELATION command, a one-to-many relationship can occur if the child database has more than one record that corresponds to a record in the parent database. Use SET SKIP TO *alias* where *alias* is the child database, so that when the SKIP command is issued, each corresponding record in the child database is skipped to before the next record in the parent database is moved. If there is more than one child database, *alias* can be a list of child databases.

If a browse window is opened after a one-to-many relationship has been established, the parent browse will display pseudo-records for each related child record. Establishing a one-to-many relationship is most useful in reporting. To remove a one-to-many relationship, issue SET SKIP TO without the alias argument.

Example The following program sets a one-to-many relationship between two files. The common field is Clicode.

```
Use CLIENTS ORDER CODE IN 1
USE SALES IN 2
SET RELATION TO CLIENTS.Clicode INTO SALES
SET SKIP TO SALES
LIST Clicode, Name, B.Amount
Record #  CLICODE   NAME          B.AMOUNT
1         A01       JIM JONES     50.00
1         A01       JIM JONES     200.00
2         A02       RUTH DOE      150.00
2         A02       RUTH DOE      50.00
3         A03       HARRY CAREY   100.00
```

See also SET()

SET SKIP OF

```
SET SKIP OF MENU menu name expL
SET SKIP OF PAD pad name OF menu name expL
SET SKIP OF POPUP popup name expL
SET SKIP OF BAR expN|system menu option OF popup name expL
```

Description This command controls access to the options of a menu or pop-up.

Operational rules The SET SKIP OF command allows you to effectively turn on or off any option in a menu or pop-up that supports a SKIP FOR clause. At any point that the logical expression *expL* is true (.T.) the MENU *menu name*, PAD *pad name* OF *menu name*, POPUP *popup name*, or BAR *expN|system menu option* OF *popup name* will be disabled and cannot be selected.

If you use the Menu Builder to create your custom menus, you may not have to use these commands at all. The Menu Builder automatically generates the commands that disable options if you specify an expression in the Skip For... option.

See also SKPBAR(), SET()

SET SPACE

```
SET SPACE ON|OFF
```

Description This command controls whether a space is printed between expressions when using the ? or ?? commands.

Operational rules If SET SPACE is ON a space between fields or expression displayed with the ? or ?? commands. The default setting for this command is ON.

Example

```
x = "Fox"
y = "Pro"
SET SPACE ON
? x,y
Fox Pro
SET SPACE OFF
? x,y
FoxPro
```

See also SET()

SET STATUS

```
SET STATUS ON|OFF|TIMEOUT TO [expN]
```

Description This command controls the display of a DOS-style status bar and the amount of time that messages are displayed in the Windows-style status bar.

Operational rules When SET STATUS is ON, a DOS-style status bar showing current drive, current database, current record/total record and Insert, NumLock, and CapsLock settings is displayed at the bottom of the screen. The status bar is turned off with SET STATUS OFF. Use SET STATUS BAR to display the Windows-style status bar.

Use the TIMEOUT TO clause to control the length of time that messages are displayed in the Windows-style status bar. The number of seconds that a message is displayed can be specified with the *expN* parameter. The default is 5 seconds. Issuing the command SET STATUS TIMEOUT TO with no parameter resets the default. The default setting is OFF.

See also SET STATUS BAR, SET BRSTATUS, SET()

SET STATUS BAR

```
SET STATUS BAR ON|OFF
```

Description This command controls the appearance of the Windows-style status bar at the bottom of the screen.

Operational rules When SET STATUS BAR is ON, a Windows-style status bar is displayed at the bottom of the main FoxPro window. The status bar automatically displays the Insert, NumLock, and CapsLock key settings and can also display the time (SET CLOCK STATUS) and system messages. The default setting is ON.

SET STEP

```
SET STEP ON|OFF
```

Description This command controls activation of the Trace window.

Operational rules Once the Trace window has been opened you can step line by line through the executing program. The Trace window displays the command lines before and after the executing line.

See the FoxPro User Interface chapter (chapter 1) for more information on using the Trace window. The default setting is OFF.

See also SET ECHO, SET()

SET SYSMENU

SET SYSMENU ON|OFF|AUTOMATIC|TO [*menu popup list*]|TO [*menu pad list*]|TO [DEFAULT]|SAVE|NOSAVE

Description This command controls access to the FoxPro system menu.

Operational rules The FoxPro system menu is available for access at any time except when executing a program. The system menu FoxPro's default menu. Each pad, pop-up and bar of the system menu is assigned a bar number that can be used to create a custom menu while incorporating parts of the system menu. SET SYSMENU OFF simply removes the menu bar from the screen and access to the menu; use SET SYSMENU ON to restore it. If you use the Menu builder to create custom menus, the Quick Menu feature creates an exact replica of the FoxPro system menu using all of its bars. The following options can be used in creating and managing a custom menu:

ON Allows access to the system menu. You must use Alt to access the menu if it is not displayed.

OFF Turns off access to the system menu

AUTOMATIC Allows the system menu to be accessed during program execution.

TO *menu popup list* You can add a subset of menu pop-ups to the main FoxPro menu bar by including a menu pop-up list or pad list. The menu pop-up or pad list can contain any combination of menu pop-up or pad names separated by commas.

TO [DEFAULT] Issuing SET SYSMENU TO without any arguments disables the main FoxPro menu bar. If you modify the main menu bar or its pop-ups, you can restore it to the default configuration by issuing SET SYSMENU TO DEFAULT. You can specify a default configuration with SET SYSMENU SAVE.

SAVE Issuing SET SYSMENU SAVE saves the current menu system as the default configuration. If you modify the menu system after issuing SET SYSMENU SAVE, you can restore the previous configuration by issuing SET SYSMENU TO DEFAULT.

NOSAVE Issuing SET SYSMENU NOSAVE returns the main menu bar and its pop-ups to the default FoxPro startup configuration.

The default setting is AUTOMATIC.

Example Issuing the following command removes all menus from the main FoxPro menu bar except the File and Window menus.

```
SET SYSMENU TO _MFILE, _MWINDOW
```

See also SET()

SET TALK

```
SET TALK ON | OFF | WINDOW [window name] | NOWINDOW
```

Description This command determines if the results of FoxPro commands are displayed.

Operational rules When SET TALK is ON, commands like APPEND FROM, COPY, PACK, STORE, SUM, and SELECT (SQL) display information about their processing status. It is recommended that SET TALK be ON when working from the command window. In programs, many times this information is not desired output, so in programs you will probably want to SET TALK OFF.

Use the command SET TALK WINDOW to direct "talk" to the system message window. Including *window name* will direct the information to a user-defined window. The window does not have to be activated before using it in SET TALK WINDOW. If *window name* does not exist, FoxPro uses the system message window. The command SET TALK NOWINDOW resets the talk display back to the default system message window. The default setting is ON.

See also SET NOTIFY, SET ODOMETER, SET()

SET TEXTMERGE

```
SET TEXTMERGE [ON|OFF] [TO [filename] [ADDITIVE]] [WINDOW
window name] [SHOW|NOSHOW]
```

Description This command controls the evaluation of database fields and expressions that are surrounded by text merge delimiters.

Operational rules The \ and \\ and TEXT ... ENDTEXT commands output text to the screen, printer, or file. To display the contents of a memory variable or field, the expression should be surrounded with the text merge delimiters. If TEXTMERGE is set OFF, the delimiters are ignored, and the expressions are output literally.

Use SET TEXTMERGE TO *filename* to direct \ and \\ and TEXT ... ENDTEXT output to a file. Use the keyword ADDITIVE to append the data to the end of a file. Use the WINDOW *window name* clause to direct the output to a named window. Use the NOSHOW clause to suppress screen output. To return to displaying output on the screen, use the SHOW clause. The default setting is OFF.

Examples The first part of the program outputs information with SET TEXTMERGE ON, the second part with SET TEXTMERGE OFF. Note that when SET TEXTMERGE is OFF the expression within the delimiters is not evaluated.

```
** Mailing.PRG
** program that creates a form letter to each name in the data-
base
USE Maillist ORDER Mzip
SET TEXTMERGE TO Invite
SET TEXTMERGE ON
\Dear <<Maillist.fname>>,
\
```

```
\Please come to our party Saturday night at 8:00 p.m.
\Yours, Corky

SET TEXTMERGE OFF
\Dear <<Maillist.fname>>,
\
\Please come to our party Saturday night at 8:00 p.m.
\Yours, Corky
```

When run, the program displays:

```
Dear Harry,
Please come to our party Saturday night at 8:00 p.m.
Yours, Corky

Dear Maillist.fname,
Please come to our party Saturday night at 8:00 p.m.
Yours, Corky
```

See also \ and \\, SET TEXTMERGE DELIMITERS, SET()

SET TEXTMERGE DELIMITERS

`SET TEXTMERGE DELIMITERS [TO` *`expC1`* `[,` *`expC2`*`]]`

Description This command sets the delimiters used with the \ and \\ and TEXT ... ENDTEXT commands to evaluate database fields and expressions.

Operational rules The \ and \\ and TEXT ... ENDTEXT commands output text to the screen, printer or file. To display the contents of a memory variable or field, the expression should be surrounded with the text merge delimiters. To change the delimiter characters, use SET TEXTMERGE DELIMITERS TO *expC1, expC2*, where *expC2* is the right delimiter.

If *expC2* is omitted, *expC1* is used for both delimiters. To restore the default delimiters, issue the command without TO *expC1*. The default setting is << >>.

See also \ and \\, SET TEXTMERGE, SET()

SET TOPIC

`SET TOPIC TO [`*`expC|expL`*`]`

Description This command determines which help text is initially displayed when HELP is activated.

Operational rules The command SET TOPIC TO *expC* allows you to specify which topic of the .DBF-style help file is displayed when either the HELP command is issued or you select Contents... from the Help menu. SET TOPIC TO is ignored when using Windows-style help. *expC* is the name of the help topic to display. If the topic does not exist in the current help file, FoxPro will display the topic which closely matches *expC*.

If you use an expression with *expL*, FoxPro will display the text of the first topic that results to true (.T.) in the expression. Unlike the SET HELPFILTER command, displaying a help topic with SET TOPIC TO still allows you to view the text of other topics outside of the *expC\expL expressions.*

See also HELP, SET HELPFILTER, SET()

SET TRBETWEEN

```
SET TRBETWEEN ON|OFF
```

Description This command controls the tracing of a program in the Trace window.

Operational rules A program can be displayed in the Trace window while executing. If SET TRBETWEEN is ON, each line of the program is displayed and the program line about to be executed is highlighted. If SET TRBETWEEN is OFF, only those program lines that have break points will be highlighted during program execution.

The Trace window has an option of Trace Between Breaks. Setting that option on is the same as issuing the SET TRBETWEEN ON command and turning it off the same as issuing the SET TRBETWEEN OFF command. See the FoxPro User Interface chapter (chapter 1) for more information on using the Trace window.

See also The FoxPro User Interface, SET()

SET TYPEAHEAD

```
SET TYPEAHEAD TO expN
```

Description This command determines the number of keystrokes FoxPro saves in its buffer.

Operational rules The typeahead buffer stores characters input by the keyboard until evaluated by FoxPro. *expN* can be within the range of 0 to 128. SET TYPEAHEAD works only when SET ESCAPE is ON. Set the typeahead buffer to 0 to deactivate INKEY() and ON KEY. The CLEAR command can be used to clear the keyboard typeahead buffer. The default setting is 20.

See also CLEAR, INKEY(), ON KEY, SET()

SET UDFPARMS

```
SET UDFPARMS TO VALUE | REFERENCE
```

Description This command determines whether memory variables and arrays are passed to a procedure or user-defined function by value or by reference.

Operational rules If SET UDFPARMS TO is VALUE, variables that are passed to a procedure or user-defined function can be changed in the program, yet the variable's original value in the calling program isn't changed. If an array is passed only the first element of the array is passed by value. To pass an entire array when SET UDFPARMS TO is VALUE, preface the array name with @.

If SET UDFPARMS TO is REFERENCE and the value of the passed variable is changed, the original value in the calling program is also changed. If an array is passed, the entire array is passed to the procedure or user-defined function. The default setting is TO VALUE.

Examples

```
* PARMS.PRG
SET UDFPARMS TO VALUE
```

```
mvalue = 10
? changit(mvalue)
? mvalue
? "Here is the difference"
SET UDFPARMS TO REFERENCE
? changit(mvalue)
? mvalue
```

When run, the program displays:

```
20
10
Here is the difference
20
20

FUNCTION changit
PARAMETERS mvalue
mvalue = mvalue * 2
```

See also PROCEDURE, FUNCTION, SET()

SET UNIQUE

```
SET UNIQUE ON|OFF
```

Description This command controls whether or not database records with duplicate key values are included in an index.

Operational rules An index can be created that contains only one record for each key of the index expression. For example, if the index key field is STATE, only one record for each STATE field value will be included in the index. When the unique index is active, only those records in the index are available.

A unique index can be created by issuing SET UNIQUE ON and using the INDEX command to create the index. The INDEX command supports the optional keyword UNIQUE that can be used to create unique indexes even if SET UNIQUE is OFF.

An index file that is created while SET UNIQUE was ON retains its UNIQUE form when reindexed whether SET UNIQUE is ON or OFF. Furthermore, records added to the database file are not added to the index file if they include a key value already residing in the index file. A UNIQUE index file can be changed to a standard index file by the commands SET UNIQUE OFF, INDEX ON, and to restore the duplicate records, REINDEX. The default setting is OFF.

See also INDEX, REINDEX, SET()

SET VIEW

```
SET VIEW ON|OFF
SET VIEW TO filename | ?
```

Description This command controls the View window and restores the FoxPro environment.

Operational rules The SET VIEW ON command displays the FoxPro View window. The View window can also be displayed by selecting View from the Window menu or with the SET command. Use SET VIEW OFF to close the View window.

The SET VIEW TO *filename* command uses a view (.VUE) file to restore an environment setting created with the CREATE VIEW command. If the argument ? is used in place of *filename*, FoxPro will display the Open File dialog with a list of available view files to open.

See also SET, CREATE VIEW, SET()

SET WINDOW OF MEMO

`SET WINDOW OF MEMO TO` *`window name`*

Description This command specifies a window in which memo fields are edited.

Operational rules To edit a memo field within a user-defined window, move the cursor to the memo field and press Ctrl-Home, Ctrl-PgUp, Ctrl-PgDn, or double-click the memo field. The TO *window name* must be defined before the memo field can be edited.

See also @ ... EDIT, MODIFY MEMO, SET()

4
FoxPro functions

Functions perform many tasks in FoxPro. Functions can be used to change the value of variables and expressions, open low-level files, perform financial and statistical operations, and lock records and databases. Unlike FoxPro commands, however, each function returns a value, in the same way that a formula returns a value. There are many functions of many types, but in general they fall into one of the following categories:

- String-manipulation functions
- Arithmetic functions
- Date functions
- Screen-handling functions
- File-handling functions

In this chapter, the functions are listed in alphabetical order, each displaying its proper syntax. Each function is followed by a short description, and then details for using it. The conventions used in this chapter are:

- All functions and optional clauses are displayed in uppercase.
- All optional clauses are enclosed in brackets, [ ].
- Multiple choice clauses are separated by a pipe, |. Only one option can be used.
- All required and optional arguments are in lowercase italics. The expression type of each parameter is very important. Character expressions are identified by *expC*, numeric by *row*, *col*, and *expN*, date by *expD*, and logical by *expL*. Parameters defined by *filename* must contain a valid DOS directory, path, and filename. Any other type of parameter can be any valid FoxPro expression. Some functions require more than one parameter of the same type. These are identified sequentially.
- Some functions support an indefinite list of parameters that can be repeated. Those parameters are followed by ellipses (...).

%

```
expN1 % expN2
```

Description This function returns the remainder of one numeric expression divided by another.

Operational rules The % operator can be helpful in finding every *n*th occurrence of a number. For instance, in the sequence 1, 6, 11, 16, etc., each of the numbers has a modulo of 1 when *expN2* is 5. *expN2* cannot be a 0 because a denominator of zero is an infinite number. If *expN2* is negative, the result will be a negative number. This function returns a numeric value.

Examples

```
? 5 % 2
1
? 11 % 3
1
```

See also MOD()

&

```
& memvar [. expC]
```

Description This function is used for macro substitution.

Operational rules The macro substitution can be used with a character memory variable or array element, or as a prefix or a suffix to a literal string. Macro substitution treats the contents of *memvar* as a literal when it is preceded with the ampersand (&). This forces FoxPro to evaluate the contents of *memvar* rather than the variable expression itself. For example the commands

```
mfile = "STUDENTS.DBF"
USE &mfile
```

The use of & forces FoxPro to replace *mfile* with STUDENTS.DBF before the command is completely processed. If & is not used, FoxPro will search for a database named *mfile*. When referencing files in FoxPro, you can use a naming expression in place of macro substitution. A naming expression works like macro substitution but can only pass character strings and in some cases is significantly faster than using &. A naming expression is used simply by enclosing the string with parentheses (). For example, the previous commands can be replaced with:

```
mfile = "STUDENTS.DBF"
USE (mfile)
```

Macro substitution is primarily used for replacing a keyword or command in *memvar*. The following example shows an index tag being created using macro substitution:

```
USE STUDENTS
mtag = "UPPER(Lname)"
INDEX ON &mtag TAG Lname
```

This creates an index tag *Lname* in the current multiple index file.

When the macro is used as a prefix to *expC*, it must be followed by a period (.) to show where the macro ends and a literal or different macro begins. For example, the following commands show a macro and literal used together:

```
mpath = "C:\WORK\"
USE &mpath.STUDENTS.DBF
```

The following example shows two macros used in the same command:

```
mpath = "C:\WORK\"
mfile = "STUDENTS.DBF"
USE &mpath.&mfile
```

You can use macro substitution in any command or function that accepts a character string literal.

Examples The following examples show the use of macro substitution in evaluating FoxPro Commands

```
mfilt = "FOR Lname = 'Jones'"
LOCATE &mfilt

mfilt = "UPPER(State) = 'CA'"
SET FILTER TO &mfilt
```

See also EVALUATE()

$

expC1 $ expC2

Description This function is used to determine if one expression occurs in another.

Operational rules This function will return true (.T.) if the expression *expC1* is found within the expression *expC2*; otherwise false (.F.) is returned. This function is case-sensitive meaning upper and lowercase values are respected. The expressions used in *expC1* and *expC2* can be any character type variable, array element, database character field, or memo field.

Using this function can be extremely slow if used on a memo field or on a database with thousands of records. The function returns a logical value.

Examples The first example assumes the STUDENTS.Notes field is a memo field. The second example shows you how to reference both expressions as uppercase.

```
LIST FIELDS notes FOR "this student has one" $ STUDENTS.Notes

LIST FIELDS notes FOR "THIS STUDENT HAS ONE" $
UPPER(STUDENTS.Notes)
```

See also AT()

ABS()

ABS(*expN*)

Description This function returns the absolute value of *expN*.

Operational rules The ABS() function can be used to circumvent an error from occurring when taking the square root of a negative number, showing the number of days between two dates, or to display a negative number as positive, as in an outstanding balance on a bill. This function returns a numeric value.

Examples

```
mvalue = 64
? SQRT(ABS(mvalue))
8.00
? ABS({9/9/89}-{12/25/89})
107
```

See also SQRT()

ACOPY()

ACOPY(*array1*, *array2* [, *expN1* [, *expN2* [, *expN3*]]])

Description This function copies one array to another.

Operational rules If only *array1, array2* arguments are specified, all elements of *array1* are copied one-to-one to *array2*. If the destination array *array2* has not been initialized, FoxPro will automatically create it.

The optional argument *expN1* specifies the element number where copying is to start. The argument *expN2* specifies the number of elements to be copied. If *expN2* is 1, all elements starting with *expN1* are copied. *expN3* specifies the element number of the destination array where copying is to begin.

If the arrays are two-dimensional, the AELEMENT() function can be used to return the number of a particular row and column. This can be helpful when using *expN1* or *expN2*. This function returns a numeric value. The value is the number of elements copied, or –1 if no elements were copied.

Example This example loads the records of the STUDENTS database into an array and copies the array to another. The students database contains 50 records.

```
USE STUDENTS
COPY TO ARRAY st_rec
mcopy = ACOPY(st_rec, st_rec2)
? mcopy
50
```

See also AELEMENT()

ACOS()

ACOS(*expN*)

Description This command returns the arc cosine (the inverse cosine) of an angle.

Operational rules The ACOS() function is used in calculating the degrees of an angle when the lengths of two of the sides are known. The angle is specified with *expN*. The RTOD() function converts the return value, which is given in radians, to degrees. Therefore, the function

RTOD(ACOS(*expN*))

is equal to

ACOS(*expN*)*180/PI().

The argument *expN*, must be between –1 and 1. Keeping in mind that the cosine represents the x-axis value at any point, the ACOS( ) function always returns a value between 0 and pi (approximately 3.1416).

If you use memory variables as the argument, the function then uses 20-place numeric accuracy. You can change the number of decimal points displayed in the answer with the SET DECIMALS command. The function returns a numeric value.

Examples

```
? ACOS(1)
0
? RTOD(ACOS(0))
90
```

See also RTOD( ), ASIN( ), COS( ), PI( ), SIN( ), SET DECIMALS

ADEL( )

ADEL(*array*, *expN* [,2])

Description This function deletes an array element, row or column.

Operational rules When an element is deleted from *array*, all elements below it are moved back and their value changed to false (.F.). If the array is two-dimensional, the function will delete a row or column from the array. *expN* specifies the row to delete and the optional argument. Use the optional argument *,2* to delete a column. This function returns a numeric value. The value is 1 if the deletion is successful; otherwise it returns –1.

Example The example displays a four-element array of team names where the second element is deleted.

```
? teams(1), teams(2), teams(3), teams(4)
Cubs  Giants  Dodgers  Braves
mdel = ADEL(teams,2)
? mdel
1
? teams(1), teams(2), teams(3), teams(4)
Cubs  Dodgers  Braves .F.
```

See also AELEMENT( )

ADIR( )

ADIR(*array* [, *expC1* [, *expC2*]])

Description This function copies information about files into an array.

Operational rules The ADIR( ) function places the file information in the array specified with *array*. If the destination array has not been initialized, FoxPro will automatically create it. The array size is increased automatically to hold the file information of all files that match the specified skeleton.

ADIR() is best used with two-dimensional arrays, as the column returns five pieces of information about a file. If the array is one-dimensional, use AELEMENT() to find the corresponding number for a particular row and column pair. The information copied is:

Column #	Information
1	filename
2	File size
3	File date
4	File time
5	File attributes (Archive, Hidden, Read only, System)

The optional expression *expC1* specifies a file skeleton such as *.DBF or BUDGET.*. If *expC1* is omitted, the skeleton *.* is used.

The optional expression *expC2* specifies additional information that can be returned. The letter *D* in the expression returns information about subdirectories. The letter *H* returns information about hidden files, and *S* returns information about system files. This function returns a numeric value.

Example

```
mdir = ADIR(mfiles,"*.frx")
? mdir
3
? mfiles(1,1), mfiles(1,2), mfiles(1,3), mfiles(1,4),
mfiles(1,5)
STUDENT.FRX      3916         07/12/91        10:50:12   .A...
? mfiles(2,1), mfiles(2,2), mfiles(2,3), mfiles(2,4),
mfiles(2,5)
CLASSES.FRX      5114         09/01/91        12:20:44   .A..R.
```

See also AELEMENT(), AINS()

AELEMENT()

`AELEMENT(array, expN1 [, expN2])`

Description This function returns the number of an array element.

Operational rules Several FoxPro functions (such as ADEL(), AINS() and ASORT()) require that elements of two-dimensional arrays be referenced by their element number instead of their row and column number subscripts. AELEMENT() converts the row and column number to this number.

If the array is one-dimensional, only the argument *expN1* is needed. In that case the function simply returns *expN1*, as long as *expN1* is not greater than the array's dimension. The expression *expN2* is required for two-dimensional arrays. *expN2* references the column subscript of the array. An array element can be referenced by its element number or subscripts. This function returns a numeric value.

Example This first example will locate the element of a one-dimensional array; the second a two-dimensional array. The third example shows how to store the value of an array element to a variable.

```
DIMENSION teams(4)
teams(1) = "Cubs"
```

```
teams(2) = "Giants"
teams(3) = "Dodgers"
teams(4) = "Braves"
DISPLAY MEMORY LIKE teams
TEAMS Pub  A
( 1, 1)   C    "Cubs"        (element number 1)
( 1, 2)   C    "Giants"      (element number 2)
( 1, 3)   C    "Dodgers"     (element number 3)
( 1, 4)   C    "Braves"      (element number 4)
mwhere = AELEMENT(teams,3)
? mwhere
3
DIMENSION teams(2,2)
teams(1,1) = "Cubs"
teams(1,2) = "Giants"
teams(2,1) = "Dodgers"
teams(2,2) = "Braves"
DISPLAY MEMORY LIKE teams
TEAMS Pub  A
( 1, 1)   C     "Cubs"        (element number 1)
( 1, 2)   C     "Giants"      (element number 2)
( 2, 1)   C     "Dodgers"     (element number 3)
( 2, 2)   C     "Braves"      (element number 4)
mwhere = AELEMENT(teams,2,1)
? mwhere
3
myteam = teams(2,1)   && Subscript
? myteam
Dodgers
myteam = teams(3)     && Element
? myteam
Dodgers
```

See also AELEMENT(), AINS(), ADEL(), DIMENSION

AFIELDS()

AFIELDS(*array*)

Description This function copies the structure of the current database into an array.

Operational rules The AFIELDS() function places the field information in the array specified with *array*. If the destination array has not been initialized, FoxPro will automatically create it; otherwise the array size is increased automatically to hold the information.

AFIELDS() is best used with two-dimensional arrays, as the column returns four pieces of information about a file. If the array is one-dimensional, use AELEMENT() to find the corresponding number for a particular row and column pair. The information copied is:

Column #	Information
1	Field name
2	Field type
3	Field length
4	Number of decimal places

This function returns a numeric value. The value returned is the number of fields in the database.

Example

```
USE STUDENTS
mfields = AFIELDS(mstruc)
? mfields
8
? mstruc(1,1), mstruc(1,2), mstruc(1,3), mstruc(1,4)
NAME  C   25     0
? mstruc(2,1), mstruc(2,2), mstruc(2,3), mstruc(2,4)
GPA   N   -5     2
```

See also AELEMENT()

AFONT()

`AFONT(array, expC [, expN]])`

Description This command copies font information to an array.

Operational rules The AFONT() function copies the information of all installed Windows fonts to the specified array. The array will not include printer specific fonts and does not have to be declared before calling AFONT(). If the array already exists, it is resized to hold all font names. Calling AFONT() with no parameters simply places the names of all installed Windows fonts into *array* and returns a value of true (.T.)

You can specify a font name with *expC* to get information on a single font. If the font specified is only available in certain point sizes, such as 8-point or 9-point, the array will contain an element for each available size of the font, and the function returns true (.T.). If the font is scalable or True Type, the array will contain one element with a value of –1, and the function returns true (.T.). To determine if a specific font size is available, specify the size in expN.

If the font specified in *expC* is available in the size specified in *expN*, the array will contain a single element with a value of true (.T.) and the function will return a value of (.T.). This function returns a logical value. The value is true (.T.) if the specified request is successful; otherwise it returns false (.F.)

Example The first example loads an array with the names of all installed Windows fonts. The second example requests the available point sizes for a specific font.

```
mgetfont = AFONT(mFonts)
? mgetfont
.T.
? mfonts[1]
Arial
? mfonts[5]
Erie
? mfonts[9]
FoxFont

mgetfont = AFONT(mfonts,"FoxFont")
? mgetfont
.T.
```

```
?  mfonts[1]
7
? mfonts[2]
9
```

See also GETFONT(), WFONT()

AINS()

`AINS(`*array*`)` *expN* `[,2])`

Description This command inserts an element, row or column into any array.

Operational rules When an element is inserted into *array*, all elements below it are moved down. If the arrays are two-dimensional, the function defaults to inserting row *expN*. Use the optional argument ,2 to insert a column. This function returns a numeric value. The value is 1 if the insertion is successful; otherwise it returns –1.

Example The example displays an array of team names where a third element is inserted.

```
? teams(1), teams(2), teams(3), teams(4)
Cubs  Giants  Dodgers  Braves
mins = AINS(teams,2)
? mins
1
DISPLAY MEMORY LIKE teams
TEAMS Pub  A
( 1, 1)   C    "Cubs"              (element number 1)
( 1, 2)        .F.                 (element number 2)
( 1, 3)   C    "Giants"            (element number 3)
( 1, 4)   C    "Dodgers"           (element number 4)
( 1, 5)   C    "Braves"            (element number 5)
```

See also AELEMENT(), ADEL()

ALEN()

`ALEN(`*array* `[,` *expN*`])`

Description This function returns the number of elements, rows or columns in an array.

Operational rules If the *array* is the only argument, the total number of elements is returned. If *expN* is 1, the function returns the number of rows. If *expN* is 2, it returns the number of columns. An *expN* of 0 is equivalent to not using the argument.

Example

```
DIMENSION mstuff(2,3)
? ALEN(mstuff)
6
```

See also AELEMENT(), DIMENSION

ALIAS()

`ALIAS([`*expN* `|` *expC*`])`

Description This function returns the alias name of a specified work area.

Operational rules The ALIAS() function with no arguments returns the alias name of the database in the current work area. A different work area can be specified by its number with *expN* or by the alias of the database with *expC*.

Use the IN keyword with the USE command to choose the work area before opening a file. The valid work areas are 1 through 25 in the Standard version, or 1 through 225 in the Extended version. The filename is the default alias, although you can provide a different one by using the ALIAS keyword with the USE command. This function returns a character value.

Examples

```
USE JOURNAL IN 1
USE ACCOUNT IN 2 ALIAS COA
? ALIAS(1)
JOURNAL
? ALIAS(2)
COA
```

See also SELECT, USE

ALLTRIM()

ALLTRIM(*expC*)

Description This function returns a character string with all leading and trailing spaces removed.

Operational rules The ALLTRIM() function is useful when comparing strings and also when combining character expressions. This function returns a character value.

Examples

```
? ALLTRIM(Lname) + " " + ALLTRIM(Fname)
John Smith

mstring1 = " Hello"
mstring2 = " Hello "
? mstring1 = mstring2
.F.
? ALLTRIM(mstring1) = ALLTRIM(mstring1)
.T.
? ALLTRIM(mstring1) + ", John"
Hello, John
```

See also TRIM()

ANSITOOEM()

ANSITOOEM(*expC*)

Description This function converts a character string from Windows ANSI to DOS ASCII characters.

Operational rules The ANSITOOEM( ) function is used to convert Windows ANSI characters to a DOS ASCII equivalent. Specify the string to convert with *expC*. The companion function is OEMTOANSI( ) which converts ANSI to ASCII. This function is useful in converting FoxPro for Windows text files to FoxPro for DOS. This function returns a character value.

Example This example converts a character using the Windows Arial font to a DOS character set equivalent.

```
? ANSITOOEM("Y")
Y
```

See also OEMTOANSI(), CHRTRAN()

ASC()

ASC(*expC*)

Description This function returns the ASCII value of a character expression.

Operational rules The ASC( ) function is used to show the ASCII number of a character. If the argument is a string of more than one character, the function returns the number of the first character of the string.

Each key on a computer keyboard has a number that corresponds to it. These numbers are called ASCII codes (pronounced as-kee), which stands for American Standard Code for Information Interchange. Almost all microcomputers use the ASCII codes when storing information.

See the CHR() function described in this chapter for a table of ASCII codes. You can also look up ASCII codes using the ASCII Codes window available from the FoxPro System Menu. Following the ASCII chart, "A" is number 65, while "a" is number 97. The first 32 numbers represent characters such as the backspace (BS) and escape (ESC) which cannot be entered as a character expression. This function returns a numeric value.

Examples

```
? ASC("a")
97
mvalue = "A"
? ASC(mvalue)
65
```

See also CHR( )

ASCAN()

ASCAN(*array*, *expr* [, *expN1* [, *expN2*]])

Description This function searches an array for a given expression.

Operational rules The ASCAN( ) function returns the matching element number. If no match is found, the function returns 0. If SET EXACT IS ON, *expr* must be the same length as the matching array expression. Otherwise, matches are made based on the number of characters of *expr*. Use the optional argument *expN1* to define the array element to begin searching at. Use *expN2* to define the number of elements to be searched.

Example

```
? teams(1), teams(2), teams(3), teams(4)
Cubs  Giants  Dodgers  Braves
? ASCAN(teams,"G")
2
SET EXACT ON
? ASCAN(teams,"G")
0
```

See also AELEMENT(), SET EXACT

ASIN()

ASIN(*expN*)

Description This function returns the arcsine (the inverse sine) of an angle.

Operational rules The ASIN() function is used in calculating the degrees of an angle when the lengths of two of the sides are known. The angle is specified with *expN*. The RTOD() function converts the answer, which is given in radians, to degrees. Therefore, the function

RTOD(ASIN(*expN*))

is equal to

ASIN(*expN*)*180/PI().

The argument *expN* must be between –1 and 1. Keeping in mind that the sine represents the y-axis value at any point, the ASIN() function always returns a value between –pi/2 to pi/2. If you use memory variables as the argument, the function then uses 20-place numeric accuracy. You can change the number of decimal points displayed in the answer with the SET DECIMALS command. This function returns a numeric value.

Examples

```
? ASIN(PI())
0
? RTOD(ASIN(PI()))
90
```

See also ACOS(), PI(), SIN(), SET DECIMALS

ASORT()

ASORT(*array* [, *expN1* [, *expN2* [, *expN3*]]])

Description This function sorts an array.

Operational rules The ASORT() function sorts an array specified with *array*. The array can be sorted in ascending or descending order. If it is a two-dimensional array, it is sorted by the rows so that the row number changes, but the column number remains the same. Use the optional argument *expN1* to define the place to start sorting. The default is 1.

If the array is two-dimensional, *expN1* represents the column number that gets sorted (the default is column 1). Use *expN2* to define the number of elements to be sorted. If the array is two-dimensional, *expN2* represents the row number to start sorting at. If *expN2* is –1 or omitted, the function sorts all elements from the starting position through to the end. The default order is ascending. To sort in descending order, use any nonzero number for *expN3*. This function returns a numeric value. The value is 1 if the sort is successful; otherwise it returns –1.

Examples

```
? mcharm(1,1), mcharm(2,1), mcharm(3,1)
Heart  Moon   Clover
? mcharm(1,2), mcharm(2,2), mcharm(3,2)
Pink  Yellow  Green
=ASORT(mcharm)
? mcharm(1,1), mcharm(2,1), mcharm(3,1)
Clover  Heart  Moon
? mcharm(1,2), mcharm(2,2), mcharm(3,2)
Green  Pink   Yellow
```

In the example above, the two-dimensional array, mcharm, is sorted with ASORT(). The array was originally defined as:

Row, column	1	2
1	Heart	Pink
2	Moon	Yellow
3	Clover	Green

When sorted with the ASORT() function, the array becomes sorted by column 1, the name of the symbol:

Row, column	1	2
1	Clover	Green
2	Heart	Pink
3	Moon	Yellow

To sort alphabetically by color, use the optional argument *expN1*. The function ASORT (mcharm, 2) would result in the following sort:

Row, column	1	2
1	Clover	Green
2	Heart	Pink
3	Moon	Yellow

See also ASCAN()

ASUBSCRIPT()

ASUBSCRIPT(*array, expN1, expN2*)

Description This function returns a row or column subscript given an array element number.

Operational rules FoxPro functions such as ASCAN() return an element number. To convert that number to the corresponding row and/or column, use ASUBSCRIPT(). This function is the opposite of the AELEMENT() function, which returns the element number given the row and column subscript.

If the array is one-dimensional, use a 1 in *expN2*. In that case the function simply returns *expN1*, as long as *expN1* is not greater than the array's dimension. Place a 1 in expression *expN2* to return the row subscript. When *expN2* is 2, it returns the column subscript. This function returns a numeric value.

Example

```
DIMENSION teams(2,2)
DISPLAY MEMORY LIKE teams
( 1, 1)    C     "Cubs"       (element number 1)
( 1, 2)    C     "Giants"     (element number 2)
( 2, 1)    C     "Dodgers"    (element number 3)
( 2, 2)    C     "Braves"     (element number 4)
? ASUBSCRIPT(teams,3,1)
2
```

See also AELEMENT(), DIMENSION

AT()

AT(*expC1*, *expC2* [, *expN*])

Description This function returns the position where one string appears within another.

Operational rules The AT() function searches the character expression *expC2* for an occurrence of *expC1*. The character string searched and the character string searching for can be either an expression or a memo field. The return value is the starting location of *expC2*. If the expression is not found in *expC2*, the return value is 0.

Unlike the ATC() function, AT() is case-sensitive meaning upper and lowercase values are respected. The optional argument *expN* can be specified to locate the *expN*th occurrence of *expC1* in *expC2*. This function returns a numeric value.

Example

```
? AT("Street","5 Main Street")
8
? AT("Street","5 Main STREET")
0
? AT(" ","5 Main Street",2)
7
```

The following example shows how the AT() function can be used in conjunction with the SUBSTR() function to extract last names from fields that contain both the first and last names. The arguments of the SUBSTR() are SUBSTR(*string*, *start number*, *n*). Therefore, the function states, "extract part of the Name field, starting at the position of the space, and going until the field ends:"

```
USE CLIENTS
LIST OFF Name
Name
John Smith
Bonnie Miller
```

```
Tom Jones
LIST OFF SUBSTR(Name, AT(" ",Name))
Smith
Miller
Jones
```

See also AT(), SUBSTR()

ATAN()

`ATAN(expN)`

Description This function returns the arc tangent (the inverse tangent) of an angle.

Operational rules The ATAN() function is used in calculating the degrees of an angle when the lengths of two of the sides are known. The angle is specified with *expN*. The RTOD() function converts the answer, which is given in radians, to degrees. Therefore, the function RTOD(ATAN(*expN*)) is equal to ATAN(*expN*)*180/PI().

The tangent represents the $^{sine}/_{cosine}$ at any point on a circle. Therefore, the ATAN() function always returns a value between –pi/2 to pi/2, representing a quadrant I or IV angle. This function returns a numeric value.

Examples

```
? ATAN(0)
0        (radians)
? ATAN(1)*180/PI()
45       (degrees)
```

See also COS(), SIN(), RTOD()

ATC()

`ATC(expC1, expC2 [, expN])`

Description This function returns the position where one string appears within another without being case-sensitive.

Operational rules The ATC() function searches the character expression *expC2* for an occurrence of *expC1*. The character string searched and the character string searching for can be either an expression or a memo field. The return value is the starting location of *expC2*. If the expression is not found in *expC2*, the return value is 0.

Unlike the AT() function, ATC() is not case-sensitive meaning upper and lowercase values are ignored. The optional argument *expN* can be specified to locate the *expNth* occurrence of *expC1* in *expC2*. The *ATC()* function is equivalent to the following function:

`AT(UPPER(expC), UPPER(expC))`

This function returns a numeric value.

Example

```
? ATC("street","5 Main Street")
8
```

See also AT()

ATCLINE()

```
ATCLINE(expC1, expC2)
```

Description This function returns the position where one string appears within another without being case-sensitive.

Operational rules The ATCLINE() function searches the memo field or expression *expC2* for an occurrence of *expC1*. The character string searched and the character string searching for can be either an expression or a memo field. The return value is the starting location of *expC2*. If the expression is not found in *expC2*, the return value is 0. Unlike the ATLINE() function, ATCLINE() is not case-sensitive meaning upper and lowercase values are ignored.

The line number returned is determined by the value of SET MEMOWIDTH even if *expC2* is not a memo field. If SET MEMOWIDTH is 20, more lines will occur than if it is set to 80. The ATCLINE() function is equivalent to the following function:

```
ATLINE(UPPER(expC), UPPER(expC))
```

This function returns a numeric value.

See also ATLINE(), SET MEMOWIDTH

ATLINE()

```
ATLINE(expC1, expC2)
```

Description This function returns the position where one string appears within another.

Operational rules The ATLINE() function searches the character expression *expC2* for an occurrence of *expC1*. The character string searched and the character string searching for can be either an expression or a memo field. The return value is the starting location of *expC2*. If the expression is not found in *expC2*, the return value is 0. Unlike the ATCLINE() function, ATLINE() is case-sensitive meaning upper and lowercase values are respected. This function returns a numeric value.

Example The following example assumes that the database has a memo field named Notes:

```
STORE ATLINE("12/15/90",NOTES) TO Memoln
8
? MLINE(NOTES,MEMOLN)
Phone call 12/15/90: discussed lease option
```

See also MLINE()

ATN2()

```
ATN2(expN1, expN2)
```

Description This function returns the arc tangent (the inverse tangent) of specified sine and cosine values.

Operational rules The ATN2() function returns the arc tangent from a set of x and y coordinates. *expN1* is the x coordinate and *expN2* is the y coordinate. Because both x and y are given, the quadrant can be calculated. Therefore, unlike the ATAN() function, the result will be between –pi and pi. The result of *expN1/expN2* must be between –pi and +pi.

Examples

```
? ATN2(1,0)
0        (radians)
? RTOD(ATN2(1,-1))
-  45    (degrees)
```

See also ATAN(), RTOD()

BAR()

```
BAR()
```

Description This function returns the bar number of the most recent selection from a pop-up menu.

Operational rules Each bar in a pop-up menu is numbered using the DEFINE BAR command. BAR() returns zero if no pop-up menu is active. This function returns a numeric value.

See also ACTIVATE POPUP, DEFINE POPUP, DEFINE BAR

BETWEEN()

BETWEEN(*expr1, expr2, expr3*)

Description This function determines if an expression is equal to or lies between two other expressions.

Operational rules The BETWEEN() returns true (.T.) if *expr1* is greater than or equal to *expr2*, and *expr1* is less than or equal to *expr3*; otherwise false (.F.) is returned. All expressions in the arguments must be of the same type (numeric, character, logical or date). The BETWEEN() function is equivalent to the following criteria selection:

expr1 >= *expr2* AND *expr1* <= *expr3*

This function returns a logical value.

Examples

```
? BETWEEN(5,2,9)
.T.
USE CLIENTS
LIST FOR BETWEEN(AMT, 100,500)
Record #   CLIENT    AMT
4          Smith     300
6          Miller    450
7          Jones     100
```

See also MAX(), MIN()

BOF()

BOF([*expN* | *expC*])

Description This function determines if the record pointer is at the beginning of a database.

Operational rules The BOF() function returns true (.T.) when the record pointer is at the top of a file and is then moved one record back. This function is useful in programs where the database is being read in reverse order.

The SKIP command moves the record pointer forward one record, and SKIP –1 moves the pointer backward one record. The top record in a nonindexed file is record number one. The top record in an indexed file is the first record in the index. The two situations where the BOF() returns .T. are:

- When the pointer is at the top record, and SKIP –1 is issued.
- When the top record is being edited, and the user presses PgUp.

If no file is opened in the current work area, BOF() returns false (.F.). BOF() is determined for the current work area if no argument is supplied. To test the condition of BOF() in another work area specify the work area number with *expN* or the database alias with *expC*. This function returns a logical value.

Examples

```
USE MAILLIST
GOTO TOP
SKIP -1
? BOF()
.T.

* Scan.prg
GOTO BOTTOM
DO WHILE !BOF()
     ? Lname,Fname
     SKIP - 1
ENDDO
```

See also EOF(), SKIP

CAPSLOCK()

`CAPSLOCK([expL])`

Description This function turns on and off the CapsLock key (to all uppercase or back to normal).

Operational rules CAPSLOCK(.T.) switches the CapsLock on, and CAPSLOCK(.F.) switches the CapsLock off. If *expL* is given, CAPSLOCK() returns the mode before the change. If *expL* is not specified, CAPSLOCK() returns the state of the CapsLock key without changing mode. This function returns a logical value.

Examples

```
? CAPSLOCK(.T.)
.T.      CapsLock Turns on.
? CAPSLOCK()
.T.      If the CapsLock is still on.
? CAPSLOCK(.F.)
.T.      CapsLock Turned off.
```

See also NUMLOCK(), INSMODE()

CDOW()

`CDOW(`*`expD`*`)`

Description This function returns the name of the day, given a date expression.

Operational rules The three ways to enter a date as an argument are:

- Enclose the date in curly brackets: {12/5/89}
- Use the *CTOD()* function: *CTOD("12/5/2010")*
- Use a field name or memory variable.

The date is assumed to be in the 1900s when two digits are used for the year. An invalid date as the argument generates an error message. This function returns a date value.

Examples

```
? CDOW({9/6/60})
Tuesday

? CDOW(CTOD("12/25/89"))
Monday
```

See also CTOD(), DTOC()

CDX()

`CDX(`*`expN1`*` [, `*`expN2`*` | `*`expC`*`])`

Description This function returns the name of a compound index file in a specified work area.

Operational rules The CDX() function is used to return the filename of any compound indexes opened in the current work area. Structural compound indexes are opened automatically when the database is opened. If another compound index is opened with the SET INDEX command, each successive index file is given an order number, depending on the order that it was opened. *expN1* must be specified to determine which index filename to return. If a database has a structural compound index, or one or more compound indexes, the following applies:

- If *expN1* is 1 and the database has a structural index file, the name of the structural index file is returned. Otherwise the name of the first opened compound index file is returned.
- If *expN1* is 2 and the database has a structural index file, the name of the first compound index filename opened with SET INDEX or specified in USE ... INDEX. Otherwise the name of the second opened compound index file is returned.
- If *expN1* is 3 and the database has a structural index file, the second compound index filename is returned and so on. Otherwise the name of the third opened compound index file is returned.
- If *expN1* is greater than the number of open compound index files, the null string is returned.

CDX() returns the name of appropriately numbered multiple indexes open in the current work area, unless a work area argument is provided. Use *expN2* to specify the work area number and *expC* to specify the database alias. If no index file is open in the designated area, CDX() returns a null string. If the designated alias name does not exist, CDX() returns an error message.

If SET FULLPATH is ON, the return value will contain a fully qualified drive and path name of the index file. The CDX() function is identical to the MDX() function. Use TAG() to return the tag names from within an index. This function returns a character value.

Examples This example assumes the STUDENTS.DBF file has a structural compound index.

```
SET FULLPATH ON
USE STUDENTS
SET INDEX TO C:\WORK\STUD2.CDX
? CDX(1)
C:\WORK\STUDENTS.CDX

SET FULLPATH OFF
? CDX(2)
STUD2.CDX
```

See also TAG(), SET INDEX, chapter 1, The FoxPro User Interface

CEILING()

`CEILING(`*`expN`*`)`

Description This function returns an integer that is greater than the argument, unless the argument is an integer.

Operational rules If the argument *expN* is a negative number, it returns a number closer to zero. This function is useful in cases where you must round up all numbers that have decimal places. This function returns a numeric value.

Examples

```
? CEILING(5.2)
6

? CEILING(-5.6)
-5
```

See also FLOOR(), ROUND()

CHR()

`CHR(`*`expN`*`)`

Description This function returns the ASCII character of the specified number.

Operational rules The CHR() function returns the character corresponding to *expN*. CHR() can be used to send printer control codes to a printer. Each key on a computer keyboard has a number that corresponds to it. These numbers are called ASCII codes (pronounced as-kee). Almost all microcomputers use the ASCII codes when storing information. The CHR() function is useful for displaying special characters on the computer and printer, such as graphics characters, the bell tone, and printer control codes.

Table 4-1 shows the codes for the numbers 0 through 127, which are standard among all ASCII computers. Following this chart, you can see that CHR(65) is an A, while CHR(97) is a. The first 32 numbers represent characters, such as the backspace (BS) and escape (ESC), which cannot be printed. Therefore the CHR() of numbers between 1 and 32 are blank. This function returns a character value.

Table 4-1 Standard ASCII codes that correspond to CHR(0) through CHR(127).

0 NUL	16 DLE	32 SP	48 0	64 @	80 P	96 ‘	112 p
1 SOH	17 DC1	33 !	49 1	65 A	81 Q	97 a	113 q
2 STX	18 DC2	34 "	50 2	66 B	82 R	98 b	114 r
3 ETX	19 DC3	35 #	51 3	67 C	83 S	99 c	115 s
4 DOT	20 DC4	36 $	52 4	68 D	84 T	100 d	116 t
5 ENQ	21 NAK	37 %	53 5	69 E	85 U	101 e	117 u
6 ACK	22 SYN	38 &	54 6	70 F	86 V	102 f	118 v
7 BEL	23 ETB	39 ‘	55 7	71 G	87 W	103 g	119 w
8 BS	24 CAN	40 (	56 8	72 H	88 X	104 h	120 x
9 HT	25 EM	41)	57 9	73 I	89 Y	105 i	121 y
10 LF	26 SUB	42 *	58 :	74 J	90 Z	106 j	122 z
11 VT	27 ESC	43 +	59 ;	75 K	91 [	107 k	123 {
12 FF	28 FS	44 ,	60 <	76 L	92 \	108 l	124 |
13 CR	29 GS	45 –	61 =	77 M	93]	109 m	125 }
14 SO	30 RS	46 .	62 >	78 N	94 ^	110 n	126 ~
15 SI	31 US	47 /	63 ?	79 O	95 _	111 o	127 DEL

Examples

```
? CHR(65)
A
? CHR(7) + "That answer is invalid, try again." && message
beeps
That answer is invalid, try again.
```

See also ASC()

CHRSAW()

`CHRSAW([expN])`

Description This function determines if the keyboard buffer contains a character.

Operational rules The CHRSAW() function returns true (.T.) if a character is present in the keyboard buffer, and false (.F.) if not. CHRSAW() doesn't affect the keyboard buffer contents. The optional argument *expN* forces the function to wait *expN* seconds before evaluating the buffer. This function returns a logical value.

Example

```
@ 15, 1 SAY "Enter Your Selection: " GET mchoice
IF !CHRSAW(60)
   ? "Wake up!! Hurry up and choose a selection!"
ELSE
   READ
ENDIF
```

See also INKEY(), READKEY()

CHRTRAN()

CHRTRAN(*expC1*, *expC2*, *expC3*)

Description This function changes a character expression by replacing all occurrences of characters found to match a character in the second character expression with the corresponding character in the third character expression.

Operational rules The CHRTRAN() functions translates the character expression *expC1* using the expressions *expC2* and *expC3*. If *expC2* has more characters than *expC3*, the extra characters in *expC2* are deleted from *expC1*. If *expC2* has fewer characters than *expC3*, then the extra *expC3* characters are ignored. This function returns a character value.

Examples

```
? CHRTRAN("hill","hi","ma")        && "h" replaced with "m", "i"
with "a"
mall
? CHRTRAN("Ken is glad.","gl","s")
Ken is sad.
```

CMONTH()

CMONTH(*expD*)

Description This function returns the name of the month, given a date expression.

Operational rules The three ways to enter a date as an argument are:

- Enclose the date in curly brackets: {12/5/89}
- Use the CTOD() function: CTOD("12/5/2010")
- Use a field name or memory variable.

The date is assumed to be in the 1900s when two digits are used for the year. An invalid date as the argument generates an error message. This function returns a character value.

Examples

```
? CMONTH({9/6/60})
September
? CMONTH(CTOD("12/25/89"))
December
```

See also CTOD(), DOW(), DTOC()

CNTBAR()

`CNTBAR(`*`expC`*`)`

Description This command returns the number of options in pop-up.

Operational rules The CNTBAR() function returns the number of options defined in pop-up *expC*. A pop-up is created and named with the DEFINE POPUP command, and activated with ACTIVATE POPUP. This command returns a numeric value.

Example

```
DEFINE POPUP list MARGIN RELATIVE SHADOW
DEFINE BAR 1 OF list PROMPT "Add a record"
DEFINE BAR 2 OF list PROMPT "Edit a record"
DEFINE BAR 3 OF list PROMPT "Goto a record"
DEFINE BAR 4 OF list PROMPT "Browse records"
? CNTBAR("list")
4
```

See also ACTIVATE POPUP, DEFINE POPUP

CNTPAD()

`CNTPAD(`*`expC`*`)`

Description This command returns the number of options in a menu.

Operational rules The CNTPAD() function returns the number of pads defined in menu *expC*. A menu is created and named with the DEFINE MENU command, and activated with ACTIVATE MENU. The argument *expC* is the name of the menu. This command returns a numeric value.

Example

```
DEFINE main
DEFINE PAD options OF main PROMPT "Options"
DEFINE PAD reports OF main PROMPT "Reports"
? CNTPAD("main")
2
```

See also ACTIVATE MENU, DEFINE MENU

COL()

`COL()`

Description This function returns the current column number position of the cursor.

Operational rules The COL() function is used in conjunction with the @ ...SAY/GET command that places a display in a particular position on the screen or printed page. The @ ... SAY/GET command places the display on the screen using the following syntax:

```
@ row, col SAY expression
```

For instance, the command:

```
@ 5,30 SAY "HI THERE"
```

would display the words HI THERE on the fifth row on the screen, in column 30. The cursor is then positioned at the end of the expression, so the COL() function would return 38 after printing the expression. This allows you to use the COL() function to display an expression on the screen relative to another expression. This function returns a numeric value.

Examples The following program prints a message after the expression *Mstring* (assuming it is of variable lengths). If *Mstring* places the cursor too far to the right, the program places the message on the next line; otherwise it is placed right next to *Mstring*:

```
@ 5,30 SAY Mstring
IF COL() > 68
   @ 5, COL() SAY "Y)es or N)o"
ELSE
   @ 6, 30 SAY "Y)es or N)o"
ENDIF
```

This program prints a 5-character string continuously until it reaches the end of the screen:

```
DO WHILE COL() < 75
   @ 10, COL() SAY Mstring
ENDDO
```

The operator $ can also be used with the @ ... SAY/GET command interchangeably with COL(). For instance the following commands are valid:

```
@ 5,30 SAY Mstring
@ 5, $ SAY "Y)es or N)o"
```

The difference between COL() and $ is that COL() can also be used in a conditional statement, as in the two previous examples.

See also PCOL(), PROW(), ROW()

COS()

```
COS(expN)
```

Description This function returns the cosine of an angle, given in radians.

Operational rules The cosine represents the x-axis value at any point on a circle, so it is always between –1 and 1. In Quadrant I, COS(*expN*) decreases from 1 to 0. In Quadrant II, COS(*expN*) decreases from 0 to –1. In Quadrant III, COS(*expN*) increases from –1 to 0. In Quadrant IV, COS(*expN*) increases from 0 to 1. The argument *expN* must be between 0 and 2pi. This function returns a numeric value.

Examples

```
? COS(PI())
0
? COS(0)
1
```

See also SIN(), TAN()

CPCONVERT()

```
CPCONVERT(expN1, expN2, expC)
```

Description This function converts a character expression from one code page to another.

Operational rules The CPCONVERT() function returns the value of *expC* converted from code page *expN2* to code page *expN1*. Use the CPCONVERT() function when moving database fields, program source-code files and text files across different FoxPro platforms. See the chapter on Cross-platform and international capabilities (chapter 11) for more detail on code pages. This function returns a character value.

Example

```
mchar = "Ø"
mnewchar = CPCONVERT(1, 2, mchar)
? mnewchar
æ
```

See also Chapter 11, Cross-platform and international capabilities, CPCURRENT(), OEMTOANSI()

CPCURRENT()

```
CPCURRENT([1])
```

Description This function returns the current code page setting.

Operational rules The CPCURRENT() function returns the current FoxPro or operating system code page setting. A code page setting must be set in the FoxPro startup configuration file. If no code page is specified in the configuration file, CPCURRENT() returns a value of 0. If the CODEPAGE = setting in your startup file is set to AUTO, or you include the optional 1 clause, CPCURRENT() returns the current operating system code page. This function returns a numeric value. See the chapter on Cross-platform and international capabilities (chapter 11) for more detail on available code page settings.

See also Chapter 11, Cross-platform and international capabilities

CPDBF()

```
CPDBF([expC | expN])
```

Description This function returns the code page for a database file.

Operational rules When a database file is created or modified, the database structure is marked with the current code page. The CPDBF() function with no argument returns the code page for the database in the current work area. A different work area can be specified by its number with *expN* or by the alias of the database with *expC*. A value of 0 is returned if no database is active in the specified work area. This function returns a numeric value. See the chapter on Cross-platform and international capabilities (chapter 11) for more information on code pages.

See also Chapter 11, Cross-platform and international capabilities

CTOD()

`CTOD(expC)`

Description This function converts a character expression, entered as a string that looks like a date, into a date type expression.

Operational rules Variables that are date type can be used to calculate the difference between two dates. For instance, subtracting 5/1/89 from 5/20/89 gives 19, the number of days between the two dates.

The character expression in the arguments must be MM/DD/YY, unless the format has been changed with SET DATE or SET CENTURY. The date is assumed to be in the 1900s when two digits are used for the year; otherwise you must enter four digits for the year. Any date between January 1, 1582, and December 31, 9999, can be used.

You can also create or reference a date type expression by placing curly braces, {} around the date expression. This function returns a date value.

Examples

```
? CTOD("12/25/89") - CTOD("9/6/89")
110
? {12/25/89} - {9/6/89}
110
```

The following program uses the CTOD() function to create a blank date type variable for input with the @ ... SAY/GET command.

```
Bdate = CTOD(" / / ")
@ 5,1 SAY "Enter Date:" GET Bdate
```

The following program uses the curly brackets to create a blank date type variable for input with the @ ... SAY/GET command.

```
Bdate = {  /  /  }
@ 5,1 SAY "Enter Date:" GET Bdate
```

See also DATE(), DTOC()

CURDIR()

`CURDIR([expC])`

Description This function returns the current directory of the specified drive.

Operational rules The optional parameter *expC* is a valid drive letter. If the optional parameter is not specified, then CURDIR() gives thc current directory of the default drive. If no such drive exists, the function returns a null string. If no directory is in use (i.e., you are in the root), the function returns \. This function returns a character value.

Examples

```
&& if we are currently in C:\FOXPRO25\
? CURDIR()
\FOXPRO25\
? CURDIR("D")
\DATA\
```

See also FULLPATH()

DATE()

```
DATE()
```

Description This function returns the current system date.

Operational rules The system date is kept through DOS, and can be set with the DATE command at the DOS prompt. Many computers come with battery clocks that keep the system date current at all times. The SET CENTURY and SET DATE commands change the way that the date is displayed. The default is MM/DD/YY. This function returns a date value.

Examples

```
? DATE()
05/29/89
? {12/25/89} - DATE()
210
```

The following program uses the DATE() function to create a date type variable for input with the @ ... SAY/GET function.

```
Mdate = DATE()
@ 5,1 SAY "Enter Date:" GET Mdate
```

See also SET DATE, SET CENTURY, CTOD()

DAY()

DAY(*expD*)

Description This function returns the number of the day in a month, given a month.

Operational rules The three ways to enter a date as an argument are:

- Enclose the date in curly brackets: {12/5/89}
- Use the CTOD() function: CTOD("12/5/2010")
- Use a field name or memory variable.

The date is assumed to be in the 1900s when two digits are used for the year. An invalid date returns a value of 0. This function returns a numeric value.

Examples

```
? DAY({9/6/91})
6
? DAY(CTOD("12/25/92"))
25
```

See also CTOD(), DOW(), MONTH()

DBF()

DBF([*expC* | *expN*])

Description This function returns the name of the database file in a specified work area.

Operational rules The DBF() function with no arguments returns the actual DOS filename of the database in the current work area. A different work area can be specified by its number with *expN* or by the alias of the database with *expC*. The ALIAS() function can be used to return the database alias name.

Use the IN keyword with the USE command to choose the work area before opening a file. The valid work areas are 1 through 25 in the Standard version, or 1 through 225 in the Extended version. The filename is the default alias, although you can provide a different one by using the ALIAS keyword with the USE command. This function returns a character value.

Examples

```
USE JOURNAL IN 1
USE ACCOUNT IN 2 ALIAS COA
? DBF()
C:\WORK\JOURNAL.DBF

? DBF("COA")
C:\WORK\ACCOUNT.DBF
```

See also USE, ALIAS()

DDEAbortTrans()

DDEAbortTrans(*expN*)

Description This function terminates an asynchronous DDE transaction.

Operational rules The DDEAbortTrans() function returns true (.T.) if the asynchronous transaction specified with *expN* is terminated. Terminating an asynchronous transaction allows FoxPro to continue program execution without waiting for the DDE server application. An asynchronous transaction is created by specifying a user-defined function to be executed by a response from a server application.

The value specified with *expN* is the transaction number returned by the DDEExecute(), DDEPoke() or DDERequest() functions when the transaction is sent to the server application. This function returns a logical value. See the chapter on Using DDE and OLE in FoxPro (chapter 12) for more information on DDE capabilities.

See also Chapter 12, Using DDE and OLE in FoxPro, DDEExecute(), DDEPoke(), DDERequest()

DDEAdvise()

DDEAdvise(*expN1, expC1, expC2, expN2*)

Description This function creates a DDE link.

Operational rules The DDEAdvise() function is used to create a notify or automatic DDE link to an item name in a DDE server application. When a notify link is created, the server application notifies FoxPro that the item name has been modified. If an automatic link is created, the server application notifies FoxPro for Windows that the item name has been modified and passes the new data to FoxPro.

A DDE channel number must be specified with *expN1*. A DDE channel is created using the DDEInitiate( ) function. Specify the item name with *expC1*. This can be a document name or an array of spreadsheet cells. Item names are determined by the DDE server application. Use *expC2* to specify a user-defined function to be executed when a link is established and the item name specified in *expC1* is modified. When the user-defined function is executed, FoxPro will pass the following parameters in order:

Channel Number The channel number of the server application.

Action ADVISE when the link is being updated; TERMINATE when the link is closed.

Item The item name

Data New data is returned if an automatic link is established; otherwise the null string (" ") is returned.

Format The data format

Advise Status The link type

Specify the link type with *expN2*. The value of *expN2* must be 0 for a manual link, 1 for a notify link, or 2 for an automatic link. If *expN2* is 0, the user-defined function specified in *expC2* will not be executed after a link is established. This function returns a logical value. See the chapter on FoxPro Programming (chapter 5) for information on creating a user-defined function.

See also Chapter 12, Using DDE and OLE in FoxPro, DDEInitiate( ), DDETerminate( )

DDEEnabled( )

```
DDEEnabled([expL1 | expN [, expL2]])
```

Description This function controls processing of DDE channels.

Operational rules The DDEEnabled( ) function is used to enable, disable or check the status of DDE processing. The DDEFunction( ) with no arguments returns the status of all DDE processing. If true (.T.) is returned, all DDE functions are enabled and active; otherwise false (.F.) is returned indicating that all DDE functions have been disabled. Use the single *expL1* argument to enable or disable all DDE processing. Specify true (.T.) to enable processing or false (.F.) to disable processing. The function returns true if the operation was successful; otherwise false is returned.

Use the single *expN* argument to determine the DDE status of a specific DDE channel. A DDE channel is created using the DDEInitiate( ) function. If true is returned, DDE functions for the specified channel are enabled and active; otherwise false is returned indicating that DDE functions for the specified channel have been disabled. You can enable or disable DDE functions for a specific channel by specifying the channel with *expN* and a value of .T. or .F. with *expL2*. True enables DDE processing and false disables DDE processing. This function returns a logical value.

See also Chapter 12, Using DDE and OLE in FoxPro, DDEAbortTrans( ), DDEInitiate( ), DDEAdvise( )

DDEExecute( )

```
DDEExecute(expN, expC1 [, expC2 [, expC3]])
```

Description This function sends a DDE command to a Windows application.

Operational rules The DDEExecute() function is used to send a DDE command to a Windows application. A DDE channel must be opened with the DDEInitiate() function before this function can be used.

Specify the DDE channel with *expN*. The command sent to the application is specified with *expC1* and must be a valid command for the server application. Use the optional argument *expC2* to specify the format for sending the command. The default value is CF_TEXT if *expC2* is not specified. Use the optional *expC3* argument to specify a user-defined function that will be executed after the DDE request is sent. The following parameters are sent to the user-defined function in order:

Channel Number The channel number of the server application.

Action XACTCOMPLETE is returned if the function was successful; otherwise XACTFAIL is returned.

Item The item name

Data The data requested

Transaction Number The DDEExecute() transaction number.

When a user-defined function is executed an asynchronous link is made. If *expC3* is not used, FoxPro waits for the period specified with the DDESetOption() function. This function returns a logical value. True (.T.) is returned if the receiving application successfully executes the command; otherwise false (.F.) is returned. See the chapter on FoxPro Programming (chapter 5) for information on creating a user-defined function.

See also Chapter 12, Using DDE and OLE in FoxPro, DDEInitiate(), DDESetOption()

DDEInitiate()

`DDEInitiate(expC1, expC2)`

Description This function establishes a DDE link.

Operational rules The DDEInitiate() function is used to establish a DDE link between FoxPro and another Windows application that can support DDE operations. If a link is established, you can use other DDE commands to request data from the Windows application. DDE channels that are created with the DDEInitiate() function must be closed using the DDETerminate() function.

Use *expC1* to specify the application to start. This is usually the filename, such as WINWORD.EXE or EXCEL.EXE. Use *expC2* to specify the DDE topic. The topic specified in *expC2* must be one that is supported by the DDE application. See your software application documentation for more information on DDE topics.

This function returns a numeric value. The value returned is the DDE link that was initiated. If the value returned is –1, the link could not be established. If the application cannot be started, FoxPro will ask you if you want to open the application manually.

See also Chapter 12, Using DDE and OLE in FoxPro, DDETerminate()

DDELastError()

`DDELastError()`

Description This function returns a number corresponding to the most recent DDE error.

Operational rules The DDELastError() function returns a value based on the last DDE function used. If the command was successful, DDELastError() returns 0. Otherwise, it can return any of the following errors:

Error	Reason
1	Service busy
2	Topic busy
3	Channel busy
4	No such service
5	No such topic
6	Bad channel
7	Insufficient memory
8	Acknowledge timeout
9	Request timeout
10	No DDEInitiate()
11	Client attempted server transaction
12	Execute timeout
13	Bad parameter
14	Low memory
15	Memory error
16	Connect failure
17	Request failure
18	Poke timeout
19	Could not display message
20	Multiple synchronous transactions
21	Server died
22	Internal DDE error
23	Advise timeout
24	Invalid transaction identifier
25	Unknown

This function returns a numeric value. All DDE functions return a value of –1 if the function was unsuccessful. All DDE functions can be tested with the DDELastError() function.

See also Chapter 12, Using DDE and OLE in FoxPro

DDEPoke()

```
DDEPoke(expN, expC1, expC2 [, expC3 [, expC4]])
```

Description This function is used to exchange data in a DDE link.

Operational rules The DDEPoke() function is used to send data to an application over an open DDE channel. The DDE channel is specified with *expN*. A DDE channel is created using the DDEInitiate() function. Use *expC1* to specify the item to send the data to. The specified item must be one that is supported by the DDE application. See your software application documentation for more information on DDE items. Use *expC2* to specify the data to send.

Use the optional argument *expC3* to specify the format for sending the data. The default value is CF_TEXT if *expC3* is not specified. Use the optional *expC4* argument to specify a user-defined function that will be executed after the DDE request is sent. The following parameters are sent to the user-defined function in order:

Channel Number The channel number of the server application.

Action XACTCOMPLETE is returned if the function was successful; otherwise XACTFAIL is returned.

Item The item name

Data The data requested

Format The data format

Transaction Number The DDEPoke() transaction number.

This function returns a logical or numeric value. True (.T.) is returned if the data was sent; otherwise false (.F.) is returned. If a user-defined function was specified, a transaction number is returned, provided the data was sent; otherwise –1 is returned.

See also Chapter 12, Using DDE and OLE in FoxPro, DDEInitiate()

DDERequest()

```
DDERequest(expN, expC1 [, expC2 [, expC3]])
```

Description This function is used to exchange data in a DDE link.

Operational rules The DDERequest() function is used to request data from an application over an open DDE channel. The DDE channel is specified with *expN*. A DDE channel is created using the DDEInitiate() function. Use *expC1* to specify the item to request the data from. The specified item must be one that is supported by the DDE application. See your software application documentation for more information on DDE items.

Use the optional argument *expC2* to specify the format for sending the data. The default value is CF_TEXT if *expC2* is not specified. Use the optional *expC3* argument to specify a user-defined function that will be executed after the DDE request is sent. The following parameters are sent to the user-defined function in order:

Channel Number The channel number of the server application.

Action XACTCOMPLETE is returned if the function was successful; otherwise XACTFAIL is returned.

Item The item name

Data The data requested

Format The data format

Transaction Number The DDERequest() transaction number.

This function returns a character or numeric value. The requested data is returned if the request was successful; otherwise a null string ("") is returned. If a user-defined function was specified, a transaction number is returned if the request was successful; otherwise –1 is returned.

See also Chapter 12, Using DDE and OLE in FoxPro, DDEInitiate()

DDESetOption()

```
DDESetOption(expC [, expN | expL])
```

Description This function changed DDE response settings.

Operational rules The DDESetOption() function is used to change or check the value of TIMEOUT and SAFETY options for DDE functions. When you issue a DDE function, FoxPro waits a specified number of milliseconds for a response from the DDE server application. The default value for TIMEOUT is 2000. To change the TIMEOUT value, specify *expC* as TIMEOUT and *expN* as the new value. To check the current TIMEOUT value, do not include *expN*.

The SAFETY option is used to control the display of a dialog that appears when the DDEInitiate() function is unsuccessful. When you issue the DDEInitiate() function and the requested application cannot be started, FoxPro presents a dialog asking if you want to start the application manually. To disable the dialog, specify *expC* as SAFETY and *expL* as false (.F.). Specify true to enable the dialog. To check the current SAFETY value, do not include *expL*. This function returns a logical or numeric value.

See also Chapter 12, Using DDE and OLE in FoxPro, DDEInitiate()

DDESetService()

`DDESetService(expC1, expC2 [, expC3 | expL])`

Description This function changes DDE service names and settings.

Operational rules The DDESetService() function is used to define and change DDE service names for FoxPro. Within Windows, FoxPro can act as a DDE server application and send data to other Windows applications. Use the DDESetTopic() function to define and modify topic settings that can be used to send data to other applications.

The DDE service name for FoxPro is FOXPRO, which supports a single topic of SYSTEM. The item names supported by the SYSTEM topic are described below:

Topic name	Returns
TOPICS	Available topic names
FORMATS	Supported formats
STATUS	BUSY or READY
SYSITEMS	Item names

The *expC1* parameter is used to define a new service name or change the default service name. The *expC2* parameter specifies the function to apply to the service name defined in *expC1*. Listed below are the valid values for expC2 and their associated functions.

- **ADVISE** Returns the current notification status, or changes the notification status, for the specified service name. Specify true (.T.) in the optional argument *expL* to enable client notification, or false (.F.) to disable client notification. If *expL* is not used, the current notification status for the specified service is returned.
- **DEFINE** Defines a new DDE service name.
- **EXECUTE** Returns the current execution status, or enables or disables DDE execution requests, for the specified service name. Specify true (.T.) in the optional argument *expL* to enable client DDE command execution, or false (.F.) to disable command execution. If *expL* is not used, the current execution status for the specified service is returned.
- **POKE** Returns the current poke status, or changes the poke status, for the specified service name. Specify true (.T.) in the optional argument *expL* to enable client

poke requests, or false (.F.) to disable client poke requests. If *expL* is not used, the current poke status for the specified service is returned.

- **RELEASE** Releases the specified service name. Releasing a service name also releases all topics associated with the service name.
- **REQUEST** Returns the current request status, or changes the request status, for the specified service name. Specify true (.T.) in the optional argument *expL* to enable client requests, or false (.F.) to disable client requests. If *expL* is not used, the current request status for the specified service is returned.
- **FORMATS** Specifies the data format for the service. When FORMATS is used, a valid format must be specified with *expC3*. If *expC3* is not specified, the default format CF_TEXT is used.

This function returns a logical value.

See also Chapter 12, Using DDE and OLE in FoxPro

DDESetTopic()

`DDESetTopic(expC1, expC2 [, expC3])`

Description This function defines topic names for a DDE service.

Operational rules The DDESetTopic() function is used to define or change DDE topic names for FoxPro. Within Windows, FoxPro can act as a DDE server application and send data to other Windows applications. Use the DDESetService() function to define and modify service settings that can be used to send data to other applications.

The service name is specified with *expC1*. The topic name to define or remove is specified with *expC2*. If *expC2* contains a value, the topic is defined. If *expC2* contains a null string (" "), the topic is released.

Use the optional argument *expC3* to specify a user-defined function that is executed when a DDE client application sends a request to the topic *expC2*. If *expC3* is not specified, the topic *expC2* is automatically removed. The following parameters are sent to the user-defined function in order:

Channel Number The channel number of the server application.
Action ADVISE, EXECUTE, INITIATE, POKE, REQUEST or TERMINATE
Item The item name
Data The data sent from the DDE client
Format The data format
Advise Status The link type

The values that are sent to the user-defined function for the item, data and advise status parameters are dependent on the value of the action parameter. Those values are listed below.

If action is	Item is	Data is	Advise status is
INITIATE	null string	Topic name	null string
TERMINATE	null string	null string	null string
POKE	Item name	New data	null string
REQUEST	Item name	null string	null string
EXECUTE	null string	New command	null string
ADVISE	Item name	null string	Link type

This function returns a logical value. True (.T.) is returned if the user-defined function is successful in handling the DDE request; otherwise false (.F.) is returned.

See also Chapter 12, Using DDE and OLE in FoxPro, DDESetService()

DDETerminate()

`DDETerminate(`*expN*`|`*expC*`)`

Description This function closes a DDE channel.

Operational rules The DDETerminate() function is used to close a DDE channel that was opened with the DDEInitiate() function. Specify the channel to close with *expN*, or the service name with *expC*. When a DDE service is closed, all related channels are also closed. This function returns a logical value. True (.T.) is returned if the channel is successfully closed; otherwise false (.F.) is returned.

See also Chapter 12, Using DDE and OLE in FoxPro, DDEInitiate()

DELETED()

`DELETED([`*expC* `|` *expN*`])`

Description This function determines if the current record in a specified database is marked for deletion.

Operational rules The DELETED() function will return true (.T.) if the current record of the current work area is tagged for deletion; otherwise false (.F.) is returned. You can check the DELETED() status of a record in another work area by specifying the database alias with *expC* or its work area number with *expN*. A record can be marked for deletion in one of three ways:

- By using the *DELETE* command.
- By pressing Ctrl-T while in Edit or Browse mode.
- Clicking on the Delete box while in Edit or Browse mode.

While there are deleted records in a database, the SET DELETED ON command can be used so that all deleted records are ignored when listing, reporting, editing, etc. Records that are marked for deletion can be undeleted with the RECALL command and can also be removed from the database with the PACK command. This function returns a logical value.

Examples

```
SELECT 1
USE JOURNAL
USE COA IN 2
GOTO 5
? DELETED()
.F.
DELETE
? DELETED()
.T.
```

```
RECALL
? DELETED()
.F.
? DELETED("COA")
.T.
```

See also PACK, RECALL, SET DELETED

DIFFERENCE()

```
DIFFERENCE(expC1, expC2)
```

Description This function returns a numeric value that represents the phonetic difference between the two character strings.

Operational rules The DIFFERENCE() function returns a value between 0 and 4 depending on how similar the two expressions are; the closer the expressions are spelled the higher the value. The character expressions to compare are specified with the *expC1* and *expC2* arguments.

The DIFFERENCE() function compares the SOUNDEX() codes of each character of the two strings. If the SOUNDEX() codes are the same, DIFFERENCE() returns a 4. If none of the characters in the SOUNDEX() codes match, DIFFERENCE() returns a value of 0. Each character in common returns a value of 1. This function is useful in searching a database for a character string when the exact spelling is unknown. This function returns a numeric value.

Examples

```
? DIFFERENCE("HUMBUG","HAMBURGER")
3
? DIFFERENCE("TINY","LITTLE")
1
USE CLIENTS
LIST Lname FOR DIFFERENCE("BALISTRERI",Lname) > 3
Record #  LNAME
4         Balestreros
8         Balistreri
10        Balosteri
20        Balestri
```

See also SOUNDEX()

DISKSPACE()

```
DISKSPACE()
```

Description This function returns the number of bytes available on the default disk drive.

Operational rules The DISKSPACE() function can be useful in determining if there is enough free disk space available for certain FoxPro file operations. Two of these functions are the PACK command and the MODIFY STRUCTURE command. Use DISKSPACE() before running either of these two commands. You can change the default drive with the SET DEFAULT command. This function returns a numeric value.

Examples This example shows you how to use the HEADER(), RECCOUNT() and RECSIZE() functions to compute the size of a database and determine if enough disk space is available to PACK the database. The PACK command requires minimum disk space of 2 times the size of the file.

Example

```
* Compute the size of the database
msize = HEADER() + (RECCOUNT() * RECSIZE() + 1)
IF DISKSPACE() < msize * 2.5
   ? "There is not enough room to run the PACK routine"
ELSE
   PACK
ENDIF
```

See also HEADER(), RECCOUNT(), RECSIZE()

DMY()

DMY(*expD*)

Description This function converts a date to the character string of DD Month YY, where the month is spelled out.

Operational rules The DMY() function returns a character string which shows the day as a one or two-digit number, the month is spelled out, and the year is two digits. To show the year as four digits, use the SET CENTURY ON command. For example, the date 5/15/89 would be displayed as 15 May 89 in the DMY() format. This function returns a character value.

Examples

```
? DMY({9/6/89})
6 September 89
SET CENTURY ON
? DMY(CTOD("12/25/89"))
25 December 1989
```

See also CTOD(), SET CENTURY, MDY()

DOW()

DOW(*expD*)

Description This function returns the numeric value of the day of the week, given a date expression.

Operational rules The three ways to enter a date as an argument are:

- Enclose the date in curly brackets: {12/5/89}
- Use the CTOD() function: CTOD("12/5/2010")
- Use a field name or memory variable.

The date is assumed to be in the 1900s when two digits are used for the year. This function returns a numeric value number ranging from 1 (Saturday) to 7 (Sunday).

Examples

```
? DATE()
01/26/93
? DOW(DATE())
3
```

See also CTOD(), DATE()

DTOC()

DTOC(*expD* [, 1])

Description This function converts a date expression to a character string.

Operational rules The DTOC() function converts a valid date expression supplied in *expD* to a character expression in MM/DD/YY format. The date is assumed to be in the 1900s when two digits are used for the year; otherwise you must enter four digits for the year. Any date between January 1, 100, and December 31, 9999, can be used.

The DTOC() function is useful in converting a date string when it needs to be used in a character expression. The optional argument ,1 causes the date to appear in YYYYMMDD form, which is very useful for indexing date fields by DTOC(). Notice that indexing by the DTOC() function without the optional argument does not sort dates in chronological order (05/01/90 will come before 12/31/89). This function returns a character value.

Examples

```
? DTOC(DATE())
02/20/89
mhead = "Date" + DTOC(DATE()) + "    MONTHLY REPORT"
? mhead
Date: 02/20/89  MONTHLY REPORT
USE SALES
INDEX ON DTOC(SALES_DAT,1) + PONUM TO SALESDAT
LIST SALES_DAT, PONUM
Record #  SALES_DAT PONUM
3         12/27/89  A1001
4         12/27/89  A1001
1         12/27/89  B2000
5         12/29/89  A2001
2         01/03/90  A1005
7         01/03/90  B2002
6         01/05/90  A1001
8         01/05/90  A2001
```

See also SET DATE, CTOD()

DTOR()

DTOR(*expN*)

Description This function converts a number, representing an angle measured by degrees, into radians.

Operational rules Fractions of a degree, usually represented by minutes and seconds, must be represented by decimals. For instance, 45 minutes should be depicted as .75 degrees. Use the SET DECIMALS command to change the number of decimals which appear in the answer. The RTOD() function is used to conversely change radians to degrees.

Examples

```
? DTOR(50)
87
DTOR(PI()/2)
.03
```

See also ACOS(), RTOD(), SET DECIMALS

DTOS()

`DTOS(`*`expD`*`)`

Description This function converts a date to a character expression in the format YYYYMMDD.

Operational rules The DTOS() function is useful when you need to index on both a date and character string added together. The DTOS() function returns a character in the YYYYMMDD format regardless of the SET CENTURY COMMAND. When entering the expression, you can use a field, memory variable, or date entered using { }. This function is equivalent to the DTOC() function used with the optional argument of 1. This function returns a character value.

Examples

```
? DTOS({12/25/89})
19891225
USE CHECKS
INDEX ON DTOS(Chkdate) + Acct
LIST Chkdate, Acct
Record #  Chkdate   Acct
3         12/27/89  A1001
4         12/27/89  A1001
1         12/27/89  B2000
5         12/29/89  A2001
2         01/03/90  A1005
7         01/03/90  B2002
6         01/05/90  A1001
8         01/05/90  A2001
```

Notice that the DTOC() function (without the optional parameter) could not be used in place of DTOS() for this index, because the dates in January would precede the dates in December.

See also CTOD(), DTOC()

EMPTY()

`EMPTY(`*`expr`*`)`

Description This function determines whether an expression is empty.

Operational rules The EMPTY() function returns true (.T.) if *expr* is empty; otherwise false (.F.) is returned. Each type of expression evaluates as empty according to the following table of values:

Data type	**Is empty when**
Character	No characters
Numeric	0
Date	" // "
Logical	.F.
Memo	No contents
General	No contents

This function returns a logical value.

Example

```
USE SALES
LIST FOR EMPTY(CHKDATE) OR EMPTY(ACCT)
Record #   Chkdate    Acct
1            /  /       A1001
4          12/27/91
7            /  /
```

EOF()

```
EOF([expN | expC])
```

Description This function determines if the record pointer is at the end of a database.

Operational rules The EOF() function returns true (.T.) when the record pointer is at the end of a file and is then moved one record forward. The SKIP command moves the record pointer forward one record. The last record in a nonindexed file is the record number returned by RECCOUNT(). The last record in an indexed file is the record reached with the command GO BOTTOM. When SKIP is issued to go one record past this record, the record number becomes RECCOUNT() + 1, and EOF() is set to .T. The two situations where the EOF() returns .T. are:

- When the pointer is at the end record, and SKIP is issued.
- When the bottom record is being edited, and the user presses PgDn.

If no file is opened in the current work area, EOF() returns false (.F.). EOF() is determined for the current work area if no argument is supplied. To test the condition of EOF() in another work area specify the work area number with *expN* or the database alias with *expC*. If the pointer is already at the end of file, and the SKIP command is issued again, FoxPro returns an "End of file encountered" error message. This function returns a logical value.

Examples

```
USE MAILLIST
GOTO BOTTOM
SKIP
? EOF()
.T.
GOTO TOP
```

```
* Scan.prg
DO WHILE !EOF()
     ? Lname,Fname
     SKIP 1
ENDDO
```

See also BOF(), SKIP

ERROR()

```
ERROR()
```

Description This function returns the number corresponding to the error that has just occurred.

Operational rules The ERROR() function will return a value of 0 unless the ON ERROR command has been issued. The ON ERROR command is given at the beginning of a program, but waits until an error occurs before performing. When ON ERROR is triggered by an error, the command can call a program, a procedure, or a user-defined function. The syntax for the command is ON ERROR *command.*

The ERROR() function can be used in conjunction with the program that ON ERROR branches to. The program can display different directions to the user, depending on the error that has occurred. The MESSAGE() function can also be helpful in this routine, as it displays the error message that would appear if the ON ERROR command was not present.

If the ON ERROR command is not active, the `Cancel, Suspend, Ignore?` error message is displayed when an error is encountered. To clear the number returned by ERROR(), use the RETURN or RETRY command. This function returns a numeric value.

Examples The following program calls an error routine command named Errtrap:

```
Mailprog.PRG
ON ERROR DO Errtrap
USE MAILLIST
SET PRINT ON
SCAN
   ? Lname, Fname
ENDSCAN

Errtrap.PRG
SET PRINT OFF
DO CASE
   CASE ERROR() = 126 OR ERROR() = 125
      WAIT WINDOW "Please put your printer on line."
      SET PRINT ON
      RETRY
   CASE ERROR() = 114
      WAIT WINDOW "The index is corrupted, please reindex the file"
      RETURN TO MASTER
      OTHERWISE
      WAIT "The following error has occurred: " + MESSAGE()
      RETURN TO MASTER
ENDCASE
```

The routine Errtrap checks for a printer error (126 or 125) which signifies that the printer is off-line. If that is the case, the program pauses until the user sets the printer on. Error 114 reports a corrupted index file, so the user is instructed to reindex the file. All other error codes return the user to the main program that called Mailprog.PRG.

See also ON ERROR, MESSAGE(), RETRY, Diskette Appendix E: FoxPro Error Messages

EVALUATE()

`EVALUATE(`*`expC`*`)`

Description This function evaluates a character expression and returns the result.

Operational rules The EVALUATE() function performs a similar type of macro substitution as the & function, and in some cases is faster. Unlike the & function, EVALUATE() cannot translate a command. EVALUATE() can be used with a character string literal, expression, memory variable, or database field of any type. The expression to evaluate is specified in *expC*.

The EVALUATE() function is also similar to the TYPE() function but returns the result of an expression rather than the type of expression. This function can return a character, numeric, date, logical, or memo field value.

Examples

```
x = 1
y = 2
z = EVALUATE("x + y")
? z
3
? TYPE(z)
N

a = "x + y"
x = 1
y = 2
? EVALUATE(a)
x + y
? TYPE(a)
N
? EVALUATE("a")
3
? TYPE("a")
C
```

See also &, TYPE()

EXP()

`EXP(`*`expN`*`)`

Description This function returns the exponential *e* raised to the *expN* power.

Operational rules The value of *e* is approximately 2.7182818. The EXP() function is the inverse of the natural logarithm LOG(). The value specified with *expN* can be a numeric field or memory variable, or the actual value. This function returns a numeric value.

Examples

```
? EXP(1)
2.72
SET DECIMALS TO 6
? EXP(1)
2.7182825
```

See also SET DECIMALS, LOG()

FCHSIZE()

FCHSIZE(*expN1*, *expN2*)

Description This function changes the size of a low-level file opened with FOPEN() or FCREATE().

Operational rules The FCHSIZE() function is used to increase a file's size or truncate the file after a specified byte. When a low-level file is successfully opened with FOPEN() or FCREATE() a file handle is returned. That file handle is specified with the argument *expN1*.

The second argument *expN2* is used to specify the new size in bytes. If *expN2* is less than the original size, the file will truncated (cut-off) at *expN2* bytes. When the size of a file is increased, FoxPro will allocate disk sectors for the file on the drive that the file was opened or created on. Since FCHSIZE() doesn't initialize the new file space, the space can contain previous data. Be sure to manage the new file space.

The return value is either the new size of the file in bytes or –1 if FCHSIZE() is unsuccessful. A return value of –1 can be caused by referencing an invalid file handle with *expN1*, referencing a file that is read-only, or insufficient disk space.

Examples This example creates a low-level file, writes a string of 32 characters, and then truncates the file to 10 characters.

```
mcreate = FCREATE("TEMP.TXT")
? mcreate
2
mwrite = FPUTS(mcreate,"Now is the time for all good men")
? mwrite
32
mchange = FCHSIZE(mcreate,10)
? mchange
10
mclose - FCLOSE(mcreate)
? mclose
.T.
SET HEADINGS OFF
TYPE temp.txt
Now is the
```

See also FOPEN(), FCLOSE()

FCLOSE()

FCLOSE(*expN*)

Description This function closes a low-level file that has been opened with FOPEN() or FCREATE().

Operational rules The FCLOSE() function is used to save a low-level file to disk. FCLOSE() returns a value of true (.T.) if the file is successfully closed; otherwise false (.F.) is returned. A "file handle" is assigned using the FCREATE() or FOPEN() functions. The file handle must be passed in the parameter *expN* when using the FCLOSE() function. This function returns a logical value.

Examples

```
mhandle = FOPEN("MAINFRAM.DTA")
? mhandle
1
mclose = FCLOSE(mhandle)
? mclose
.T.
```

See also FOPEN(), FCREATE()

FCOUNT()

FCOUNT([*expN* | *expC*])

Description This function returns the number of fields in a database.

Operational rules The FCOUNT() function returns the number of fields in the current database unless another work area is specified. *expN* specifies the work area number and *expC* the database alias. This function returns a numeric value.

Examples

```
SELECT 1
USE JOURNAL
USE COA IN 2
? FCOUNT()
5
? FCOUNT(2)
10
```

See also FIELD()

FCREATE()

FCREATE(*expC* [, *expN*])

Description This function creates a low-level file and opens it for use.

Operational rules The FCREATE() function creates a new low-level file and opens it for writing data to. The DOS filename for the file is specified with *expC*. If a file named *expC* already exists, it is overwritten.

The FCREATE() function returns a number, called the file's handle. If the file cannot be created, FCREATE() returns –1. The optional argument *expN* allows you to set a DOS attribute. The available attributes are:

Value	Attribute
0	Read / Write (default)
1	Read only
2	Hidden
3	Read only / Hidden
4	System
5	Read only / System
6	System / Hidden
7	Read only / Hidden / System

This function returns a numeric value.

Examples

```
mhandle = FCREATE("LISTED.DTA")
? mhandle
1
```

See also FCLOSE(), FOPEN(), FWRITE()

FEOF()

`FEOF(`*`expN`*`)`

Description This function determines whether the file pointer is at the end of a low-level file that has been opened with FOPEN() or FCREATE().

Operational rules The FEOF() function returns true (.T.) if the file pointer is at the end of the file. The FCREATE() and FOPEN() functions are used to open low-level files. The argument *expN* specifies the file handle number of the file to check for the end of file condition. This function returns a logical value.

Examples

```
mhandle = FOPEN("MAINFRAM.DTA")
? mhandle
1
mtop = FSEEK(mhandle,2) && Go to end of file
? mtop
0
? FEOF(mhandle)          && If true, then the file is empty
.T.
```

See also FOPEN(), FCREATE(), FSEEK()

FERROR()

`FERROR()`

Description This function returns a number corresponding to the most recent low-level file function error.

Operational rules The FERROR() function returns a value based on the last low-level function used. If the command was successful, FERROR() returns 0. Otherwise, it can return any of the following errors:

Error	Reason
2	File not found.
4	Too many files open.
5	Access denied.
6	Invalid file handle given.
8	Out of memory.
25	Seek error.
29	Disk full.
31	Error opening file or general failure.

All low-level file functions return a value of –1 if the function was unsuccessful. The following functions can all be tested with the FERROR() function: FCHSIZE(), FCREATE(), FOPEN(), FCLOSE(), FSEEK(), FEOF(), FFLUSH(). This function returns a numeric value.

Examples

```
* Create.prg
mhandle = FCREATE("LISTFILE.DTA")
IF mhandle = -1    && Unsuccessful
   DO CASE
      CASE FERROR() = 4
         WAIT WINDOW "Too many files are open."
      CASE FERROR() = 5
         WAIT WINDOW "Access to the disk is denied"
      CASE FERROR() = 8
         WAIT WINDOW "Insufficient memory to open the file"
      CASE FERROR() = 29
         WAIT WINDOW "Insufficient disk space to open the file"
      OTHERWISE
         WAIT WINDOW "An error has occurred"
   ENDCASE
ELSE
   WAIT WINDOW "File opened successfully"
ENDIF
```

See also FOPEN(), FCREATE(), FSEEK(), FEOF(), FCHSIZE(), FFLUSH()

FFLUSH()

FFLUSH(*expN*)

Description This function flushes the contents of a low-level file from memory to disk.

Operational rules The FLUSH() function flushes the memory buffers of all low-level file data, and writes it to disk. The FCREATE() and FOPEN() functions are used to open low-level files. The argument *expN* specifies the file handle to flush. It is a good idea to use this function when closing a file, because it reduces the chance of data loss if the computer is shut down before exiting FoxPro. This function returns a logical value.

See also FCLOSE()

FGETS()

`FGETS(expN1 [, expN2])`

Description This function returns a character string from a file opened with one of the low-level file operations.

Operational rules The FGETS() function returns a number of characters from a low-level file. The *expN* argument is the file handle to read from. If the number of characters to return is not specified in *expN2*, FGETS() returns the next 254 bytes, or the bytes between the file pointer and next carriage return, whichever is shorter.

If a carriage return is encountered, the file pointer is positioned at the next byte following the carriage return. The FGETS() function does not include any carriage returns encountered and ignores all line feed characters after a carriage return. This function returns a character value.

Examples

```
mopen = FOPEN("WORDS.TXT")
? mopen
2
msize = FSEEK(mopen,0,2)
? msize
32
mgets = FGETS(mopen,msize)
? mgets
Now is the time
mclose = FCLOSE(mopen)
```

See also FREAD(), FSEEK()

FIELD()

`FIELD(expN1 [, expN2 | expC])`

Description This function returns the name of the specified field, designated by the number.

Operational rules The FIELD() function returns the name as an uppercase string. Fields are ordered numerically as they are added or moved. *expN* specifies which field of the current database to return. If the number in the argument is greater than the number of fields in the database, or no database is open in the specified work area, FIELD() returns a null string (" ").

FIELD() returns the field name of a database in the current work area. To return the field name of a database in another work area specify the work area number with *expN* or the database alias with *expC*. This function returns a character value.

Examples

```
USE MAILLIST
? FIELD(1)
LNAME
```

```
Showfld.prg
SET TALK OFF
USE MAILLIST
FOR i = 1 TO FCOUNT()
   ? FIELD(i)
ENDFOR
```

```
Showfld output
LNAME
FNAME
ADD
CITY
ST
ZIP
```

See also FCOUNT()

FILE()

FILE(*expC*)

Description This function determines if a file exists.

Operational rules The FILE() function returns true (.T.) if the file specified in *expC* exists in the default directory or along the FoxPro path. The name of the file is not case-sensitive, but the extension must be included. Unless the drive and directory are entered in the character expression, the function searches the default drive and directory. This is the default drive when starting FoxPro. The default drive and directory can be changed after entering FoxPro, using SET DEFAULT, and the search path can be changed using SET PATH. This function returns a logical value.

Examples

```
? FILE("MAILLIST.DBF")
.T.

? FILE("D:\FILES\JOURNAL.DBF")
.T.
Openfile.PRG
SET TALK OFF
IF FILE("MAILLIST.DBF")
   USE MAILLIST
ELSE
   WAIT WINDOW "The MAILLIST.DBF file cannot be found."
   QUIT
ENDIF
```

See also SET DEFAULT, SET PATH

FILTER()

FILTER([*expN* | *expC*])

Description This function returns the current filter condition on a database.

Operational rules The FILTER( ) function returns the filter condition as a string. The filter condition for all currently open files can also be seen with the DISPLAY STATUS command. FILTER( ) returns the filter condition of the current database. To return the filter condition of a database in another work area specify the work area number with *expN* or the database alias with *expC*. This function returns a character value.

Examples

```
USE MAILLIST IN 1
SET FILTER TO ZIP = "92"
SELECT 2
? FILTER(1)
ZIP = "92"
```

See also SET FILTER

FKLABEL()

FKLABEL(*expN*)

Description This function returns the name which has been given to the specified function key.

Operational rules The SET FUNCTION command allows you to program the function keys. You can program 9 function keys (F2 through F10), 9 Shift-function keys, and 10 Ctrl-function keys.

The SET FUNCTION command can be issued one of two ways. The more common is SET FUNCTION *key label* TO *command*. (For instance, SET FUNCTION F2 TO "Modify Command"). The second way is SET FUNCTION *expN* TO *command*, where each key is designated by a number. (For instance, SET FUNCTION 1 TO "Modify Command"). The FKLABEL( ) function returns the function key assigned to each number.

The F1 key is not assignable, because it is used as the Help key. Therefore, the numbers start with F2=1, F3=2, and so forth. This function returns a character value.

Examples

```
? FKLABEL(1)
F2
```

See also SET FUNCTION, FKMAX( )

FKMAX()

FKMAX( )

Description This function returns the maximum number of programmable function keys and function key combinations.

Operational rules The SET FUNCTION command allows you to program the function keys. The maximum number of programmable keys is 28: 9 function keys (F2 through F10), 9 Shift-function keys, and 10 Ctrl-function keys. Function keys F11 and F12 are not programmable through FoxPro. This function is used primarily with applications that are not going to be run on typical IBM-compatible keyboards. This command returns a numeric value.

Examples

```
? FKMAX()
28
```

See also SET FUNCTION, FKLABEL()

FLOCK()

`FLOCK([`*expN* `|` *expC*`])`

Description This function attempts to lock a database file.

Operational rules The FLOCK() function returns true (.T.) if a file lock has been placed on the current database. Locking a database prevents any other users from modifying the database, yet remains available for read-only operations such as viewing or reporting. A database locked with the FLOCK() function will remain locked until it is closed or the UNLOCK command is issued. Individual records of a database can be locked with the RLOCK() function. Single records do not need to be locked if the database has been locked.

The FLOCK() function will attempt to lock the database based on the SET REPROCESS setting. If SET REPROCESS is 0 and the initial lock attempt fails, FoxPro will continue the lock attempt until the Esc key is pressed. The FLOCK() function simply returns false (.F.) if the lock attempt fails and does not generate any type of error.

FLOCK() attempts to lock the current database. To lock a database in another work area specify the work area number with *expN* or the database alias with *expC*. This function returns a logical value.

Examples

```
USE STUDENTS IN 1
USE CLASSES IN 2
mlock = FLOCK()
? mlock
.T.
mlock = FLOCK("CLASSES")
? mlock
.F.
```

See also RLOCK(), SET REPROCESS, SET EXCLUSIVE

FLOOR()

`FLOOR(`*expN*`)`

Description This function returns an integer that is less than or equal to the argument.

Operational rules The FLOOR() function is useful in cases where you must round down all numbers that have decimal places. Negative numbers return a number less than the argument by rounding to the next smaller number. This function returns a numeric value.

Examples

```
? FLOOR(5.2)
5
? FLOOR(5.6)
```

```
5
? FLOOR(- 5.2)
-6
? FLOOR(- 5.6)
-6
```

See also CEILING(), ROUND()

FONTMETRIC()

`FONTMETRIC(expN1 [, expC1, expN2 [, expC2]])`

Description This function returns information on the font used in the current output window.

Operational rules The FONTMETRIC() returns a value for specific attributes of the font used in the current output window. The values returned can be used to determine specific locations of text display functions. When the FONTMETRIC() function is called with no arguments, the default font for the current output window is assumed. The following values are returned for *expN1*:

Attribute value returned	When expN1 is
Character height in pixels	1
Character ascent in pixels	2
Character descent in pixels	3
Space between lines in pixels	4
Extra leading in pixels	5
Average character width in pixels	6
Maximum character width in pixels	7
Font weight	8
Italic (0 = no, nonzero = yes)	9
Underlined (0 = no, nonzero = yes)	10
Strikeout (0 = no, nonzero = yes)	11
First character defined in font	12
Last character defined in font	13
Default character	14
Word break character	15
Pitch and family	16
Character set	17
Overhang	18
Horizontal aspect for font device	19
Vertical aspect for font device	20

To determine the attributes of a specific font, specify the font name in *expC1*, the font size in *expN2* and the font style in *expC2*. When a font is specified and the style parameter *expC2* is omitted, the standard font style is used. Font style characters can be combined to create different styles. The available font styles that can be used are listed below:

Character	Font Style
B	Bold
I	Italic

Character	Font Style
N	Normal
O	Outline
Q	Opaque
S	Shadow
-	Strikeout
T	Transparent
U	Underline

See your Windows documentation for more information on font attributes and the values returned by the FONTMETRIC() function. This function returns a numeric value.

See also TXTWIDTH(), SYSMETRIC(), WFONT()

FOPEN()

```
FOPEN(expC [, expN])
```

Description This function opens a file for low-level functions.

Operational rules The FOPEN() function is a low-level function that opens a file. The FOPEN() function returns a number, called the file handle. Designate the name of the file to open using the parameter *expC*. If the file cannot be opened, FOPEN() returns –1.

The optional argument *expN* allows you to set read-write privileges for the open file. The default value for *expN* is 0.

expN	Status
0	Read Only (default)
1	Write Only
2	Read/Write
10	Read Only
11	Write Only
12	Read/Write

This function returns a numeric value.

Examples

```
* Files.prg
mhandle = FOPEN("LISTED.DTA")
IF mhandle > 0
   = FWRITE(mhandle, "This file contains a list of names")
ELSE
   WAIT "The requested file could not be opened."
ENDIF
```

See also FCREATE(), FWRITE()

FOUND()

```
FOUND([expN | expC])
```

Description This function determines if a record was successfully located using the FIND, SEEK, LOCATE, or CONTINUE commands.

Operational rules The FOUND() function returns true (.T.) if a record was located using FIND, SEEK, LOCATE, or CONTINUE and is not at the end of the file. All of the positioning commands listed above move the record pointer to the first record that matches their search criteria. The FIND and SEEK commands require the database to be indexed on the search criteria, and are much faster than the LOCATE command.

FOUND() returns the search status of the current database. You can use FOUND() on a database in another work area by specifying the work area number with *expN* or the database alias with *expC*. This function returns a logical value.

Examples

```
USE MAILLIST ORDER Lname
SEEK "smith"
? FOUND()
.F.
SEEK "SMITH"
? FOUND()
.T.    && Because the index expression is "UPPER(Lname)"
```

This example uses FOUND() and CONTINUE to count records

```
LOCATE FOR Lname = "SMITH"
DO WHILE FOUND()
   mcnt = mcnt + 1
   CONTINUE
ENDDO
? mcnt
3
```

This example uses a relationship to list records in the parent database of a one-to-many relationship. In this example all STUDENT (the parent) records not having a record in CLASSES (the child) are listed.

```
USE STUDENTS IN 1
USE CLASSES ORDER Stuno IN 2
SET RELATION TO Stuno INTO CLASSES
LIST STUDENTS.Lname FOR !FOUND("CLASSES")
```

See also CONTINUE, FIND, LOCATE, SEEK

FPUTS()

```
FPUTS(expN1, expC [, expN2])
```

Description This function writes a character string into a file or communications port that has been opened with one of the low-level file operations. The character string has a carriage return and line feed placed at the end.

Operational rules The first parameter *expN1* is the file handle. FPUTS() begins writing the character string specified with *expC* at the byte where the file pointer is positioned. The optional third parameter *expN2* is the number of bytes to be written. FPUTS() returns the number of bytes written to the file.

This function is equivalent to the FWRITE() function, except it always appends a carriage return and line feed to the end of the string. This function returns a numeric value.

Examples

```
mopen = FOPEN("TEMP.TXT")
? mopen
2
mput = FPUTS("Now is the time")
? mput
17    && 15 characters plus carriage return and line feed
mput = FPUTS("for all good men")
? mput
18    && 16 characters plus carriage return and line feed
mclose = FCLOSE(mopen)
? mclose
.T.

SET HEADINGS OFF
TYPE temp.txt
Now is the time
for all good men
```

See also FWRITE(), FREAD()

FREAD()

FREAD(*expN1*, *expN2*)

Description This function returns a character string from a file opened with one of the low-level file operations.

Operational rules The first parameter *expN1* is the file handle. FREAD() always starts reading from the file at the byte where the file pointer is positioned. The second parameter *expN2* is the number of bytes to be returned. The FREAD() function returns the bytes specified, or the bytes between the file pointer and end of file, whichever is shorter.

This function is much like the FGETS() function with the optional number of bytes parameter, except that FREAD() includes carriage returns when they are within the specified number of bytes. This function returns a numeric value.

Examples

```
mopen = FOPEN("WORDS.TXT")
? mopen
2
msize = FSEEK(mopen,0,2)
? msize
32
mgets = FGETS(mopen,msize)
? mgets
Now is the time
```

```
for all good me
mclose = FCLOSE(mopen)
```

See also FGETS()

FSEEK()

FSEEK(*expN1*, *expN2* [, *expN3*])

Description This function moves the file pointer within a file that has been opened with one of the low-level file operations.

Operational rules The first parameter *expN1* is the file handle. The second parameter *expN2* is the number of bytes to move the pointer. To move the pointer forward, use a positive number; move backward with a negative number.

If the third parameter *expN3* is not used, FSEEK() moves the pointer starting at the beginning of the file or comm port. To move it from a different position, use the following values as the third parameter:

Value	Position
0	Start from beginning of the file (default)
1	Start from current file pointer position
2	Start from the end of the file

This function returns a numeric value.

Examples

```
mopen = FOPEN("WORDS.TXT")
? mopen
2
msize = FSEEK(mopen,0,2)
? msize
32
```

See also FREAD()

FSIZE()

FSIZE(*expC1* [, *expN* | *expC2*])

Description This function returns the byte length of a specified field.

Operational rules The FSIZE() function can be used with any type of field. Date, Logical, Memo, and General type fields have a fixed field length. The field to check is specified in the parameter *expC1*.

FSIZE() returns the size of a specified field in the current database. You can use FSIZE() on a database in another work area by specifying the work area number with *expN* or the database alias with *expC2*. This function returns a numeric value.

Examples

```
USE MAILLIST IN 1
USE ACCOUNTS IN 2
```

```
? FSIZE("LNAME")
20
? FSIZE("CNO","ACCOUNTS")
5
```

See also RECSIZE()

FULLPATH()

FULLPATH(*filename1* [, *expN* | *filename2*])

Description This function returns the drive and path name of a specified file.

Operational rules The FULLPATH() function searches the FoxPro path for *filename1*. The path setting can be changed with the SET PATH command. Including a numerical value in the optional argument *expN* forces FULLPATH() to search the DOS path rather than the FoxPro path. If the file does not exist in the designated path, FULLPATH() returns the name of the specified file together with the current default directory. The default directory can be changed with the SET DEFAULT command. If a second file *filename2* is included, the function returns the path relative to the two files, *filename1* and *filename2*. This function returns a character value.

Examples

This first example returns the location of the MAILLIST database file, assuming it is in C:\WORK\DATA.

```
SET DEFAULT TO C:\WORK
SET PATH TO C:\WORK\DATA
? FULLPATH("MAILLIST.DBF")
C:\WORK\DATA\MAILLIST.DBF
```

In the second example, the value returned contains the path of SET DEFAULT, since the MAILLIST database, assuming it is in C:\WORK\DATA, could not be located along the FoxPro path.

```
SET PATH TO C:\FOXPRO25
SET DEFAULT TO C:\
? FULLPATH("MAILLIST.DBF")
C:\MAILLIST.DBF
```

In the last example, the value returned is the path and name of the first file argument, relative to the second file argument. In this case, the ACCOUNTS database is in C:\WORK.

```
SET PATH TO C:\WORK;C:\WORK\DATA
? FULLPATH("MAILLIST.DBF","ACCOUNTS.DBF")
C:\WORK\MAILLIST.DBF
```

See also SET DEFAULT, SET PATH

FV()

FV(*expN1*, *expN2*, *expN3*)

Description This function returns the future value of an investment.

Operational rules The FV() function returns the future value of fixed periodic payments with a compounded interest rate. This is the function that answers the question, "If I put $250 a month in an account that pays 10 percent interest, how much will I have at the end of 10 years?" The three parameters are payment *expN1*, interest rate *expN2*, and payment period *expN3*.

As with all of the FoxPro financial functions, keep in mind that if the rate is given as an annual percentage rate (as it most often is), and the periods are monthly (as they most often are), then the interest rate must be divided by 12, and the term must be in months (years times 12). Payments are assumed to be made at the end of each period. If the payments are made at the beginning of each period, the formula to calculate the future value is:

```
FV(pmt,rate,term)*(1+rate)
```

The term must be at least one. The following formula is used to calculate the future value:

```
pmt * (((1+rate)^term)-1/rate)
```

Examples This example calculates the future value of periodic payments of $250 for 10 years placed in an account paying 10 percent interest, compounded monthly:

```
? FV(250,.1/12,10*12)
51211.24
```

See also PAYMENT(), PV()

FWRITE()

FWRITE(*expN1*, *expC* [, *expN2*])

Description This function writes a character string to a file that has been opened with one of the low-level file operations.

Operational rules The first parameter *expN1* is the file handle. FWRITE() writes the character string at the byte where the file pointer is positioned. The optional third parameter *expN2* is the number of bytes to be written. FWRITE() returns the number of bytes written to the file. This function is equivalent to the FPUTS() function, except that FPUTS() always appends a carriage return and line feed to the end of the string. This function returns a numeric value.

Examples

```
mopen = FOPEN("TEMP.TXT")
? mopen
2
mwrite = FWRITE(mopen,"Now is the time")
? mwrite
15
mwrite = FWRITE(mopen,"for all good men")
? mwrite
16
mclose = FCLOSE(mopen)
? mclose
.T.
```

See also FPUTS()

GETBAR()

GETBAR(*expC, expN*)

Description This function returns the location number of an option in a pop-up.

Operational rules The GETBAR() function is used to determine the position of an option in a pop-up. Pop-ups are defined with the DEFINE POPUP command and the pop-up options are defined with DEFINE BAR. Each option in the pop-up has a bar number. Pop-up options can be added, removed or even rearranged if the MOVER clause was included when the pop-up was defined.

The two parameters used in this function are the pop-up name, specified with *expC*, and the pop-up option, specified with *expN*. GETBAR() returns the bar number of the option in pop-up position *expN*. The value specified in *expN* should be between 1 and maximum number of options in the pop-up. This function returns a numerical value.

Example This example defines a pop-up and its options and then removes one of the options.

```
DEFINE POPUP list FROM 5,5
DEFINE BAR 1 OF list PROMPT "This is option 1"
DEFINE BAR 2 OF list PROMPT "This is option 2"
DEFINE BAR 3 OF list PROMPT "This is option 3"
DEFINE BAR 4 OF list PROMPT "This is option 4"
? GETBAR("list",3)   && The third pop-up position
3    &&  is BAR 3.
RELEASE BAR 3 OF list
? GETBAR("list",3)   && The third pop-up position
4    &&  is now BAR 4 which moved up.
```

See also DEFINE POPUP, DEFINE BAR

GETDIR()

GETDIR([*expC1* [, *expC2*]])

Description This function displays the Select Directory dialog.

Operational rules The GETDIR() function is used to display the Select Directory dialog and returns the character string of the selected directory. If no directory is selected, a null character (" ") is returned. The optional parameter *expC1* can be used to specify the directory to be displayed when the dialog appears.

If no directory is specified, or the directory does not exist, the current default directory is initially displayed. An optional prompt can be specified with *expC2* that is displayed on the dialog window. This function returns a character value.

Example

```
mdir = GETDIR("C:\WORK","Save this file to:")
? mdir
C:\WORK\DATA
```

See also GETFILE(), GETEXPR()

GETENV()

`GETENV(expC)`

Description This function returns the status of a specified DOS environment setting.

Operational rules DOS has a group of commands that change the DOS working environment. These commands include PROMPT, which changes the appearance of the DOS system prompt, and PATH, which tracks the subdirectories that should be searched when a command is issued. Your DOS manual has a list of these commands. They are often automatically issued through the AUTOEXEC.BAT file.

The *expC* argument must be given as a string or string variable. It can be upper or lowercase, but must match the particular DOS system command. This function returns a character value.

Examples The function in the first example checks the existing path set up in the DOS working environment. The second example checks for the location of the Windows directory.

```
? GETENV("PATH")
C:\;C:\DOS;C:\WP
? GETENV("COMMAND")
COMMAND.COM

? GETENV("WINDIR")
C:\WINDOWS
```

See also OS()

GETFILE()

`GETFILE([expC1] [, expC2] [, expC3] [, expN])`

Description This function displays the Open File dialog box.

Operational rules The GETFILE() function displays the Open File dialog, allowing the user to choose a file from the list. GETFILE() returns the name of the file chosen, returned as a character string. If no file is chosen, or Cancel is selected, a null string (" ") is returned.

The first optional parameter *expC1* can be one or more extensions that determine the types of files to be listed. If more than one extension is listed, separate them with semicolons (;). The extension parameter must be surrounded by quotes ("). To display all files in the directory, use the null string (" ") for this parameter. To display all files that have no extension, use the semicolon. The second optional argument *expC2* is a message to display on the dialog box.

When the Open File dialog is displayed, two push button options are available: Open and Cancel. The GETFILE() function allows you to change the prompt of the Open push button and also add a third push button. The optional argument *expC3* is used to replace the Open push button with *expC3*. The optional argument *expN* specifies the number and type of push buttons that appear in the Open File dialog.

The following list details which buttons appear when the *expN* argument is 0, 1 or 2 and the *expC3* argument is not used:

Value	Buttons available
0	Cancel (default) Cancel

Value	Buttons available
1	New Open Cancel
2	None Open Cancel

If *expN* is 1 and the push button selected is New, the string returned is the directory plus Untitled. This function returns a character value.

Examples

```
mdbf = GETFILE("DBF","CHOOSE A FILE")
IF !EMPTY(mdbf)
   USE (mdbf)
ENDIF

mdbf = GETFILE("DBF","Choose a file to Browse","Browse")
IF !EMPTY(mdbf)
   IF "Untitled" $ mdbf
      CREATE (mdbf)
   ELSE
      USE (mdbf)
      BROWSE
   ENDIF
ENDIF
```

See also LOCFILE(), PUTFILE()

GETFONT()

`GETFONT()`

Description This function displays the Windows font dialog box.

Operational rules The GETFONT() function displays the Window font dialog, allowing the user to select a font from a list of available fonts. The value returned is a string which contains the font name, font size and font style. Each font attribute is separated by a comma. If no font is selected, or Cancel is selected, a null string (" ") is returned. This function returns a character value.

Example

```
newfont = GETFONT()
? newfont
LotusLineDraw,11,B
```

See also WFONT()

GETPAD()

`GETPAD(expC, expN)`

Description This function returns the name of a menu pad from a user-defined or system menu.

Operational rules The GETPAD() function is used to determine the position of a pad in a menu. Menus are defined with the DEFINE MENU command and the pads options are defined with DEFINE PAD. Each option in the menu has a pad name. Pads on a menu can be added, removed, or even rearranged.

The two parameters used in this function are the menu name, specified with *expC*, and the pad option, specified with *expN*. GETPAD() returns the pad number of position *expN*. The value specified in *expN* should be between 1 and maximum number of pads in the menu. This function returns a numerical value.

Examples

```
? GETPAD("_MSYSMENU"",2) && The second pad of the system menu
_MSM_EDIT
RELEASE PAD _MSM_EDIT OF _MSYSMENU

? GETPAD("_MSYSMENU"",2) && The second pad of the system menu
_MSM_DATA                 &&   has changed
```

See also DEFINE MENU, DEFINE PAD

GOMONTH()

GOMONTH(*expD*, *expN*)

Description This function returns the date given a specified date and the number of months after that date.

Operational rules The GOMONTH() function returns the date *expN* months after *expD*. If *expN* is negative, the function subtracts the months from the date. This function returns a date value.

Examples

```
mwedding = {9/16/90}
maildate = GOMONTH(WEDDATE,-2)
? maildate
07/16/90
```

HEADER()

HEADER([*expN* | *expC*])

Description This function returns the size of the header record for a specified database file.

Operational rules The HEADER() function returns the length of a database header in bytes. A database header contains information about the database including field names and lengths, and whether the database uses a structural compound index or memo field.

This function can be used in conjunction with the RECSIZE() and RECCOUNT() functions to find the total number of bytes used by a file. The following formula will return the number of bytes used by the data in the database:

```
HEADER() + (RECCOUNT() * RECSIZE()) + 1
```

HEADER() returns the size of the header for the current database. You can use HEADER() on a database in another work area by specifying the work area number with *expN* or the database alias with *expC*. This function returns a numeric value. See the DISKSPACE() function in this chapter for an example on using HEADER() to determine the size of a database.

See also DISKSPACE(), RECSIZE()

IDXCOLLATE()

```
IDXCOLLATE([cdx file,] expN1 [, expN2 | expC])
```

Description This function returns the collation sequence of the specified index file or tag.

Operational rules The IDXCOLLATE() function returns the collation sequence of the controlling index file. Multiple compound index (.CDX) and single index (.IDX) files can be used with a single database. Each index is opened with the USE or SET INDEX commands. Single index files contain only one index expression while compound index files can contain multiple index expressions, or tags.

The *expN1* argument determines which index file or tag to use when determining the IDXCOLLATE() expression. The controlling index file is determined by:

- Single index files.
- Structural compound index file.
- Other compound index file.

If the optional *cdx file* argument is used, IDXCOLLATE() returns the collation sequence for the first tag in the specified compound index file. Tags are numbered in the order they were created in the multiple index file.

IDXCOLLATE() returns the collation sequence of a database in the current work area. To return the collation sequence of a database in another work area, specify the work area number with *expN* or the database alias with *expC*. This function returns a character value.

Examples

```
USE STUDENTS    && Assumes a .CDX
? IDXCOLLATE(1)
MACHINE
? IDXCOLLATE(2)
UNIQWT
```

See also SET COLLATE, chapter 11, Cross-platform and international capabilities

IIF()

```
IIF(expL, expr1, expr2)
```

Description This function, immediate if, evaluates a logical expression and returns a value based on the result.

Operational rules The IIF() function evaluates the logical expression *expL* and if true (.T.) returns the first expression *expr1*; otherwise it returns the second expression *expr2*. A simple explanation of this function is to use the English translation, "If this condition is true, do this; otherwise do that." The expressions, *expr1* and *expr2* can be character, numeric, logical, or date. However, both expressions must be of the same type.

Unlike the IF ... ENDIF command, IIF() can be issued from the Command window and can even be used in reports for conditional printing. However, in some cases the IF ... ENDIF command must be used, because the IIF() function cannot be used to issue commands based on a condition.

Conditional statements usually use one or more of the following operators:

=	equal
<	less than
<=	less than or equal to
>	greater than
>=	greater than or equal
! or <>	not equal
$	substring search
AND	Both conditions must be true.
OR	Either condition may be true.

For instance, ? IIF(Sex="F","FEMALE","MALE") states, "If the variable Sex equals F, then display FEMALE; otherwise display MALE." Following is an example of the IF command replaced by the one-line IIF() function:

```
IF Results = "P"
   ? "Positive"
ELSE
   ? "Negative"
ENDIF
```

or as an IIF() function:

```
? IIF(Results = "P","Positive","Negative")
```

In instances where more than two conditions must be run, you can nest IIF() functions. An example is a grading application where (in English): "If score >= 90, then return A; otherwise, if score >= 80, then return B; otherwise return a C." (In this case, C is the lowest grade possible). The comparable FoxPro function for this case is:

```
IIF(Score >= 90,"A",IIF(Score >= 80,"B","C"))
```

Examples The following are all valid uses of the IIF() function:

```
IIF(Grade > 70, "PASS","FAIL")    (contents of a report column)
? IIF(Sex = "M","Male",IIF(Sex = "F","Female",""))
Tax = IIF(State = "CA" AND Taxable = "Y",Price*.06,0)
```

See also IF ... ENDIF

INKEY()

```
INKEY([expN] [, expC])
```

Description This function returns a number that represents the most recent key pressed on the keyboard or mouse click, in the typeahead buffer.

Operational rules The INKEY() functions returns a number between 0 and 255 that represents the ASCII code of a key press or mouse click. 0 is returned if no key is pressed. When the INKEY() function is used, the key that the user presses is not displayed on the screen, as with all other interactive commands. Also, INKEY() can detect the exact keystroke pressed (such as a Ctrl key combination, or an arrow key). If the user has typed several characters, the INKEY() function returns the first character in the typeahead buffer, and removes it from the buffer.

The optional numeric argument *expN* determines how long in seconds INKEY() pauses to receive the keystroke. If there is no argument, INKEY() reads the most recent key pressed. The second parameter *expC* is used to detect a mouse click or hide the cursor. To detect a mouse click, include M in *expC*. If M is included in *expC*, INKEY() returns the value 151 for a single mouse click. There is no INKEY() value for a double mouse click. *expC* can be any combination of the following:

M	Detect a single mouse click
H	Hides the cursor
S	Shows the cursor
E	Evaluate a keyboard macro character

If both H and S are included, the last character takes precedence. If the keyboard character in the buffer is assigned to a macro, including E forces INKEY() to return a value corresponding to the first keystroke assigned to the macro. If the macro contains more than one character, use the INKEY() function with E as many times as necessary to get the value of each keystroke in the macro. Not including E forces INKEY() to return the value of the keystroke(s) that activated the macro.

INKEY() does not return the values of Alt function key combinations because these keystrokes are handled by the macro interpreter. Function keys and their Ctrl and Shift combinations are represented by negative numbers. Alt key combinations with letters are also negative, and there is no differentiation between uppercase and lowercase with Alt keys.

If the key pressed is between 40 and 126, the CHR() function of the INKEY() displays the character pressed. For instance, the function

```
CHR(INKEY(20))
```

returns the letter A if uppercase A (INKEY() value 65) is pressed. Table 4-2 lists all FoxPro INKEY() return values. This function returns a numeric value.

Table 4-2 INKEY return values.

Key	Alone	Shift	Ctrl	Alt
F1	28	84	94	104
F2	–1	85	95	105
F3	–2	86	96	106
F4	–3	87	97	107
F5	–4	88	98	108
F6	–5	89	99	109
F7	–6	90	100	110

F8	–7	91	101	111
F9	–8	92	102	112
F10	–9	93	103	113
F11	133	135	137	139
F12	134	136	138	140
1	49	33	–	120
2	50	64	33	121
3	51	35	–	122
4	52	36	–	123
5	53	37	–	124
6	54	94	30	125
7	55	38	–	126
8	56	42	–	127
9	57	40	–	128
0	48	41	–	19
a	97	65	1	30
b	98	66	2	48
c	99	67	3	46
d	100	68	4	32
e	101	69	5	18
f	102	70	6	33
g	103	71	7	34
h	104	72	127	35
i	105	73	9	23
j	106	74	10	36
k	107	75	11	37
l	108	76	12	38
m	109	77	13	50
n	110	78	14	49
o	111	79	15	24
p	112	80	16	25
q	113	81	17	16
r	114	82	18	19
s	115	83	19	31
t	116	84	20	20
u	117	85	21	22
v	118	86	22	47
w	119	87	23	17
x	120	88	24	45
y	121	89	25	21
z	122	90	26	44
INS	22	22	146	162
HOME	1	1	29	151
DEL	7	7	147	163

Table 4-2 Continued.

Key	Alone	Shift	Ctrl	Alt
END	6	6	23	159
PGUP	18	18	31	153
PGDN	3	51	30	161
UP	5	5	141	152
RIGHT	4	4	2	157
LEFT	19	19	26	155
DOWN	24	24	145	160
ESCAPE	27	27	27	1
ENTER	13	13	10	28
BSPACE	127	127	127	14
TAB	9	15	148	165

Examples The program below pauses and waits for the user to press a key. The program responds with three different displays, depending if the ↑, ↓, or other key is pressed.

```
mkey = INKEY(20)
DO CASE
   CASE mkey = 5
      ? "Going UP!"
   CASE mkey = 24
      ? "Going DOWN!"
   OTHERWISE
      ? "Please press the ↑ or ↓!"
ENDCASE
```

See also ON KEY, CHR(), READKEY()

INLIST()

`INLIST(`*`expr1, expr2`*` [, `*`expr3...`*` ])`

Description This function determines if an expression is contained in a list of given expressions.

Operational rules The INLIST() function returns true (.T.) if the first expression *expr1* is in the list of expressions starting with *expr2*. All expressions in the arguments must be of the same type (numeric, character, or date). The INLIST( ) function is equivalent to the following criteria selection:

```
expr1 = expr2 OR expr1 = expr3 OR . . .
```

This function returns a logical value.

Examples

```
mfruit = "apple"
? INLIST(mfruit,"pear","banana","orange")
.F.
```

```
USE CLIENTS
LIST FOR INLIST(AMT, 100, 250, 500)
Record #  CLIENT    AMT
4         Smith     100
6         Miller    100
7         Jones     500
```

INSMODE()

`INSMODE([expL])`

Description This function turns on and off the Insert key (to insert mode or back to overwrite mode).

Operational rules INSERT(.T.) switches the Insert mode on, and INSERT(.F.) switches it off. If *expL* is given, INSERT() returns the mode before the change. If *expL* is not specified, INSERT() returns the state of the Insert key without changing mode. This function returns a logical value.

Examples

```
? INSERT(.T.)
.T.    (if Insert was already on)
? INSERT()
.T.    (if the Insert is on)
```

See also CAPSLOCK(), NUMLOCK()

INT()

`INT(expN)`

Description This function returns a numeric expression, truncated at the decimal point.

Operational rules The INT() function returns only the integer portion of *expN* and ignores all numbers that are right of the decimal point. To round numbers to zero decimal places, use the ROUND() function. The INT(5.6) is equal to 5, while the ROUND(5.6,0) is equal to 6. This function returns a numeric value.

Examples

```
? INT(5.2)
5
? INT(5.6)
5
? INT(- 5.6)
-5
```

See also ROUNT(), CEILING(), FLOOR()

ISALPHA()

`ISALPHA(expC)`

Description This function determines if a given character expression begins with a letter.

Operational rules The ISALPHA() function returns true (.T.) if the first character of *expC* is an upper or lowercase letter, a through z. All other cases return false (.F.). Use the ISDIGIT() function to determine if an expression begins with a number. The function that tells whether a variable is a character string or a numeric (or other type), is the TYPE() function. This function returns a logical value.

Examples The following program allows the user to edit a record. The user can pull up the record by entering the record number, or a last name for seeking. The ISALPHA() function checks whether the first character of the seek string begins with a letter or a number. If it is a number, the GOTO record number command is used; otherwise, a SEEK is performed.

```
ACCEPT "Enter a name or record number " TO Search
IF ISALPHA(Search)
   SEEK Search
ELSE
   GOTO VAL(Search)
ENDIF
BROWSE
```

See also ISDIGIT(), TYPE(), ISLOWER()

ISCOLOR()

```
ISCOLOR()
```

Description This function determines if the computer has the ability to display color.

Operational rules The ISCOLOR() function returns true (.T.) if the computer has a color graphics adapter. This function can be used in programs that will be run on several computers. By determining the value of ISCOLOR(), the program can set screen colors on or ieave them off. This function returns a logical value.

Examples The following program checks whether there is a color adapter and sets the color accordingly.

```
IF ISCOLOR()
   SET COLOR SET TO COLOR
ELSE
   SET COLOR SET TO MONOCHROME
ENDIF
```

See also SET COLOR

ISDIGIT()

ISDIGIT(*expC*)

Description This function determines if a given character expression begins with a digit (0–9).

Operational rules The ISDIGIT() function returns true (.T.) if the first character of *expC* is a number, 0 through 9. All other cases return false (.F.). Use the ISALPHA() function to determine if an expression begins with a character. The function that tells whether a variable is a character string or a numeric (or other type), is the TYPE() function. This function returns a logical value.

Example

```
ACCEPT "Enter a name or record number " TO Areacode
IF !ISDIGIT(Areacode)
   WAIT WINDOW "Area Code must begin with a number"
ENDIF
```

See also ISDIGIT(), TYPE()

ISLOWER()

`ISLOWER(`*`expC`*`)`

Description This function determines if the first character of a given character expression is a lowercase letter.

Operational rules The ISLOWER() function returns true (.T.) if the first character of *expC* is a lowercase letter, a through z. All other cases return false (.F.). This function returns a logical value.

Examples

```
? ISLOWER("John")
.F.
? ISLOWER("john")
.T.
? ISLOWER("")
.F.
? ISLOWER("55")
.F.
```

See also ISUPPER()

ISUPPER()

`ISUPPER(`*`expC`*`)`

Description This function determines if the first character of a given character expression is an uppercase letter.

Operational rules The ISUPPER() function returns true (.T.) if the first character of *expC* is an uppercase letter, A through Z. All other cases return false (.F.). This function returns a logical value.

Examples

```
? ISUPPER("John")
.T.
? ISUPPER("john")
.F.
? ISUPPER("")
.F.
? ISUPPER("55")
.F.
```

See also ISLOWER()

KEY()

```
KEY([cdx file,] expN1 [, expN2 | expC])
```

Description This function returns the key expression that the specified index file or tag was created with.

Operational rules The KEY() function returns the index expression of the controlling index file. Multiple compound index (.CDX) and single index (.IDX) files can be used with a single database. Each index is opened with the USE or SET INDEX commands. Single index files contain only one index expression while compound index files can contain multiple index expressions, or tags.

The *expN1* argument determines which open index file or tag to use when determining the KEY() value. The controlling index file is determined by:

- Single index files.
- Structural compound index file.
- Other compound index file.

If the optional *cdx file* argument is used, KEY() returns the index key expression for the first tag in the specified compound index file. Tags are numbered in the order they were created in the multiple index file.

KEY() returns the index expressions of a database in the current work area. To return the index expressions of a database in another work area, specify the work area number with *expN* or the database alias with *expC*. This function returns a character value.

Examples

```
USE STUDENTS    && Assumes a .CDX
? KEY(1)
UPPER(LNAME)
? KEY(5)
STATE
```

See also USE, SET INDEX, INDEX, ORDER()

LASTKEY()

```
LASTKEY()
```

Description This function returns a number that represents the most recent key entered on the keyboard.

Operational rules The LASTKEY() function, like the INKEY() function, can detect the exact keystroke entered (such as a Ctrl key combination, or an arrow key). The LASTKEY() function is different than INKEY(), however, in that it reads the key pressed in the last interactive command, such as READ, while INKEY() pauses to receive the keystroke (or captures it during a noninteractive command). The READKEY() function, which also captures keystrokes, is different in that it is only used with full-screen commands, and it returns a different value depending on whether data was changed or not.

For values 0 through 255, the number is the ASCII value that corresponds to the keystroke. Function keys and their Ctrl, Shift, and Alt combinations are represented by negative numbers. The values returned by LASTKEY( ) are the same returned by the INKEY( ) function. Table 4-2 lists all FoxPro INKEY( ) return values. This function returns a numeric value.

Examples The following program instructs the user to press Escape to abort the program and return to the main menu. The LASTKEY( ) function reads whether that key was pressed. The following keys (and their LASTKEY( ) values) can be used to exit a full-screen command without the user having to press Enter through each field: PgDn (3), PgUp (18), Ctrl-End (23), and Esc (27):

```
* Mailing List Program
mprn = "P"
msort = "A"
@ 1,1 SAY "Press ESC to Return to Main Menu"
@ 3,1 SAY "Display on Printer or Screen? (P/S) " GET mprn
@ 5,1 SAY "Sort by Zip or Alpha? (A/Z) " GET msort
READ
IF LASTKEY( ) = 27
   CLEAR
   WAIT WINDOW "Returning to Master Menu" NOWAIT
ELSE
   DO MAILLIST
ENDIF
```

See also ON KEY, INKEY( ), READKEY( )

LEFT()

LEFT(*expC*, *expN*)

Description This function returns a specified number of characters from a character string, beginning with the first character.

Operational rules The LEFT() function returns a substring of *expC*. This can be helpful in retrieving first initials of names, or printing variables on forms where there is not enough room for the entire string to print. The LEFT( ) function is the same as the SUBSTR( ) function where the beginning position is 1.

If *expN* is larger than the length of the *expC*, the result is the string itself. If the number is 0, LEFT() returns the null string (" "). This function returns a character value.

Example

```
? LEFT("California",5)
Calif
? LEFT("California",0)
      (a null string)
mdate = "11-Nov-89"
? LEFT(mdate,2)
11
? LEFT("Hello",9)
Hello
```

See also SUBSTR(), RIGHT()

LEN()

```
LEN(expC)
```

Description This function returns the number of characters in a string.

Operational rules The LEN() function returns the number of characters in the specified string *expC*. If *expC* is a database field, LEN() returns the full length of the field, unless a memo field is specified. Specifying a memo field forces LEN() to return the number of characters stored in the memo field. Use LEN(ALLTRIM(*expC*)) to return the length of the data in a database field other than a memo field. A null string returns a length of 0. This function returns a numeric value.

Example The following example assumes that Lname is the name of a field that is 25 characters long.

```
? Lname
Smith
? LEN(Lname)
25
? LEN(TRIM(Lname))
5
```

See also TRIM()

LIKE()

```
LIKE(expC1, expC2)
```

Description This determines if one character expression matches another.

Operational rules The LIKE() function returns true (.T.) if the character expression *expC1* is contained in the character expression *expC2*. The first character expression can include any combination of the two wild cards:

- * Represents any group of characters.
- ? Represents any one character.

For instance, the string SM?TH represents SMITH, SMOTHERS, SMITHSONIAN, and SMYTHE.

Unlike in DOS, which uses the same wild card operators, the asterisk (*) can be placed anywhere within the string. DOS only allows the asterisk at the end of the string. For instance, SM*TH represents both SMITH and SMOOTH.

The function is case-sensitive, so SM?TH does not match Smith. The SOUNDEX() function is like this function, except it compares the SOUNDEX() codes attributed to each character expression to estimate how much the two strings sound alike. This function returns a logical value.

Examples

```
? LIKE("Go?f","Golfing")
.T.
? LIKE("GO?F","GOOFIER")
.T.
```

```
? LIKE("GO?F?","GOOFIEST")
.F.
? LIKE("Go?f","GOOFIER")
.F.
USE Clients
LIST Lname, Fname FOR LIKE("J*NSON",LNAME)
Record #  Lname      Fname
4         JOHNSON    JILL
8         JONSON     JANE
10        JANSONS    JAMES
20        JENSON     JULIE
```

See also SOUNDEX()

LINENO()

```
LINENO([1])
```

Description This function returns the number of the next line of a program that is about to be executed.

Operational rules The LINENO() function is useful in debugging programs. LINENO() can be used with the ON ERROR command when an error is trapped to determine which program line the error occurred. The value of LINENO() is determined by the number of program lines in the executing program, including blank lines, comments and program lines separated with a semicolon (;). This function returns a numeric value.

Examples The following program calls an error routine command named Errtrap:

```
Mailprog.prg
ON ERROR DO Errtrap
USE MAILLIST
SCAN
   ? Lname, Fname
ENDSCAN
Errtrap.prg
CLEAR
? "An error has just occurred. The error is:",MESSAGE()
? "and it occurred on line", LINENO()
WAIT
RETURN TO MASTER
```

The routine Errtrap is automatically called any time an error occurs. The MESSAGE() function displays the error message, while LINENO() shows the line number that the error occurred in. The user then returns to the main program that called Mailprog.prg.

See also ON ERROR

LOCFILE()

LOCFILE(*expC1* [, *expC2*] [, *expC3*])

Description This function returns the name and path of a specified file.

Operational rules The LOCFILE() function returns the path along with the name of the file specified with *expC1*. If the file cannot be located along the FoxPro path, the Open File dialog is displayed, allowing the user to locate the file. If no file is chosen, the function returns a null string (" "). The first parameter, *expC1*, can include a path or not. If the file is not found in the designated path, FoxPro searches the default directory and then the FoxPro path.

The second parameter, *expC2*, might be one or more file extensions that determine the types of files to be listed. If more than one extension is listed, separate them with semicolons (;). The extension parameter must be surrounded by quotes ("). To display all files in the directory, use the null string (" ") for this parameter. DOS wild cards (* and ?) can be used in the file extension list.

The third optional parameter *expC3* is a message to display on the dialog box. This parameter must be a character string. Use the function GETFILE() to bring up the Open File dialog box automatically. This function returns a character value.

See also GETFILE()

LOCK()

LOCK([*expN* | *expC1*] | [*expC2*, *expN* | *expC1*])

Description This command attempts to lock a record in the current database.

Operational rules The LOCK() function returns true (.T.) if a record lock has been placed on a database record. Locking a record prevents any other users from modifying the record, yet remains available for read-only operations such as viewing or reporting. A record locked with the LOCK() function will remain locked until the database is closed or the UNLOCK command is issued.

You can attempt to lock more than one record in a single database by specifying each record number in *expC2*. Each record to lock must be separated by a comma. If all of the records specified are locked, LOCK() returns true. If even one of the records cannot be locked, false is returned and none of the specified records is locked. SET MULTILOCKS must be ON to attempt a multiple record lock.

The LOCK() function will attempt to lock the database based on the SET REPROCESS setting. If SET REPROCESS is 0, and the initial lock attempt fails, FoxPro will continue the lock attempt until the Esc key is pressed. The LOCK() function simply returns false (.F.) if the lock attempt fails and does not generate any type of error.

LOCK() attempts to lock a record in the current database. To lock the record of a database in another work area, specify the work area number with *expN* or the database alias with *expC*. This function returns a logical value.

Examples

```
USE MAILLIST
GO 10
? LOCK()
.T.
? SYS(2011)
Record Locked
UNLOCK
```

```
? SYS(2011)
Record Unlocked
```

See also RLOCK(), FLOCK(), SYS(2011)

LOG()

`LOG(`*`expN`*`)`

Description This function returns the number *e* base *x*, or natural logarithm.

Operational rules *e* is approximately 2.7182818. The LOG() function returns e^x or, in English: *e* raised to the *x* power. A zero or negative value returns an error message. The EXP() function is the inverse of the natural logarithm. This function returns a numeric value.

Examples

```
? LOG(5)
1.61
? LOG(- 5)
error message
? LOG(2.7182818)
1.02
```

See also EXP()

LOG10()

`LOG10(`*`expN`*`)`

Description This function returns the base-10 exponent of a numeric expression *x*. This is called a command logarithm.

Operational rules The LOG10() function returns a value in the following formula:

```
expN = 10^x
```

For instance, the logarithm of 100 is 2, because 10^2, or 10 * 10, is 100. A zero or negative value returns an error message. This function returns a numeric value.

Examples

```
? LOG10(5)
0.70
? LOG10(100)
2.00
```

To calculate the antilog of an expression:

```
mvalue = LOG10(3) + LOG10(3)
.95
? 10^ mvalue
9
```

See also EXP()

LOOKUP()

`LOOKUP(field1, search expr, field2 [, expC])`

Description This function searches the current database for the first occurrence of a specified expression in a specified field.

Operational rules The LOOKUP() function searches the database for a record where the field *field2* is equal to *search expr*. The value to return is specified with *field1*. If the database being searched has an active index, the LOOKUP() function uses the index to search for the expression. If the database has a compound index tag that matches the search expression, the tag name should be provided with *expC* to speed up the search process.

If a matching record is located, the FOUND() function returns true (.T.) and the value of field1 is returned. Otherwise, FOUND() returns false (.F.) and a value equal to an empty field is returned. This function returns a character, numeric, logical or date value.

Example The first example searches the *Lname* field of the STUDENTS database for JOHNSON, and displays the contents of the *Ssn* field for the record found.

```
USE STUDENTS
? SAY LOOKUP(Ssn,"JOHNSON",Lname)
555-55-5555
```

The next example uses the index tag "LNAME" to speed up the search:

```
? SAY LOOKUP(Ssn,"SMITH",Lname,"LNAME")
222-22-2222
```

See also LOCATE, FOUND(), EMPTY()

LOWER()

`LOWER(expC)`

Description This function converts a character string to lowercase letters.

Operational rules The companion function is UPPER(), which converts all letters in the expression to uppercase. Numbers and other nonalphabetical characters are not affected. This function returns a character value.

Examples

```
? LOWER("Hello")
hello
? LOWER("HELLO")
hello
```

To convert a string to proper case (first letter uppercase, and all other letters lowercase):

```
Fname = "JOHN"
? UPPER(LEFT(Fname,1)) + LOWER(SUBSTR(Fname,2))
John
```

See also UPPER(), SUBSTR(), PROPER()

LTRIM()

`LTRIM(expC)`

Description This function removes all leading spaces from a character string.

Operational rules The companion function is TRIM(), which removes all trailing blanks from an expression. The LTRIM() function is often used to trim off leading spaces created by the STR() function which converts numbers to a character string. This function returns a character value.

Examples

```
? LTRIM(" Hello")
Hello
? LEN(TRIM(LTRIM(" Hello ")))
5
Donation = 500
? "Thank you for the donation of $" + LTRIM(STR(Donation)) + "
to us."
Thank you for the donation of $500 to us.
```

See also TRIM(), STR(), RTRIM()

LUPDATE()

`LUPDATE([expN | expC])`

Description This function returns the date that a database was last updated.

Operational rules The LUPDATE() function returns the last update date of the current database, unless a work area argument is provided. To return the expression of a database in another work area, specify the work area number with *expN* or the database alias with *expC*. This function returns a date value.

Examples

```
USE MAILLIST
? "This file was last updated on ", LUPDATE()
This file was last updated on 02/02/93

WAIT WINDOW "Last updated on: " + DTOC(LUPDATE())
```

See also DBF(), RECCOUNT()

MAX()

`MAX(expr1, expr2 [, expr3 ...])`

Description This function compares a list of expressions, and returns the largest value. The arguments can be numeric, character, or date.

Operational rules When the arguments are dates, the later date is considered greater. When the arguments are strings, its value is designated by its ASCII code value. Therefore, S is greater than A, and a is greater than Z. To calculate the maximum value of a field in a

FoxPro file, use the MAX argument of the CALCULATE command. This function returns a character, numeric or date value.

Examples

```
Maxwage = 45000
Income = 60000
? MAX(Maxwage,Income)
60000
? MAX("Apple","Banana")
Banana
? MAX("Pear","banana")
banana
```

The following function displays 12/25/89 until the system date is set to a date later than December 25, 1989:

```
? MAX(DATE(),{12/25/89})
12/25/89
```

See also MIN()

MCOL()

MCOL([*expC*])

Description This function returns the column position of the mouse pointer.

Operational rules The MCOL() function returns the column position of the mouse pointer in the active screen or window. If MCOL() is used without any argument, the value returned is relative to the FoxPro desktop screen or a user-defined window if one is active.

Use *expC* to specify a user-defined window for checking the column location of the mouse pointer. If the window *expC* does not exist, an error will occur. MCOL() will return –1 if the mouse pointer is outside the coordinates of the specified window. If *expC* is the name of a Browse window, MCOL() will return 0 when the mouse pointer is located on the left border of the window. This function returns a numeric value.

See also MROW()

MDOWN()

MDOWN()

Description This function determines if the mouse button is being pressed.

Operational rules The MDOWN() function returns true (.T.) when the left mouse button is being pressed; otherwise false (.F.) is returned. This function returns a logical value.

MDX()

MDX(*expN1* [, *expN2* | *expC*])

Description This function is identical to the CDX() function. See the description of CDX() in this chapter.

MDY()

`MDY(`*`expD`*`)`

Description This function converts a date to a string that looks like a date in the written format Month Day, Year (such as September 16, 1990).

Operational rules The MDY() function returns a character string with only two digits for the year, unless SET CENTURY is ON. The three ways to enter a date as an argument are:

- Enclose the date in curly brackets: {12/5/89}
- Use the *CTOD()* function: *CTOD("12/5/2010")*
- Use a field name or memory variable.

The date is assumed to be in the 1900s when two digits are used for the year; otherwise you must enter four digits for the year. Any date between January 1, 1582, and December 31, 9999, can be used. This function returns a character string.

Examples

```
? MDY(DATE())
September 16, 89
SET CENTURY ON
? MDY({09/16/89})
September 16, 1989
HEADING = "Date: " + MDY(Repdate) +"    MONTHLY REPORT"
? HEADING
Date: February 20, 1989    MONTHLY REPORT
```

See also SET CENTURY, CTOD(), DATE(), DMY()

MEMLINES()

`MEMLINES(`*`memo field`*`)`

Description This function returns the number of lines in the memo of the current record.

Operational rules The argument is the name of the memo field and can include an alias. MEMLINES() returns the number of lines of the memo at the current record, so the pointer must be set at the desired record.

The number of lines in a memo field is affected by the setting of the SET MEMO WIDTH command. FoxPro automatically word wraps the memo according to the value specified with SET MEMOWIDTH. The default is 50 characters. If the memowidth is changed, the number of MEMLINES() returned may also change. This function returns a numeric value.

Examples

```
USE MAILLIST
? MAILLIST.Comments
   Joe's Garage is one of our happiest clients.
They may always be used as a referral, although try not to give
their name out more than once a month.

? MEMLINES(Comments)
3
```

```
SET MEMOWIDTH TO 30
? MAILLIST.Comments
   Joe's Garage is one of
our happiest clients. They may
always be used as a referral,
although try not to give their
name out more than once a
month.

? MEMLINES(Comments)
6
Mfield = "Comments"
? MEMLINES(&Mfield)
6
```

See also MLINE(), SET MEMOWIDTH

MEMORY()

```
MEMORY()
```

Description This function returns the amount of conventional memory available in the current application.

Operational rules The MEMORY() function returns the amount of conventional RAM available and does not include any expanded memory. The value returned by MEMORY() is in kilobytes, where 1 kilobyte is equal to 1024 bytes. This function is identical to the SYS(12) function, but SYS(12) returns a character string in bytes. This function always returns a numeric value of 640.

Examples

```
? MEMORY()
60
? MEMORY() * 1024
61440
```

See also SYS(12), RUN|!

MENU()

```
MENU()
```

Description This function returns the name of the most recent menu activated.

Operational rules Menus are defined with the DEFINE MENU command and activated with ACTIVATE MENU. The MENU() function returns the name of the menu in uppercase and will return a null string ("") if no menu has been activated. The PAD() function can be used to return the name of the pad most recently chosen from a menu. This function returns a character value.

Examples

```
ON SELECTION MENU _MSYSMENU DO prompt WITH MENU(),PAD()
```

```
PROCEDURE prompt
PARAMETERS mmenu,mpad
WAIT WINDOW "You have selected "+mpad+" from the "+mmenu+"
menu."
```

See also ACTIVATE MENU, DEFINE MENU, PAD()

MESSAGE()

```
MESSAGE([1])
```

Description This function returns the message corresponding to the error that has just occurred.

Operational rules The MESSAGE() function can be used with the ON ERROR command to return the message corresponding to a FoxPro ERROR() number. Unlike ERROR() which requires you to set an ON ERROR trap, the MESSAGE() function can be called at any time. If an ON ERROR command has been issued, including the optional parameter 1 will return the program line number that the error occurred on, rather than the error message itself.

The RETURN and RETRY commands do not clear the value of MESSAGE(). This function returns a character value.

Examples The following program calls an error routine command named Errtrap:

```
Mailprog.prg
ON ERROR DO Errtrap
USE MAILLIST
SCAN
   ? Lname, Fname
ENDSCAN

Errtrap.prg
WAIT CLEAR
WAIT WINDOW "The error " + MESSAGE() + " has just occurred."
RETURN TO MASTER
```

See also ON ERROR, ERROR(), RETURN

MIN()

```
MIN(expr1, expr2 [, expr3 ...])
```

Description This function compares a list of expressions and returns the smallest value. The arguments can be numeric, character, or date.

Operational rules The MIN() function compares the given expressions, *expr1*, *expr2*, *expr3*..., and returns the smallest one. When the arguments are dates, the earliest date is considered less. When the arguments are strings, its value is designated by its ASCII code value. Therefore, A is less than K, and Z is less than a. To calculate the minimum value of a field in a FoxPro file, use the MIN argument of the CALCULATE command.

Examples

```
Minwage = 45000
Income = 60000
? MIN(Maxwage,Income)
45000
? MIN("Apple","Banana")
Apple
? MIN("apple","Banana")
Banana
```

The following function displays today's date until the system date is set beyond December 25, 1989. It will display that date from then on:

```
? MIN(DATE(),{12/25/89})
09/16/89
```

See also MAX()

MLINE()

MLINE(*memo field, expN1* [, *expN2*]

Description This function returns a specific line of text in the memo field of the current record.

Operational rules The MLINE() function returns a character string from the specified memo field. The arguments are the name of the memo field and the line number to be returned.

If the optional third argument *expN2* is used, the offset from the beginning of the memo field is used for finding the line to return. This is most often used in conjunction with _mline system variable. _mline tracks the offset from line one of the memo each time that MLINE() is called. Using _mline as the optional third argument (and 1 as the second argument, *expN1*) greatly speeds up the performance of the MLINE() function.

The number of lines in a memo field is affected by the setting of the SET MEMO WIDTH command. FoxPro automatically word wraps the memo according to the value specified with SET MEMOWIDTH. The default is 50 characters. When the memowidth is changed, the memo is automatically set with the new margin, so the value of MLINE() returned might also change. This function returns a character value.

Examples

```
USE MAILLIST
? Comments
   Joe's Garage is one of our happiest clients. They may always
be used as a referral, although try not to give their name out
more than once a month.

? MLINE(Comments,2)
used as a referral, although try not to give their name out
more than once a

SET MEMOWIDTH TO 50
? Comments
   Joe's Garage is one of our happiest clients.
```

```
They may always be used as a referral, although try not to
give their name out more than once a month.

? MLINE(Comments,2)
They may always be used as a referral, although try not to
```

The following program allows the user to print a memo field on a 4-inch-long index card. If the field is too long, it pauses and lets the user put a new card in the printer.

```
USE MAILLIST
SET MEMOWIDTH TO 55
Line = 1
DO WHILE Line < MEMLINES(Comments)
   ??? MLINE(Comments,Line)
   Line = Line + 1
   IF Line = 20
      EJECT
      WAIT WINDOW "Put a new index card in"
      Line = 1
   ENDIF
ENDDO
```

See also SET MEMOWIDTH

MOD()

MOD(*expN1*, *expN2*)

Description This function returns the remainder of two expressions (*modulo*).

Operational rules The MOD() divides *expN1* by *expN2* and returns the remainder. This function can be helpful in finding every *n*th occurrence of a number. For instance, in the sequence 1, 6, 11, 16, etc., each of the numbers has a modulo of 1 when *expN2* is 5. *expN2* cannot be a 0 because a denominator of zero is an infinite number. If *expN2* is negative, then MOD() returns a negative answer. This function returns a numeric value.

Examples

```
? MOD(5,2)
1
? MOD(11,- 3)
-1
```

See also FLOOR()

MONTH()

MONTH(*expD*)

Description This function returns the number of a month, given a date expression.

Operational rules The three ways to enter a date as an argument are:

- Enclose the date in curly brackets: {12/5/89}
- Use the *CTOD()* function: *CTOD("12/5/2010")*
- Use a field name or memory variable.

The date is assumed to be in the 1900s when two digits are used for the year; otherwise you must enter four digits for the year. Any date between January 1, 1582, and December 31, 9999, can be used. This function returns a numeric value.

Examples

```
? MONTH({9/6/89})
9
? MONTH(CTOD("12/25/89"))
12
```

See also CTOD(), DAY()

MRKBAR()

MRKBAR(*expC*, *expN*)

Description This function determines if a menu or pop-up option is marked.

Operational rules The MRKBAR() function returns true (.T.) if bar *expN* of pop-up *expC* has been marked with a check mark. This function returns a logical value.

See also SET MARK OF

MRKPAD()

MRKPAD(*expC1*, *expC2*)

Description This function determines if a menu pad is marked.

Operational rules The *MRKPAD()* function returns true (*.T.*) if a menu pad *expC2* of menu *expC1* has been marked with a check mark. This function returns a logical value.

See also SET MARK OF

MROW()

MROW([*expC*])

Description This function returns the row position of the mouse pointer.

Operational rules The MROW() function returns the row position of the mouse pointer in the active screen or window. If MROW() is used without any argument, the value returned is relative to the FoxPro desktop screen or a user-defined window if one is active.

Use *expC* to specify a user-defined window for checking the row location of the mouse pointer. If the window *expC* does not exist, an error will occur. MROW() will return –1 if the mouse pointer is outside the coordinates of the specified window. If *expC* is the name of a Browse window, MROW() will return 0 when the mouse pointer is located on the left border of the window. This function returns a numeric value.

See also MCOL()

MWINDOW()

MWINDOW([*window name*])

Description This function determines if the mouse pointer is positioned over a specified window, or returns the name window that the mouse pointer is positioned over.

Operational rules The MWINDOW() function returns true (.T.) if the mouse pointer is positioned over window *window name*. If the MWINDOW() function is called without specifying a window, the function returns the name of the window that the mouse pointer is positioned over. The null string (" ") is returned if the mouse pointer is over the FoxPro desktop screen. This function returns a logical or character value.

See also MCOL(), MROW()

NDX()

```
NDX(expN1 [, expN2 | expC])
```

Description This function returns the name of an open single index file in the current work area.

Operational rules Each single index file (.IDX) is given an order number, depending on the order that it was opened. The SET INDEX and USE commands open the indexes. The first file in the list is the master index, or 1. The SET ORDER command can be used to change the order of currently opened index files.

If the number in *expN1* is larger than the number of index files open, then NDX() returns a null string. NDX() returns the index of a database in the current work area. To return the index of a database in another work area, specify the work area number with *expN2* or the database alias with *expC*. Use CDX() or MDX() to return the names of compound index files. This function returns a character value.

Examples

```
USE MAILLIST INDEX Name,Zip,Code
? NDX(1)
NAME.NDX
SET ORDER TO 2
? NDX(1)
ZIP.NDX
```

See also SET INDEX, SET ORDER, USE

NUMLOCK()

```
NUMLOCK([expL])
```

Description This function turns on and off the NumLock key.

Operational rules NUMLOCK(.T.) switches the NumLock on, and NUMLOCK(.F.) switches it off. If *expL* is given, NUMLOCK() returns the mode before the change. If *expL* is not specified, NUMLOCK() returns the state of NumLock without changing mode. This function returns a logical value.

Examples

```
? NUMLOCK(.T.)
.T.    (if NumLock was already on)
```

```
? NUMLOCK()
.F.     (if NumLock is off)
```

See also CAPSLOCK(), INSMODE()

OBJNUM()

`OBJNUM(var [, expN])`

Description This function returns a GET's object number.

Operational rules When the @ ... SAY/GET and @ ... EDIT commands are used, each object (field, check box, push button, pop-up, etc.) is numbered in the order that the cursor passes through it when a READ is issued. OBJNUM() returns the number, given the variable or field name in *var*. The optional argument *expN* is the READ level of the object. This function returns a numeric value.

See also @ ... SAY/GET, READ

OCCURS()

`OCCURS(expC1, expC2)`

Description This function returns the number of times one character string occurs within another character string.

Operational rules The OCCURS() function returns the number of times that *expC1* occurs within *expC2*. If *expC1* does not occur within *expC2*, the function returns zero. This function returns a numeric value.

Examples

```
? OCCURS("p","apple")
2
? OCCURS(" ",City)     && where City is "San Juan Capistrano"
2
```

See also AT(), $, INLIST()

OEMTOANSI()

`OEMTOANSI(expC)`

Description This function converts a character string from ASCII to an ANSI equivalent.

Operational rules The OEMTOANSI() function is used to convert DOS ASCII characters to the Windows ANSI equivalent. Specify the string to convert with *expC*. The companion function is ANSITOOEM() which converts ANSI to ASCII.

This ANSITOOEM() function is useful in converting FoxPro for MS-DOS text files to FoxPro for Windows. This function returns a character value.

See also ANSITOOEM()

ON()

`ON(expC1 [, expC2])`

Description This function returns the command that has been assigned to a FoxPro ON event command.

Operational rules The ON() function is used to determine the command that has been assigned to the following ON event commands:

```
ON ERROR
ON ESCAPE
ON KEY
ON KEY LABEL
ON PAGE
ON READERROR
ON SHUTDOWN
```

The first parameter, *expC1*, specifies the ON event. The valid expressions are:

Command	**expC1 value**
ON ERROR	ERROR
ON ESCAPE	ESCAPE
ON KEY	KEY
ON KEY LABEL	KEY
ON PAGE	PAGE
ON READERROR	READERROR
ON SHUTDOWN	SHUTDOWN

The second parameter, *expC2*, is used to specify those keys programmed with ON KEY LABEL. This function returns a character value.

Examples

```
ON KEY LABEL F2 DO Msort.prg
? ON("KEY","F2")
do msort.prg

ON SHUTDOWN DO Shutitdown
? ON("SHUTDOWN")
do Shutitdown
```

See also ON ERROR, ON ESCAPE, ON KEY, ON KEY LABEL, ON PAGE, ON READERROR

ORDER()

ORDER([*expN1* | *expC* [, *expN2*]])

Description This function returns the name of the controlling index file or tag for the current database.

Operational rules The ORDER() function returns the controlling index name or tag that was set with the USE ... ORDER or SET ORDER commands. A database can have multiple single or compound indexes open at any time yet only one index can be active. If no index tags are active, the null string (" ") is returned.

ORDER() returns the controlling index tag of a database in the current work area. To return the index tag of a database in another work area, specify the work area number with *expN2* or the database alias with *expC*. This function returns a character value.

Examples

```
USE MAILLIST INDEX Name,Zip,Code
? ORDER()
Name

SET ORDER TO 2
? ORDER("MAILLIST")
Zip

morder = ORDER("MAILLIST")
SET ORDER TO
SET ORDER TO morder
```

See also SET ORDER, USE

OS()

```
OS([1])
```

Description This function returns the name and version of the operating system that FoxPro is running on.

Operational rules Including the optional argument 1 returns the version Windows version number. This function returns a character value.

Examples

```
? OS()
DOS 5.00
? OS(1)
Windows 3.10
```

See also VERSION(), GETENV()

PAD()

```
PAD()
```

Description This function returns the name of the pad most recently selected from a bar menu.

Operational rules The PAD() function returns the name of only the most recent pad activated in uppercase. Menus are defined with the DEFINE MENU command and activated ACTIVATE MENU. This function returns a character value.

Examples This example assumes that a bar menu has been recently activated. The options are Print Report, Listing, and Labels:

```
? PAD()
Labels
```

See also ACTIVATE MENU, DEFINE MENU, DEFINE PAD

PADC() | PADL() | PADR()

```
PADL(expr, expN [, expC])
PADR(expr, expN [, expC])
PADC(expr, expN [, expC])
```

Description These functions return a string padded with characters to the left, right, or centered.

Operational rules The PADL() function pads from the left, PADR() from the right, and PADC() displays the expression centered in the padding.

The expression *expr* will be expanded to a length of *expN*, after padding is complete. If *expN* is less than the length of *expr*, then the function truncates it to that length. The optional argument *expC* defines the character to use for padding. If it is omitted, a space is used. This function returns a character value.

Examples

```
? PADL("This is the Title",60,"-")
-------------------------------------------This is the Title
? PADR("This is the Title",60)
                                           This is the Title
? PADC("This is the Title",60,"-")
                     -----------------This is the Title------------
```

See also STUFF(), LTRIM(), RTRIM()

PARAMETERS()

```
PARAMETERS()
```

Description This function returns the number of parameters passed to the last procedure or function called.

Operational rules Programs can call other user-defined functions or procedures. Functions and procedures can receive parameters passed to them using the PARAMETER command. You can pass less parameters to a function or procedure than are defined in a PARAMETER statement. This function is useful in procedures and functions to determine if a variable number of parameters are passed. This function returns a numeric value.

Examples

```
DO Mcount with 1,2,3
? PARAMETERS()
3

PROCEDURE mcount
PARAMETERS c1,c2,c3,c4
```

See also FUNCTION, PROCEDURE, PARAMETERS

PAYMENT()

```
PAYMENT(expN1, expN2, expN3)
```

Description This function returns the fixed payment on a loan of *expN1* at an interest rate of *expN2* for *expN3* periods. This is the function that answers the question, "What will be my monthly payment on a $75,000, 30-year fixed loan with a 10% interest rate?"

Operational rules The PAYMENT() function returns the amount of the periodic payment assuming the interest rate and term are in periodic amounts. Because most fixed loans have monthly periods, the interest and term often must be adjusted. For instance, suppose if the payments are to be made monthly, but the interest rate and term are given in annual terms, such as a 10% annual rate for 30 years. In this case, divide the annual interest rate by 12 and multiply the yearly term times 12. FoxPro uses the following formula to calculate the PAYMENT():

```
princ * (int/(1-(1+int)/^-n))
```

where

```
princ = principal
int = interest rate
n = term
```

As with all financial functions dealing with annuities (fixed payments), payments are assumed to be made at the end of each period. The formula to calculate the term if the payments are made at the beginning of each period is:

```
PAYMENT(expN1,expN2,expN3)/(1+expN2)
```

This function returns a numeric value

Example This function calculates the monthly payment on a 30-year fixed rate loan of $75,000 at a 10% interest rate:

```
Pmt = PAYMENT(75000,.1/12,3012)
? Pmt
658.18
```

The next formula calculates the total paid over the 30 years: pmt term 12. Running this calculation is not advised for those with weak stomachs or newly purchased homes:

```
? Pmt * 12 * 30
236944.32
```

See also PV(), FV()

PCOL()

```
PCOL()
```

Description This function returns the column number position where the printer head currently is.

Operational rules The PCOL() function is used in conjunction with the @ ... SAY/GET command that places a display in a particular position on the screen or printed page. The @ command places the display on the screen using the following syntax:

```
@ row,col SAY expression
```

For instance, the command:

```
@ 5,30 SAY "HI THERE"
```

would display the words HI THERE on the fifth row on the screen, in column 30. When the command SET DEVICE TO PRINT has been given, all @ ... SAY commands are sent to the printer.

After each @ ... SAY, the cursor is then positioned at the end of the expression. Therefore, the PCOL() function would return 38 after printing the expression in the example. This allows you to use the PCOL() function to display an expression on the screen relative to another expression. This function returns a numeric value.

Examples The following program prints a message after the expression Mstring (assuming it is of variable lengths). If Mstring places the cursor too far to the right, the program places the page number on the next line; otherwise it is placed right next to Mstring:

```
SET DEVICE TO PRINT
@ 5,30 SAY Mstring
IF PCOL() < 68
   @ 5, PCOL() SAY "Page: "+PAGNUM
ELSE
   @ 6, 1 SAY "Page: "+PAGNUM
ENDIF
```

This program prints a string continuously until it reaches the end of the screen:

```
DO WHILE PCOL() < 75
   @ 10, PCOL()+ SAY Mstring
ENDDO
```

The operator $ can also be used with the @ ... SAY/GET command interchangeably with PCOL(). For instance, the following commands are valid:

```
@ 5,30 SAY Mstring
@ 5, $ SAY "Y)es or N)o"
```

The difference between PCOL() and $ is that PCOL() can also be used in a conditional statement, as in the last two examples. Also, $ can be used to relatively address the screen or printer, while PCOL() can only be used with the printer, and COL() can only be used with the screen.

See also COL(), PROW()

PI()

```
PI()
```

Description This function returns the number pi (approximately 3.1415926).

Operational rules The value of PI() is used in engineering and drafting calculations, often in conjunction with trigonometric functions (COS(), SIN(), ACOS(), etc.) The ratio between the circumference of a circle and its diameter is always pi. Because it is a constant, there are no arguments to the PI() function. The function is usually entered in formulas, such as:

```
PI() * 3^2
```

which is the area of a circle with a radius of 3. The following:

```
COS(PI())
```

is the cosine of a half circle. This function returns a numeric value.

Examples

```
SET DECIMALS TO 5
? PI()
3.14159
```

The formula below calculates the area of a circle with a 5 inch radius:

```
? PI() * 5^2
78.53982
```

See also COS(), SIN(), TAN()

POPUP()

```
POPUP()
```

Description This function returns the name of the most recent pop-up menu activated.

Operational rules The command that activates a pop-up menu is ACTIVATE POPUP. A pop-up menu is a menu that pops up on the screen with a specific message. The POPUP() function returns the name of only the active pop-up menu. Once the menu is deactivated, it is erased from the screen, and the screen is restored to its previous contents.

To create a pop-up menu, you must use the command DEFINE POPUP. This command assigns the coordinates and prompts of the menu. To create a pop-up menu where the user can make selections, use the DEFINE BAR command in conjunction with DEFINE POPUP. The companion function, BAR(), returns the number of the bar most recently chosen. This function returns a character value.

Examples

```
? POPUP()
MAIN
```

See also ACTIVATE POPUP, DEFINE POPUP, DEFINE BAR

PRINTSTATUS()

```
PRINTSTATUS()
```

Description This function determines if the printer is on-line.

Operational rules The PRINTSTATUS() function returns true (.T.) if the printer is ready (on-line); otherwise it returns false (.F.). If the print device is not ready to accept output, those FoxPro commands that have a TO PRINT clause and the ??? command will generate an error when issued.

The PRINTSTATUS() function is controlled by the setting of SET PRINTER TO. If SET PRINTER is TO an ASCII file, PRINTSTATUS() will always return true unless the file cannot be accessed. The four main reasons that the printer is not on-line are:

1. The printer is not turned on.
2. The printer's on-line toggle is not on.

3. The cable between the printer and computer is disconnected.
4. The computer is not set to send output to the correct printer port.

The SYS(13) function can also be used to check the status of the printer. This command returns a logical value.

Examples The following program checks the print status before running a report to the printer:

```
IF !PRINTSTATUS()
   ? "The printer is not on or is not connected. Please turn "
   ? "it on-line, and try to run this option again. "
ELSE
   REPORT FORM Maillist TO PRINT
ENDIF
```

See also SET PRINTER, SYS(13)

PRMBAR()

PRMBAR(*expC, expN*)

Description This function returns the prompt text of a specified pop-up bar.

Operational rules The PRMBAR() function returns the prompt text of bar *expN* of pop-up *expC*. The pop-up bar is given a prompt using the DEFINE BAR command. The pop-up is named with DEFINE POPUP. The null string (" ") is returned if the bar has no prompt and any hot keys and other special characters in the prompt are not returned with this function. This function returns a character value.

Example

```
DEFINE POPUP list
DEFINE BAR 1 OF list PROMPT "Action 1"
DEFINE BAR 2 OF list PROMPT "Action 2"

? PRMBAR("LIST",1)
Action
```

See also DEFINE POPUP, DEFINE BAR

PRMPAD()

PRMPAD(*expC1, expC2*)

Description This function returns the prompt text of specified menu pad.

Operational rules The PRMPAD() function returns the prompt text of pad *expC2* of menu *expC1*. The menu pad is given a name using the DEFINE PAD command. The menu is named with DEFINE MENU. Hot keys and other special characters in the prompt are not returned with this function.

The null string (" ") is returned if the pad has no prompt and, any hot keys and other special characters in the pad are not returned with this function. This function returns a character value.

Example

```
DEFINE MENU main
DEFINE PAD list OF main PROMPT "Record List"
DEFINE PAD report OF main PROMPT "Report \<List"

? PRMPAD("MAIN",2)
Report List
```

See also DEFINE PAD

PROGRAM()

PROGRAM([*expN*])

Description This function returns the name of the current program being executed, or the last executing program when the last error occurred.

Operational rules The PROGRAM() function always returns the name of the executing program until an error occurs. If an ON ERROR trap has been set, PROGRAM() returns the name of the program in which the error occurred, even while executing an ON ERROR program.

The optional parameter *expN* is used to specify a program level. If it is used, the PROGRAM() function will return the name of the program at that level. For example, if the master program (level 1) calls one procedure (level 2), which in turn calls another (level 3), the value of PROGRAM(2) would be the first procedure called by the master program: level 2. This can be useful in determining how many program levels have been executed (FoxPro supports 32 levels.) If *expN* is 0 or 1, the master program is returned. If *expN* is greater than the number of program levels running, the null string ("") is returned. This function returns a character value.

Examples

```
Mailprog.PRG
ON ERROR DO Errtrap WITH PROGRAM()
USE MAILLIST
SET PRINT ON
SCAN
   ? Lname, Fname
ENDSCAN

Errtrap.PRG
PARAMETERS mprogname
WAIT WINDOW "An error has occurred in " + mprogname
```

See also ON ERROR, MESSAGE(), LINENO()

PROMPT()

PROMPT()

Description This function returns the prompt text of the most recently selected menu pad or pop-up.

Operational rules The PROMPT() function returns the prompt text from a selected menu pad, or the prompt text of a selected pop-up bar. If Esc is pressed to exit a menu or pop-up, the null string (" ") is returned. The BAR() function can be used to get the bar number of a selected pop-up bar and the POPUP() function can be used to return the name of the selected POPUP(). This function returns a character value.

Examples

```
? PROMPT()
Run Report
```

See also ACTIVATE POPUP, DEFINE POPUP, DEFINE BAR

PROPER()

PROPER(*expC*)

Description This function converts a character string so that the first letter of each word is capitalized and all the rest are lowercase.

Operational rules The companion functions are UPPER() and LOWER(), which convert all letters in the expression to upper or lowercase. Numbers and other nonalphabetical characters are not affected. This function returns a character value.

Examples

```
? PROPER("JULIE ANN SMITH")
Julie Ann Smith
```

See also LOWER(), UPPER()

PROW()

PROW()

Description This function returns the row number position where the printer head currently is.

Operational rules The PROW() function is used in conjunction with the @ ... SAY/GET command that places a display in a particular position on the screen or printed page. The @ command places the display on the screen using the following syntax:

@ *row,col* SAY *expression*

For instance, the command:

```
@ 5,30 SAY "HI THERE"
```

would display the words HI THERE on the fifth row on the screen, in column 30. When the command SET DEVICE TO PRINT has been given, all @ ... SAY commands are sent to the printer.

After each @ ... SAY, the cursor is then positioned at the end of the expression. Therefore, the PROW() function would return 5 after printing the expression in the example. This allows you to use the PCOL() function to display an expression on the screen relative to another expression. This function returns a numeric value.

Examples The following program prints a phone directory. Each name uses two lines: one for the name, and one for the phone number. Each time printer head reaches the 55th line, the program ejects a page, and reprints the title:

```
USE Maillist
SET DEVICE TO PRINT
@ 1,1 SAY "Phone Listing "
SCAN
   IF PROW() > 55
      EJECT
      @ 1,1 SAY "Phone Listing "
   ENDIF
   @ PROW()+2,1 SAY Fname + Lname
   @ PROW()+1,1 SAY Phone
ENDSCAN
```

The operator $ can also be used with the @ ... SAY/GET command interchangeably with PROW(). For instance, the following commands are valid:

```
SCAN
   @ $+2,1 SAY FNAME + LNAME
   @ $+1,1 SAY PHONE
ENDSCAN
```

The difference between PROW() and $ is that PROW() can also be used in a conditional statement, as in the two examples above. Also, $ can be used to relatively address the screen or printer, while PROW() can only be used with the printer, and ROW() can only be used with the screen.

See also COL(), PCOL(), ROW()

PUTFILE()

PUTFILE([*expC1*] [, *expC2*] [, *expC3*])

Description This function displays the Save As dialog box and returns the directory and file entered.

Operational rules The PUTFILE() function returns the chosen filename as a character string. If Cancel was selected or Esc pressed, a null string (" ") will be returned. The first optional parameter *expC1* is a message to display at the top of the dialog box. The second optional parameter *expC2* is the default filename to display in the text box. The third parameter, *expC3*, is the extension to be used as the default of the filename.

If more than one extension is listed, separate them with semicolons (;). The first extension is the one that will be appended, however. The PUTFILE() function is very useful in allowing a user to select the drive, directory, and filename of a file about to be created. This function returns a character value.

Examples This example queries the user for a filename and then copies 10 records in SDF format.

```
mfile = PUTFILE("Name of ASCII file","MAILLIST","DTA")
IF !EMPTY(mfile)
```

```
   COPY TO (mfile) TYPE SDF NEXT 10
ENDIF
```

See also GETFILE(), COPY TO

PV()

PV(*expN1*, *expN2*, *expN3*)

Description This function returns the present value on a loan with fixed payments at an interest rate of *expN2* for *expN3* periods.

Operational rules The PV() function returns the amount of the present value assuming the interest rate and term are in periodic amounts. Because most fixed loans have monthly periods, the interest and term often must be adjusted. For instance, if the payments are monthly, but the interest rate and term are annual, divide the annual interest rate by 12 and multiply the yearly term times 12. FoxPro uses the following formula to calculate the PV():

```
pmt * ((1   (1 + int)^ -n))/int
```

where

```
pmt = periodic payment
int = interest rate
n = term
```

As with all financial functions dealing with annuities (fixed payments), payments are assumed to be made at the end of each period. The formula to calculate the term if the payments are made at the beginning of each period is:

PV(*expN1*,*expN2*,*expN3*) * (1+*expN2*)

This function is the companion to PAYMENT(), which returns the payment given principal, interest and term. The PV() function answers the question, "How much can I borrow if my loan will be 30-year fixed, 10% interest rate, with a monthly payment of $500?" This function returns a numeric value.

Example The following example calculates the principal on a 30-year fixed rate loan with payments of $500 at a 10% interest rate. Because the interest and term are in annual figures, the arguments in the PV() formula divide the annual interest by 12 and multiply the annual term times 12:

```
? PV(500,.1/12,30*12)
56975.41
```

The next example calculates the principal left on the same loan after 2 years of payments:

```
? PV(500,.1/12,2*12)
10835.43
```

RAND()

RAND([*expN*])

Description This function returns a number between 0 and 1 that changes each time you request the function.

Operational rules The optional numeric argument *expN* is used as a seed to create a new random number sequence. The default seed is 100001. Although this function is named after the "random" expression, the sequence of numbers returned from a series of RAND()'s is always the same if started from the same seed. However, if you use a negative number as the argument, the seed is taken from the system clock.

Although the number returned by RAND() is less than 1, you can get larger numbers. First choose the highest and lowest numbers you would like to generate. Create a formula that multiplies RAND() by the highest minus lowest number, and then adds the lowest number.

```
RAND()     A random number
RAND()*5+1          A number between 1 and 6.
```

The RAND() function is used in some statistical modeling applications as well as computer games. (Random numbers are often used to ensure that the game does not start the same way every time.) This function returns a numeric value.

Example

```
? RAND()
0.47
? RAND()
0.80
? RAND()
0.88
```

The following sequence starts with a seed taken from the system clock:

```
? RAND(-5)     (do this only once)
0.55
? RAND()
0.62
? RAND()
0.53
```

RAT()

RAT(*expC1*, *expC2* [, *expN*])

Description This function returns the position where one character string appears within another character string, starting from the end of the string.

Operational rules The RAT() function returns the position that character expression *expC1* first occurs in character expression *expC2*, beginning from the end, or right, of *expC2*. The function is very useful for finding key words within comments or addresses, or for finding the last word in a full name or address. If *expC1* does not exist in *expC2*, the null string (" ") is returned.

The optional third argument, *expN*, searches for the *expN*th occurrence (backwards) of *expC1* in *expC2*. The RAT() function is the reverse of the AT() function. This function returns a character value.

Example

```
? RAT(" ","555 Main Street")
9
```

The example below shows how RAT() can be used in conjunction with the SUBSTR() function to extract last names from fields that contain the entire name. The arguments of SUBSTR() are SUBSTR(*string,start number*).

```
USE CLIENTS
LIST OFF NAME
NAME
Mr. John Smith
Bonnie Miller
Mr. and Mrs. Tom Jones
LIST OFF SUBSTR(NAME, RAT(" ",NAME)+1)
Smith
Miller
Jones
REPLACE ALL LNAME WITH SUBSTR(NAME, RAT(" ",NAME)+1)
```

See also AT(), SUBSTR()

RATLINE()

RATLINE(*expC1, expC2*)

Description This function returns the line number where one character string occurs within another, beginning with the last line.

Operational rules The RATLINE() function searches the character expression *expC2* for an occurrence of *expC1*, beginning from the end, or right, or *expC2*. The character string searched and the character string searching for can be either an expression or a memo field. If the expression is not found in *expC2*, the return value is 0. RATLINE() is case-sensitive, meaning the upper and lowercase values of each expression are respected.

The line number returned is determined by the value of SET MEMOWIDTH even if *expC2* is not a memo field. If SET MEMOWIDTH is 20, more lines will occur than if it is set to 80. This function returns a numeric value.

Example The following example assumes that the database has a memo field named Notes:

```
STORE RATLINE("camp fund",NOTES) TO Memoln
? Memoln
12
? MLINE(NOTES,MEMOLN)
Phone call 12/15/90: probably the last time we discuss the camp
fund
```

See also ATLINE(), SET MEMOWIDTH, MLINE()

RDLEVEL()

RDLEVEL()

Description This function returns the current READ level.

Operational rules Multiple READ levels can occur when @ ... SAY/GETs and a READ are issued while another READ is active. FoxPro supports up to 5 READ levels. This function returns a numeric value.

See also @ ... SAY/GET, READ

READKEY()

`READKEY([expN])`

Description This function returns a number that represents the most recent key pressed to exit an editing command, or how a READ was terminated.

Operational rules The value returned by READKEY() is determined by the previous editing or READ command. The following FoxPro commands determine the value of READKEY():

APPEND
BROWSE
CHANGE
CREATE
EDIT
INSERT
MODIFY
READ

The commands listed above require some combination of keystrokes to exit their respective editing window. Each exiting key combination returns a different value. Table 4-3 lists all FoxPro READKEY() return values. Notice that there are only codes for those keystrokes that exit from a full-screen command.

Table 4-3 READKEY return values.

Key	No-update	Update
Backspace, ← Ctrl-H, Ctrl-S	0	256
→, Ctrl-D, Ctrl-L	1	257
Home, Ctrl-A	2	258
End, Ctrl-F	3	259
↑, Ctrl-E, Ctrl-K Shift-Tab	4	260
↓, Ctrl-X, Tab Ctrl-Enter, Ctrl-J	5	261
PgUp, Ctrl-R	6	262
PgDn, Ctrl-C	7	263
Ctrl-U	10	266

Ctrl-N	11	267
Esc, Ctrl-Q	12	–
Ctrl-End, Ctrl-W	14	270
Enter, Ctrl-→	15	271
Ctrl-M		
Ctrl-Home, Ctrl-J	33	289
Ctrl-PgUp, Ctrl- -	34	290
Ctrl-PgDn, Ctrl-^	35	291
F1	36	292

READKEY(), like the INKEY() function, can detect the exact keystroke pressed (such as a Ctrl key combination, or an arrow key), unlike other interactive commands, such as READ and ACCEPT. The READKEY() function is different than INKEY(), however, in that it only reads the key pressed in the last full-screen command (such as BROWSE or READ), while INKEY() pauses to receive the keystroke (or captures it during a noninteractive command).

The value returned by READKEY() is different depending on whether any data was changed during the command. The LASTKEY() function, which also captures keystrokes, is different in that it is used with any type of interactive command, such as ACCEPT, and it returns the same value whether or not data was changed. This function returns a numeric value.

Examples The program below instructs the user to press Esc to abort the program and return to the main menu. The READKEY() function reads whether that key was pressed.

```
*  Mailing List Program
DO WHILE .T.
   mprn = "P"
   msort = "A"
   @ 1,1 SAY "Press ESC to Return to Main Menu, PgDn for Help"
   @ 3,1 SAY "Display on Printer or Screen? (P/S) " GET mprn
   @ 5,1 SAY "Sort by Zip or Alpha? (A/Z) " GET msort
   READ
   IF READKEY() = 12     && if ESC, return to menu
      CLEAR
      ? "Returning to Master Menu"
      RETURN
   ENDIF
   IF READKEY() = 7 OR READKEY() = 263     && if PgDn, run Help
      CLEAR
      DO Helper.prg
      LOOP
   ENDIF
   DO Maillist.prg
   EXIT
ENDDO
```

See also ON KEY, INKEY(), LASTKEY()

RECCOUNT()

```
RECCOUNT([expN | expC])
```

Description This function returns the number of records in a database file.

Operational rules The RECCOUNT() function returns the number of records in a database file from the database header. This is the same number received by running the COUNT command without any options. However, the COUNT command takes a much longer time to return the same answer.

RECCOUNT() always returns the total number of records, regardless of whether any of the status of any data filtering commands, such as SET DELETED ON or SET FILTER TO. RECCOUNT() returns the number of records for the database in the current work area. To return the record count of a database in another work area, specify the work area number with *expN* or the database alias with *expC*. This function returns a numeric value.

Examples The example here assumes that JOURNAL.DBF has 20 records and that COA.DBF has 8 records:

```
USE COA IN 1
USE JOURNAL IN 2
? RECCOUNT()
20
? RECCOUNT(2)
8
? RECCOUNT("COA")
8
```

See also DBF(), RECSIZE()

RECNO()

```
RECNO([expN | expC])
```

Description This function returns the number of the current record.

Operational rules The RECNO() function returns the record number of the current record, except in the following occasions:

RECNO() value	when
0	no current file
1	no records in database
1	record pointer is at BOF()
RECCOUNT()+1	record pointer is at EOF()

RECNO() returns the record number for the database in the current work area. To return the record number of a database in another work area, specify the work area number with *expN* or the database alias with *expC*. This function returns a numeric value.

Examples

```
USE COA
? RECCOUNT()
8
```

```
GO 5
? RECNO()
5
GO BOTTOM
? RECNO()
8
SKIP
? RECNO()
9
```

See also DBF(), RECSIZE()

RECSIZE()

```
RECSIZE([expN | expC])
```

Description This function returns the size of a record in the database file.

Operational rules The RECSIZE() function returns the length of a record, which is the total of the lengths of each field plus 1. This is the number displayed during the CREATE or MODIFY STRUCTURE commands. The following formula returns the number of bytes used by the data in the database:

```
RECCOUNT() + RECSIZE() + 1
```

All database files have a header record at the top of the file. The length of the header record is returned with the HEADER() function.

RECSIZE() returns the size of a record for the database in the current work area. To return the record size of a database in another work area, specify the work area number with *expN* or the database alias with *expC*. This function returns a numeric value.

Examples

```
USE MAILLIST
LIST STRUCTURE
Structure for database: MAILLIST.DBF
Number of data records: 6
Field     Field name     Type        Width
1         LNAME          Character   10
2         FNAME          Character   10
** Total **       21
? RECSIZE()
21
filesize = HEADER + (RECSIZE() * RECCOUNT() + 1)
? filesize
225
```

See also RECCOUNT(), HEADER()

RELATION()

```
RELATION(expN1 [, expN2 | expC])
```

Description This function returns the expression used in setting a relation.

Operational rules The RELATION() function returns a specified relation as a character string. The parameter *expN1* specifies which relation, relative to the order they were created with the SET RELATION command, to return. The relationships for all currently open files can also be seen with the DISPLAY STATUS command.

RELATION() returns the relations for the database in the current work area. To return the relations of a database in another work area, specify the work area number with *expN2* or the database alias with *expC*. This function returns a character value.

Examples

```
USE MAILLIST IN 1
USE STATENAM ORDER STATE_ZIP IN 2
SET RELATION TO STATE INTO STATENAM
SET RELATION TO ZIP INTO STATENAM
? RELATION(1)
STATE
? RELATION(2)
ZIP
? RELATION(1,"STATNAM")
   && null string
```

See also SET RELATION

REPLICATE()

REPLICATE(*expC*, *expN*)

Description This function returns a character string that contains a specified number of repeated characters.

Operational rules The REPLICATE() function returns a string of characters *expC* replicated *expN* times. This function is useful when creating lines for report headings and section breaks. The character string can be more than one character, but the resulting string exceeds the amount of available memory. The SPACE() function is equivalent to using REPLICATE() with " " as the character argument. This function returns a character value.

Examples

```
? REPLICATE("-",40)
----------------------------

? REPLICATE("yeah ",3)
yeah yeah yeah

? REPLICATE("* ",10)
* * * * * * * * * *
```

See also SPACE()

RGBSCHEME()

RGBSCHEME(*expN1* [, *expN2*])

Description This function returns an RGB color pair or color pair list from a color scheme.

Operational rules The RGBSCHEME() function returns the numeric values of RGB color pairs and color pair lists. It is similar to the SCHEME() function, which returns letters for the color pairs. The *expN1* argument specifies the number of the color scheme for which you want a complete RGB color listing. Ten RGB color pairs are returned. You can use the optional second argument *expN2* to return a single RGB color pair from a color scheme. *expN2* specifies the position of the RGB color pair in the color scheme. This function returns a character value.

Examples

```
? RGBSCHEME(1)
RGB(0,0,0,255,255,255),RGB(0,0,0,192,192,192)...

? RGBSCHEME(1,5)
RGB(0,0,0,128,128,128)

? SCHEME(1)
N/W*,N/W*,N/W*.W+/RB,N/W,W+/N,W+/N,N/N,N/W*,W/W*,

? SCHEME(1,4)
W+/RB
```

See also SCHEME()

RIGHT()

RIGHT(*expC*, *expN*)

Description This function returns a specified number of characters from a character string, starting from the right.

Operational rules The RIGHT() function returns a substring of *expC*. This can be helpful in retrieving first initials of names, or printing variables on forms where there is not enough room for the entire string to print.

The RIGHT() function is the same as the SUBSTR(*string,startnumber,length*) function where the start-number is *expN*, and the length is to the end of the string. If *expN* is larger than the length of the *expC*, the result is the string itself. If the number is 0, RIGHT() returns the null string (" "). This function returns a character value.

Example

```
? RIGHT("California",5)
ornia
? RIGHT("California",0)
   (null string)
mdate = "11-Nov-89"
? RIGHT(mdate,2)
89
? RIGHT("Hello",9)
Hello
```

See also LEFT(), SUBSTR()

RLOCK()

```
RLOCK([expN | expC1] | [expC2, expN | expC1])
```

Description This function is identical to the LOCK() function. See the description of LOCK() in this chapter.

ROUND()

```
ROUND(expN1, expN2)
```

Description This function returns a number rounded to a specified number of decimal places.

Operational rules The ROUND() function returns the number specified in *expN1* rounded to *expN2* decimal places. To truncate at the decimal (always rounding down), use the INT() function. Numbers display with less decimal places (see SET DECIMAL TO), but they calculate the decimals that do not show.

If the second argument *expN2* is a negative number, the number rounds to multiples of 10, 100, etc. For instance, rounding to –1 places returns a multiple of 10, and rounding to –2 places returns a multiple of 100. This function returns a numeric value.

Example

```
? ROUND(5.22,0)
5
? ROUND(5.29,1)
5.3
? ROUND(- 5.22,0)
-5
? ROUND(8,- 1)
10
? ROUND(125,- 2)
100
```

See also INT(), SET DECIMAL

ROW()

```
ROW()
```

Description This function returns the row number where the cursor is currently positioned.

Operational rules The ROW() function is used in conjunction with the @ ... SAY/GET command that places a display in a particular position on the screen or printed page. The @ command places the display on the screen using the following syntax:

```
@ row,col SAY expression
```

For instance, the command:

```
@ 5,30 SAY "HI THERE"
```

would display the words HI THERE on the fifth row on the screen, in column 30.

After each @ ... SAY, the cursor is then positioned at the end of the expression. Therefore, the ROW() function would return 5 after printing the expression in the example. This allows you to use the ROW() function to keep track of the rows displayed on the screen. This function returns a numeric value.

Examples The following program displays a list of information on the screen. Each name can use one or two lines: If the name does not have a phone number, the program does not print one. Each time the screen fills with names down to row 22, the program pauses, and waits for the user to press a key to continue.

```
USE MAILLIST
@ 1,1 SAY "Mailing List "
SCAN
   IF ROW() > 22
      WAIT
      CLEAR
      @ 1,1 SAY "Mailing List "
   ENDIF
   @ ROW()+2,1 SAY Fname + Lname
   IF Phone <> ""
      @ ROW()+1,1 SAY Phone
   ENDIF
   SKIP
ENDSCAN
```

The operator $ can also be used with the @ ... SAY/GET command interchangeably with ROW(). For instance, the following commands are valid:

```
SCAN
   @ $+2,1 SAY FNAME + LNAME
   @ $+1,1 SAY PHONE
ENDSCAN
```

The difference between ROW() and $ is that ROW() can also be used in a conditional statement, as in the two previous examples. Also, $ can be used to relatively address the screen or printer, while PROW() can only be used with the printer, and ROW() can only be used with the screen.

See also COL(), PCOL(), PROW()

RTOD()

`RTOD(expN)`

Description This function converts a number representing an angle measured by radians into degrees.

Operational rules The number to convert is specified in *expN*. Fractions of a degree, usually represented by minutes and seconds, are to be represented by decimals. For instance, 45 minutes is depicted as .75 degrees. The DTOR() function is used to conversely change degrees to radians. Use the SET DECIMALS command to change the number of decimals that appear in the answer. This function returns a numeric value.

Examples

```
? RTOD(PI()/2)
90
? X1 = 45.75
45.75
? RTOD(X1)
2621.28
```

See also ACOS(), DTOR(), SET DECIMALS

RTRIM()

RTRIM(*expC*)

Description This function removes all trailing spaces from a string.

Operational rules The RTRIM() function is often used to trim off the blanks at the end of a field, because the display commands do not do this automatically. It is also often used with the SEEK command to ensure that there are no blanks at the end of the search target string.

The only command that automatically trims trailing spaces when displaying expressions is the LABEL command. The companion function to RTRIM() is LTRIM(), which removes all leading spaces from an expression. RTRIM() is identical to the TRIM() function. Use the ALLTRIM() function to remove both leading and trailing blanks from a string. This function returns a character value.

Examples The first example shows how fields are displayed when the RTRIM() is not used. The second example shows how RTRIM(), when used in conjunction with a comma, leaves one space between the two strings. The third example shows how RTRIM(), when used in conjunction with a plus sign, leaves no spaces between the two strings:

```
USE MAILLIST
? FNAME,LNAME
John   Smith

? RTRIM(FNAME),LNAME
John   Smith

? RTRIM(FNAME)+LNAME
JohnSmith
```

See also LTRIM(), TRIM(), ALLTRIM

SCHEME()

SCHEME(*expN1* [, *expN2*])

Description This function returns a color pair or color pair list from a color scheme.

Operational rules The SCHEME() function returns the color pairs and color pair lists, in letters, of a color scheme. It is similar to the RGBSCHEME() function, which returns RBG values for the color pairs.

The *expN1* argument specified the number of the color scheme for which you want a complete color scheme listing. Ten color pairs are returned. You can use the optional second argument *expN2* to return a single color pair from a color scheme. *expN2* specifies the position of the color pair in the color scheme. This function returns a character value.

Examples

```
? SCHEME(1)
N/W*,N/W*,N/W*,W+/RB,N/W,W+/N,W+/N,N/N,N/W*,W/W*,+

? SCHEME(1,4)
W+/RB

? RGBSCHEME(1)
RGB(0,0,0,255,255,255),RGB(0,0,0,192,192,192)...

? RGBSCHEME(1,5)
RGB(0,0,0,128,128,128)
```

See also RGBSCHEME()()

SCOLS()

```
SCOLS()
```

Description This function returns the number of console columns available on the FoxPro desktop.

Operational rules A standard console displays 80 characters across the screen. However, some video drivers change the number of display columns, usually allowing more than 80 characters to be displayed. This function can be very useful in determining how screens are centered or reports and other listings will be displayed. This function returns a numeric value.

See also SROWS()

SECONDS()

```
SECONDS()
```

Description This function returns the number of seconds since midnight.

Operational rules Divide the value returned from the SECONDS() function by 60 to get the number of minutes since midnight. Divide the value returned by the function by 3600 to get the number of hours since midnight. This function returns a numerical value. The value returned is in seconds, with thousandths to the right of the decimal point.

Examples This example shows you how to use the SECONDS() function to determine how long a process took.

```
mstart = SECONDS()
COUNT
mend = SECONDS()
mtotal = mend - mstart
WAIT WINDOW "The COUNT process took " + ALLTRIM(STR(mtotal)) +
"seconds."
```

See also TIME(), SYS(2)

SEEK()

```
SEEK(expr [, expN | expC])
```

Description This function searches the current database for a given expression.

Operational rules The SEEK() function returns true (.T.) if the expression is found; otherwise it returns false (.F.). If found, the record pointer is moved to the record that matches; otherwise it is moved to the end of the file (EOF()). SEEK() uses the master index to search for expr. The expression must be of the same type as the key expression of the master index. If an index order is not set, an error occurs.

Using the SEEK() function is similar to using the SEEK command and checking the value of FOUND(). SEEK() performs the search on the database in the current work area. To search a database in another work area specify the work area number with *expN* or the database alias with *expC*. This function returns a logical value.

Examples The example is a program that looks for a name in an indexed database, and edits the record that matches. If no records match, a message is displayed. Notice that the SEEK() function replaces the use of the SEEK command followed by the FOUND() function.

```
USE MAILLIST ORDER Mailname
ACCEPT "Enter Last Name of Person to Edit " TO Mlname
IF SEEK(Mlname)
   BROWSE
ELSE
   WAIT WINDOW "NO MATCHING RECORDS FOUND!"
ENDIF
```

See also FOUND(), SEEK

SELECT()

```
SELECT([0 | 1])
```

Description This function returns the number of the current work area, or the number of the highest work area that is not being used.

Operational rules The SELECT() function is used to determine the current or highest available work area. The use of this function can ensure that the area being selected is not currently being used. SELECT() (and SELECT(0)) returns the current work area number. SELECT(1) returns the highest available work area.

The SELECT() function is affected by the setting of SET COMPATIBLE. If SET COMPATIBLE is ON, the SELECT() function returns the number of the highest available work area. The SELECT command is used to change the active work area. This function returns a numeric value.

Examples The following example opens two files, and then opens a third file named Batch in the next available work area:

```
USE COA IN 10
USE JOURNAL IN 2
? SELECT()
```

```
1
? ALIAS(10)
COA
USE BATCH IN SELECT()
```

See also SET COMPATIBLE, SELECT, USE

SET()

`SET(`*`expC`*` [, 1])`

Description This function returns the current status of a particular SET command.

Operational rules The argument *expC* is the name of the SET command. The optional argument 1 can be used to return a secondary setting for those SET commands that have both an ON/OFF and TO clause.

The value returned by the SET() function is dependent on what the specified SET command does. The SET() function cannot be used on SET DISPLAY—see SYS(2006)—and SET VIEW. This function returns a character or numeric value. See Appendix in the help file disk for a complete table of SET() return values.

Examples

```
? SET("MEMOWIDTH")
60
? SET("STATUS")
ON
? SET("Carry")
OFF
```

See also FoxPro SET Commands

SIGN()

`SIGN(`*`expN`*`)`

Description This function returns a number that represents whether the argument is a positive number, negative number, or zero.

Operational rules The SIGN() evaluates the value of *expN* and returns a 1 for positive numbers, a –1 for negative numbers, and a 0 for zero. This function returns a numeric value.

Examples

```
? SIGN(55)
1
? SIGN(0)
0
? SIGN(-55)
-1
```

See also ABS()

SIN()

`SIN(`*`expN`*`)`

Description This function returns the sine of an angle.

Operational rules The SIN() function evaluates *expN* as the angle. The sine represents the y-axis value at any point of the circle with radius pi/2. Therefore it is always between –1 and 1. It is often better to use memory variables as the argument, because the function then uses 20-place numeric accuracy. You can change the number of decimal points displayed in the answer with the SET DECIMALS command. This function returns a numeric value.

Examples

```
? SIN(0)
0
? SIN(PI()/6)
.5
```

See also ASIN(), ACOS(), COS()

SKPBAR()

`SKPBAR(expC, expN)`

Description This function determines whether a pop-up option has been disabled.

Operational rules The SKPBAR() function returns true (.T.) if bar *expN* of pop-up *expC* has been disabled with the SET SKIP OF command. Pop-ups are defined with the DEFINE POPUP command and each pop-up option is defined with the DEFINE BAR command. This command returns a logical value.

See also DEFINE POPUP, DEFINE BAR, SET SKIP OF

SKPPAD()

`SKPPAD(expC1, expC2)`

Description This function determines whether a menu pad has been disabled.

Operational rules The SKPPAD() function returns true (.T.) if menu pad *expC2* of menu *expC1* has been disabled with the SET SKIP OF command. Menus are defined with the DEFINE MENU command and each menu pad is defined with the DEFINE PAD command. This command returns a logical value.

See also DEFINE MENU, DEFINE PAD, SET SKIP OF

SOUNDEX()

`SOUNDEX(expC)`

Description This function returns a value based on the phonetic representation of a character expression.

Operational rules The SOUNDEX() function returns a four-digit code, which represents the phonetic value of the expression. SOUNDEX() is not case-sensitive (upper and lowercases are ignored). This function can be used to determine if two character strings are phonetically alike. The value returned is made up of the following:

The first digit is the first character of the string. After the first digit of the string, all occurrences of the letters a, e, h, i, o, u, w, and y are ignored. Then it assigns a number to the remaining letters:

```
b, f, p, and v = 1
c, g, j, k, q, s, x, z = 2
d, t = 3
l = 4
m, n = 5
r = 6
```

If two letters next to each other have the same code, it only uses the code of the first letter. If the first character of the string isn't a letter, SOUNDEX() returns 0000. The companion function, DIFFERENCE(), calculates the difference between the SOUNDEX() codes of two strings.

Examples

```
? SOUNDEX("HUMDINGER")
H535
```

You can index a file on the soundex code of a name to help look up names when you do not know the exact spelling:

```
USE CLIENTS
INDEX ON SOUNDEX(Lname) TO Clisound
SEEK SOUNDEX("Balisteri")
? FNAME,LNAME
John Ballestros
```

See also DIFFERENCE()

SPACE()

SPACE(*expN*)

Description This function returns a string of spaces.

Operational rules The SPACE() function returns a string of *expN* blank spaces. This function is often used to initialize a character variable, or to pad a string on the left so that it displays at a certain position. The maximum value specified with expN is limited by available memory. This function returns a numeric value.

Examples The example displays the character string in the center of an 80-character screen. The PADC() function performs this same function:

```
Title = "Income Projection"
Padding = (80/2)-LEN(Title)/2  && PAD=screen/2title-length/2
? SPACE(Padding) + Title
Income Projection
```

See also LEN()

SQRT()

SQRT(*expN*)

Description This function returns the square root of a specified numeric expression.

Operational rules A negative argument returns an error message, as it is impossible to take the square root of a negative number. Either the ABS() or IIF() functions can be used to circumvent this problem:

```
SQRT(ABS(value))   && Square root of the absolute value
IIF(value<0,0,SQRT(value))    && 0 if Amount < 0
```

This function returns a numeric value.

Examples
```
? SQRT(100)
10.00
? SQRT(ABS(-100))
10.00
```

See also ABS(), IIF()

SROWS()

`SROWS()`

Description This function returns the number of console rows available on the FoxPro desktop.

Operational rules A standard console displays 25 rows down the screen. However, some video drivers can change the number of available rows. This function returns a numeric value.

Examples
```
* Using standard Windows VGA driver
? SROWS()
35.25

* After changing to Windows SVGA driver
? SROWS()
45.25
```

See also SCOLS()

STR()

STR(*expN1* [, *expN2* [, *expN3*]])

Description This function returns the a character string equivalent of a specified numeric expression.

Operational rules The STR() function evaluates the numeric expression *expN1* and returns a character string equivalent. The length argument *expN2* represents the length of the string, including decimal points and places, to return. If *expN2* is not specified, the return length is 10 characters.

The decimal argument *expN3* represents the number of digits left of the decimal point. If the number has more decimal places than requested, STR() rounds it. The default length is 10. The default decimal places is 0. The companion function is the VAL() function, which converts a character string to a numeric value. This function returns a character value.

Example

```
? STR(5,6,2)
5.00
? STR(5,6)
5
```

The following example uses the LTRIM() function (trim off leading blank spaces) to left justify a number.

```
mowe = 500
? "You have 10 days to send the $" + LTRIM(STR(mowe)) + " that
you owe."
You have 10 days to send the $500 that you owe.
```

See also VAL()

STRTRAN()

`STRTRAN(`*`expC1, expC2`*` [, `*`expC3`*`] [, `*`expN1`*`] [, `*`expN2`*`])`

Description This function replaces the occurrences of *expC2* in *expC1* with *expC3*.

Operational rules STRTRAN() performs a "find and replace" function using the following arguments: STRTRAN(*expression to replace in, string to find, string to replace it with*).

The optional first numeric argument *expN1* tells the function to replace at the *expN1*th occurrence of *expC2* in *expC1*. If it is omitted, the function starts at the first occurrence. The optional second numeric argument *expN2* tells the function to replace *expN2* times. If it is omitted, the function replaces all occurrences of *expC2*. This function returns a character value.

Example In the following example, all occurrences of Los Angeles are replaced with L.A. in order to save room for more comment space:

```
USE MAILLIST
LIST COMMENTS FOR "LOS ANGELES" $ COMMENTS
Record #  COMMENTS
4         OUR DEALER IN LOS ANGELES
6         CONTACT TO LOS ANGELES POLITICIANS
8         VOTED "LOS ANGELES MAN OF THE YEAR"
REPLACE ALL Comments WITH STRTRAN(Comments,"LOS ANGELES",
"L.A.")
LIST COMMENTS FOR "L.A." $ COMMENTS
Record #  COMMENTS
4         OUR DEALER IN L.A.
6         CONTACT TO L.A. POLITICIANS
8         VOTED "L.A. MAN OF THE YEAR"
```

See also STUFF()

STUFF()

`STUFF(`*`expC1, expN1, expN2, expC2`*`)`

Description This function replaces a specified number of characters in a given character expression.

Operational rules The STUFF() function removes the *expN2* number of characters from *expC1*, starting at position *expN1*. Then it takes *expC2*, and places it within *expC1* at the *expN1* position. If *expN1* is greater than the length of *expC1*, then STUFF() appends *expC2* to the end of *expC1*. If *expN2* is zero, then no characters are eliminated from *expC1*, and *expC2* is simply inserted into the string. The STUFF() function is not supported in memo fields. This function returns a character value.

Example

```
mstring = "I am happy"
? STUFF(mstring,6,0,"very ")
I am very happy
? STUFF(mstring,6,5,"hungry")
I am hungry
```

To replace all occurrences of the word Exxon with Arco in a character field named Desc:

```
SET FILTER TO "Exxon" $ Desc
REPLACE ALL Desc WITH STUFF(Desc,AT("Exxon",Desc),5,"Arco")
```

See also REPLACE, STRTRAN(), LEFT(), SUBSTR()

SUBSTR()

SUBSTR(*expC*, *expN1* [, *expN2*])

Description This function returns a specified number of characters from a given character expression.

Operational rules The SUBSTR() function returns the rest of *expC*, starting at the position *expN1*. If the third argument is given, the SUBSTR() function returns a substring of *expN2* characters. When no third argument is entered, the answer ends at the last character of *expC*. If the third argument is larger than the number of characters left in the string, then the third argument is ignored.

If the number is 0, the function returns the null string. If the second argument is larger than the number of characters in *expC*, an error occurs. This is also true of negative numbers in the argument. This function returns a character value.

Example

```
? SUBSTR("California",5,3)
for
?SUBSTR("California",5)
fornia
? SUBSTR("California",0)
   (a null string)
mdate = "11-Nov-89"
? SUBSTR(mdate,4,3)
Nov
```

See also LEFT(), RIGHT()

SYSMETRIC()

SYSMETRIC(*expN*)

Description This function returns the value of a Windows display element.

Operational rules The SYSMETRIC() function can be used to accurately determine the size and attributes of windows, menus, and controls. When *expN* is between 1 and 34, the value returned by SYSMETRIC() is a pixel size. The value returned will vary among different video cards and drivers.

The table below describes what is returned for each value of *expN*.

Display element returned	**When *expN* is**
Maximum window width	1
Maximum window height	2
Width of sizable window frame	3
Height of sizable window frame	4
Width of scroll arrows on vertical scroll bar	5
Height of scroll arrows on vertical scroll bar	6
Width of scroll arrows on horizontal scroll bar	7
Height of scroll arrows on horizontal scroll bar	8
Height of window title	9
Width of nonsizable window frame	10
Height of nonsizable window frame	11
Width of DOUBLE or PANEL window frame	12
Height of DOUBLE or PANEL window frame	13
Thumb width on horizontal scroll bar in text editing windows	14
Thumb height on vertical scroll bar in text editing windows	15
Minimized window icon width	16
Minimized window icon height	17
Maximum cursor width	18
Maximum cursor height	19
Single line menu bar height	20
Maximized window width	21
Maximized window height	22
Kanji window height	23
Minimum sizable window width	24
Minimum sizable window height	25
Minimum window width	26
Minimum window height	27
Window controls width	28
Window controls height	29
1 if a mouse is present; otherwise 0	30
1 if Windows debugging version; otherwise 0	31
1 if mouse buttons are swapped; otherwise 0	32
Half-height window bit-map width	33
Half-height window bit-map height	34

Consult your Window documentation for more information on Windows display elements. This function returns a numeric value.

See also TXTWIDTH()

SYS()

Description The FoxPro SYS() functions each return information regarding system status. The argument is a number that designates the type of information to be obtained. The result of many SYS() functions can also be determined with other FoxPro functions. Unless otherwise indicated, all SYS() functions return a character value.

Due to space limitations, all SYS() function descriptions can be found in Appendix F in the help file.

TAG()

```
TAG([cdx file,] expN1 [, expN2 | expC])
```

Description This function returns the tag names from a compound index, or single index file.

Operational rules Each tag in a compound index file is given an order number, depending on the order that it was created. Use TAG() to return the tag names from within an index. The *expN1* parameter specifies which tag to return, in the order they were created. Use CDX() to return index file names. You only need to use the *cdx file* argument if more than one multiple index file is open.

TAG() returns the tag names of a database in the current work area. To return the tag names of a database in another work area, specify the work area number with *expN2* or the database alias with *expC*. This function returns a character value.

See also CDX()

TAN()

```
TAN(expN)
```

Description This function returns the tangent of a specified angle.

Operational rules A circle is marked with points in radians (0 to pi). The cosine represents the x-axis value at any point, and the sine represents the y-axis value at any point. The tangent, therefore, is SIN(*expN*)/COS(*expN*). This ratio can be any number other than PI()/2 or 3PI()/2, which have sine values of 0. This function returns a numeric value.

Examples

```
TAN(0)
0
TAN(30*PI/180)
.5
```

See also COS(), SIN()

TARGET()

```
TARGET(expN1 [, expN2 | expC])
```

Description This function returns the database alias of a relation target.

Operational rules The TARGET() function returns the alias name of a database target as specified with SET RELATION ... INTO. The argument expN1 specifies which alias to return if multiple relationships have been set. The relationships for all currently open files can also be seen with the DISPLAY STATUS command.

TARGET() returns the target alias of the database in the current work area. To return the target alias of a database in another work area, specify the work area number with *expN2* or the database alias with *expC*. This function returns a character value.

Examples

```
USE MAILLIST IN 1
USE STATENAM INDEX STATENAM IN 2
SELECT 1
SET RELATION TO STATE INTO STATENAM
? TARGET(1)
STATENAM
? TARGET(1,"B")
   && returns null string
```

See also SET RELATION, RELATION()

TIME()

```
TIME([expN])
```

Description This function returns the system time as a character string.

Operational rules The system time is kept through DOS and can be set with the TIME command at the DOS prompt. Many computers come with battery clocks that keep the system time current. The TIME() format is hh:mm:ss. Use the optional *expN* argument to include hundredths of a second. *expN* can be any numerical value. Use the SET HOURS command to determine whether the time is displayed in a 12-hour or 24-hour clock format. This function returns a character value.

Examples

```
? TIME()
16:35:36
? TIME(1)
17:42:32.58
```

See also DATE(), SET HOURS

TRANSFORM()

```
TRANSFORM(expr, expC)
```

Description This function returns an expression formatted with a PICTURE or FORMAT template.

Operational rules The PICTURE and FORMAT codes are used to display numbers, strings, logicals, and dates in a set format. They are usually used in conjunction with the @ ... SAY/GET command. Examples of a few picture formats:

Variable	Format	Will print as
5000	"###,###.##"	$5,000.00
5000	"$ ####.#"	$5000.0
"hello"	"@!"	HELLO

The *expr* argument is the expression to transform, and *expC* is any valid FoxPro PICTURE or FORMAT code. The TRANSFORM() function allows these picture formats to be used in commands other than @ ... SAY/GET. This command is often used with any of FoxPro's display commands, and in the report generator. This function returns a character value.

Example

```
mvalue = 66000
? mvalue
66000
? TRANSFORM(mvalue,"###,###.##")
66,000.00
mpicture = "$ #,###,###"
? TRANSFORM(mvalue,mpicture)
$66,000
```

See also @ ... SAY/GET

TRIM()

TRIM(*expC*)

Description See the RTRIM() function.

TXTWIDTH()

TXTWIDTH(*expC1* [, *expC2*, *expN* [, *expC3*]])

Description This function returns the length of a character expression based on the average width of a specified font.

Operational rules The TXTWIDTH() function returns the length of the expression specified with *expC1*. This function is useful when centering an expression that uses a proportional font. Use *expC2* to specify a font. If no font is specified, the value returned is determined by the current output window font. A font size can be specified with *expN* and a font style with *expC3*. The available font styles that can be used are listed below:

Character	Font Style
B	Bold
I	Italic
N	Normal
O	Outline
Q	Opaque

S	Shadow
-	Strikeout
T	Transparent
U	Underline

This function returns a numeric value.

See also FONTMETRIC(), SYSMETRIC()

TYPE()

`TYPE(expC)`

Description This function returns the data type of a specified expression.

Operational rules The TYPE() function evaluates the contents of *expC* and returns one of the following codes:

Code	Type of variable
C	Character
N	Numeric
D	Date
L	Logical
M	Memo
U	Undefined

The value of *expC* can be a literal or an expression, and is "typed" accordingly. This function returns a character value.

Examples

```
USE MAILLIST
? TYPE("ZIP")      && The ZIP field is character
C
? TYPE("PHONE")    && The PHONE field is numeric
N
mphone = "PHONE"   && Evaluates the expression
? TYPE(mphone)
N

mexpr = "x + y"
? TYPE(mexpr)      && Unknown type
U
x = 1
y = 2
? TYPE(mexpr)      && Becomes a numeric expression (x=1 and
y =2)
N
```

See also EVALUATE()

UPDATED()

`UPDATED()`

Description This function determines if any @ ... GET values were changed.

Operational rules The UPDATED() function returns true (.T.) if any GET field or object was changed during the active READ; otherwise false (.F.) is returned. The UPDATED() function returns false immediately following a SHOW GETS command. This function returns a logical value.

Examples The following program has a Lookup Address option. If the user changes anything on the address screen, the information is saved back to the database:

```
USE MAILLIST ORDER MAILNAME
@ 3,1 SAY "Lookup Address Screen"
@ 6,1 SAY " Name:" GET NAME
@ 7,1 SAY "Address:" GET ADD
@ 8,1 SAY " City: " GET CITY
@ 9,15 SAY "State: " GET STATE
@ 9,25 SAY "Zip: " GET ZIP
READ CYCLE
IF UPDATED()
   GATHER MEMVAR MEMO
ENDIF
```

See also READKEY(), SHOW GETS

UPPER()

UPPER(*expC*)

Description This function converts all the letters in a string to uppercase letters.

Operational rules The companion function is LOWER(), which converts all letters in the expression to lowercase. Numbers and other nonalphabetical characters are not affected. This function returns a character value.

Examples

```
? UPPER("Hello")
HELLO
? UPPER("hello")
HELLO
```

See also LOWER()

USED()

USED([*expN* | *expC*])

Description This function determines whether a database is currently being used in the specified work area.

Operational rules The USED() function returns true (.T.) if database alias *expC* is currently open in any work area, or work area *expN* is in use.

Examples

```
USE COA IN 10
USE JOURNAL IN 2
```

```
? USED(2)
.T.
? USED("C")
.F.
```

See also SELECT(), ALIAS()

VAL()

VAL(*expC*)

Description This function returns the numeric value of a specified character expression.

Operational rules The VAL() function converts *expC* to a numeric string, assuming *expC* is composed of numbers. If *expC* has no numbers in it, the function returns zero. VAL() reads the numeric characters in the string until it reaches a nonnumeric character.

The companion function is the STR() function, which converts a numeric value to a string. The SET DECIMALS command can be used to change the number of decimal places displayed. This function returns a numeric value.

Example

```
? VAL("5")
5.00
? VAL("500 West Street")
500
```

See also STR(), SET DECIMALS

VARREAD()

VARREAD()

Description This function returns the name of the variable or array element being edited in the current GET object.

Operational rules This function can be used to pass the current GET object to a custom help system. If a Browse or Edit window is active, VARREAD() returns the name of the field that the cursor is on. This function returns a character value.

Examples The following program displays context-sensitive help.

```
USE MAILLIST
ON KEY LABEL F1 DO Helpit.prg
@ 1,1 SAY "Press F1 to get help for a particular field"
@ 3,1 GET Code
@ 4,1 GET Desc
READ CYCLE

Helpit.Prg
DO CASE
   CASE VARREAD() = "CODE"
      ? "Help for Code Field"
   CASE VARREAD() = "DESC"
      ? "Help for Desc Field"
```

```
ENDCASE
RETURN
```

See also @ ... SAY/GET, READKEY(), SYS(18)

VERSION()

```
VERSION([1])
```

Description This function returns the version number of FoxPro currently being used.

Operational rules The version is always the same as the number displayed at the FoxPro sign-on message. The optional argument 1 returns the build date and serial number of your current version. This function returns a character value.

Examples

```
? VERSION()
FoxPro 2.5 (X)
? VERSION(1)
FoxPro 2.5 (X) [Feb 04 1993 08:34:02] Serial # xx-xxx-xxxx-xxxxxxxx
```

See also OS()

WBORDER()

WBORDER([*window name*])

Description This function determines if a specified window has a border.

Operational rules The WBORDER() function returns true (.T.) if window *window name* has a border; otherwise false (.F.) is returned. If the optional argument is not given, the value returned is relative to the current output window. All user-defined windows have a border unless the NONE clause is used with the DEFINE WINDOW command. This function returns a logical value.

See also DEFINE WINDOW

WCHILD()

WCHILD([*window name*] [*expN*])

Description This function returns the number or names of child windows for a specified parent window.

Operational rules It is possible to place a window (the child) inside of another window (the parent). To do this, use the IN or IN WINDOW clause in any of the commands that allow a window to be placed within another. The child window must be smaller than the parent and stay within the parent window's boundaries.

If no argument is given, WCHILD() returns the number of child windows for the current output window. Specify *window name* to return the number of child windows for any active window. Use the optional argument *expN* to return the names of all child windows, rather than the number of child windows. *expN* can be any positive value. This function returns a character or numeric value.

See also WPARENT( ), DEFINE WINDOW

WCOLS()

`WCOLS([window name])`

Description This function returns the number of columns available in the specified window.

Operational rules If no argument is given, the function returns the number of columns in the current output window. Otherwise, use the name of an active window as the optional argument. The value returned is based on the font used for the current or specified output window. This function returns a numeric value.

See also WROWS( )

WEXIST()

`WEXIST(window name)`

Description This function determines if a specified window exists.

Operational rules The WEXIST( ) function returns true (.T.) if the window *window name* has been defined in memory; otherwise false (.F.) is returned. A window only has to be defined, and not activated, to exist. Use the WVISIBLE( ) function to see if a window is currently activated. This function returns a logical value.

See also WVISIBLE( )

WFONT()

`WFONT(expN [, window name])`

Description This function returns font attributes for the specified window.

Operational rules The WFONT( ) function returns the font name, font size, or font style of the current output window. Use the optional *window name* argument to return the values for the specified window. This function returns a character or numeric value based on the following:

expN	Value returned
1	Font of the current or specified window
2	Font size of the current or specified window
3	Font style of the current or specified window

See also TXTWIDTH( ), SYSMETRIC( )

WLAST()

`WLAST([window name])`

Description This function returns the name of the last active window, or determines if the specified window was active prior to activating the current window.

Operational rules The *WLAST( )* function returns the name of the last active output window, if no window name argument is provided. If a window is specified, *WLAST( )* returns true (.T.) if *window name* was the last active window; otherwise false (.F.) is returned. This function returns a character or logical value.

Examples

```
ACTIVATE WINDOW w1
? WONTOP()
w1
ACTIVATE WINDOW w2
? WONTOP()
w2
? WLAST()
? w1
? WLAST("w2")
.F.
```

See also WEXIST(), WONTOP()

WLCOL()

`WLCOL([`*`window name`*`])`

Description This function returns the top-left column position of the current or specified output window.

Operational rules The WLCOL() function returns the location of the top-left corner of the current output window, if no window name argument is provided. If a window is specified, WLAST() returns the value for the specified window. The screen column location is relative to the FoxPro desktop screen. This function returns a numeric value.

See also WLROW()

WLROW()

`WLROW([`*`window name`*`])`

Description This function returns the top-left row position of the current or specified output window.

Operational rules The WLROW() function returns the location of the top-left row of the current output window, if no window name argument is provided. If a window is specified, WLROW() returns the value for the specified window. The screen row location is relative to the FoxPro desktop screen. This function returns a numeric value.

See also WLCOL()

WMAXIMUM()

`WMAXIMUM([`*`window name`*`])`

Description This function determines if a window is maximized to its largest size.

Operational rules The WMAXIMUM() function returns true (.T.) if the specified window has been maximized; otherwise false (.F.) is returned. A user-defined window can only be maximized if it has been defined with the ZOOM clause of the DEFINE WINDOW command. If no window argument is given, the value returned is relative to the current output window. This function returns a logical value.

See also DEFINE WINDOW, WMINIMUM()

WMINIMUM()

WMIMIMUM([*window name*])

Description This function determines if a window is minimized to its smallest size.

Operational rules The WMINIMUM() function returns true (.T.) if the specified window has been minimized; otherwise false (.F.) is returned. A user-defined window can only be minimized if it has been defined with the MINIMIZE clause of the DEFINE WINDOW command. If no window argument is given, the value returned is relative to the current output window. This function returns a logical value.

See also DEFINE WINDOW, WMAXIMUM()

WONTOP()

WONTOP([*window name*])

Description This function returns the frontmost window, or determines if a specified window is frontmost.

Operational rules If no argument is given, the function returns the name of the frontmost window as a character string. The optional argument is the name of a particular window. When the argument is used, the function returns true (.T.) if the specified window is frontmost. This function returns a character or logical value.

See also DEFINE WINDOW, WEXIST(), WOUTPUT()

WOUTPUT()

WOUTPUT([window name])

Description This function returns the current output window, or determines if a specified window is the current output window.

Operational rules If no argument is given, the function returns the name of the current output window. The optional argument is the name of a particular window. When the argument is used, the function returns true (.T.) if the specified window is the current output window.

The current output window is always the last window activated with the ACTIVATE WINDOW command. If the FoxPro desktop screen is the current output window, the null string (" ") is returned. This function returns a character or logical value.

See also WONTOP(), WEXIST()

WPARENT()

WPARENT([*window name*])

Description This function returns the name of the parent window of a specified child window.

Operational rules It is possible to place a window (the child) inside of another window (the parent). The child window must be smaller than the parent and stay within the parent window's boundaries. If no argument is given, WPARENT() returns the parent window name of the current window. For other windows, use the name of the child window as the argument. If there is no parent window, the null string (" ") is returned. This function returns a character value.

See also WCHILD()

WREAD()

`WREAD([`*`window name`*`])`

Description This function determines if a specified window is used in the current READ.

Operational rules The WREAD() function returns true (.T.) if the window is involved in the READ; otherwise false is returned (.F.). If no window name is specified, the value returned is relative to the current output window.

Multiple windows can be involved in a single READ if the @ ... SAY/GETs issued before the current READ are placed on different windows or the window names are specified in the WITH clause of the READ command. This command returns a logical value.

See also READ, RDLEVEL()

WROWS()

`WROWS([`*`window name`*`])`

Description This function returns the number of rows available in the specified window.

Operational rules If no argument is given, the function returns the number of rows in the current window. Otherwise, use the name of the window as the optional argument. The value returned is based on the font used for the current or specified output window. This function returns a numerical value.

See also WCOLS()

WTITLE()

`WTITLE([`*`window name`*`])`

Description This function returns the title of a specified window.

Operational rules If no argument is given, the function returns the title of the current output window. The optional argument is the name of a particular window. When the argument is used, the function returns the title of *window name*. The title of a user-defined window is specified with the TITLE clause of the DEFINE WINDOW command. This function returns a character value.

See also DEFINE WINDOW, WONTOP()

WVISIBLE()

`WVISIBLE(`*`window name`*`)`

Description This function determines if a specified window is currently activated and not hidden.

Operational rules The WVISIBLE() function returns true (.T.) if the specified window has been activated and is visible on the screen; otherwise false (.F.) is returned. Use the name of the window as the argument.

A user-defined window is activated with the ACTIVATE WINDOW command. The WVISIBLE() function will return false if a window is activated with ACTIVATE WINDOW ... NOSHOW or is hidden with the HIDE WINDOW command. This function returns a logical value.

See also ACTIVATE WINDOW, DEFINE WINDOW, WEXIST()

YEAR()

`YEAR(`*`expD`*`)`

Description This function returns the number of the year, given a date expression.

Operational rules The YEAR() function always returns the year with the century, regardless of the current SET CENTURY setting. The three ways to enter a date as an argument are:

- Enclose the date in curly brackets: {12/5/89}
- Use the CTOD() function: CTOD("12/5/2010")
- Use a field name or memory variable.

This function returns a numeric value.

Examples

```
? YEAR({9/6/89})
1989
? YEAR(CTOD("12/25/89"))
1989
```

See also DAY(), MONTH()

5

FoxPro programming

In this chapter, we address the subject of programming. The primary intent of this book is to provide information in a reference-based manner. We've presented all commands and functions in other chapters, and many of them are used here. For a more in-depth survey of FoxPro programming, you might wish to acquire an additional book, although the material here might be adequate for your needs.

First we discuss the editor, and then our attention turns toward programming, mentioning a few basics. Finally, we present and analyze in detail an example program for managing a mailing list database.

Since the early days of dBase II, programming in a database language has rapidly evolved from being somewhat awkward to being sophisticated and powerful. The main idea was to allow a sequence of commands (normally executed from the command window) to be executed in succession, while providing some programming constructs for decision making and control. This is still true, but the tools at the programmer's disposal have improved a great deal.

Using the FoxPro editor

FoxPro has its own built in editor for editing program files. The editor can be invoked in two ways: Issue the command MODIFY COMMAND (followed by a filename) at the command window, or select or create a file from the File menu. To save a little bit of typing when at the command window, remember that you need to type only the first four letters of the command, so MODI COMM will work, as well as MODIFY COMMAND.

To create a program file from the File menu, choose New and then Program. To open an existing file, choose Open and go to the Type box to choose Program. You can then choose the desired program file from a list.

If you wish to use another program with which to edit your files, such as Microsoft Word or Lotus Ami Pro, you can modify the CONFIG.FPW file. Add the additional line TEDIT = /N *editor*, where *editor* is the name of the program you wish to use to edit files (e.g., WINWORD.EXE or AMIPRO.EXE).

Editing keys

Basic cursor keys function as you would expect when editing files. A table appears below for all editing keys:

Key	Description
Arrow keys	Move left, right, up, down.
Ctrl-→	Move one word to the right.
Ctrl-←	Move one word to the left.
Home	Go to the beginning of the line.
End	Go to the end of the line.
Tab	Go to the next tab.
Shift-Tab	Go to the previous tab.
PgUp	Move up one screen.
PgDn	Move down one screen.
Ctrl-Home	Go to the beginning of the file.
Ctrl-End	Go to the end of the file.
Ctrl-Backspace	Delete word.
Ins	Toggle insert/typeover modes.
Esc	Exit editor without saving work.

All other editing is done through the Edit menu. Through this menu you can "cut and paste" and find occurrences of certain strings or a particular line. To use the Cut and Paste commands, you need to select text. To do this, highlight the area by holding down the Shift key and pressing the arrows to highlight, or if you have a mouse, double-click it and drag it over the area. To delete an area, simply highlight it and then select Cut from the Edit menu. See chapter 1 for more information on using the Edit menu.

Indentation

You can set the editor to indent automatically when you edit files. After pressing Return on a line, the cursor appears immediately below the first nonspace character in the previous line. If you then press the ← key, the cursor will jump back to the end of the previous line, and not move to the empty space to the left. Just remember that pressing Shift-Tab allows you to move to the left, specifically to the previous tab setting. If you forget this, you could easily become annoyed. Use the Auto indent option from the Edit Preferences menu to turn indentation ON or OFF.

Copying and moving text

For both copy and move text, first go to the beginning of the desired block of code. Highlight the area (using the mouse or Shift-arrow combinations). After the entire area is highlighted, pull up the Edit menu.

To copy the text, choose Copy. This places the text in the *clipboard*, a temporary storage location in memory. Then move to the area that you want the text copied to, and choose Paste. This places the text from the clipboard at the cursor's position. The text stays in the clipboard until something else is placed there, so you can call the Paste command more than once to copy something several times.

To remove the text, choose Cut. This places the text in the clipboard, and deletes it from the current area of the file. Then move to the area that you want the text moved to, and choose Paste. As with the Copy command, this places the text from the clipboard at the cursor's position.

Other features

The Go To Line option allows you to jump to the specified line number of the program and continue editing. This is useful when compiling programs because FoxPro notifies you on what line number the error occurred. You can print your program while it is open by simply opening the File menu and choosing Print.

Modular-design programming

In programming, it's often easier to complete a large task by breaking it down into smaller, more manageable tasks. This is known as *modular programming*. Each module of a program is dedicated to performing one operation, which makes designing and debugging much easier.

To execute a program from the command menu, enter the DO command followed by the desired file name. If the file has been modified, it is compiled first. Within your programs, you can also include DO commands, having programs call other subprograms, while all public variables are still retained in memory for use of the subprograms.

A more structured approach is to use procedures. A *procedure* is found in a program file that does not necessarily bear its name, as in the aforementioned method. A procedure begins with the keyword PROCEDURE followed by the procedure name. The lines of code to execute are next, and the procedure is terminated by a RETURN statement. For example, a procedure to print "Hello world" is as follows:

```
PROCEDURE Hello
        ? "Hello World"
RETURN
```

To execute this within a program, include the line DO Hello. Then there's another species of animals called *procedure files*. We won't go into detail about these here, but basically they are files of procedures that your programs can call with the DO command, after first setting SET PROCEDURE TO followed by the name of the file that contains all the procedures. A procedure file is simply a .PRG file containing any number of functions and procedures.

Setting up the FoxPro environment

When the highest-level program is executed, usually the first lines of programming code set up the environment. These include CLEAR ALL, to release existing variables in memory and close any open files, and any SET commands. Several SET commands are available; these can be found in chapter 3. SET commands allow you to control the way other commands or display functions work. Failure to control settings can lead to problems.

Memory variables

After setting up the environment, you need to initialize any global variables. You can initialize memory variables in two ways. You can either use the assignment statement (*x* = 0) or the STORE command (STORE 0 TO *x*). The STORE method might seem more verbose, but it offers the advantage of having the ability to assign the same value to more than one variable at a time. To assign *x*, *y*, and *z* to 0 using assignment statements, you would enter:

```
x = 0
y = 0
z = 0
```

Using the STORE command instead, you could enter the following:

```
STORE 0 TO x,y,z
```

Memory-variable arrays are a very useful feature of FoxPro. They can be either one- or two-dimensional arrays. The number of elements in the array must be included in the declaration. For example, to declare an array *names* for 20 entries and 2 elements (last name and first name) for those 20 entries, enter:

```
DECLARE names[20,2]
```

You can now make the following assignments to the names array:

```
name[1,1] = "Lambert"
name[1,2] = "Julie"
```

The elements of an array can have different types. You can copy the contents of a record to an array using the COPY TO ARRAY command. Similarly, new records can be added by inserting values into an array and using the APPEND FROM ARRAY command. These two commands allow you to shorten up the length of your programs a bit by performing several actions in just one statement.

Memory variables and fields

One concern for first-time programmers is using field names from data files and memory variables together in programs. Naming a memory variable the same name as a field can lead to confusion. The important thing to remember is that STORE and = assignment statements change the value of memory variables only. To change the value in a field, you must use the REPLACE command. The format of the REPLACE command is:

```
REPLACE field WITH value
```

where *value* is a constant or expression of variables or fields. Observe the following program excerpt:

```
USE NAMES
STORE "Fred" to m.fname
REPLACE Names.Fname WITH m.fname
? Names.Fname
```

Assume the field Fname exists in the database NAMES.DBF. The file is open and is at the first record. Fred is initialized to the memory-variable name. The field name in the current record is replaced with the contents of the memory variable name, Fred. Good database programming style dictates that you precede memory variables with a lowercase m and a period (m.), so as to avoid confusion.

Decision making

The two tools available to facilitate decision making are IF statements and CASE statements. The IF command uses the following format:

```
IF condition
      list of commands
ENDIF
```

The IF statement processes the commands between the IF and ENDIF only if the *condition* is true (.T.). It's considered good programming style to indent (3 or 4 spaces) all the commands between the IF and ENDIF statements. IF statements can also have ELSE statements within them. The format for this type of command would be:

```
IF condition
      list of commands
ELSE
      list of commands
ENDIF
```

In this case, the commands between the IF and ELSE are performed if the *condition* is true (.T.); otherwise, the commands between the ELSE and ENDIF are performed. The DO CASE command uses the following format:

```
DO CASE
   CASE condition
      list of commands
   CASE condition
      list of commands
   CASE condition
      list of commands
      .
      .
ENDCASE
```

The DO CASE statement processes the commands after the first CASE condition that's true (.T.). This command is useful in situations where several conditions can exist, such as choosing one of five options from a menu. For more information on the IF ... ENDIF and DO CASE commands, see chapter 2, FoxPro commands.

Loops

The three looping mechanisms are DO WHILE ... ENDDO, FOR ... ENDFOR, and SCAN ... ENDSCAN. The DO WHILE command uses the following format:

```
DO WHILE condition
     list of commands
ENDDO
```

The DO WHILE statement keeps processing the commands between the DO and ENDDO until the *condition* is no longer true (.T.). The FOR command uses the following format:

```
FOR memvar = expN1 TO expN2
      list of commands
ENDFOR
```

The FOR statement keeps processing the commands between the FOR and ENDFOR a set number of times (from *expN1* to *expN2*). The SCAN command uses the following format:

```
SCAN
      list of commands
ENDSCAN
```

The SCAN statement moves through a database file and processes the commands between the SCAN and ENDSCAN for each record in the file. This command can use a scope or FOR condition statement to process only records that match a specified condition. Again, for more information, look these statements up in chapter 2.

A sample application

Here's a sample application, a database named People, to introduce some typical programming techniques. It contains mailing list information, phone numbers, the date the information was entered, and a numeric field for a dollar amount of potential business to be obtained. The structure is as follows:

Field	Field name	Type	Width	Dec
1	lname	Character	20	
2	fname	Character	15	
3	address	Character	30	
4	city	Character	20	
5	state	Character	2	
6	zip	Character	10	
7	phone	Character	14	
8	ent_date	Date	8	
9	poten	Numeric	8	2

The file uses a structural compound index file with a tag of Lname, indexed on the expression UPPER(Lname). Use INDEX ON UPPER(*Lname*) TAG LNAME to create the index, which will create the compound index file PEOPLE.CDX. To improve readability in the program listings provided, the conventions used for capitalization are:

- All FoxPro keywords are in uppercase.
- Memory variables and field names are in lowercase.
- Procedures and files begin with a capital letter followed by lowercase letters.

A simple program for maintaining the file

Before going on to a modular-designed program, here is a single program file that handles opening the People database, adding records, editing records, and running a report. The program isn't as sophisticated as the application that follows it, but it does contain many of the basic commands and standards used in FoxPro programs:

```
Pmain.prg:
* Set-up environment
SET TALK OFF
* Open People database
USE People ORDER Name
* Repeat Until "Exit" is selected from menu
m.choice = "0"
DO WHILE m.choice != "4"
    CLEAR
    TEXT
       PEOPLE DATABASE PROGRAM
       1) Insert Entries
       2) Edit Entries
       3) Run a Report
       4) Exit
    ENDTEXT
    ACCEPT "        Enter Selection: " TO m.choice
    CLEAR

    DO CASE
       CASE m.choice = "1"
          APPEND
          * Find name in index, and edit
       CASE m.choice = "2"
          ACCEPT "Enter Last Name of Record to Edit " TO
          name
          SEEK m.name
          EDIT
          * Turn on print mode if desired, and list report
       CASE m.choice = "3"
          ACCEPT "List to Screen or Printer? (S/P) " TO m.prnt
          IF UPPER(m.prnt) = "P"
          SET PRINT ON
                ENDIF
                REPORT FORM Plist
                IF UPPER(m.prnt) = "P"
          SET PRINT OFF
                ELSE
          WAIT
                ENDIF
   ENDCASE
ENDDO
QUIT
```

Notice the comments that introduce each section of the program. Comment lines must begin with asterisks (*). You can also use asterisks in front of a line of code that you temporarily want the program to ignore, such as SET PRINT ON. It is very important to comment your programs, no matter how simple they can seem. Comments not only help you when going back to the program to edit or add additional features, but they are essential in helping someone else understand your coding.

The SET TALK OFF command at the top of Pmain.prg is needed so that FoxPro does not display each memory variable as it is assigned. This also suppresses the TALK messages displayed during commands such as INDEX, REPLACE, and SEEK.

Next, the USE command opens the database along with the index file, ensuring that the data is in alphabetical order. The memory variable m.choice holds the number of the menu option that the user chooses. Following good programming standards, we initialize the memory variable by making it equal to a constant, in this case zero.

The command `DO WHILE m.choice != 4` ensures that the menu isn't being displayed after each option is run, until the user presses 4 as the selection. The ! symbol means NOT in FoxPro, so != means NOT EQUAL. It can also be written as NOT=, <>, or #. The TEXT command then displays all text between TEXT and ENDTEXT. In this case, the text is the menu. The ACCEPT command displays the prompt for the user's selection and waits for input. The memory variable m.choice becomes equal to whatever the user types.

You should use the DO CASE command instead of IF ... ENDIF because it's more efficient in instances where more than two conditions exist. In this case, there are three possible conditions (DO CASE statements). The first case, `m.choice = "1,"` simply calls the APPEND command. This is a very simplistic way to add records, as it calls the plain-looking Append screen. The more sophisticated application in the next section sets up a custom-designed screen for inserting records.

The second case, `m.choice = "2,"` asks the user for the last name of the record to be edited. Because the database is indexed on Lname, we use the SEEK command to find the name. Using the SEEK command (which requires an indexed file) can be much faster than using the LOCATE command, especially with large databases. Notice that there are no provisions in case the user types in a name that is not found in the database. If this happens, the Edit command will be positioned at the end-of-file record. The editing program in the next section includes a routine that handles this situation.

The third case, `m.choice = "3,"` turns on the printer if the user so desires. It then calls a report that has already been formatted from the Report menu. The reports name is Plist. This report lists all records in the database in alphabetical order (because the index is open).

The rest of this chapter covers a program that handles many of the same functions as this simple program. However, the latter program is much more sophisticated. The main menu uses pop-up menus, the editing screens use custom designed screens instead of the basic Edit command layout, and the reports allow the user to build a criteria for filtering out names. Because each of the modules takes many lines of programming, the application is broken up into separate .PRG files, starting with the Main menu program.

The Main program

In the highest-level program (the one executed first that calls other subprograms), the environment for the entire application is set up, and the main menu is put into action. The program is first listed, and then discussed.

```
Main.prg:
* Set-up environment
SET TALK OFF
SET HEADING OFF
```

```
SET STATUS OFF
SET SCOREBOARD OFF
SET BELL OFF
CLEAR ALL
* Open People database
USE People ORDER Name
* Do menu definition
DO Main_Menu
* Repeat Until "Exit" is selected from menu
READ VALID BAR() != 8
SET SYSMENU TO DEFAULT
RETURN

PROCEDURE Main_Menu
SET SYSMENU AUTOMATIC
DEFINE PAD Main OF _MSYSMENU PROMPT "People Database"
ON PAD Main OF _MSYSMENU ACTIVATE POPUP people
DEFINE POPUP people MARGIN RELATIVE SHADOW
DEFINE BAR 1 OF people PROMPT "Insert Entries"
DEFINE BAR 2 OF people PROMPT "Edit Entries"
DEFINE BAR 3 OF people PROMPT "Delete Entries"
DEFINE BAR 4 OF people PROMPT "Report"
DEFINE BAR 5 OF people PROMPT "Labels"
DEFINE BAR 6 OF people PROMPT "Pack"
DEFINE BAR 7 OF people PROMPT "\-"
DEFINE BAR 8 OF people PROMPT "Exit"
ON SELECTION POPUP people DO Main_Opt
RETURN
PROCEDURE Main_Opt
DO CASE
   CASE BAR() = 1
      DO Insert
   CASE BAR() = 2
      DO Edit
   CASE BAR() = 3
      DO Delete
   CASE BAR() = 4
      DO Report
   CASE BAR() = 5
      DO Labels
   CASE BAR() = 6
      DO Packem
   CASE BAR() = 8
      CLEAR READ
      RETURN TO MASTER
ENDCASE
RETURN
```

The first executed command, CLEAR ALL, releases memory variables (if they exist) from memory, closes all files, and sets the work area to 1. In other words, any leftover garbage from previous work is cleaned up.

The SET commands used are the typical ones that many applications use. They ensure that FoxPro messages are not printed on the display to mess up the screen, that column headings do not appear when using the LIST command, and that the somewhat annoying BELL is turned OFF. Next, the USE command opens the database for adding, editing, or listing records.

Now we discuss the menu system. The Main.prg example changes the FoxPro system menu. The SET SYSMENU AUTOMATIC command allows the menu bar to be active during program execution. The three components of the menu are the definition, the activation, and the actions to take based on the menu's result.

The definition is put in procedure Def_Main. The DEFINE PAD command defines the pads that will be available in the menu. The DEFINE POPUP command names the pop-up menu of each pad and gives the placement and dimensions of the menu. DEFINE BAR is used to describe the options available in each menu pad. For BAR 7, the \- forces a line between the sixth and eighth options and cannot be selected. ON SELECTION POPUP determines what procedure to execute after an option has been selected. If no DO procedure follows, the course of action to take is to do nothing, and execution of the program continues following the line in which the menu was activated.

Since the system menu is being used *(_msysmenu)*, no ACTIVATE POPUP command is required. If the system menu is not used, the ACTIVATE POPUP command must be issued to display the menu options. The actions to take appear in procedure Main_opt. The function BAR() contains the value of the bar last selected. Typically a CASE statement appears to select the course of action next.

Once the menu has been defined, a READ command is issued which puts the program into a "wait" state. The READ won't be terminated until the Exit option (BAR 8) is selected from the menu. Program execution will continue at the statement following the READ command once the menu READ is terminated. Finally, the menu is returned to its default state after the READ is terminated with the command SET SYSMENU TO DEFAULT.

The Insert program

The Insert program allows you to insert new records into the database. The program follows:

```
Insert.prg:
PRIVATE m.continue, m.yn
m.continue = .T.
m.yn = ""
DEFINE WINDOW again FROM 10,26 TO 14,54
DEFINE WINDOW insert FROM 6,10 TO 19,60
ACTIVATE WINDOW insert
* Repeat forever
DO WHILE m.continue
   * Initialize variables
   SCATTER MEMVAR BLANK
   STORE "" TO m.yn
   * Obtain values
   @ 1,1 SAY "Last Name:" GET m.lname
   @ 2,1 SAY "First Name:" GET m.fname
   @ 3,1 SAY "Address:" GET m.address
   @ 4,1 SAY "City:" GET m.city
```

```
    @ 5,1 SAY "State:" GET m.state PICTURE "!!"
    @ 6,1 SAY  "Zip:" GET m.zip PICTURE "99999-9999"
    @ 7,1 SAY  "Phone:" GET m.phone PICTURE "(999) 999-9999"
    @ 8,1 SAY  "Entry Date:" GET m.ent_date
    @ 9,1 SAY  "Potential:" GET m.poten PICTURE "99999.99"
    @ 11,1 SAY "Press ESC To Abort"
    READ
    * See if Escape was pressed
    IF LASTKEY() = 27
       EXIT
    ENDIF
    * Add new record
    APPEND BLANK
    * Replace field values
    * This can also be accomplished with the INSERT INTO command
    REPLACE lname WITH m.lname, fname WITH m.fname, ;
       address WITH m.address, city WITH m.city, ;
       state WITH m.state, zip WITH m.zip, ;
       phone WITH m.phone, ent_date WITH m.ent_date ;
       poten WITH m.poten
    * See if user wants to continue insertions
    WAIT WINDOW "Insert Another? (Y/N)" TO m.yn
    IF UPPER(m.yn) <> "Y"
       m.continue = .F.
    ENDIF
ENDDO
RELEASE WINDOW insert
RETURN
```

The first command, PRIVATE, is used to hide the name of the variables m.continue and m.yn in case they're used in a higher-level program. The variables are then initialized.

Windows are used here for a clean-looking entry screen. The first two lines define two windows, Again and Insert, and give their coordinates. Each time this program is executed from the main menu, the windows are redefined. This does not hurt anything, but we could have had the definitions appear in the Main program so they are only executed once.

Next, the Insert window is activated. Now when information is printed to the screen, it is bounded by the window, and coordinates are now relative within the window and not the entire screen. In other words, @ 0,0 appears at 0,0 within the window, but is at 7,11 on the main desktop screen.

A DO WHILE loop appears next. The variable m.continue is used as the condition to determine when to exit the loop. The variable is logical and initiated as true (.T.). The loop is exited when the value of m.continue is false (.F.), an EXIT command is issued, or a RETURN statement is encountered.

Next, the SCATTER MEMVAR command is used to create a memory variable from each field in the People database. The BLANK keyword causes the variables to have null (or blank) values. Each variable created is the same type and length of its corresponding field. The program is structured to allow many insertions to be made without having to go back to the main menu.

@ ... Say/GETs are used to obtain the new record's values. The PICTURE clauses are used to format variables into their desired appearances. The READ command activates the GETs for editing.

It's nice to allow users the opportunity to abort an operation if the users change their minds or press the wrong key. The LASTKEY() function returns the ASCII value of the last key that was pressed in exiting a READ. You can check if Escape was pressed and, if so, exit the loop and return to the main menu. Escape's ASCII value is 27.

Pressing Escape doesn't always halt program execution. It depends where you are in the program. Pressing Escape in a READ exits the READ. Pressing Escape when selecting a pop-up menu option deactivates the menu. If SET ESCAPE is ON, the program will be interrupted.

After obtaining user input, you can now create a new record to hold the data. The APPEND BLANK command creates an empty record at the end of the database, which becomes the current record. The REPLACE command is employed to transfer the values in the memory variables into the proper fields in the record. Several fields in a record, separated by commas, can be replaced at once. You can also accomplish this using the SCATTER and GATHER commands. In the program, note that semicolons appear at the end of the line. The semicolons tell FoxPro that the command continues on the next line.

Finally, the user is given the opportunity to insert another record. A WAIT WINDOW is activated and the user is prompted to add another record. If the answer is not Y for yes, the variable m.continue is given the value of false. This will force the DO WHILE loop to exit and return to the main menu. Otherwise, the end of the loop is encountered and the program loops back to the top and obtains the next record.

An alternative Insert program demonstrating the use of arrays can be found in the help file.

The Edit program

With the Edit program, you can retrieve and modify existing records. Here is the program:

```
Edit.prg:
PRIVATE m.recnum, m.reccnt
DEFINE WINDOW edit FROM 6,10 to 19,60
DEFINE WINDOW key FROM 4,35 TO 21,75
ACTIVATE WINDOW key
* Repeat forever
DO WHILE .T.
   * Clear part of window
   @ 2,0 CLEAR TO 15,36
   STORE 0 TO m.recnum
   STORE SPACE(20) TO m.lname
   * Get desired name
   @ 0,1 SAY "Enter Last Name:" GET m.lname
   @ 15,1 SAY "Press ESC To Abort"
   READ
   * See if Escape was pressed.
   IF LASTKEY() = 27
```

```
      EXIT
   ENDIF
   m.lname = ALLTRIM(m.lname)
   SEEK m.lname
   * Error if not found
   IF !FOUND()
      WAIT WINDOW "Not Found! Press Any Key To Continue."
      LOOP
   ENDIF
   * List all matches
   DO WHILE lname = m.lname
      @ 2,0 CLEAR TO 15,36
      @ 1,0
      m.reccnt = 0
      SCAN WHILE lname = m.lname AND m.reccnt < 10
         LIST NEXT 1 TRIM(lname)+", "+TRIM(fname)
         m.reccnt = m.reccnt + 1
      ENDSCAN
      IF lname = m.lname
         ?
         WAIT
      ENDIF
   ENDDO
   @ 13,0 SAY " Enter Record # To Edit:" GET m.recnum RANGE
1,RECCOUNT()
   @ 15,0 SAY " Press ESC To Abort"
   READ
   * See if Escape was pressed.
   IF LASTKEY() = 27
      EXIT
   ENDIF
   * Goto the record, assign fields to memory variables.
   GOTO m.recnum
   SCATTER MEMVAR
   ACTIVATE WINDOW edit
   @ 1,1 SAY " Last Name:" GET m.lname
   @ 2,1 SAY " First Name:" GET m.fname
   @ 3,1 SAY " Address:" GET m.address
   @ 4,1 SAY " City:" GET m.city
   @ 5,1 SAY " Sate:" GET m.state PICTURE "!!"
   @ 6,1 SAY " Zip:" GET m.zip PICTURE "99999-9999"
   @ 7,1 SAY " Phone:" GET m.phone PICTURE "(999) 999-9999"
   @ 8,1 SAY " Entry Date:" GET m.ent_date
   @ 9,1 SAY " Potential:" GET m.poten PICTURE "99999.99"
   @ 11,1 SAY "Press ESC To Abort"
   READ
   * See If Escape was pressed.
   IF LASTKEY() = 27
      EXIT
   ENDIF
   REPLACE lname WITH m.lname, fname WITH m.fname, ;
```

```
      address WITH m.address, city WITH m.city, ;
      state WITH m.state, zip WITH m.zip, ;
      phone WITH m.phone, ent_date WITH m.ent_date, ;
      poten WITH m.poten
   DEACTIVATE WINDOW edit
ENDDO
CLEAR WINDOWS
```

Two windows are defined. One is for editing the variables, and one for selecting which record to edit.

After the window is activated, a DO WHILE .T. loop appears so the users can edit records for as long as they want. The window is cleared of its previous contents, and the user is prompted to enter the last name of the person to look up. Like Insert, the program returns if the Escape key is pressed.

Next, m.lname is trimmed to remove leading and trailing spaces, which is very important for string comparisons. The default in string comparisons is to compare the two strings only up to the length of the string on the right. For example, if the user types in the following at the Command window:

```
? "program" = "pro"
.T.
```

a value of true is returned. FoxPro considers these two strings equivalent. However, the following returns false:

```
? "program" = "pro   "
.F.
```

because the spaces are not ignored.

The SEEK command also functions this way. If m.lname = "D," SEEK goes through the database indexed on lname and stops at the first occurrence of a last name beginning with D. This is useful if the user is unsure of the spelling or doesn't want to type in a long name. He can enter just the first few letters.

After executing a SEEK, the function FOUND() is true if SEEK found a match; otherwise, it's false. If no names match the m.lname pattern, the WAIT WINDOW command will display an error message. After a key is pressed, the window is deactivated and LOOP causes the flow of the program to jump to the instruction immediately following DO WHILE .T..

The next part is a bit tricky. If SEEK was successful, the DO WHILE Lname = m.lname loop is executed. The idea here is to list all the records that match m.lname. Because the database is indexed on the last name, all the records that meet the lname = m.lname condition will appear one after another.

First, part of the window is cleared, the cursor is positioned @ 1,0 in the window, and a counter, m.reccnt, is set to 0. A SCAN WHILE loop then appears within the DO WHILE loop. The SCAN WHILE loop is used here in the following:

```
SCAN WHILE condition
   :
ENDSCAN
```

and it has the same meaning as:

```
DO WHILE condition AND !EOF()
   :
   SKIP
ENDDO
```

The SCAN's condition in the Edit program is to loop as long as the lname field in the current record equals m.lname up to 10 times by keeping track of m.reccnt. Within the SCAN WHILE loop, one record's lname and fname fields are displayed, and the record counter (m.reccnt) is incremented.

If m.reccnt is equal to 10, the loop exits. A check is made to see if lname equals the new current record. If so, more records are going to have to be displayed, so a line is skipped and a WAIT is issued to allow the user to see the existing records so far.

Although you're now outside the SCAN WHILE loop, we are still inside the DO WHILE loop. Because Lname = m.lname, the process repeats; the window is cleared, and the next 10 records are scanned, and so on.

After listing all matching records, the user can select which person to edit by their record number. The @ ... SAY/GET statement uses the RANGE clause to ensure that nonexistent record numbers aren't entered. RECCOUNT() is equal to the number of records in the database.

If the Escape key isn't pressed, you'll GOTO the record number chosen by the user. Next, memory variables are assigned the values in these fields. The rest should look familiar; it's similar to Insert. The Edit window is activated, and the values are edited and replaced. Encountering ENDDO causes the program flow to jump back to the top of the loop, where another entry can be retrieved.

An alternative Edit program demonstrating the use of arrays can be found on the help file disk.

The Delete program

The Delete program is very similar to Edit. The program appears here:

```
DELETE.prg:
PRIVATE m.recnum, m.reccnt, m.yn
* Initialize
STORE SPACE(15) TO m.fname
STORE 0 TO m.reccnt
DEFINE WINDOW delete FROM 6,15 to 10,60
DEFINE WINDOW key FROM 4,35 TO 21,75
ACTIVATE WINDOW key
DO WHILE .T.
   @ 2,0 CLEAR TO 15,36
   * Initialize variables
   STORE SPACE(20) TO m.lname
   STORE "N" to m.yn
   STORE 0 TO m.recnum
   @ 0,1 SAY "Enter Last Name:" GET m.lname
   @ 15,1 SAY "Press ESC To Abort"
```

```
    READ
    * See if Escape key was pressed.
    IF LASTKEY() = 27
       EXIT
    ENDIF
    m.lname = TRIM(m.lname)
    SEEK m.lname
    * Error if not found
    IF !FOUND()
       WAIT WINDOW "Not Found! Press Any Key To Continue."
       LOOP
    ENDIF
    * List all matches
    DO WHILE lname = m.lname
       @ 2,0 CLEAR TO 15,36
       @ 1,0
       m.reccnt = 0
       SCAN WHILE lname = m.lname AND m.reccnt < 10
          LIST NEXT 1 TRIM(lname)+", "+TRIM(fname)
          m.reccnt = m.reccnt + 1
       ENDSCAN
       IF lname = m.lname
          ?
          WAIT
       ENDIF
    ENDDO
    @ 13,0 SAY " Enter Record # To Delete:" GET m.recnum RANGE 1,RECCOUNT()
    @ 15,0 SAY " Press ESC To Abort"
    READ
    * See if Escape was pressed
    IF LASTKEY() = 27
       EXIT
    ENDIF
    * Goto the record, assign fields to memory variables.
    GOTO m.recnum
    m.lname = lname
    m.fname = fname
    * Last chance prompt
    ACTIVATE WINDOW delete
    @ 0,1 SAY TRIM(lname)+", "+TRIM(fname)
    @ 2,1 SAY "Delete: Are You Sure? (Y/N):" GET m.yn PICTURE "!"
    READ
    IF UPPER(m.yn) = "Y"
       DELETE
    ENDIF
    DEACTIVATE WINDOW delete
ENDDO
```

Again, it's similar to Edit, only the selected record is to be deleted and not edited. The prompt "Are You Sure?" appears with the record in the Delete window to verify the user's selection.

Keep in mind that when records are deleted, they're only marked for deletion. They're physically removed from the database only when a PACK is performed.

The Report program

Both the Report and Labels program try to emphasize how to use previously created reports in programs using scoping, and how to obtain the criteria with which to filter those reports. The Report program follows:

```
Report.prg:
PRIVATE m.criteria, m.dest
* Initialize variables
SCATTER MEMVAR BLANK
STORE 0 TO m.poten1
STORE 99999.99 TO m.poten2
STORE "" TO m.criteria, m.dest
* Get criteria
DO Crit
* Get destination
DO Dest
REPORT FORM Peorep FOR &criteria &dest
CLEAR
RETURN
```

When memory variables are declared in FoxPro, they can be accessed by the program in which they were declared, or by the subprograms that the current program calls. If a memory variable is declared in a subprogram that was called, the program that called it cannot access the variable.

This point is mentioned here because in Report two subprograms are called: Crit (to obtain criteria) and Dest (to select the print destination). You want Crit to return a criteria you can use in this program. Because you aren't using procedures with parameter passing, the memory variables must be declared here. The Crit program is discussed later.

After Crit is executed, the memory variable m.criteria contains the criteria for the report. To use this information, the FOR &criteria clause is used with the REPORT FORM command. Note that criteria is preceded with an ampersand (&), making m.criteria a macro. This macro means "substitute &criteria with the contents of m.criteria, and execute this statement." For example, if mac = "DO MAIN," typing &mac at the command window executes Main.

Next, Dest is executed to select where to output the report, to the screen or printer. The variable m.dest contains the destination for the report and is added as a clause to the REPORT FORM command. Assume that a report exists called Peorep, created with the Report Writer.

The Label program

The Labels program is exactly like the Report program, except that the REPORT FORM command is replaced with a LABEL FORM command, assumed to already exist.

```
Labels.prg:
PRIVATE m.criteria, m.dest
```

```
* Initialize variables
SCATTER MEMVAR BLANK
STORE 0 TO m.poten1
STORE 99999.99 TO m.poten2
STORE "" TO m.criteria, m.dest
* Get criteria
DO Crit
* Get destination
DO Dest
REPORT FORM Peorep FOR &criteria &dest
CLEAR
RETURN
```

Procedures

This section lists procedures that are called from the Edit, Delete, Report and Label programs. The Packem program is a brief program that uses the PACK command to remove those records marked for deletion from the database.

```
Packem.Prg:
CLEAR
SET TALK ON
WAIT WINDOW "One moment, please..." NOWAIT
PACK
SET TALK OFF
CLEAR
RETURN
```

Recall that in Main.prg you SET TALK OFF. Packing can take quite a while for large databases. Not seeing anything change on the screen for a long time can sometimes cause anxiety. SET TALK ON allows users to see the process take place. Afterwards the talk is set off again.

Crit allows users to set a filter condition that's entered into the memory variable criteria. The program follows:

```
Crit.prg:
DEFINE WINDOW crit FROM 6,10 TO 21,60
ACTIVATE WINDOW crit
@ 0,1 SAY " ENTER CRITERIA:"
@ 2,1 SAY " Last Name:" GET m.lname
@ 3,1 SAY "First Name:" GET m.fname
@ 4,1 SAY " Address:" GET m.address
@ 5,1 SAY " City:" GET m.city
@ 6,1 SAY " State:" GET m.state PICTURE "!!"
@ 7,1 SAY " Zip:" GET m.zip PICTURE "99999-9999"
@ 8,1 SAY " Phone:" GET m.phone PICTURE "(999) 999-9999"
@ 9,1 SAY "Entry Date:" GET m.ent_date
@ 10,1 SAY " Potent >=:" GET m.poten1 PICTURE "99999.99"
@ 11,1 SAY " Potent <=:" GET m.poten2 PICTURE "99999.99"
@ 13,1 SAY "Press ESC To Abort"
READ
```

```
* See if Escape was pressed
IF LASTKEY() = 27
   DEACTIVATE WINDOW crit
   RETURN TO MASTER
ENDIF
* Trim all variables
m.lname = TRIM(m.lname)
m.fname = TRIM(m.fname)
m.address = TRIM(m.address)
m.city = TRIM(m.city)
m.state = TRIM(m.state)
m.zip = TRIM(m.zip)
m.phone = TRIM(m.phone)
* For each variable, check and see if it was used,
* and if so, add it to criteria
DO CASE
   CASE !EMPTY(m.lname)
      m.criteria = m.criteria + "Lname = m.lname AND"
   CASE !EMPTY(m.fname)
      m.criteria = m.criteria + "Fname = m.fname AND"
   CASE !EMPTY(m.city)
      m.criteria = m.criteria + "City = m.city AND"
   CASE !EMPTY(m.state)
      m.criteria = m.criteria + "State = m.state AND"
   CASE !EMPTY(m.zip)
      m.criteria = m.criteria + "Zip = m.zip AND"
   CASE !EMPTY(m.phone)
      m.criteria = m.criteria + "Phone = m.phone AND"
   CASE !EMPTY(m.ent_date)
      m.criteria = m.criteria + "Ent_date = m.ent_date AND"
   CASE m.poten1 > 0
      m.criteria = m.criteria + "Poten >= m.poten1 AND"
   CASE m.poten2 < 99999.99
      m.criteria = m.criteria + "Poten <= m.poten2 AND"
ENDCASE
* Get rid of last " AND"
m.criteria = LEFT(m.criteria, LEN(m.criteria)-6)
DEACTIVATE WINDOW crit
RETURN
```

The first part of the program isn't anything new. There are two variables, poten1 and poten2, allowing a "from" and "to" pair of values to be entered.

Here's how it works. Only those memory variables where an entry has been made are counted toward the criteria. If more than one field is filtered on, the filter conditions are connected with the word AND.

After the input is read, all string variables are trimmed to remove trailing spaces. The CASE statement checks each variable to see if it has an entry. An entry will exist if the length of the variable is greater than 0. If an entry exists, it's added to criteria. AND appears at the end of all the strings to allow the conditions to be joined together.

The last AND is removed by the LEFT() function. LEFT() takes the substring of criteria, starting at the left and continuing for length of criteria minus 6 characters, the length of " AND ." The Dest program selects the destination for report output.

```
Dest.prg:
* Destination menu
DO Def_Dest
ACTIVATE POPUP dest
RETURN
PROCEDURE Def_dest
DEFINE POPUP dest FROM 10,55 TO 16,70
DEFINE BAR 1 OF dest PROMPT " PRINT TO"
DEFINE BAR 2 OF dest PROMPT "\-"
DEFINE BAR 3 OF dest PROMPT " Screen"
DEFINE BAR 4 OF dest PROMPT " Printer"
DEFINE BAR 5 OF dest PROMPT " Abort"
ON SELECTION POPUP dest DO Destpop
RETURN
PROCEDURE Destpop
DO CASE
   CASE BAR() = 3
      m.dest = "PREVIEW"
   CASE BAR() = 4
      m.dest = "TO PRINT"
   CASE BAR() = 5
      RETURN TO MASTER
ENDCASE
DEACTIVATE POPUP
RETURN
```

The pop-up menu is similar to the Main program's main menu. If Screen or Printer is selected, the appropriate REPORT FORM or LABEL FORM clause is assigned to the variable m.dest. The variable is then appended to a command using macro substitution. The last option allows the user to abort the entire operation, and returns control to the main program via RETURN TO MASTER.

DEACTIVATE POPUP deactivates the most recently activated pop-up menu, in this case the menu Dest.

Documenting your programs

You can document your application using FoxDoc, which is supplied with FoxPro. FoxDoc is an application-documentation utility that you can use to provide summary and cross-reference information on all the files contained in your application. If FoxDoc is installed in the FoxPro directory, you can access it from the Program menu.

6

Using the Screen Builder

You can use the FoxPro Screen Builder to easily create custom data entry screens and dialogs that once took days to program. It provides an easy-to-learn template that can have you editing your data in no time. If you're using FoxPro to develop database applications, you can use the Screen Builder to build interfaces that do most of the work.

The first section of this chapter details the Screen Builder tools, menu, and layout operations. Following that is a simple exercise that shows how to create a custom data entry screen using the Screen Builder.

What the Screen Builder does

The Screen Builder provides a template you can use to set up and control editing objects, and display text and graphics. FoxPro stores all screen information in a database file with an extension of .SCX and uses the screen database to generate a source-code file for you to run. The end result is a program that's written for you.

The objects that you place on your screen template let you see exactly how a particular screen will look when the program is executed. Within the Screen Builder, each editing object, called a GET, can be controlled by a code snippet. A code snippet is simply a procedure that's executed when a particular GET object is entered or exited, or when all GET objects are activated with a READ.

When a program is generated from a screen database, the resulting code is a program that contains the following:

- Setup code
- @ ... SAY/GET commands
- The READ command
- Cleanup code
- Code snippet functions and procedures

Because the source code generated from a screen file doesn't contain any special commands that you as a programmer or developer cannot use, you don't have to use the Screen Builder to take advantage of FoxPro's powerful command language. However, if you've spent many hours laboring away at a custom data entry screen, you will find that you can accomplish the same task using the Screen Builder in a fraction of the time.

Starting the Screen Builder

You can enter the Screen Builder in two ways:

- From the Command window, issue either CREATE SCREEN (to create a new screen) or MODIFY SCREEN (to modify an existing screen), followed by the file name of the screen.
- From the File menu, choose New... to start a new screen, or Open... to open an existing screen.

When you open a screen, a screen design window appears (see Fig. 6-1) and the Object and Screen menu pads are added to the main menu.

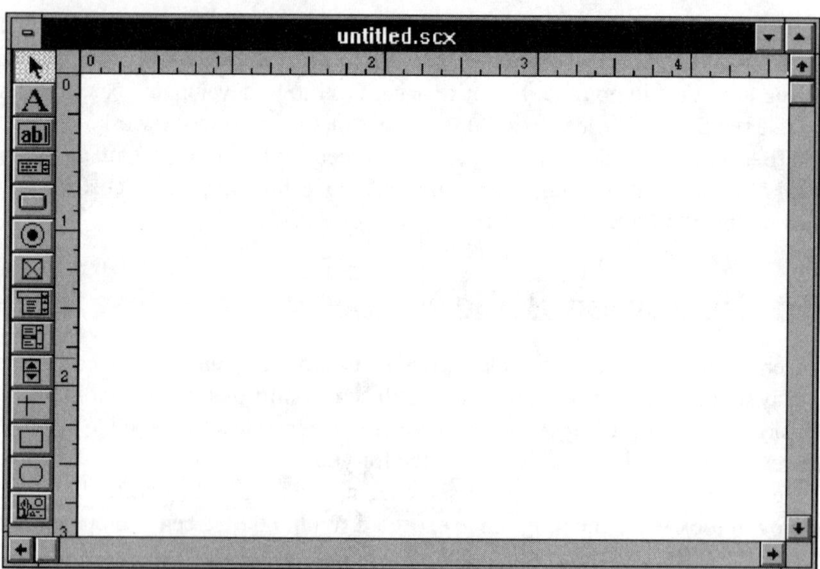

6-1 A screen design window.

Designing a custom screen

Screen objects

You can use a screen template to position objects that will be displayed or edited when the program is executed. Objects can be one of four types:

Fields Fields or memory variables to display or edit.

Controls Push buttons, radio buttons, check boxes, pop-ups, spinners, or lists.

Text Any text on the screen, such as prompts and headings.

Graphics Boxes, lines, or pictures.

The screen builder toolbox appears at the left of the screen design window, and is used to select an object and place it on the screen layout. The toolbox is detailed later in this chapter.

Selecting and moving objects

Once an object has been placed on the screen layout, you can select it and move it. An object must be selected before it can be moved. To select an object, position the mouse pointer over an object and click. The object appears with handles on each side. To move the object, simply drag the object to the desired position using the mouse or arrow keys. To deselect an object, click the mouse outside the object, or click on the selection pointer tool in the toolbox.

Selecting and moving multiple objects

Often, you must select or move a group of objects. This can be accomplished in two ways: by selecting each object individually or all objects at once. The latter option is the easiest, and is done by surrounding the objects to be selected with a marquee (a dashed line). To do this, follow these steps:

1. Using the mouse, position the cursor at a point outside the objects to be selected and not within any other object.
2. Click the mouse. The mouse pointer changes to a "hand," signifying the starting position of the marquee.
3. Move the mouse to drag the marquee around the group.
4. Release the mouse. All objects in the marquee area are now selected.

Use the mouse to move the selected objects to the desired location. Select Undo from the Edit menu to return the objects to the previous location. To select multiple objects without using a marquee, simply hold down the Shift key while selecting the objects.

If you accidentally include an object you don't want to in a group of selected objects, you can deselect that single object by pressing the Shift key and clicking on the object with the mouse. To deselect all objects, simply click the mouse outside of the selected objects, or click on the selection pointer tool in the toolbox.

Editing objects

You can delete screen objects by selecting them and pressing the Delete key. You can also use standard FoxPro editing functions such as Cut, Copy, and Paste on all screen objects. If more than one screen design window is open, you can copy an object from one screen and paste the object into another screen.

Once a field or object has been placed on the screen, you can resize it. To resize an object you must first select it with the mouse. A set of handles appears around the selected object. Each handle determines the direction of sizing: horizontal, vertical, or diagonal. Using the mouse, resize the object by placing the mouse pointer over the desired handle, click, and drag the object. Release the mouse button to fix the new size.

Using the keyboard, hold down the Shift key and use any combination of arrow keys to size the object. Click outside the selected object or on the selection pointer tool to fix the new size. Objects can be sized in increments relative to the type of ruler being used. The attributes of each object (such as color, font, and fill type) can be changed using the Object menu. The Object menu is described later in this chapter.

Controlling objects

After an object is placed on the screen layout, a dialog will appear. Each object dialog is used to define the appearance and control of the object. Once an object has been placed on the design screen, you can activate its control dialog by double-clicking on the object with the mouse. Object dialogs are detailed later in this chapter.

Code snippets

You can use code snippets to control the action of screens and objects. A code snippet can be a simple FoxPro expression or an entire procedure. Code snippets are defined using the dialog shown in Fig. 6-2. When the code snippet dialog appears, enter the procedure or expression in the text box. Use the Procedure/Expression radio button to specify whether the code snippet is a procedure or a FoxPro expression.

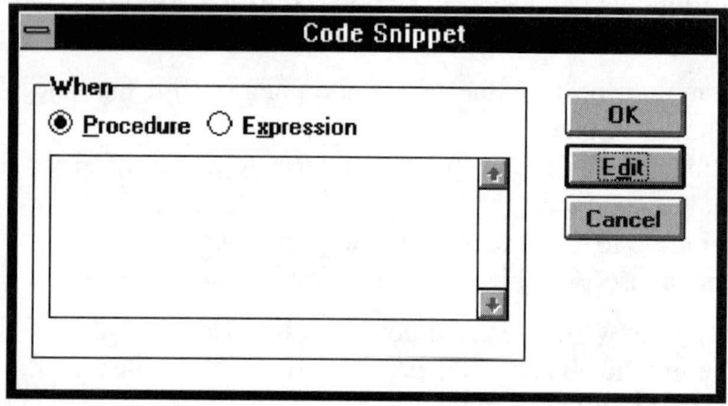

6-2 Code Snippet dialog.

If you're creating a procedure, do not enter a PROCEDURE statement or a procedure name because code snippets that are procedures are given a unique procedure name. If you want to call a user-defined procedure or function, enter the name of the procedure or function in the text box, followed by parentheses, and select Expression.

If you select Procedure and you want to open a full editing window, select the Edit push button. An editing window will appear, and you must select OK to activate the window. The code snippet dialog won't appear if the procedure editing window is already open.

Commenting objects

You can enter comments for each object on the screen design window using the Comments dialog that appears when you select the Comment button. Any comments entered are stored with the screen file and aren't included in the generated source-code file.

The Screen toolbox

The screen toolbox shown in Fig. 6-3 contains the tools necessary for placing objects on the screen layout. To select an object, position the mouse pointer over an object tool and click. The

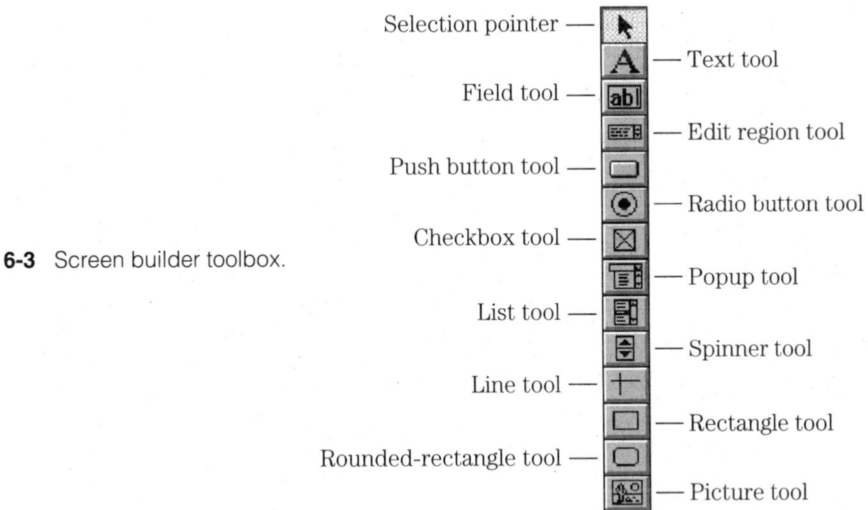

6-3 Screen builder toolbox.

mouse pointer will change to reflect the type of object selected: a vertical line for text objects, crosshairs for objects that require sizing, or a representation of the object selected.

To place the selected object on the screen layout, move the mouse pointer to the desired location and click. Depending on the object selected, a dialog might appear, allowing you to enter control codes and snippets. Once an object has been defined, the mouse pointer returns to a pointer tool (its default state).

Selection pointer tool

Click on the Selection pointer tool to deselect (or invert) any selected objects and return the mouse pointer to its default state.

Text tool

Use the Text tool to place literal text objects on the screen. Once Text has been selected, place the mouse pointer over the screen layout, click, and begin typing the desired letters using the keyboard. Click on the Selection pointer tool to fix the text object in place. Pressing the Enter key while editing a text object will add a carriage return at the end of the current text line.

Field tool

Use the Field tool to place a text editing field (GET) or text display object (SAY) on the screen. After selecting the Field tool, the mouse cursor changes to crosshairs so you can size the field. Place the mouse pointer over the screen layout, click the pointer at the top left position of the field, and drag the mouse to the bottom right position of the field. Release the mouse to fix the field object. A field can be sized to edit or display more than one line of data. Use the Field dialog shown in Fig. 6-4 to format the object expression and controls.

Input Field/Output Field When Output Field is selected, the expression is displayed on the screen and cannot be edited. Use Input Field to allow editing of the expression.

Input.../Output... You must enter an Input expression (GET) when the Input Field radio button is selected, or an Output expression (SAY) when the Output Field radio button is selected. Type the expression in the text box or select the Input/Output push button to activate the Choose Field/Variable dialog shown in Fig. 6-5. From this dialog, select a database field or memory variable to edit. The dialog displays the type (character, numeric, etc.) of expression that can be created.

Format... You can format expressions with codes to control the display of an expression or the type of data entered. Enter the appropriate format code(s) in the text box or select the Format... push button to display the Format dialog shown in Fig. 6-6. The codes entered correspond to the PICTURE and FORMAT codes detailed in the @ ... SAY/GET section of chapter 2.

Select Field on Entry When checked, all text in the field will be selected when the cursor enters the field.

Refresh Output Field If the Output Field radio button is selected, select Refresh Output Field to update the screen if the value of the expression has changed. The update occurs only when a SHOW GETS command is issued.

Initially Disable Field When checked, the field will be disabled when the READ command is issued and the editing cursor cannot access the field.

Range If Output Field is selected, use the Lower and Upper options to specify the lowest and highest value that can be entered into the field. The Range expression must match the Output Field expression. For example, if the Output Field is a date expression, the Lower and Upper range values must be date expressions.

When... Selecting When activates the Code Snippet dialog. A When expression or procedure is used to control access into a field. See the WHEN clause of @ ... SAY/GET in chapter 2 for more information.

Valid... Selecting Valid activates the Code Snippet dialog. A Valid expression or procedure is used to validate the information entered into a field. See the VALID clause of @ ... SAY/GET in chapter 2 for more information.

Message... Selecting Message activates the Code Snippet dialog. A Message expression or procedure is displayed on the screen when the editing cursor moves into the field. See the MESSAGE clause of @ ... SAY/GET in chapter 2 for more information.

Error... Selecting Error activates the Code Snippet dialog. When a field fails validation, an input error message is displayed. You can override the default FoxPro input error message by entering a custom expression or procedure. See the ERROR clause of @ ... SAY/GET in chapter 2 for more information.

Comment... Enter comments for the object.

Select OK to save the field attributes. Selecting Cancel will discard any changes to the object.

See also @ ... SAY/GET

Edit region tool

Use the Edit region tool to place a scrolling edit field (GET) on the screen. An edit region is similar to a normal GET field, except that a scroll bar is placed to the right of the area to allow scrolling multiple lines of data.

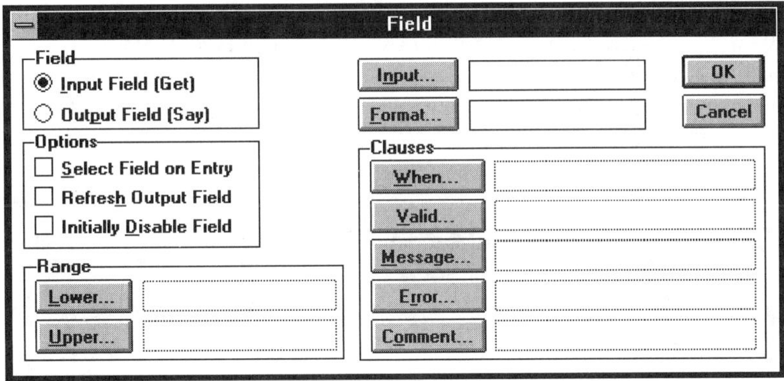

6-4 Screen Field dialog.

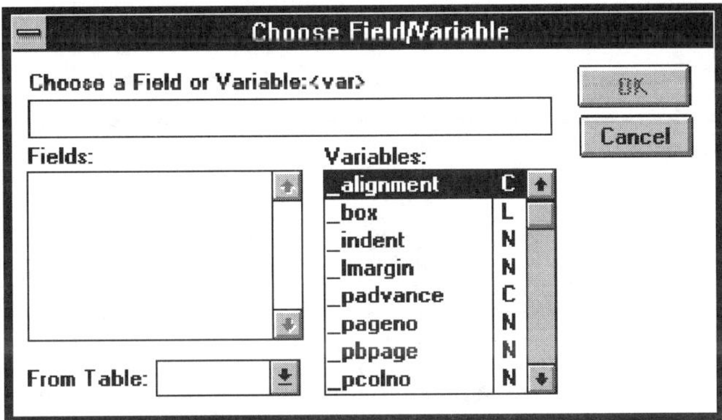

6-5 Choose Field/Variable dialog.

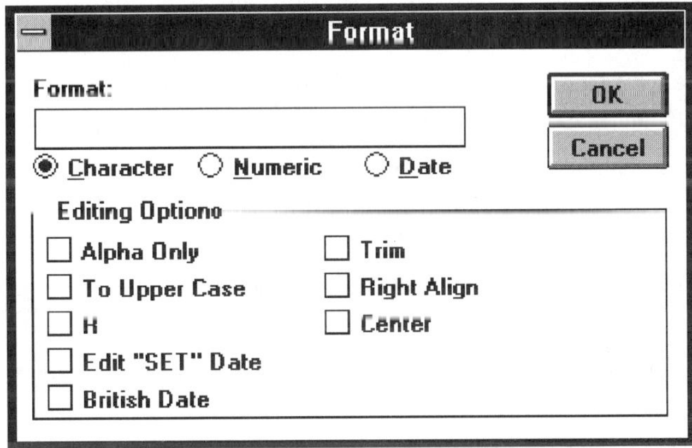

6-6 Format dialog.

After you select the Edit region tool, the mouse cursor changes to crosshairs so you can size the region. Place the mouse pointer over the screen layout, click the pointer at the top left position of the region, and drag the mouse to the bottom right position of the region. Release the mouse to fix the edit region object. An edit region can be sized to edit or display more than one line of data. Use the Edit Region dialog shown in Fig. 6-7 to format the object expression and controls.

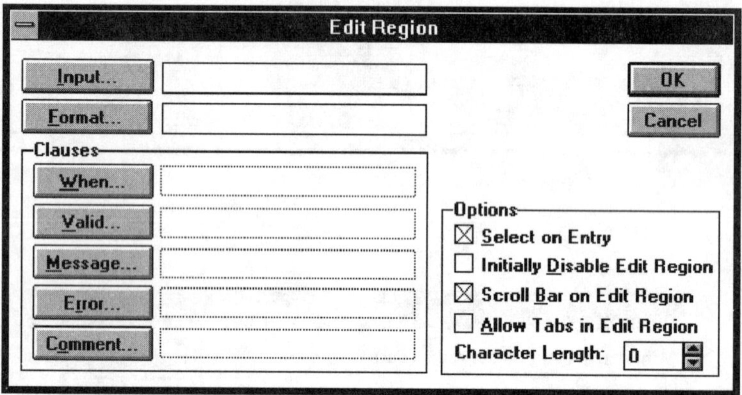

6-7 Edit Region dialog.

Input... You must enter an Input expression (GET) for the object. Type the expression in the text box or select the Input push button to activate the Choose Field/Variable dialog shown in Fig. 6-5. From this dialog select a database field or memory variable to edit. The dialog displays the type (character, numeric, etc.) of expression that can be created.

Format... You can format expressions with codes to control the display of an expression or the type of data entered. Enter the appropriate format code(s) in the text box or select the Format... push button to display the Format dialog shown in Fig. 6-6. The codes entered correspond to the PICTURE and FORMAT codes detailed in the @ ... SAY/GET section of chapter 2.

Select on Entry When checked, all text in the edit region will be selected when the cursor enters the field.

Initially Disable Edit Region When checked, the field will be disabled when the READ command is issued and the editing cursor cannot access the field.

Scroll Bar on Edit Region When checked, a scroll bar is placed to the right of the editing region. The scroll bar is active only when the data entered in the edit region is more than what can be displayed.

Allow Tabs in Edit Region When checked, Tab characters can be entered in the edit region. If this option is selected, the user must press Ctrl-Tab to exit the edit region.

Character Length Enter the maximum number of characters that can be entered in the edit region.

When.., Valid..., Message..., Error..., Comment... These options are described under the Field tool section above.

Select OK to save the field attributes. Selecting Cancel will discard any changes to the object.

See also Field tool, @ ... SAY/GET, @ ... EDIT

Push button tool

Use the Push button tool to create a set of normal, picture, or invisible push button objects that can be used for editing data, selecting an option, or activating a control. Normal push buttons appear as gray boxes with shadow borders and text prompts, and are normally used to close an editing screen, giving the user an option of OK or Cancel.

Picture push buttons are similar to normal push buttons. However, the prompts are displayed as bitmap or icon images. Invisible buttons have no text prompts. Use the Push Button dialog shown in Fig. 6-8 to format the object expression and controls.

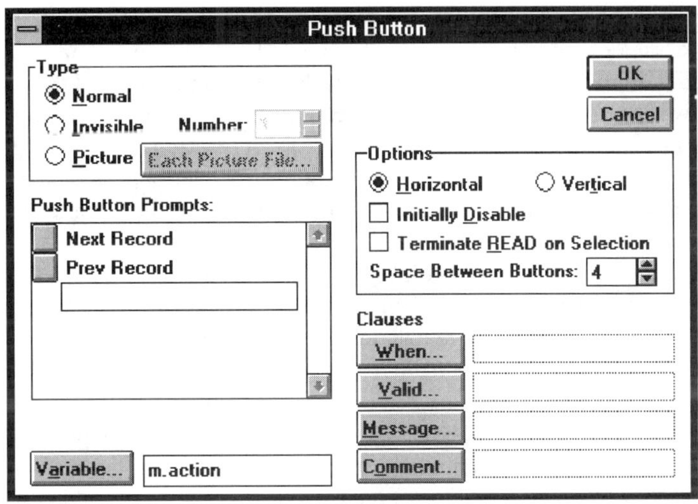

6-8 Push Button dialog.

Normal/Invisible/Picture Determines the type of button set. If Invisible is selected, enter the number of buttons in the Number text box. If Picture is selected, use the Picture button to locate a bitmap or icon image file for each button prompt.

Push Button Prompts Enter the text to appear for each button in the set. If the button type is Picture, enter the appropriate bitmap or icon image file for each button in the set. This option is disabled if the button type is Invisible.

Variable... When a push button is selected, its value is stored to a database field or expression. Enter the field or expression in the text box, or select Variable... to activate the Choose Field/Variable dialog shown in Fig. 6-5. From this dialog, select a database field or memory variable to edit. The value stored to the memory variable can be either the numeric value of the push button or the button's text prompt.

Horizontal/Vertical When Horizontal is selected, the push button prompts will appear on the screen from left to right. Selecting vertical places the push button prompts from top to bottom.

Initially Disable When checked, the object will be disabled when the READ is issued and the editing cursor can't access the object.

Terminate READ on Selection When checked, activating any push button in the set will cause FoxPro to attempt to terminate the READ. The READ VALID clause then determines whether or not the READ is terminated.

Space Between Buttons Enter the number of spaces, in pixels, between each push button prompt.

When..., Valid..., Message..., Comment... These options are described under the Field tool section above.

Select OK to save the object attributes. Selecting Cancel will discard any changes to the object.

You can easily change the order of the push button prompts once they've been entered. To change the order of the prompts using the keyboard, hit the Tab key until the prompt list is highlighted. Use the ↑ or ↓ keys to highlight the desired prompt and then use Ctrl-↑ or Ctrl-↓ to move the prompt to the desired location. Using a mouse, simply position the mouse pointer over the double-arrow mover control to the left of the desired prompt. Click the mouse and drag the prompt to the desired location. To delete a push button from the list, select the desired prompt using the actions described above, and press the Delete key. Move off of the prompt to update the list.

You can assign hot keys to each push button prompt, to allow the user to activate a single push button control with one keystroke. When entering the text for a push button, precede the desired hot key letter with \<. For example, to give the Next Record push button a hot key of "R," enter the prompt as Next \<Record. When the program is executed, pressing Alt plus the hot key letter (R) while the editing cursor is anywhere on the screen will cause the push button control to be executed. Hot keys can't be assigned to picture or invisible push buttons.

You can also use push button hot keys to define a single push button as the default or escape push button. When a default push button exists, pressing Ctrl-Enter while the cursor is anywhere on the screen other than a push button activates the default button. When an escape push button exists, pressing Esc while the cursor is anywhere on the screen other than a button activates the escape button. To define a default push button, preface the push button prompt with \!. A default push button is surrounded by a solid black line. To define an escape push button, preface the push button prompt with \?. Picture or invisible push buttons can't be defined as default or escape buttons.

While the entire push button set is created with one @ ... GET command, each button is a single object. This allows you to control the appearance and availability of each button in the set using the SHOW OBJECT and SHOW GET commands.

See also Field tool, @ ... GET - Push Buttons, SHOW OBJECT, SHOW GET

Radio button tool

Use the Radio button tool to create a set of normal or picture radio button objects that can be used for editing data, selecting an option, or activating a control. Each normal radio button option is preceded by an empty circle, and the selected option appears with a bullet inside the circle. Use radio buttons to select an option from a list of multiple options.

Picture radio buttons are similar to normal radio buttons. However, the prompts are displayed as bitmap or icon images and the selected option appears indented. Use the Radio Button dialog shown in Fig. 6-9 to format the object expression and controls.

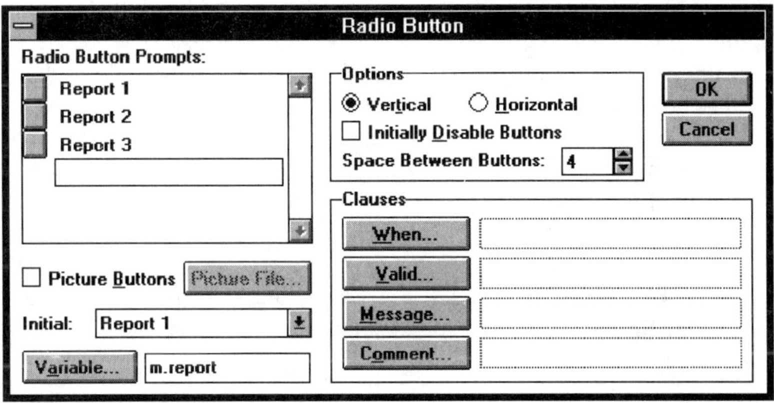

6-9 Radio Button dialog.

Radio Button Prompts Enter the text to appear after each button in the set. If the button type is Picture, enter the appropriate bitmap or icon image file for each button in the set.

Picture Buttons Select this option to use picture radio buttons. Use the Picture File push button to select an appropriate bitmap or icon image file for each button.

Initial This pop-up contains a list of all the radio button options and allows you to select which button is initially selected.

Variable... When a radio button is selected, the value of the radio button is stored to a database field or memory variable. Enter the field or variable name in the text box, or select Variable... to activate the Choose Field/Variable dialog shown in Fig. 6-5. From this dialog, select a database field or memory variable to edit. The value stored to the expression can be either the numeric value of the radio button, or the button's text prompt.

Horizontal/Vertical When Horizontal is selected, the radio button prompts will appear on the screen from left to right. Selecting vertical places the radio button prompts from top to bottom.

Initially Disable Buttons When checked, the object will be disabled when the READ is issued and the editing cursor can't access the object.

Space between Buttons Enter the number of spaces, in pixels, between each radio button prompt.

When..., Valid..., Message..., Comment... These options are described under the Field tool section above.

Select OK to save the object attributes. Selecting Cancel will discard any changes to the object.

You can change the order of the radio button prompts easily once you've entered them. To change the order of the prompts using the keyboard, Tab until the prompt list is highlighted. Use the ↑ or ↓ keys to highlight the desired prompt and then use Ctrl-↑ or Ctrl-↓ to move the prompt to the desired location. With a mouse, simply position the mouse pointer over the double-arrow mover control to the left of the desired prompt. Click the mouse and drag the prompt to the desired location. To delete a radio button from the list, select the desired prompt using the actions described above and press the Delete key. Move off the prompt to update the list.

You can also assign hot keys to each radio button prompt, which allows the user to activate the control with one keystroke. When entering the text for a radio button prompt, precede the desired hot key letter with \<. For example, to give the Report 3 radio button a hot key of t, enter the prompt as Repor\<t 3. When the program is executed, pressing Alt plus the hot key letter (t) while the editing cursor is anywhere on the screen causes the control to be executed. Hot keys cannot be assigned to picture radio buttons.

While the entire radio button set is created with one @ ... GET command, each button is a single object. This allows you to control the appearance and availability of each button in the set using the SHOW OBJECT and SHOW GET commands.

See also Field tool, @ ... GET - Radio Buttons, SHOW OBJECT, SHOW GET

Check box tool

Use the Check box tool to create a normal or picture check-box object that can be used for editing data, selecting an option, or activating a control. A normal check-box option is preceded by an empty square and, when the object is selected, an X appears inside the square. Check boxes are normally used to turn on or off a particular action.

A picture check box is similar to a normal check box; however, the prompt is displayed as a bitmap or icon image and appears indented when selected. Use the Check Box dialog shown in Fig. 6-10 to format the object expression and controls.

Check Box Prompt Enter the text to appear after the check box. If the check box type is Picture, enter the appropriate bitmap or icon image file for each button in the set.

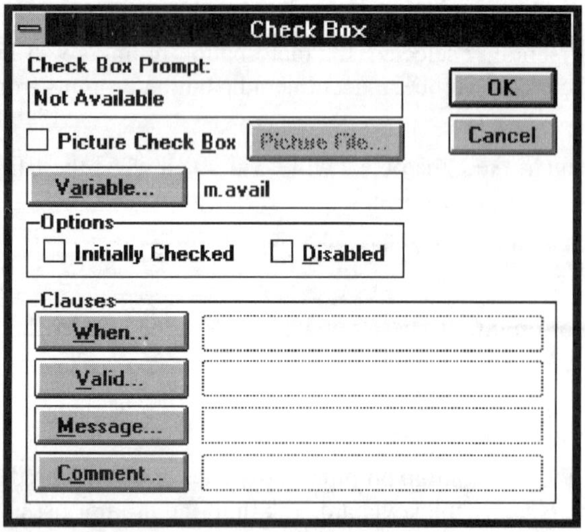

6-10 Check Box dialog.

Picture Check Box Select this option to use a picture check box. Use the Picture File push button to select an appropriate bitmap or icon image file for the check box.

Variable... When a check box is selected, its value is stored to a database field or memory variable. Enter the field or variable name in the text box, or select Variable... to activate the Choose Field/Variable dialog shown in Fig. 6-5. From this dialog select a database field or memory variable to edit. The value stored to the expression can be numeric or logical. If the check box isn't selected, the value is 0 or false (.F.). If the check box is selected, the value is 1 or true (.T.).

Initially Checked When checked, the check box will be checked when the READ is issued and the value of the expression will be 1 or true.

Disabled When checked, the object will be disabled when the READ is issued and the editing cursor can't access the object.

When..., Valid..., Message..., Comment... These options are described under the Field tool section above.

Select OK to save the object attributes. Selecting Cancel will discard any changes to the object.

You can also assign a hot key to a check box prompt, which allows the user to activate the control with one keystroke. When entering the text for a check-box prompt, precede the desired hot key letter with \<. For example to give the check box Not Available a hot key of A, enter the prompt as Not \<Available. When the program is executed, pressing Alt plus the hot key letter (A) while the editing cursor is anywhere on the screen causes the control to be executed. Hot keys cannot be assigned to picture check boxes.

See also Field tool, @ ... GET - Check Boxes

Popup tool

Use the Popup tool to create a pop-up object to either edit data or select an option. The pop-up is displayed as a rectangle with an underlined arrow to the right. When the pop-up is selected, the box opens, allowing you to select one of the options in the pop-up. Use the Popup dialog shown in Fig. 6-11 to format the object expression and controls.

List Popup/Array Popup When List Popup is selected, the Popup Prompts scrolling list allows you to enter all of the items to be displayed in the pop-up. Use Array Popup to fill the pop-up list with the elements of an array.

Initial If List Popup is selected, select the item from the pop-up that's initially displayed in the pop-up control.

Variable... When a pop-up item is selected, the value of the selection is stored to a database field or memory variable. Enter the field or variable name in the text box, or select Variable... to activate the Choose Field/Variable dialog shown in Fig. 6-5. From this dialog select a database field or memory variable to edit. The value stored to the expression can be either the numeric value of the item in the pop-up, or the item's pop-up text prompt.

Initially Disable Popup When selected, the object will be disabled when the READ is issued and the editing cursor can't access the object.

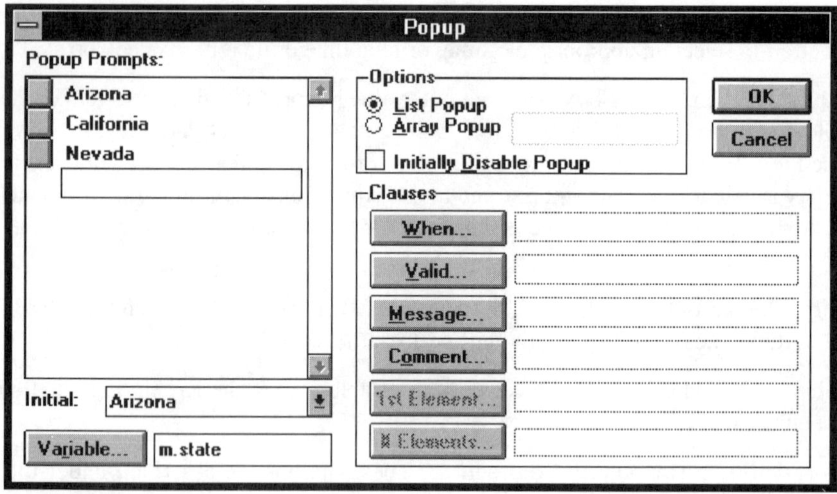

6-11 Popup dialog.

1st Element... If the pop-up is an Array type, you can use this option to specify which element of the array is to be the first item in the pop-up list. Selecting 1st Element... activates the code snippet dialog.

 # Elements... If the pop-up is an Array type, you can use this option to specify the number of elements of the array to be included in the pop-up list. Selecting # Elements... activates the code snippet dialog.

When..., Valid..., Message..., Comment... These options are described under the Field tool section above.

Select OK to save the object attributes. Selecting Cancel will discard any changes to the object.

If the pop-up is a List type, you can easily change the order of the pop-up options once they've been entered. To change the order of the options using the keyboard, hit the Tab key until the prompt list is highlighted. Use the ↑ or ↓ keys to highlight the desired prompt, then use Ctrl-↑ or Ctrl-↓ to move the option to the desired location. Using a mouse, simply position the mouse pointer over the double-arrow mover control to the left of the desired prompt. Click the mouse and drag the option to the desired location. To delete a pop-up option from the list, select the desired option using the actions described above, and press the Delete key. Move off of the option to update the list.

You can assign hot keys to each pop-up option, which allows the user to select an option once the pop-up control has been opened. When entering the text for a pop-up option, precede the desired hot key letter with \<. For example to give the pop-up option California a hot key of C, enter the prompt as \<California.

See also Field tool, @... GET - Popups

List tool

Use the List tool to create a scrolling-list object that can be used for editing data or selecting an option from the list. The list is displayed with a scroll bar on the right side. Lists are primarily used for selecting a value from a large list of options.

After selecting the List tool the mouse cursor changes to crosshairs so you can size the list object. Click the pointer at the top left position of the list and drag the mouse to the bottom right position of the list. Release the mouse to fix the field object. Use the List dialog shown in Fig. 6-12 to format the object expression and controls.

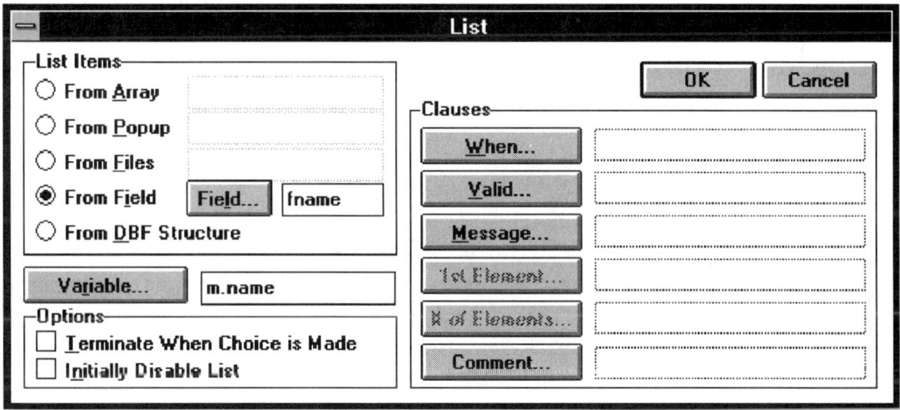

6-12 List dialog.

List Items This determines the source of information displayed in the list.

From Array The list is filled from the elements of a specified array. Enter the array name in the text box.

From Popup The list is filled from the options of a predefined pop-up. Enter the popup name in the text box.

From Files This list is filled with DOS file information. Enter the drive, directory, and file specification in the text box.

From Field The list is filled with records of a database. The fields to display are specified in the text box. Select the Field button to display the Expression Builder.

From DBF Structure The list is filled with the structure of a specified database file. Enter the name of the database in the text box.

Variable... When an item is selected from the list, the value of the selection is stored to a database field or memory variable. Enter the field or variable name in the text box, or select Variable... to activate the Choose Field/Variable dialog shown in Fig. 6-5. From this dialog select a database field or memory variable to edit. The value stored to the expression can be either the numeric value of the item in the list, or the item's text prompt.

Terminate When Choice is Made When checked, selecting an option from the list will cause FoxPro to attempt to terminate the READ. The READ VALID clause then determines whether or not the READ is terminated.

Initially Disable List When checked, the object will be disabled when the READ is issued and the editing cursor can't access the object.

1st Element... If the list is defined as From Array, you can use this option to specify which element of the array is to be the first item in the list. Selecting 1st Element... activates the code snippet dialog.

 # Elements... If the list is defined as From Array, you can use this to specify the number of elements of the array to be included in the list. Selecting # Elements... activates the code snippet dialog.

When..., Valid..., Message..., Comment... These options are described under the Field tool section above.

Select OK to save the object attributes. Selecting Cancel will discard any changes to the object.

See also Field tool, @ ... GET - Lists

Spinner tool

Use the Spinner tool to create a spinner object that can be used for editing numeric data. The value of a spinner is changed by clicking on the up or down arrow controls, or by entering a value in the text box. Spinners are primarily used to change a numeric value.

After selecting the Spinner tool the mouse cursor changes to crosshairs so you can size the control. Click the pointer at the top left position of the control and drag the mouse to the bottom right position of the control. Release the mouse to fix the spinner object. Use the Spinner dialog shown in Fig. 6-13 to format the object expression and controls.

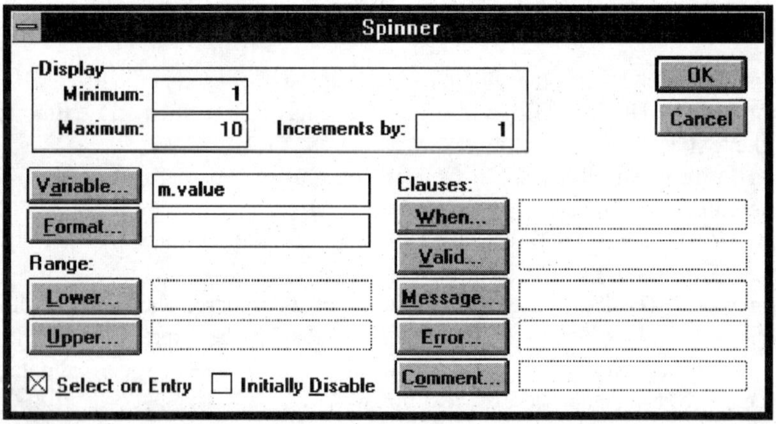

6-13 Spinner dialog.

Variable... The value of the spinner is stored to a database field or memory variable. Enter the field or variable name in the text box, or select Variable... to activate the Choose Field/Variable dialog shown in Fig. 6-5. From this dialog select a database field or memory variable to edit. The value stored to the expression is always the numeric value of the control.

Format... You can format expressions with codes to control the display of an expression or the type of data entered. Enter the appropriate format code(s) in the text box or select the Format... push button to display the Format dialog shown in Fig. 6-6. The codes entered correspond to the PICTURE and FORMAT codes detailed in the @ ... SAY/GET section of chapter 2.

Minimum Enter the minimum value that can be selected when the down arrow control is used.

Maximum Enter the maximum value that can be selected when the up arrow control is used.

Increments by Enter a number that determines the incremental value when the up or down arrow controls are used. The value can be positive or negative.

Range Use this option to control keyboard input of the spinner text box. The Upper and Lower values should correspond to the Minimum and Maximum values of the display.

Select on Entry When checked, all text in the spinner text box will be selected when the cursor enters the text box.

Initially Disable When checked, the object will be disabled when the READ is issued and the editing cursor can't access the field.

When..., Valid..., Error..., Message..., Comment... These options are described under the Field tool section above.

Select OK to save the field attributes. Selecting Cancel will discard any changes to the object.

See also Field tool, @ ... GET - Spinner

Line tool

Use the Line tool to place a vertical or horizontal line object on the screen. After selecting the Line tool the mouse cursor changes to crosshairs so you can size the object. Click the pointer at the top left position of the line and drag the mouse up or down to create a vertical line, left or right to create a horizontal line. Release the mouse to fix the line object. The pen width of the line object is determined by the Object menu Pen setting, which is discussed later in this chapter. To enter comments for the object, double-click on the object to activate the Comment dialog.

See also @ ... TO

Rectangle tool

Use the Rectangle tool to place a box or rectangle object on the screen. After selecting the Rectangle tool, the mouse cursor changes to crosshairs so you can size the object. Click the pointer at the top left position of the rectangle and drag the mouse to the bottom right position of the rectangle. Release the mouse to fix the rectangle object. The pen width of the rectangle object is determined by the Object menu Pen setting, which is discussed later in this chapter. To enter comments for the object, double-click on the object to activate the Comment dialog.

See also @ ... TO

Rounded-rectangle tool

This option is similar to the Rectangle tool. However, the corners of the object are rounded rather than square. After the object is fixed, double-click on the object to select a corner style or to enter comments for the object.

See also @ ... TO

Picture tool

Use the Picture tool to place a bitmap or icon image on the screen. After selecting the Picture tool the mouse cursor changes to crosshairs so you can size the object. Click the pointer at the top left position of the picture and drag the mouse to the bottom right position of the picture. Release the mouse to fix the picture object. The Screen Picture dialog shown in Fig. 6-14 is used to select a picture file and format the picture display.

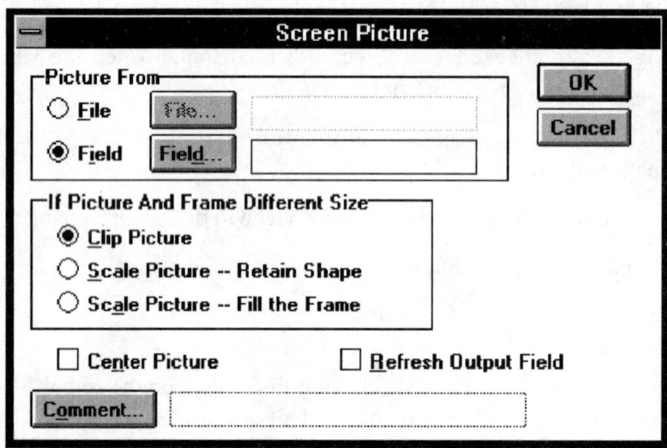

6-14 Screen Picture dialog.

File/Field When File is selected, enter the name of a bitmap or icon image file in the text box, or use the File... button to locate a bitmap or icon image file. When Field is selected, enter the name of a FoxPro general field in the text box, or select Field... to activate the Choose Field/Variable dialog shown in Fig. 6-5.

Clip Picture When selected, the picture's original dimensions are retained and only that portion of the picture that fits in the object's frame is displayed, beginning at the top left corner of the frame.

Scale Picture - Retain Shape When selected, the picture's original dimensions are scaled to fit inside the frame, while filling the frame as much as possible.

Scale Picture - Fill the Frame When selected, the picture is sized to fill the entire frame. This may cause distortion in the picture.

Center Picture When checked, the contents of the general field will be centered within the picture frame. This is useful when images stored in a general field are smaller than the frame size. This option is only available when Field is selected.

Refresh Output Field You can use this option to update the picture object if the contents of the general field change (such as moving the record pointer). The update only occurs when a SHOW GETS command is issued.

Comment... Enter comments for the picture object.

Select OK to save the object attributes. Selecting Cancel will discard any changes to the object. If the picture object is using a general field and the contents of the general field is an OLE object other than a bitmap or icon picture, the picture will be displayed as an icon representing the application to which the OLE object belongs.

See also @ ... SAY - BMPs & OLE Objects

The Screen menu

The Screen menu shown in Fig. 6-15 contains all the tools necessary for designing the screen layout.

6-15 The Screen Menu.

Layout... Open All Snippets Ctrl+S
Show Position Ruler/Grid... Snap to Grid
Object Order...
Quick Screen...

Screen Layout...

The dialog shown in Fig. 6-16 is used to control and define the type of screen displayed, its name and title, window size and position, and allows you to create setup and cleanup procedures for the screen code.

Title Use the text box to define a title for the window. The title is displayed in the title bar.

Name Use the text box to define a reference name for the window. If no name is entered, FoxPro creates a unique name in the screen code.

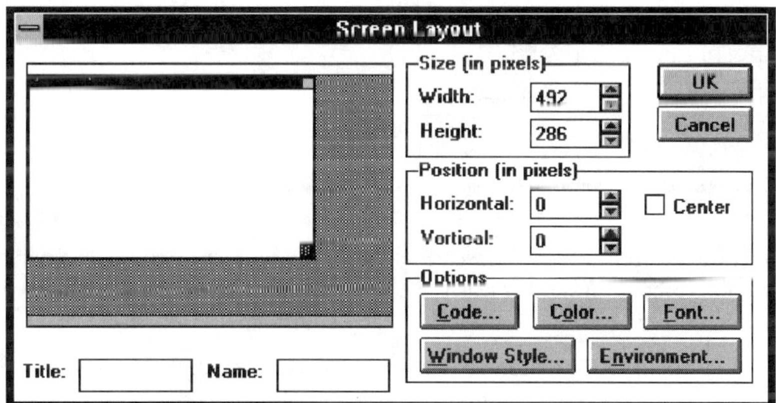

6-16 Screen Layout dialog.

Width Enter the width of the window in pixels.

Height Enter the height of the window in pixels.

Horizontal position Enter the column, in pixels, at which the top left corner of the window will be displayed.

Vertical position Enter the row, in pixels, at which the top left corner of the window will be displayed.

Center When checked, the screen will be centered in the middle of the main FoxPro window or another user-defined window. Otherwise, enter a row and column position for the top left corner of the window.

Color This allows you to select a background color for the screen. When Automatic is selected, the background color is taken from the current Windows color scheme. You can use the Wallpaper option to select a bitmap or icon image to display as the window background. The image that is selected will be duplicated as many times as necessary to fill the entire background.

Font... Use the Windows Font dialog to select a default font for the screen. The default font determines the font used when adding any new objects to the screen.

Window Style... Displays the dialog shown in Fig. 6-17 which allows you to set certain attributes of the window. Table 6-1 shows the attributes available for each type of window. The type of windows available are Desktop, User, System, Dialog, and Alert. Each window type has certain predefined characteristics that cannot be modified. A User window is the most flexible, as all attributes can be changed. See the DEFINE WINDOW command in chapter 2 for more information on window attributes.

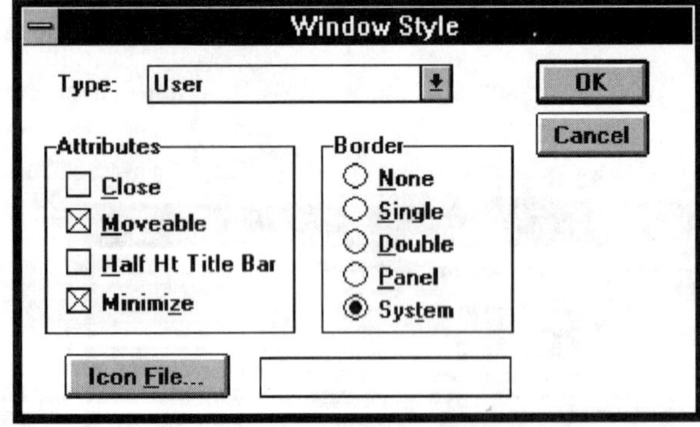

6-17 Window Style dialog.

Environment... Selecting Save causes FoxPro to save the current environment settings with the screen. If the environment was previously saved, select Restore to restore the original environment settings, or Clear to remove any environment settings.

Code... Selecting the Code button activates the Screen Code dialog, which is used to define screen code snippets. The When, Valid, Activate, Deactivate, and Show Gets options activate the Code Snippet dialog shown in Fig. 6-2.

Table 6-1 Window types and settings.

Window type	Attributes	Border
Desktop	Close	None
	Move	
	Minimize	
User	All options available	All options available
System	Close	System
	Move	
	Minimize	
	Half Ht Title Bar	
Dialog	Move	Double
	Close	
Alert	Move	Double

Setup Code Opens an editing window for screen setup code. Select OK to activate the editing window. Setup code is placed at the top of the source-code file and is executed first.

Cleanup and Procedures Opens an editing window for screen cleanup code and screen procedures. Select OK to activate the editing window. Cleanup code consists of all commands starting from the top of the snippet window and ending at the first PROCEDURE or FUNCTION statement. Cleanup code is placed after the READ command in the source-code file and is executed after the READ is terminated. Place any user-defined functions after the cleanup code.

When... A screen When procedure or expression is executed before the READ command is issued. It's similar to the WHEN clause of the GET command. If the procedure or expression returns false (.F.), the READ won't be executed, and the editing screen will not be activated. See the READ command in chapter 2 for more information on the WHEN clause.

Valid... A screen Valid procedure or expression is executed when the user attempts to terminate the READ. A read can be terminated by selecting a terminating control, pressing Ctrl-W or Escape, or by issuing the CLEAR READ command. If the Valid procedure or expression returns false (.F.), the READ won't be terminated. See the READ command in chapter 2 for more information on the VALID clause.

Activate... A screen Activate procedure or expression is executed when the window is activated. A window is first activated when the READ command is issued. See the READ command in chapter 2 for more information on the ACTIVATE clause.

Deactivate... A screen Deactivate procedure or expression is executed when the window is deactivated. A window is normally deactivated by selected Close from the window's control menu. If the expression or procedure returns true (.T.), the READ is terminated.

Show... A screen Show procedure or expression is executed when the READ window is first activated, and whenever a SHOW GETS command is issued.

The Screen Layout dialog also contains a what-you-see-is-what-you-get (WYSIWYG) display of the current screen design. This display is relative to the current display driver and the dimensions of the screen layout. The screen layout in the display carries the same attributes as defined in the screen layout, including dimensions, location, and colors.

You can use the WYSIWYG display to move and size the screen layout without using the Size and Position controls. To change the size of the screen layout, simply click the mouse pointer over the shaded box at the bottom right corner of the screen and drag the mouse to change the screen size. The position of the screen window can be changed by clicking on any portion of the window border or title bar and dragging the window to the desired position.

Screens can also be sized without activating the Screen Layout dialog. To change the size of a screen layout, click the mouse pointer over the shaded box at the bottom right corner of the screen window (not the screen layout window) and drag the mouse to change the screen size. Select OK to save the screen attributes and return to the screen design. Selecting Cancel will discard any changes to the screen layout.

Open All Snippets

Opens an editing window for all screen object and screen layout code snippets that are defined as Procedure. Pressing the Shift key before selecting the Screen menu changes this option to Close All Snippets.

Shortcut key Ctrl-S

Show Position

Use Show Position to display the coordinates of the mouse pointer or the size of the currently selected object. When no objects are selected, Show Position tracks the mouse and displays the coordinates of the mouse pointer relative to the screen dimensions and the current ruler being used. When an object is selected, the position and size of the object are displayed. The values displayed are relative to the screen dimensions and the current ruler being used.

The Show Position information is displayed in the status bar at the bottom of the main FoxPro window. Show Position is active when a check mark appears to the left of the menu option. Select Show Position again to turn the function off.

Ruler/Grid

This option displays the Ruler/Grid dialog. Use the Ruler/Grid dialog to format the screen builder ruler display and associated functions.

Ruler Select a unit of measurement for the ruler. The screen builder ruler isn't displayed when No Rulers is selected. Selecting Character displays a ruler that is equal to the average font width for the current screen font.

Ruler Lines Selecting Yes places horizontal and vertical ruler lines over the screen layout.

Grid Determines the number of pixels that an object can be moved when the Snap to Grid function is on.

Snap to Grid

When Snap to Grid is on (a check mark appears to the left of the menu option), objects that are sized or moved using the mouse will be automatically aligned to the closest grid line, relative to the current ruler being used. When Snap to Grid is off, objects can be sized or moved one pixel at a time. Select Snap to Grid again to turn the function off or press the Ctrl key while sizing or moving an object to ignore the current Snap to Grid setting.

Object order

Use this option to change the order of the editing (GET) objects on the screen. The Object Order dialog contains a list of all editing objects on the current screen layout. To change the order, simply click on the double-arrow mover control to the left of the object expression and drag the object to the desired location. Using the keyboard, press the Tab key until the first item in the list is selected. Use Ctrl-↑ or Ctrl-↓ to drag the object to the desired location.

By default, the order of screen objects is determined by the order in which they are added to the screen. Selecting the By Row button will automatically order the objects on the screen from left to right and top to bottom. Selecting the By Column button will automatically order the objects on the screen from top to bottom and left to right.

Quick Screen...

The Quick Screen option is used to easily fill the screen with field objects from a selected database, and is only available when the screen layout is empty. The Quick Screen dialog shown in Fig. 6-18 is displayed.

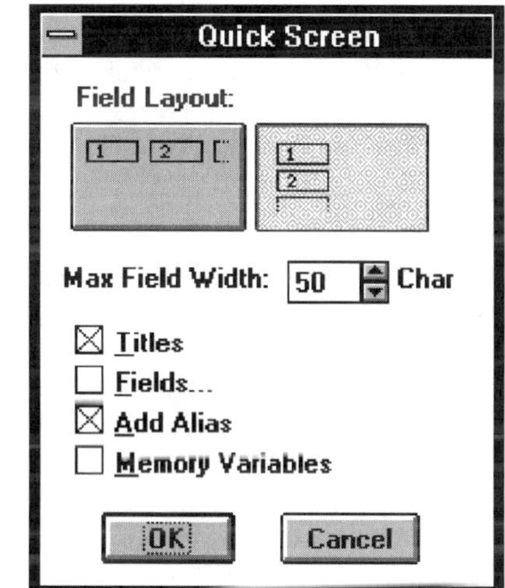

6-18 Quick Screen dialog.

Field Layout When the left button is selected, the field objects will be placed on the screen from left to right. Selecting the right button places the field objects from top to bottom.

Maximum field width Specifies the maximum length that any field object created with Quick Screen can be. The value only applies if any selected fields are greater than the value entered in the text box.

Titles When checked, this option places column headings at the top or left side of the screen. The column headings are text objects that correspond to the field names.

Fields... Displays the field picker dialog, allowing you to select certain fields to place on the screen.

Add Alias When checked, the expression of each field object consists of the alias of the database the field belongs to, a period, and the field expression. Use Add Alias if the screen contains multiple field objects that have the same field name but different aliases. This option is only enabled when the Memory Variables option is unchecked.

Memory Variables When checked, the expression of each field object consists of the memory variable identifier (m), a period, and the field expression. Use memory variables if you want the editing screen to change the value of memory variables rather than database fields. Selecting this option overrides the Add Alias option.

Select OK to add the objects to the screen layout.

The Object menu

Use the options in the Object menu to control the appearance and style of objects on the screen layout.

Align to Grid

Selecting Align to Grid when one or more screen objects is selected will cause those objects to be aligned to the nearest horizontal and vertical grid lines.

Shortcut key Ctrl-T

Bring to Front

Selecting Bring to Front when one or more screen objects is selected causes those objects to be moved to the front of the screen. This is useful when line or text objects need to be placed on top of field or control objects. Bringing an object to the front forces any overlapping objects to appear behind the selected object.

Shortcut key Ctrl-G

See also Send to Back

Send to Back

Selecting Send to Back when one or more screen objects is selected causes those objects to be moved to the back of the screen. This is useful when line or text objects need to be placed behind field or control objects. Sending an object to the back forces any overlapping objects to appear on top of the selected object.

Shortcut key Ctrl-J

See also Bring to Front

Center

This option positions a selected object in the middle of the screen, relative to the size of the screen's window dimensions. If multiple objects are selected, each object will be centered. If you want to center a group of objects and keep the relative spacing of each object the same, use Group to first group the objects into one object then select Center.

See also Group

Group

Selecting Group allows you to select multiple objects and group them together as one object to be manipulated. This is useful when you want to move many objects the same distance.

See also Ungroup

Ungroup

Selecting Ungroup ungroups a set of grouped objects, returning them to their single object state.

See also Group

Font...

Selecting Font... displays the Windows font dialog. Use the Font dialog to change the font attributes for the selected object. Refer to your Windows documentation for more information on changing a font.

Text Alignment

Use the Text Alignment options to adjust the alignment and spacing of text within a text object.

Fill

This option allows you to fill selected rectangle and rounded line objects with a variety of different patterns.

Pen

Use the Pen options to adjust the width of the line used for line, rectangle and rounded objects.

Mode

Use the Mode options on text, line, rectangle, and rounded-rectangle objects. When Mode is set to Opaque, any objects behind the selected object will not show through the selected object. When Mode is to Transparent, any objects behind the selected object will show through the selected object.

Fill Color

Use Fill Color to select a background color for the following screen objects:

Object	Affects
Text	Nothing
Field	Background color of the field
Editing region	Background color of the region
Push button	Nothing
Radio button	Background of the radio button circle
Check box	Background of the check box square
Popup	Background color of the options
Scrolling list	Background color of the options
Spinner	Background color of the value

Normal and picture push buttons cannot be given a fill color since they are always displayed in the default Windows color.

Pen Color

Use Pen Color to select a foreground color for the following screen objects:

Object	Affects
Text	All text in the object
Field	Text displayed in the field
Editing region	Text displayed in the region
Push button	Nothing
Radio button	Foreground of the radio button circle and the text of each prompt
Check box	Foreground of the check box square and the text of the prompt
Popup	Text of the options displayed in the popup
Scrolling list	Text of the options displayed in the list
Spinner	Text displayed in the value box

Normal and picture push buttons cannot be given a pen color since they are always displayed in the default Windows color.

Saving the screen

Once the screen design is complete, you must save the screen file. Do this by selecting Save from the File menu, pressing Ctrl-W, or by double-clicking on the window control bar.

If you're saving the screen for the first time, FoxPro will display an alert asking if you want to save the environment information. If you select Yes, the status of all work areas, indexes, and relations is stored with the screen. When a screen file that contains a saved environment is opened, FoxPro will restore the environment automatically.

Generating screen code

Once the screen design is complete, you must create a source code file. The source code file is a FoxPro program that, when executed, will display your customized screen and activate all controls. FoxPro uses a FoxPro program (GENSCRN.PRG) to create a source code file from a screen file. The resulting file contains:

- FoxPro setup code
- User-defined setup code
- Window definitions
- @ ... SAY/GET commands
- The READ command
- User-defined cleanup code
- FoxPro cleanup code
- User-defined procedures and functions
- FoxPro defined functions

To generate a source-code file, select Generate... from the Program menu to display the Generate Screen dialog shown in Fig. 6-19 (the More> push button must be selected to expand the Generate Screen dialog.). This option is only available when a Screen Builder window is active and frontmost.

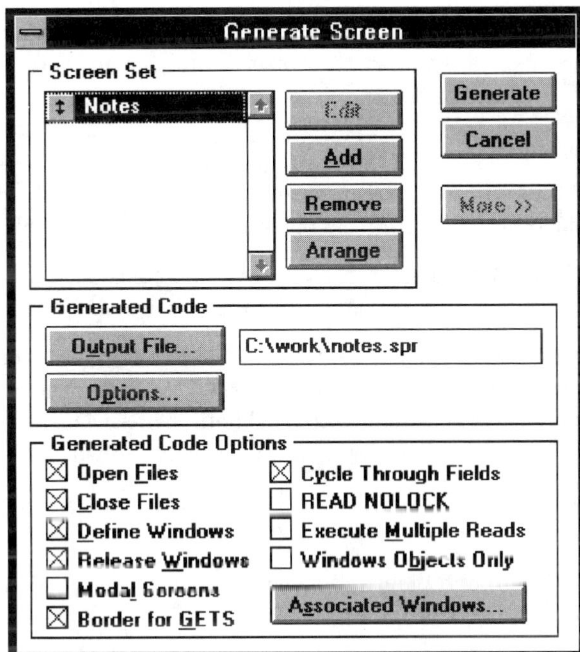

6-19 Generate Screen dialog.

Screens

FoxPro has the ability to generate code for multiple screens into one source code file. These are called *screen sets*. When the Generate Screen dialog is activated, all open Screen Builder design windows are automatically added to the screen list. Use the Add and Remove push buttons to add more screens to the set or to remove any screens from the list.

The order in which the screens are displayed in the list determines the activation sequence of the windows. The screen at the end of the list is activated first, and the screen at the top of the list is activated last. You can change the order of screens by clicking on the double-arrow mover control and dragging the screen to the desired location. To change the order of screen with the keyboard, use the ↑ or ↓ keys to highlight the desired screen, then press Ctrl-↑ or Ctrl-↓ to drag the screen to the desired location.

Although the position of a screen window is defined in its screen layout, you can change the position at this time with the Arrange button, which activates the Arrange Screens dialog. The Arrange Screens dialog contains a graphical representation of the video display and the position of all screens involved in the screen set. You can use the methods described earlier in the Screen Layout section to change the position of the screen(s). Once the arrangement is complete, select OK to save the changes. The position of all windows will be stored in memory and override, but not change, the defined position contained in each screen file. Select Cancel to discard any previous actions.

Specifying code options

You can use the Generated Code Options to specify what predefined commands are included in the source-code file.

Open Files When checked, the screen code will contain the commands to restore the environment that was saved with any of the screens in the set.

Close Files When checked, the screen code will contain the commands to close all open databases when the program is exited.

Define Windows When checked, the screen code will contain the commands to define each window in the set. Turn this option off if the window is defined before the program is executed.

Release Windows When checked, the screen code will contain the commands to release all windows that were defined in the screen code.

Modal Screens When checked, the screen code will contain the MODAL clause on the READ statement. When a READ MODAL command is issued, any window not involved in the READ cannot be activated until the READ is terminated. Use the Associated Windows to specify windows that can be activated when a READ MODAL is in effect.

Border for Gets When checked, all field controls will be displayed with a border around the field area.

Cycle through Fields When checked, the screen code will contain the CYCLE clause on the READ statement.

READ NOLOCK When checked, the screen code will contain the NOLOCK clause on the READ statement.

Execute Multiple Reads When checked, the screen code will contain a separate READ statement for each window and its controls in the set. In this instance, only one window is activated at any time and terminating one READ will cause the program to display the next window, activate the controls, and execute another READ command.

Windows Objects Only By default, FoxPro will generate code for all objects in the screen file. If any screen in the set contains objects created in FoxPro for MS-DOS, select

Windows Objects Only to generate a source code file that contains only FoxPro for Windows objects. See chapter 12 for more information on other FoxPro platforms.

Associated Windows... Displays the Associated Windows dialog, which is used to define a list of window names that can be activated when a READ MODAL is in effect. It isn't necessary to list windows that are part of the screen set. When associated windows are identified, the screen code will contain a WITH *windowlist* clause on the READ statement. You should include in this list the name of any window that needs to be activated and that isn't part of the screen set. This includes browse windows, memo field editing windows, and FoxPro desk accessory windows (i.e., Calendar, Calculator). See chapter 2 for more information detailing the READ command and its clauses.

See also Chapter 2, FoxPro commands, chapter 11, Cross-platform and international capabilities

Specifying the output

By default, the screen code-file name is the first screen in the list with an extension of .SPR. You can change the name of the output file by entering it in the text box, or select Output File... to activate the Save As dialog. If you prefer to save the screen code as a program so that it can be used as a user-defined function, change the extension from .SPR to .PRG.

The screen code that's eventually created contains a number of commenting sections (provided by the Screen Generator program) and information on who generated the source code file. The style of this information can be changed by selecting Options..., which displays the dialog shown in Fig. 6-20.

Developer Information The text entered in the Author, Company, Address, City, State, and Zip text boxes is contained at the top of the source-code file.

Comment Style Selecting Box Around Comments will cause the Screen Generator to place solid boxes around the comments that are generated. Selecting Asterisks Around

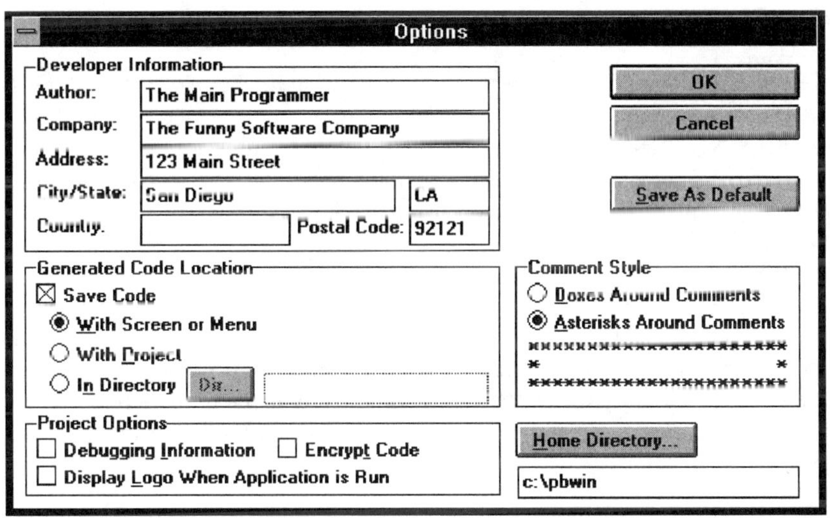

6-20 Screen Options dialog.

Comments will cause the Screen Generator to place asterisks (*) around the comments that are generated. This won't affect any comments that you may have entered into any screen code snippets.

Home Directory If a drive and directory are entered in the text box, all code that's generated to open database files (the USE command) will contain a path relative to the Home Directory setting and the location of the databases in the environment settings.

Save as Default When selected, all settings specified in the dialog will be saved to the resource file if OK is selected.

Select OK to save the information in this dialog, or Cancel to discard and return to the Generate dialog.

Creating the screen-code file

When all options have been set, select OK to begin generating the source-code file. A progress indicator is displayed while the file is being created.

The Screen Generator program

FoxPro uses a program, GENSCRN.PRG, to read the contents of a screen file and create a source-code file. The name and location of the Screen Generator are stored in the system memory variable _genscrn.

Because the screen generator program is written in FoxPro, it can be customized to your needs. If you change the name of the Screen Generator program, be sure to change to the value of _genscrn, either in the CONFIG.FP file or at the Command window, before attempting to generate a source-code file.

See also Diskette Appendix D

Screen Generator directives

Screen generator directives are used to control the way that the Screen Generator program evaluates certain expressions in the screen file, and they are also used to include certain READ and DEFINE WINDOW clauses that aren't available through the Screen Builder. All Screen Generator directives must be placed at the beginning of the screen setup code.

#INSERT

```
#INSERT filename
```

When used, the contents of filename are inserted into the source-code file at the point that the directive is encountered. The specified file must be an ASCII text file and exist along the FoxPro path. If the file cannot be located, a comment is added to the screen code at the #INSERT location, specifying that the Screen Generator could not locate the file.

#ITSEXPRESSION

```
#ITSEXPRESSION expC
```

Defines a single character that tells the Screen Generator to treat all expressions after the character as expressions rather than literals. For example, if a screen is given a title of Titlevar, the generated code would look like:

```
DEFINE WINDOW mywind TITLE "Titlevar"
```

Using #ITSEXPRESSION ^ and placing the ^ character before the title of the window in the Screen Layout dialog would cause the generated code to look like:

```
DEFINE WINDOW mywind TITLE Titlevar
```

In the second case, the title of the window would be replaced by the contents of the variable Titlevar when the program is run. This directive is primarily used for format codes and window titles.

#NAME

`#NAME` *`snippet name`*

This is used to assign a name to a code snippet procedure. By default, all code snippet procedures are given a unique name by the Screen Generator.

```
FUNCTION _qea0tx99s     &&  m.order VALID
HELP
```

Use the #NAME directive followed by a valid snippet name at the beginning of the code snippet to provide a name for the procedure. For example, beginning the same procedure displayed above with #NAME help_func would generate the following:

```
FUNCTION HELP_FUNC     &&  m.order VALID
HELP
```

#NOREAD

`#NOREAD [PLAIN]`

When used, the generated source code will contain no READ statement. This is useful for creating simple dialog screens where no editing is involved. Using the PLAIN keyword will create a source-code file with @ ... SAY/GET/EDIT commands only.

#READCLAUSES

`#READCLAUSES` *`clauses`*

The valid clauses are:

```
TIMEOUT
SAVE
OBJECT
NOMOUSE
COLOR
```

All clauses must be contained on the same line. See the READ command in chapter 2 for more information on READ clauses.

#REDEFINE

The screen source-code file contains the commands to define each window involved in the screen set. By default, the window definition code is inside an IF ... ENDIF statement that checks for the existence of the window before defining it. Placing the #REDEFINE directive in the screen will cause the Screen Generator to generate the source code without the IF ... ENDIF statements.

#SECTION

```
#SECTION 1 | 2
```

If the screen set contains an environment setting and the Open Files option is checked, the code required to restore the environment is generated before any setup code. Use the #SECTION 1 directive to have all setup code following the directive to be placed before the environment code. Also, you must include a #SECTION 1 statement to include a PARAMETER statement for a screen program. The #SECTION 2 directive forces all code following the directive to be generated after the window definition code and before the @ ... SAY/GET code.

#TRAN SNIPPET ONLY

When transporting screens across different platforms, you can use the #TRAN SNIPPET ONLY directive to force the transporter to move code snippets only for any updated objects. See chapter 12 for more information on transporting FoxPro screens across different platforms.

#WCLAUSES

```
#WCLAUSES clause1, clause2, ...
```

Any DEFINE WINDOW clause can be specified with #WCLAUSES and will be added to the window definition code of the screen in which the directive is in. This directive is evaluated only when the Define Windows option is checked in the Generate dialog.

#WNAME

```
#WNAME expC
```

If no window name is specified in the Name option of the Screen Layout, FoxPro provides a unique name for the window. Using the #WNAME directive will replace all occurrences of *expC* with the unique window name.

A Screen Builder example

This section shows how to create a custom screen set for a database of high school students. Figure 6-21 shows an example of how the finished entry screens will look. The Screen Builder makes it easy to create screen layouts by providing a "view screen" that lets you move information around, add prompts and boxes, and add other embellishments without

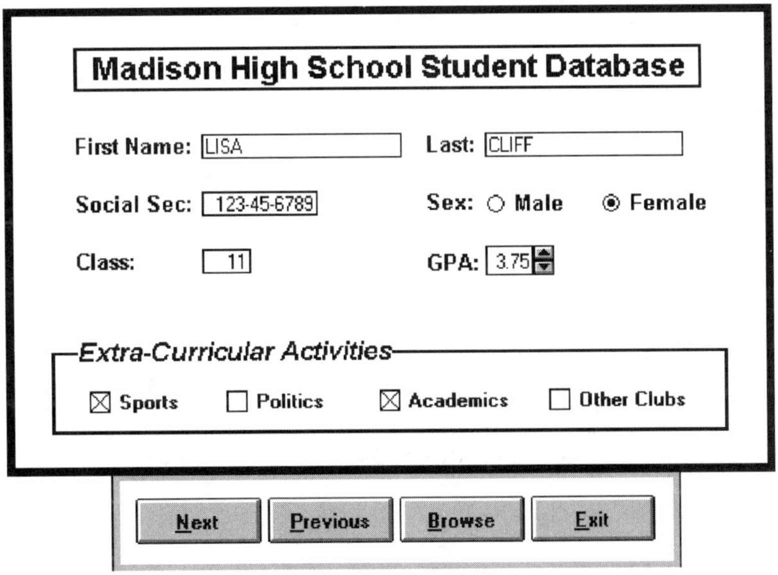

6-21 A screen set created with the Screen Builder.

using the normal FoxPro programming commands. In addition, you can place controls (push buttons, radio buttons, pop-up menus, check buttons, spinners, or lists) and graphical images on the screen. To create the screen in the next section, follow these steps:

1. Enter the Screen Builder and load the fields.
2. Move the fields around and change the prompts.
3. Attach formatting statements to the fields.
4. Create sections that use push buttons and check boxes.
5. Generate the Screen Code file.

The database to be used in the Screen Builder is MADISON.DBF. Create this file with the following structure:

Field Name	Type	Width	Dec
FNAME	Character	15	
LNAME	Character	15	
SOC_SEC	Numeric	9	
GPA	Numeric	4	
SEX	Numeric	1	
CLASS	Numeric	4	
SPORTS	Logical	1	
POLIT	Logical	1	
ACAD	Logical	1	
OTHER	Logical	1	

Make sure that this file is open before entering the Screen Builder. Remember that you can enter the Screen Builder from either the File menu or by entering the commands in the Command window. For this example type CREATE SCREEN in the Command window and press Enter. A screen design window titled Untitled.SCX appears, and the Screen and Object menus will be added to the menu bar.

Designing the screen

Loading fields Because this example creates a data entry screen, it begins with the command that loads some or all fields from the current file. To load the first six fields in the database:

1. Choose the Quick Screen option from the Screen menu.
2. Check the Fields... box.
3. From the dialog box that appears, choose the first six fields from the database by moving to the field with the ↓ key and then pressing Enter.
4. The fields selected should now be: Lname, Fname, Soc_Sec, GPA, Sex, and Class.
5. Choose OK to exit the dialog box, and then OK again to exit the Quick Screen box.

The six fields should now be loaded into the top left corner of the screen. Now move the field and text objects to the center of the screen. Draw a marquee around all of the objects and use the arrow keys or the mouse to move the objects.

Changing and adding text The next step is to change the text prompts in front of each field. To enter the first prompt:

1. Click on the Text tool in the screen toolbox.
2. Position the text pointer over the Fname text object and click.
3. Type First Name:. Use the Delete key to remove the other characters.
4. Click on the selection pointer tool to deselect the object.

Type in the rest of the text so that all prompts reflect those of Fig. 6-22. Remember, if a text object isn't placed exactly where you want, you can select it and drag it to the correct spot.

Now add a text heading to the screen. Click on the Text tool and place the cursor near the top center of the screen. Click the mouse to activate the text object and type in MADI-

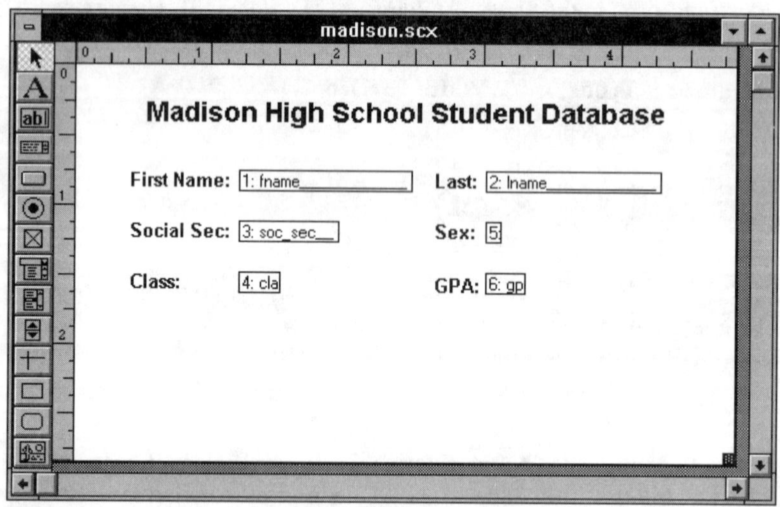

6-22 The screen with modified text objects.

SON HIGH SCHOOL STUDENT DATABASE. Click on the selection pointer tool to fix the object. You can easily change the font of the object by selecting the object and then selecting Font from the Object menu. Select an appropriate font, size, and style for the text. The font used for the heading in Fig. 6-22 is Arial, 14-point bold.

Placing a box on the screen To place the box around the heading, click on the rectangle line tool and position the mouse pointer above and to the left of the MADISON HIGH SCHOOL STUDENT DATABASE heading. Click the mouse and drag the box down and to the right, surrounding the area with a single-line box. Release the mouse button to fix the box object. To change the box to a different pen style, select Pen from the Object menu and select the desired pen.

Formatting the fields to be edited You can specify data editing options for each editing object on the screen. This places restrictions on what the user can enter for that particular field or memory variable.

The first format placed in the example is to restrict the first and last names to all uppercase letters. To start, double-click on the Fname field object (not the text label). Choose the Format... push button. From the checklist of editing options, choose To Upper Case. Finish by pressing OK to exit the Format... options, and then OK again to exit the screen Field dialog. Repeat this step with the Lname field.

The format for Social Security Number is entered as a template of 999-99-9999. The 9 forces the entry to be numeric, and the hyphens act as a "mask" in the entry area. See the @ ... SAY/GET section in chapter 2 for a list of all format template options. Double-click on the Soc_Sec field object. Place the cursor in the Format... text box and enter 999-99-9999. Finish by pressing OK twice.

Now format the Class field object to display a message in the status bar when the cursor enters the field. Double-click on the Class field object. Choose the Message... option. Change the radio button to Expression. In the text box enter "Type a year between 1956 and 1998" (include the quotes). Press Ctrl-Tab to exit. Finish by pressing OK through both screens.

Adding editing controls First add a radio button control for the SEX field. A radio button is a good choice for a Sex field because the value can only be one of two choices (male or female). Remove the SEX field object by selecting it and pressing the Delete key. Select the Radio Button tool from the toolbox. Position the mouse pointer over the screen (near the Sex text object) and click the mouse. Once the screen Radio Button dialog appears, follow the steps listed below to create the object.

1. Enter two radio button prompts: Male and Female.
2. Enter the expression SEX in the Variable text box.
3. Select OK to save the radio button object.

Now add some check box controls for the SPORTS, POLIT, ACAD and OTHER fields. These fields have been defined as Logical and can have one of two values, true or false. Select the Check Box tool from the toolbox. Position the mouse pointer over the screen at bottom left and click the mouse. Once the screen Check Box dialog appears, follow the steps listed below to create the object.

1. Enter the check box prompt as Sports.
2. Enter the expression SPORTS in the Variable text box.
3. Select OK to save the check box object.

Repeat the steps above for the POLIT, ACAD and OTHER fields. Place all four check boxes left to right along the bottom of the screen. When all check boxes have been placed, enter a text label of Extra-Curricular Activities centered above the check box objects. Finally, add a box around the objects and position the Extra-Curricular Activities: over the label. See Fig. 6-23 for an example.

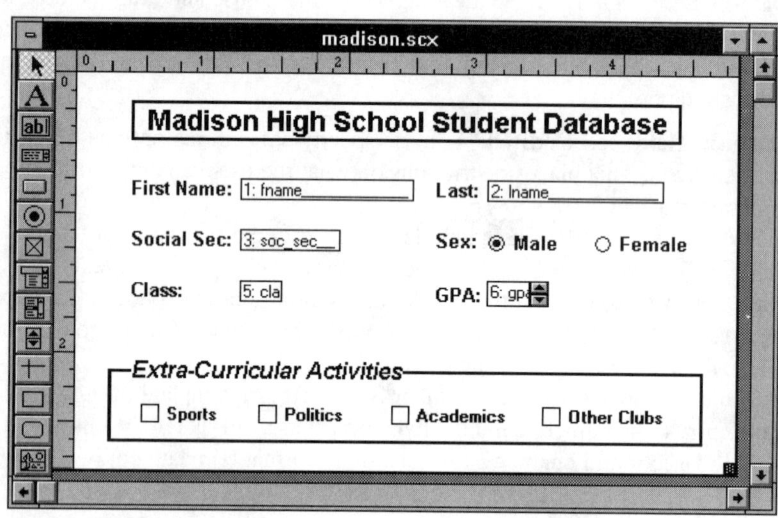

6-23 Controls on the screen.

Now change the GPA field object to a spinner control. A spinner control allows you to control the value of a numeric expression. Remove the GPA field object. Select the Spinner tool from the tool bar. Position the mouse pointer near the GPA text label and click the mouse. Once the screen Spinner dialog appears, follow the steps listed below to create the object.

1. Enter the expression GPA in the Variable text box.
2. Enter a value of 1 in the Minimum text box, a value of 5 in the Maximum text box, and a value of .25 in the Increments by text box.
3. Select OK to save the spinner object.

Changing the screen attributes When you create a FoxPro screen layout, the default window style is a user-defined window with a title bar. Follow the steps listed below to create a window with no title bar.

1. Select Screen Layout from the Screen menu.
2. Select the Window Style button.
3. From the Window Style dialog, change the border to Double and turn off (uncheck) all Attributes settings.
4. Select OK to save the window style.

From the Screen Layout dialog, enter the name Students in the Name text box. Change the Horizontal position to 87 and the Vertical position to 26.

To ensure that the MADISON database is open when the screen code is executed, use the Setup code to enter the commands open the database.

1. Choose Code... from the Screen Layout dialog. This activates the Screen Code dialog.
2. Select Screen Setup Code... and then OK. This activates the Setup code window where you can place initial commands.
3. In the editing window, type the command USE Madison.
4. Save the Setup code by selecting Close from the File menu, pressing Ctrl-W, or double-clicking on the window control bar.

Saving the screen

To save the MADISON.SCX file:

1. Choose Save from the File menu, press Ctrl-W, or double-click on the window control bar.
2. When the Save As dialog appears, enter the name MADISON in the text box. It isn't necessary to enter the .SCX extension of the screen file name.
3. Select OK to save the screen. FoxPro will now ask you if you want to save the en vironment. Select No.

Creating a second screen

When executed, the MADISON screen created above will allow the user to edit and view certain fields of the Madison database. Now create a second screen that, when combined with the editing screen, will allow the user to move the record pointer through the database and also close the editing screen.

The second screen is called a "control" screen; it contains controls for moving through the database, without being specific to any database. By putting the controls on a separate screen, the control screen can be used with other editing screens.

Setup The control screen panel is named CONTROL.SCX. To create it, enter CREATE SCREEN CONTROL from the Command window. Follow the steps listed below to setup the second screen.

1. Select Screen Layout... from the Screen menu and enter Control in the Name text box.
2. Select Window Style... and change the border to Double. Turn off all Attributes settings. Select OK to save the style settings.
3. Size the screen by entering a value of 50 in the Height box and 310 in the Width box. For the position of the screen, enter a value of 163 in the Horizontal box and 306 in the Vertical Box.
4. Select OK to save the screen layout. The screen design window change to reflect the new settings.

Controls The controls used in the second screen will be normal push buttons. Follow the steps listed below to create the controls for the push buttons for the control screen.

1. Select the Push Button tool from the toolbox. Place the mouse pointer over the screen and click.
2. In the screen Push Buttons dialog enter the following prompts:

```
\<Next
\<Previous
\<Browse
\<Exit
```

3. Assign the push button action to the variable m.control by entering the variable name in the Variable text box.
4. Select the Valid... check box to activate the code snippet dialog. Change the snippet to a Procedure and enter the following code:

```
DO CASE
     CASE m.control = 1
       SKIP
     CASE m.control = 2
       SKIP -1
     CASE m.control = 3
       BROWSE NORMAL
     CASE m.control = 4
       CLEAR READ
ENDCASE
SHOW GETS
```

5. Save the code snippet and select OK at the Push Button dialog to save the control attributes.

m.control is the name of a numeric memory variable that holds the user's selection. If the user chooses the first push button (Next Record), m.control is one, and so on. If the variable has been declared as a character, it's equivalent to the prompt chosen. If the variable has not been declared before the screen is run, FoxPro creates it as a numeric variable with a value of 0.

Push buttons default to being laid out horizontally, although you can choose a Vertical orientation instead. You can also change the spacing between the buttons. To define a default push button, enter \! before the prompt. See chapter 2 for more information on the commands used in the code snippet.

See also Chapter 2, FoxPro Commands

Generating code

Once the screens have been designed, you must generate a program that can run them. In this example, the two screens are generated into one program named MADISON.SPR. To generate the code for MADISON.SPR, do the following:

1. Save the CONTROL.SCX screen.
2. Open the MADISON.SCX file.

3. Choose Generate... from the Program menu. The screen list should contain both the MADISON and CONTROL screens.
4. Under Generated Code Options, turn off the Open Files check box. The MADISON.SCX screen contains the necessary commands to open the database.
5. The output file is given the same name as the first screen file, with an extension of .SPR. The Generate... dialog should now match that of Fig. 6-24.
6. Select the Generate push button to create the source-code file.

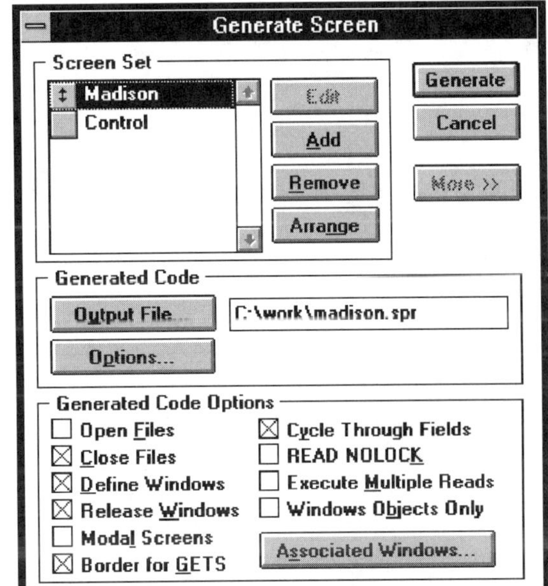

6-24 Generate dialog.

The program that has been generated, MADISON.SPR, contains all of the directives to display the screens and activate the GETs created in the Screen Builder. Run the source-code file by entering the command DO MADISON.SPR in the command window.

The screen code

The source code that is generated from the previous example can be found in the help file disk included with the book.

7
Using the Menu Builder

You can use the FoxPro Menu Builder to create custom menus that replace the System menu and also remove the need to write programs to create a menu system.

The first section of this chapter details the Menu Builder menu and layout operations. Following that is a simple exercise that shows how to create a custom menu using the Menu Builder.

What the Menu Builder does

The Menu Builder provides a template that is used to design a menu structure to replace the FoxPro System menu. FoxPro stores all menu information in a database file with an extension of .MNX and uses the menu database to generate a source code file for you to run. The end result is a program that's written for you.

When a program is generated from a menu database, the resulting code is a program that contains the following:

- Setup code
- Menu definition commands
- Cleanup code
- Code-snippet functions and procedures

Because the source code generated from a menu file doesn't contain any special commands that you as a programmer or developer cannot use, you don't have to use the Menu Builder to take advantage of FoxPro's powerful command language. However, if you have spent many hours laboring away at a custom menu system, you'll find that you can accomplish the same task using the Menu Builder in a fraction of the time.

Starting the Menu Builder

You can enter the Menu Builder in two ways:

- From the Command window, issue either CREATE MENU (to create a new menu) or MODIFY MENU (to modify an existing menu), followed by the file name of the menu.
- From the File menu, choose New... to start a new menu, or Open... to open an existing menu.

When you open a menu, a menu design window will appear (see Fig. 7-1) and the Menu menu pad is added to the main menu.

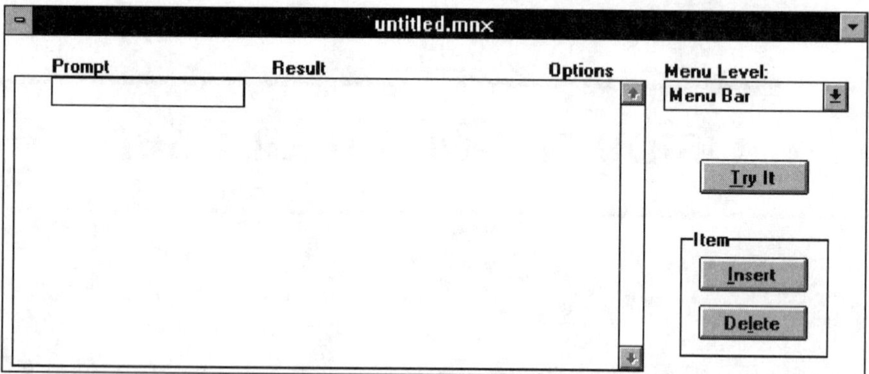

7-1 A menu design window.

Designing a custom menu

You can use a menu template to specify the levels of the menu. When you create a menu template, the first level of prompts (top to bottom on the layout) define the system menu pads (left to right on the screen). These are the Menu Bar prompts. Lower-level prompts assigned to each pad determine the options to be displayed in the pop-up when a menu pad is selected.

Menu prompts

The text assigned to a menu prompt determines what is displayed for each menu option. To assign a prompt, place the cursor in the Prompt text box and enter the text.

Hot keys can be assigned to each menu prompt by prefacing the desired hot key letter with \<. At the Menu Bar level, you activate hot keys by pressing the Alt key and then the hot key letter. Once a pop-up is activated, you can activate options that have hot keys by entering the option's hot key letter.

Menu results

Each menu option must have a result. A result determines what action is taken when a menu prompt is selected. At the Menu Bar level, the following results are available:

Command Enter a valid FoxPro command that will be executed when the pad is selected.

Pad Name Enter a pad name for the menu option. Pad names can be user defined, or a FoxPro pad name. If no pad name is specified, FoxPro will give the menu pad option a unique name. Specifying a pad name allows you to control menu behavior with commands such as ON SELECTION PAD.

Submenu Use Submenu to define the options that will be displayed in a pop-up when the pad is selected. Select Edit to define the submenu options.

Proc. Create a procedure that will be executed when the pad is selected. Select Create to edit the procedure. If the procedure has already been created, the option will be displayed as Edit.

The options available for submenus are:

Command Enter a valid FoxPro command that will be executed when the pad is selected.

Bar # Enter a user-defined or valid FoxPro menu bar number. Each option of the default FoxPro menu has an associated bar number. To emulate a FoxPro function, specify its bar number. If the bar number is user defined, you must enter the appropriate ON SELECTION BAR command in the cleanup code of the menu. FoxPro menu bar numbers can be found in help file included on disk with the book.

Submenu Use Submenu to define the options that will be displayed in a pop-up when the pad is selected. Select Edit to define the submenu options. Since this will be a submenu of a submenu, the first level will be displayed with a right triangle. Selecting that item will display this submenu.

Proc. Allows you to create a procedure that will be executed when the pad is selected. Select Create to edit the procedure. If the procedure has already been created, the option will be displayed as Edit.

See also ON SELECTION PAD, ON SELECTION BAR

Menu prompt options

The Options check box to the right of each menu item displays the dialog shown in Fig. 7-2, which lets you determine certain characteristics of the menu option. The following options are available:

Comment Enter any comments for the menu option. Comments are not included in the resulting source code file.

Shortcut... Displays the dialog shown in Fig. 7-3. This allows you to enter a set of keystrokes that can be used to select the menu pad. At the Menu Pad level, the keyboard shortcut should be defined to match any assigned hot key. For example, if the Menu Pad option was defined with a hot key of R, the key label should be entered as Alt-R. Submenu options can be assigned shortcut keys of any combination. Any text entered in the Key Text text box will be displayed to the right of the menu option. The Key Text information is ignored at the Menu Bar level.

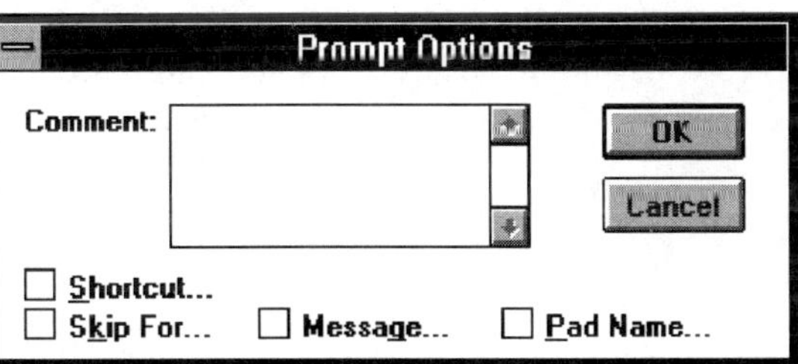

7-2 Menu prompt options dialog.

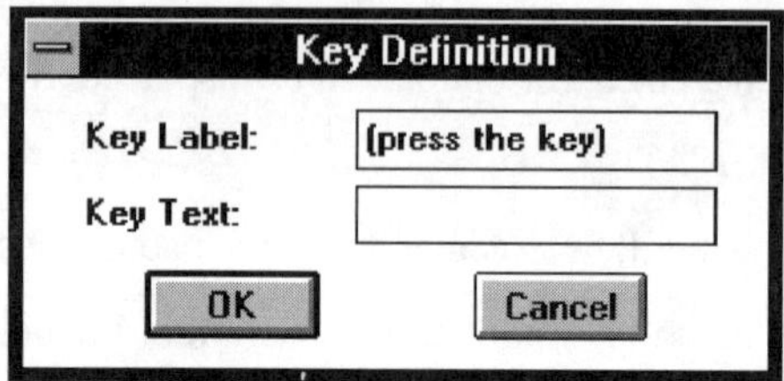

7-3 Menu prompt key shortcut dialog.

Skip For... When selected, the Expression Builder is activated. The Skip For expression must equate to a logical value (true or false). If a Skip For expression is assigned to a menu pad option, that option will be disabled whenever the expression evaluates to true (.T.). Menu pads can also be disabled using the SET SKIP OF command.

Mark... When selected, a character dialog appears. Select a character to be displayed to the left of the option when the option's SET MARK OF setting is true. See chapter 3 for more information on the SET MARK command.

Pad Name...\Bar #... At the Menu Bar level, use Pad Name to assign a pad name to the menu option if the result is Command, Submenu or Procedure. Pad names can be user defined, or a FoxPro pad name. Assigning a pad name allows you to control menu behavior with commands such as ON SELECTION PAD. At the submenu level, use Bar # to assign a valid FoxPro menu bar number. FoxPro menu bar numbers can be found in help file included on disk with the book.

See also SET SKIP, SET MARK

Try It

Selecting Try It will replace the FoxPro System menu with a replica of the items contained in the menu template. Selecting a menu option will display the assigned result in the Try It dialog. Select Done to restore the system menu and return back to the menu builder.

Inserting and deleting menu prompts

Use the Insert and Delete buttons on the menu template to insert and delete options from the menu design. To insert a new option, place the cursor at the desired position and select Insert. A new prompt line appears with the text "New Item." To delete a menu prompt, place the cursor on the desired prompt and select Delete. If the menu result is a submenu, FoxPro will ask if you want to delete the associated submenu.

The Menu menu

When a menu template is opened, a Menu option is added to the system menu. The Menu menu shown in Fig. 7-4 contains the tools necessary to define the placement of the menu, and for entering code snippets.

General Options...
Menu Bar Options...

Try It Ctrl+T

Insert Item Ctrl+I
Delete Item Ctrl+E

Quick Menu

7-4 The Menu menu.

General Options...

The dialog shown in Fig. 7-5 is used to define a menu procedure, define setup and cleanup code, and to specify the location of the menu in the system menu.

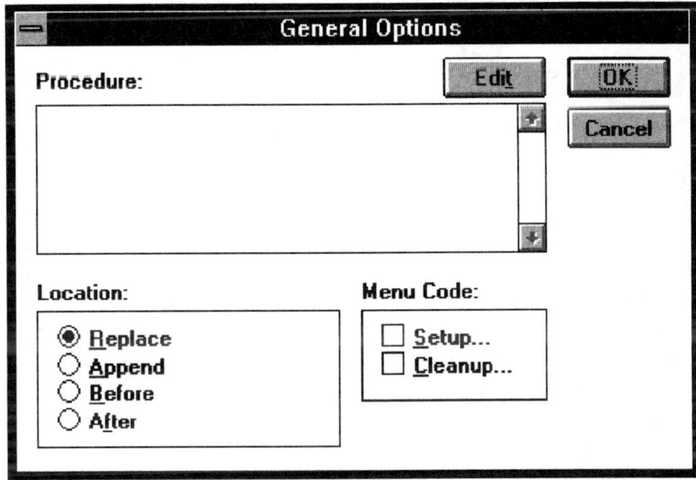

7-5 Menu General Options dialog.

Procedure Enter a procedure that will be executed when any option from the menu is selected. Select the Edit button to open a full editing window.

Location This determines the location of the custom menu relative to the FoxPro system menu.

> **Replace** Replaces the FoxPro system menu with the contents of the user-defined menu.
> **Append** Adds the user-defined menu to the end of the FoxPro system menu.
> **Before** Places the user-defined menu before a system menu option.
> **After** Places the user-defined menu after a system menu option.

Setup... Opens an editing window for entering menu setup code. Select OK from the General Options dialog to access the editing window. Menu setup code is placed at the beginning of the generated source code file and can be used to set up the necessary environment before the menu structure is defined.

Cleanup... Opens an editing window for entering menu cleanup code. Select OK from the General Options dialog to access the editing window. Menu cleanup code is placed after all menu definition commands in the generated source code file and can be used to enter any ON SELECTION type commands. Similar to the Screen Builder, you can also enter user-defined procedures for the menu.

Menu Options...

This option will change according to the level at which the menu layout is at. At the Menu Bar level the option is Menu Options. If the menu layout is at the submenu level, the option will contain the pad name of the submenu. All information entered in the dialog is relative to the current menu level—either the Menu Bar or a submenu of the Menu Bar. The dialog shown in Fig. 7-6 is displayed.

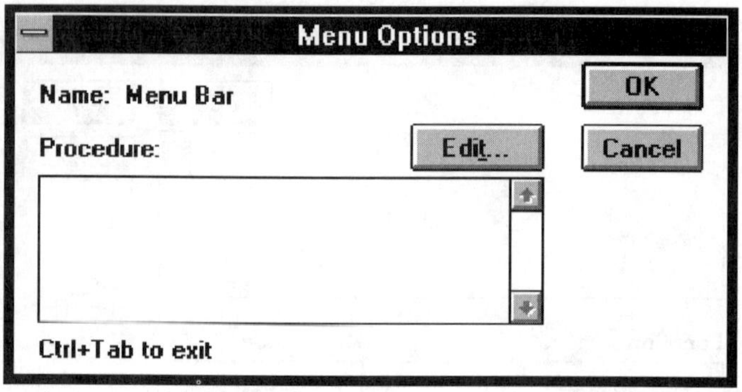

7-6 Menu Menu Options dialog.

Name Displays the pad name of the menu prompt that's currently selected. If the name is Menu Bar, options are being defined for all pads of the menu and the name cannot be changed. At the submenu level, the pad name is displayed and all options in the dialog are relative to that pad. The name can be changed at the submenu level.

Procedure Enter a procedure that will be executed when an option from the menu pop-up is selected. Select the Edit... button to open a full editing window.

Try It

The Try It function is detailed in the Menu prompt options section above.

Shortcut key Ctrl-T

Insert Item

The Insert Item function is detailed in the Menu prompt options section above.

Shortcut key Ctrl-I

Delete Item

The Delete Item function is detailed in the Menu Prompt Options section above.

Shortcut key Ctrl-E

Quick Menu

This option creates an exact duplicate of the FoxPro System menu, with the exception of the Run menu. Quick Menu is only available when the menu template is empty.

Saving the menu

Once the menu design is complete, you must save the menu file. Do this by selecting Save from the File menu, pressing Ctrl-W, or double-clicking on the window control bar.

Generating the menu code

Now that the menu design is complete, you must create a source-code file. The source-code file is a FoxPro program that, when executed, will replace the FoxPro system menu with your customized menu.

FoxPro uses a FoxPro program (GENMENU.PRG) to create a source-code file from a menu file. The resulting file contains:

- FoxPro setup code
- User-defined setup code
- Menu definition code
- User-defined cleanup code
- FoxPro cleanup code
- User-defined procedures and functions
- FoxPro-defined functions

To generate a source-code file, select Generate... from the Program menu to display the Generate Menu dialog shown in Fig. 7-7. This option is only available when a Menu Builder window is active and frontmost.

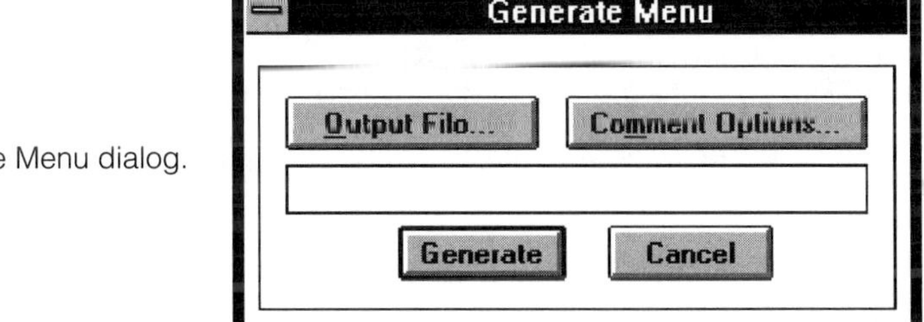

7-7 Generate Menu dialog.

Specifying the output

By default, the menu code file name is the name of the menu template with an extension of .MPR. You can change the name of the output file by entering it in the text box, or select Output File... to activate the Save As dialog. If you prefer to save the menu code as a program, change the extension from .MPR to .PRG.

The menu code that is eventually created contains a number of commenting sections (provided by the Menu Generator program) and information on who generated the source-code file. The style of this information can be changed by selecting Comment Options..., which displays the dialog shown in Fig. 7-8.

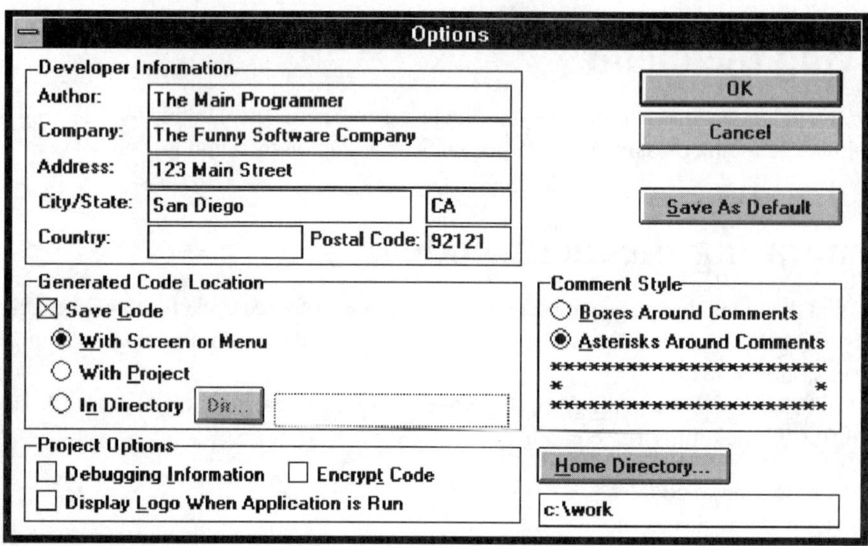

7-8 Comment Options dialog.

Developer Information The text entered in the Author, Company, Address, City, State, and Zip text boxes is contained at the top of the source-code file.

Comment Style Selecting Box Around Comments will cause the Screen Generator to place solid boxes around the comments that are generated. Selecting Asterisks Around Comments will cause the Screen Generator to place asterisks (*) around the comments that are generated. This won't affect any comments that you may have entered into any screen code snippets.

Home Directory If a drive and directory are entered in the text box, all code that's generated to open database files (the USE command) will contain a path relative to the Home Directory setting and the location of the databases in the environment settings.

Save as Default When checked, all settings specified in the dialog will be saved to the resource file if OK is selected.

Select OK to save the information in this dialog, or Cancel to discard and return to the Generate dialog.

Creating the menu-code file

When all options have been set, select OK to begin generating the source-code file. A progress indicator is displayed while the file is being created.

The Menu Generator program

FoxPro uses a program, GENMENU.PRG, to read the contents of a menu file and create a source code file. The name and location of the Menu Generator are stored in the system memory variable _genmenu.

Because the menu generator program is written in FoxPro, it can be customized to your needs. If you change the name of the Menu Generator program, be sure to change to the value of _genmenu, either in the CONFIG.FP file or at the Command window, before attempting to generate a source code file.

See also Diskette Appendix E.

Menu Generator directives

Menu generator directives are used to control the way that the Menu Generator program evaluates certain expressions in the menu file. All Menu Generator directives must be placed at the beginning of the menu setup code.

#INSERT

```
#INSERT filename
```

When used, the contents of *filename* are inserted into the source code file at the point that the directive is encountered. The specified file must be an ASCII text file and exist along the FoxPro path. If the file cannot be located, a comment is added to the menu code at the #INSERT location, specifying that the Menu Generator could not locate the file.

#NAME

```
#NAME snippet name
```

This is used to assign a name to a code-snippet procedure. By default, all code-snippet procedures are given a unique name by the Menu Generator.

```
FUNCTION _qea0tx99s
REPORT FORM names TO PRINT
```

Use the #NAME directive followed by a valid snippet name at the beginning of the code snippet to provide a name for the procedure. For example, beginning the same procedure displayed above with #NAME repo_func would generate the following:

```
FUNCTION REPO_MENU
REPORT FORM names TO PRINT
```

A Menu Builder example

This section shows how to create a custom menu to accompany the screen built in chapter 7 for Madison High School. Figure 7-9 shows an example of how the finished menu will look. The Menu Builder makes it easy to create custom menus for moving around data and selecting tasks. To create the menu in the next section, follow these steps:

1. Enter the Menu Builder.
2. Create the menu bar.
3. Create a submenu for each menu option.
4. Assign commands and procedures to be run for each pop-up option.
5. Generate the Menu Code file.

Data Maintenance Printouts Reports Exit
Add Records
Edit a Record
Delete a Record
Browse

7-9 A menu created with the Menu Builder.

The database to be used in the Menu Builder is MADISON.DBF, the same file used in the previous chapter. If you haven't created it yet, do so with the following structure:

Field Name	Type	Width	Dec
FNAME	Character	15	
LNAME	Character	15	
SOC_SEC	Numeric	9	
GPA	Numeric	4	
SEX	Numeric	1	
CLASS	Numeric	4	
SPORTS	Logical	1	
POLIT	Logical	1	
ACAD	Logical	1	
OTHER	Logical	1	

Designing the menu

Defining menu pads Because this example creates a menu bar with submenus, the first step is to assign prompts and results to each pad in the main menu.

1. At the Prompt box, enter \<Data Maintenance. The \< causes the letter D to be a hot key.
2. Press the ↓ key to get to the next prompt area. Leave Submenu as the Result default, because this pad brings up a submenu pop-up. Also, don't go into the Create Result section, because the pop-up is created in the next section of this exercise.
3. Enter the other three prompts: \<Printouts, \<Reports, and \<Exit.
4. At this point, the Menu Builder screen should look like Fig. 7-10.

In the example above, all four results should be set to Submenu.

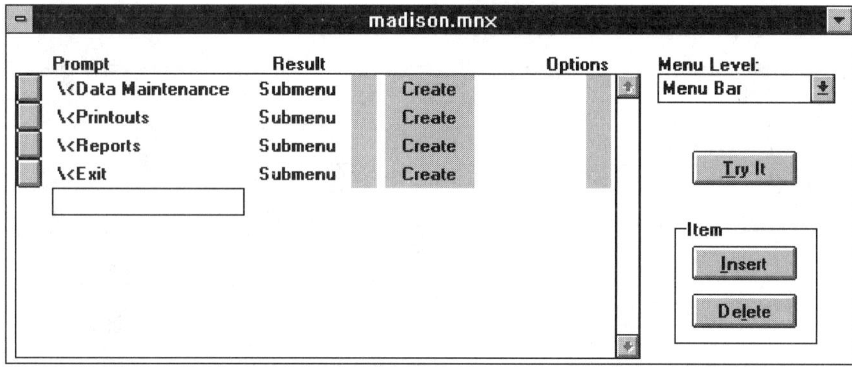

8-10 The menu with the menu bars entered.

Defining a submenu option The next step is to set up the pop-up menu for the first pad, Data Maintenance. To enter the first pop-up:

1. Click on the submenu Create button for the Data Maintenance option. It now shows an area for designing the first pop-up.
2. At the Prompt box, enter \<Add Records.
3. Leave Command as the Result default, because this pad runs a command.
4. In the Result box, type in the command APPEND BLANK. When this pop-up bar is chosen, the APPEND BLANK command will be executed.

Defining a submenu procedure The next step is to write a procedure that's run every time that Edit a Record is chosen from the Data Maintenance pop-up.

1. Press the ↓ key to get to the next prompt.
2. At the Prompt box, enter \<Edit a Record.
3. Change the Result to Proc.
4. Now click on Create, which brings up a text area for entering a procedure. Type in the following procedure:

```
ACTIVATE SCREEN
CLEAR
ACCEPT "Enter a Last Name to Search for: " TO m.lname
LOCATE FOR UPPER(Lname) = UPPER(m.lname)
IF FOUND()
   DO Madison.SPR
ELSE
   WAIT WINDOW "No match found"
ENDIF
```

5. Press Ctrl-W when done.
6. Press the ↓ key and enter the third prompt \<Delete a Record.
7. Leave Command as the default, and in the Result box type in the command DELETE.
8. Press the ↓ key and enter the fourth prompt \<Browse.
9. Leave Command as the default, and in the Result box, type in the command BROWSE.
10. At this point the Menu Builder screen should look like Fig. 7-11.
11. Return to the menu bar level by selecting Menu Bar from the Menu Level pop-up.

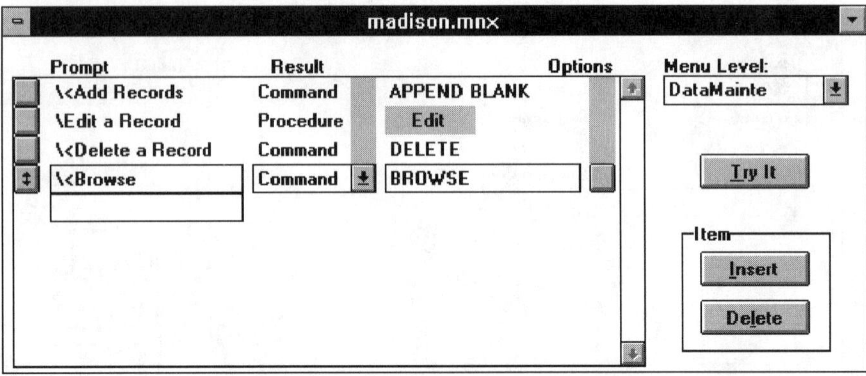

7-11 The menu with submenus added.

Setting up the Printouts submenus Setting up the Printout and Submenu pop-ups are essentially the same step as that of Data Maintenance. To enter the Printouts pop-up:

1. Move to the Printouts option and click on the submenu Create option.
2. At the prompt box, enter the following prompts and results:

Prompt	Result	Enter
\<Mailing Labels	Command	LABEL FORM Madison TO PRINT
\<Listing	Proc.	
		ACTIVATE SCREEN
		CLEAR
		LIST Fname,Lname,Class,GPA
		WAIT

3. Return to the menu bar level by selecting Menu Bar from the Menu Level pop-up.

Setting up the Reports submenus The Report submenu takes advantage of a few of the options. To enter the Report pop-up:

1. Move to the Reports option and click on the submenu Create option.
2. At the prompt box, enter the following prompts and results:

Prompt	Result	Enter
\<Summary	Command	REPORT FORM MADSUM TO PRINT
\<Detail	Command	REPORT FORM MADDET TO PRINT

3. Click on the Summary Options check box to activate the Prompt Options dialog.
4. Choose the Shortcut... check box.
5. At the Key Label box, press Alt-S and then choose OK. Choose OK again to exit the dialog box. When the menu is run, you can choose the Summary bar with either the S hot key or the Alt-S shortcut key.
6. Click on the Detail Options check box to activate the Prompt Options dialog..
7. Choose the Skip For... check box.
8. Enter the following logical expression: !FILE("MADDET.FRX").

9. Choose OK, and then choose OK again to exit the dialog. The Detail bar will be disabled if the report form MADDET.FRX is not found.
10. Return to the menu bar level by selecting Menu Bar from the Menu Level pop-up.

Defining the Exit option The Exit option is simply a command that quits FoxPro.

1. Move to the Exit submenu option and change the Result to Command.
2. At the Result box, enter QUIT. The option should look like this:

Prompt	**Result**	**Enter**
\<Quit	Command	QUIT

Saving the menu

To save the MADISON.MNX file:

1. Choose Save from the File menu, press Ctrl-W, or double-click on the window control bar.
2. When the Save As dialog appears enter the name MADISON in the text box. It is not necessary to enter the .MNX extension of the menu file name.
3. Select OK to save the screen.

Generating code

Once the menu has been designed, you must generate a program that defines the menu and displays it. To generate the code for MADISON.MPR, do the following:

1. Choose Generate... from the Program menu.
2. The output file is given the same name as the menu file, with an extension of .MPR. The Generate... dialog is shown in Fig. 7-7.
3. Select the Generate push button to create the source-code file.

The program that has been generated, MADISON.MPR, contains all of the commands to define and display the menu. Run the source-code file by entering the command DO MADISON.MPR in the command window.

The menu code

The source code that is generated from the previous example can be found in the help file disk included with the book.

8
Using the RQBE window

The first SQL (structured query language) command to be added to FoxPro is the SELECT command, which was introduced with version 2.0. SELECT is a very powerful command that can take the place of many FoxPro commands. For instance, one SELECT command can perform the function of five commands such as USE, SET FILTER TO, SET INDEX, BROWSE, and SET RELATION.

The SELECT command is quite complex, and it takes awhile to learn all of its clauses and features. However, FoxPro has a window which allows you to easily put together the pieces of the command. This RQBE (Relational Query By Example) window lets you set filters, the FOR conditions, the output format (browse, display, report format, labels, etc.), index order, and relations.

The first section of this chapter details the RQBE window and its options. Following that is a simple exercise that shows how to create a custom query.

What the RQBE window does

The RQBE window provides a template that is used to create a SELECT statement, which can then be used to query one or more databases. The results returned by the query are dependent on user-defined criteria. FoxPro stores all query information in a file with an extension of .QPR

None of the source code generated from a query file contains any special commands that you as a programmer or developer cannot use, so you don't have to use the RQBE window to take advantage of FoxPro's powerful SQL command set.

Starting the RQBE window

You can open an RQBE window in two ways:

- From the Command window, issue either CREATE QUERY (to create a new query) or MODIFY QUERY (to modify an existing query), followed by the file name of the query.
- From the File menu, choose New... to start a new query, or Open... to open an existing query.

If you're starting a new query and no database is selected, the Open File dialog will appear, prompting you to select a database for the query. When you open a query, the RQBE window appears (see Fig. 8-1) and the RQBE menu pad (see Fig. 8-2) is added to the main menu.

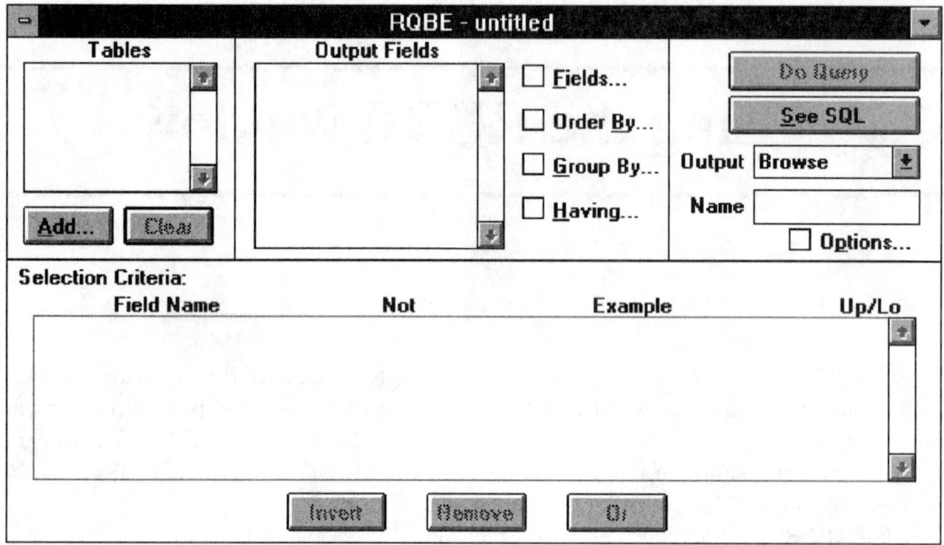

8-1 An RQBE window.

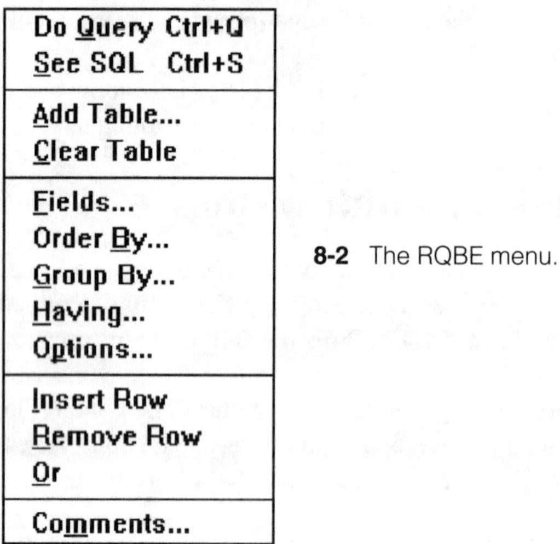

8-2 The RQBE menu.

Designing a query

Databases

The database files that are involved in the query are listed in the Databases list. To query data in multiple databases, use the Add option to activate the Open File dialog, where you can select additional databases.

If more than one database is involved in the query, the nature of the relation between the files must be specified. When more than one database is added to the query, the RQBE Join Condition dialog, shown in Fig. 8-3, appears. Follow these steps to join two or more databases:

1. Select, from the left pop-up, a field from the database that was just added.
2. From the center pop-up, select a comparison operator. These are discussed later in the chapter.
3. From the right pop-up, select a field from another database in the query that is common to the field selected in the left pop-up.
4. Turn the Ignore Upper/Lower Case checkbox on if you don't want the join to be case sensitive, where upper and lowercase values are respected.
5. Select OK to save the join condition.

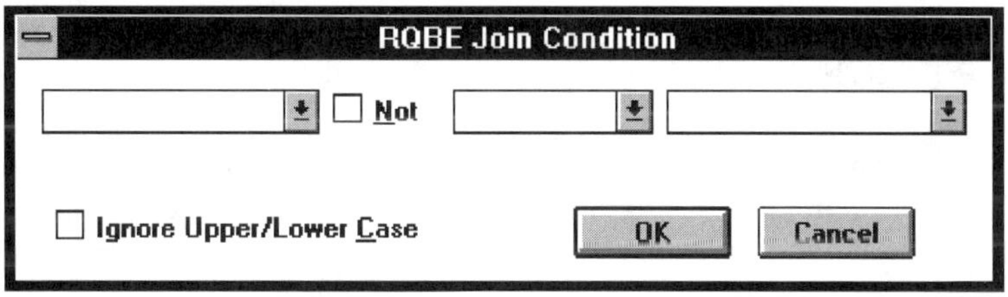

RQBE Join Condition

Not

Ignore Upper/Lower Case

OK

Cancel

8-3 RQBE Join Condition dialog.

When two databases are joined, their join condition appears in the Selection Criteria box at the bottom of the Query window. To change a join condition, simply select it from the list and change the value.

Use the Clear option to remove a database from the query. If all databases are cleared, all other options of the query are also cleared.

Output fields

This list displays the fields that will be included in the query result file. Use the double-arrow mover control to change the order of the fields. To change the Output Fields list, select the Fields... check box, which displays the Select Fields dialog shown in Fig. 8-4.

To include a field in the output, select the desired field from the Table Fields list and move it to the Selected Output list by highlighting the desired field and selecting Move. Mouse users can select a field by double-clicking on the desired field.

FoxPro functions and expressions can also be part of the query output. To choose a function, activate the Functions pop-up and choose one of the listed functions (all functions except COUNT() can be performed on numeric fields only). An alternate method for entering functions is to move to the text box in the Functions/Expressions box and enter the function. To place the function in the Selected Output list, choose Move. You cannot select memo or general fields for the output. The following functions can be included in the query output:

COUNT()
SUM()
AVG()
MIN()
MAX()

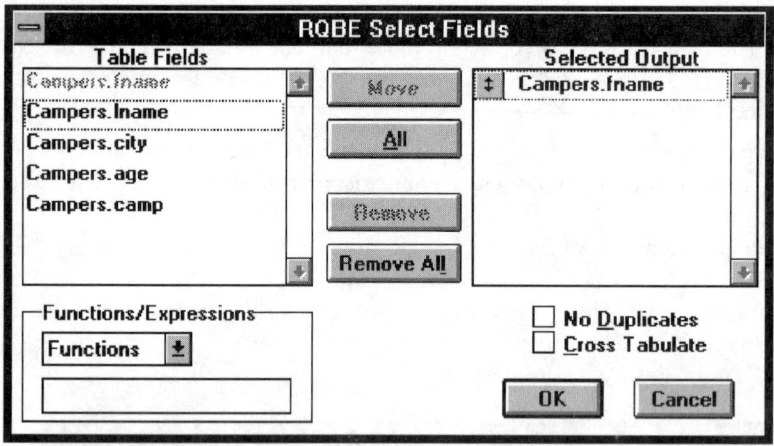

8-4 RQBE Select Fields dialog.

To adjust the order of the Selected Output fields, highlight the desired field. Then use either Ctrl-↑ or Ctrl-↓, for the direction to move the field. To adjust the order using the mouse, click on the double-arrow mover control at the left of the field and drag the field to the new location.

The No Duplicates check box allows you to eliminate any duplicate records from the output. Duplicate records are defined as records that have identical entries in just the fields shown in the Selected Output list.

The Cross Tabulate check box allows you to output the query results in cross-tabular format for use in a report or graph. At least three fields or expressions must be in the Selected Output list before this option is enabled. Those three items must be the X axis, Y axis, and cell value for the graph. FoxPro uses the program GENXTAB.PRG to format the graph results.

Sorting the query result

The Order By... option displays a dialog which allows you determine the order in which the query result is sorted. You can choose from any of the selected output fields, and the result can be in ascending or descending order.

If desired, you can use multiple fields in the sort order. This is most often needed when the primary field is not unique and many records share the same primary key. If you choose multiple keys and the fields must then be reordered, highlight the desired field. Then use either Ctrl-↑ or Ctrl-↓, for the direction to move the field. To adjust the order using the mouse, click on the double-arrow mover control at the left of the field and drag the field to the new location. To remove a particular field, click on the desired field and select Remove.

Grouping the query result

The Group By... option displays a dialog which allows you to specify fields to group the query result on. You can choose from any field of all databases involved in the query. If the query is grouped, only one record per group will appear in the query result.

Use the Having... option to define criteria that a grouping must match to be included in the query result.

Specifying the output result

The results that are generated from a query can be viewed, stored in a table, or sent to a report or label. The following options are available from the Output pop-up:

Browse Displays the query result immediately following query execution. This data resides in memory and cannot be saved.

Report/Label Sends the query result to a specified report or label form. Use the Options... check box to set the environment for the report or label.

Table/DBF Stores the query result in a FoxPro database file. Use the Save As dialog to select an existing database or to create a new database. Running this type of query performs a function similar to the COPY TO *file name* FOR *criteria* command.

Cursor Stores the query result in a cursor memory file. This is the same as selecting Browse, but the results aren't displayed. The Cursor output creates a temporary file that contains just the output fields and records that match the criteria. The file appears in the View window and can be used for browsing, reporting, etc. When the database is closed, the file is not saved on disk.

Graph Sends the query result to the Microsoft Graph graphing application.

If the Report/Label option is chosen, the Options... check box should then be selected. This brings up the RQBE Display Options dialog as shown in Fig. 8-5. The dialog allows one of the following three radio buttons to be selected: Screen Display, Report, or Label. If Report or Label is chosen, the form name must be selected. To choose an existing form, select the Form Name check box to bring up the file list of form names. If the form has not been created yet, enter a name in the text box below the check box.

You can set many of the report or label form options in this dialog box. There are check boxes for Preview, Summary, Report Heading, and Pause Between Screens. If Quick Report is chosen, an RQBE quick report can be created and saved right from this dialog.

The output default is for the display to be sent to the screen. To send to the printer, choose the To Printer check box (you can then choose whether to suppress the console display). To send to file, choose the To File check box and choose an existing file name or enter a new name in the text box. See the Database Report section in chapter 1 for more information on printing reports.

Selection criteria

The bottom half of the RQBE screen is the area where selection criteria is entered. To specify a selection, do the following:

1. Choose a field from the Field Name pop-up.
2. Choose the type of comparison (Like, Exactly Like, More Than, Less Than, Between, or In).
3. Enter the criteria example.
4. If desired, choose the Up/Lo check box that tells the RQBE to ignore differences between uppercase and lowercase.

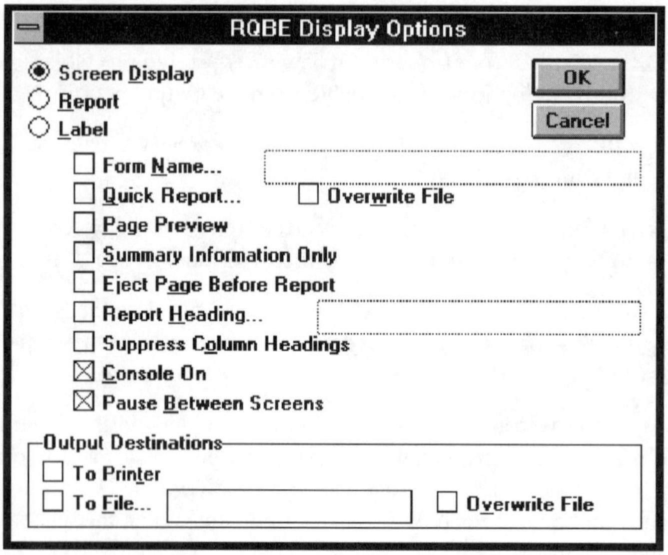

8-5 RQBE Display Options dialog.

When choosing the field, the pop-up that appears allows you to choose a field name from any of the databases involved in the query. If the <expression...> option is chosen, the Expression Builder dialog appears, which allows you to choose a Math, String, Logical, or Date function. If the NOT box is checked, the query finds the opposite of the criteria asked for.

Comparison types After the NOT box, one of the following comparison types must be chosen:

Like Works like the equal sign with SET EXACT OFF. When searching on character fields, if the example is *n* characters long, it only searches on the first *n* characters of the field. For instance, in the criteria of City LIKE "S", because the example is one letter long, it compares against just the first letter of City, finding records from San Diego, San Jose, etc.

Exactly Like Works like the equal sign with SET EXACT ON. When searching on character fields, the example must be exactly the same number of characters as the field. For instance, if the field name is City and the example is "San Diego", no records would be found because the City field is 15 characters wide. For a San Diego record to match, the criteria would have to be City EXACTLY LIKE "San Diego   ".

More than Works like the greater-than sign (>). With character fields, this finds letters that come after the example. For example, Name MORE THAN "R" would find records whose company names begin with the letters S through Z. Remember that lowercase letters are greater than uppercase, unless case is being ignored.

Less Than Works like the less than sign (<). With character fields, this finds letters that come before the example.

Between Works like *field >= expr AND field <= expr* without having to use two lines of criteria. The example must be a range separated with the word AND. The example can be numeric or character, but if it's character, the example expressions must be surrounded by quotes. For instance, Amount BETWEEN 5000 AND 8000 would find all records with amounts greater than or equal to 5000 and less than or equal to 8000.

In Works like *field $ value list*. The example can be a list of values separated with commas. For example, City IN "San Diego", "La Jolla" would find all records from San Diego or La Jolla.

Entering the example The example is the expression used in the comparison. If it's a character, the quotes are not necessary unless the Between comparison is being used.

Multiple criteria If multiple lines of criteria are used, the default is that they are connected with AND. This creates a *selective search* where both criteria must be true for a record to be found. The alternate method is to use an OR connection, also called a nonselective search. In OR searches, either criteria can be true for a record to match. To create a nonselective connection, enter the first criterion and then choose Or from the dialog. This separates the two lines of criteria with an OR divider line.

Editing criteria To delete a criterion, highlight that row and choose Remove. To place a criterion over an existing criterion, move to the row where the new criterion is to be placed, and choose Insert. To rearrange the order of criteria, use the double-arrow mover control to drag the criteria to the desired location. Using the keyboard, highlight the criterion to move, hold down Ctrl, and press ↑ or ↓ in the direction to move.

Viewing the SELECT statement

FoxPro uses the query criteria to generate a SELECT statement, which is simply a FoxPro command. The See SQL option displays the SELECT command for your query in a window. This allows you to copy the SELECT statement and paste it into a program. The statement displayed in the window cannot be modified.

Executing the query

Once the query has been defined, use the Do Query option to execute the query and create the result set. Once a query has been saved, it can be executed by issuing the command DO query, where query is the file name of the RQBE file.

Comments

You can add comments to the RQBE window by selecting Comments from the RQBE menu. You can enter information in the displayed dialog concerning the nature of the RQBE file. The comment text is not included in the SELECT statement.

Saving the query

Once the query design is complete, you must save the RQBE file. This can be done by selecting Save from the File Menu, pressing Ctrl-W, or double-clicking on the window's control menu.

An RQBE example

This section uses the COMPANY.DBF database in examples of several queries in the RQBE window. The database holds records of companies that have made purchases at a computer store. The Amount field contains the total of all purchases per client. If you're following along with this exercise, create the COMPANY database file and add the following records:

Record #	NAME	CODE	CITY	AMOUNT
1	Joe's Tacos	A01	San Diego	1000
2	Jill's Advertising	A02	La Jolla	5000
3	Computers R Us	B01	San Diego	8000
4	Sausedo Systems	A05	San Jose	6000
5	Jetson Electronics	B02	Glendale	0

To run a query, the following steps will be taken:

1. Open the RQBE window.
2. Specify the database(s) to be used in the query.
3. Select fields to appear in the query results.
4. Change output format and order, if desired.
5. Specify selection criteria.
6. Execute the query.

Create the Company query

At the command window, type CREATE QUERY COMPANY and press Enter. You are now in the RQBE window and the RQBE menu is active. If COMPANY.DBF is already open, the RQBE window will automatically choose it as the data file.

Specifying the output fields

The default is for all fields to display in the query output. In this example, all fields are selected, so no changes are required.

Specifying the output order

The default is for all fields to display in order of record number. In this example, the database is ordered alphabetically by Client Name. Choose the Order By... check box. This brings up the Order By dialog box. Double-click on the Name field.

Specifying the output to format

In this example, the Browse screen is used for the output, so no changes are made.

Selection criteria

Follow the steps described above to create the following criteria:

Field name	NOT	Comparison	Example	Up/Lo
COMPANY.CITY	[ ]	Like	San Diego	[ ]

Below are examples of other criteria and the records that would be found with each:

Criteria	Records
CITY Like S	From any city beginning with S
CITY Like S AND NAME Like J	Where City begins with S *and* company Name begins with J
CITY Like S OR NAME Like J	Where City begins with S *or* company Name begins with J
AMOUNT Between 5000 and 10000	Between 5000 and 10000
CODE In A01,B01,C01	Where the code is A01, B01, or C01

The RQBE window should now look like the example in Fig. 8-6.

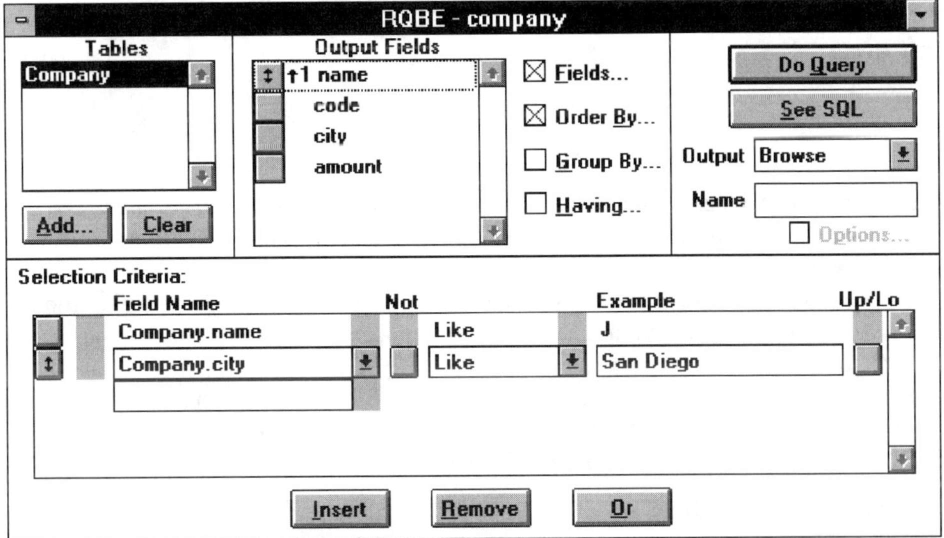

8-6 RQBE Comments dialog.

The SQL SELECT command

The RQBE window constructs an SQL SELECT command. Each option modifies the clauses used in the command. Choose See SQL to see the syntax used for the query. An example of a SELECT command constructed by the RQBE window is:

```
SELECT *;
   FROM COMPANY;
   WHERE COMPANY.NAME = "J";
   AND COMPANY.CITY = "San Diego";
   INTO CURSOR COMPANY_A
   BROWSE NOMODIFY PREFERENCE COMPANY_A
```

For more information on the syntax of the SELECT (SQL) command, see the listing in chapter 2.

Running the query

To run the query, choose Do Query. The output is in browse mode, unless you have chosen a different format. Before the output is displayed, the number of records selected and the time it took to run the query are displayed in the status bar at the bottom of the screen.

Joining multiple databases

Multiple databases can be used in the RQBE window. A relationship must be set between the fields that join the two files together. Unlike the SET RELATION command, which also joins files together, indexes do not have to be created or open for the join option to work.

An example of a file that could be joined to COMPANY.DBF is a data file named TAXES.DBF, which tracks the sales tax being charged in the following cities:

Record #	City	Tax
1	San Diego	.06
2	La Jolla	.07
3	San Jose	.05

To see the sales tax next to the record of each company, the files can be joined. The City field is the shared field, which is used for joining the records. Shared fields do not have to have the same name.

To join the files, choose Add from the RQBE window. Choose Taxes.DBF from the list of files. The Join Condition dialog box then appears. Choose the first pop-up, which lists the fields from the Taxes file. Choose Taxes.City. Leave LIKE as the comparison default. In the last pop-up, choose Company.City. The files are now connected by the City fields. Now choose Do Query. The Browse screen now shows the corresponding tax from TAXES.DBF next to each record in the Company file.

See also SELECT (SQL)

9
Using the Report Writer and Label Designer

The FoxPro Report Writer tool is used to easily create custom reports and labels for output. It provides an easy-to-learn template that can have you printing reports and labels in no time. Unlike FoxPro for MS-DOS, FoxPro for Windows uses the same interface and tools to create both report and label layouts.

The first section of this chapter details the Report Writer tools, menu, and layout operations. Following that is a simple exercise that shows how to create a custom report.

What the Report Writer does

The Report Writer provides a template that is used to set up and control report and label output definition files. FoxPro stores all report information in a database file with an extension of .FRX and all label information in a database file with an extension of .LBX. The report and label database files are used to generate the output results. The objects that you place on your report template let you see exactly how a particular report will look when it is printed.

Starting the Report Writer

You can enter the Report Writer in two ways:

- From the Command window, issue either CREATE REPORT or CREATE LABEL to create a new report or label layout. To modify an existing report or label, issue either MODIFY REPORT or MODIFY LABEL, followed by the file name of the screen.
- From the File menu, choose New... to start a new report or label, or Open... to open an existing report or label.

If you are creating a new label, you will be presented with a dialog containing a list of standard layouts to choose from. The layouts are taken from those that are defined in the current resource file, normally FOXUSER.DBF, and defines the starting format for the label. If no layouts are found in the current resource file, the dialog will not appear. When you open a report or label, a design window appears (see Fig. 9-1) and the Report menu pad is added to the main menu.

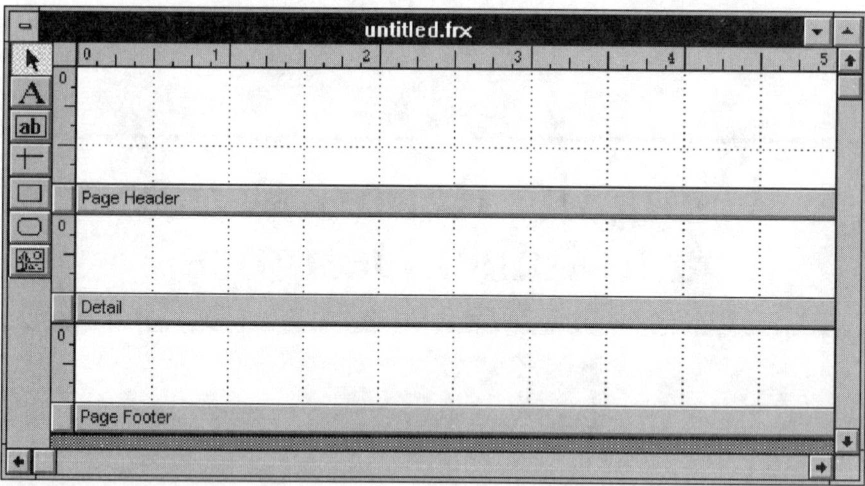

9-1 A report design window.

The Report layout

When a new report or label is opened, the layout has three bands: page header, detail, and page footer. Each band is separated by a horizontal bar called the Band Separator Bar, and the band name is displayed on the bar. Other bands will become available as you add objects to the layout, or by choosing options from the Report menu. Following is a description of the layout bands:

Title The title band contains information that appears at the top of the report. It can be a simple title or a paragraph. Information in the Title band is printed only once.

Page header A page header appears at the top of each page of the report. Your page header might include the date, the title, and the page number. Some of this information is fixed, and some is variable.

Group header If you break items on the report into groups, each group can have a heading to identify it.

Detail The detail band makes up the body of the report. This information comes directly from records in your database(s), or from calculations performed on those records. If this information is grouped, the detail band can also contain group headers and footers.

Group footer A group footer can contain summaries and/or subtotals for each group listed under a group heading.

Page footer Page footers perform the same function as page headers, but do so at the bottom of the page. You might prefer to list page numbers, for instance, at the bottom as a footer.

Summary The summary appears once at the end of the report. It can contain summary information taken from calculations or text.

Figure 9-2 contains an example of all bands on a report layout. To the left of each Band Separator Bar is the move button that is used to control the size of the band. To change the

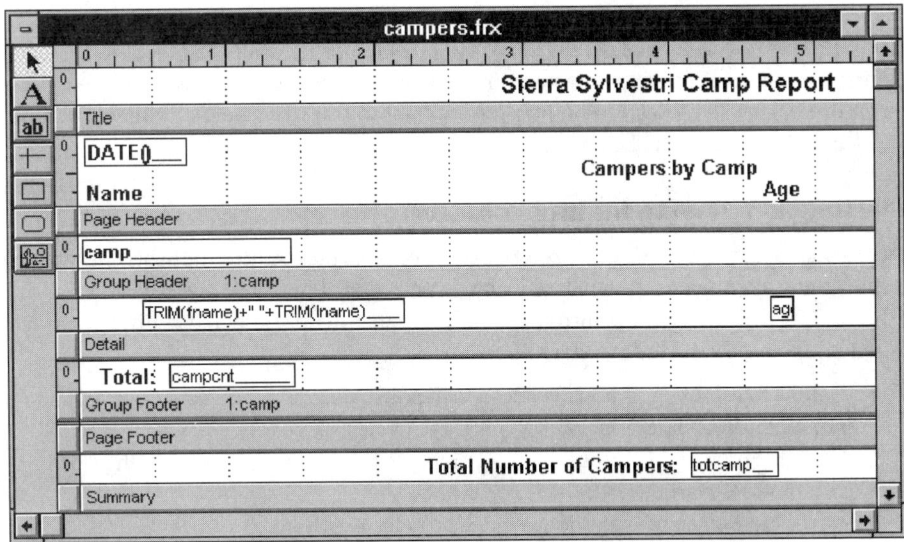

9-2 A report layout with bands.

size of the band, place the mouse pointer over the move button (the mouse pointer will change to a double-arrow), click, and drag the band to the desired point. You can also change the band size by double-clicking on the move button to activate the band dialog. Use the spinner control in the band dialog to change the size of the band. Selecting Constant Band Height ensures that the size of the band will not change, even when the report contains blank lines or large amounts of data.

The size of a band is controlled by other bands and objects within the band. A report band can never be sized smaller than the objects within the band. When the size of a band is changed, all other bands are moved up or down respectively.

Designing a custom report

Report objects

A report template is used to layout objects that will be printed on the report. Objects can be one of three types:

Fields Database fields, memory variables, or FoxPro expressions.

Text Any text on the report, such as prompts and headings, etc.

Graphics Boxes, lines, or pictures.

The report writer toolbox appears at the left of the report design window, and is used to select an object and place it on the report layout. The toolbox is detailed later in this chapter.

Selecting and moving objects

Once an object has been placed on the report layout, you can select it and move it. An object must be selected before it can be moved.

To select an object, position the mouse pointer over an object and click. The object appears with handles on each side. To move the object, simply drag the object to the desired position using the mouse or arrow keys. To deselect an object, click the mouse outside the object, or click on the selection pointer tool in the toolbox. To select all objects in a band, simply double-click on the Band Separator Bar.

Selecting and moving multiple objects

Often, you must select or move a group of objects. This can be accomplished in two ways: by selecting each object individually, or by selecting all objects at once. The latter option is the easiest and is done by surrounding the objects to be selected with a *marquee* (a dashed line). To do this, follow these steps:

1. Using the mouse, position the cursor at a point outside the objects to be selected and not within any other object.
2. Click the mouse. The mouse pointer changes to a "hand," signifying the starting position of the marquee.
3. Move the mouse to drag the marquee around the group.
4. Release the mouse. All objects in the marquee area are now selected.

Use the mouse to move the selected objects to the desired location. Select Undo from the Edit menu to return the objects to the previous location. To select multiple objects without using a marquee, simply hold down the Shift key while selecting the objects.

If you accidentally include an object you don't want to in a group of selected objects, you can deselect that single object by pressing the Shift key and clicking on the object with the mouse. To deselect all objects, simply click the mouse outside of the selected objects, or click on the selection pointer tool in the toolbox.

Editing objects

You can delete report objects by selecting them and pressing the Delete key. You can also use standard FoxPro editing functions such as Cut, Copy, and Paste on all report objects. If more than one report design window is open, you can copy an object from one report and paste the object into another report.

Once a field or object has been placed on the report, you can resize it. To resize an object you must first select it with the mouse. A set of handles appears around the selected object. Each handle determines the direction of sizing: horizontal, vertical, or diagonal. Using the mouse, resize the object by placing the mouse pointer over the desired handle, click, and drag the object. Release the mouse button to fix the new size. Using the keyboard, hold down the Shift key and use any combination of arrow keys to size the object. Click outside the selected object or on the selection pointer tool to fix the new size. Objects can be sized in increments relative to the type of ruler being used.

The attributes of each object, such as color, font, and fill type, can be changed using the Object menu. The Object menu is described later in this chapter.

Controlling objects

After an object is placed on the report layout, a dialog will appear. Each object dialog is used to define the appearance of the object. Once an object has been placed on the report layout, you can activate its control dialog by double-clicking on the object with the mouse. Object dialogs are detailed later in this chapter.

Commenting objects

You can enter comments for each object on the report layout window using the Comments dialog that appears when you select the Comment button. Any comments entered are stored with the report file and aren't included in the report output.

The Report toolbox

The report toolbox shown in Fig. 9-3 contains the tools necessary for placing objects on the report layout. To select an object, position the mouse pointer over an object tool and click. The mouse pointer will change to reflect the type of object selected: a vertical line for text objects or crosshairs for objects that require sizing.

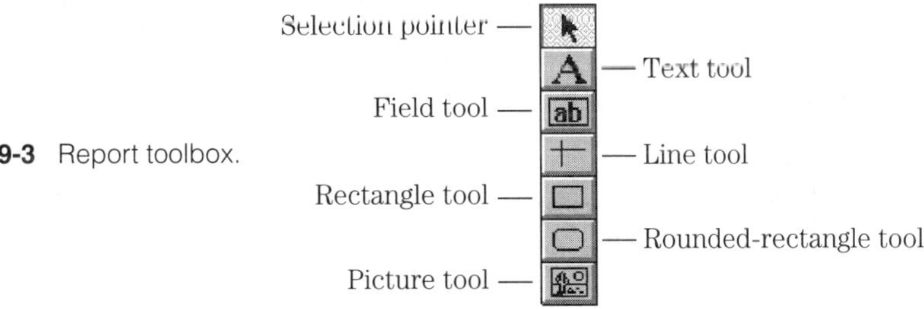

9-3 Report toolbox.

To place the selected object on the report layout, move the mouse pointer to the desired location and click. Depending on the object selected, a dialog might appear, allowing you to enter formatting codes. Once an object has been defined, the mouse pointer returns to a pointer tool (its default state).

Selection pointer tool

Click on the Selection pointer tool to deselect (or invert) any selected objects and return the mouse pointer to its default state.

Text tool

Use the Text tool to place literal text objects on the report. Once Text has been selected, place the mouse pointer over the report layout, click, and begin typing the desired letters using the keyboard. Click on the Selection pointer tool to fix the text object in place. Pressing the Enter key while editing a text object will add a carriage return at the end of the current text line.

Once the text object is in place, double-click on the object to activate the Text dialog. Use the Text dialog to control when and where the object is printed on the report. Selecting Print When... displays the Print When dialog shown in Fig. 9-7. The options on the Print When dialog are discussed later in this section.

The two position options, Top and Bottom, are used to determine the position of the object should any other object above it spill over. Selecting Top ensures that the object's position stays relative to the top of the band. All position options are disabled if the object's size covers more than one report band.

Field tool

Use the Field tool to place a database field or expression object on the report. After selecting the Field tool, the mouse cursor changes to crosshairs so you can size the object. Place the mouse pointer over the report layout, click the pointer at the top left position of the field, and drag the mouse to the bottom right position of the field. Release the mouse to fix the field object. A field can be sized to display more than one line of data. Use the Report Expression dialog shown in Fig. 9-4 to format the object expression.

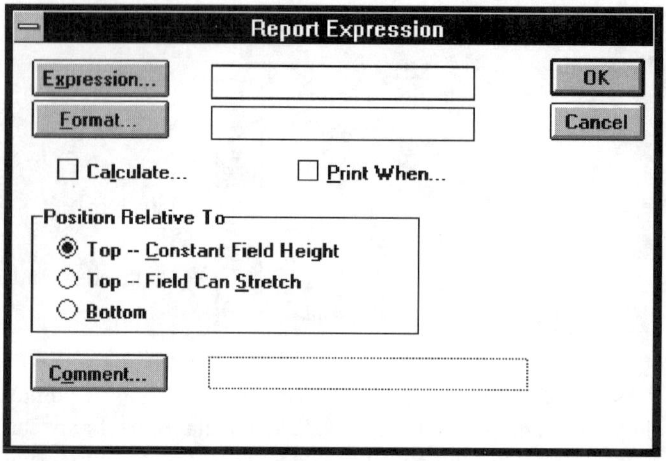

9-4 Report Expression dialog box.

Expression... Defines the expression that is displayed on the report. Type the expression in the text box or select the Expression... push button to activate the Expression Builder. See chapter 1 for more information on the Expression Builder.

Format... Expressions can be formatted with codes to control the display of an expression. Enter the appropriate format code(s) in the text box or select the Format... push button to display the Format dialog shown in Fig. 9-5. Eleven characters (listed next) can be used to indicate a format. Any other characters typed in the Format text box will appear themselves in the format on your report.

Format characters	Description
A	Displays only alphabetic characters.
L	Displays only logical data.
N	Displays only letters and digits.
X	Displays any character.

9	Displays only digits for character data. Displays digits and signs for numeric data.
#	Displays digits, blanks, and signs.
$	Displays fixed dollar sign in front of numeric value.
$$	Displays floating dollar sign in front of numeric value.
*	Displays asterisks in front of numeric value. Can be used with $ for check protection.
.	Specifies decimal point position.
,	Separates digits left of the decimal point.

Below the Format text line, four radio buttons determine whether the field appears as a Character, Numeric, Date, or Logical field.

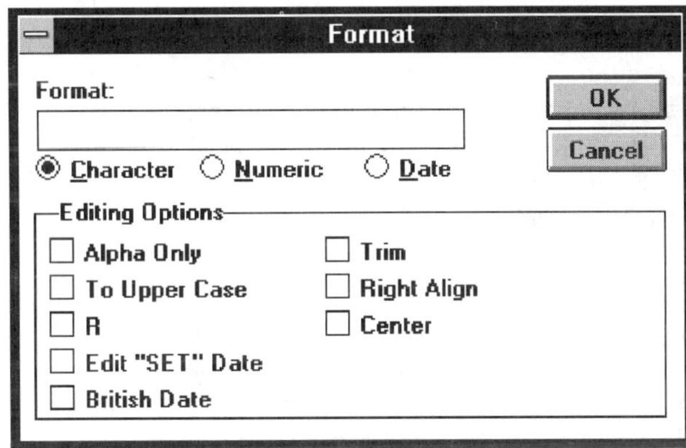

9-5 Format dialog box.

The bottom half of the dialog box contains Editing Options. These change according to which radio button is currently selected. The formatting options for each type of field are listed here.

Character The following are formatting options for character fields:

Alpha Only Displays only alphabetic characters.
To Upper Case Converts all characters to uppercase.
R Displays nonformat characters, but does not store them.
Edit "SET" date Uses current SET DATE format to edit date data.
British Date Edits data as a European (British) date (dd/mm/yy).
Trim Removes leading and trailing blank spaces.
Right Align Prints data flush right in field.
Center Centers data in field.

Numeric field The following are formatting options for numeric fields:

Left Justify Left justifies all data in field.
Blank If Zero Does not print if field output is 0.
(Negative) Displays negative numbers in parentheses.
Edit "SET" Date Uses current SET DATE format to edit date data.

British Date Edits data as a European (British) date (dd/mm/yy).

CR if Positive CR (credit) appears after the number if the number is positive.

DB if Negative DB (debit) appears after the number if the number is negative.

Leading Zero Prints all leading zeros.

Currency Displays currency format (as specified in View or SET CURRENCY command).

Scientific Displays data in scientific notation.

Date field The following are options for formatting date fields:

Edit "SET" Date Edits data using the current SET DATE format.

British Date Edits data as a European (British) date (dd/mm/yy).

No editing options are available for logical data.

Calculate Displays the Calculate Field dialog shown in Fig. 9-6, which is used to create a computed field. Computed fields are used to calculate a value, and that value can then be displayed on the report. If a calculation is selected for a field, the value of the calculation is reset to the field's initial value at the end of the report, unless a specific reset point has been selected from the Reset pop-up. This selection of radio buttons allow you to determine what type of calculation is performed on the field:

Nothing No computation is performed.

Count Counts the number of times the field itself appears within the Reset group, and not the expression of the field.

Sum Computes the additive sum of the field's expression.

Average Computes the average of the field's expression.

Lowest When selected, the lowest value that the field had is displayed.

Highest When selected, the highest value that the field had is displayed.

Std. Deviation When selected, the field will display the square root of the variance for the field values.

Variance When selected, the variance between each value of the field and the average of all field values.

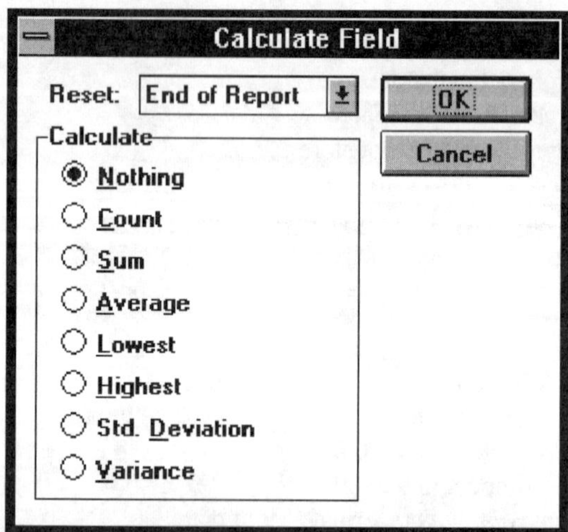

9-6 Calculate dialog box.

Print When... Displays the Print When dialog shown in Fig. 9-7. The options in this dialog are used to control selective printing of an object.

Print Repeated Values When Yes is selected, the field will always be printed. When No is selected, the field is only printed when the value of the expression changes.

In First Whole Band of New Page/Column When checked, the object is printed in the first band of a new page or column that is not carried over from a previous page or column. This option is only available when the object is in a group or detail band, and can only be turned off when the Print Repeated Values option is No.

When This Group Changes When checked, the object is printed only when the expression for the selected group changes. This option is only available when the object is in a group band, and can only be turned off when the Print Repeated Values option is No.

When Detail Overflows to New Page/Column When checked, the object is printed when the detail band overflows to a new page or column.

Print Only When Expression is True Selecting this option activates the Expression Builder. If an expression is entered, the object will only be printed when the expression evaluates to true (.T.), and all other options in this dialog, except for Remove Line if Blank, are disabled.

Remove Line if Blank When checked, the line on which the object is located will not be printed if the object expression is blank. If other objects are included on the same line, the line will be printed. All options in the Print When dialog, except for Print Only When Expression is True, are disabled if the object's size covers more than one report band.

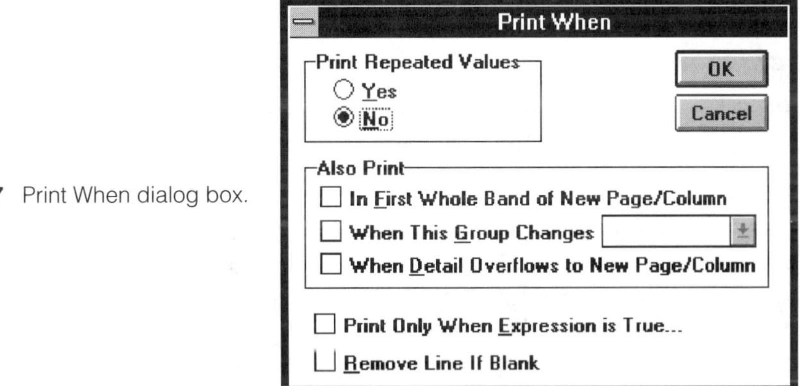

9-7 Print When dialog box.

Position Relative To These options determine the position of the object in the band.

Top - Constant Field Height When selected, the object will maintain its position in the band, even if other objects above it overflow their position.

Top - Field Can Stretch When selected, the object will be "stretched" down the report if the length of the expression is greater than the specified height and width. For example, if the expression is a database memo field containing 4,000 characters and the width of the expression is 70, only one line of the memo field will be displayed unless this option is on.

Bottom When selected, causes the object to be "pushed" down the report if any objects next to or above it have been set to Field Can Stretch.

All position options are disabled if the object's size covers more than one report band.

Comment... Enter comments for the object.

Select OK to save the field attributes. Selecting Cancel will discard any changes to the object.

Line tool

Use the Line tool to place a vertical or horizontal line object on the report. After selecting the Line tool, the mouse cursor changes to crosshairs so you can size the object. Click the pointer at the top left position of the line and drag the mouse up or down to create a vertical line, left or right to create a horizontal line. Release the mouse to fix the line object. The pen width of the line object is determined by the Object menu Pen setting, which is discussed later in this chapter.

Once the line object is in place, double-click on the object to activate the Rectangle/Line dialog. Use the Rectangle/Line dialog to control when and where the object is printed on the report. Selecting Print When... displays the Print When dialog shown in Fig. 9-7. The options on the Print When dialog are discussed above under the Field tool section.

The three position options, Top, Stretch With Band, and Bottom, are used to determine the position of the object should any other object above it spill over. Selecting Top ensures that the object's position stays relative to the top of the band. Stretch With Band is only available when the object is a vertical line, and forces the object to stretch when its band also stretches. All position options are disabled if the object's size covers more than one report band.

See also Field tool

Rectangle tool

Use the Rectangle tool to place a box or rectangle object on the report. After selecting the Rectangle tool the mouse cursor changes to crosshairs so you can size the object. Click the pointer at the top left position of the rectangle and drag the mouse to the bottom right position of the rectangle. Release the mouse to fix the rectangle object. The pen width of the rectangle object is determined by the Object menu Pen setting, which is discussed later in this chapter.

Once the rectangle object is in place, double-click on the object to activate the Rectangle/Line dialog. Use the Rectangle/Line dialog to control when and where the object is printed on the report. Selecting Print When... displays the Print When dialog shown in Fig. 9-7. The options on the Print When dialog are discussed above under the Field tool section.

The three position options, Top, Stretch With Band, and Bottom, are used to determine the position of the object should any other object above it spill over. Selecting Top ensures that the object's position stays relative to the top of the band. Stretch With Band is only available when the object is a vertical line, and forces the object to stretch when its band also stretches. All position options are disabled if the object's size covers more than one report band.

See also Field tool

Rounded-rectangle tool

This option is similar to the Rectangle tool. However, the corners of the object are rounded rather than square.

Once the rectangle object is in place, double-click on the object to activate the Rectangle/Line dialog. Use the Rectangle/Line dialog to select a corner style for the object, and to control when and where the object is printed on the report. Selecting Print When... displays the Print When dialog shown in Fig. 9-7. The options on the Print When dialog are discussed above under the Field tool section.

The three position options, Top, Stretch With Band, and Bottom, are used to determine the position of the object should any other object above it spill over. Selecting Top ensures that the object's position stays relative to the top of the band. Stretch With Band is only available when the object is a vertical line, and forces the object to stretch when its band also stretches. All position options are disabled if the object's size covers more than one report band.

See also Field tool

Picture tool

Use the Picture tool to place a bitmap or icon image on the report layout. After selecting the Picture tool the mouse cursor changes to crosshairs so you can size the object. Click the pointer at the top left position of the picture and drag the mouse to the bottom right position of the picture. Release the mouse to fix the picture object. The Report Picture dialog shown in Fig. 9-8 is used to select a picture file and format the picture display.

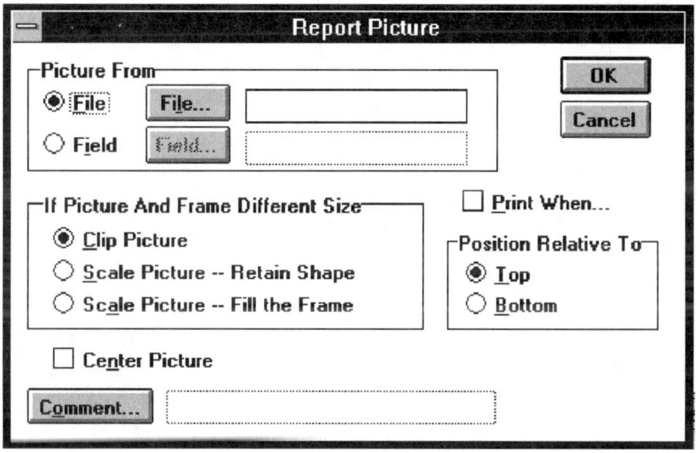

9-8 Report Picture dialog box

File/Field When File is selected, enter the name of a bitmap or icon image file in the text box, or use the File... button to locate a bitmap or icon image file. When Field is selected, enter the name of a FoxPro general field in the text box, or select Field... to activate the Choose Field/Variable dialog shown in Fig. 7-5.

Clip Picture When selected, the picture's original dimensions are retained and only that portion of the picture that fits in the object's frame is displayed, beginning at the top left corner of the frame.

Scale Picture - Retain Shape When selected, the picture's original dimensions are scaled to fit inside the frame, while filling the frame as much as possible.

Scale Picture - Fill the Frame When selected, the picture is sized to fill the entire frame. This may cause distortion in the picture.

Center Picture When checked, the contents of the general field will be centered within the picture frame. This is useful when images stored in a general field are smaller than the frame size. This option is only available when Field is selected.

Print When... Displays the Print When dialog shown in Fig. 9-7. The options in this dialog are detailed in the Field tool section above.

Position Relative To These options determine the position of the object in the band. Selecting Top ensures that the object's position stays relative to the top of the band. All position options are disabled if the object's size covers more than one report band.

Comment... Enter comments for the picture object.

See also Field tool

The Report menu

The Report menu shown in Fig. 9-9 contains all the tools necessary for designing the report layout.

Page Layout...
Page Preview... Ctrl+I

Show Position
Ruler/Grid...
Snap to Grid

Title/Summary...
Data Grouping...
Variables...

Quick Report...

9-9 Report menu.

Page Layout...

The dialog shown in Fig. 9-10 is used to define the layout of the printed page, assign printers and fonts, and save or restore a report environment.

Columns Determines the number of columns in the report, or the number of labels across the page.

Left margin Determines the left margin setting.

Column width Determines the width of each column in the report, or width of each label. This option can only be changed when the number of columns is greater than 1.

Space between columns Determines the number of spaces between each column in the report, or the space between each label. This option can only be changed when the number of columns is greater than 1.

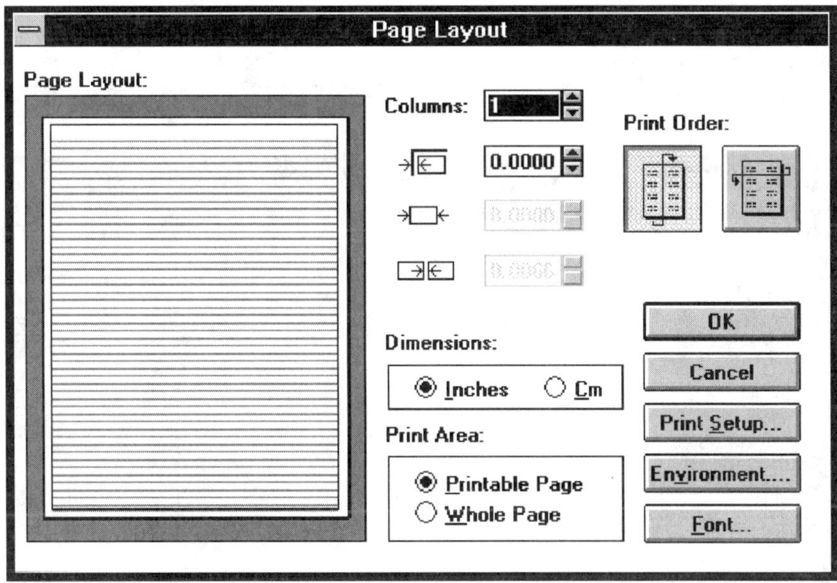

9-10 Page Layout dialog box.

Dimensions When Inches is selected, all values displayed in the Columns, Left margin, Column width, and Space between columns spinners are in inches. The values are displayed in centimeters when Cm is selected.

Print Area Determines the available printing space for the report or label. When Printable Page is selected, the printing area is within the margins for the current printer. Select Whole Page for more printing space.

Print Order Determines the order that columns are printed. If the left button is selected, report columns and labels are printed top to bottom and left to right. If the right button is selected, report columns and labels are printed left to right and top to bottom.

Print Setup... Displays the Windows Print Setup dialog. Use this dialog to select a printer, orientation, and paper source for the report or label. Changing the default or specific printer also causes the FoxPro Print Setup to reflect the same settings. You must save the report environment if you want the selected printer settings to stay with the report.

Environment Save/Restore/Clear Selecting Save causes FoxPro to save the current environment settings with the report. If the environment was previously saved, select Restore to restore the original environment settings or Clear to remove any environment settings.

Font... Use the Windows Font dialog to select a default font for the report. The default font determines the font used when adding any new objects to the report layout.

The Report Layout dialog also contains a what-you-see-is-what-you-get (WYSIWYG) display of the current report design. This display is relative to the current display driver and the dimensions of the report layout. Select OK to save the report layout attributes and return to the report design screen. Selecting Cancel will discard any changes to the report layout.

Page Preview...

Displays the report in a window (see Fig. 9-11), which allows you to see an actual representation of the report while it's being created. All data is displayed in correct locations and styles.

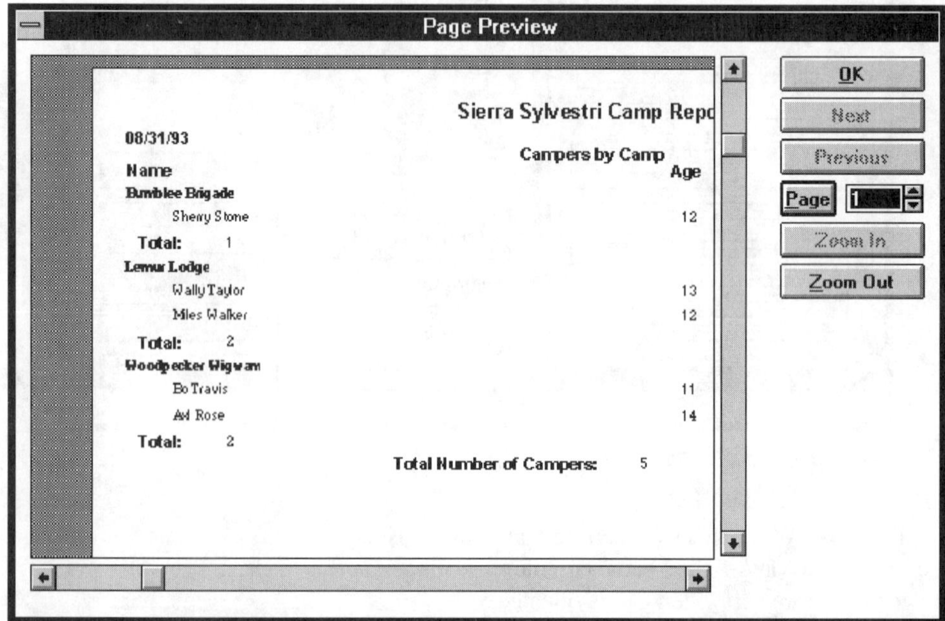

9-11 Page Preview of a report.

Select Next to see more pages of the report, or Previous to scroll backwards. To view a specific page, select the desired page number using the spinner control and select Page to view the page.

Use the Zoom In and Zoom Out controls to see a section of the page, or the entire page. The same functions can be accomplished by clicking the mouse pointer (looks like a magnifying glass) anywhere on the page graphic.

Shortcut key Ctrl-I

Show Position

Use Show Position to display the coordinates of the mouse pointer or display the size of the currently selected object. When no objects are selected, Show Position tracks the mouse and displays the coordinates of the mouse pointer relative to the report layout dimensions and the current ruler being used. When an object is selected, the position and size of the object are displayed. The values displayed are relative to the report layout dimensions and the current ruler being used.

The Show Position information is displayed in the status bar at the bottom of the main FoxPro window. Show Position is active when a check mark appears to the left of the menu option. Select Show Position again to turn the function off.

Ruler/Grid

This option displays the Ruler/Grid dialog. Use the Ruler/Grid dialog to format the report layout ruler display and associated functions.

Ruler Select a unit of measurement for the ruler.

Ruler Lines Selecting Yes places horizontal and vertical ruler lines over the report layout.

Grid Determines the number of pixels that an object can be moved when the Snap to Grid function is on.

Snap to Grid

When Snap to Grid is on (a check mark appears to the left of the menu option), objects that are sized or moved using the mouse will be automatically aligned to the closest grid line, relative to the current ruler being used. When Snap to Grid is off, objects can be sized or moved one pixel at a time. Select Snap to Grid again to turn the function off or press the Ctrl key while sizing or moving an object to ignore the current Snap to Grid setting.

Title/Summary...

This option lets you add title and summary bands to the report. The dialog box shown in Fig. 9-12 is subdivided into two sections:

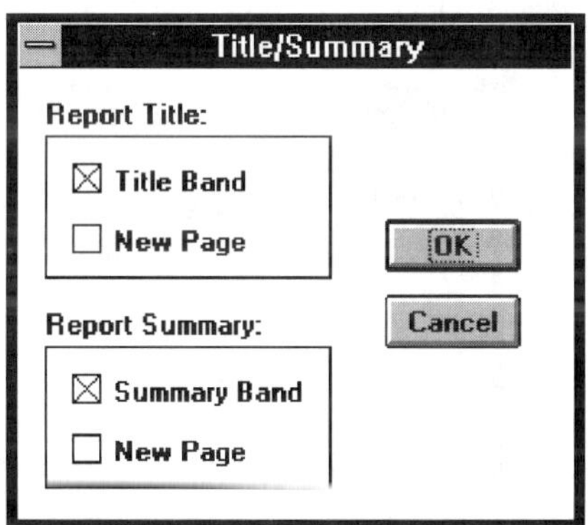

9-12 Title/Summary dialog box.

Report Title In the dialog box, check Title Band if you want to add a title. Because your title can be anything from a word to pages of introductory paragraphs, you can check the New Page box if you want the title to print on a separate report.

Report Summary The Summary check box works the same way. If it is checked, you can also check the New Page box if you want the summary to print on a separate page at the end of the report.

Choose OK to confirm your selections, or Cancel to exit the dialog box without making changes. A Title and/or Summary band will be added to the report layout window, and you can add desired objects.

Data Grouping...

This option lets you group records on the report. To do this properly, you must index or sort the database on the same expression you want to use for the grouping. Otherwise, groups will be separated as they occur in the database. When you choose Data Grouping..., the Group dialog box appears. The Group dialog box contains a list of all report grouping expressions, along with controls for adding, editing, and deleting groups. Choose Add to activate the Group Info dialog box (see Fig. 9-13) with the following options:

Group... Activates the Expression Builder. Enter a valid expression for grouping.

New Column When checked, a new column is started when the group changes. This option is only available to reports with more than one column, and labels.

New Page When checked, each distinct group will begin on a new page. In this case, page headers and footers print as usual.

New Page (Page No.=1) When checked, each distinct group will begin on a new page and the page number counter is reset to 1.

Reprint Header on Subsequent Pages When checked, the group footer will be printed on each page that begins with this group. Otherwise, the page header, if any, will print at the top of each page.

If Less Than *expN* Below Header, Begin New Page When checked, the distance specified with *expN* determines how far from the bottom of the page a group header can be printed. Use the spinner control to enter a value for *expN*. The value can be in either inches (when Inches is selected), or centimeters (when Cm is selected).

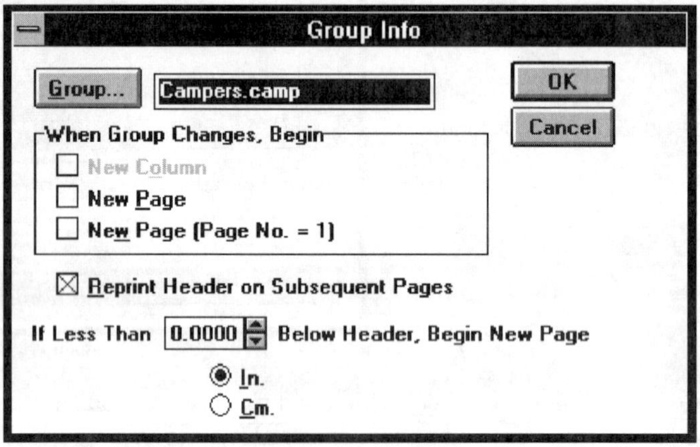

9-13 Group Info dialog box.

Choose OK when your selections are complete. You can add up to 20 groups to a report, with each group breaking down records within the higher group.

To change or delete a group, select the group in the Group box and choose Change or Delete. To change the order of groups, click on double-arrow mover control and drag the group to the desired location. Choose OK when you are ready to see your group bands in the report layout.

Variables...

This option lets you create variables to use in the report. When you choose Variables..., a dialog box appears that contains a list of all report variables, along with controls for adding, editing, and deleting variables. Choose Add to activate the Variabled Definition dialog box (see Fig. 9-14) with the following options:

Variable Name Enter the name for the variable in the text box.

Value to Store Enter the value to store to the variable in the text box. Selecting the Value to Store push button will activate the Expression Builder. See chapter 1 for more information on the Expression Builder.

Initial Value A report variable must be initialized with a value before any calculation is performed on the variable. Enter the value in the text box, or select the Initial Value push button to activate the Expression Builder.

Release after Report When checked, the variable will be released from memory after the report is finished printing. If the variable isn't released, it can be referenced after the report is printed, following standard variable initialization rules.

Reset The pop-up contains options for selecting a point to reset the variable back to its initial value. If the report contains one or more group bands, those group expressions will appear in the Reset pop-up.

Calculate Report variables can be used to calculate a value, and that value can then be displayed on the report. If a calculation is selected for a variable, the value of the calculation is reset to the variable's initial value at the end of the report, unless a specific reset point has been selected from the Reset pop-up. This selection of radio buttons allow you to determine what type of calculation is performed on the variable:

Nothing When selected, no calculation is performed and the value of the variable will always be its initial value.

Count Counts the number of times the variable itself appears within the Reset group, and not the expression of the variable.

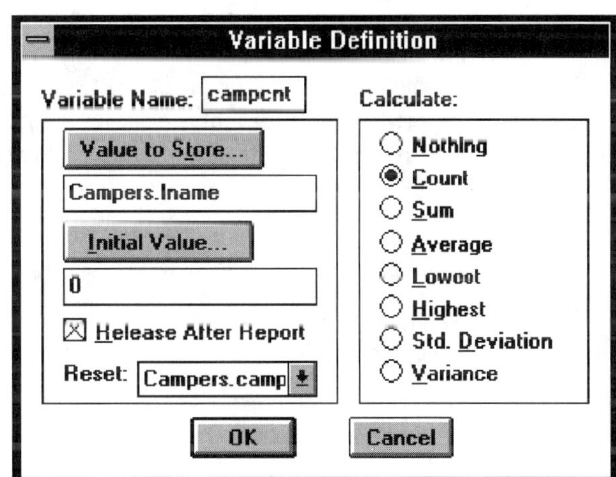

9-14 Variable Definition dialog box.

Sum Adds the values of the variable's expression.

Average Computes the average of the variable's expression.

Lowest When selected, the lowest value that the variable had is displayed.

Highest When selected, the highest value that the variable had is displayed.

Std. Deviation When selected, the variable will display the square root of the variance for the variable values.

Variance When selected, the variance between each value of the variable and the average of all values.

Choose OK to save the variable definition and return to the Report Variables dialog. Any new variables are added to the Variables list.

To change the definitions of an existing variable, highlight the desired variable in the list and select Change. This displays the Variable Definition dialog. To remove a variable from the report, highlight the desired variable in the list and select Delete. To change the evaluation order of variables, click on double-arrow mover control and drag the variable to the desired location.

Quick Report...

If the report layout is empty, you can use the Quick Report option to create a report using a few simple dialogs. The Quick Report dialog shown in Fig. 9-15 is displayed.

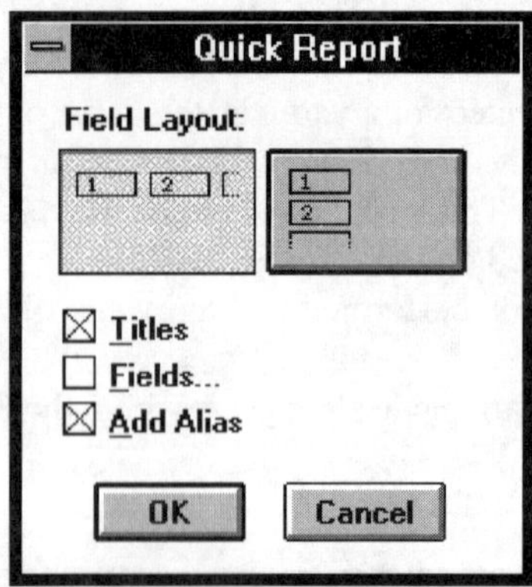

9-15 Quick Report dialog box.

Field Layout When the left button is selected (column layout), the field objects will be placed on the report from left to right. Selecting the right button (form layout) places the field objects from top to bottom. In column layout, any fields that do not fit on the page are omitted. In form layout, the Detail band stretches to accommodate all the fields.

Titles When checked, places column headings at the top or left side of the report layout. The column headings are text objects that correspond to the field names of the database.

Fields... Displays the field picker dialog allowing you to select certain fields to place on the report. See chapter 1 for more information on the field picker dialog.

Add Alias When selected, the expression of each field object consists of the alias of the database the field belongs to, a period (.), and the field expression. Use Add Alias if the report contains multiple field objects that have the same field name but different aliases.

FoxPro places date and page number objects on a quick report. The date is placed at the bottom left and the page number at the bottom right of the report Page Footer.

The Object menu

Use the options in the Object menu to control the appearance and style of objects on the report layout.

Align to Grid

Selecting Align to Grid when one or more report objects is selected will cause those objects to be aligned to the nearest horizontal and vertical grid lines.

Shortcut key Ctrl-T

Bring to Front

Selecting Bring to Front when one or more report objects is selected causes those objects to be moved to the front of the report layout. This is useful when line or text objects need to be placed on top of field objects. Bringing an object to the front forces any overlapping objects to appear behind the selected object.

Shortcut key Ctrl-G

See also Send to Back

Send to Back

Selecting Send to Back when one or more report objects is selected causes those objects to be moved to the back of the report layout. This is useful when line or text objects need to be placed behind field objects. Sending an object to the back forces any overlapping objects to appear on top of the selected object.

Shortcut key Ctrl-J

See also Bring to Front

Center

This option positions a selected object in the middle of the report layout, relative to the size of the layout's window dimensions. If multiple objects are selected, each object will be centered. If you want to center a group of objects and keep the relative spacing of each object the same, use Group to first group the objects into one object then select Center.

See also Group

Group

Selecting Group allows you to select multiple objects and group them together as one object to be manipulated. This is useful when you want to move many objects the same distance.

See also Ungroup

Ungroup

Selecting Ungroup ungroups a set of grouped objects, returning them to their single object state.

See also Group

Font...

Selecting Font... displays the Windows Font dialog. Use the Font dialog to change the font attributes for the selected object. Refer to your Windows documentation for more information on changing a font.

Text Alignment

Use the Text Alignment options to adjust the alignment and spacing of text within a text object.

Fill

This option allows you to fill selected rectangle and rounded line objects with a variety of different patterns.

Pen

Use the Pen options to adjust the width of the line used for line, rectangle and rounded objects.

Mode

Use the Mode options on text, line, rectangle, and rounded-rectangle objects. When Mode is set to Opaque, any objects behind the selected object will not show through the selected object. When Mode is to transparent, any objects behind the selected object will show through the selected object.

Fill Color

Use Fill Color to select a background color for field objects.

Pen Color

Use Pen Color to select a foreground color for text, line, and field objects.

Saving the report

Once the report design is complete the report file must be saved. This can be done by selecting Save from the File Menu, pressing Ctrl-W, or double-clicking on the window control bar.

If the report is being saved for the first time, FoxPro will display an alert asking if you want to save the environment information. If Yes is selected, the status of all work areas, indexes and relations is stored with the report file. When a report file is opened that contains a saved environment, FoxPro will restore the environment automatically.

Running a report

Once you've created and saved a report, you can run it by selecting Report from the Database or Run menus, or by issuing the command REPORT FORM. Both menu options give you a dialog with a variety of options available to print the report to a printer, display it on screen, or send the report to an ASCII file. See chapter 1 for a description of the Database and Run menus, and chapter 2 for a description of the REPORT FORM command.

See also Chapter 1, The FoxPro user interface, REPORT FORM

Running a Label

Once you've created and saved a label, you can run it by selecting Label from the Database or Run menus, or by issuing the command LABEL FORM. Both menu options give you a dialog with a variety of options available to print the label to a printer, display it on screen, or send the label to an ASCII file. See chapter 2 for a description of the LABEL FORM command.

See also LABEL FORM

A Report Writer example

This section shows how to create a simple report. Because there are so many ways to create easy or complex reports, this example cannot cover all of them. The database to be used in the Report Writer example is the CAMPERS.DBF file used in chapter 6. To create the report in the next section, follow these steps:

1. Enter the Report Writer and load the fields.
2. Move the fields around and change the expressions.
3. Print the report.

Make sure that the Campers.DBF file is open before entering the Report Writer. Remember that you can enter the Report Writer from either the File menu or by entering the commands in the Command window. For this example type CREATE REPORT in the Command window and press Enter. A report layout design window titled Untitled.FRX appears and the Report menu is added to the menu bar.

Designing the report

For this example you will create a report that lists all campers alphabetically by camp and shows each camper's age. Call the report "Sierra Sylvestri Camp Report." To enter this title, choose Title/Summary from the Report menu. Check the Title Band box and choose OK.

Now create the title text. Click on the Text tool and place the mouse pointer over the report layout inside the title band. Click the mouse to activate the text bar and begin entering the text. When you finish entering text, click on the selection pointer tool to fix the text object.

The title will look better in the center of the page. Select the title text object and choose Center from the Object. The title might not look like it is in the center of your screen, but FoxPro knows to center it between the right and left margins of the report.

Pretend this is a very long report, and that you want to see today's date at the top of each page.

1. Click on the Field tool and place the mouse pointer over the page header band. Click the mouse. The mouse pointer changes to crosshairs. Drag the pointer down and to the right to size the field. Release the mouse button to activate the Report Expression dialog. Choose Expression... to activate the Expression Builder.
2. Open the Date pop-up and choose DATE( ) from the list.
3. Choose OK in the Expression Builder and the Report Expression dialog box.
4. Choose Page Preview from the Report menu. You can see that today's date is now showing where DATE( ) expression was placed on the report. Choose OK to return to the layout window.

Add two more headers that you will want to see at the top of each page. The left column of the report should be headed "Campers by Camp" and the right column will be "Age." Use the Text tool to create the text objects.

To group the campers by camp, you must first be sure the database is indexed on the Camp field. Use File New Index to create an index tag for the Campers database. Choose Database Setup and make sure a key appears to the left of the index tag name, indicating the index is active. If it is not, use the Setup dialog to activate the Camp index order. To create the Camp grouping:

1. Choose Data Grouping... from the Report menu.
2. Choose Add, and the Group Info dialog box appears.
3. Pick Group... to bring up the Expression Builder.
4. Select Camp from the field list and choose OK.
5. Choose OK again in the Group Info box, and again in the Group box.

Creating a data grouping causes records to be grouped, but it does not automatically print the name of each group. To do that, you must add the camp field to the grouping band:

1. Click on the Field tool and place the field object in the camp group band.
2. Pick Expression... to open the Expression Builder.
3. Select Camp from the Expression Builder.
4. Choose OK and return to the layout window.

In each group, you want to list the campers' first and last names in the detail band:

1. Click on the Field tool and place the field object in the detail band.
2. Pick Expression... to open the Expression Builder.
3. Choose TRIM( ) from the String pop-up.
4. Choose Fname from the fields list.
5. Move the cursor to the right of the right parenthesis and type + " " +.
6. Choose Lname from the fields list.

This expression trims the blank spaces from the end of the Fname field, adds a space, and adds the Lname field. Without the TRIM( ) function, names would look like this:

```
Bo      Travis
Sherry  Stone
```

Choose OK to return to the layout window. Press Ctrl-I to choose Page Preview, and you will see the names are showing correctly.

Add the Age field using the Field tool and the Expression Builder. If you forgot to place the field object in the right position first, select the Age field and use the arrow keys to put it where it belongs. Now press Ctrl-I to see the report. It should look like Fig. 9-11.

Now add an expression to the group footer band that will display the total number of campers in each camp. Click on the Text tool and place the cursor in the group footer band. Enter the text Total. Click on the selection pointer tool to fix the text. Follow these steps to create the report variable to use for the count expression:

1. Select Variables... from the Report menu. The Report Variables dialog is displayed. Select Add to display the Variable Definition dialog box.
2. Enter CAMPCNT in the Variable Name text box. This is the name of the variable.
3. Select the Value to Store push button, which displays the Expression Builder. Select lname from the fields list and select OK to save the expression.
4. Enter 0 in the Initial Value text box.
5. Select Count from the Calculate options.
6. Select campers.camp from the Reset pop-up.
7. Select OK from the Variable Definition dialog and OK again from the Report Variables dialog. See Fig. 9-14 for an example.

You now need to assign the variable CAMPCNT to a report expression. Click on the field tool and place the cursor in the group footer band. Enter CAMPCNT in the Expression text box. Select OK to save the expression. See Fig. 9-16 for an example of how the finished report should now look. When you want to print a report, use the Report option in the Database menu.

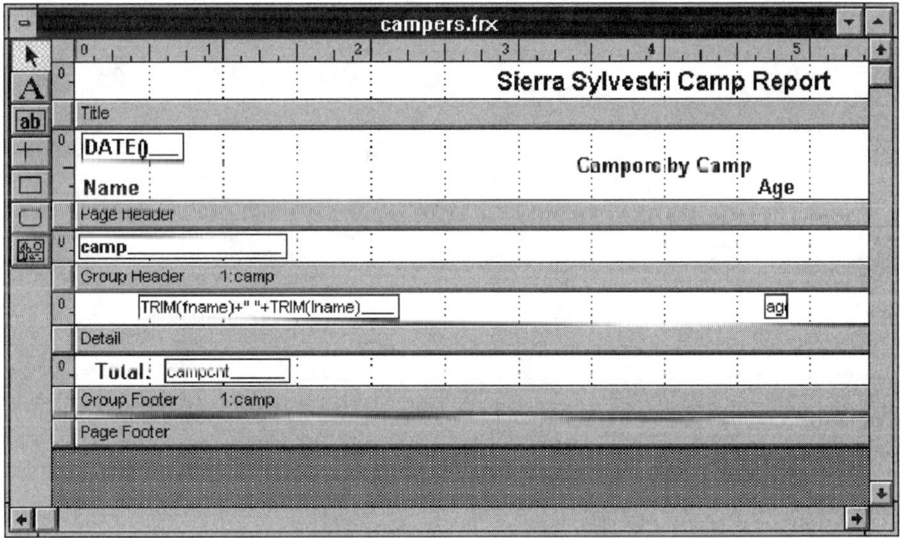

9-16 Sierra Sylvestri Camp Report example report layout.

Saving the report

To save the MADISON.FRX file:

1. Choose Save from the File menu, press Ctrl-W, or double-click on the report's window control bar.
2. When the Save As dialog appears enter the name MADISON in the text box. It is not necessary to enter the .FRX extension of the report file name.
3. Select OK to save the report. FoxPro will now ask you if you want to save the environment. Select No.

10
Using the Project Manager

The FoxPro Project Manager is used as a central control tool when building an application. A FoxPro application can consist of any number of programs, screen sets, menus, queries, databases, and libraries. The Project Manager gives you the tools necessary for managing each piece of your application.

What the Project Manager does

The Project Manager provides a template that you can use to design and control the pieces of a FoxPro application. When building a FoxPro application, the Project Manager is the first step. When your application is complete, you have one single file that includes all the pieces necessary to run the application.

FoxPro stores all project information in a database file with an extension of .PJX and uses the project database to generate an application for you to run. A FoxPro project file contains the following information:

- The name and location of every file of the application
- Object code of all source code files
- Screen set options
- File versions

Once you've defined all the pieces, the Project Manager can be used to build a single application file.

Starting the Project Manager

You can enter the Project Manager in two ways:

- From the Command window, issue either CREATE PROJECT (to create a new project) or MODIFY PROJECT (to modify an existing project), followed by the file name of the project.
- From the File menu, choose New... to start a new project, or Open... to open an existing project.

When you open a project, a project window appears (see Fig. 10-1) and the Project menu pad is added to the main menu.

Designing a project

The main program

The first step in creating a project is to add the main (or first) application program to the project. This is accomplished by selecting Add from the project window. From the Add File dialog shown in Fig. 10-2, select the type of file to add to the project. The main program is executed first when the application is run. If the main file you desire does not exist, select New from the Add File dialog to create a new program, screen, menu, query, report, or label file.

The main program appears in the project list with a bullet next to it. To change the main program, select Set Main from the Project menu.

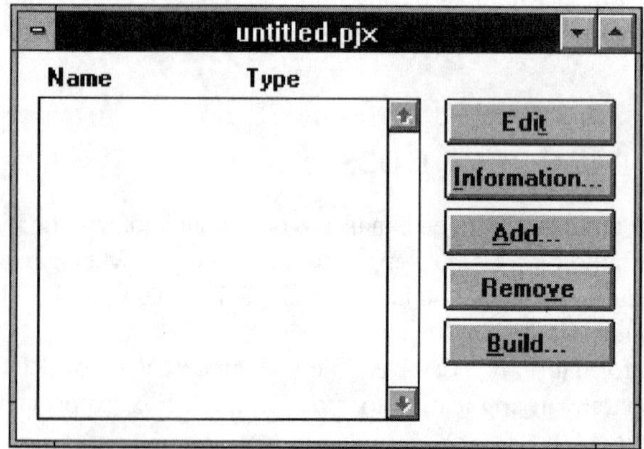

10-1 A project window.

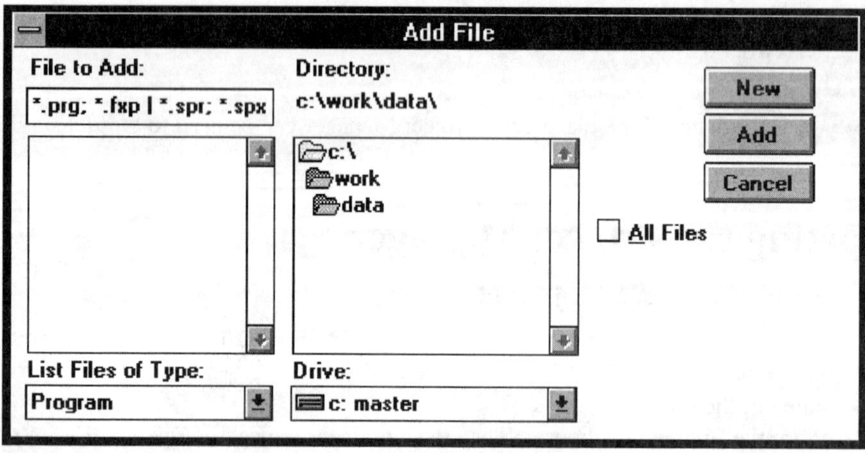

10-2 File to Add dialog box.

Adding other files

Once the main file has been added, you can manually add other files that participate in the application. This can be accomplished by selecting Add from the project and then selecting the type and name of file to add. The following file types can be included in a project:

File type	What it does
Program	Adds a FoxPro program source-code file.
Screen	Adds a FoxPro screen set.
Menu	Adds a FoxPro menu.
Query	Adds a FoxPro query.
Report	Adds a FoxPro report.
Label	Adds a FoxPro label.
Library	Adds a FoxPro API library.
Format	Adds a FoxPro format file.
Table/DBF	Adds a FoxPro database.
Index	Adds a FoxPro index.
File	Adds any type of DOS file.
Application	Adds a FoxPro application file.

Editing project files

You can edit files in the project by highlighting a file and selecting Edit, which opens an editing window for the selected file. The following list details what happens for each type of file and the corresponding FoxPro command:

Program Opens a program editing window (MODIFY COMMAND).

Screen Displays the Edit Screen Set dialog shown in Fig. 10-3. To edit a screen in the list, select the desired screen and press the Edit button, or double-click on a screen in the list (MODIFY SCREEN). The Edit Screen Set dialog is detailed in chapter 7.

Menu Opens a menu design editing window (MODIFY MENU).

Query Opens an RQBE editing window (MODIFY QUERY).

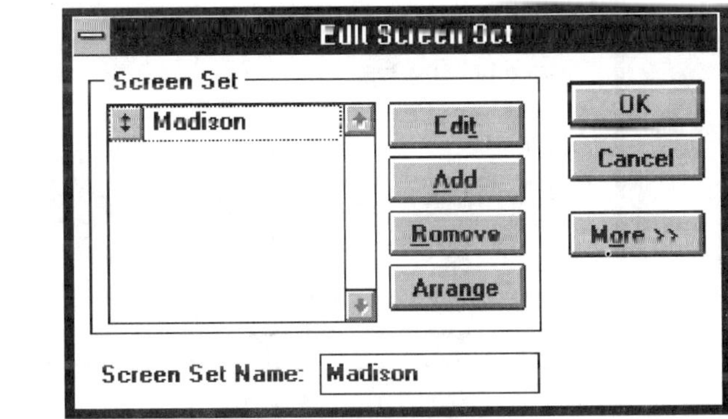

10-3 Edit Screen Set dialog.

Report Opens a report layout editing window (MODIFY REPORT).

Label Opens a label layout editing window (MODIFY LABEL).

Library Cannot be edited.

Format Opens a text file editing window (MODIFY FILE).

Database Opens a browse window (BROWSE LAST).

Index Cannot be edited.

File Opens a text file editing window (MODIFY FILE) if the file is an ASCII file. Non-FoxPro files cannot be edited.

Application Opens a project window of the application's project (MODIFY PROJECT).

Removing files from the project

To remove a file from the project, select a file from the files list and select Remove from the project window. A dialog prompting you to remove the selected file from the project will appear. If Yes is selected, the file is removed.

Viewing project file information

You can use the File Information dialog shown in Fig. 10-4 to view information on selected files in the project. To activate the File Information dialog, select a file in the project and select Information... from the project window. This dialog displays the name and location of the file, the type of file (e.g., Report, Menu), current and last build date, and all symbol references in the file. Only the name is displayed for screen files.

The symbols list displays all arrays, procedures or files that are either defined or called in the file. Use the Next and Previous buttons to scroll through all the files in the project without closing the File Information dialog.

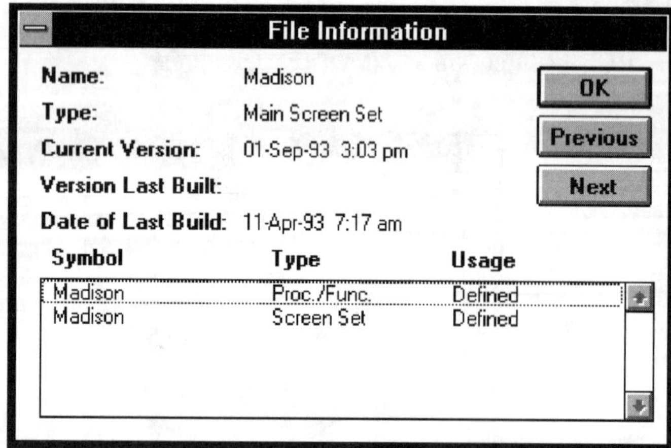

10-4 Project File Information dialog.

The Project menu

The Project menu shown in Fig. 10-5 contains the tools necessary for maintaining a project file.

Options...

Displays the Project Options dialog shown in Fig. 10-6, where you can specify information about the project.

Developer Information The text entered in the Author, Company, Address, City, State and Zip text boxes can be used to track developer information and is included at the top of all screen- and menu-generated source-code files.

Generated Code Location These options allow you to determine the location where menu and screen code will be generated. If With Screen or Menu is selected, the generated code is stored in the same location as the menu or screen file. If With Project is selected, the generated code is stored in the same location as the project file.

Select In Directory if you want to store the generated code in a location other than the menu, screen or project. The current default directory is initially selected. Enter the drive

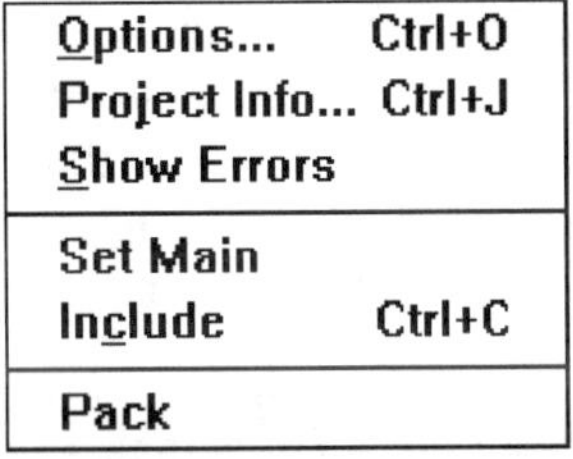

10-5 The Project menu.

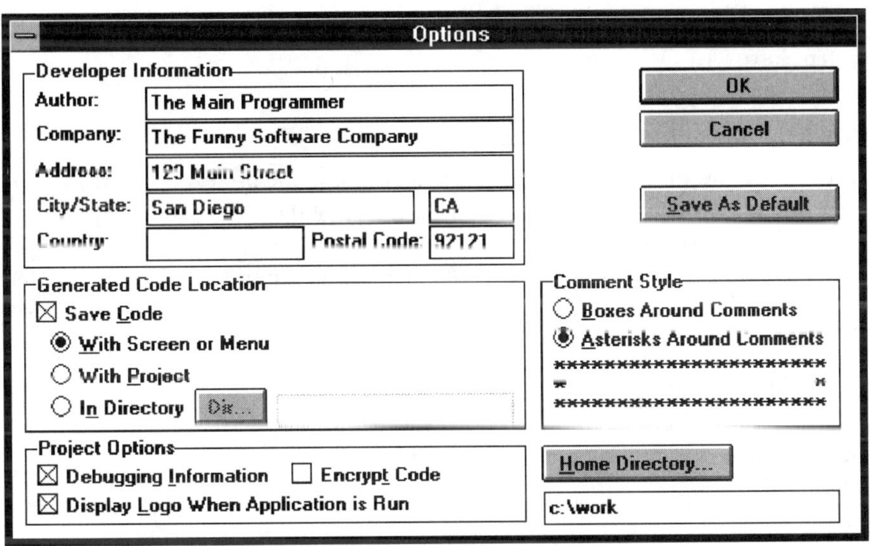

10-6 Project Options dialog.

and directory in the Directory text box, or select the Dir push button to activate the Select Directory dialog.

Project Options Selecting the Debugging Information check box causes FoxPro to include the information necessary to trace program execution in the Trace window when an application is run. If Debugging Information is not selected, the size of each compiled source code file will be reduced by approximately two bytes per executable program line. Debugging Information is always selected by default.

Selecting the Encrypt Code check box causes FoxPro to encrypt, or "scramble," the compiled code that is included in the application. Encrypting an application provides a certain level of security so that an individual cannot view the application and read the program code.

Select Display Logo When Application is Run to display the FoxPro startup logo on execution. The logo displays when the application is executed using the FoxPro runtime libraries from the FoxPro Distribution Kit.

Comment Style Selecting Box Around Comments will cause the screen and menu generators to place solid boxes around the comments that are generated. Selecting Asterisks Around Comments will cause the screen and menu generators to place asterisks (*) around the comments that are generated. This won't affect any comments that you may have entered into any screen code or menu code snippets.

Home Directory This is the directory in which the project file resides. If any files included in the project reside in a different directory, FoxPro uses the Home Directory setting to determine a relative directory path to those files. If a project file is moved and opened, a dialog appears prompting you to change the home directory. Select Yes if you plan on keeping the project in the new location.

Save as Default When selected, all settings specified in the dialog will be saved to the resource file if OK is selected. The default settings are then applied to all new projects.

Select OK to save the information in this dialog, or Cancel to discard.

Shortcut key Ctrl-O

Project Info...

Select Project Info to see a status of all files included in the project. The Project Information dialog (see Fig. 10-7) displays the name and path of the project file, the date it was last built, and file information.

The Type list displays each type of file included in the project. The Out of Date column contains the number of files that have been modified since the project file was last built. The Totals column indicates the total number of files in the project.

Shortcut key Ctrl-J

Show Errors

Displays a list of errors that may have occurred when the project file was rebuilt or an application was created. The list of errors is stored in an ASCII text file with the same name as the project with an extension of .ERR.

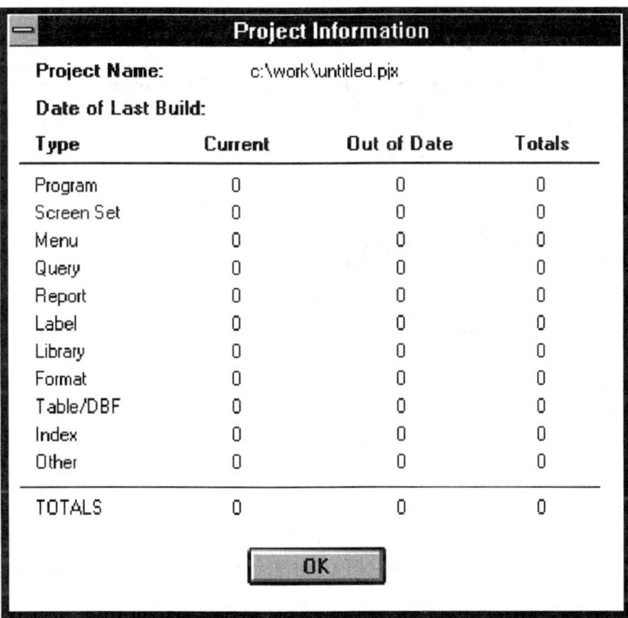

10-7 Project Information dialog.

Set Main

Makes the selected file the main application file. Set Main is only available when a program, screen, or menu file is selected. The main file is executed first when the application is run.

Exclude/Include

Excludes the selected file from the application. Excluded files appear in the project window with an O character next to the file type and aren't included in the generated application. Exclude is changed to Include when the selected project file displays the excluded character.

Both non-FoxPro executable files and other FoxPro applications are automatically excluded from the application. If a database is included in an application, the database can be opened and viewed in the application, but cannot be modified.

Shortcut key Ctrl-C

Pack

Deletes removed files from the project file database and packs the project database. If you are adding and deleting a lot of files from a project, use Pack on occasion to reduce the size of the project database and memo field files.

Saving the project

Once the project is complete, the project file must be saved. This can be done by selecting Save from the File Menu, pressing Ctrl-W, or double-clicking on the window control bar.

Building the project

When you are ready to build your application, select Build from the project window. This displays the Build Option dialog shown in Fig. 10-8. The Build Option dialog is used to rebuild a project file or create an application.

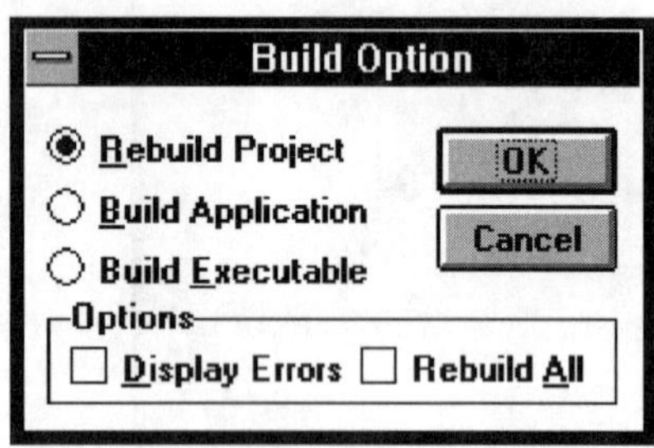

10-8 Build Option dialog box.

When creating a new project, you should only add the main program file to the project and then select Build. FoxPro will then attempt to find all of the source code and library files that are referenced and automatically add those files to the project file.

FoxPro stores the compiled object code of each source file in the project database. When a project is rebuilt or an application is built, any modified files since the last build date are recompiled. The following describes the options on the Build Option dialog:

Rebuild Project Rebuilds the project file. All files that were modified since the last project build date are updated and source code files for all screen and menu project files that were modified since the last build date are regenerated. After a project is rebuilt, the Project Information dialog (see Fig. 10-7) should show no Out of Date files.

Build Application Builds an application file (.APP) from the project. The Save As dialog appears prompting you for the name and location of the application file. You should always save the application file in the same location as the project.

Build Executable Builds an executable file (.EXE) from the project. The Save As dialog appears prompting you for the name and location of the EXE file.

Display Errors When checked, FoxPro will automatically display the error file after the project or application has been built. See Show Errors in this chapter for more information on the error file.

Rebuild All When checked, all files in the project are updated. Screen and menu code is generated for all screen and menu files.

When a project is built, FoxPro automatically adds referenced files to the project. For example, if Main.PRG contains the following commands:

```
* Main.PRG
USE Students
DO Edit.SPR
```

FoxPro will attempt to locate the Edit screen set and add it to the project. If a referenced file or procedure cannot be found, or a file already in the project cannot be found, the Locate File dialog (see Fig. 10-9) is displayed with the following options:

Locate Displays the Open File dialog which allows you to "show" the project where the file is. The name and location of the file is stored with the project.

Ignore Ignores the file error and continues rebuilding. Any file that cannot be located is displayed in the error file.

Remove Removes the file reference from the project. Remove should only be selected when the project contains a file that no longer exists.

Cancel Aborts the build process and returns control to the project window. Selecting Cancel resets the project build date to the date and time prior to the current build.

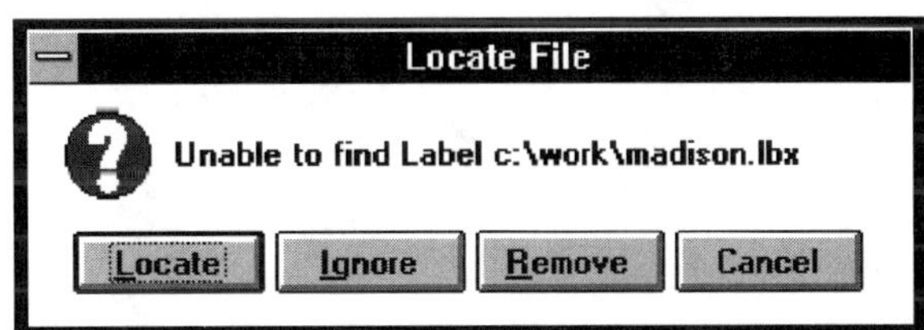

10-9 Locate File dialog box.

Creating applications

The project Build options are also used to create an application for distribution. Building an application simply combines all of the included project files into one file. Using the dialog shown in Fig. 10-8, select whether to build an application (.APP) file, or runtime executable (.EXE) file. The Build Executable option is only available if the FoxPro for Windows Distribution Kit has been installed.

When you choose to build an application or executable file, the FoxPro Save As dialog will appear, prompting you for the name of the file. The filename defaults to the name of the project file with an extension of .APP or .EXE.

Application files can be run in FoxPro by selecting Application from the Run menu and then selecting the appropriate application. Running an application on a computer that does not have FoxPro installed requires the FoxPro for Windows runtime library file, available with the Distribution Kit. When you distribute an application to another computer, be sure that all excluded project files that the application needs are included in the distribution.

11
Cross-platform and international capabilities

With FoxPro version 2.5a, you can develop applications on any supported platform and run those applications on any other platform, unchanged. At press time FoxPro 2.5a is available for both DOS and Microsoft Windows. Versions for the Macintosh and Unix operating systems are planned for later release.

FoxPro defines an application that can run on multiple platforms as a *cross-platform application*. The first part of this chapter provides some insight into the cross-platform capabilities of FoxPro 2.5a.

FoxPro 2.5a also provides the capability to translate accented characters in database and text files, and international indexing support. The functions are available through a variety of code page and collation sequence settings. The second part of this chapter provides an overview of FoxPro's international capabilities.

Developing cross-platform applications

Three different approaches can be taken when you decide to develop a cross-platform application:

1. Develop the application on one platform to run on any other platform unchanged.
2. Develop the application on one platform and transport the application's screens, menus, reports, and labels to another platform. This method allows you to take advantage of certain features available to each platform.
3. Develop the application with a platform specific interface, while leaving your procedure code unchanged.

Each approach has its pros and cons. The two platforms that FoxPro currently supports are very different in terms of interface issues: Windows is a graphical interface; DOS is a character interface. The platform that a developer chooses to work in and support will depend on a number of issues that only the developer can answer.

The three approaches are discussed below. Since this book is for FoxPro for Windows, the approaches are detailed using FoxPro 2.5a for Windows as the primary development environment.

Approach 1

Using FoxPro for Windows, the same application can be run under FoxPro for MS-DOS with no changes. Assuming that none of the pieces of the Windows application were developed in FoxPro for MS-DOS, the placement and appearance of screen and report objects may not be very good. Picture buttons and graphics cannot be displayed on the DOS side. This approach is better suited for going from DOS to Windows, not Windows to DOS.

Approach 2

After development in FoxPro for Windows, transport your files to FoxPro for MS-DOS and change the application interface. If your Windows application uses any type of graphic control or display, these need to be replaced with the proper DOS control. This approach poses one basic problem: coming back to Windows will require you to pay attention to the Transport process.

Approach 3

Taking this approach means that after developing a Windows application, you will redevelope the same application interface under DOS. Both platforms have the option of generating platform specific code for screen sets.

The FoxPro transporter

The screen shown in Fig. 11-1 is the same screen designed in chapter 6, but running under FoxPro 2.5a for MS-DOS. The Madison.SCX file was *transported* to MS-DOS and modified.

As stated in chapter 6, screen file information is stored in a FoxPro database. When a screen is modified, FoxPro checks to see if any new objects have been added to the screen file from a different platform, and also if any objects from the current platform have been changed on another platform. If so, the Transporter dialog shown in Fig. 11-2 is displayed.

```
Madison High School Student Database

First Name:  LISA                  Last:  CLIFF
Social Sec:  123-45-6789           Sex:   ( ) Male      (•) Female
Class:       11                    GPA:   3.75

Extra-Curricular Activities
[X] Sports    [ ] Politics    [X] Academics    [ ] Other Clubs
```

11-1 The Madison screen running under DOS.

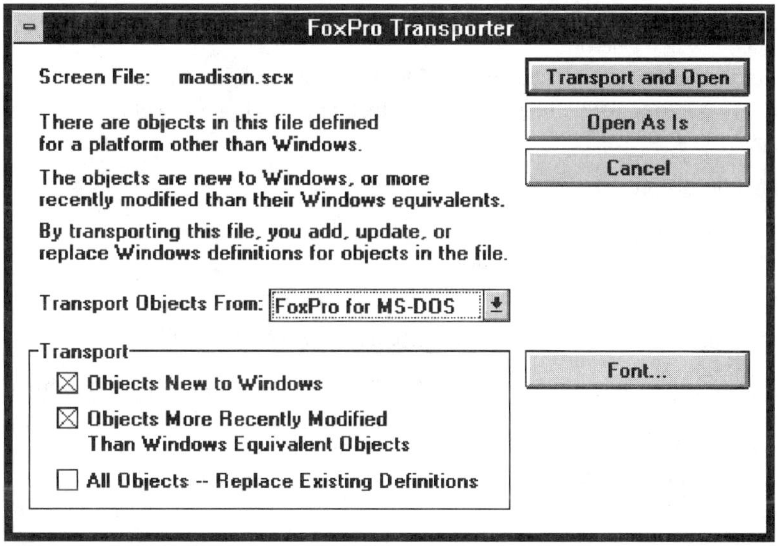

FoxPro Transporter

Screen File: madison.scx

There are objects in this file defined
for a platform other than Windows.

The objects are new to Windows, or more
recently modified than their Windows equivalents.

By transporting this file, you add, update, or
replace Windows definitions for objects in the file.

Transport Objects From: FoxPro for MS-DOS

Transport

☒ Objects New to Windows

☒ Objects More Recently Modified
Than Windows Equivalent Objects

☐ All Objects -- Replace Existing Definitions

Transport and Open

Open As Is

Cancel

Font...

11-2 Transporter dialog box.

The Transport Objects From pop-up will display the platform from which the new or modified objects were created. The Transport box gives you the options of adding any new objects to the screen, updating equivalent objects, or redefining all objects. Selecting the Open As Is push button will leave the screen unchanged for the current platform.

When transporting applications across different platforms you need to pay attention to three important pieces: screen, report, and label files. These three types of files can contain objects that cannot be displayed in DOS. The Transporter dialog will appear any time a screen, report, or label file has been modified on one platform and then opened on another. The process of transporting a file is accomplished with a FoxPro program, TRANSPORT.PRG.

Transporting objects

When you convert FoxPro for Windows screen, report, and label files, you are going from a graphical environment to a character mode environment. Since FoxPro for MS-DOS doesn't support fonts or graphical images, among other things, the transporter must convert these types of objects to similar DOS objects. This section details the conversion of objects that occurs when any screen, report, or label file is transported from Windows to DOS.

When any screen, report, or label is transported:

- Object coordinates, which in Windows are based on pixels and fractions, are converted to DOS character text coordinates.
- Objects with different fonts, styles, and sizes are converted to single-spaced text characters. Fonts are not supported in FoxPro for MS-DOS.
- Objects that are grouped are no longer grouped.
- Rounded-rectangle objects are converted to DOS rectangle objects.

- Any text object that contains more than one line of text is broken into separate objects for each line of text.
- Picture objects are not transported, since they are not supported in FoxPro for MS-DOS.
- The Pen setting for rectangle, rounded-rectangle, and line objects are converted as follows:

Windows Pen value	DOS line type
1,6	Single
2	Double
4	Panel

Along with the actions described above, when any screen file is transported:

- All rectangle, line, and text object color settings are transported. Some Windows color settings, such as a red foreground, may cause the DOS object to blink or be displayed as high-intensity.
- Spinner control objects are converted to standard GET fields, with numeric formatting controls.
- Picture push buttons are converted to DOS character push buttons. The file name of the bitmap or icon image used in the push button becomes the text label for the DOS button.
- Picture radio buttons are converted to DOS character push buttons. The file name of the bitmap or icon image used in the push button becomes the text label for the DOS button.

Along with the actions described earlier, when any report file is transported:

- Reports with more than one column are converted to a single column, since FoxPro for MS-DOS doesn't support multicolumn reports. Any extra column headers and footers are added to the report page header and footer, respectively.
- If any report object's Remove Line if Blank setting is checked on, the DOS report's Suppress Blank Lines setting is turned on.
- The Top-Field Can Stretch setting for group header and footer objects is ignored, since this function is not supported by FoxPro for MS-DOS.
- The Group Overflow setting for objects with Print Repeated Values set to No is ignored, since this function is not supported by FoxPro for MS-DOS.

Along with the actions described earlier, when any label file is transported:

- Labels with a single column are converted to 80-column labels.
- Rectangles and line objects are not converted, since FoxPro for MS-DOS labels can only be comprised of expressions.
- Expressions on the same line are converted to a single expression, since FoxPro for MS-DOS labels can only have one expression per label line.

Using transporter directives

The FoxPro transporter supports directives that can be used to determine which platform objects are transported to. Transporter directives are similar to screen and menu generator directives, but are placed in the Comment snippet of an object.

The four transporter directives are: #WINOBJ for FoxPro for Windows, #DOSOBJ for FoxPro for MS-DOS, #MACOBJ for FoxPro for Macintosh, and #UNIXOBJ for FoxPro for Unix. Placing a generator directive in the Comment snippet of an object ensures that that object will be transported only to the platform that matches the directive. For example, if you have objects on a FoxPro for Windows screen that you don't want transported to any other platform, place the #WINOBJ directive in the Comment snippet of those objects.

There is also a screen generator directive, #TRAN SNIPPET ONLY, that can be used to transport screen snippet code only. See chapter 6, Using the Screen Builder, for more information on using screen generator directives.

International capabilities

As stated at the beginning of this chapter, FoxPro for Windows version 2.5a provides the capability to translate accented characters in database and text files, and provides international indexing and sorting. These functions are provided by using a variety of code pages and collation sequences.

Character sets and code pages

The standard ASCII character set is used for determining the value of all alphabetical letters stored in a computer. The letters A–Z are given the values 65–90, and the letters a–z are given the values 97–122. The value of accented characters is different among American and international ASCII character sets. And some operating systems, such as Microsoft Windows, use an implementation of the ANSI character set.

FoxPro provides the capability to automatically translate accented characters in a database by using code pages. A code page is based on the operating system of the computer in use, and is used to translate accented ASCII characters from the code page that the characters are stored in the database to the current code page in use on the computer. FoxPro supports the following code pages:

Code Page	Platform
437	U.S. MS-DOS
850	International MS-DOS
852	EE MS-DOS
865	Nordic MS-DOS
866	Russian MS-DOS
1250	Windows EE
1251	Russian Windows
1252	Windows ANSI

The Windows ANSI code page, 1252, is in use when you are using FoxPro for Windows, and the MS-DOS code page, 437, is in use when you are using FoxPro for MS-DOS. Remember that code pages are based on the operating system in use, and cannot be changed.

How code paging affects your files

Translation occurs on character and memo fields in databases, and program and text files. If you open a file that was created with a code page other than what you are using, FoxPro will automatically translate accented characters (if any) to your code page. If you make any changes to a translated file, the changes are translated back to the code page of the file, and not yours. You can prevent automatic translation of specific fields in a database using the SET NOCPTRANS command, which is detailed in chapter 2.

Activating cross-platform translation

In FoxPro, code page translation is activated by specifying a CODEPAGE = *expr* statement in your startup configuration file. The value of *expr* can be either AUTO, or a supported code page number from the table above. There is no FoxPro command that you can use to activate code paging. The AUTO setting ensures that data and text is translated correctly to the current system code page. If for some reason you need to translate to a different code page, specify the desired code page number in *expr*. You can use the CPCURRENT() function (see chapter 4) to check the current code page setting.

Once code paging is active, any new database, program, or text file that is created is marked with the current system code page (if AUTO is specified). You can use the DISPLAY STATUS command to view the current system code page, along with the default code page of any open database files.

The dialog shown in Fig. 11-3 appears whenever you attempt to open a database file that does not have a code page marking so that it can be marked. The scrolling list option will default to the CODEPAGE setting specified in your configuration file.

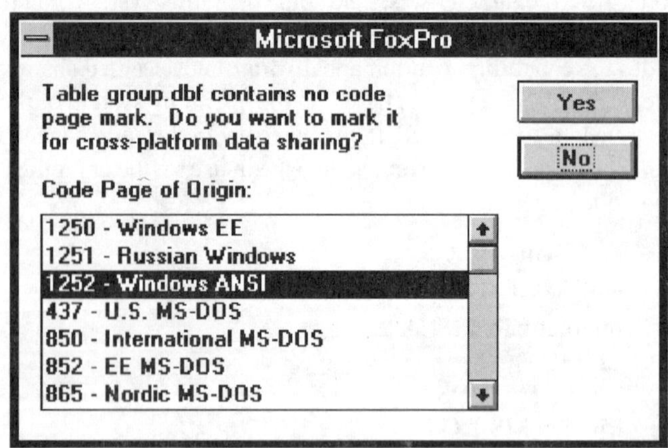

11-3 Code page mark dialog box.

The translation of program and text files requires an extra step. If you open a program or text file using the Open... option from the File menu, you must check the Other Code Page option on the Open dialog (see Fig. 1-17). If you open a program or text file using the MODIFY COMMAND|FILE commands, you can specify a code page to translate to using the AS expN clause. When a program or text file is translated, it looks the same as it would in the code page it was created with. When you save a program or text file, you can specify a new code page to be stored with the file. Using the Save As... option in the File menu, check the Change Code Page option on the Save As dialog (see Fig. 1-18). If you choose to save the file, the dialog shown in Fig. 11-3 appears, allowing you to select a new code page for the file.

Collation sequences

Collation sequences can be used to control the order of database records that contain accented characters when using the INDEX and SORT commands. When a collation sequence is active, the resulting order of records is determined by the "weight" of accented characters. The languages that FoxPro supports and their associated collation sequences are detailed under SET COLLATE section of chapter 3. A collation sequence can be set:

- By specifying a COLLATE = statement in the startup configuration file.
- By using Collation Sequence popup in the International panel of the View window. This popup is only enabled if a CODEPAGE setting has been specified in the startup configuration file.
- By using the SET COLLATE command.

Collation sequences can only be used if the file FOXPRO.INT is in the default FoxPro directory.

How a collation sequence affects ordering

Using either the MACHINE or UNIQWT collation sequences is similar to indexing or sorting records on the UPPER() or LOWER() value of an expression. The MACHINE setting is what earlier versions of FoxPro would use. The UNIQWT setting determines the order after removing a character's accent. The GENERAL setting is not case sensitive and determines the order based on the sound value of an accented character.

FoxPro will always order records by the ASCII value of the index or sort expression. Therefore, the final order of records is determined by two things: the current code page in use and the collation sequence used when indexing or sorting records. The only way to truly know the order in which records will appear is to know the ASCII value of each character in the current code page.

12
Using DDE and OLE in FoxPro

As a true Windows application, FoxPro for Windows can take advantage of certain functions that allow you to share information between FoxPro and other Windows applications. The first is Dynamic Data Exchange, or DDE. DDE functions can be used to programmatically send and receive data between applications. The second is Object Linking and Embedding, or OLE. OLE can be used to link or store other files from other Windows application in a FoxPro database.

This chapter is designed to provide you with a fundamental understanding of DDE and OLE and how they can be used in FoxPro. Consult your Windows documentation for further information not discussed here.

Using DDE

Dynamic Data Exchange is used by Windows applications to send and receive data requests. Applications exchange information by talking to each other. The application that initiates the DDE request is considered the client application; it will receive the data. The application that responds to the DDE request is considered the server application; it sends the requested information back. In a FoxPro application, you might send a request to a Microsoft Word document to do a mailmerge. On the other hand, a FoxPro application can receive a data query from Microsoft Excel and return the results of the query. To initiate a DDE conversation in FoxPro you need three things: an application service name, a topic, and an item. The application service name is usually the name of the application's executable (.EXE) file name, such as WINWORD.EXE. Most applications that support DDE have a variety of service names relating to specific operations of the application. A DDE topic identifies the subject of the conversation, and is usually a filename. This might be a Word document name or an Excel spreadsheet name. Most DDE applications also have a topic name of Service, which can be used for requesting general information or sending commands to the server application. An item identifies a certain element of the topic. For instance, a topic could be a number of cells from an Excel spreadsheet.

Using FoxPro as a DDE client

The following sections provide information on how to setup a FoxPro application to act as a DDE client so that you can request data from other DDE applications.

Creating a link

A DDE conversation is initiated using the DDEInitiate( ) function. Either a notify or automatic link can be created. When a notify link is established, the application to which you linked will notify FoxPro whenever data changes. When an automatic link is established, the application that you linked to will send the requested data automatically when it changes.

Before you attempt to initiate a DDE link, you must first start the other application (if it is not already active). Through FoxPro, you can use the RUN command to launch a Windows application. For example, issuing the following command:

```
RUN /N WINWORD.EXE
```

would launch Microsoft Word for Windows. If you attempt to initiate a DDE link and the other application is not open, FoxPro will present a dialog asking you if you want FoxPro to attempt to launch the application. You can control the display of this dialog using the DDESetOption( ) function.

Once an application is open, you can attempt to open a DDE channel to the application. A DDE channel is used to identify a DDE link for communications. For example, issuing the following:

```
x = DDEInitiate("WINWORD","SYSTEM")
```

would attempt to initiate a DDE channel with Word for Windows, concerning the System topic. The example shown above can generally be used to open a channel with another Windows application.

If the link is successful, a numeric value, corresponding to the DDE channel that was opened, is returned. Otherwise, –1 is returned. In some cases, your DDE requests will fail. By using the DDELastError() function, you can determine what caused the failure. See chapter 4 for more information on using the DDELastError( ) function.

Requesting data from a link

Once a link has been established, the DDERequest( ) function can be used to request data from the linked application. If the request is successful, the requested information will be returned to FoxPro. See chapter 4 for more information on using the DDERequest( ) function.

Terminating a link

The DDETerminate( ) function is used to terminate a DDE link and close the conversation channel. See chapter 4 for more information on using the DDETerminate( ) function.

Remotely controlling applications

Once a link has been established, you can remotely control the application by using the DDEExecute( ) function. This allows you to open documents, print documents, change values, or even run a menu option. For example, the following function can be used to tell Microsoft Word to maximize itself:

```
max = DDEExecute(x, "[AppMaximize]")
```

where x is the channel name that was established earlier (see the initiate example above). Each application that supports DDE may have its own set of DDE execution commands. Refer to your application's software documentation for more information.

Controlling the link

As explained earlier, the DDE link can be either a notify or automatic link. Once a link has been established, you can use the DDEAdvise() function to establish an automatic link for each item. The DDEAdvise() function passes a user-defined function that will be executed whenever a data item in the link changes. See chapter 4 for more information on using the DDEAdvise() function.

Once a DDE function has been issued, FoxPro waits a period of two seconds for a response from the linked application. If no response is sent, the DDE function fails. You can change the timeout value using the DDESetOption() function, which is detailed in chapter 4.

You can create an asynchronous DDE link that will continue with program execution while waiting for a response to a DDE request. An asynchronous link is created by passing a user-defined function as one of the DDERequest() function parameters. When the response comes back, FoxPro will execute the specified user-defined function. You may want to create this type of link in situations where you know a response may take some time.

Using FoxPro as a DDE server

While you can use DDE functions in the command window to request data, FoxPro can only act as server in passive mode; this means that you must write a server program to act on any DDE requests from other DDE applications.

The following sections provide information on how to setup a FoxPro application to act as a DDE server so that other DDE applications can request data from FoxPro tables or even send commands to your application.

Defining a service

Before a DDE application can initiate a conversation with FoxPro, a DDE service must be defined, and the supported service types must be specified. Using the DDESetService() function, FoxPro will begin waiting for DDE calls from other applications. In the following example, the parameter FoxWin is used to define a DDE service for FoxPro.

```
x = DDESetService("FoxWin","DEFINE")
```

The DEFINE parameter is used to define FoxWin as the DDE server. Once a service is defined, you may need to specify the DDE actions that your application will support. A FoxPro DDE server, by default, can accept initiate, terminate, and requests calls from another DDE application, and can also accept execute, poke, and advise actions if you define them using the DDESetService() function.

A FoxPro server application continues to monitor DDE requests until it is terminated with a release function. For example, issuing the following:

```
done = DDESetService("FoxWin","RELEASE")
```

would release the DDE service FoxWin that was defined earlier. See chapter 4 for more information on using the DDESetService() function.

Defining topics

Once a service is defined, you need to define topics using the DDESetTopic() function. Service topics determine what action is taken when FoxPro receives a DDE request, and are defined by specifying a topic name and a user-defined function to be executed. For example, issuing the following:

```
x = DDESetTopic("FoxWin","System","Sys_func")
```

defines the System topic for the FoxWin service. Whenever FoxPro receives a DDE call for the System topic, the user-defined function Sys_func would be executed.

You can define as many system topics as you like for any single DDE service. You may also want to define a "catch-all" topic in case FoxPro receives a DDE call with an unknown topic, or if you want to use a single user-defined function to process all DDE calls. This can be done by defining a null topic. For example, defining the following topic:

```
x = DDESetTopic("FoxWin","","Unknown_func")
```

would cause the FoxPro DDE server to execute the Unkown_func function when it receives an undefined DDE call to the FoxWin service. See chapter 4 for more information on using the DDESetTopic() function.

Handling responses

When a FoxPro DDE service receives a DDE call, the type of action must be evaluated and a response made. As discussed earlier, when you define service names and topic names, you must provide the name of a user-defined function to be executed when a topic is called. The user-defined functions that you specify will receive a certain number of parameters and must conform to FoxPro programming standards. The user-defined function should only return a value of true (.T.) or false (.F.), and not any requested data (requested data is sent back to the DDE client using the DDEPoke() function). Your DDE server may receive simultaneous calls to the same topic. In this case, you will need to handle the FoxPro environment accordingly.

A server example

The following is a simple DDE server program for FoxPro. The premise of the program is that a DDE client will initiate a DDE conversation to either open a database, send data back to the client, or change the value of record in the database. The database to be used, NAMES, contains two fields: FIRST and LAST.

```
* Program is SERVER.PRG
serv1 = DDESetService("FoxWin","DEFINE",.T.)
```

```
serv2 = DDESetService("FoxWin","EXECUTE",.T.)
serv3 = DDESetService("FoxWin","POKE",.T.)
topic = DDESetTopic("FoxWin","","Eval_call")

Procedure Eval_call
* This procedure is known as a callback function
PARAMETERS channel,action,item,data,format,status
PRIVATE execute_ok
execute_ok = .T.
= DDEEnabled(.F.)
DO CASE
   CASE action = "INITIATE"
      USE NAMES IN 1
   CASE action = "REQUEST"

      DO CASE
         CASE UPPER(item) = "NEXT10"
            COPY TO ARRAY maData NEXT 10
         CASE UPPER(item) = "ALL"
            COPY TO ARRAY maData
      ENDCASE
      = DDEPoke(channel,item,maData)

   CASE action = "POKE"
      REPLACE &item WITH &data
   CASE action = "EXECUTE"
      &data
   CASE action = "TERMINATE"
      CLOSE DATA
   OTHERWISE
      execute_ok = .F.
ENDCASE
= DDEEnabled(.T.)
RETURN execute_ok
```

The example program, SERVER.PRG, is designed to accept DDE initiate, request, poke, and terminate actions from another DDE client application. In the first part of the program, the service name and topics are defined using DDESetService() and DDESetTopic(). Since the example accepts POKE and EXECUTE calls, those services must be defined (remember, a DDE server only accepts initiate, terminate, and request actions by default). A "catch-all" topic is defined, so that a single function (Eval_call) can be used to process all DDE calls to the FoxWin service.

The Eval_call procedure, known as a callback procedure, is used to process DDE calls to the FoxWin service. The PARAMETERS statement contains six parameters that will be passed to the procedure when it is executed. The first parameter, channel, is the DDE channel over which the call is made. The second parameter, action, is the type of action that the DDE client is requesting and will be one of the following: ADVISE, EXECUTE, INITIATE, POKE, REQUEST, or TERMINATE. The third parameter, item, is the data item that the client is requesting, if the DDE call is a request. The fourth parameter, data, contains data to use in a poke or execute call. The fifth parameter, format, determines the format of the data item. The sixth parameter, status, is used to advise the server of the link status. These parameters and their values are further detailed under DDESetTopic() in chapter 4.

The DDEEnabled(.F.) function is issued to disable DDE processing while a call is evaluated. At the end of the procedure, it is issued again to enable DDE processing. The execute_ok variable will be used to determine if the processing was successful or not, and its value (true or false) will be returned to the DDE client.

The first step is to determine the type of call that was made. Since this is a catch-all procedure, a DO CASE statement is used to process the action value. If the value of action is INITIATE, a call has been made to initiate a DDE conversation with the FoxWin service. In this case, the command is issued to use the NAMES database.

If the value of action is REQUEST, the DDE client is requesting that data from the NAMES database be sent back to the client application. Since different requests can be made, another DO CASE statement is used to process the request item, which is contained in the item parameter. If the value of item (UPPER() is used here) is NEXT10, the command is issued to copy the next 10 records of the database into the array maData. If the value is ALL, all records are copied into the array. Once the data is extracted, the DDEPoke() function is used to send back the data.

If the value of action is POKE, the DDE client is requesting that an element of the NAMES database (determined by the value of the item parameter) be changed to reflect the value contained in the data parameter. In this case, the command is issued to replace the value for the current record.

If the value of action is EXECUTE, the DDE client is attempting to execute a valid FoxPro command. In this case, the command (again, determined by the value of the data parameter) is combined with the macro command (&) and is executed. If the value of action is TERMINATE, the DDE client is requesting that the DDE conversation be terminated. In this case, the command is issued to close the NAMES database.

Finally, if no valid request is processed (using the OTHERWISE statement), the variable execute_ok is changed to false. The last line of the procedure returns the value of execute_ok to the DDE client application.

See also DDEAbortTrans(), DDEAdvise(), DDEEnabled(), DDEExecute(), DDEInitiate(), DDELastError(), DDEPoke(), DDERequest(), DDESetOption(), DDESetService(), DDESetTopic(), DDETerminate()

Using OLE

Object Linking and Embedding is used to link or embed data from other Windows applications into FoxPro database files. This data could be a word processing document, a spreadsheet, a sound file, or even a bitmap picture. Any file that is created by a registered OLE application can be stored in a FoxPro database file. An OLE server is defined as the application that creates and modifies the object file. An OLE client, such as FoxPro, can make reference to the original file, and even store a copy of it. FoxPro cannot act as an OLE server.

OLE data can only be stored in a general field of a FoxPro database and, in some cases, be used in reports or data-entry screens. When data is linked to a FoxPro database, only a reference to the data item is saved, and not the actual contents of the file. When data is embedded in a FoxPro database, the entire contents of the file is stored in the database file. The link information or data object is stored in the associated .FPT file of the database.

To link or to embed

The biggest disadvantages to embedding OLE objects is disk space. When you embed an object in a FoxPro general field, you are in effect duplicating the document, and using up valuable disk space. Because you are simply creating a copy of the file and storing it in a FoxPro database, you lose all parental rights to the original file, so any changes made to the file won't be reflected in any embedded copies. When you link an object, any changes that are made to the document in its server application are mirrored in the link. Linking is also a good choice if you need to share the file among different FoxPro database files.

Accessing OLE in FoxPro

Most OLE operations can be performed with options on the Edit menu when a general field editing window is open and frontmost. The Paste and Paste Special options can be used to place data from the Windows clipboard into the general field, while the Insert Object option can be used to select an OLE object file that already exists on disk. Since all of the Edit menu functions used for OLE are detailed in chapter 1, The FoxPro user interface, this section is designed to provide details on how to store and edit OLE objects.

Inserting OLE objects

As discussed earlier, you can either link or embed OLE objects. OLE objects can exist on the Windows clipboard, or can be an existing file. While embedding is pretty straightforward (you store a copy of the document in the database), linking has a few more tricks. When you use the Edit menu Paste Special option, you can either paste the entire object (embed) or create a link to the object.

When an OLE link is created, FoxPro stores information concerning the object in the appropriate general field. This information is later used to access the server application and open the document when you want to make changes to the object from FoxPro. A link always refers back to the parent document, so moving or renaming the document will break the link. If a link is broken, you can use the Edit menu Change Link option to fix the link.

Once an OLE object is placed in a FoxPro database, you can open a general field editing window to view the contents of the field. What you will see is determined by what type of object is in the field. If the field contains a Paintbrush picture or similar type of graphic image, you will see the image. However, if the object is some type of word processing document or spreadsheet, you will see an icon that represents the object's server application.

Editing and running OLE objects

Once an OLE object has been attached to a FoxPro database, you can activate the object's server application to execute the object's primary OLE verb. An OLE verb determines what action is taken, such as Edit or Run. The primary OLE verb for most OLE objects is Edit. To edit an OLE object that is stored in a general field, open a general field editing window and double-click on the object. This will launch the object's server application and place the object or document in the application's editing window. For objects such as sound files, double-clicking on the object will play the sound stored in the sound file.

When a general field editing window is open and frontmost, the Edit menu option directly under Insert Object changes to reflect the type of object stored and the available OLE verbs for that object. For instance, if the object is a Paintbrush picture, the option is displayed as Edit Paintbrush Picture Object. Selecting this menu option performs the same action as double-clicking on the object. If the object is a Windows sound file, the option might be displayed as Sound Object, along with a submenu of other actions, such as Play and Edit.

Using FoxPro commands

Two FoxPro commands, APPEND GENERAL and MODIFY GENERAL, can be used in place of the Edit menu options to place and view OLE objects into a FoxPro database. These commands allow you to add OLE features to your FoxPro application.

The APPEND GENERAL command is similar to using the Insert Object option from the Edit menu, and is used to import an OLE object or document into a specified general field for the current database record. The CLASS clause of the APPEND GENERAL command is used to tell FoxPro what OLE class the object belongs to. An OLE class determines the server application used to execute the object's OLE verb. For example, the file BIRDS.BMP could be created using Paintbrush and embedded in a FoxPro database file with the following statement:

```
APPEND GENERAL picture BIRDS.BMP
```

In this case, attempting to edit the picture would cause Paintbrush to be executed. If later you decide to use a different graphics application for editing your bitmap files, you could issue the following command:

```
APPEND GENERAL picture BIRDS.BMP CLASS graphics
```

This statement would register the OLE object with a new server. You must specify a class that belongs to an OLE server that is registered in the Windows Registration editor. Consult your Windows documentation for more information.

See also Chapter 1, The FoxPro user interface

Appendix
Using the Help file

Included on disk with this book is a Windows help-file version of the text. The help file is contained in the self-extracting file MASTER.EXE and requires 3MB of disk space to install.

Installing the help file

To install the help file to your hard drive, change to your FoxPro directory and type B:MASTER, where B: is the drive that contains the disk. This creates the file MASTER.HLP in the current directory.

Accessing and using the help file

To access the help file from the Windows Program Manager, select Help Contents from the Program Manager menu. Once a help screen appears, select File Open, locate the MASTER.HLP file, and select OK. to access the help file from within FoxPro for Windows, enter the command:

```
SET HELP TO C:\FOXPROW\MASTER.HLP
```

where C:\FOXPROW is the directory that the file was installed in. If you want to add the help file as an icon to your FoxPro group, use the Program Manager File New option to add a new Program Item. Select Browse and locate the MASTER.HLP file that was installed following the instructions above.

Refer to your Windows documentation for more information on using and navigating through a Windows help file.

Some extra stuff

You'll find a few extra things in the help file that aren't in the book. These include:

- Appendix B, Controlling FoxPro with CONFIG.FPW
- Appendix C, FoxPro error messages
- Appendix D, FoxPro system memory variables
- Appendix E, FoxPro SET() return values
- Appendix F, FoxPro SYS() functions

Index

E

Q

R

S

Other Bestsellers of Related Interest

FoxPro 2.5 for Windows Inside & Out
A hands-on learning method that includes lots of examples, exercises, and illustrations. Learn how to use the querying, sorting, indexing, and reporting capabilities of this powerful database. 742 pages.
ISBN # 0-07-881898-2 $27.95 Paper

Microsoft FoxPro 2.5 Applications Programming,
An advanced applications development toolbox for FoxPro programmers. Applicable to FoxPro for DOS, Windows, Mac, and Unix. An updated guide for experienced FoxPro programmers to cover enhancements in version 2.5. 384 pages.
ISBN # 0-8306-4568-3 $24.95 Paper

The Green PC: Making Choices that Make a Difference
Takes a candid no-holds-barred look at how computing affects our environment and what computer users can do to reverse the growing problem of computer-generated pollution. 192 pages.
ISBN # 0-8306-4311-7 $9.95 Paper

Stacker: An Illustrated Tutorial, 2nd Edition
A complete user's guide to the disk-doubling data compression software from STAC Electronics. Covers all the new features of Stacker for Windows and DOS, Version 3.0. 176 pages.
ISBN # 0-8306-4487-3 $19.95

DoubleSpace: An Illustrated Tutorial
The only guide to DOS 6's data compression utility. A must for and DOS 6 user. Gives DOS 6 users the knowledge and tools they need to dramatically increase their hard disk storage capacity with this data compression utility. 160 pages
ISBN # 0-8306-4629-9 $15.95 Paper

SuperStor: An Illustrated Tutorial
Describes in step-by-step detail how to install and setup SuperStor 2.1 and SuperStor Pro 1.01 on any system running DOS or Windows. Allows users to take full advantage of SuperStor capabilities without bogging down in the minutiae of data compression and memory management. 160 pages
ISBN # 0-8306-4529-2 $16.95 Paper

DISK WARRANTY

This software is protected by both United States copyright law and international copyright treaty provision. You must treat this software just like a book, except that you may copy it into a computer in order to be used and you may make archival copies of the software for the sole purpose of backing up our software and protecting your investment from loss.

By saying "just like a book," McGraw-Hill means, for example, that this software may be used by any number of people and may be freely moved from one computer location to another, so long as there is no possibility of its being used at one location or on one computer while it also is being used at another. Just as a book cannot be read by two different people in two different places at the same time, neither can the software be used by two different people in two different places at the same time (unless, of course, McGraw-Hill's copyright is being violated).

LIMITED WARRANTY

Windcrest/McGraw-Hill takes great care to provide you with top-quality software, thoroughly checked to prevent virus infections. McGraw-Hill warrants the physical diskette(s) contained herein to be free of defects in materials and workmanship for a period of sixty days from the purchase date. If McGraw-Hill receives written notification within the warranty period of defects in materials or workmanship, and such notification is determined by McGraw-Hill to be correct, McGraw-Hill will replace the defective diskette(s). Send requests to:

Customer Service
Windcrest/McGraw-Hill
13311 Monterey Lane
Blue Ridge Summit, PA 17294-0850

The entire and exclusive liability and remedy for breach of this Limited Warranty shall be limited to replacement of defective diskette(s) and shall not include or extend to any claim for or right to cover any other damages, including but not limited to, loss of profit, data, or use of the software, or special, incidental, or consequential damages or other similar claims, even if McGraw-Hill has been specifically advised of the possibility of such damages. In no event will McGraw-Hill's liability for any damages to you or any other person ever exceed the lower of suggested list price or actual price paid for the license to use the software, regardless of any form of the claim.

MCGRAW-HILL, INC. SPECIFICALLY DISCLAIMS ALL OTHER WARRANTIES, EXPRESS OR IMPLIED, INCLUDING, BUT NOT LIMITED TO, ANY IMPLIED WARRANTY OF MERCHANTABILITY OR FITNESS FOR A PARTICULAR PURPOSE.

Specifically, McGraw-Hill makes no representation or warranty that the software is fit for any particular purpose and any implied warranty of merchantability is limited to the sixty-day duration of the Limited Warranty covering the physical diskette(s) only (and not the software) and is otherwise expressly and specifically disclaimed.

This limited warranty gives you specific legal rights; you may have others which may vary from state to state. Some states do not allow the exclusion of incidental or consequential damages, or the limitation on how long an implied warranty lasts, so some of the above may not apply to you.

Disk Instructions

This disk contains the sample code and help files for Microsoft FoxPro 2.5 for Windows (Book #0609918) (c) 1994 by John C. Fitzsimmons and Robin Stark. These files demonstrate the FoxPro commands, functions, and features, and provide on-line help. The instructions for accessing these files are in file **README.TXT**. You will need to open this file and read it before proceeding.

IMPORTANT

Read the Disk Warranty terms on the previous page before opening the disk envelope. Opening the envelope constitutes acceptance of these terms and renders this entire book-disk package nonreturnable except for replacement in kind due to material defect.